A History of Women's Writing in Germany, Austria and Switzerland

This book is the first full-length account in English of women's writing in Germany, Austria and Switzerland to offer both an introduction to and a chronological overview of women's writing in German-speaking countries from the Middle Ages to the present day. It will appeal both to students and to scholars of German literature, and to a wider readership interested in women's writing and gender studies wishing to learn about the diversity and development of writing by women in Germany, Austria and Switzerland. The sixteen chapters, written by experts in their field, are designed to dovetail into a comprehensive account of women's writing over a thousand-year period. Extensive guides to further reading, and a detailed guide to more than three hundred writers and their works, together with an index for cross-referencing, form an integral part of the volume.

JO CATLING is Lecturer in German Literature and Language at the University of East Anglia. She has written on Rilke, and on German women artists and writers, as well as translating Walter Haug, *Literaturtheorie im deutschen Mittelalter*, published in English as *Vernacular Literary Theory in the Middle Ages* (1997).

A History of
Women's Writing
in Germany, Austria
and Switzerland

Edited by
JO CATLING

CAMBRIDGE
UNIVERSITY PRESS

PUBLISHED BY THE PRESS SYNDICATE OF THE UNIVERSITY OF CAMBRIDGE
The Pitt Building, Trumpington Street, Cambridge, United Kingdom

CAMBRIDGE UNIVERSITY PRESS
The Edinburgh Building, Cambridge CB2 2RU, UK   http://www.cup.cam.ac.uk
40 West 20th Street, New York, NY 10011–4211, USA   http://www.cup.org
10 Stamford Road, Oakleigh, Melbourne 3166, Australia

First published 2000

Printed in the United Kingdom at the University Press, Cambridge

Typeface TEFFLexicon 9/13 pt   *System* QuarkXPress®   [SE]

A catalogue record for this book is available from the British Library

ISBN 0 521 44482 9 hardback
ISBN 0 521 65628 1 paperback

To my parents

Contents

List of contributors

Angelika Bammer teaches at Emory University (Atlanta, Georgia, USA) in the Graduate Institute of Liberal Arts. Her research interests are reflected both in courses on history and fiction, nationalism, geographies of identity, feminist theory, gender and writing, and in publications on questions of gender and history, feminist theory, women writers, and women's film. She is the author of *Partial Visions: Feminism and Utopianism in the 1970s* (1991), and editor of *Displacements: Cultural Identities in Question* (1994). Current research projects include 'Ways of forgetting: issues of history, memory, and representation', 'Being German, or the ambivalence of attachment' – a project combining issues of nation, identity and the body within the context of modern Germany – and two collaborative projects on landscape and memory, and identifications and modernity.

Elizabeth Boa is Professor of German at the University of Nottingham. Her publications include *Critical Strategies: German Fiction in the Twentieth Century* (co-author J. H. Reid), *The Sexual Circus: Wedekind's Theatre of Subversion*, and *Kafka: Gender, Class and Race in the Letters and Fictions*. She has also written extensively on contemporary women's writing and edited, with Janet Wharton, the proceedings of the 1994 Women in German Studies Nottingham Conference on *Women and the Wende: Social Effects and Cultural Reflections of the German Unification Process* (1994).

Petra Boden is *Wissenschaftliche Miterarbeiterin* at the Zentrum für Literaturforschung, part of the Geisteswissenschaftliche Zentren Berlin. Her research interests include the academic history of the GDR, the history of socialist literature in Germany – particularly women's writing in the *Vormärz* period – and are reflected in articles in the *Lexikon Sozialistischer Literatur: Ihre Geschichte in Deutschland bis 1945* (ed. Simone Barck et al.; 1994) and in the books *Der Germanist Julius Petersen 1878–1941: Bibliographie, systematisches*

Nachlaßverzeichnis und Dokumentation (co-author Bernhard Fischer; 1994) and
*Atta Troll tanzt noch: Selbstbesichtigungen der literaturwissenschaftlichen Germanistik
im 20. Jahrhundert* (co-author Holger Dainat; 1997).

Agnès Cardinal was born and educated in Switzerland, studied in
England, and now teaches Comparative Literary Studies at the University of
Kent at Canterbury. Her publications include a book on Robert Walser and
articles on Swiss writers as well as on Irmtraud Morgner and Berta Lask. She
is currently working on French and German women's war literature and is co-
editor of the forthcoming *Oxford Anthology of Women's Writing on the First World
War*.

Jo Catling is Lecturer in German at the University of East Anglia,
Norwich. Her research interests in the field of gender and creativity include
German and European women's writing and translation, twentieth-century
German poetry (particularly Rilke), and women artists. These interests are
reflected in a number of articles on Rilke and women writers and artists, e.g.
in the *Jahrbuch der deutschen Schillergesellschaft*, *Blätter der Rilke-Gesellschaft*, and
Women Writers in the Age of Goethe series. Further publications include the
translation of Walter Haug, *Vernacular Literary Theory in the Middle Ages*
(1997).

Sonja Hilzinger is currently Visiting Professor at the Universities of
Mainz and Dortmund. Research interests include, as well as the
Enlightenment and realist novels, the literature of the Weimar Republic and
the GDR; exile literature; German-Jewish writing, modern German poetry
and gender studies. Books published include *'Als ganzer Mensch zu leben ...'
Emanzipatorische Tendenzen in der neueren Frauen-Literatur der DDR* (1985); *Christa
Wolf* (1986); *'Das siebte Kreuz' von Anna Seghers. Texte, Daten, Bilder* (ed.; 1990),
Anna Seghers: 'Die Heimkehr des verlorenen Volkes'. Ein Lesebuch (ed.; 1996);
*Anekdotisches Erzählen in Historiographie, Publizistik und Literatur des 18.
Jahrhunderts* (1997); *Anna Seghers* (1998).

Patricia Howe is Senior Lecturer in German at Queen Mary and
Westfield College, University of London, and specializes in nineteenth-
century literature, especially the narrative, on which she has published
widely.

Margaret C. Ives has recently retired as Reader in German Studies at
Lancaster University, where she was for many years also Head of Department.
After working on the medieval mystics, notably Mechthild von Magdeburg,
she returned to her original research interests in the Classical Age of German

literature and for ten years, starting in 1987, organized an annual Day School on Women Writers of the Age of Goethe, the proceedings of which have been published in a series of Occasional Papers. In collaboration with Professor A. J. Harper (Strathclyde University) she is author of the study *Sappho in the Shadows*, dealing mainly with women poets of the Goethe era.

Anna K. Kuhn is Professor of German and Women's Studies at the University of California, Davis. She has published a book on the dramatist Frank Wedekind; her book *Christa Wolf: From Marxism to Feminism*, published by Cambridge University Press, was the first English-language study of this important writer. Together with Barbara Wright, she recently co-edited a volume entitled *Playing for Stakes: German-Language Drama in Social Context*. She has also published essays on such topics as the New German Cinema film-makers Rainer Werner Fassbinder and Margarethe von Trotta, the politics of the *Wende*, GDR literature, and women's autobiographical writings. Her current fields of interest include feminist and gender theory, gender and nationhood, minority discourse, and German cultural studies.

Karen Leeder is Faculty Lecturer in German at the University of Oxford and Fellow and Tutor in German at New College, Oxford. She has published widely on modern German poetry and the poetic tradition, including most recently *Breaking Boundaries: A New Generation of Poets from the GDR* (1996) and the chapter 'Modern German Poetry' in the *Cambridge Companion to Modern German Culture* (ed. Eva Kolinsky and Wilfried van der Will; 1998).

Margaret Littler is Senior Lecturer in German at the University of Manchester and specializes in post-war women's writing and feminist theory. In addition to publications on Alfred Andersch, she is the editor of *Gendering German Studies: New Perspectives on German Literature and Culture* (1997) and has published widely on German women's writing since 1945.

Judith Purver is Senior Lecturer in German at the University of Manchester. Research specialisms include German Romanticism; the *Vormärz*; women's writing of the eighteenth and nineteenth centuries; and German cultural history with special reference to the reception of Romanticism, to literature and the theatre in Dresden, and to aspects of architectural restoration. Publications include *Hindeutung auf das Höhere: A Structural Study of the Novels of Joseph von Eichendorff* (1989) and numerous articles on the above areas and entries on Eichendorff in the *Literaturlexikon: Autoren und Werke deutscher Sprache* (ed. Walther Killy; 1989) and the *Deutsche Biographische Enzyklopädie* (ed. Walther Killy; 1996).

Lesley Sharpe is Professor of German at the University of Exeter and has published extensively on eighteenth-century German literature. Her most recent monographs are *Friedrich Schiller: Drama, Thought and Politics* (1991) and *Schiller's Aesthetic Essays: Two Centuries of Criticism* (1995). She is currently Germanic Editor of the *Modern Language Review*.

Ricarda Schmidt is Senior Research Fellow in German at the University of Manchester, where she works on post-1945 women writers from East and West Germany and Austria, literary theory, and E. T. A. Hoffmann, on which subjects she has published numerous articles, in addition to the book *Westdeutsche Frauenliteratur in den 70er Jahren* (2nd edn 1990).

Almut Suerbaum is Fellow and Tutor in German at Somerville College, Oxford. Her principal research interests and publications are in medieval German literature, especially fictional literature of the twelfth and thirteenth centuries.

Helen Watanabe-O'Kelly is a Fellow of Exeter College and Professor of German at the University of Oxford. She has published extensively on German literature and court culture, especially in the early modern period, and has also edited *The Cambridge History of German Literature* and (with Pierre Béhar) *Spectaculum Europaeum: Theatre and Spectacle in Europe 1580–1750 – a Handbook*.

Sabine Werner-Birkenbach studied Germanistik, art history and publishing in Mainz. Her doctoral dissertation, *Hugo Ball und Hermann Hesse – eine Freundschaft, die zur Literatur wird. Kommentare und Analysen zum Briefwechsel, zu autobiographischen Schriften und zu Balls Hesse-Biographie*, appeared in 1995. She has published numerous articles and reviews on twentieth-century women writers, including Emmy Hennings, Selma Meerbaum-Eisinger and Rose Ausländer. She is currently working as a freelance editor.

Chris Weedon is Reader in Critical and Cultural Theory at the University of Wales, Cardiff. She has published widely in the areas of women's writing, feminist theory, critical and cultural theory and cultural politics. Her books include *Feminist Practice and Poststructuralist Theory* (1987); *Cultural Politics: Class, Gender and the Postmodern World* (with Glenn Jordan; 1995); *Postwar Women's Writing in German* (1996) and *Feminism, Theory and the Politics of Difference* (1999).

Anthony Vivis is a freelance translator and writer based in Norwich. His translations of contemporary German plays, e.g. by Kroetz, Karge and

Sperr, have been widely performed on stage and screen. His version of Gerhart Hauptmann's *The Weavers* was performed at the Gate Theatre, London in 1996 and will shortly be published by Oberon, together with his translation of *The Rats*. He has co-translated poems by Sarah Kirsch (*The Brontës Hats*, 1991 and *T*, 1995, with Wendy Mulford) and by Rose Ausländer (*Mother Tongue*, 1995). Recent translations of contemporary drama by women include Elfriede Jelinek's *Clara S.: A Musical Tragedy* for the Goethe-Institut (also scheduled for publication by Oxford University Press in the forthcoming volume *Modern European Plays by Women*, ed. Alan Barr), and Gerlind Reinshagen's *Leben und Tod der Marilyn Monroe*.

Acknowledgements

This project came into being while I held the post of Research Fellow in Arts in the Department of German at the University of Durham. I am grateful to the University, and my colleagues there, for allowing me the time and space to establish the connections without which such a collaborative volume could not have been produced. In particular I should like to thank Professor Patrick Bridgwater, Waltraud Coles, Jo Tudor, and Catherine and Kevin Hilliard, not forgetting their son Sam, without whom we should never have met Eva Ibbotson. Among the many other friends and colleagues who helped to make my years in Durham 'eine kurze / Goldene Zeit beinah der Gerechtigkeit' (to quote Brecht) I am grateful to Lynne Pearce; Pat Waugh; and last but by no means least, Caroline Mason.

A special mention is due to WIGS (Women in German Studies), founded in 1988, without which this project would have been unimaginable, and which by its very existence has had a profound impact on German studies in the UK today; in particular I should like to thank Margaret Ives for her continued interest and support, and for the Day Schools in Women Writers of the Age of Goethe at the University of Lancaster, at one of which this project in its present collaborative form may be said to have been conceived; Helen Watanabe-O'Kelly, for supporting the idea and putting me in touch with Cambridge University Press; Patricia Howe and Ricarda Schmidt, for providing congenial spaces in London and Manchester for us to 'meet and talk' about the initial shape of the project; Elizabeth Boa, for continued enthusiasm and, when faced with the thankless task of providing a Postscript, for her willingness continually to update as we were overtaken by events in German-speaking countries – not least German reunification! I am grateful too to Joyce Crick and to Juliet Wigmore for their active and supportive interest in the project. The US-based WiG (Women in German) has also been an invaluable source of contacts and information; and I am grateful to Professor Linda Dietrick at the University of Winnipeg, Canada for her interest in the project, and especially for generously making available her list of works in English translation, not all of which were known or accessible to me in the UK.

I should further like to thank Eva Ibbotson of Newcastle, daughter of Anna Gmeyner and well-known author in her own right, for her spontaneous hospitality at our fortuitous meeting in Jesmond, for the books of *Exilliteratur*, and for putting me in touch with Lisette Buchholz of the Persona-Verlag and thus with Heike Klapdor-Kops, both of whom I should like to thank here for their interest and support. Thanks are also due to Beate Schmeichel-Falkenberg (whose acquaintance I owe to a similarly serendipitious meeting with her late mother); her active engagement in the field of *Exilliteratur* enabled her to put me in touch with Sonja Hilzinger, for whose swift response I remain extremely grateful.

In Norwich, I should like to acknowledge the assistance of the EUR Research Committee Special Travel Fund at the University of East Anglia for funding to attend the WiG Special Session in Potsdam and the opportunity this presented to meet like-minded American colleagues, and for supporting research trips to the Deutsches Literaturarchiv in Marbach and the Europäisches Übersetzer-Kollegium in Straelen. I should like to take this opportunity to thank Klaus Birkenhauer, Regina Peeters and Karin Heinz at the EÜK, and all the ever-helpful *MitarbeiterInnen* at the Deutsches Literaturarchiv – particularly Jutta Bendt for her interest in the project. Special thanks are also due to Sabine Werner-Birkenbach for all the *Frauengespräche* and her generous hospitality in Marbach on numerous occasions.

I am further grateful to the EUR Research Fund, and especially to the British Centre for Literary Translation at UEA, for financial support for the translation of the three German chapters in the book, and particularly to the translator Anthony Vivis for agreeing to undertake it, for his continued interest and support for the project as a whole, and his assistance in tracking down elusive translations (especially of contemporary drama) for the bibliography. Thanks are also due to the former and current directors of the BCLT, Terry Hale and Peter Bush, for information on recent English translations of German women's writing.

Less formally, I should like to thank my EUR colleagues Professors Max Sebald and Clive Scott, Keith Harvey, and Christine Wilson of the

BCLT for their encouragement and support during difficult times. I am also grateful to my students at UEA, particularly the Contemporary German Women's Writing class of 1996, for their consideration, understanding and enthusiasm during the later stages of the project. Thanks also to Serena Inskip for making springtime workspace and other home comforts available; Margot Paterson deserves a special mention here for her continuing support and interest as well as practical help.

I should also like to thank Camilla Ullmann (daughter of Regina Ullmann); Joachim W. Storck and Evelyn Grill; in Oxford Ray Ockenden, Richard Sheppard, and Jill Hughes of the Taylorian; Gene Rogers and Derek Krueger in the US; Liz Harvey, Margaret Dériaz, and all the other friends and colleagues who have been supportive and encouraging of this project during its many stages.

At Cambridge University Press, I am extremely grateful to Kate Brett and Linda Bree for their initial and continuing enthusiasm for the project, and especially for their patience and perseverance, as well as for their practical and editorial support and many valuable comments and suggestions.

The editor wishes to thank the Deutsches Literaturarchiv, Marbach for the cover picture and Prof. Dr. Alexander Böhm of Rockenberg, Germany for permission to use it.

Anna Kuhn would like to thank Azade Seyhan and, in particular, Heike Hofmann for the fruitful conversations that helped crystallize her thoughts about Turkish women's writings.

Karen Leeder and the editor are grateful to the Aufbau-Verlag for permission to reproduce the poem 'Unterm Schutt' in chapter 13, p. 206, from Inge Müller, *Irgendwo; noch einmal möcht ich sehn: Lyrik, Prosa, Tagebücher*, ed. Ines Geipel, Berlin: Aufbau, 1996.

Margaret Littler wishes to acknowledge the generous support of the DAAD for a grant in support of a visit to Germany for research on chapter 11.

Lesley Sharpe is grateful to the British Academy for awarding her a grant under their Small Grants in the Humanities scheme to enable the essential library work for chapter 3.

Chris Weedon wishes to acknowledge the generous support of the Alexander von Humboldt-Stiftung which enabled her to do the primary research and writing for chapter 7.

Finally, last but not least, the editor wishes to thank all the contributors to this volume for bearing with her – and each other – during the prolonged gestation of the book and the shifts in direction that this has sometimes entailed, and especially for the vast amount of scholarship and research – textual, bibliographical and biographical – each has contributed, not all of which could ultimately be included even in the ambitious scope of our 'Bio-bibliography', but which will, it is to be hoped, continue to bear fruit in many other projects on women's writing in Germany, Austria and Switzerland in the years to come.

J. M. Catling

Introduction

Die Frauen lebten lange, ohne zu schreiben,
dann begannen sie zu schreiben ...
mit ihrem Leben und um ihr Leben.

    CHRISTA WOLF (ed.), *Karoline von Günderrode: Der Schatten eines Traumes* (1981), p. 5

Women lived for a long time without writing; then they
began to write ... with their lives and for their lives.

A History of Women's Writing in Germany, Austria and Switzerland –
the title for this volume is at once both self-explanatory and controversial, ambitious yet necessarily modest in terms of what can be achieved
in the scope of one volume. It cannot of course claim to provide an
exhaustive analysis; where it breaks new ground for the English-speaking reader is in offering both an introduction to and an overview of the
whole field, from the medieval mystic setting down her visions in
Latin on the banks of the Rhine, to the immigrant writers of post-unification Germany and beyond, whose mother tongue may not necessarily be German, but Turkish or Czech. It is intended to appeal not
only to students and scholars of German literature, who I hope by now
no longer have to ask – as previous generations have done, contemplating their reading lists or library shelves – 'why are there no women
authors in German?' (sic), but also to a wider readership interested in
women's writing and gender studies wishing to inform themselves
about the diversity and development of writing by women in German-speaking countries. This definition, which formed part of the original
working title of the project, is intended to cover not only literature
from Austria and Switzerland, as well as the former GDR and West
Germany, but also writing by women from earlier periods when the

boundaries of the German-speaking world were very different from what they are today.

In the present volume, individual chapters are designed to dovetail in such a way as to provide a chronological overview of writing by women in the German-speaking world, divided into four broad chronological sections. The markers used, for reasons of convenience rather than ideology, as Elizabeth Boa discusses in the postscript to this volume, are landmarks familiar from more conventional German literary history. (This has the advantage of providing points of orientation, which coincide with classification systems in most humanities libraries, thus facilitating further research.)

As one of the purposes of this volume is to open up the field of women's writing in German for further research, an extensive – though necessarily select – bibliography of secondary and background works, and suggestions for further reading, has been provided by the contributors to accompany their chapters. Footnotes and references within individual chapters, meanwhile, have been kept to a minimum; all bibliographical material has been grouped together at the end of the volume. The bibliographies by subject and by chapter are followed by a 'bio-bibliography' of individual writers, arranged alphabetically rather than chronologically. This gives details of dates and principal works by individual writers, together with translations where available, and (where appropriate) references to secondary material; finally, the index provides the necessary cross-referencing.

The genesis of this volume may be traced back to a series of lectures I devised one summer term in Oxford in the late 1980s on 'German Women Authors'. This was in turn provoked by the notable, even glaring, absence of books by German women writers on the otherwise generously stocked shelves of the college libraries with which I was most familiar. Those eight introductory lectures (which rapidly developed into a participatory seminar), spanning the period from the Middle Ages to the present day, are present as a kind of ghost or palimpsest beneath the chronological layout of the present volume. Conversations with colleagues and contacts at conferences of the then recently founded Women in German Studies (WIGS) and at Margaret Ives's 'Women Writers of the Age of Goethe' Day Schools in Lancaster, and subsequently in the Deutsches Literaturarchiv in Marbach, and in the USA, created the initial concept of a collaborative and multi-perspective project, with contributors from Britain, the USA and Germany, both East and West. This project was code-named

'"Invisible Writing": German Women of Letters Through the Ages', a programmatic working title which has, happily, been superseded as women's writing has acquired a higher profile and greater visibility, both with its readers and within the academy. Things have changed, then, and for the better; the study of women's writing is now an accepted (if not established) part of the curriculum, feminist scholarship in English- and German-speaking countries has moved on apace, and women writers are no longer systematically overlooked in standard works of reference and literary history. In this context it is gratifying to note that both Helen Watanabe-O'Kelly's *Cambridge History of German Literature* and Eda Sagarra and Peter Skrine's *Companion to German Literature: From 1500 to the Present* include significant numbers of women writers, in stark contrast to earlier volumes of this kind; furthermore, the relevant volumes devoted to German literature in the *Dictionary of Literary Biography* also contain substantial entries on individual women writers.

Along the way, too, the Berlin Wall fell; the concept of Germany, and thus 'German literature', acquired a new dimension, and the book an extra chapter, reflecting the momentous historical changes and the 'elation and despair' (to use the original working title for that chapter) which German (re)unification has meant for women, and for women writers, particularly those from the former GDR.

While the title of the volume and indeed its constituency of contributors have undergone modification, the project has remained faithful to the original aim of providing an introduction to, and survey of, writing by women in German-speaking countries from the Middle Ages to the present day. Its purpose is twofold: firstly to give the lie to the idea – based on the necessarily restricted range of '*master*pieces' (sic) which tends to make up the canon of German literature studied outside German-speaking countries – that 'there are no German women authors', by examining the works of women writers who seem by definition to be 'little known'; and, secondly, to examine why this should be so. Was it the case, for example, that women in nineteenth-century Germany did not produce literary works (in contrast to their counterparts in, say, nineteenth-century England)? – or is there, rather, a problem of reception, so that the literary output is present, but has remained undiscovered or been deliberately ignored or suppressed?

A survey of writers such as the present one does not of itself necessarily imply a feminist approach: however, in setting out to answer these questions, any gender-orientated study inevitably touches on the issue of what

Toril Moi calls *Sexual/Textual Politics*. A number of German and American scholars, mostly (though not exclusively) women, for example Silvia Bovenschen, Gisela Brinker-Gabler, Inge Stephan and Sigrid Weigel, Barbara Becker-Cantarino, Ruth-Ellen Boetcher-Joeres, Elke Frederiksen (to name but a few), have been devoting themselves to these questions since the 1980s, establishing the basis for an alternative or parallel 'FrauenLiteraturGeschichte' (women('s) literature history) – to use the inevitable, and somewhat unwieldy, German compound which has arisen as a kind of shorthand for this activity. While there are some excellent compilations of specialist articles in German on women's writing through the ages, on both German and other literatures – notably Gisela Brinker-Gabler's admirable two-volume *Deutsche Literatur von Frauen* (1988) and Hiltrud Gnüg and Renate Möhrmann's *Frauen-Literatur-Geschichte* (1985) – there is no work which attempts a survey of all periods of German literature from this viewpoint in English at present.

The present volume does not seek to produce an alternative, feminist, canon, but rather – as the original project title suggests – to make visible German women of letters to a wider audience. In this spirit, it fleshes out the bare bones of the indispensable bibliographical tools now available, such as the *Lexikon deutschsprachiger Schriftstellerinnen 1800–1945* (edited by Gisela Brinker-Gabler, Karola Ludwig and Angela Wöffen) and Elke Frederiksen's *Bio-bibliographical Guide to Women Writers of Germany, Austria and Switzerland*. The present volume should provide a complement to existing anthologies of German women's writing in both German and English, such as Gisela Brinker-Gabler's pioneering 1978 anthology of German women's poetry, *Deutsche Dichterinnen vom 16. Jahrhundert bis zur Gegenwart* and Jeannine Blackwell and Susanne Zantop's *Bitter Healing*, which makes selected works of *German Women Writers 1700–1830* (its subtitle) available to an English-speaking readership, many for the first time. It is to be hoped that the general outline which this volume seeks to present will be filled out in due course by more detailed studies of particular periods, such as Chris Weedon's 1997 *Postwar Women's Writing in German*, or Margaret Ives and Tony Harper's volume on the eighteenth and nineteenth centuries, *Sappho in the Shadows*, as well as by volumes with a more European or comparative perspective, such as Helena Forsås-Scott's *Textual Liberation*.

The term 'FrauenLiteraturGeschichte', like the title of this volume, raises the question of history. While the use made of historical landmarks and epochs of conventional literary history as a kind of guiding thread running through this volume might suggest otherwise, in fact, inasmuch as the concept of history is taken to mean a continuous narrative of development, or diachronic progress, the 'history of women's writing' cannot be said to be a history at all. As Elizabeth Boa notes in the Postscript, the attempt to compile a history of women's writing is more like the 'criss-cross work of darning', or the making of a patchwork quilt (as Elaine Showalter notes in a different context) than the spinning of a continuous thread. Any 'development', if this term applies at all, proceeds by fits and starts. Tracing a history of women's writing is, then, an enterprise of continual recovery, of teasing out threads or picking up pieces, a work of making and mending: at all events, a slow and laborious process seemingly undertaken by each age afresh, sometimes, though not always, accompanying significant historical or political developments. Thus, for example, the plethora of anthologies of women's writing in the early years of the twentieth century may be explained by the growing awareness of 'the woman question' which precedes and accompanies the women's suffrage movements. In similar vein, what would in earlier ages no doubt have been referred to as the flowering of women's writing in recent decades has its origins in the emancipatory women's movements from the 1970s onwards. The struggle to find a voice of their own (it is no accident that the German for voice, *Stimme*, also means vote) is evoked in the title of Barbara Becker-Cantarino's investigation of the development of women's literature – and literacy – between 1500 and 1800, *Der lange Weg zur Mündigkeit* (The long road: coming of age), where *Mündigkeit* (the age of majority) appears to be cognate with *Mund*, meaning 'mouth'.

The foundations for the reclamation or perhaps reconstruction of a female literary tradition have, however, been laid by German women writers themselves. As an illustration of this, it may be worth tracing briefly here one example, that which gives rise to the epigraph by Christa Wolf above: Karoline von Günderrode. Born in Karlsruhe in 1780, she published a number of poems and dramas under a male pseudonym – Tian – before committing suicide in Winkel am Rhein in 1806. Part of the loose grouping of Romantic writers, including the Arnims and Brentanos, she was engaged in a correspondence with her friend Bettine Brentano (better known after her marriage to a fellow writer as Bettina von Arnim), which Bettine used as the basis for her epistolary biographical novel *Die Günderode*. The letter form, which she also used for her similarly fictionalized *Briefbiographien* of Goethe (whom she almost literally worshipped as a young woman) and of her brother, the poet Clemens Brentano, is a genre which she virtually inherited from her grandmother Sophie von La Roche, a 'founding mother' of the novel in Germany. Her *Die Geschichte des Fräuleins von Sternheim* (*The History of Lady Sophia Sternheim*) pre-dates – and had a major influence on – Goethe's *Die Leiden des jungen Werther* (*The Sorrows of Young Werther*) as an epistolary novel in the Richardson style.

If Bettine, with all the advantages that coming from a literary family meant for an aspiring woman writer, played a large part in rescuing the work of her less fortunate, though arguably more talented, friend Günderrode from an undeserved oblivion, it is to the scholarly enterprises of a later generation of writers from the GDR that we owe, at least in part, the current reputation of that generation of Romantic writers. Christa Wolf, together with her husband Gerhard, has edited works by, and written about, Bettine, Günderrode and others; an essay on Bettine, 'Nun ja! Das nächste Leben geht aber heute an', accompanies a 1983 Insel reissue of *Die Günderode*, and this is preceded by her own work of compiling and editing a volume of Karoline von Günderrode's works, *Der Schatten eines Traumes* (1979). This volume is prefaced by an essay with the same evocative title ('the shadow of a dream'), from which the epigraph above is quoted. Wolf's interest in this constellation of Romantic poets, who have been compared with the Bloomsbury group in the complexity of their interrelationships, although the Lake poets might provide a more contemporary comparison, is also reflected directly in her own 1979 narrative, *Kein Ort Nirgends* (*No Place on Earth*). She in turn cites the older GDR writer Anna Seghers's mentioning of Günderrode in letters as a source of her own fascination with this era. Nor is such interest in women writers of an earlier generation an isolated example; further instances are Sigrid Damm's recent biographical novels, or Sarah Kirsch and Elke Erb's editions of Annette von Droste-Hülshoff in 1986 and 1989 respectively. Kirsch indeed goes further, weaving into her own poetry references to her literary antecedents: Bettina von Arnim, 'die Droste' and even the Brontë sisters, giving rise to the title of a volume of English translations of her poems, *The Brontës Hats*.

The work of reclamation and recovery, and the conscious establishing of a 'weibliche (= female) Tradition', is thus nothing new. Nevertheless, the examples of Bettine and Günderrode raise a number of points about gender, genre and literary recognition, or 'finding a voice'.

One problem facing women writers until very recently was the difficulty of being recognized – and thus of being published – in their own right, or indeed under their own name: like Karoline von Günderrode, or indeed George Eliot and George Sand, many took refuge behind a male pseudonym. There are two interrelated problems here: finding a voice, and finding an appropriate literary form in which to express it. The relatively restricted, narrowly circumscribed social roles women 'enjoyed' for much of the time-span covered by this volume makes the notion of self-expression, taken for granted by writers today, somewhat ambivalent. For long periods of history, women were not expected – or indeed allowed – to participate in the public sphere, so that the whole notion of 'publication', presenting oneself to a literary (or literal) audience, becomes fraught with ambiguity.

There is, then, a question of genre, as well as of gender, to be addressed here. The most 'public' of the three traditional literary genres – epic, lyric and dramatic – is the drama, a form which has traditionally dominated the German literary canon from the mid-eighteenth to the close of the nineteenth century. It will come as no surprise, then, that drama is the hardest sphere for women to penetrate, and, as a number of the contributors to this volume have pointed out, it is the sphere in which the smallest number of women have been active as writers, with fewer still achieving lasting recognition.

Traditionally, women's sphere has been seen as the private or domestic one, and accordingly, women writers are seen to fare better in prose fiction, which in nineteenth-century English literature becomes almost a female prerogative, and which gives much more scope to the depiction of a 'private sphere'. In the 'Age of Goethe' (an epithet which speaks volumes!), as we have seen, Sophie La Roche and Bettine Brentano achieve a certain prominence in this genre; however, the form the novel takes on in Bettine's hands, with its quasi-autobiographical diary- and letter-like outpourings, is perhaps indicative of where the women of the Romantic generations, at least, found their true medium. It is in the intimate yet practical sphere of this *Briefkultur* (letter-writing culture) that German women writers of the 'modern' era first achieve a form of eminence, communicating without primary thought of publication, and yet writing for a select readership of like-minded individuals. The epistolary form, then, gives scope for blending autobiography with philosophy, conversation with criticism, and allows for a variety of perspectives to be presented via an 'invisible' narrator: it is small wonder that it proved such a popular form among women novelists of the eighteenth and early nineteenth century.

The most intimate genre of all, of course, is generally considered to be lyric poetry, although as an essentially personal genre, it is also arguably the most difficult in which to achieve recognition. Indeed, almost the only woman writer represented in the canon – Annette von Droste-Hülshoff (1797–1848), or 'die Droste', as she is affectionately but perhaps patronisingly known – typically owes her position to a short story rather than to her main activity, poetry.

One may conjecture that, given the obstacles they encounter and the disincentives to seeking publicity, women writers through the ages have tended to favour more intimate forms and less traditional genres, such as letters and diaries, fragmentary or more 'open' forms, which may be seen as indicative of a (subconscious) unease with the prevailing traditional genres of their age. On the one hand, such unconscious unconventionality may go some way towards accounting for the lack of recognition experienced by many writers – male as well as female – who find themselves excluded or marginalized by the dominant cultural code; on the other hand, however, such cutting across the boundaries of traditional genres may be seen as an opportunity for opening up new, less formal possibilities of expression, some of which may only now be bearing fruit.

In attempting to explain the apparent dearth of women authors in the German literary canon, then, we find ourselves somewhat in the position of Virginia Woolf contemplating women and fiction in *A Room of One's Own*, inevitably led beyond a merely literary evaluation of well-known works to an inquiry into the social and historical circumstances governing the production and reception, and thus the 'visibility' or otherwise, of women's writing. Furthermore, the role of patriarchal culture in the suppression or ignoring of women's writing, together with the limited opportunities open to women, is now more widely acknowledged than has often been the case in the past, and is perhaps also more readily articulated by women writers themselves, as the superficially light-hearted example below demonstrates.

In these introductory remarks I have tried to draw attention to some of the obstacles which the women writers whose works will be discussed in this volume have faced, and – to the extent that their works are available for us to read today – overcome. By way of illustration, and in answer to the question which formed the starting point for this project, we may quote the Jewish writer Mascha Kaléko. Writing in American exile in the mid-twentieth century, she comments on the problem of *Die Leistungen der Frau in der Kultur* (women's cultural achievements) thus:

Zu deutsch: 'Die klägliche Leistung der Frau'.
Meine Herren, wir sind im Bilde.
Nun, Wagner hatte seine Cosima
Und Heine seine Mathilde.
Die Herren vom Fach haben allemal
Einen vorwiegend weiblichen Schatz
Was uns Frauen fehlt, ist 'Des Künstlers Frau'
Oder gleichwertiger Ersatz.

(KALÉKO, In meinen Träumen läutet es Sturm, 1981, p. 96)

I.e.: 'A woman's pitiful contribution'.
Yes, gentlemen, we're in the picture.
Well now, Wagner had his Cosima
And Heine his Mathilde.
All professional men can call upon
A mainly female helpmate
We women, though, have no 'artist's wife'
Or any substitute of equal weight.

(translated by Anthony Vivis)

That this is not a new problem, or one which has entirely disappeared, should emerge as one of the recurring and unifying threads in the 'patchwork quilt' of the varied and multifaceted history of women's writing in German-speaking countries from the Middle Ages to the present day which this volume seeks to present.

Note on translations

As this book is aimed not just at *GermanistInnen* but at non-readers of German, care has been taken to include translations wherever possible. However, the 'making visible' of translations is a task even more complex than the uncovering of 'invisible writing', and as translation is both a continuous and a continual enterprise, some omissions are inevitable. The practice followed in this volume is to provide a translation of every German term or title mentioned in the text. Where a work has been translated into English, this is denoted by italicization of the translated title (in the case of poems and short stories, where a title would not normally be italicized, it is shown by the use of inverted commas and upper case). Where no translation is available, an English equivalent is given, in lower case and without inverted commas.

As far as possible, details of available translations are listed in the bibliography under the entry for the writer in question. It must be stressed, however, that this cannot claim to be comprehensive; there is a likelihood that some translations (particularly those published in the United States) will have slipped through the net.

All translations of quotations in the text are by the author of that chapter, or, in rare cases, by the editor, except where otherwise stated.

Beginnings to 1700

MARGARET IVES *and*
ALMUT SUERBAUM

1

The Middle Ages

According to Katharina M. Wilson in her excellent anthology *Medieval Women Writers*, for both men and women in the Middle Ages several conditions had to be fulfilled before literary productivity could take place. These included at least a certain level of education, leisure, access to the materials necessary for writing, patronage or other means of financial independence, and – true for writers in every century – something to communicate. 'For women writers', continues Wilson, 'an added pre-requisite often entails the freedom from childbearing and repeated pregnancies' (Wilson, p. ix). It is not therefore surprising that many of the earliest achievements by women of letters in German-speaking countries, whether in Latin or the vernacular, should spring from the ambience of the cloister. In the convents of the religious orders girls were taught to read the Psalter and to copy passages from the Bible, both of which presupposed instruction in Latin. In the seclusion of her cell or during the silences of the daily office a nun would have ample time to reflect on her own life and the mysteries of religion and, with a little encouragement, might indeed begin to write.

In some cases, the convents produced highly trained female scribes, some of whom emerge as rather striking personalities. One of the earliest known female scribes who copied a book of Latin sermons in the second half of the twelfth century, known as the *Guda-Homiliar* (now held in Frankfurt) identifies herself in a rubric: 'Guda, peccatrix mulier, scripsit et pinxit hunc librum' (Guda, a sinful woman, wrote and illuminated this book). Despite the self-deprecating humility, this is a confident statement at a time when most scribes, whether women or men, remained anonymous; Guda is clearly aware of the importance and value of her work, and adds a picture of herself in the illuminated initial D – one of the earliest self-portraits of an artist.

A similar tribute to such an achievement, this time by a contemporary, is paid to Gisela von Kerssenbrock, a Cistercian nun from Rulle in Northern Germany, who must have spent years of her life producing a lavishly illustrated gradual, now commonly known as *Codex Gisle* in recognition of her achievement. On the first folio, one of her contemporaries noted shortly after her death:

> Istud egregium librum scripsit, illuminavit,
> notavit, impaginavit, aureis litteris et
> pulchris imaginibus decoravit venerabilis
> ac devota virgo Gysela de Kerzenbroeck in sui memoriam
> Anno Mccc cuius anima requiescat in sancta pace.
> Amen.

> The venerable and pious Gisela of Kerssenbrock wrote,
> illuminated, annotated, paginated this excellent book
> and decorated it with gold letters and beautiful
> pictures, so that she might be remembered. AD 1300.
> May her soul rest in holy peace. Amen.

Not only this note but also the illuminations testify to the self-confidence of the nun who trusted she would be remembered by her own work: on the pages for Christmas and Easter, the two most important feast days and therefore the most lavishly decorated, she inserts the figures of kneeling nuns, one of whom is clearly identified in a rubric as 'Gisle'.

Gisela of Kerssenbrock and Guda are thus examples of women with sufficient education to be able to produce Latin liturgical manuscripts, but despite the high degree of literacy shown here, women did not normally have access to Latin learned traditions, which were the prerogative of the monasteries and hence equally inaccessible to most lay men. Nevertheless, there are female writers who defy the general trend.

The significance of Latin and a knowledge of the classical canon can be seen in the work of Hrotsvit (also known as Roswitha) von Gandersheim, who has the distinction of being the first known Christian dramatist. Probably born in the fourth decade of the tenth century, she was a Saxon of noble lineage who entered the religious life at an early age and became a canoness of the abbey of Gandersheim in the Harz mountains. Here she also became acquainted with the works of Horace, Ovid, Statius, Lucan, Boethius, Terence and Virgil as well as with the early Christian Fathers and the Vulgate. Then – following, as she tells us, an inner compulsion which she perceived to be a gift of God – she too sought to express herself in Latin, the language of liturgy, learning and culture, and wrote some eight legends, six plays, two epics and a short poem, all of them inspired by her Christian faith and sense of mission. Her two epics depict Otto the Great (912–73) as an exemplary Christian ruler and his queens Edith and Adelheid as embodiments of Christian virtue. Although she describes herself as a weak woman of little scholarship, she is in all probability adopting here again the traditional medieval modesty topos in such utterances, since her material is wide-ranging and possesses a self-confident authority.

The entry for Hrotsvit in the *Oxford Companion to German Literature* (p. 732, under the alternative version of her name, Roswitha) lists her as the author of six Latin plays 'intended as a Christian substitute for the comedies of Terence'. This statement needs elucidation. In one very important aspect these plays – *Gallicanus, Dulcitius, Callimachus, Abraham, Pafnutius* and *Sapientia* – can all be regarded as anti-Terentian tirades, not so much in style and structure as in content and message. Hrotsvit was incensed by the portrayal of women by the Latin dramatist as lewd, lascivious creatures forever seeking the attention of men and certainly no strangers to seduction. Her aim, as she tells us in a preface, is to establish a counter-model, that of the chaste Christian virgin, who can withstand all temptation, preferring martyrdom to the sacrifice of her integrity. Thus, in *Dulcitius*, three Christian maidens – Agape, Chionia, and Irene – refuse to honour pagan gods at the request of the Emperor Diocletian and foil the advances of their torturer, Dulcitius, who consequently has them put to death. In *Callimachus*, Drusiana, a respectable married lady, prays for death when confronted by the lustful Callimachus, and her wish is immediately granted. In *Abraham* and *Pafnutius* the theme is varied slightly. Abraham here is not the Biblical patriarch, but a hermit who has brought up a niece, Maria, in the silence and solitude of the desert. Nevertheless, when temptation comes her way, she is deceived and dishonoured and becomes a prostitute. Having tracked her down to a brothel, Abraham dons a disguise and seeks to win her back, asserting that God's grace and mercy are open to all who genuinely repent. In *Pafnutius* two harlots are similarly reclaimed for God by two saintly male anchorites. Christian women, then, should aspire to be pure vessels for the reception of the Holy Spirit after the example of the Blessed Virgin, but – failing that – can draw solace from the story of Mary Magdalene, do penance and find salvation.

It must be emphasized that, for Hrotsvit, the figures of Mary and the reformed Mary Magdalene genuinely represented a higher concept of womanhood. This in itself was not so startlingly original, since Jerome (342–420) had influenced much medieval thinking with his well-known condemnation of women as daughters of Eve, and his famous dictum 'mors per Evam, vita per Mariam' was understood, when applied to women, to mean that through vows of chastity and abstinence they could indeed redeem their fallen nature. What is particularly striking about Hrotsvit's work is the assurance with which she proclaims that women have undeservedly been cast in the role of sinners, their natural inclination being to value integrity in both the physical and moral sense. Although in *Abraham* and *Pafnutius* it is acknowledged that men, too, can be chaste, in other plays the male characters are depicted as being at the mercy of their carnal appetites. Dulcitius is so ablaze with passion that, attempting to enter the prison of the virtuous Christian sisters after nightfall, he mistakenly embraces pots, pans and culinary utensils and becomes covered in dirt and grime. Even worse, Callimachus plans to violate the tomb of Drusiana, although – of course – he is prevented from doing so. Elsewhere in Hrotsvit's dramas it is the women who transform their would-be seducers and convert them into true Christians. A good example is *Gallicanus*, where the eponymous pagan general is inspired by Constantia, daughter of the Emperor Constantine, to give up his hopes of marrying her and, like her, adopt a vow of chastity. All this may not appeal greatly to modern tastes, but it has to be seen in the context of its time as a powerful campaign for the enhancement of the status of women.

Such a campaign was not without its dangers. Hrotsvit tells us that she sometimes had to blush with shame because, in the course of her dramatic dialogues, she occasionally had to depict the distasteful passions of forbidden love and reproduce unseemly conversations. The hint of necrophilia in *Callimachus* is a case in point; there are also lines in *Abraham* that speak of the desire of an old man for a young woman, while in *Dulcitius* there are vivid descriptions of the hapless man's encounter with the kettle!

From an inserted introductory letter to her benefactors it is evident that Hrotsvit only completed this collection of plays after she had gained the express approval of her mentors, who praised and encouraged her. Since there was no established theatre in the tenth century, her plays were probably not performed. That even these moves towards Christian drama were, however, highly controversial is highlighted by remarks included in the *Hortus deliciarum* (Garden of delights) by Herrad of Hohenburg in

the late twelfth century. A compendium of reading matter for the education of nuns, compiled by the abbess of a convent in Alsace and famous for
the way in which it integrates text, illustration and musical notation into
an overall programme of the essentials of Christian doctrine as well as for
the many minute details of everyday life contained within its structure, it
voices strong reservations against the introduction of religious drama on
the grounds that there is potential here for liturgical seriousness to
degenerate into frivolous play.

Nevertheless, Hrotsvit may justifiably be seen as a pioneer of German
drama. Her works were rediscovered in 1501 by the humanist Conrad
Celtis, and it is interesting that her two major themes – the woman who
cannot be forced to surrender her integrity, and the penitent who finds
salvation – foreshadow well-known classical works, such as Lessing's
'domestic tragedy' *Emilia Galotti* (1772) and the 'Gretchen tragedy' of
Goethe's *Faust*. Her own memory lives on in contemporary drama in Peter
Hacks's re-interpretation of her comedies, *Rosie träumt* (1975). She went on
to compose a short history of the convent of Gandersheim, where she had
spent most of her life, and a life of Emperor Otto I. This piece of commissioned official biography shows most clearly the esteem in which she
must by then have been held, and in dealing with contemporary matters,
Hrotsvit had to rely on her own individuality as a writer – an existence
which, despite all acknowledged difficulties, she clearly enjoyed.

The distinction of being the first woman to write in German whose
name has come down to us belongs to 'Frau Ava'; in an epilogue to her
writings, she reveals that she is the mother of two sons, one of whom had
predeceased her. She may be identical with the highly respected ancho-
ress Ava whose death in 1127 is recorded in the annals of the monastery at
Melk. If so, this is another example of a woman for whom the seclusion of
the religious life offered the freedom to write, although the epilogue also
stresses the encouragement and advice received from her sons. Her
oeuvre, written for a lay audience interested in devotional reading, but
unable to do so in Latin, consists of a group of five narrative poems which
together form a history of human salvation through time. She begins
with the life of St John the Baptist, the precursor of Christ, moves on to a
vividly narrated life of Christ, and concludes – in short poems on the
seven gifts of the Holy Spirit, the Anti-Christ and the Last Judgement –
with a vista of the end of the world and the possibility of salvation. The
centrepiece, the life of Christ, is based mainly on the accounts of the Gospels as they would have been read out in church during the year, but Ava's

narrative has certain distinctive characteristics; she focuses, with obvious interest, on the female figures, selecting the Biblical stories of Christ's encounters with women in preference to other episodes. Her narrative style is vivid, especially when she describes gestures and settings, giving us the first German account of the ox and ass surrounding the manger in the Nativity scene. At times, the way in which she evokes images appears reminiscent of religious drama.

In an Age of Faith such as the Middle Ages, the claim that one had a God-given talent to depict the lives of the saints and martyrs or to proclaim the Gospel had to be respected. Similarly, a woman who claimed to be inspired by the Holy Spirit could not be dismissed out of hand, even if her revelations challenged traditional notions. An outstanding example of such inspiration is Hildegard von Bingen (1098–1179), sometimes known as the 'Sibyl of the Rhine'. Of noble birth, she reports in an autobiographical fragment that she experienced her first visions at the age of three and, clearly a gifted child, she was placed by her parents at the age of eight in a convent of the Benedictine order where she received her education. In 1136 she was unanimously chosen as Mother Superior and some five years later, in 1141, took the decisive step of revealing her prophetic insights to the world. A voice told her to write down what she had seen in her visions: she was reluctant at first to do so, but then fell into a debilitating illness, from which she only recovered when she resolved to follow her inner compulsion. Employing a scholarly monk to help her with Latin grammar, she began work on her first book *Scivias* (Know the ways), and during a visit of Pope Eugene to Trier sent him some extracts from the manuscript, which obtained his blessing. Armed with this authority, she completed *Scivias*, which she divided into three parts, the first containing visions of God the Father as creator of the universe, the second concentrating on Christ and His message of salvation, and the third – on the analogy of the Trinity – focusing on the power of the Holy Spirit to shape and transform our lives. After this Hildegard went from strength to strength. Her second great religious work, the *Liber vitae meritorum* (Book of life's merits), was finished between 1158 and 1163 and is a treatise on the Christian virtues in contrast to worldly sins and vices. The *Liber divinorum operum* (Book of divine works), compiled between 1163 and 1173, is, on the other hand, a mystic insight into the nature of the Universe, in which the fully harmonious human being, the crown of God's creation, draws strength from the natural world which, in turn, is spiritualized and lifted back to God. Her interest in plants and animals, coupled with her keen powers of observation, also enabled her to produce two scientific manuals, the first, *Physica* (Physics), being a handbook on nature, while the second and better-known *Causae et Curae* (Causes and cures), a textbook on medicine, contributed to her reputation as a physician and healer. Recognized in her own lifetime as a person of great spirituality and wisdom, she did not hesitate to comment on contemporary events or to rebuke kings and princes. According to Hozeski, in the preface to his English translation of *Scivias*, Hildegard foresaw 'that the abuse of political power and the corrupt government of the episcopal electors and princely abbots was exasperating the Germans and that the volatile situation would eventually burst into flames such as the Reformation or the Thirty Years War' (Hozeski, p. xxx). Hozeski also quotes the opinion of the Dominican theologian Matthew Fox that, had she been a man, Hildegard would have been one of the most famous people in the history of humanity.

Be that as it may, *Scivias* certainly has the authoritative tone of a new Revelation. The visions are followed by detailed commentaries: the finale is apocalyptic in its prophecy. At the end of the world, according to Hildegard, the elements will be destroyed: 'fire will burst forth, the air will be dissolved, water will pour forth, the land will shake, flashes of lightning will seethe, claps of thunder will clash loudly, mountains will be torn asunder, forests will fall down, and whatever is mortal in the air or in the water or on the land will give back its life' (Hozeski, p. 367). For all their force and power, however, Hildegard maintains that she received her messages not in a state of ecstasy, but from a deep source within her soul. As she writes in a famous letter, 'I do not hear these things with my external ears; nor do I perceive them by the thoughts of my heart, nor by any combination of my five senses – but rather in my soul, with my external eyes open, so that I have never suffered the weakness of ecstasy in them, but alertly see them by day and by night' (Wilson, p. 123). In this she differed from other religious women who, particularly in the following century, experienced in dreams or trance-like states what they describe as a rapturous union with Divine Love.

Foremost among these ecstatic visionaries writing in Germany is Mechthild von Magdeburg, who was probably born sometime between 1207 and 1212 and who died at Helfta in 1282. Unlike Hildegard, she was not formally professed as a member of a religious order, but settled in Magdeburg as a beguine, and wrote not in Latin, but in the vernacular. Her sole work, *Das fließende Licht der Gottheit* (*Flowing Light of the Divinity*), is an extraordinary collection of poems, prayers, aphorisms and dialogues between the soul and her Divine Lover. Mechthild, too, writes out of a profound conviction that God Himself had chosen her as a new apostle. In answer to a monk who expressed astonishment at her audacity, she asked him if he could explain 'how it came about that the apostles themselves, who were at first so timid and afraid, grew to be so bold after they had received the Holy Spirit'. Like Hildegard, she claims that she was commanded to write her book. It is not, however, an easy book to follow. It has, she says, to be read at least nine times, and always with due reverence and humility. Its central message is that it is natural for the soul to crave God, but God Himself also craves the human soul, and in the highest states of ecstasy a mystic union becomes possible. In such states, she writes, 'eye shines to eye, spirit flows to spirit, hand seeks hand, mouth seeks mouth, and one heart greets another'. God's love for the soul is indeed overwhelming, and Mechthild struggles to find adequate images. Thus, as her title suggests, God is an ever-flowing radiance, an ever-buoyant flood-tide, the Divine illuminates the soul as sunlight shining upon gold or water, the Divine music is a music to which all hearts must dance. This is, even for its time, bold and unconventional language, and it offended a good many people. Mechthild's passionate evocation of the Divine courtship led to accusations of obscenity, and towards the end of her life she was obliged to seek refuge in the Cistercian convent at Helfta, where she found other mystics of a similar persuasion. Her work, originally written in Low German, was later translated into Middle High German by Heinrich von Nördlingen and in this form was undoubtedly known to both Margarete and Christine Ebner (see p. 23 below).

Different though these two remarkable women were, Hildegard and Mechthild do share certain features. Like Hrotsvit, both denigrate their authorship. Hildegard tells us that she is 'a poor little female' and Mechthild often describes herself as 'a sinful woman' who is ashamed that she cannot find better words to express heavenly splendours. There may, however, be subtle irony at work here. By conceding their weakness, both women acknowledge the structure of the patriarchal society in which they lived, while at the same time evoking scriptural sanction for their activities. It is precisely because, as women, they are of low degree and thus more humble and obedient that the Holy Spirit has deigned to reveal to them new ways of truth and love. Both could cite here the words of the Magnificat (Luke 1: 46–55), and as Barbara Newman has pointed out in her excellent study on Hildegard, *Sister of Wisdom* (1987), Mary the Mother of God occupies a central place in Hildegard's theology. Versed as she was in liturgy and Church tradition, Hildegard seems to have seen some of the topoi of theological debate not as abstract concepts, but as larger-than-life allegorical figures, many of them female. Sapientia (Wisdom), Caritas (Divine Love) and Ecclesia (the Church) are all personified in her writings, and all are grouped round the pivotal figure of Mary, by whom 'the Word became flesh and dwelt among us, full of grace and truth' (John 1: 14). It is through the purity, humility and obedience of Mary that the Incarnation, and hence the Redemption, is possible. Following on from this it is only through a feminine response to the Divine Nature that Creation itself comes into being. Hence Sapientia is identified with the great creative force flowing throughout the universe which gives birth to all things; Caritas is depicted as a female figure responsive to God and, like Ecclesia, often pregnant with generations to come; and all three, together with Mary, can be taken as what Newman calls 'cosmic theophanies of the feminine; and the purpose of the feminine is to manifest God in the world' (Newman, p. 160).

If Hildegard thus draws the attention of her contemporaries to the feminine principle inherent in the Divine mystery, Mechthild von Magdeburg personalizes it in the account of her own relationship with God. Her God is no stern authoritarian, sitting in judgement. He is, rather, an ardent wooer of the human soul, delighted if the latter reciprocates his feelings. As one of Mechthild's poems expresses it, 'You (i.e. the soul) are a light before my eyes, a harp to my ears.' Or again, the soul is said by God to 'taste like the grape, to have the fragrance of balm, to shine like the sun' and to be 'the rose on the thornbush'. Yet not all human souls surrender to these endearments. Indeed, only the truly humble can be truly receptive, and these are much more likely to be women rather than men. Mechthild is often quite emphatic that it is difficult for men *per se* to find God. 'Alas!' she laments in one of her frequent outbursts 'here is one thing that many a man of excellent education and clever natural talent finds impossible, and that is to dare to surrender himself to the power of naked Divine Love. . .'

Although subsequently canonized by the Church, it is easy to see why Hildegard, Mechthild and other women mystics provoked so much controversy. Both Hildegard and Mechthild speak out very strongly against the male-dominated Church establishment of their day, which they condemn as corrupt and anti-Christian. One of Hildegard's most terrifying visions concerns 'a woman of such exquisite sweetness and of such rare and delightful beauty that the human mind could by no means comprehend it'.

This is Ecclesia, who is dressed 'in a shining robe of white silk and wrapped in a mantle trimmed with the most precious gems – emerald, sapphire and pearls . . . Yet her face was spattered with dust and her robe torn . . . her mantle had lost its elegance, and her shoes were blackened with mud.' In her anguish and distress Ecclesia complains that she has been betrayed by 'my foster-fathers – the priests! – they who should have made me beautiful in every part have despoiled me in all!' (Newman, p. 241). Mechthild is no less extreme. 'Alas! Crown of Holy Church, how tarnished you have become! Your precious stones have fallen from you because you are weak and you disgrace the holy Christian faith. Your gold is sullied in the filth of unchastity, for you have become destitute and do not know true love . . . Whoever does not know the way to hell, let him behold the depraved priesthood, how its path goes straight to hell with women and children and other public sins' (Wilson, p. 170).

Another vivid source of controversy is the explicit sexual language. It may well be that medieval times were not as prudish or as squeamish as our own. Hildegard, in her medical treatises, writes quite openly about menstruation and other gynaecological topics, although admittedly in Latin. Yet her vision of Ecclesia assaulted by Antichrist, again in Latin, verges on the pornographic. 'That feminine figure which I had formerly seen before the altar in the sight of God now appeared to me again, so that this time I could see her below the navel as well. For from her navel down to the place where a woman's sex is recognized, she had variegated scaly patches, and in place of her privy parts there appeared a monstrous black head with fiery eyes, asses' ears, and the nose and mouth of a lion gaping wide, horribly gnashing and sharpening its terrible iron teeth' (Newman, p. 245). Nevertheless, given the traditions of medieval iconography, this is probably less difficult to take than Mechthild's erotic descriptions of divine love-play. 'For He then steals away with her to a secret place . . . for He wishes to play games with her, games that the body does not understand, nor the peasant at his plough, nor the knight at his tournament, nor even his loving mother Mary. And after this ecstasy the soul sighs with all her might, so that the whole body is shaken.'

Neither Hildegard nor Mechthild is an isolated example. A book of visions by Hildegard's contemporary and fellow Benedictine Elisabeth von Schönau extols Mary as a paradigm for all Christians, even portraying her at one point as a priest at the altar. Elisabeth also wrote a life of St Ursula which contributed to the widespread veneration of that saint in the Cologne area. In the convent of Helfta, as already mentioned, Gertrud von Helfta, Gertrud von Hackeborn, and Mechthild von Hackeborn all wrote treatises on the religious life, stressing in particular the virtues of obedience and humility and initiating the adoration of the Sacred Heart as a special form of Christian devotion. All these works are in Latin. A little later, at Engelthal, the Dominican nun Christine Ebner recorded the lives and mystical visions of her sister nuns in a German work, *Von der Gnaden Überlast* (On the over-abundance of grace), while at the abbey of Medingen, near Donauwörth, Margarete Ebner – no relation of the former – corresponded with the priest Heinrich von Nördlingen on spiritual matters, and, through him, became very influential among the *Gottesfreunde* (friends of God), a religious community with adherents in Strasbourg and Basel. From all this it can be seen that women made a very substantial contribution to religious thought and practice during the medieval period and in doing so explored many forms of literary expression. History, biography, theology and medicine are among the scholarly topics covered by their works, while the prophetic visions and rhapsodic flights of the soul towards Heaven, whatever their cause or origin, resulted in devotional poetry and meditation of outstanding beauty and eloquence. Yet, as the Age of Faith receded, much was overlooked or forgotten. Even today, their views are not always regarded as acceptable. The attempt, from Hildegard onwards, to work out a theology of the feminine which sees certain aspects of the great drama of Creator and Creation as essentially female is still regarded in some circles as verging on heresy or even blasphemy. Nevertheless, its presence as an underground current in German mysticism, literature and thought cannot be questioned. When, at the end of *Faust II*, Goethe evokes 'das Ewig-Weibliche' (the Eternal Feminine) he is again acknowledging that receptivity to the divine Creator expressed in humility, reverence, loving-kindness and service – that is to say, those values which are held to be female prerogatives – is the only sure way of achieving spiritual significance. (It is of course ironic that Faust, in his very masculine goal-orientated striving, fails to understand this as he rushes headlong through life.) When, in the early twentieth century, Rilke speaks of 'the eternal torrent' (Leishman's translation of 'die ewige Strömung') in the *Duineser Elegien* (*Duino Elegies*; 1923), or uses the metaphor of the dance in some of the *Sonette an Orpheus* (*Sonnets to Orpheus*), this may be seen as a continuation of a long line of contemplatives and charismatics, linking back to Mechthild von Magdeburg's unequivocal assurance of God as the fountain-head of all being and inexhaustible source of joy. 'I will dance if you will lead' she exclaims. 'I leap up into the Divine.' It is a supreme expression of that superbly confident religious faith which must constantly find new outlets for itself in language and music.

Apart from the religious houses, the secular courts are the other important sphere in which German literature developed, and again, women play their part, even if not in quite the same way as in France. From Carolingian times onwards, women exerted their influence as patrons of literature, and in the period of Hrotsvit's life, we can see a whole group of important female patrons: Adelheid, the second wife of Otto I, supported Ekkehard IV of St Gall, while her daughter Mathilde, as abbess of Quedlinburg, commissioned important manuscripts and a chronicle of the Saxons, dedicated to her; Gerberga, the niece of Otto I, was not only Hrotsvit's abbess, but also acted as her friend and adviser. In the twelfth century, with the rise of secular literature as courtly entertainment in France, it is again female patrons – often French-born wives of German noblemen – who are influential in introducing these new developments into Germany, but whereas in France, noblewomen are writers as well as patrons, there is no evidence for women taking such an active role as writers in Germany.

Around 1170, the cleric Konrad was commissioned by Mathilde, wife of Henry of Brunswick (= Heinrich der Löwe) and daughter of Eleanor of Aquitaine, to translate the *Chanson de Roland* into German. This is more than the desire of an educated noblewoman for appropriate reading matter, since the genre of the *chanson de geste* had been used in France as a literary means to justify political power of the ruling family; through her mother, Mathilde was almost certainly aware of the way in which literary patronage could be used thus to enhance the importance of the secular courts.

In the development of French courtly literature, the central concept is that of *amour courtois* (courtly love). The love-relationship is expressed in images and metaphors drawn from the contemporary social structures of feudal service, so that the lady assumes the part of the liege-lord in whose power it lies to grant favours and acknowledge the service of the vassal. Although the theme itself is quickly taken up in German literature, it is adapted only in forms which suppress the potential tension between such an elevated image of the all-powerful feudal lady, and the actual political and social reality of male domination over women. Whereas in France women could occasionally wield considerable political power in their own right, and were also able, as writers and poets (for example Marie de France or the *trobadora* Beatriz de Diaz), to comment on the problems of women, or, as rulers and patrons, to feature as the supreme judge in cases of fictional amorous disputes, there is no evidence for parallel developments in Germany. On the whole, women appear to have been restricted to a more passive role until much later, so that the first woman to achieve similar independence within a courtly setting is Elisabeth von Nassau-Saarbrücken. After the death of her husband in 1429, she governed the duchy of Saarbrücken until 1438, when her son was old enough to take over. During the same period, she also engaged in literary activity and translated four French *chansons de geste* into German prose. Again, family connections provided the source and perhaps the inspiration, because the French versions of these *chansons* had been copied for Elisabeth's mother, Margarethe of Vaudémont and Joinville, in 1405, and Elisabeth later revised and corrected her translation checking it against another French copy procured by her son in Paris. In literary terms, Elisabeth's four epics are not much more than faithful renditions which follow her French – verse – sources closely in most details, even where references to rhyme and verse no longer make sense in German prose. While her prime interest was clearly to introduce these stories – about the knight *Herpin* and his sons, the two brothers *Loher und Maller*, *Hug Schapel*, the ficticious heir to the Carolingian throne, and *Sibille*, the innocent wife of Charlemagne maliciously persecuted by her husband – to the court at Saarbrücken, in so doing, she laid the foundations of a new genre which had already enjoyed a head start in France, that of the prose romance.

These beginnings were developed further by Eleonore of Austria (also known as Eleonore of Scotland, since she is the daughter of James I of Scotland). Her translation of the French *Pontus et Sidonie* was undertaken 'to please her husband Sigismund', and to assist him in his attempt to emulate the example of the Italian courts by attracting humanist scholars and writers. Her achievements were acknowledged by Andreas Silvius Piccolomini, one of the most important German humanists at the time. *Pontus und Sidonia*, the love-story of the prince of Galicia and his future bride, quickly achieved widespread literary success, and its special appeal lies not so much in the adventures of the chivalrous hero as in the extended and often vivid depictions of courtly ceremony and everyday life. Pontus is well-bred, courteous and possesses exquisite table manners, and he marks the shift towards a truly modern novel which features an early aristocrat instead of the traditional knight.

Compared to their French counterparts, German women took much longer to assert their creative influence, but when Elisabeth of Nassau-Saarbrücken and Eleonore of Austria began their work, they helped to introduce to German literature the genre of the prose romance, precursor of the novel which was to prove so overwhelmingly successful in centuries to come.

2
_____

Women's writing in the early modern period

The material

Our picture of writing by women in this period is necessarily determined by the texts which have come down to us. In a period when only those manuscripts which had a legal, political or bureaucratic relevance were systematically preserved, it is a matter of pure chance if writing by women is preserved in manuscript form. While there are more manu-script letters, diaries and chronicles in court and convent archives than was formerly thought, it is published writing by women which had the greatest chance of survival. But women usually had no access to printers or publishers – indeed it is questionable whether it was considered suit-able for them to publish their work at all – so it needed the agency of a male relative or mentor, often only after the writer's death, for their work to get into print. The poetry of Catharina Regina von Greiffenberg was first published thanks to her guardian, step-uncle and later husband Hans Rudolf von Greiffenberg, Sibylle Schwarz was published thanks to her tutor Samuel Gerlach and it was a grandson who published the work of Margaretha Susanna von Kuntsch. In the two latter cases publication was posthumous, so the writers had no control whatever over the pub-lished form of their work. It is at least probable that the male relatives or mentors instrumental in the publication edited and emended the texts, so that the final product does not have the status of the oeuvre of a mod-ern woman writer. We must also assume that these male editors selected which works to publish and that they may have suppressed material which did not conform to the forms and themes considered suitable for women. Sometimes a male writer gives an intimation of activity by women in an area where it is in general unsuspected. In his account of the work of the Mastersingers entitled *Von der Musica* and preserved in manuscript in Breslau, Wolfhart Spangenberg tells of one Susanna Granerin, the daughter of a Mastersinger, who composed a song each New Year and in her will left money to the Mastersingers' guild in Strasbourg.

Even where women published their work, it can be difficult nowadays to establish its authorship. Women took refuge under pseudonyms, for example Aramena, the still unknown author of the novel *Die Durchlauchtigste Margaretha von Oesterreich* which appeared in Hamburg in 1716. Women's work also frequently appeared under men's names, for example, the contributions of Sibylle Ursula von Braunschweig-Lüneburg to her more famous brother Anton Ulrich's novels.

One must in general be aware of the existence of a writer before either looking for or finding work by that writer – the problem of the invisibility of women. Until Birgit Neugebauer came on an occasional poem by an unknown poet who signed herself 'Agnes Heinhold / Geborne Schickartin' in the prefatory material to the published text of Sibylle Schuster's play *Ophiletes*, no one knew of the existence of Heinhold. Neugebauer then unearthed a further sixteen, mostly published, writings by Heinhold and made them available in 1991, and it is likely, now that scholars are aware of Heinhold's existence, that more will come to light. Systematic searching will undoubtedly reveal authors hitherto unknown to us.

It can therefore be seen that the printed material actually known to us at present represents only an unknown proportion of what women actually wrote.

Social and historical factors

Since pregnancy accounted for the high mortality of women between the ages of twenty and fifty when compared to men, female biology must be taken into account when discussing literary production. The physical exhaustion caused by multiple pregnancies, miscarriages and difficult labours and the emotional exhaustion caused by the constant deaths of infants and children also account for the fact that most writing by women is the work either of childless women such as Greiffenberg or of widows such as Elisabeth von Braunschweig-Lüneburg or Anna Ovena Hoyers. Even those women who were childless were fully occupied with the endless tasks of early modern housekeeping. Many women, it is clear, simply did not have the leisure or the conditions in which to write.

We must also ask whether they were literate in the first place. Around five to ten per cent of the total population in sixteenth- and seventeenth-century Germany is estimated as being literate, though it is not always easy to define what literate means. While this percentage varied from region to region and increased as the period progressed, we can assume that literacy was highest among upper-class men and lowest among lower-class women. In her pioneering study of reading material for German girls in this period, *The Maiden's Mirror*, Cornelia Niekus-Moore shows how girls were educated with the sole aim of making them better wives and mothers. This was true of girls of all social classes. Girls of the aristocracy and middle class were more likely to be educated at home than sent to school and where girls did go to school – something which was usually only possible in the towns anyway – a few hours a day for a maximum of two years was often considered sufficient. Knowledge in general, apart from a knowledge of housekeeping, was considered unnecessary, indeed burdensome to girls. The only social class to provide a more thorough education for its daughters was, according to Niekus-Moore, 'the educated and learned bourgeoisie, the families of pastors, teachers, scholars, and government officials' (*The Maidens' Mirror*, p. 50).

There was furthermore the fact that Latin was the learned language of the age, the language of science, of educated discourse, even of literature, and that well into the eighteenth century the majority of all writing published in the German-speaking world was in Latin. Few women knew Latin and if they tried to learn it were told, as Kuntsch was by her parents in the 1660s, that this was more suitable for a great lady than for a middle-class girl, whereupon they had to give it up again. Since all educated men of the period wrote in Latin, sometimes instead of but virtually always as well as in German, one whole aspect of the literary life of the period was by definition closed to women. Women were also debarred from undertaking the kind of travel which was a standard part of the education of young men who aspired to learning.

But what of the Renaissance? Surely this meant an opening up of learning and a dissemination of it via the printing-press, a new stress on the individual and his or her development and a questioning of time-honoured assumptions? Surely the ideals of learning for its own sake and artistic endeavour embraced both men and women equally? It is well known that the Renaissance in France, Italy, England, Spain and other countries produced numerous learned and cultivated women. But education only made women into writers if, as Katharina Wilson says, they had 'some financial independence, access to source materials and books, some encouragement and/or religious, political or social zeal' (Wilson, *Women Writers of the Renaissance and Reformation*, p. xvii).

North of the Alps in the German-speaking world, Agrippa of Nettesheim (1486–1535) was the first German Humanist to sum up the debate on women, their abilities and their rights in his *De nobilitate et praecellentia foeminei sexus* (1509). His title, 'On the Nobility and Pre-eminence of the Female Sex', already announces his belief that women, far from being inferior beings to men, are in fact superior. Women are capable of learning and of literary production and Agrippa is able to support this with quotations from the Bible and the Ancients. A scholar of even greater prestige, namely Erasmus of Rotterdam (1467?-1536), took the debate further in such dialogues as *The New Mother* in which he has a feminist argue women's superiority, *A Girl with no Interest in Marriage*, in which a girl wants to be a nun, and *The Abbot and the Learned Lady*, where a woman who loves learning is contrasted with a boorish ignorant abbot who wants to stamp out learning everywhere (Jordan, *Renaissance Feminism*, pp. 56f.). The learned lady of the dialogue is usually identified as Margaret More Roper, the daughter of Erasmus's friend Thomas More, and among the examples of other learned women she mentions are the Pirckheimer girls in Germany.

Barbara Pirckheimer was the eldest child of Dr Johannes Pirckheimer and the sister of the distinguished Humanist Willibald Pirckheimer. At the age of twelve she was sent to the convent of the sisters of St Clare in Nuremberg, the so-called Klarakloster, noted for its learning and holiness and as a school for patrician girls. Here she took the veil around 1483 and by 1485 at the latest she had adopted the name of Caritas. She was a woman of great learning, adept in Latin, well known to the Humanists of her day, with many of whom she corresponded. In 1503 she was elected abbess of the convent. Three of her younger sisters who had also become nuns served their convents in the same capacity. Willibald's friend the Humanist Conrad Celtis saw Caritas, with whom he corresponded in Latin, as the German counterpart of the learned women he had encountered in Italy. Since the Latin writings of the medieval nun Hrotsvit von Gandersheim had been discovered in Regensburg in 1494, Celtis was able to refer to Caritas as the 'new Hrotsvit' as part of a German nationalist effort to prove Germany the equal of Italy intellectually. While Caritas was not the only German woman to be admitted to Humanist circles – we might mention Conrad Peutinger's wife Margarethe and his two daughters Juliana and Konstanze – unlike the Peutinger women her position as a nun gave her an independence and a standing which they lacked.

But in the German-speaking world the Renaissance led to the Reformation and Caritas Pirckheimer herself provides an excellent illustration of the negative effects of the Reformation on those women seeking an intellectual life. The Reformation was indeed a movement intended by Luther and other early Reformers to empower the ordinary person in the pew, to take religion out of the exclusive control of a priestly class and to open it up even to the unlettered believer, to put the Bible in the vernacular into the hands of all and to stress the importance of the laity over the clergy as enunciated in the doctrine of the priesthood of all believers. Such an apparently democratic movement, it seems, must have empowered women. But Luther's radical ideas with regard to church organization did not necessarily extend to political or social structures, as can be seen in his condemnation of the Peasants' Revolt in 1525. Luther gave marriage such a central importance in his moral and social teaching that he went so far as to present marriage and childbearing as the only destiny for women in *Ein Sermon von dem ehlichen Stand* (A sermon on the married estate; 1519); and *Vom ehelichen Leben* (On married life; 1522), though he was well aware that child-bearing could lead to the death of the mother, as the 1525 *Predigt vom Ehestand* (Sermon on the married estate) shows. The celibate life of clerics and nuns was frowned upon and the convents were to be thrown open. If we bear in mind that the convent was the only space available to women where they could be completely free of their biology and where they were not just allowed but encouraged to read, write, study and pray, we can see what a retrograde step this was for them.

By 1524 the Klarakloster was fighting for its existence in Reformation Nuremberg. In the memoirs she wrote in German, the so-called *Denkwürdigkeiten*, Caritas Pirckheimer chronicles the pressures and harassment to which her convent was subjected and which she as abbess had to withstand. Through the agency of Melanchthon in 1525 the convent was allowed to continue in existence but was doomed to extinction because of a prohibition against the admission of novices. Nor could the nuns receive the sacraments according to the old rites. Caritas died there in 1532 aged sixty-six, a woman whose learning was made possible by her life as a nun.

In general, the Reformation reduced women's participation in public life, in the guilds, in trade, etc. and restricted their sphere to the home, to child-bearing and rearing and household management. Simultaneously the Reformation re-affirmed the father as head of the household, almost as the priest within his own household. He therefore was to be the sole fount of knòwledge for his wife, should she need instruction. In consequence only those women who came from an intellectual family, in whose discussions and reading they were allowed to participate, had a chance of acquiring learning. Examples are Sibylle Schwarz, who was allowed access to the professors of Greifswald University who were her father's friends, and Maria Cunitz (1610–64), the remarkable astronomer who was the daughter of an astronomer and clearly engaged in astronomical research with her husband.

But were there not important women Reformers? Certainly there were women who worked and fought to further the cause of the Reformation. We might mention Katharina Zell (1497/8–1562) in Strasbourg, one of the first women to marry a Reformed priest, and Argula von Grumbach in Bavaria, who wrote a number of Reformation pamphlets in 1523–4. There was also Elisabeth, Duchess of Braunschweig-Lüneburg, who wrote and worked publicly for Reform during the years of her Regency, 1540–5, as did many lesser women, who tried to convert their friends, disseminate pamphlets, etc. As the sixteenth century progressed, however, the formation of theological faculties in the new Protestant universities meant that religious interpretation was taken back into professional and therefore male hands and was carried on in an institution to which women by definition were not admitted. One of the main complaints of Anna Ovena Hoyers was precisely the exclusion of women from theological debate.

The Reformation in the German-speaking world ensured, however, that at least one book in the vernacular was accessible to women – the Bible. German women were never forbidden to read the Bible for themselves as English women were in the Act of Parliament promulgated in 1543.

On the positive side, we might single out two institutions which actually fostered writing by women, particularly in the latter half of our period: these were the courts and, from the middle of the seventeenth century, the more progressive language academies or 'Sprachgesellschaften'.

Women and literature

As well as the social and historical factors mentioned above, there were literary constraints on women too. Apart from their lack of access to the classics in an age which legitimized vernacular literature by basing it on that of the ancient world, which drew its forms and themes from ancient writers and which made constant elegant allusion to them, there was a series of prohibitions, both written and unwritten, as to what women might write, indeed as to what they might read (Niekus-Moore, *The Maiden's Mirror*, p. 189). The drama, where it was not the province of such male institutions as the Catholic orders and the boys' grammar schools, partook of the morally dubious nature of the stage. The novel purveyed lies and was furthermore a dangerous foreign import. Secular love poetry, based as it was on Petrarch or on the Latin poets, contravened conventions about the sexual purity of women. If we put all these factors together, it is obvious what the bulk of writing by women must consist of: predominantly verse and within that, religious verse and occasional poetry; in the realm of prose, non-fiction and autobiographical writing, with novels only making their appearance from the second half of the seventeenth century. Drama is the genre where women's contribution is smallest. Let us now examine each of these areas in turn.

As just mentioned, verse is the pre-eminent genre employed by women. Poems can be small in scale and unpretentious in theme and form; they do not need the long-term concentrated work of a novel or the co-operation of actors and the existence of a theatre before they can be realized. They are complete in themselves, they can be produced in private and even women had familiar models to emulate: Biblical psalms in translation, hymns in the vernacular, satirical verse on broadsheets, didactic verse in emblems and on gravestones, folksongs, as well as the occasional poetry familiar to all at weddings, christenings and in funeral sermons. Of all forms poetry was the one women could most easily practise in private and without censure.

While the patchy nature of the known extant material must be taken into account, the multiplicity of forms which women's verse takes in this period is indicative of the fact that each poet is embarking on a unique journey by an unauthorized route and without companions, with no sense of a tradition to fall back on. The family likeness, the common images, the line of development one can see from one generation of male poets to the next, from Opitz to Gryphius to Hofmannswaldau to Günther, for example, is wholly lacking from one female poet to the next. To illustrate this we shall look briefly at the work of four female poets: Anna Ovena Hoyers, Sibylle Schwarz, Catharina Regina von Greiffenberg and Margaretha Susanna von Kuntsch.

As we know from Becker-Cantarino's research, Anna Ovena Hoyers was born in the Duchy of Schleswig-Holstein-Gottorp as the daughter of Hans Ovens, was orphaned young and was a considerable heiress when she married Hermann Hoyers in 1599 at the age of fifteen. The marriage appears to have been a happy one and she bore her husband at least nine children. He died in 1622 and in the course of the next ten years, Hoyers lost a large part of her fortune through law-suits and taxes. It was, however, her deviant religious views which led to her unsettled existence from 1632 and her ultimate refuge in Sweden. Central to her life during the years after her husband's death was her involvement with non-conformist groups. Such 'alternative' Christians, usually led by one charismatic figure, came together in small groups to practise a much more individualistic and mystical Christianity than the orthodox churches, of whatever persuasion, were prepared to allow. The movement towards Reform, itself so revolutionary and anti-orthodox in the early Reformation years, had hardened into two institutionalized churches, Lutheran and Calvinist. By Hoyers's day, each of them had evolved a set of official beliefs and practices of which the theological faculties in the new Protestant universities were the guardians. The same faculties pronounced on which sects and writings were to be banned as heretical. It is clear that by the 1620s Hoyers was reading a great deal of such banned material which circulated secretly among believers.

By 1623 a group of believers had collected round the lay preachers Nicolaus Knutzen Tetzing and Hartwig Lohmann on Hoyers's estate at Hoyersworth. They were both called to order by the Lutheran authorities and had to flee, first to other towns in Schleswig-Holstein and afterwards to Denmark. Hoyers was able to remain in the area under the protection of the Dowager Duchess Augusta of Schleswig-Holstein-Gottorp and carried on holding private prayer meetings and worship as before. On the death of her uncle in 1630 she lost her last family protector and from 1632 seems to have moved around in North Germany. We know that she was in Sweden by 1643, accompanied by five of her children, though the exact date of her arrival there is not certain, and that by now her financial circumstances were straitened. However, in 1648 she came under the protection of Maria Eleonora, Queen Mother of Sweden, who allowed her to live on one of her estates until her death in 1655.

As a life history of a woman and a non-conformist in the early modern period her story would be fascinating in itself. Even more interesting is that her emergence as a non-conformist in religious matters also marked her emergence as a writer. Her first publication was the verse dialogue *Gespräch eines Kindes mit seiner Mutter* (Conversation of a child with his mother), which appeared in 1628. Her second was her verse rendering of the Book of Ruth, which appeared in Sweden in 1634. Today she is chiefly known for her *Geistliche und weltliche Poemata* (Religious and secular poems), an anthology which contains the two above-mentioned works as well as twenty-one others and which appeared in Amsterdam in 1650. A Stockholm manuscript put together by her sons Caspar and Friedrich Wilhelm after her death contains a further forty-seven poems.

Hoyers's oeuvre covers a wide range of forms and themes. The *Gespräch eines Kindes* is a conversation between mother and child on the topic of 'the path to true piety', as the subtitle has it. The verse dialogue *Einfältige Wahrheit* (Simple truth) is a satire on those clerics who far from seeking Truth, chase her away, while the Low German *De Denische Dorp-Pape* (The Danish village priest) mocks those clerics who prefer to live well rather than fulfil their duties as clergymen – a familiar Reformation topic. Many of Hoyers's shorter poems are in fact hymn texts, with an indication of the melody or with actual musical notation accompanying them. Clearly these were to be used by a congregation as part of their worship and are characterized by a clarity and simplicity of diction, a heartfelt piety and a regularity of form reminiscent of Luther himself. She indeed saw herself as standing in direct descent from Luther, both in her criticism of clerical abuse and in her composition of hymns for actual liturgical use. More characteristic of Hoyers's own century than of Luther's are the many poems in which she plays on her own name or initials, on letters of the alphabet or on the name of Jesus, and her oeuvre also includes occasional poems, for instance, to members of the Swedish royal family or to religious leaders.

Hoyers's short-lived contemporary Sibylle Schwarz (1621–38) led a very different life. She was born in Greifswald as the daughter of a lawyer of standing and education who served at the court of Boguslav XIV in Stettin and later became mayor of Greifswald. The Thirty Years War meant that Schwarz and her siblings spent the years 1627–31 not in Greifswald but in Fretow on the coast. They returned to Greifswald in 1631 and since her father had many acquaintances among the professors of Greifswald University, Schwarz's basic schooling was supplemented by Johann Schöner, Professor of Medicine and Mathematics, and by Samuel Gerlach, who afterwards edited her poems. It is clear that in her studies and in her poetry, which she must have begun to write at about the age of ten, she had the full support of her widowed father and of her brother. Influenced by Martin Opitz, the great renewer of German literature in the seventeenth century, with whom her mentor Gerlach was in contact, she began to translate foreign poets and knew enough Latin and Dutch to understand Ovid and Heinsius respectively. By the time of her death at the age of only seventeen, Schwarz had written some eighty poems, a fragment of a drama entitled *Susanna* and part of a pastoral novel. Her poems, showing skilful use of such forms as the sonnet and the alexandrine, deal with a much wider range of themes than was usual for women, even later in the century. Of course she writes religious verse and occasional poetry but there are many poems on the theme of friendship and, surprisingly for a woman and a young woman at that, at least a quarter of her verse is Petrarchist love poetry. It would appear that when a talent such as that of Schwarz is given the necessary encouragement and education it can vie with the poetry of male contemporaries.

The poetry of Catharina Regina von Greiffenberg makes this point even more forcefully. This Austrian Protestant aristocrat lost her father at the age of seven, whereupon her step-uncle Hans Rudolf von Greiffenberg became her guardian. He was also her first teacher and taught her the classical languages as well as French, Italian and Spanish. She read works on ancient and modern history, law, politics, astronomy, alchemy, theology and philosophy as well as the European literature of her day. Her Protestantism meant that she and her family had to make long journeys to attend services at important religious festivals, usually to Western Hungary. After the death of her younger sister and only sibling, Greiffenberg had what she considered an important mystical revelation at Easter 1651 in Pressburg (Bratislava). This revelation, which she referred to thereafter as her 'Deoglori-Licht' (the light of God's glory), marked her birth as a writer. She became a member of the so-called 'Ister-Gesellschaft', a loose association of people with literary interests who met socially and which included many women. Among her friends in the educated Protestant aristocracy was Johann Wilhelm von Stubenberg, a notable translator from French and Italian who had widespread connections with the intelligensia of his day. She showed him her poems; he acted as her literary mentor and adviser and put her in contact with the poet and scholar Sigmund von Birken (1626–81), who had settled in Nuremberg in 1659. Nuremberg was the centre of a group of Protestant poets devoted to the pastoral mode and to metrical experimentation who had formed themselves into the language society called 'Der Pegnesische Blumenorden'. This friendship with Birken, from which 150 letters sur-

vive, was one of the most important elements in Greiffenberg's development as a writer.

Meanwhile Hans Rudolf, her step-uncle, had declared his long-stand-
ing wish to marry her and put her under great pressure to agree, though
he was almost thirty years her senior. They were too nearly related for this
marriage to be lawful in Austria and when Greiffenberg finally gave in,
they had to be married in Bayreuth in 1664. After their return to their
estates at Seisenegg in Austria in 1665, however, Hans Rudolf had to
spend a year in prison on a charge of unlawful cohabitation. It was during
Greiffenberg's years at Seisenegg from 1664 until 1677 that most of the
letters to Birken were written. They bear witness to a deeply religious
woman who longed for the solitude and the leisure to pursue her studies,
her writing and her devotions, but who was constantly forced to abandon
them either to help run the house and estate or to entertain the loud jolly
company her husband enjoyed. Greiffenberg's mother died and then her
husband in 1677. The estate had already been sold but on her husband's
death the purchaser refused to pay the two-thirds of the purchase price
still owing. Greiffenberg was all but destitute and it was only when she
finally got her mother's inheritance that she was able to move to Nuremberg where she lived from 1680 until her death in 1694.

Of all women writers in the early modern period Greiffenberg is the
only one to be the subject of sustained research and discussion. This has
centred above all on her collection of poems entitled *Geistliche Sonette,
Lieder und Gedichte* (Sacred sonnets, songs and poems), published in 1662 by
Hans Rudolf with the help of Birken and apparently without Greiffenberg's knowledge. These poems are remarkable by any standard. Greiffenberg's characteristic method is to present the concrete in vividly sensuous
terms and then to interpret it in spiritual ones, teasing out the religious
significance. The physical world is seen as a set of ciphers which have to be
decoded to arrive at the spiritual meaning. To do this she employs such
tightly controlled forms as the sonnet and pushes language to its boundaries by creating unexpected compounds and by the use of emphatic
prefixes. One is reminded of Gerard Manley Hopkins, who was driven by
the same urge to express the unexpressible and who finds himself having
to mould and distort language in the same way.

In 1662 Greiffenberg wrote the short pastoral piece *Tugend-übung Sieben
Lustwehlender Schäferinnen*, a conversation between seven shepherdesses on
the subject of virtue, and in 1663 she began the lengthy poem *Sieges-Seule
der Buße und des Glaubens*, a call to repentance and faith to ward off the

Turkish threat, though she did not publish it until 1675. From her own point of view and that of her contemporaries her principal achievement as a writer was not her poems but her four extensive series of religious meditations in prose, interspersed here and there with poems, on the incarnation and early life of Jesus (1678), His suffering and death (1683), His teachings and miracles (1693) and His life and prophecies (1693).

Greiffenberg was fortunate to have had the friendship and advice of Birken for twenty years, for Birken actively furthered the writing of many women, corresponded with them, drew them into the pursuits of the literary societies (the so-called 'Sprachgesellschaften') and clearly valued their company and their ideas. Under his leadership, 20 per cent of the 'Pegnesischer Blumenorden' consisted of women, all of them active writers (Brandes, 'Baroque Women Writers', p. 54). Typical of Birken was the way he brought his old pupil, the novelist Duke Anton Ulrich von Braunschweig-Wolfenbüttel, into contact with Greiffenberg. Birken let her see the first part of Anton Ulrich's novel *Aramena* in manuscript and Anton Ulrich later asked Greiffenberg to write a preface for the third part.

Margaretha Susanna von Kuntsch had no such like-minded associates to encourage her literary endeavours. We know from her own account of her life printed with her collected poems and taken from her *Leichenpredigt* or funeral sermon that, though her father as a court official in Altenburg in Saxony belonged to the educated middle class, she herself was merely taught 'all that a true Christian and virtuous woman needed to know'. She explains that though her own inclinations led her to learn Latin and French and other branches of knowledge, her parents were more far-sighted than she and decided that such occupation was more suited to a great lady than to a woman of the middle rank and so she had to give up her studies. At eighteen she married Christoph von Kuntsch, also an official of the Altenburg court. With the exception of a period of three years at the beginning of her married life, she spent the rest of her days in Altenburg where she had grown up. It is clear that she was well known in her own narrow circle for her verse but it is thanks to her grandson, the poet Christoph Gottlieb Stockmann, that her collected poems were published in 1720 under the title *Sämmtliche Geist- und weltliche Gedichte*, with a preface by the well-known writer Christian Friedrich Hunold (1681–1721), known as Menantes. Most of her poetry takes exactly that form we outlined above as virtually pre-determined in the case of a woman writer of the period: it consists either of religious verse on Biblical or other pious topics or of occasional poetry, written for funerals, weddings and birthdays or in the form of tributes to acquaintances and friends. There are, for instance, thirty poems written one each year on her husband's birthday, there are poems on Biblical texts and on the pious literature she has been reading as well as playful poems written for the weddings of friends. What strikes the reader is the extent to which her mind is preoccupied with the theme of death to a degree unusual even for a Baroque poet. Not only is there a large number of references to death, even in the birthday poems for her husband, and of poems on the topic itself but a heart-rending intensity is revealed in her treatment of the subject. Remarkable in this regard is the series of poems on the deaths of her own children, whose names and precise ages to the day she lists in her *curriculum vitae*. She had fourteen pregnancies of which only one child, her daughter Margaretha Elisabeth, lived to adulthood. Two of the pregnancies ended in miscarriages, two were stillbirths, two were premature and no less than five others died at less than a year old. Two others died aged seven and nine respectively. While she uses the common rhetoric of lament and consolation, followed by acquiescence in God's will, she does not conceal the agony of her loss which each death increased. Her poem on the death of her fifth son Chrisander on 22 November 1686 takes as its starting point the story of the painter Timantes who, when asked to depict Agamemnon's pain at the loss of Iphigenie, simply painted a veil. In a skilfully turned poem she compares the courage needed by the warrior Agamemnon in battle with the far greater courage needed to cope with the loss of his child, and then contrasts herself, now the mother of nine dead children, both to Agamemnon and to Timantes, who like herself, is attempting to depict grief in art. If he was unable to limn the pain of another, how can she present her own heartbreak? She ends her poem: 'Dumb pain must bear witness to my sorrow.'

As we saw in the case of Kuntsch, women frequently wrote accounts of their own lives as part of a lively tradition of autobiography in the seventeenth century. We also saw how these accounts were frequently included in printed funeral sermons as exemplars for the reader, who in many cases were intended in the first instance to be the children of the deceased (see Bepler, 'Women in German Funeral Sermons', pp. 393f.). Women's autobiography also played an essential part in that movement towards a more inward piety within Lutheranism which came to be known as Pietism. As Jeannine Blackwell has pointed out, such collections of spiritual autobiographies as Gottfried Arnold's *Unpartheyische Kirchen- und Ketzer-Historie* (Impartial history of belief and unbelief; 1688), Johann Heinrich Reitz's

Historie der Wiedergeborenen (History of the Anabaptists; 1717) and Erdmann Heinrich von Henckel's *Letzte Stunden* (Last hours; 1746), consisted to a large extent of the life-stories of women, in which they related their visions and prophecies as well as their daily lives and the story of their conversion. It is clear that these women were active in various non-conformist religious groups throughout the seventeenth century, something we have already seen in the case of Hoyers. Blackwell points out that in the seventeenth century women's visions were tolerated since it was believed that, after all, they were the irrational sex. However, they walked a tightrope between being recognized as prophets and being condemned as witches whose visions came from the devil (Blackwell, 'Herzensgespräche mit Gott', pp. 271f.).

One of the best-known of these spiritual autobiographies is that of the noblewoman Johanna von Merlau, more commonly known by her married name of Johanna Eleonore Petersen. She tells the story of her life up to the birth of her first son in vivid detail: the early death of her mother; her father's cruelty; her service with a deranged and homicidal noblewoman; her time as a lady-in-waiting at court, an environment she found unbearably frivolous; her subsequently broken engagement to a godless soldier; her difficulties in being allowed to marry the man of her choice, who was socially beneath her; how her father finally consented to her marriage to another social inferior, the pastor Johann Wilhelm Petersen, an associate of Spener's, the founder of Pietism. For her this outward narrative is the framework for what really concerns her, namely, her spiritual development. She learns to depend absolutely on God and to see His hand in all things and as her spirituality becomes more and more inward and her own inclinations more ascetic, she finds the social role she is required to play, for instance, at court, deeply distasteful. We are reminded of Greiffenberg's wish to withdraw from society to pray and meditate. Had either of these women belonged to a different religious grouping, the convent would have been the obvious refuge. Johanna von Merlau, however, has to marry and her struggle to accomplish this and yet remain true to her religious ideals constitutes a constant thread in her narrative. Once she is married to Petersen and can express her spirituality in sympathetic surroundings, she then develops visionary and prophetic gifts. As an exploration of emotions and spirituality and in its insistence on their primacy over the happenings of daily life, this autobiography anticipates the eighteenth century.

A very different sort of autobiography is that of the Jewish woman

Glickl bas Judah Leib (often known under the German version of her name as Glückel von Hameln) who wrote seven volumes of memoirs in Yiddish, partly after her first husband's death in 1689 and partly at a later stage in her life, between 1715 and 1719. She addresses her memoirs ostensibly to her children but maintains that her intention is not didactic. Rather she is writing in order to commune with herself, to have someone to talk to in the loneliness of her widowhood. The sheer length of her account means that the reader is given a full and detailed picture of the customs, religious observance and daily life of the German Jewish community of her day. She displays the same piety, the same trust in God, the same resignation in adversity as her Christian contemporaries, but in contrast to them was clearly treated by her husband as an equal partner in his business with whom he discussed every negotiation, every financial deal, to such an extent that she was able to take over the business on his death.

Prose fiction by women in this period takes second place behind the autobiographical writings just discussed. Even though the early novel in the form of the prose romance was a female preserve, with such writers as Elisabeth von Nassau-Saarbrücken discussed in the previous chapter, in the sixteenth and seventeenth centuries women were not supposed to read, still less to write novels. In his *Frauenzimmer Gesprächsspiele* (Conversational diversions for women; 1647–; vol. I, pp. 236f.), a sort of encyclopaedia for women in the form of conversations or debates on a whole range of topics, Harsdörffer, one of the Nuremberg group mentioned above and the co-founder of the so-called 'Pegnesischer Blumenorden', has his discussants rehearse the arguments relating to this issue. Julia, for instance, maintains that since the novel is a form of literature which actually purveys lies, women are particularly susceptible to corruption by it. After all, Eve's corruption by the deceitful serpent has already proved that. Harsdörffer gives the last word, however, to Angelika, who maintains that any woman who can run a household has as much power of discernment as the ruler of a country and can therefore distinguish a virtuous book from an evil one and that even novels fall into these two categories. Virtuous books present wise and true precepts in a pleasing and digestible manner. The debate is decided in favour of Angelika. Not all educators and theorists were as open-minded as Harsdörffer, however, and it is not surprising that so few women wrote novels in this period.

Foremost among them is Sibylle Ursula von Braunschweig-Lüneburg (1629–71), a daughter of the noted scholar, writer and bibliophile Duke August von Braunschweig-Lüneburg (1579–1666), virtually all of whose children, male or female, were engaged in literary and artistic pursuits and who made his court at Wolfenbüttel into a noted cultural centre. Sibylle Ursula was educated with her brothers and shared her literary interests particularly with her favourite, the novelist Anton Ulrich von Braunschweig-Lüneburg (1633–1714). When he went on his Grand Tour he engineered a correspondence between his sister and the French novelist Madeleine de Scudéry. Sibylle Ursula delayed marrying to devote herself to her writing. Among other things she translated one of the Latin writings of the Spanish Humanist Juan de Vives into German and wrote a five-act play and a series of spiritual meditations (*Geistliches Kleeblatt*, 1655) but it is for her contribution to the novel that she is chiefly known today. After a period of intense interest on her part in the contemporary French novel in which she translated La Calprenède's *Cassandre* in 1656 and his *Cléopâtre* in 1659 and wrote to Madame de Scudéry to send her *Clélie* when it first appeared, she set out to emulate these works in a novel of her own called *Aramena*. The manuscript of the first version of this work in her hand, preserved in her father's library at Wolfenbüttel, is undated and breaks off in the middle of a sentence in the second book (Brandes, 'Studierstube', p. 244). It is thought that when Sibylle Ursula married belatedly in 1663 at the age of thirty-four she handed her work over to her brother who revised and reordered parts of it, added to it and gave it to his old tutor Sigmund von Birken to edit. The novel which later became famous as *Die Durchlauchtige Syrerin Aramena* (Aramena, the noble Syrian lady) appeared under Anton Ulrich's name. Sibylle Ursula's marriage was disastrous: her first three children died, she became gravely ill from syphilis contracted from her husband and died in her fourth childbed in 1671.

Another female novelist whose work sometimes became swallowed up in that of her male collaborator is Maria Katharina Heden, née Frisch (1633?-1692), better known as Maria Katharina Stockfleth after her marriage in 1669 to the Lutheran pastor Heinrich Arnold Stockfleth. At the time of her marriage she had already made a name as a poet and was a member of the female language society, the 'Ister-Nymphen'. In the year of their marriage she and her husband published the first volume of the pastoral novel *Die Kunst-und Tugend-gezierte Macarie* (The artistic and virtuous Macarie), in which to an extent they describe their own love story. The novel tells the history of the shepherd Polyphilus who sets off to find honour and falls in love with the beautiful and learned Macarie. Before he can win her, however, he must first learn to see through the sham glamour of court life and the emptiness of power before he can retreat to the community of shepherds and live a life of virtue and literary endeavour with his beloved Macarie. If the first part was the work of both the Stockfleths, the second part, which appeared in 1673, was written by Maria Katharina alone and is generally agreed to be both more profound in its ideas and of much greater literary merit than the first part on which the couple collaborated.

If there is little prose fiction by women in this period, there is even less drama. The only milieu which was at all propitious in this regard was the court. Sibylle Ursula's five-act play has already been mentioned. It is untitled and not quite finished but is modelled on the martyr dramas of the age in which a virtuous woman, exposed to the untrammelled lust and unscrupulous wiles of an evil man, is prepared to lose her life rather than her virtue. In the matter of dramatic composition Sibylle Ursula had someone in her own family to emulate, namely her stepmother, Sophie Elisabeth von Mecklenburg-Güstrow (1613–76). Sibylle Ursula's mother died when she was five, and a year later, in 1635, her father Duke August took Sophie Elisabeth as his third wife. Though only twenty-two at the time of her marriage, she took her role as step-mother to four young children, as wife of a man of learning and artistic interests and as consort to the ruler of a duchy very seriously. As well as bearing him three more children, Sophie Elisabeth corresponded with the composer Heinrich Schütz and with Harsdörffer in Nuremberg. She brought Sigmund von Birken and the grammarian and literary theorist Justus Georg Schottelius to Wolfenbüttel as tutors to her children and step-children, in whose education she took a close interest. She herself composed and wrote and was a central figure in the cultural life of the court.

As a writer she anticipated Sibylle Ursula and Anton Ulrich's interest in the novel by translating an episode from Honoré d'Urfé's *Astrée* which she entitled *Die histori der Dorinde* (The tale of Dorinde; 1641–52). She was also the author of a considerable quantity of religious verse. In addition, each year between 1652 and 1656, with the exception of 1653, she wrote and sometimes also composed the music for a theatrical presentation in honour of her husband's birthday. The first of these is a short opera: there is the libretto and the music for a ballet on the theme of Time, there are the scenarios and the music for three masquerades, in which a costumed procession of the ducal family and courtiers, a ballet or short opera and a banquet are all linked together in one presentation. Lastly there is the five-act prose drama *Ein Freudenspiel von dem itzigen betrieglichen Zustande in der Welt* (A comedy on the present deceitful way of the world; 1656). Hans-Gert Roloff, the editor of a modern edition of Sophie Elisabeth's dramatic works, surmises that three other works preserved in manuscript in Wolfenbüttel may also be at least in part her work (Roloff, 'Absolutismus und Hoftheater', p. 125). In his discussion of *Ein Freudenspiel* in the same article Roloff points out that the Duchess is here using drama to analyse and pass judgement on one of the burning issues of her day: the exercise of power by an Absolutist prince within the framework of a virtuous life and Christian precepts. Sophie Elisabeth sets up two princes and two courts, the one Machiavellian, scheming, violent and unscrupulous, the other peace-loving, just and honourable and shows how, in spite of a series of intrigues, virtue wins out in the end. It is an allegorical and didactic drama which is doubly fascinating because it reflects with great subtlety the political theories of the day and because it is written by the consort of a ruler to be performed in front of him and his court by, among others, his own children, future rulers and consorts of rulers themselves.

Of course Sophie Elisabeth is not the only noble lady to write plays and court festivities nor Wolfenbüttel the only court at which women played a central role. But much material in manuscript form is still to be unearthed in court archives. It is clear too that our picture of dramatic activity by women may be extended by investigation of the role they played in the professional companies of strolling players, as for example in Becker-Cantarino's discussion of Catharina Elisabeth Velten (c. 1650–1715) (*Der lange Weg*, pp. 306f.) and by examination of such works as *Ophiletes* (1685), the tragedy by Sibylla Schuster, of whom up to now little is known.

Given the difficulties faced by sixteenth- and seventeenth-century women who wanted to write, it seems almost a miracle that they wrote at all. The dawning of a new age, in which women might officially be acknowledged to have talents which could be trained and furthered, in however limited a way, is marked by the appearance at the beginning of the eighteenth century of three works by men which celebrated women writers: Christian Franz Paullini's *Das Hoch- und Wohl-gelahrte Teutsche Frauenzimmer* (The learned German lady; 1705), Johann Caspar Eberti's *Eröffnetes Cabinet Deß Gelehrten Frauenzimmers* (A treasury of learned ladies; 1706) and Georg Christian Lehms's *Teutschlands Galante Poetinnen* (Germany's gallant poetesses; 1715). With a considerable admixture of nationalist feeling, the three authors want to prove that German women are as capable of learning and literary talent as those of any nation. The Enlightenment is on the horizon.

Part II

The eighteenth and nineteenth centuries

3
_____

The Enlightenment

The period covered in this chapter saw the decisive emergence of the female writer and of a female reading public. Literacy expanded considerably in the German states during the eighteenth century, including literacy among women, whose education had frequently been neglected, and the reading of imaginative literature as a leisure activity gained respectability among the expanding middle classes. Whereas at the beginning of the period even literate women rarely read anything beyond household manuals or works of religious edification, by the end of the eighteenth century male commentators were voicing concern about the sorry effects of the *Lesewut* (reading mania) that had gripped the female middle classes.

The period 1720 to 1789 was a time of change in the traditional image of woman and the roles ascribed to her. In the first half of the century, it was fully accepted that men should have authority over women and that in the hierarchy of the household women should be subordinate. In the predominantly rural and small-town communities in the German states the nuclear family had not yet developed and women were important to the economic success of the extended household (see Hausen); the skill, industry, thrift and practical sense of the German *Hausmutter* were greatly prized. While old prejudices against women's weakness and ignorance survived – as late as the 1720s theological treatises were being written on whether women had souls – the early Enlightenment saw attempts to assert their educability and the potential of at least some women to show intellectual gifts equal to men's (see Blochmann). Thus popular channels of Enlightenment thinking, for example the moral weeklies modelled on English periodicals such as *The Spectator* and *The Tatler*, took up the cause of the improvement of education and the expansion of edifying reading for women (see Martens). By the end of the century the ideal middle-class woman was *gebildet*, acquainted with a range of imaginative and informative literature, though anything but *gelehrt*, academic or learned.

Yet by the end of the century women found themselves in a new kind of straitjacket. The ideal image of woman was now based on the mother of the nuclear family, a social unit that was becoming increasingly the norm as town life and the professional middle class expanded. The wife of the lawyer, professor, administrator or magistrate was not economically active but rather responsible for the good management of the household and for the creation of domestic warmth and harmony. She was now to be more of a companion to her husband, and a source of basic education and emotional stability to their children. The nature of the relationship between the sexes became the subject of intense discussion. Secular ideas based on the emerging scientific disciplines and supported by theories of education and political and social development (those of Rousseau being perhaps the most influential) displaced old religious prejudices against women but introduced new stereotypes. The relationship between the sexes was held to be one of complementarity, and accompanying this notion was an increasingly rigid conception of the contrasting sets of attributes of the sexes, often known as *Geschlechtscharaktere*. Anatomy, physiology and anthropology were used to support the notion that women were essentially different from men not only in body but also in mind and should pursue only those activities compatible with their calling (*Bestimmung*) as *Gattin, Hausfrau und Mutter* (spouse, housewife and mother). The resulting theories of the separate spheres of male and female activity, which determined the relations between the sexes well into the twentieth century, sprang from this intense preoccupation with gender roles in the later part of the eighteenth century. Thus, while literacy and reading among women greatly increased in the second half of the century, new culturally determined restrictions were being placed on the exercise of that literacy. Literature itself reflected those cultural changes in the development of new female stereotypes such as the *schöne Seele* (beautiful soul) or the innocent child of nature.

The great expansion of the reading public in Germany brought an intensive preoccupation on the part of male writers with aesthetics and the poetological assumptions underlying literary creation. Though women were writing and publishing in ever greater numbers by the last decades of the century, recognition of their achievements was hampered by the changing theories of literature, from the idea of poetry as a craft that could be learned to the more inspirational model culminating in the *Geniekult*. As the emphasis shifted increasingly to the psyche of the artist and to the particular confluence of conscious and unconscious, of reason and imagination in the act of creation, so women were increasingly excluded. Women might show evidence of skill and talent within the lesser genres but genius, the divine spark, tended to be regarded as vouchsafed exclusively to men (see Battersby, esp. pp. 70–112). Women writers in the eighteenth century constantly had to manoeuvre for the space left them by male writers and literary arbiters, basing the justification for their participation in literary activity on the didactic value of their work. While they are represented in the lyric and the drama, women particularly exploited the novel, the didactic short story and the lively and well-written letter, forms that were more fluid and lower in the hierarchy of genres, and their exponents therefore arguably less of a threat to male writers.

The two Zs

It is against the background of the earlier Enlightenment's greater openness to the notion of women's neglected poetic and intellectual potential that we should examine the contrasting lives and experience of the two most honoured women poets of that period, Christiana Mariana von Ziegler and Sidonia Hedwig Zäunemann. Christiana Mariana von Ziegler grew up in a wealthy and prominent Leipzig family. By the age of twenty-seven she was a widow twice over and had lost also the two children from her marriages. Having returned to her parental home in Leipzig, she was in the position as a wealthy widow to make that home a meeting place for the literary and musical world. She furnished Bach, who came to take up his position as Kantor of the Thomasschule in 1723, with the texts for a number of his cantatas. One of the literary figures she helped to prominence was the young scholar Johann Christoph Gottsched, who was determined to raise the status of German language and literature by a programme of reform. She made contributions to Gottsched's journal for women, *Die vernünftigen Tadlerinnen* (The rational critics), and supported his reforms, and he in turn saw to it that she was given public recognition. She was the first woman to be made a member of the 'Deutsche Gesellschaft', a society formed to promote excellence in language and literature along Gottschedian lines, and won its poetry prize in 1732 and 1734. Her first collection of poetry, *Versuch in Gebundener Schreib-Art* (An exercise in verse), was published in 1728. In 1731 she published a collection of letters, *Moralische und Vermischte Send-Schreiben*.

An einige Ihrer guten und vertrauten Freunde gestellet (Moral and miscellaneous missives. Addressed to several of her good and close friends), and in 1739 *Vermischte Schriften in gebundener und ungebundener Rede* (Miscellaneous writings in verse and prose).

Ziegler's facility with verse is combined with vigour and versatility, wit and humour. Her collections of poems range from religious verse to occasional poems, pastoral poems and satirical and didactic verse. Amid this wide range of themes and styles she makes women's writing her subject on a number of occasions. Her poems in *Die vernünftigen Tadlerinnen* lend support to Gottsched's campaign in the journal to encourage female education and participation in literature. More than once she makes fun of intemperate male reactions to the challenge from women to men's monopoly of the arts:

> Glaubt, daß Apollo wird die schönen Musen schützen,
> Rast nur mit ungestüm, brüllt gleich dem Höllenhund:
> Sie werden ungestört am schönen Pindus sitzen.
>
> (*Die vernünftigen Tadlerinnen*, supplement p. 3)

> Be assured that Apollo will protect the fair Muses. You may rave wildly and bellow like the hound of hell – they will sit undisturbed on fair Pindus.

Ziegler herself had to suffer a good deal of ridicule and invective the more she came to prominence. It is clear that she considered women every bit as intellectually competent as men, as we can judge from her reply to a female friend whose daughter shows an interest in learning:

> Wir bringen ja eben sowohl fünff Sinnen mit auf die Welt, wie jenes [Geschlecht], Verstand und Vernunfft werden unter beyderley Geschlechten von der Natur ausgetheilet, und das Gedächtnis wird uns zur Mitgifft von Ihr mit angerechnet ...
>
> (*Send-Schreiben*, p. 8)

> We also bring five senses into the world as men do; understanding and reason are distributed by nature among both sexes and memory is also granted by her as part of our dowry ...

In this same letter she even goes as far as to suggest that women should not be excluded from professional and public life, the reward most men have from their studies. This was a profoundly revolutionary idea, however, and if she had clung to it she would no doubt have lost the sympathy of the male supporters on whom she and all women who wished to publish depended. Her address to the 'Deutsche Gesellschaft' on whether women should be allowed to study makes clear that women seek only the chance to exercise their God-given talents and not to enter into competition with men for public offices. Whether or not the exposure she received and the propaganda that was made with her for the reform programme of the 'Deutsche Gesellschaft' turned her away from poetry in the end, as has been suggested, the fact remains that she published no more after her third marriage in 1741 (cf. Heuser).

Sidonia Hedwig Zäunemann specifically refers to the encouragement she received from the example of Christiana Mariana von Ziegler. Brought up in an educated middle-class family, she rebelled in both word and deed against the roles she felt were forced on women. Her main collection of poetry, *Poetische Rosen in Knospen* (Poetic rosebuds; 1738), shows her fluency and versatility in the German language. It contains many conventional religious and occasional poems but also indicates her conscious adoption of unconventional *personae*. Gisela Brinker-Gabler aptly identifies in Zäunemann's self-presentation a longing for the heroic, itself a radical transgression of the boundaries set for the female writer. She first came to fame as the result of a poem written in praise of Prince Eugene and his Hussars. Her life too reflected this desire for expansion out of the conventional female roles. The daughter of a notary, she often donned men's clothing to ride her horse alone to visit her sister in Ilmenau. It was on one such ride that she drowned while crossing a bridge. The poem to which she draws particular attention in *Poetische Rosen in Knospen*, 'Das Ilmenauische Bergwerk' (The Ilmenau mines), arose from her pioneering visit to the copper and silver mines in Ilmenau. It conveys the excitement of her voyage of discovery with a compelling immediacy:

> O wie vergnügt bin ich! wie frölich fahr ich aus!
> Weg Spielen, Tanzen, Scherz und Schmücken;
> Das Bergwerk kan mich nur erquicken;
>
> *(Poetische Rosen p. 579)*
>
> What pleasure I feel, with what joy I set out! Away with gaming,
> dancing, frivolity and adornments, only the mine can enliven me;

Like Mariana von Ziegler, who was honoured by Leipzig University, Zäunemann was crowned a poet by Göttingen University (in 1738), a significant public honour and an indication of how far in this period literature still belonged to the academic world.

Drama and theatre

In the first half of the eighteenth century two women were of decisive importance in laying the foundations of a renaissance of the German theatre. Both were allies of the dominant literary arbiter, Gottsched, but both were superior to him in imagination and literary talent. The first was the actress-manager Caroline Neuber, whose work was vital in creating the conditions for the emergence of a theatre of literary value, and the second Gottsched's wife, Luise (née Culmus), whose translations and original comedies pointed the way towards a high German comedy. Caroline Neuber was the daughter of an Erfurt lawyer, whose harshness drove her to flee from home in 1717 with her suitor, later her husband, Johann Neuber, and join the Spiegelberg troupe of actors. Theatrical life in Germany at the time was divided between the court theatres, where French and Italian opera dominated and interest in indigenous theatre was negligible, and the travelling companies (*Wanderbühnen*). These latter catered for the limited artistic demands of their audiences with a mixture of low comedies and historical costume dramas (the *Haupt- und Staatsaktion*), with comic interludes provided by the ubiquitous comic figure, whether the Italianate Harlekin or the indigenous Hanswurst. There were few fixed texts; the actors worked to a scenario and improvised in accordance with it.

The life of the actor or actress was extremely insecure. Competition between the travelling companies was fierce, and actresses had a dubious moral reputation; in the court theatres they provided a source of mistresses for the ruling aristocracy. Even before she met Gottsched, Frau Neuber had already begun to try to raise the quality of the theatre by using fixed texts, though she was reputedly a very skilled extemporizer. Gottsched had taken upon himself the reform of the theatre, with the aim of bringing literary drama and the stage together in Germany in order to create the conditions for a flowering of German drama based on classical principles, to which end he encouraged translations of the works of the French classical stage to supply the company with plays. Caroline Neuber provided the perfect ally for him. Not only did she subject herself and her company to the discipline of learning fixed texts, and verse texts to boot, but she tried to introduce a less florid acting style to complement the elevated tone of the plays. Eduard Devrient credits her with the creation of the first German school of acting (Devrient, p. 99); she tried also to improve the reputation of theatre people and of acting as a serious profession.

For all her reforming zeal, though, Frau Neuber remained flexible. The reformed repertoire was not large enough to sustain the troupe, so she retained some of the old plays, cleansed of their vulgarity and of some of their low comedy. Yet it was a daring enterprise to challenge and educate the taste of the theatre-going public. Audiences began to desert her, and a few years later she broke with Gottsched. His determination to publish his *Deutsche Schaubühne*, the collection of translations and original plays that formed the basis of the reformed repertoire, was intended to bring the new repertoire to the reading public and so educate taste through reading. However, this undermined the viability of companies, who in the transitional phase from extemporized to text-based theatre still jealously guarded 'their' plays. Frau Neuber's own plays, the majority short *Vor-* or *Nachspiele*, were rarely published for this very reason. The revival of German theatrical life from the 1740s onwards is nevertheless a tribute to the efforts of Caroline Neuber, and if by her last years on the stage her style seemed old-fashioned this is proof of how far the reforms had been successful. She remained forward-looking and had an eye for young talent, staging the young Lessing's first comedy, *Der junge Gelehrte* (The young scholar), in 1748. She ended her days, though, in very reduced circumstances, dependent on the charity of well-wishers.

The reputation of Luise Adelgunde Victorie Gottsched has suffered by association with her domineering husband, partly because she was allowed to exercise her talents only in ways that served him and because the unjust derision of Gottsched's ideas that began in his day and dominated nineteenth-century literary criticism precluded a just appraisal of his wife's talents. As the daughter of a Danzig doctor, Luise Culmus enjoyed a much wider and more intellectually adventurous education than most girls of her station, learning English, French, geography, mathematics and music from members of her family. Her correspondence with Gottsched before their marriage shows her maturity, intelligence and willingness to learn, but also – and this quality is evident to the end of her life – her subordination of all her talents and energies to him. Despite his vigorous advocacy of women's education in *Die vernünftigen Tadlerinnen*, Gottsched was ruthless in exploiting his able wife, whose own literary work was always kept strictly secondary to the work he set her. Frau Gottsched worked constantly on translations from the French and English, which made works such as Addison's and Steele's *Spectator* and parts of Bayle's dictionary available to German readers, and also produced a tragedy (though *Panthea* can hardly be seen as more than a paper exercise in tragedy) and four original comedies which, with her adaptation *Die Pietisterey im Fischbeinrocke oder die Doktormäßige Frau* (*Pietism in Petticoats*; 1736), represent her most important literary works.

These were all written within the constraints imposed by her husband's theory of comedy set out in his *Versuch einer critischen Dichtkunst* (Attempt at a critical art of poetry). For Gottsched comedy was primarily satirical and aimed to ridicule human shortcomings with the purpose of correcting them and encouraging wisdom and virtue. He also demanded a certain realism in speech, commensurate with the lower social standing of comic, as opposed to tragic, figures. The unities must be observed, the time of the action ideally not running over about ten hours. The play must have five acts and involve an element of mystery or intrigue that is resolved at the end. Frau Gottsched's comedies, then, are examples of a form in the process of change. Her plots are, in the main, too simple to sustain a five-act play. She retains to some extent the use of comic names to denote virtues and vices, and yet in probably her best original comedy, *Das Testament* (*The Will*), she tries to move beyond black and white contrasts and point the moral in more conciliatory terms.

All of Frau Gottsched's comedies reflect the attitudes and aspirations of the educated middle class of her day. *Die ungleiche Heirath* (*The Mésalliance*) deals with marriage between the impoverished lower aristocracy and the prosperous bourgeoisie. While the pretensions of the Dorfjunker are made to look ridiculous, the chief lesson has to be learned by Herr Wilibald, who is finally persuaded that his desire to marry above himself is foolish and unnecessary in a man of his talents and wealth. In *Die Hausfranzösinn* (*The French Housekeeper*) the gullible father is hoodwinked by a family of French rogues who have taken over the running of his household and intend to use his children to extort money from him. The implication is that the sensible and unpretentious German family has virtues enough without adopting foreign manners. *Das Testament* deals with the attempts of a brother and sister to secure a handsome legacy from their wealthy aunt. Their sister, the sensible and honourable Caroline, treats her aunt with honesty and respect and is rewarded with a legacy when the will is read, though the aunt confounds them all by deciding in the end to remarry. *Der Witzling* (*The Witling*) is a lively one-act play, which defends Gottsched's linguistic and theatrical reforms by ridiculing their opponent, the pretentious Herr Vielwitz. In spite of their structural weaknesses and moralizing tendency, these plays show Frau Gottsched's potential as a writer of comedy, for she has both wit and the gift of comic invention. These qualities are also evident in her most famous adaptation, *Die Pietisterey im Fischbeinrocke*. The original French comedy, Bougeant's *La Femme docteur ou La Théologie Janséniste tombée en Quenouille*, is a satire on the Jansenists written by a Jesuit. Frau Gottsched transposes the action with complete success to Germany and aims the satire at the Pietists, who were influential in her native Danzig. So controversial was the subject matter that the play, published anonymously, was not only never performed but was actually banned in some states.

Frau Gottsched's subordination of her literary talents to her husband's concerns reflects the fact that she saw her own path in life as the exception rather than the rule. Her attitudes as reflected in her writings and in her letters are conservative. What one might tentatively say is that comedy gave her the opportunity to show some female characters as more independent and less governed by social custom than most actual women could afford to be.

No women later in the century left such a mark on theatre and drama as Frau Neuber and Frau Gottsched. Women continued to be active, however, both on the stage and as dramatists. Actresses wrote for the professional theatre and women wrote for the flourishing amateur theatrical life, but little of this work was published, and what was published usually appeared anonymously or was presented as a translation. Though research is uncovering new material, the work of women playwrights is the least accessible area of women's writing in this period because of the rareness of the texts themselves. It was not until the last decades of the eighteenth century that more plays by women began to appear in print – sentimental comedies such as Victoria Rupp's *Marianne oder der Sieg der Tugend* (Marianne or the triumph of virtue; 1777), domestic tragedies such as Christiane Caroline Schlegel's *Düval und Charmille* (1778) and historical dramas such as Sophie Eleonore Kortzfleisch's *Lausus und Lydie* (1776) and Emilie von Berlepsch's *Eginhard und Emma* (1787). However, these plays and the bulk of women's writing for the theatre before 1800 received no contemporary critical attention and made no recorded theatrical impact. It was not until well into the nineteenth century that the work of women dramatists became essential to the theatrical repertoire.

The emergence of letter-writing

The period 1720 to 1789 saw the large-scale expansion of letter-writing, with both men and women conducting vast correspondences, often with people they never met face to face. The letter became a demanding and cultivated form of writing in an age in which the development of the affective life and the cult of friendship brought an increased need to communicate thoughts and feelings. The Pietist tradition had also left a legacy of reflection and self-examination that found expression in the letter. As a culture of letter-writing emerged, women were frequently encouraged to put their literary talents to use in this activity and they often excelled at the spontaneous, lively, communicative letter. Both Gottsched and, more influentially, Gellert saw women as having the simplicity and directness of style to make the letter combine naturalness and literary value. Of the vast quantities of letters written by women, only a small fraction survives. These, however, provide increasing evidence as the century progresses of the accomplishment of women in this genre; and this becomes even more apparent in the Romantic period.

The letter assumed a special place in women's lives. Naturally, the cultivation of a correspondence was confined to the aristocracy and the prosperous middle classes. Even here, however, women's lives were often extremely circumscribed. Letters provided then as now a means of maintaining friendships. Travel for women was uncommon and difficult and letters helped to enlarge the world for female correspondents. They also gave women the opportunity to report and reflect on their daily existence and relationships and thus provided a means of self-expression. The letter created also a small public for its writer, for apart from such private matters as love letters, it was rarely written for the recipient only, but was passed round, read aloud in excerpts and passages were even copied.

We can see the change in the possibilities of the letter as a communication of the personality and affective life if we look at the first published collection of letters by a German woman. Christiana Mariana von Ziegler's *Moralische und vermischte Send-Schreiben* (Moral and mixed missives) of 1731 were intended by her as a kind of signpost to other women. In fact they still owe much to an older school of letter-writing that laid stress on discussion of an issue and logical composition. The recipients of the letters are not named because the interest is in the issues rather than in the personalities – whether girls should be allowed to study, how to bring up children, whether quarrels over rank are important, whether it is important for sons to be sent abroad. The letters combine a lively style with practical wisdom but by comparison with letters written later in the century are anything but personal confessions. Ziegler was concerned to show that women could write a sensible, intelligent and entertaining letter.

While Ziegler was publishing that first collection, young Luise Culmus had embarked on her correspondence with her future husband, Gottsched. These letters were recognized as fine examples of the genre by her husband but she forbade publication during her lifetime. They show a serious but also witty and intelligent correspondent, whose letters are written in a precise and elegant style. They already have the quality of *Natürlichkeit* that Gellert was later to demand, meaning a style free from cumbersome mannerisms. Her early letters show her eagerness to learn from her prominent suitor, her willingness to respond to his guidance in the matter of her reading and also her deference to his opinion. While responding in a lively manner to all his reading suggestions, she is quickly put in her place if she oversteps the mark and she accepts this.

In her later letters to her friend Dorothea von Runckel Frau Gottsched shows a much greater need to unburden herself. She expresses her melancholy and disappointment with the restraint that already characterized her youthful letters:

> Mein Leben ist nichts als ein abwechselndes Leiden, bald am Cörper, bald am Gemüthe. Mein Sommer ist vorbey; der rauhe Herbst sammlet die Früchte der verstrichenen Jahreszeiten, und ich sehne mich nicht in den herbeyeilenden Winter mich lange aufzuhalten.
>
> (*Briefe*, vol. III, p. 149)
>
> My life is nothing but alternate suffering of body and spirit. My summer is past; the rough autumn gathers the fruits of the seasons past and I have no desire to linger long into the rapidly approaching winter.

A new tone and expressive power in the letter form was reached in the correspondence of Meta Klopstock née Moller, who met Klopstock, the young poet of *Der Messias* (The Messiah) in 1751, married him in 1754 and died in childbirth only four years later. Yet such was the resonance for the next generation of their relationship that she became almost a mythical figure. Meta Moller came from a well-situated Hamburg family. While her two elder sisters made conventional marriages, Meta opted for the unusual course of marrying for love a man who had no recognized profession. Though she never strove to be learned, she was well-read and intelligent, and her letters and posthumously published writings show her own, sadly undeveloped, poetic talent. All of her letters reflect her ability to capture her mood and to speak with an arresting directness to the recipient, but it is in her correspondence with Klopstock that we see her creating in the letter form a method of capturing an intense emotional relationship. What gave the Klopstock–Meta relationship its power for future generations was the combination of romantic love and religious sentiment. Their letters, and hers to him in particular, are evidence of a communion of souls in which the reciprocity of love is woven together with Christian spirituality. Meta Klopstock had the rare talent of finding words to express her happiness, while not disguising the pain she felt at their frequent separations:

> Ich weis nicht wie das gehen soll, ich muß schon wieder schreiben! Gottlob daß mir dies nur noch bleibt! Wie unendlich süsser aber würde es seyn wenn du bey mir wärst! Du fehlst mir niemals mehr also wenn ich des Abends zu Hause komme, denn ich hole itzt alle die Besuche nach, die ich deinetwegen versäumt habe. O wie unbeschreiblich süß war das, wenn ich wuste, daß ich dich in meiner Stube fand!

(META KLOPSTOCK, Briefwechsel, vol. I, p. 166)

> I do not know what's the matter with me but I have to write yet again! Thank goodness that at least I still have that. But how infinitely sweeter it would be to have you with me! I miss you most of all when I come home in the evening, for I am catching up now on all the visits I neglected on your account. O how inexpressibly sweet it was to know that I would find you in my room!

Klopstock's own letters are raised to a much higher level of poetic and expressive power through Meta, whom he often refers to as his Clärchen, after Richardson's *Clarissa*, a novel they both greatly admired. Meta helped to establish a correspondence between her husband and the English novelist some few months before her death and her letters to Richardson show how even in a foreign language she was able to convey spontaneity and depth of feeling:

> Though I love my friends dearly, and though they are good, I have however much to pardon except in the single Klopstock alone. *He* is good, really good, good at the bottom, in all his actions, in all the foldings of his heart. I know him; and sometimes I think if we knew others in the same manner the better we should find them. For it may be that an action displeases us which would please us, if we knew its true aim and whole extent. None of my friends is *so* happy as I am; but no one had the courage to marry as I did. They have married, – as people marry; and they are happy, – as people are happy.

(Briefwechsel vol. II, p. 440)

Another prolific letter-writer is Anna Luise Karsch, who goes down in literary history as the first German woman to make a living by writing.

Better known for her patriotic odes, religious and occasional poems and for her gift of rapid improvisation, she fascinated Berlin society when she was brought there in 1761 from her native Silesia. Few of her letters were published in her life-time, and yet they, in some critics' view more than the majority of her verses, show her literary talent in a power of expression that is both moving and concrete.

Born into humble circumstances, and neglected by her mother on account of her plainness, she was taught to read and write as a child by a great-uncle. Divorced by her first husband (in possibly the first divorce among subjects of her station in Prussia), she was forced to leave her home and her two children, while already expecting a third child. Under family pressure she then married a tailor who drank, fathered four children and beat her. Through commissions for occasional poems she began to use her extraordinary facility for writing verses to supplement her meagre income. Her odes in praise of Frederick the Great's victories in the Seven Years War brought her some local fame and through patrons she was brought to Berlin, her husband having been bundled off to the army. The emergence of this *Naturtalent* aroused great curiosity in Berlin. She gained the support of the philosopher Sulzer and of the poets Ramler and Gleim, the latter a constant friend and adviser in spite of the difficulties caused in the early months of their relationship by her unrequited love for him. It was he who attached to her the name of the German Sappho and tried to secure her financial future by having an edition of her collected poems printed in 1764. It brought in 2,000 Thalers, more than any literary work before it, though that windfall did not in fact guarantee her an easy life and she frequently suffered acute shortages of money thereafter.

The designation of Anna Luise Karsch as a *Naturtalent* sprang from the longing in some literary circles for a poetry that was not the product of learned deliberation and the study of rules, and from the desire to believe in a pre-civilized world, where poetry sprang spontaneously from the lips of the poet. Her letters to Sulzer describing her earlier life are stylized to fit that idealized vision of country life. Once introduced by Gleim to the language of rococo dalliance, Karsch takes this into her poetry and her letters to him. Yet it is clear that for her this is not mere role-playing, and her own emotions break through the gallant language. When Gleim makes it clear that he does not intend an actual romantic involvement her pain is evident in her directness:

> Sagen Sie von Ihrer kalten Freundschaft, was Sie wollen. Das Wort
> Liebe war eher als das Wort Freundschaft, und mir dünkt, es führt so

viel Süßes bei sich, daß ich ihm Vorzug geben muß. Hüten Sie sich,
mir jemals die Liebe wieder lächerlich zu machen! Itzt, da mich der
Nahrungskummer nicht mehr anspornt zu dichten, itzt kann nichts
so allmächtig sein, mich zu begeistern, als eben die Liebe.

(Gedichte, p. 107)

Say what you like about your cold friendship. The word love was there
before the word friendship, and to me it has such sweetness in it that I
must give it preference. Take care never to make love ridiculous in my
eyes again! Now that I am no longer spurred on to write poetry to
provide my next meal nothing has the overwhelming power to inspire
me so much as love.

Yet her ability to make verses on any and every occasion was for others
what made her a *Naturtalent*. In fact, her most prominent poems, for
example her odes to Frederick the Great, owe more to the Baroque tradition than to any spontaneous style of her own, genuine though her veneration for the king might have been.

The arguments surrounding Anna Luise Karsch illustrate well the
poetological controversies of the day. They indicate also how difficult it
was for her contemporaries to place her and their consequent tendency to
overlook what was really of value in her work. There is much that is sec-
ond-rate in such a voluminous output and yet there are poems striking
for their wit and their remarkable feeling for the tangible things of life, as
in her 'Lob der schwarzen Kirschen' ('In Praise of Black Cherries'), and for
their poignancy:

Was wir heftig lange wünschen müssen,
Und was wir nicht zu erhalten wissen,
Drückt sich tiefer unserm Herzen ein;
Rebensaft verschwendet der Gesunde
Und erquickend schmeckt des Kranken Munde
Auch im Traum der ungetrunkne Wein.

('AN DEN DOMHERRN VON ROCHOW', *Gedichte*, p. 69)

What we have to wish for long and hard and what we do not know how
to hold on to impresses itself more deeply on our hearts. The healthy
man is wasteful with the juice of the grape; to the lips of sick man the
wine he cannot drink tastes refreshing even in his dreams.

Sophie La Roche and the emergence of the woman novelist

Sophie La Roche is a key figure in the emergence of the German woman of
letters. Her first novel, *Geschichte des Fräuleins von Sternheim* (*The History of*

Lady Sophia Sternheim; 1771), was a huge success and made her famous. She was also, with Anna Luise Karsch, one of the first German women whose writing was an important source of income for her family and thus her career brings us into the period when a reading public was forming, whose interests and tastes increasingly shaped what was offered by publishers. Though famous in her day, Sophie La Roche was neglected after her death by the nineteenth-century literary historians whose judgements formed the canon of eighteenth-century works, because much of her output was primarily for women readers and was often didactic in intention. Yet her energy and range are impressive. In addition to writing several novels, two of which, *Das Fräulein von Sternheim* and *Rosaliens Briefe an ihre Freundin Mariane von St. Altenburg* (Rosalia's letters to her friend Mariane von St. Altenburg), were particularly influential, she was one of the first female editors of a women's journal, *Pomona für Teutschlands Töchter* (Pomona. For Germany's daughters), wrote extensive accounts of her travels when travel writing was still in its infancy in Germany, and engaged in a vast correspondence. However, it is true that her style seemed old-fashioned as time passed and her range of tone and expression was limited. She reached a pinnacle of literary achievement with her first work, *Das Fräulein von Sternheim*, in which didacticism and literary skill were most successfully combined.

Sophie La Roche enjoyed the benefits of being brought up in an academic family, the daughter of a doctor, who taught her to read and write. Her education was supplemented in her teens by an Italian doctor, Gian Lodovico Bianconi, a friend of her father, to whom she became engaged and who instructed her in mathematics, singing, Italian and art. The marriage plans foundered on religious differences between Bianconi and Sophie's father. Her reading and literary interests were further cultivated by her cousin Christoph Martin Wieland, later to become one of the most prominent writers of the German Enlightenment, to whom she was engaged for a time. Though again no marriage ensued, Wieland later brought her to the public eye by encouraging her to finish and publish her first novel. At the age of twenty-three she agreed to marry Georg Michael Frank La Roche, *Hofrat* at the court of the Elector of Mainz and adopted son of Count Stadion, first minister of the Elector. One of Sophie's main functions was to entertain with informed conversation about such topics as literature, and her curiosity, her facility in moving from one subject to another and her quick response to new impressions were developed within this court environment. She constantly returns in her work to her belief that women should acquire through suitable reading a store of useful knowledge about the world around them. In this respect she belongs to the Enlightenment tradition, despite all the sentimental qualities of her works. For her and her heroines, moral goodness goes hand in hand with a character-building awareness of the world.

La Roche's first novel, *Geschichte des Fräuleins von Sternheim*, appeared anonymously in 1771, edited by Wieland. The popularity in Germany of the novels of Samuel Richardson, in which for the first time a woman's experience and perspective were explored (albeit by a male writer), laid the foundations for its enormous success with both male and female readers. The moral weeklies had created a taste for Moral Tales (*Moralische Erzählungen*), a tradition of popular didactic writing that continued well into the nineteenth century. *Das Fräulein von Sternheim* also bears the mark of Rousseau's condemnation of the decadence of civilization in its contrasting pictures of court and country life and in its concentration on the heart-searchings of the central figure, a feature that also links the novel to the strong German Pietist tradition of introspection and self-examination. It satisfied contemporary demands for a measure of realism, some depth of psychological motivation and an appeal to the emotions, while providing outer action that was fast-moving and exciting. It is fitting that the first great novelistic success for a woman should come from a novel in letter form, for, leaving aside the influence of Richardson, the letter was, as we have seen, a type of writing in which women in the eighteenth century excelled and which gained from naturalness and liveliness of style.

Sophie von Sternheim is the product of a *mésalliance*. Her father is an ennobled officer, her mother a member of an old aristocratic family. For her, as for her parents, true aristocracy is an aristocracy of the heart, which shows itself in philanthropy and the careful stewardship of one's estates. An orphan at eighteen, Sophie is brought to the court of D. by her aunt and uncle, who aim to make her the Prince's mistress in order to influence a legal case affecting their wealth. Sophie attempts to cling to the principles of her upbringing while not being experienced enough to see how she is being compromised. After seeking rescue in what turns out to be a sham marriage to the rake Derby she enters a period of testing when all that she relied on is removed. However, turning her moral sensitivity into practical help for those around her, she survives even abduction to a remote part of Scotland and assault by Derby's servant to be united finally with her true soulmate, Lord Seymour.

Sophie von Sternheim is an intriguing reflection of her creator's position between Enlightenment and *Empfindsamkeit* (sensibility). While possessed of extreme moral sensitivity, Sophie does not collapse under the weight of her misfortunes. She does not pine away but rather seeks useful activity. However, the heroine's refusal to abandon her belief in good works and in her duty to perform them cannot disguise the fact that she is essentially powerless to control her own life. We are meant to see the happy ending as a vindication of goodness and courage by a benevolent providence, but La Roche also reveals, probably contrary to any conscious intention, the vulnerability of a woman without male protectors.

La Roche's subsequent novels are less successful in balancing moral didacticism with excitement, immediacy and narrative skill. Her next novel, *Rosaliens Briefe* (1779–81), though very popular, already has a more prescriptive tone. Where she is perhaps particularly interesting, bearing in mind tendencies in modern women's fiction, is in her creation in various novels and stories of women's utopias. The story *Der schöne Bund* (A beautiful alliance; 1789) deals with the promise of four girls from differing backgrounds to stand by one another in their future lives. One of them, uncharacteristically for her time, devotes herself to scholarship. This then is the feminine counterpart to the contemporary cult of idealistic male friendships. Marriage as a partnership of equals, as we see it at the end of *Das Fräulein von Sternheim,* occurs again in *Erscheinungen am See Oneida* (Scenes on Lake Oneida; 1798), the story of a young French couple attempting to create a new life in America. By such examples we see Sophie La Roche trying to stretch the frontiers of female experience and activity.

Sophie La Roche can claim to have made a significant contribution to developing forms of writing in three further areas – the women's journal, travel writing and the moral tale, the first two being still in their infancy at the time she began her work. Her travel writing documents journeys to countries such as France, Switzerland, Holland and England, and combines information, anecdote and personal impressions in an easy, mellifluous style. She published numerous *moralische Erzählungen*, some of which depart from the purely predictable. In *Liebe, Mißverständnis und Freundschaft* (Love, misunderstanding and friendship; 1786), for example, she tells the story of Elisa, who though engaged to a man she loves becomes convinced that their temperaments are not suited and that she will fail to hold his affection in future years. Instead of marrying she begins a school for girls with a young widow and is entirely fulfilled by this activity – another female utopia, created by a widow who is glad to be free and a woman who commits herself to celibacy in pursuit of her vocation.

Das Fräulein von Sternheim was the first in a growing number of novels by women. The next generation of women writers was encouraged by the example of Sophie La Roche. However, few novels by women in the eighteenth century, interesting evidence though they may supply about attitudes and depictions of women, come close to her achievement. The *Frauenroman* (woman's novel) became a platform on which an ideal of womanhood was constantly being set up but rarely being explored with realism. The intense preoccupation with women's role and education, and with the nature of *Geschlechtscharaktere*, is reflected in the novels of the following decades, many of which take up again the theme of virtue on trial and patience in suffering. The prime example of the novel as vehicle for a deeply conservative view of woman is *Elisa, oder das Weib wie es seyn sollte* (1795; Elisa, or what women should be like), usually attributed to Wilhelmine Karoline von Wobeser (though external evidence suggests the possibility of a male author or a man working with a woman – see Gallas and Heuser, pp. 114–31). Elisa is forced by family pressure to renounce her true love and enter into a marriage with a cold, boorish tyrant, who squanders their fortune and entertains a mistress. Elisa's goodness and complete self-effacement finally win over her husband and she dies at peace. This novel was immensely successful, went into six editions and provoked numerous variations on its themes and title. Its popularity is a reminder that although in Romantic circles a more progressive view of women was entertained, such a view was far from being shared by the majority of men or women. The exception to this generally conservative depiction of woman is in the early work of Therese Huber, in particular in *Die Familie Seldorf* (The Seldorf family; 1795/96), set before and during the French Revolution and the first novel by a German woman to be based on contemporary history, and *Luise. Ein Beitrag zur Geschichte der Konvenienz* (Luise. A contribution to the history of social propriety; 1796). Both novels show a remarkable honesty in their depiction of the heroine. Luise can be seen as a negative counterpart to Elisa. Also forced by family pressure to make an unsuitable match, she is by nature excessively sensitive and prone to illness. The stresses of her situation drive her to madness and even though she tries repeatedly to find a way of making her husband happy, both by devotion and by good sense, she is trapped and at the mercy of his selfishness, folly and brutality. Huber reveals the terrible dependency of her heroine on an indifferent husband and an insensitive family in which the daughter is a burden to be off-loaded as soon as possible.

The contemporary controversy over education for women is reflected in Helene Unger's novel, *Julchen Grünthal. Eine Pensionsgeschichte* (Julchen Grünthal. A boarding school story; 1784), another considerable popular success, which satirizes the German fashion for adopting French manners and education. The worthy but weak-willed Grünthal allows his wife to persuade him that their beautiful young daughter is buried in the country and needs the sophisticating influence of a few years at a boarding school in Berlin. The result is the loss of her simple goodness and destruction of her moral character. As well as showing a strongly anti-French and anti-court tendency, the novel reflects the contemporary fear that women are endangered morally by knowing too much. The warning example here is the head of the school, Madame Brennfeld, who combines philosophical freethinking with snobbery and a moral *insouciance* fatal to her charges. Julchen's passions are inflamed by unsuitable reading, Rousseau's *La nouvelle Héloïse* being particularly detrimental. After seducing her cousin's husband and then marrying him after his divorce, she is bankrupted by luxury and runs off with a Russian nobleman. A second novel appeared in 1798, in which the repentant Julchen is reunited with her father. Unger produced this mainly because of the stir caused by the original work and by the appearance of an anonymous sequel by another author. While Unger may be exaggerating both Julchen and Grünthal for satirical effect (Susanne Zantop sees the novel as having elements of self-parody; see Gallas and Heuser, p. 137), the novel nevertheless reflects a fear that women were constantly in danger of moral corruption from the influences outside the family and from unsuitable reading. It is instructive to compare the attitudes in these novels with the assumptions that underlie the emerging *Bildungsroman*. Women were increasingly required by the end of the century to be *gebildet*, that is cultivated and moderately well-read. However, *Bildung* as an ideal embodied in the *Bildungsroman* is primarily related to male experience and possibilities and thus the female *Bildungsroman* has seemed to some critics a contradiction in terms. Whereas the male hero goes out into the world as a kind of representative figure and grows to maturity and insight through experience, the openness to change and receptivity to life that are the preconditions of the maturing process in men are presented as problematic and even hazardous for women (see also Gallas and Heuser; Touaillon).

A contrast to the didactic tone of much fiction by women is provided by the work of Benedikte Naubert, which is only just receiving new critical attention. Her speciality became the fairy tale and, most importantly, the historical novel, which she pioneered in Germany both with her own novels and through her many translations. Her technique of presenting a fictional family history against a historical background influenced Sir Walter Scott. Her main concern as a novelist is in swiftness and abundance of action. In her early non-historical novel *Heerfort und Klärchen. Etwas für empfindsame Seelen* (Heerfort and Klärchen: A story for feeling hearts; 1779) the focus of attention is the series of misfortunes that separate and of adventures that then reunite the young lovers, a pattern she was to use many times, while setting her novels in a wide variety of countries and periods.

Women's journals

Just as in the course of the eighteenth century the woman writer gradually became thinkable, so too the woman editor emerged. Women's journals owe their existence very substantially to the moral weeklies that flourished in the first half of the century. These encouraged, as we have noted, female literacy and informative reading. In the 1720s Gottsched's journal *Die vernünftigen Tadlerinnen* uses the fiction of female editorship, an indication that it was already felt desirable that the readers should consider themselves in some kind of dialogue with other women. While numerous journals aimed at a female readership sprang up in the following decades and women were frequent contributors to them, the first journals to be edited by women for women began to appear in the late 1770s and 80s. Ernestine Hofmann edited the journal *Für Hamburgs Töchter* (For Hamburg's daughters) in 1779, though using a male persona, and Charlotte Henriette von Hezel edited the equally shortlived *Wochenblatt für's schöne Geschlecht auf das Jahr 1779* (Weekly for the fair sex for the year 1779), an intellectually broader and more ambitious publication than Hofmann's. The most popular of these early journals was *Pomona für Teutschlands Töchter*, edited by Sophie La Roche, who used primarily female contributors. It ran for only two years (1783–4) and the reasons for its discontinuation are not clearly established. Her readers were, in any event, greatly disappointed when publication ceased. *Pomona* (named after the goddess of autumn) shows the didactic and educational goals of the editor and also her skill and journalistic flair. She denies from the start that she wants to make her readers learned but they should be informed

in matters of history, geography, literature, natural history and the rudi-
ments of science so that they can understand something of the world
about them. A continuous thread running through the journal, the
'Briefe an Lina', advice to a girl preparing for marriage, were very popular
and later published separately. Some volumes were devoted to a particular country, a forward-looking experiment which indicates La Roche's
journalistic talent. She also published poems by women poets and a number of her own *moralische Erzählungen* in the journal.

The best-known female editor in the following decade was Marianne
Ehrmann, who as well as writing plays edited *Amaliens Erholungsstunden*
(Amalia's recreational hours) between 1790 and 1792 for the publisher
Cotta. After losing this post, possibly because of the controversial tenor of
some of her material, she published in her own right a shortlived journal
Die Einsiedlerin aus den Alpen (The settler from the Alps). In both these
journals we find, alongside more conventional contributions such as
serialized stories, poems and news of the latest fashions, some more
provocative considerations of women's roles. Ehrmann takes up again the
theme of the need for better education for women, claiming it does not
conflict with their *Bestimmung* (calling). She wants her readers to dare to
think for themselves, to equip themselves with *Nachdenken, Grundsätze,
Menschenkenntniß* (reflection, principles, knowledge of human nature),
qualities to which she refers repeatedly. While she is careful not to challenge the notion of woman's primary role as wife and mother, she clearly
wishes to encourage her readers to develop and exercise their own judgement. *Die Einsiedlerin aus den Alpen* is even more explicitly satirical of male
attitudes, especially those that condemn women to uselessness and thereby bring about the vanity that men then criticize. Ehrmann's journals are
unique in their period and it is tempting to overemphasize their critical
tendency. It would be the task of nineteenth-century women writers and
journalists to exploit the journal in the cause of female emancipation.
What Ehrmann's and the other, predominantly conservative, journals do
show is the extent by the end of the century of female participation in
journalism and of a literate and literature-conscious female reading
public.

4

Revolution, Romanticism, Restoration
(1789–1830)

To many German writers and thinkers the French Revolution seemed, at least initially, the dawn of a new age of freedom. For women, however, the promise of the Revolution, as of the Enlightenment, remained largely unfulfilled. Its ideals of liberty and equality were undermined by a gender-exclusive interpretation of the ideal of fraternity, or the brotherhood of man. Significantly, it is this ideal which is invoked in Schiller's 'Ode to Joy' (1785), now the European anthem. Since the political upheavals of 1989 the problematic legacy of the revolutionary decades has acquired a new topicality. An understanding of it is, therefore, essential, not least in view of the intensity of current debates on gender roles, the origins of which may be traced back to this period.

The years following the Revolution saw numerous publications concerned with gender roles and the nature and function of women. In the early 1790s three treatises advocating for women the rights claimed by men appeared almost simultaneously in different European countries. In 1791 the French dramatist Olympe de Gouges published a *Déclaration des droits de la femme*; in 1792 Mary Wollstonecraft's *Vindication of the Rights of Woman* came out in England; and in the same year a German author, Theodor von Hippel, brought out an essay entitled *Über die bürgerliche Verbesserung der Weiber* (*On Improving the Status of Women*). All three writers based their arguments on Enlightenment principles, but their demands were not met: de Gouges was guillotined, Wollstonecraft reviled, and Hippel's polemic – the only one written by a man and published anonymously – was overtaken by a series of essays produced shortly afterwards by Schiller, Wilhelm von Humboldt and Friedrich Schlegel.

These essays were concerned not with the rights and status of women, but with gender characteristics, and they exerted a decisive influence on attitudes to women well into the twentieth century. This is particularly the case with the writings of Schiller and Humboldt. Both developed antithetical conceptions of gender difference in terms of sexual polarity, and Schiller disseminated these in poems which enjoyed great popularity among the German middle classes throughout the nineteenth century and beyond. The influence of German culture on other countries enabled these ideas to gain widespread currency elsewhere, too. This is shown, for instance, by 'The Literary Lady', a translation of Schiller's disparaging poem 'Die berühmte Frau' (The famous woman) which appeared in the *Dublin University Magazine* of 1834. According to Schiller and Humboldt, women were naturally passive and emotional, lacking in the rational and analytical capacity which was seen as the prerequisite both for social action and for the creation of artistic works of genius. While the domesticated woman was idealized, those who sought political power or literary fame were censured. The Romantics, whose mode of thought tended towards the unification of opposites and the blurring of borderlines, ridiculed Schiller's vision of womanhood. 'Nur selbständige Weiblichkeit, nur sanfte Männlichkeit ist gut und schön' (Only independent femininity, only gentle masculinity is good and beautiful), wrote Friedrich Schlegel in *Über die Diotima* (On Diotima; 1795), arguing that both categories should be subordinated to the higher concept of humanity. Even Schlegel, however, falls short of postulating complete equality between the sexes: his ideas are often ambiguous or contradictory, and he ignores the practical obstacles which prevented contemporary women from achieving the independence which, in theory, he advocated for them.

These obstacles were legal, economic, educational and cultural. Legally, women were minors, dependent on their fathers before marriage and their husbands after it. As the provisions of the Prussian Civil Code of 1794 show, they lacked almost all rights, including, crucially, financial and property rights. They were excluded from business and the professions, and from participation in public forums and affairs of state. The married woman was effectively a non-person, and although divorce was possible, particularly in Protestant Prussia, the female divorcee was virtually a pariah, while Luther's teaching on marriage had made the single woman an anomaly. Employment opportunities for middle-class women were restricted to the 'respectable' occupations of teacher or governess, or the more questionable one of actress. The only alternative sources of income were needlework or, importantly, writing. In practice, very few women managed to pursue independent careers.

Since middle-class women were not being prepared for a profession their education was normally inferior to that of men. It was intended to equip them for a domestic role, with the addition of such 'accomplishments' as might make them good mothers, companionable spouses, and entertaining acquaintances. Abstract, analytical and scientific subjects were regarded as unsuitable for the female mind, and systematic study of any kind by women was rare. 'Learned women' (*gelehrt*, rather than *gebildet* = accomplished) were the butt of criticism and ridicule: the award in 1787 of a doctorate, the first gained by a woman in the humanities, to Dorothea Schlözer (1770–1825) was described by Schiller as a farce.

This reaction illustrates vividly the cultural barriers to female emancipation which existed immediately before the Revolution. Far from attempting to dismantle them after that event, the leading intellectual authorities of the age – including, besides Schiller and Humboldt, the philosophers Kant and Fichte – sought to entrench them still further by underwriting as permanent the socially conditioned dependence characteristic of late eighteenth-century German women's lives.

The era of the Napoleonic Wars, although entailing much upheaval and hardship for women, brought them at the same time a measure of autonomy as traditional social structures crumbled. This liberation was, however, of brief duration. In the conservative political climate which prevailed after the Restoration of 1815, hierarchical values were reasserted and male and female roles more sharply defined than ever. Hegel proclaimed marriage and the family to be ethical institutions, the foundations of the state and of social order. These views were echoed by theologians and government ministers alike. The family was regarded as both a natural and a moral unit, and women's place was declared to be in the home, while the middle-class male tended to spend a good deal of time outside the house, whether in professional activities or in all-male voluntary associations.

Such a cultural climate was not conducive to the development of women's self-confidence or of a strongly independent female voice in the German writing of the time. Nevertheless, it is this period that produced most of the small number of pre-twentieth century German 'women of letters' who are still at all well known. The majority of these are associated with the Romantic movement, and the continuing resonance of their names is inextricably interwoven with the fascination exercised by that movement down to the present day, while other women are known for their association with Goethe or Schiller.

There is, however, a greater diversity of women writers in this period than can be accommodated under the traditional headings of either Romanticism or Classicism. They wrote in virtually all the major genres, fictional and non-fictional: lyric, drama, prose narrative, letters, diaries, autobiography, travel writing, educational and journalistic works. They also made a significant contribution to cultural life as hostesses of salons, and as reviewers and translators. In general, these women had enjoyed an education superior to that of most women of the time: some were members of the aristocracy, while several were daughters of university professors or of prosperous Jewish families. They were well read in German and often in other modern literatures – acceptable subjects of study for women – and some knew the classics and even philosophical works. Nevertheless, their writing, unlike that of many men of the period, does not tend to the creation of grandiose theoretical edifices or overarching schemes of thought. Whatever their learning, they were discouraged from the ostentatious display of it. They concentrate instead on the specific, the concrete, and the personal, making up for gaps in their knowledge, or for its haphazard acquisition (which sometimes left them deficient in such areas as orthography and syntax), by a freshness, a spontaneity and a directness which makes much of their work still worth reading today.

Lyric poetry

The verse of Sophie Albrecht, née Baumer, exemplifies many of the characteristics of women's writing at this time. Her life, too, is not untypical: an educated middle-class background; a marriage ending in divorce; a period of relative independence and the attempt to establish a career, which was for a time successful; the eventual abandonment of creative writing; efforts to scrape a living by other means; increasing impoverishment; and final dependence on the charity of others. These typical features are, however, combined with more unusual aspects. She was under fifteen when in 1772, a year after the death of her father, a professor of medicine at the University of Erfurt, she married a physician who was also an adventurer, bookseller, theatre director and writer. She became, too, a celebrated actress while retaining her respectability: in 1774 she played the female lead in the first performance of *Kabale und Liebe* (*Intrigue and Love*) by Schiller, and became friendly with him. Her poems, stories and plays appeared in three volumes, the last in 1791. Subsequently she turned her hand to gothic novels. However, her situation steadily worsened: she was divorced in 1796 or 1798 and after 1808 published no more literary works. In old age she wrote cookery books.

Sophie Albrecht's poems convey personal emotion with frankness and simplicity and in a variety of verse forms. Many of them centre on love, often expressed in terms of absence, loss, deprivation, grief and suffering. 'An die Freiheit' (To freedom) takes up a characteristic theme of the late eighteenth century, but in contrast to poems by men interprets it in purely personal terms, omitting any political or patriotic dimension. Nevertheless, awareness is shown both of the connection between personal autonomy and creative self-expression and of the social constraints placed on women. The first and last stanzas link the return of freedom with the production of new songs, while the penultimate stanza attributes lack of emotional fulfilment to masculine domination of the sphere in which the self exists: 'Hier in dieser Männer-Zone / Grünt für mich die Myrte nicht'. (Here in this male zone the myrtle will not flourish for me).

A similar insight is demonstrated in a short poem by Sophie Mereau, née Schubart, 'An einen Baum am Spalier' ('To a Trellised Tree'). This achieves greater objectivity than Albrecht's poem to freedom, but the indirect comparison of the tree to a human form ('eine menschliche Gestalt'), cut off from the liberty of nature and compelled by an alien force to adopt a rigid, conventional pose, clearly suggests the restrictions placed on middle-class women. Mereau, born in Altenburg, Thuringia, the younger daughter of the ducal secretary, constantly chafed against these restrictions and championed love, freedom, and physical, emotional and intellectual fulfilment for women. In 1793 she married Karl Mereau, subsequently Professor of Law at the University of Jena, who had introduced her to Schiller and thereby set her literary career in train. Her house became a centre of social and cultural life, but the marriage was unhappy and the couple divorced in 1801. For the next two years Mereau supported herself and her daughter by her writing, reluctantly marrying the Romantic writer Clemens Brentano in 1803 when she became pregnant by him. She died giving birth to her fifth child in 1806, aged thirty-six.

Schiller published a number of Mereau's poems in his journals and discussed her extensively in his correspondence with Goethe. Two volumes of her poems appeared in 1800 and 1802, and a collected edition came out in 1805. The French Revolution was a defining experience for her: it forms the subject of her first published poem (1790), and is indirectly evoked in 'Feuerfarb' (Fire-colour; 1792), which was set to music in 1805 by Beethoven in his Opus 52. Fire and the colour red – the latter is never explicitly mentioned in the poem – had strong contemporary associations with the Revolution, but the poem manages to avoid offence by its 'feminized', non-violent tone which implies more than it actually states.

Another woman whose poems were set to music by contemporary composers was Wilhelmine (Helmina) von Chézy, née von Klenke, the granddaughter of the poet Anna Luise Karsch. Like many women writers of the period, she tried her hand at a wide range of genres, both fictional and non-fictional. She was also socially and politically active, and as a result frequently came into conflict with authorities. Male writers and critics have treated her with ridicule and contempt. She is, however, of interest as a chronicler of Parisian life, and some of her poems are worthy of note. One of them, dedicated to her friend Therese von Winkel, anticipates Rilke in its use of rose imagery.

The most significant woman poet of the period is Karoline von Günderrode. Born in Karlsruhe in 1780, the eldest of the six children of a court adviser and writer, she moved with her family to Hanau after her father's death in 1786 and was educated at home by her learned and poetically gifted mother, Louise. In 1797 she entered a *Stift* (Protestant cloister) for unmarried gentlewomen of slender means in Frankfurt am Main. She suffered greatly from the limitations imposed on her as a woman, longing for more education, for a physically active life such as only men were permitted, for fulfilment in love, and for association with men who were her intellectual equals. She became emotionally involved with three men in succession: Karl von Savigny (later Prussian Minister of Justice); Clemens Brentano, whose sister Gunda married Savigny; and Friedrich Creuzer, a married professor in Heidelberg whose decision to break off their affair was the catalyst for Günderrode's suicide by stabbing at Winkel on the banks of the Rhine in 1806. The ultimate cause of her death was, however, not so much an individual disappointment as the irreconcilable contradictions which characterized her life and are reflected in symbolic form in her works.

Two volumes of verse were published in her lifetime, both under the masculine pseudonym of Tian: *Gedichte und Phantasien* (Poems and fantasies; 1804) and *Poetische Fragmente* (Poetic fragments; 1805). A third volume, *Melete*, containing poems, prose pieces and dramatic fragments, was to have been published in Heidelberg under the pseudonym of Ion but was suppressed by Creuzer after her death. What remained of it was published in a limited edition in 1906. Like Mereau, she stands between

Classicism and Romanticism and cannot be definitely assigned to either. She experimented with a great variety of poetic forms and styles, from folksongs and love lyrics to philosophical poems and verse in classical metre. Mythology and exotic settings play an important role in her poems, while death is a pervasive theme and is often linked with sexuality, as in the ballad 'Don Juan'. Murder and especially suicide are frequent motifs, and there are hints of homosexuality, incest and masochism. Another constant topic in her works is the search for knowledge and truth, for instance in the poems 'Der Adept' (The adept) and 'Des Wanderers Niederfahrt' (The wanderer's descent). Both are closely related to central themes and motifs of Goethe's *Faust* (the first part of which was not published until 1808, two years after Günderrode's death) and both end with a resigned acceptance of finite human existence.

Another talented writer whose life ended in suicide is Louise Brachmann. The daughter of a local government official, she was, like Günderrode, taught at home by an educated mother. She was recommended to Schiller by the Romantic writer Novalis (Friedrich von Hardenberg), with whose sister, Sidonie, she was friendly, and like Mereau she published several poems in Schiller's journals. She first attempted suicide in 1800; subsequently both her parents, a sister, Friedrich and Sidonie von Hardenberg and their brother Erasmus all died in the space of four years. Totally impoverished, she turned to writing as a career, but was unable to gain the sponsorship of a major publisher and was obliged to be overprolific. Persistent financial difficulties, personal problems and lack of artistic recognition led her to drown herself in the Saale at Halle.

Like Günderrode, Brachmann drew on mythological subject matter in some of her poems, notably 'Antigone', which celebrates in classical hexameters the heroine's act of sacrificial love in burying her brother's corpse, thereby transgressing male law and bringing about her own destruction. While her deed may be seen as an extreme expression of traditional female behaviour, the elements of free choice and heroic defiance are stressed in the poem, which opens with an invocation of the Olympian goddesses as symbols of female power and closes with an address to Antigone as a personal role model. Another poem, 'Griechenlied' (Greek song), relates ancient Greece to the contemporary Greek struggle for independence, declaring that those who do not help the modern Greeks are not worthy to extol the ancients. Although only male figures are mentioned, heroism is again equated with sacrificial death. The theme of death is implicitly present, too, in 'Der Führer' (The guide; 1805), a poem of homage to Novalis which presents the deceased poet as a youth with a torch, a classical image of death which Novalis himself had used. In contrast to the more active tone of the poems with classical allusions, the predominant mood of two poems which use non-classical topoi, 'Das Hirtenmädchen' (The young shepherdess; 1807) and 'Klosterstille' (The tranquillity of the convent; 1819), is one of resignation.

While Brachmann, like Karsch before her, was known as the German Sappho, the Austrian poet Gabriele Baumberg was acclaimed by contemporaries as the Viennese Sappho. Born into affluent circumstances in 1766 – her father was Director of the Imperial Court Archives – she became a lady-in-waiting to the Empress in 1797, but in 1799 fell in love with the Hungarian poet and nationalist János Bacsányi (1763–1845), whom she married in 1805 and whose imprisonment and banishment she shared. Some of her poems were published in a Viennese literary journal and an edition of them, *Gedichte*, appeared in 1805, but after 1809 she was unable for political reasons to find a publisher and ceased to write.

That Baumberg had a clear conception both of her role as a woman writer and of the prejudices with which she was confronted is evident from two contrasting poems, 'Beweggründe zur Poesie' (Motives for writing poetry) and 'Widerruf' (Recantation). In the first of these she declares that she can express in poetry the emotions – specifically, love for the opposite sex – which women are not permitted to express in prose, a conviction which she puts into practice in poems such as 'Schwärmerey (Nach einem Ball)' (Rapture (After a ball)). She was, however, distressed by the notoriety that her poetry brought her, and in 'Widerruf' revokes her attempts to challenge a taboo which she now views as beneficial for women, since it protects them from the contempt of men. The renewed optimism of 'Die Glückliche' (The happy woman), written in celebration of her marriage, indicates restored confidence in writing, while the complex late poem 'Herbstblumen' (Autumn flowers) shows potential for further development which remained unrealized. Her work has now virtually disappeared from anthologies.

Some of the lyrics of Luise Hensel, on the other hand, have become common property through their inclusion in hymn books and other collections. The daughter of a Protestant pastor who died when she was twelve, she wrote patriotic songs for the Wars of Liberation against Napoleon and was introduced into artistic and aristocratic circles in Berlin where she met, among others, Clemens Brentano, on whose life she had a profound influence. He was deeply impressed by her religious poetry –

she converted to Catholicism in 1818 – but took liberties with her work, publishing his own versions of a number of her poems. Most of her poetry was written before 1820: later she undertook caring work, retiring to a convent in 1874. Her poems, simple in form and expression, convey intense religious feeling, fervent love for her brother, Wilhelm, and at times frustration at enforced female passivity, as in 'Will keine Blumen mehr' (I want no more flowers; 1814).

Brentano's treatment of Hensel's poetry is not uncharacteristic of attitudes towards women's intellectual property at this time. Friederike Brun, née Münter, published four volumes of poetry, but is chiefly remembered for one poem, 'Ich denke Dein' (I think of you), which Goethe had heard in a musical setting by Zelter, and which, rewritten by him in 1795 under the title 'Nähe des Geliebten' (The beloved's presence), was set to music by Beethoven in 1799. Marianne von Willemer was not only the inspiration for the figure of Suleika in Goethe's *West-östlicher Divan* (*West-Eastern Divan*; 1819) but also wrote several of the poems in the collection and part-authored several others. Unlike mere adaptations, this was a genuinely collaborative effort; however, the work appeared under Goethe's name alone.

Drama

Drama posed a number of problems for women writers. In the first place, it belonged essentially to the public sphere, from which women were excluded. Secondly, women's lack of knowledge of classical structures and formal requirements, conditioned by educational discrimination, proved a handicap in an area where these were regarded as prerequisites. Thirdly, the dominant literary discourses of the day, and particularly the poetics of drama, which was accorded supreme status among the genres, conflicted with the characteristics ascribed to women in contemporary discourse on gender. Besides their supposed deficiency in intellectual independence and creative power, women were declared to lack the potential for conflict, which was seen as the basis of drama: hence they appeared by definition unfitted to be dramatists. Finally, drama by women was more systematically ridiculed and trivialized, and thus marginalized, than was their work in any other genre. In this way they were further disqualified as serious rivals to men.

It is, then, hardly surprising that until fairly recently dramas by women of the period were almost wholly unknown. They existed only in

isolated copies or had been totally lost; indeed, many had never been published at all. Yet numerous dramas by women did appear in print, albeit
usually anonymously or under a pseudonym, and some were performed,
either as play readings or as theatrical productions. In several cases they
enjoyed considerable public acclaim and their authors became celebrities.
Even these women, however, faded into obscurity after their deaths, as
they were neglected both by theatre directors of later times and by literary
historians.

Virtually all the dramatists were members of the educated middle class
or the nobility. A number were actresses whose profession provided them
with access to the commercial theatre, while others moved in court circles. They wrote in a great variety of forms and their dramas range from
brief fragments to full-length plays. The bulk of their output consists of
comedies: this genre presented fewer obstacles to women than other
types of drama, since it was not obliged to aspire to the status of art, but
could be presented simply as entertainment. Nevertheless, there are a
number of plays by women which do not fall into the category of comedy
and thus implicitly make more ambitious claims.

Most dramas by women are set in the private sphere of love, marriage,
and the family. One of the most effective is the one-act comedy *Die Kriegs-
list* (The stratagem; 1792) by Sophie Mariane von Reitzenstein, née Wei-
kard (1770–1823), which concerns the efforts of a crusty general to trick his
niece, who is also his ward, into marrying the man of his choice. The characters are well drawn, the structure taut, the dialogue lively, and the heroine quick-witted and independent minded. Like most comedies, though,
this one preserves the status quo: the general, literally, has the last word.
In Elise Müller's (1782–?) *Die Kostgängerin im Nonnenkloster* (The boarder at
the convent; 1797), on the other hand, which is likewise based on the
theme of the tyranny of the older generation over the younger in the
choice of a marriage partner, women play a more active role and parental
plans are thwarted. A further variation on this theme is provided by *Sidney
und Eduard, oder Was vermag die Liebe* (Sidney and Edward, or What can love
do?; 1792) by Susanne von Bandemer, a friend of Anna Luise Karsch and
Sophie La Roche. The plot has tragic potential, since the heroine is almost
poisoned by her jealous husband, but all ends well when the latter's
tyrannical father repents his harshness. As in many of these plays, however, the happy ending is highly improbable. The same goes for the hugely successful and frequently performed comedies of Amalie Heiter, the
pseudonym of Princess Amalie of Saxony.

In contrast, several dramas present the tragic consequences that may ensue when women are denied emotional fulfilment. Schiller's sister-in-law Caroline von Wolzogen wrote an unfinished drama, *Der leukadische Fels* (The Leukadian rock; 1792), in which the heroine, faced with a forced marriage, identifies with the Greek poet Sappho, who according to legend threw herself from this rock when crossed in love. Charlotte von Stein, who is almost exclusively remembered for her association with Goethe, wrote a tragedy about another legendary female suicide, *Dido* (1796). Whereas in Virgil's *Aeneid* Dido is largely a passive victim, Stein depicts her as active, independent and a good ruler, and suggests that the people are better off under female than male rule. The drama is partly directed against the French Revolution, but also satirizes male intellectuals, one of whom was said to resemble Goethe; nevertheless, its reputation as merely the vengeful work of a woman scorned is undeserved. A second tragedy by Stein, *Die zwei Emilien* (The two Emilies), was published together with poems by her in 1803.

Charlotte von Stein's niece, Amalie von Helvig, née von Imhoff, a lady-in-waiting at the Weimar court, received encouragement from both Goethe and Schiller, even though they regarded her, along with other women writers, as a dilettante. Besides lyric and epic poetry – her best known work is the epic poem 'Die Schwestern von Lesbos' (The sisters of Lesbos; 1800) – she wrote two 'dramatic idylls': *Die Schwestern auf Corcyra* (The sisters of Corfu), which dates from 1806 and was privately performed, and a cyclical verse-drama *Die Tageszeiten* (The times of day). Both works were published in 1812. As the designation 'idyll' suggests, they evoke a harmonious world far removed from the real historical context in which they were written.

A more direct, though still idealized response to contemporary events is provided by women's patriotic dramas glorifying heroes of national history or legend. Two of the most prominent practitioners of this genre were the Austrian writers Johanna von Weißenthurn and Caroline Pichler, née Greiner, both of whom wrote for the stage. Typical examples of their work are Weißenthurn's *Hermann* and Pichler's *Heinrich von Hohenstauffen, König der Deutschen* (Heinrich von Hohenstauffen, King of the Germans), both dating from 1813. Pichler's play was received with particular enthusiasm: staged at the Hofburgtheater in Vienna, it enjoyed twenty-seven repeat performances. Other historical dramas by women centre on female protagonists, for instance *Johanna Gray* (Jane Grey; 1806) by Karoline Ludecus, *Charlotte Corday* (1804) by Christine Westphalen (1758–1840), and *Hildgund* (1805) by Karoline von Günderrode. The last two have patriotic overtones, as they deal with women who assassinate a tyrant; a parallel with Napoleon is implied. Unlike women's historical dramas about men, however, they were published anonymously or under a pseudonym and were not performed on stage, though a reading performance of Westphalen's play is documented. In neither case was the actual assassination dramatized: in Westphalen's drama the murder of Marat takes place offstage, while Günderrode's fragment ends before Hildgund's decisive act, the stabbing of Attila the Hun. Women authors avoided showing women killing men on stage, even if these were notorious for their tyranny.

Hildgund does challenge gender stereotypes, however, not only by resolving to kill Attila, but by taking his armour and weapons, thereby symbolically assuming the attributes of the warrior king. The heroine of another of Günderrode's dramas, *Mora* (1804), which is based on Nordic myth, likewise puts on a king's armour, but her challenge to convention is weaker, as she is killed in a duel. The female protagonist of Günderrode's Orphic fragment *Immortalita* is even more powerless, as she must wait for a male character to descend to the underworld and rescue her. Indeed, most of this author's dramas – *Udohla* (1805), *Magie und Schicksal* (Magic and fate; 1805), *Nikator* (1806), and her only completed play, *Mahomed, der Prophet von Mekka* (Mohammed, the Prophet of Mecca; 1805) – have male protagonists, and although women's need for self-determination is a persistent theme in her dramatic writings, Hildgund is the only female character in them who acts independently. The fact that she is not actually seen to do so indicates that even with the aid of mythical or historical settings Günderrode was unable to present unambiguously in drama a degree of female autonomy that did not exist in reality.

Historical or pseudo-historical settings were favoured by women dramatists not only as vehicles for patriotic sentiment or experiments in role reversal, but also because they were fashionable and hence likely to enhance a play's chances of success. While Schiller's later works popularized historical drama, his early play *Die Räuber* (*The Robbers*; 1781), together with Goethe's *Götz von Berlichingen* (1773), had ushered in a vogue for plays about chivalry and daring deeds: examples of such dramas by women include *Adelheit Gräfinn von Teck* (Adelheit Countess of Teck; 1799) by the actress Elise Bürger, née Hahn, which was performed in Altona and Celle, and *Karl Moor und seine Genossen nach der Abschiedsscene beim alten Thurm* (Karl Moor and his companions after the farewell scene at the old tower; 1801) by Isabella von Wallenrodt, a sequel to *Die Räuber* which provided the original with an improbable happy ending and was performed in Zagreb in 1802. Another drama by a woman based on a well-known play by a male writer is *Die That* (The deed; 1817) by Therese von Artner, which depicts the events supposedly preceding those of Adolf Müllner's hugely successful 'fate tragedy' *Die Schuld* (Guilt; 1816). While Artner's plot is highly melodramatic, her play, cast in the trochaic tetrameter usual for this genre, is interesting for its contrasting portrayal of the scope available to men and women for the exercise of free will.

Further types of drama written by women include Biblical dramas; fairy-tale plays, often with music; other musical plays and operas, notably the libretto of Carl Maria von Weber's opera *Euryanthe* (1824) by Wilhelmine von Chézy; festival pieces and dramatized proverbs; and moral plays for children, which became popular during the 1820s. Unlike other plays by women, those in the last category have no critical potential, tending merely to reinforce existing power-relations: while urging children to be hardworking and obedient to authority, they offer as a role-model for women only the figure of the devoted wife and mother, wholly confined to the domestic sphere.

Letters; the salon; diaries, autobiography, travel writing

During this period letter-writing by women reached a peak of achievement unequalled before or since. This may be ascribed in part to a new awareness of self among the Romantic generation, but in part also to the limited opportunities open to women for engaging in other types of writing. A large number of women wrote letters, but very few of these were published during the lifetime of the writers and many were lost or destroyed. Some women used letter-writing as a stepping-stone to other genres; for some, however, letters remained their only significant form of literary expression. Among this latter group are two women whose impact extends far beyond their own time: Caroline Schlegel-Schelling and Rahel Levin-Varnhagen von Ense.

Caroline Schlegel-Schelling, née Michaelis, was the daughter of a professor of Oriental Studies at Göttingen University. In 1784 she married a physician named Böhmer, who died in 1788 leaving her with three children. In 1792 she moved with her only surviving daughter, Auguste, to Mainz, where in 1793, pregnant with a child who died two years later, she was arrested for revolutionary sympathies after the collapse of the short-lived 'Republic of Mainz' and was imprisoned for a time at Königstein near Frankfurt. In 1796 she married the writer and critic August Wilhelm Schlegel and moved with him to Jena. Their household, and particularly Caroline herself, became a focal point of early Romanticism until Auguste's sudden death in 1800. In 1803 Caroline and Schlegel divorced and she married the philosopher F. W. J. Schelling. She has inspired more novels and biographies than any other figure of German Romanticism; her personality is, however, most memorably expressed in her lively and original letters, over 400 of which have survived. Varying widely in content and style, they reveal her talent for observation and her capacity for reflection, both on her own life and on her times. Her republican leanings and disregard for conventional morality were tempered by an acute awareness of the social constraints placed on women: she rejected any public parade of female erudition and consciously restricted herself to the role of collaborator in works by men. As these were published under the name of the male author alone, the precise extent of her contribution is uncertain. She did, however, write reviews, and A. W. Schlegel included in his critical writings her letters on Shakespeare's *Romeo and Juliet*.

Rahel Varnhagen was doubly subject to social restriction, both as a woman and as a Jew. Born Rahel Levin, the daughter of a well-to-do Berlin jewel merchant and banker, she claimed to be entirely self-taught, but had probably received a better-than-average, though unsystematic education which she extended by reading. From the beginning of the 1790s until the French occupation of Berlin in 1806 she entertained the city's literary and intellectual élite at regular gatherings in her parents' house. In 1814, after two failed engagements, she married Karl August Varnhagen von Ense, a Prussian diplomat and writer, and converted to Christianity. From 1819 until shortly before her death she hosted a salon in Berlin. Her outstanding conversational gifts found written expression in some ten thousand letters to over 120 correspondents. These are characterized by spontaneity, independence of thought, acute self-awareness, and penetrating observations on German culture and society. A number were published anonymously during her lifetime, and in 1834 her husband edited and published a three-volume selection of her letters and diaries, together with aphorisms and biographical anecdotes, under the title *Rahel. Ein Buch des Andenkens für ihre Freunde* (Rahel. A memorial book for her friends). This work was highly influential, especially in liberal and radical circles, and also won acclaim outside Germany. Regarded as a pioneer of women's intellectual emancipation, she articulated a vision of equality that encompassed all humankind. Her thought and writing combine impulses from the Enlightenment and Romanticism with a fervent admiration for Goethe which also pervaded the atmosphere of her salon.

Like the publication of personal letters, the salon culture of the late eighteenth and early nineteenth centuries blurred the borderline between the private and the public domain. This is particularly true of the Berlin salons, many of which were presided over by Jewish women. Rahel Varnhagen's was the most famous: here people of different gender, class, religious affiliation and profession mingled freely and exchanged ideas in an atmosphere of Romantic *Geselligkeit* (sociability). This temporary, ideal equality pointed forward to a form of society not yet achieved in reality. Even within the salons, however, there were limits to equality. The elevation of conversation to an art form, and the view that it was particularly appropriate to women, may have hindered their writing, except where letters were concerned. This seems to have been the case with Henriette Herz, née Lemos, the best-known Berlin *salonnière* after Rahel Varnhagen: she destroyed two novels and even most of her correspondence. Caroline Pichler, on the other hand, not only maintained a noted Viennese salon but produced sixty volumes of published work.

The vehicle of expression most favoured by women, however, was the private form of the diary or journal, which permitted intense self-analysis. In the German-speaking lands its development was decisively influenced by the legacy of Protestantism and especially Pietism, which encouraged introspection. A Catholic equivalent of Pietism can be found in the posthumously published diaries of Princess Amalie von Gallitzin, née von Schmettau, which combine self-reflection with openness to the world, intellectual curiosity and considerable learning. The diaries of Elisabeth von der Recke, which were likewise published after her death, display a more secularized sensibility and provide insights into the life of an eighteenth-century aristocratic woman. She also published a four-volume travel journal, *Tagebuch einer Reise durch einen Teil Deutschlands und durch Italien in den Jahren 1804 bis 1806* (Diary of a journey through part of Germany and through Italy in the years 1804–6; 1815–17), which conveys much information on the social history of the time.

Few women of this period published autobiographies during their lifetime. Two notable exceptions are Isabella von Wallenrodt, whose autobiography appeared in 1797, and Regula Engel, née Egli, a Swiss writer who in 1821 and 1828 published an account of her experiences as the wife of an officer in the French army under Napoleon. While neither work is of high intrinsic quality, both are historically significant as documents of contemporary women's lives. Regula Engel's account is partly a travel work, but also deals with childbirth and the hardships of military campaigning. Isabella von Wallenrodt's life-history is somewhat reminiscent of a popular novel: cast in the epistolary form popular in the eighteenth century, it is a long-winded and often contradictory secular confession intended to restore her public reputation. It is, however, invaluable for its detailed description of the conditions under which women writers lived and worked. Friederike Brun, too, published an autobiography, *Wahrheit aus Morgenträumen* (Truth from morning dreams; 1824), which recounts her childhood in Copenhagen. It includes a treatise on female aesthetic education, *Idas ästhetische Entwicklung* (Ida's aesthetic development), which is dedicated to Madame de Staël. Friederike Brun also acted as a salon hostess in Denmark and wrote numerous travelogues, including *Tagebuch über Rom* (Diary of Rome; 1795–6) and *Briefe aus Rom* (Letters from Rome; 1808–10), which became a best-seller and was translated into various languages. These works cross generic boundaries and, as the titles indicate, exploit private forms of female writing for public purposes.

Narrative fiction

The most accessible literary genre for women writers in the late eighteenth and early nineteenth centuries was the epistolary novel. This was partly because women were accustomed to writing letters, and partly because the works of Richardson, Rousseau and Sophie La Roche, and Goethe's *Die Leiden des jungen Werthers* (*The Sorrows of Young Werther*; 1774) had made this type of novel fashionable. Furthermore, because novels were regarded as an inferior genre and were subject to few formal rules, they presented less of an obstacle to women writers than lyric poetry or drama.

Sophie Mereau's first novel, *Das Blüthenalter der Empfindung* (The blossoming age of sentiment; 1794), is not cast in epistolary form but has a first-person male narrator. It documents the changing intellectual currents of the age and points forward to later developments. Unusually for the time at which it was written, it upholds the ideals of the French Revolution; it also contains criticism of the social position of women and of conventional marriage. In some respects it anticipates the *Bildungsroman*, and is one of the first novels of the period to depict emigration to America in search of personal freedom. Mereau's second novel, *Amanda und Eduard. Ein Roman in Briefen* (Amanda and Edward. A novel in letters; 1803), follows the epistolary tradition in its focus on characters' feelings, but resembles Romantic novels in its multi-perspectivism, mixture of genres, and presentation of love as the only true basis for marriage. It demonstrates, however, greater insight into women's real situation, and in particular their economic dependence, than do works by male writers. The Romantic motif of the *Liebestod* – Amanda's sudden death after her marriage to Eduard – forms a parallel to that of emigration at the end of Mereau's first novel and of elopement in her story *Die Flucht nach der Hauptstadt* (*Flight to the City*; 1806): all three 'escapes' reveal the incompatibility between fulfilment in love and the restrictions imposed by society. Similar themes occur in other stories by Mereau and in her essay on the French courtesan Ninon de Lenclos in her journal *Kalathiskos* (1801–2).

Unlike Mereau, Caroline Auguste Fischer, née Venturini, had no access to important literary or social circles and no close association with any major German writer. Consequently, she was almost totally forgotten. She is, however, one of the most significant women writers of the period. Highly educated, though of modest social origins – her father, who was of Italian extraction, was a court violinist at the Duchy of Brunswick, while her mother was the daughter of a local tailor – she married Christoph Johann Rudolph Christiani, court preacher and head of a German boys' school in Copenhagen, but returned to Germany in 1799, leaving her son behind; her daughter had died in infancy. Subsequently she lived with Christian August Fischer, a minor writer of anti-feminist tendencies; she married him in 1808 after the birth of their son, but was divorced shortly afterwards. Information on her later life is sparse: she attempted to support herself by writing and by opening a girls' school in Heidelberg, and around 1820 is reputed to have run a lending-library in Würzburg. After this she apparently ceased writing. She was committed to a Würzburg hospital on the grounds of mental illness in 1832 and died in poverty and obscurity in a hospital in Frankfurt.

Fischer's three major novels, *Die Honigmonathe* (The honeymoon; 1802), *Der Günstling* (The favourite; 1808), and *Margarethe* (1812), are epistolary, while the title of her collection of five stories, *Kleine Erzählungen und romantische Skizzen* (Short stories and romantic sketches; 1818), is similarly conventional. Beneath the veneer of conformity, however, her narratives offer a penetrating critique of patriarchal society and its institutions, focusing chiefly on the areas of marriage, art and court life. While relations between the sexes are their main concern, they also indict the military, racism and the absolute ruler. Criticism is voiced through the words of characters rather than the narrator and seems not to have been noticed at the time; to present-day readers, however, its radicalism is both evident and surprising.

A much better known contemporary of Fischer is Dorothea Schlegel, née Brendel Mendelssohn, the daughter of the renowned Enlightenment philosopher Moses Mendelssohn and the wife of Friedrich Schlegel. Her only original work is her unfinished novel *Florentin*, the first part of which appeared in 1801 under her husband's name; fragments of a sequel have been published posthumously. The novel has generally been regarded as derivative, but its digressive and open-ended structure – justified by the author in a 'Dedication to the Editor' which was not published with the novel – may be viewed as both genuinely Romantic and modern (cf. Inge Stephan (1991), p. 362 below), since it derives from the hero's lack of a stable identity. This can be seen as expressing the author's own uncertain identity as a Jewish woman who repeatedly changed name, status and religion: married in 1783 to the banker Simon Veit, she assumed the name Dorothea, divorced her husband in 1799 to live with Schlegel, converted to Protestantism in 1804, receiving the baptismal name Friederike, married Schlegel the same year, and converted to Catholicism in 1808. *Florentin* influenced the Romantic writers Achim von Arnim and particularly Joseph von Eichendorff, the manuscript of whose first novel, *Ahnung und Gegenwart* (Divination and the present), was corrected by Dorothea Schlegel.

Caroline de la Motte Fouqué, née Briest, the wife of the Romantic author Friedrich de la Motte Fouqué, was a far more prolific novelist than Dorothea Schlegel. An intelligent and highly educated woman, she published more than one hundred works, including twenty novels and over sixty stories, as well as poems, reviews, and non-fictional pieces. She also collaborated with her husband in editorial work and travel writing, and for a time they were Germany's most successful literary couple. Her life was marked by contradictions between what was acceptable for a woman of her class, in her own eyes as well as in those of society, and her actual circumstances, notably the breakdown of her first marriage and her status as a professional writer who, particularly after 1815, was obliged to write for money. These contradictions, characteristic of an age of transition, are mirrored in both the content and the style of her writing. Her first novel, *Rodrich* (1806–7), which probably influenced E. T. A. Hoffmann, already displays the mixture of Romanticism and realism characteristic of her later work. Her second novel, *Die Frau des Falkensteins* (The lady of Castle Falkenstein; 1810), has many of the trappings of the gothic novel, but also deals with marriage and relationships between the sexes; both elements recur frequently in her narratives. Two works, *Die Magie der Natur* (The magic of Nature; 1812), which won Goethe's approval, and *Das Heldenmädchen aus der Vendee* (The heroic girl of the Vendée nobility; 1816), one of her best historical novels, are set in revolutionary France but carry an anti-revolutionary message. Her main strengths are her flair for character drawing and vivid description, and her gift for detail. Her capacity for observation is also evident in her non-fictional works, notably *Geschichte der Moden, vom Jahre 1785 bis 1829, als Beytrag zur Geschichte der Zeit* (History of fashion, from 1785 to 1829, as a contribution to the history of the age; 1829–30), which shows originality in its insight that changes in fashion reflect intellectual and social changes.

These changes are likewise documented in the life and work of Bettina von Arnim, née Brentano, who was the sister of Clemens Brentano, wife of Achim von Arnim and granddaughter of Sophie La Roche. Although her literary career did not begin in earnest until after her husband's death in 1831, her works are closely connected with the preceding period as well as with their own time. Four may be termed epistolary novels, but unlike other works of this genre they are based on actual letters which have, however, been extensively reworked for publication. *Goethes Briefwechsel mit einem Kinde* (*Goethe's Correspondence with a Child*; 1835) caused a sensation on its appearance and was translated into several languages. *Die Günderode* (*Günderode*; 1840) and *Clemens Brentanos Frühlingskranz* (Clemens Brentano's spring garland; 1844) project a forward-looking image of Romanticism in contrast to the reactionary and narrowly denominational picture painted by opponents of the movement in the 1830s and 1840s. Arnim's combination of Romantic thought with impulses from Goethe and the Enlightenment aligns her with Rahel Varnhagen, and she is similarly regarded as having advanced the cause of women. She did not, however, address women's issues specifically, but championed the persecuted and socially disadvantaged in general. *Dies Buch gehört dem König* (This book belongs to the King; 1843), a fictitious dialogue dedicated to King Frederick William IV of Prussia, advocates far-reaching constitutional, legal, social and penal reforms and has an appendix documenting conditions in a Berlin slum. Arnim planned a comprehensive documentary study of poverty, but the uprising of the Silesian weavers in 1844 deterred her from publishing it. Her later works met with little response. No German woman of letters, however, has had a more profound effect on fellow artists, and her importance is increasingly recognized by scholars.

Other novels of interest are Caroline von Wolzogen's *Agnes von Lilien* (1798); *Cornelia* by Charlotte von Kalb (1761–1843), published posthumously in 1851; Caroline Pichler's epistolary novels, which provide insights into the lives and psychology of the educated Austrian middle class; the novels of Therese Huber, Johanna Schopenhauer, and Fanny Tarnow; and *St. Evremond* (1836), a vast historical novel by Sophie Tieck, sister of the Romantic author Ludwig Tieck. Ludwig's daughter Dorothea Tieck wrote no original works, but her translations of Shakespeare's plays in the celebrated 'Schlegel–Tieck' version are one of the most distinguished contributions by a woman to German literature in any age.

5

Women's writing 1830–1890

Whereas the Romantic movement valued qualities traditionally deemed feminine, such as the imaginative, the irrational and the poetic, this period, marked by a rapid expansion in women's writing, retreated from what it perceived as the dangerous formlessness of the Romantic period, dwelling instead on the moral. The achievements of women writers, then, owed more to individual talent than to a general raising of female consciousness or to political developments. While there were moments, for example around 1848 or at the very end of the period, when women's interests coincided with public developments, in general it was a time when men and women occupied separate spheres, and their interests and occupations were perceived as naturally opposed.

As growing industrialization separated home and work, turning the extended household into the modern nuclear family, the roles of men and women became polarized. While men worked outside the home, women stayed at home to fulfil domestic duties that were much reduced. The woman, then, was no longer the manager of 'the whole house', the self-sufficient, traditional extended household, but became instead the 'angel in the house', whose task was to create a spiritual and material refuge from the world. Though she was still seen as the embodiment of poetic qualities, these became absorbed into her domestic role. Her destiny and privilege was now to be muse and, increasingly, reader:

> Die Werke der Poesie sind so vorzugsweise *für* das schöne Geschlecht geschaffen; der Geist der Frauen nährt sich nicht an Wissenschaft und Leben; der Mann bereitet ihm aus diesen weiten Gebieten, was ihm Bildung und Genuß schafft.
>
> (GERVINUS, *Geschichte der deutschen Dichtung*, 1853)

> Works of literature are so advantageously created *for* the fair sex; woman's spirit does not nourish itself on science and life; the man

provides it with what gives it education and pleasure from these wide areas.

This renewed emphasis on woman's dependence meant that she was not in a position to fulfil Goethe's definition of the true artist as standing firmly and securely alone, and so had little chance of becoming a writer herself. However, as the conservatism of the Metternich era was punctuated by the revolutions of 1848, eventually giving way to rapid economic and industrial expansion in the second half of the century, so the conditions necessary for writing improved; some women, at least, were able to benefit from greater literacy, leisure, material and psychological rewards, and the confidence bestowed by working in a tradition.

Change, however, came slowly, erratically and, in part, accidentally. As the home was no longer run as a place of business, women had more time to educate their children and themselves – although their education was designed to make them better wives and mothers rather than to develop their intellects. They were helped inadvertently by the régime of Metternich, with its censorship, spies and restrictions on public gatherings, for these restrictions encouraged art in general to retreat from the public domain. They thus promoted 'domesticated' forms like the piano duet and the Lied, genre painting and portraiture. A passion for reading also developed, but much of the literature presented to women was restricted to that which confirmed stereotypical perceptions of the feminine. Anthologies edited to this end and sentimental tales of conversion and moral improvement were staple literary fare. Girls growing up in families where reading was a part of life, as in the older extended household, were allowed to choose their own reading matter and a lucky few, mainly in aristocratic houses, were educated alongside their younger brothers. Clearly access to education, to opportunities for reading and writing depended in these years on individual circumstances rather than on any general improvement in women's situation.

While the revolution of 1848 was a turning point, the reactionary years that followed made women's attempts to improve their lives more difficult. Growing demands for better education, working conditions and welfare met with some success, but also with many setbacks. Although the unification of Germany in 1871 brought free, secret ballots, women were still refused the vote. Radical publications for women appeared, only to be banned within a short time. The rapid growth of a female working class employed outside the home emphasized divisions between women, but also made training and welfare more urgent. Karl Marx's statement that 'social progress may be measured precisely by the social position of the fair sex (including the ugly ones)' suggests the ambivalence of even radical men. In 1878, Bebel recognized women's position as that of a social and economic proletariat, but working-class men were generally opposed to women workers' welfare organizations and unions, believing that women took men's jobs, depressed wages and ruined family life. In 1887, Helene Lange demanded proper training for teachers, but at the same time a scientific conference concluded that woman had, by nature and destiny, no capacity for intellectual pursuits. However, in 1889 the social democratic party supported women's demand for political equality, and by the end of the period there were women doctors and teachers qualified to prepare girls for university entrance.

As Marie von Ebner-Eschenbach pointed out in 1879, the German attitude to women writers still lagged behind that of the English or the French: 'The French are proud that the line of great women writers who influence the nation, is unbroken from Marie de France to Louise Ackermann. An Englishman would certainly be surprised if he heard us deny that the greatest living novelist is George Eliot . . . It is different with us.' In German, perhaps more than in many other literatures, the notion of literary excellence has traditionally been based on scholarship, on academic abstractions largely inaccessible to women because of their lack of education. Many women accepted their ignorance and dependence, and wrote only in the genres considered suitable for their temperament and constitution: lyric poetry, novels or tales, travelogues and educational tracts. The argument that they could produce only trivia because they had neither experience nor scholarship, and were unable to acquire these because they were women, therefore dependent and passive, thus became self-fulfilling.

Although internalized stereotypes of femininity or inhibitions about their lack of learning conspired to prevent them from 'conquering' the world in literature, and although men saw them as amateurs who were incapable of working within traditional genres, women made the most of the less codified, more personal forms. One of the hallmarks of their writing was their blurring of boundaries between genres and their refusal to treat one form of writing as essentially superior or inferior to another: they wrote as it seemed right or merely expedient to write. In growing numbers women writers broke through the circular argument of their dependence and ignorance by subverting or refining those forms open to them and by defying the 'rules' of men's literature.

Nevertheless it cannot be denied that, when one asks who was writing at this time, the immediate answer is: those who were educated, and these are found, primarily, among the aristocracy and the middle classes. Annette von Droste-Hülshoff and Marie von Ebner-Eschenbach, probably the best-known women writers of the period, came from aristocratic families and so enjoyed more formal education than most of their contemporaries. However, the advantages of education and leisure were offset by the disapproval of their families, who shunned publicity. This became more marked after 1850, when the declining prestige of writers caused the aristocracy to shy away from paid writing and from expressing its emotions in public. Moreover, the 1848 revolution, which prompted an increase in politically engaged writing, saw the emergence of women authors who wrote to earn a living, to draw attention to the situation of women and to establish their professional status.

Lyric poetry

Lyric poetry was the most acceptable form for women writers during this period, as in others, because it was considered to be emotional and spontaneous, rather than rational and scholarly. The writing and recitation of occasional verse was seen as a feminine accomplishment; further, by publishing their poetry in anthologies, almanacs and fashion journals, that is, collective or ephemeral media, women did not draw so much attention to themselves. But beside the many anthologies, with their traditional emphasis on love, nature and religion, in which some women appeared under abbreviated names or pseudonyms, or anonymously, there are individual collections of poems in which personal voices make an impact. These address themselves increasingly to the real nature of women's experience: in them, women could begin to confront their own identities through themes such as childhood or in portraits of themselves or of their friends; to address their problematic role as women who write; to broach the difficult area of their own sexuality, for which they had no accepted vocabulary, through explorations of the demonic, the alien and the exotic. Beyond this, some expressed themselves as social and political beings or, by celebrating the achievement of remarkable women and speaking for nameless, silent ones, put forward the idea that there is a specifically female experience and a female tradition.

Much lyric poetry of the period treats traditional themes like nature, love and religion and uses conventional imagery, rhythms and forms.

Religious poetry ranges from the devout to the sceptical. The profound, indecisive struggle between a questing, intellectual self and a desire for a simple faith emerges in the religious poetry of Droste-Hülshoff, the best-known woman writer of the age. In treating the themes of love and nature, women had to overcome the difficulty of entering a tradition in which the poet's stance is the oppositional, conquering one of men. Often the unfamiliar task of turning the passive, social self into the speaking, poetic self produces a split sensibility, expressed in imagery of mirroring or doubling. But the split is overcome by identifying with nature, especially in its more ordinary aspects, and by re-working traditional modes of expression. A significant number of collections by women writers have titles connected with flowers, especially roses, some as conventional as their titles suggest, but others, such as Louise Aston's *Wilde Rosen*, and Kathinka Zitz-Halein's *Herbstrosen. Poesie und Prosa* (Autumn roses), both published in 1846, disguising the work of radical thinkers. For Louise Otto-Peters, the public role of a radical poet resembles that of the lark singing the dawn-song of freedom; for Zitz-Halein, the eagle flying boldly towards the sun expresses progress and the owl creeping into its hole reactionary cowardice. Resistance to the stereotypical female role attracts women lyricists to images of water in which boundaries dissolve. All these natural images are used to convey public and private messages. The East offers images of alternative or extreme versions of existence: to Louise Plönnies it suggests colourful vitality and ancient splendour, while for Betty Paoli it represents freedom, escape from betrayal, and fulfilment in solitude, but to the central figure in Louise Aston's poem 'Die Türkin' (The Turkish woman) death is preferable to slavery in the harem of a man she does not love.

One of these writers, Droste-Hülshoff, is generally included in the traditional 'canon' of German literature. She owes her inclusion in part to her nature poetry, which is remarkable for its observation of minute details. Nature provides her with themes and a range of poetic voices and stances. She is known for her affinity with the Westphalian countryside, for the scientific precision of her descriptions of natural phenomena, combined with an evocation of the atmosphere of mystery associated with this province. Yet nature poetry is only one aspect of her writing. Her ballads and some of her other poetry have more recently been read especially by feminists for their revelations about her psychology and insights into her frustrated sexuality. She also explores her ambivalence towards her vocation: on the one hand she sees it as a dangerous challenge to the gods, but on the other she resents being treated like a thief breaking into Parnassus. Sometimes she writes as a consciously female self, sometimes she colludes with the social limitations on women's experience by assuming a masculine persona. Her vacillation testifies to her difficulties as a woman who writes and whose aristocratic family alternately encourages and is embarrassed by her literary interests.

Probably the most gifted woman lyricist of this period, apart from Droste-Hülshoff, from whom she drew inspiration, is the Austrian Betty Paoli (pseudonym for Elisabeth Glück). She published five collections of poems between 1841 and 1870, developing a lyrical range that moves with musicality, technical competence and rhythmic beauty through melancholy introspection, towards concern with the possibilities of art and poetry in an increasingly prosaic age. Her early poetry asserts the centrality of self, and the right to determine her own fate, but she later wonders at this independence of mind. Her early writing shows Byronic pessimism and a devotion to the poetry of her near-contemporary, Lenau, but after encountering the philosophy of Schopenhauer, she came to believe that all life is suffering and that in an age of transition life and poetry are not in harmony with each other. She became, in turn, a model for the young Ebner-Eschenbach, who sought her comments on her own poetic talents, but received instead practical hints on training the mind and the study of versification.

Much poetry records the conflict between the desire for security and the desire to break the cultural bonds that are imposed upon women. Indeed women create poetry from this division in themselves. It is the mainspring of some of their poetic tributes to famous women of the past and present. The most frequent literary subjects of these tributes are Sappho or George Sand, with both of whom, as celebrated women authors, German women writers are often compared. They also admire female figures associated with the French Revolution, as well as writing about girlhood and its relation to adult life, and about the lives of ordinary women. Female subjects, then, offer models for their own lives and visions of contingent lives. Some poets confront the self directly, as in Betty Paoli's poem 'Ich' (I; 1841) or in poems about portraits or reflections in mirrors. The self is also the starting-point for other reflections on broader issues. Ada Christen uses her own experiences as a springboard for social issues. Others express political views. Radical lyricists, like Louise Dittmar, Louise Aston and Louise Otto-Peters, celebrate the 1848 revolution uncompromisingly; others, like Zitz-Halein, acknowledge the strength of reactionary elements in society, or, like Paoli, are at first enthusiastic about the 1848 revolution in Vienna but are then horrified by the ensuing chaos.

The relationship between the woman lyricist and the male-dominated literary world remained ambiguous. Women writers were in the hands of male publishers and patrons. Individual collections and poems published by women in serious journals or in predominantly male anthologies were subject to interference, censorship and mischief, for even those men willing to promote women's writing had their own ideas about how it should be written. But women began to answer back. Paoli's poem *Censor und Setzer* (Censor and typesetter) describes the censor as Herod, searching her poems for a new Messiah, but acknowledges that even his excisions are preferable to the errors of the typesetter, who practises not the madness of censorship, but the censorship of madness.

Drama

By contrast, drama was still the genre in which it was most difficult for women writers to succeed. In the first half of the century, as in the previous era, drama represented the genre with most prestige, a public domain in which women were less than welcome. Moreover, public taste was generally conservative, and while popular dramatists pandered to this taste, more serious ones sought to extend the dramatic range by experimenting with new materials and forms. Thus radical drama by men was just as likely to fail as drama by women. But when women used unconventional forms and themes, and their dramas failed, critics attributed their failure to ignorance of the rules and unsuitable temperament. The blank verse of high tragedy was thought to be beyond them, and their dislike of conflict to incline them to conciliatory, even sentimental resolutions. The more sympathetic Heinrich Laube, director of the Burgtheater in Vienna, explained the failure of *Ruth* (1868), a 'poetic idyll' by Emilie von Binzer, as a mismatch between literary and popular taste. With its star role for the actress Charlotte Wolter, Binzer's earlier drama *Karoline Neuber* (1847) was a success, but the fickle public ridiculed the poetry of *Ruth*, and was bored by its Biblical themes and unfamiliar form. It should be remembered that drama was becoming a difficult and lifeless genre throughout the second part of the century, and that a number of male writers tried it in vain before turning to prose fiction. This may explain their mixed reactions to women dramatists: in Germany the dramatist Friedrich Hebbel kept up a running battle against women writers, but his Austrian contemporary Grillparzer discerned talent in the young Ebner-Eschenbach, and the novelist Theodor Fontane in his journalistic output reviewed Berlin productions of dramas by women as seriously as those by men.

Dramas by women writers tended to fall into two groups: there were unsuccessful, sometimes incomplete attempts at drama by women who succeeded in other genres, such as Droste-Hülshoff and Ebner-Eschenbach, and there were popular successes. In *Bertha oder die Alpen* (Bertha or the Alps; 1813) Droste-Hülshoff created a semi-autobiographical, artistic heroine, divided from other members of her sex by her reluctance to accept the traditional marriage of convenience. Through this heroine Droste-Hülshoff suggests a parallel between political power and the structure of power in the family. The drama foundered because her interest in her heroine's psychology conflicted with the dynamics of plot. She returned to dramatic form only once, with the satirical *Perdu* (1847). Ebner-Eschenbach struggled long enough with the demands of drama to have some successful productions, but most of her dramas remained unpublished. Like Droste-Hülshoff, she encountered the inability to further the movement of plot because of her exploration of character. Nor, despite her knowledge of the theatre and the advice of male mentors, was she able to create roles for specific actors. Influenced by Shakespeare and Schiller, she wrote historical drama, but the heroine of her *Maria Stuart in Schottland* (1860) is the victim not of Elizabeth's jealousy, as in Schiller's play *Maria Stuart*, but of her own uncontrollable emotions and of intrigue. Adverse criticism of this and of her *Marie Roland* (1867) led her to realize that writing from a female point of view is interpreted as incompetence, and she abandoned her attempts at drama, partly in deference to her embarrassed husband. A writer for whom drama formed a diversion from polemical pamphlets and novels is Hedwig Dohm, whose play *Vom Stamm der Asra* (Of the tribe of Asra; 1874), about men who pretend to die for love, was acclaimed by the Berlin public. It was followed by *Der Seelenretter* (The saver of souls; 1875), *Ein Schuß ins Schwarze* (Bulls-eye) and *Die Ritter vom goldenen Kalb* (The Knights of the Golden Calf; both 1879), comedies of errors in which she criticized traditional marriage, but less sharply than in her other writings.

Among the most successful dramatists of the century were the actresses Charlotte Birch-Pfeiffer and Johanna von Weißenthurn. Birch-Pfeiffer, a power before whom directors trembled, wrote a hundred dramas, which, despite the critics' insistence on their trivial, unaesthetic quality, remained popular with actors and audiences throughout the century. With her sharp ear for dialogue, talent for translating narrative into scene, and meticulous organization, she had a stronger sense of what the stage requires than many of her male contemporaries. She was criticized for reflecting fashionable political opinion and for plundering other people's writings for material. Her most successful dramas were *Dorf und Stadt* (Village and city; 1848), based on a work by the Swabian Jewish writer Berthold Auerbach (1812–1882), and *Die Grille* (The caprice; 1856), based on George Sand's *La petite Fadette* (1850). These and works like *Die Waise von Lowood* (The orphan of Lowood; 1892), based on *Jane Eyre* (1847), enabled her to smuggle interesting psychological and social problems from English and French literature into the German theatre, fulfilling her duty to conservative German morality by balancing her emancipatory ideas with the conciliatory conclusion that love overcomes emotional and social conflict. Weißenthurn brought romance into the Viennese theatre with dramas set in remote provinces of the Austro-Hungarian empire, but her later comedies showed more originality. Criticized for her sentimentality, her broad speech and the crudeness of her dramatic intrigue, she nonetheless enjoyed popularity in her day.

Narrative fiction

As narrative prose generally gained in prestige after 1850, so women's writing expanded. Indeed writers like Ebner-Eschenbach and Louise von François are credited with contributing to the move towards the novel. Narrative fiction was already the most popular form with women writers, because novels and tales paid best and women were writing to earn a living or to contribute to the family income. Much of this fiction was conventionally designed to educate women to fulfil their culturally defined role. It deals with stereotypical characters and dilemmas, in which conventional moral choices bring approval and happiness. As the conservative ideology retreated from what it saw as the excessive freedom of Romanticism, so writing came to observe overwhelmingly moral codes, often with a covert political intention. These express a belief that what is written both reflects and, in turn, affects life. The literature of the period combines a desire for the circumstantial authenticity of realism with a need to articulate a view of the world in which each person has his or her place. Since women are seen as the bearers and transmitters of morality, their writing tends to reflect traditional views of morals and society.

When, in the 1840s, women began to break out and write fiction that questioned traditional assumptions about their own roles, this was seen as particularly unnatural and reprehensible.

One narrative work from this period has a place in the traditional 'canon', namely Droste-Hülshoff's *Die Judenbuche* (*The Jew's Beech*; 1842), a story about a mysterious murder. Conventionally read as a tale about justice, its treatment of marginalized figures, like the hero and the Jew he allegedly murders, of women and of a secondary, 'folk' justice growing up alongside the established law, means that it also lends itself to a feminist reading. Droste-Hülshoff also wrote fragmentary novels – *Ledwina* (1819–26) and *Bei uns zu Lande auf dem Lande* (At our home in the country; begun 1841) – which explore aspects of female identity, especially the plight of the daughter who resists the traditional female role. Male critics still dismiss these works, which were not published until after her death, but the portrayal of illness and the fragmentation of personality in *Ledwina*, and the conflict between obligation to self and to family and society in both works, give them a place in the broad tradition of women's writing.

Ebner-Eschenbach became successful when she turned from drama to narrative fiction. She wrote numerous stories and three novels, *Bozena* (1876) about a loyal servant, *Das Gemeindekind* (*The Child of the Parish*; 1887), and *Unsühnbar* (*Beyond Atonement*; 1891), a novel of adultery sometimes compared with Fontane's *Effi Briest* (1894). The difference between her novel and Fontane's lies in the self-awareness of Ebner-Eschenbach's heroine, in her moral debate with herself, and in her self-determination, which culminates in her choosing to reveal her adultery rather than to allow her lover's son to inherit her husband's title and estates. Ebner-Eschenbach also produced novellas and tales that demonstrate her knowledge of urban and rural life, her humour and compassion. The critical emphasis on these qualities and on her idealism are sometimes emphasized at the expense of the social criticism in her work. This is partly because her female characters remain within the traditionally female spheres of home and family, and because she creates some exemplary male characters. Although she also created defiant female characters, for example in *Zwei Komtessen* (*The Two Countesses*; 1885), which attacks loveless marriages of convenience and the deficient education of girls, and recognizes the problems of talented women in patriarchal society, she did not challenge the latter directly. Yet she was hailed on her seventieth birthday as the greatest German woman writer living and awarded an address of thanks signed by 10,000 Viennese women.

Louise von François, daughter of an aristocratic Huguenot family, wrote her novels and stories solely to relieve her poverty. Her most famous novel is *Die letzte Reckenburgerin* (*The Last von Reckenburg*; 1871), whose success surprised her. Set during the Seven Years War (1756–63), its two central female figures show how the offended nature takes its revenge, the neglected one helps itself. Her second novel, *Frau Erdmuthens Zwillingssöhne* (Frau Erdmuthe's twin sons; 1873), deals with the conflict between France and Germany during the Wars of Liberation and her third, *Stufenjahre eines Glücklichen* (Stages in the life of a happy man; 1876), with events during the 1848 revolution. She constructs characters to embody moral values, especially strong female figures who gain independence and fulfilment by accepting responsibility for the well-being of others, but at the expense of personal happiness. The conflict between duty and inclination, feeling and reason, convention and independence, undoubtedly part of her own life, are central to her work.

The radical women novelists who emerged in the middle of the century were part of a larger movement towards uncovering social ills. But they were also concerned with subjects of specific interest to women, such as marriages of convenience and women's emancipation. Inspired by ideas of freedom and justice, by the rebellion of weavers and peasants, influenced by Eugène Sue's descriptions of poverty in Paris and Dickens's picture of social divisions in England, they wrote about the moral and social degradation of poverty and attempts to relieve it. Luise Mühlbach's *Ein Roman in Berlin* (A novel in Berlin; 1846) belongs to this genre, with its descriptions of urban poverty and its hope for improvement through Christian-socialist principles. But it is not clear whether Mühlbach's insistence on the innocent freedom of poverty, as opposed to the shame associated with it, is a serious belief or a subversive, alienating strategy. Her novel *Eva* (1844, republished as *Frau Meisterin*, 1859), influenced by George Sand, shows the conflict between rich and poor through the rise, fall and emigration of an industrialist and his wife. The latter is only content with her wealth when she uses it to create wealth for others. Apart from novels dealing with social conditions, Mühlbach also wrote about the situation of the woman writer in *Aphra Behn* (1849).

Fanny Lewald published her first novel, *Clementine* (1842), anonymously at the request of her family; its theme, the need to educate girls to earn their own living so that they do not need to make degrading marriages of convenience, is taken up again in *Hausgenossen* (Fellow tenants; 1856); her second novel, *Jenny* (1843), treats the oppression of women and of Jews;

Eine Lebensfrage (A vital question; 1845) advocates easier divorce; *Der dritte Stand* (The third estate; 1846) takes up the cause of poor women. Her later writings offer more conventional solutions to the problems of poverty and ignorance: for example, *Wandlungen* (Changes; 1853) is an attempt to write a classically harmonious novel, where liberal principles triumph; *Kein Haus* (Homeless; 1856) deals with homeless lovers, unable to afford to emigrate, who go mad or commit suicide. Her relationship to the emergent female tradition is ambivalent. Rahel Varnhagen and her Berlin salon play a role in *Prinz Louis Ferdinand* (1849), but her admiration for Rahel diminished shortly after writing it. *Diogena von Gräfin Iduna H* (Diogena, by Countess Iduna H.; 1847), satirizing the sentimentalities of Ida Hahn-Hahn's salon novels, caused a stir. Lewald also wrote about her own journeys in Europe and about the social and political position of women.

The career and reputation of the prolific Hahn-Hahn are divided by her conversion to Catholicism in 1850. Her early life and novels are colourful, even scandalous. The daughter of an aristocrat whose passion for the theatre ruined his family, she married her rich cousin at her family's wish, gave birth to a mentally handicapped daughter in 1829 and was divorced in the same year. She lived and travelled throughout Europe with Adolf, Baron Bystram, writing lyric poetry, accounts of her travels and numerous novels. These are set in aristocratic circles and deal with woman's desire for freedom and the exploitation and discrimination she endures. Male critics took offence at her independent female figures, like *Gräfin Faustine* (*The Countess Faustina*; 1841), with their claims to Faustian despair and their rejection of conventional roles. But liberal thinkers were equally horrified by her conversion to Catholicism in 1850, which interrupts the flow of emancipatory novels; no novels appear between *Levin* (1848) and *Maria Regina* (1860), when she was persuaded to put her talents to the use of her new faith. The larger number of novels written after her conversion tends to be dismissed, especially by feminist criticism, to which they are an embarrassment, but it is possible to discern a reworking of parallel plots with contrasting ideologies in *Zwei Frauen* (Two women; 1845) and *Zwei Schwestern* (Two sisters; 1863), both of which deal with the contrasting fates of sisters.

Apart from these serious novelists, there are many popular novelists, such as Eugenie Marlitt (Eugenie John), Ottilie Wildermuth and Johanna Spyri. The most famous outside her native Switzerland is Johanna Spyri. Reactionary, opposed to university education for women and to the women's movement, she wrote moral tales mainly for children, of which the most famous is the story of *Heidi* (1880). Popular for its warmth and humour, it has been translated and filmed many times, but was criticized at the turn of the century for its rejection of the modern world. Marlitt, a singer before being encouraged to write, became famous when her second work, *Goldelse* (1867) appeared in the periodical *Die Gartenlaube*, whose circulation doubled between 1866 and 1876 thanks to her serialized fiction. Her novels are versions of the Cinderella story with a social dimension. Although critics like Fontane considered them to be lacking in style, they have been translated into six or seven languages, and a number of her works have recently been reprinted. Wildermuth was a popular writer of Swabian tales for adults and children of humorous and Christian import.

In another vein, the adventure novels of Sophie Wörishöffer were meant to promote Bismarck's colonial aspirations among young readers. But with their accounts of escape from domestic pressure and tedium, of smugglers, castaways and explorers, of freedom and danger in the desert, the jungle or at sea, they can be read as a woman's fantasies of breaking out, comparable to the narratives of travel writers. In fact she never travelled, deriving all her knowledge of distant places from books provided by her publisher. Despite this, her stories of travel and adventure were very successful. Yet because her publishers associated this kind of novel with male writers, they compelled her to write under a series of pseudonyms which concealed the fact that she was a woman, perhaps fearing that such a revelation would detract from the books' popularity.

Non-fiction

An acceptable, but subversive form of non-fiction for women was travel writing. Travel provided a means of breaking out of the confines of women's lives, especially for the middle class, and travelogues enabled women to record their impressions in the open form of letters, diaries and reminiscences. Between the years 1830 and 1890 the scope of travel and of travel writing grew rapidly. Exploration of different parts of the German-speaking countries was frequent; England and Scotland, the subject of accounts by Emilie Berlepsch and Johanna Schopenhauer in 1802–4 and 1818, by Amely Bölte, Ida Hahn-Hahn, Fanny Lewald and Emma Niendorf in the 1840s and 50s, remained favourite destinations, as did Italy, the subject of Lewald's *Italienisches Bilderbuch* (*The Italians at Home*; 1847) and Ida Düringsfeld's *Aus Italien* (From Italy; 1851). For some, travel was a necessity: Betty Paoli travelled to earn her living as a governess and companion; for Hahn-Hahn travel brought spiritual growth, as she records in *Von Babylon nach Jerusalem* (*From Babylon to Jerusalem*), the account of her conversion to Catholicism. The first full-time woman traveller was Ida Pfeiffer, for whom writing provided the means to finance travel. After bringing up her children, Pfeiffer travelled to the Holy Land, to Iceland, twice round the world and to Madagascar, writing five books which were translated into seven languages. Her aesthetic and moral judgements remain uncompromisingly Eurocentric, but she condemns the failings of Europeans as vehemently as those of others. For all these writers, travel became a means of interrogating both their own cultures and their roles within them as women. They delighted in being able to visit places where men could not go, such as a convent or a harem, and in defeating the pessimistic expectations of their families and friends by surviving the rigours of travel.

The least acceptable theme for women was politics, but following Bettina von Arnim's *Dies Buch gehört dem König* (This book belongs to the King; 1845), depicting poverty in Berlin, political writings by women increased. (See the following chapter for a more detailed account of women's political and journalistic activities in the 'year of revolutions', 1848.) Their aim was to improve women's lives, but their strategies differed, some seeing education and improved legal and social status as steps towards complete emancipation, others seeing the right to vote as the beginning of all other improvements. Lewald pleaded for the right of women to be educated to earn a living. Her *Lage der weiblichen Dienstboten* (The situation of female servants; 1843) and *Osterbriefe für die Frauen* (Easter letters for women; 1863) appeal to women to help themselves and their female servants through education and welfare; she is particularly concerned about the welfare of the hundreds of young women from villages who streamed into Berlin every year at Easter and Michaelmas to seek domestic work, often to be cheated, robbed or fall into prostitution before they could find homes. *Für und wider die Frauen* (For and against women; 1870) expresses gratitude to John Stuart Mill, whose *Vindication of the Rights of Women* (1869) was translated into German by Jenny Hirsch as *Über die Hörigkeit der Frau* (The dependence of woman) in 1872. While advocating woman's education and need for economic independence, it emphasizes her responsibilities and condemns frivolity. Hedwig Dohm, equally well acquainted with Mill's work, believed that only the vote would improve women's lot. She wrote several polemical pamphlets, including *Der Frauen Natur und Recht* (*Women's Nature and Privilege*; 1876), in which the themes of her earlier works culminate in a plea for votes for women.

Conclusion

Although women could not agree about the best way to improve their position, or count on the support of other women, let alone of men, their friendships and rivalries built up a tradition of women's writing. One encounters collaborations, and translations of women's writing, and increasingly, women wrote autobiographies and biographies of other women. Some women absorbed the traditions of their literary families, believing that writing was not merely for their brothers: Luise Büchner was the sister of the more famous Georg, author of *Woyzeck*, but in her lifetime she was much better known; Emma Herwegh, the wife of the radical writer Georg Herwegh, also wrote; Johanna Schopenhauer was a writer and the mother of the philosopher Arthur Schopenhauer and of the writer Adèle Schopenhauer. Wilhelmine von Chézy, daughter of the writer Karoline von Klenke (née Karsch), grew up partly under the care of her grandmother Anna Luise Karsch. Inspired by the literary tradition of her family and by writers she knew, including Bettina von Arnim, Louise Brachmann, and Fanny Tarnow, Chézy published poems, translations from the French, novels and travelogues. Writers who were discouraged by their own families sometimes found encouragement from other women: François's talents were fostered by Tarnow, who in turn corresponded with Ebner-Eschenbach, a close friend of Paoli. Such friendships were selective, often accidental. Some formed part of a movement to promote women's political, social or literary independence, others were based simply on shared experience and cordiality.

They did not eliminate rivalry, such as that between Lewald and Hahn-Hahn. Nor did they exclude friendships with literary men. Although much women's writing was trivialized or dismissed by men, women also gained from friendships with male writers: Droste-Hülshoff's relationship with her young mentor, Levin Schücking, combined encouragement with interference; François was encouraged by Conrad Ferdinand Meyer; Ebner-Eschenbach received encouragement from Grillparzer and gave it to Ferdinand von Saar, Saar helped Christen to publish her first poems. Some, like Lewald and Johanna Schopenhauer, entertained both men and women writers and artists in their salons. Literary liaisons were common among radicals: Mühlbach married Theodor Mundt; Therese von

Bacheracht, who wrote fiction, was the companion of Karl Gutzkow as well as the friend and travelling companion of Lewald.

Relationships to men and their writings raise questions of value and of the so-called canon. Some women's achievements were publicly acknowledged: Droste-Hülshoff's publisher, Cotta, began to pay her the same as a man, but her canonical status was created by editors and critics who commended only those works that conformed to a male view of excellence; Ebner-Eschenbach was awarded the first doctorate given to a woman by the University of Vienna; Bertha von Suttner, whose polemical novel *Die Waffen nieder!* (*Lay down your arms!*; 1889) was an international best-seller, became the first woman to win the Nobel Peace Prize. But much women's writing was dismissed because it did not match men's writing, especially in the prestigious area of drama. On the other hand, the general retreat from drama to the novel favoured women, who wrote entertaining social novels before the form entered the so-called canon. Realism gave status to a talent for detailed observation, which came to be perceived as representative or exemplary, rather than as superfluous or trivial. Humour was more problematic, for it enabled women to endure situations against which they might otherwise have protested. Historical novels, adventure novels, children's literature by women compared so well with those by men that publishers concealed the female identity of their most popular authors. Literary history has however relegated these forms to inferior or marginal positions. The huge growth of women's writing during this period, and the manoeuvres invented by critics to marginalize it, create a need for new aesthetic criteria, not derived from writing by men, by which it may be appropriately judged.

6

Political writing and women's journals: the 1848 revolutions

By the mid-nineteenth century, women had been writing for a long time, and there was nothing new about journals aimed at a female audience. Yet newspapers written and edited by women did not appear until as late as 1848, in the context of the revolution of that year. The ground was prepared by the industrial and technological revolution around 1830, which vastly increased the opportunities for such ventures; and the mood of political optimism and hope engendered around 1848 encouraged women to find a voice of their own. The four *Frauenzeitungen* (women's journals) which were founded in fairly rapid succession used the very direct means of commentaries, reports, calls for action and biographical statements to draw attention to the subordinate position women occupied throughout society. In their journalistic work, these women writers – all of whom drew inspiration from the French novelist George Sand – found far greater scope for innovation than in traditional prose genres such as the novel or short story. Germany's first, and eponymous, *Frauen-Zeitung* appeared in Cologne on 27 September 1848. In founding it, the editor, Mathilde Franziska Anneke, was responding to the banning of the *Neue Kölnische Zeitung*, which was edited by her husband, Friedrich Anneke, together with Fritz Breust, and whose character as a journal she had helped shape. The target readership of both papers was working men and women, and the intention was that they should educate and inform themselves about their situation through political articles and commentaries on current events.

This strategy of informing and educating workers by means of literature and the press was a central concern of politically active intellectuals around the 1840s. Mathilde Franziska Anneke had emphatically formulated her own more radical standpoint as early as 1847. As the title indicates, her pamphlet *Das Weib im Konflikt mit den socialen Verhältnissen* (Women in conflict with social circumstances) was an open declaration of solidarity with the subversive Louise Aston, and, in a sense, the motto of her own life. She was firmly convinced that equality for all had to be achieved before women could be liberated from their economic and social dependence on marriage and the state, even though the subservient role of women in a society devised and ruled by men either had not been challenged, or was, at best, only explained away as a side issue. This is what Anneke was attacking in her writings. After only three issues the *Frauen-Zeitung*, too, was banned. As a result of their active participation in the spring uprisings of 1849, both she and her husband risked arrest, which they averted by emigrating to the USA. There Anneke founded the *Deutsche Frauen-Zeitung* in 1852; however, this was also soon forced to close. The fact that she had employed only women gave rise to both annoyance and male professional jealousy. Despite being based in America, she remained active in journalism as a correspondent for various American and German newspapers, reporting on such matters as the slave question and the American Civil War.

In Berlin on 1 November 1848 there appeared the first edition of the *Freischärler. Für Kunst und sociales Leben* (The irregular. A journal for art and social life), founded by Louise Aston. She herself wrote most of the articles published in this weekly journal until it was banned in December 1848. More radical than either Mathilde Franziska Anneke or her contemporaries Louise Otto-Peters and Louise Dittmar, whose journals were founded not long afterwards, Aston used the paper as a vehicle for formulating her demands for equal rights for women. 'Der demokratische Frauenclub und die Frauenemanzipation' (The democratic women's club and the emancipation of women), in Issue 1, is a passionate attack on efforts to emancipate women within the confines of 'faith in God and respect for the world'. 'The free man sins because he cannot help it' was the message in her poem 'Den Frauen' (To women) published in Issue 2; in her view, true freedom is possible only beyond the boundaries which society – i.e. church and state – sets for the individual. Her criticism of religion was strongly influenced by the unorthodox views of the philosopher Ludwig Feuerbach, and forms a backdrop to all her ironic, sarcastic and embittered commentaries on current events in politics and culture. In her novels, Louise Aston was unable to free herself from a cliché-ridden style, and they remain at the level of popular fiction. In her journalistic work, however, where she could express her own experiences of being marginalized and rejected, she brooked no compromise. This resulted in her second expulsion from Berlin, and moreover – since she openly put into practice in her own life what she preached about independence and freedom from prejudiced notions of virtue and morals – led to her being cold-shouldered by other less radical women, such as Louise Otto-Peters.

Shortly thereafter, Louise Otto-Peters in turn founded a weekly *Frauen-Zeitung*, which first appeared on 21 April 1849. Her previous work on other newspapers (Robert Blum's *Vorwärts* and *Sächsische Vaterlandsblätter*, or Ernst Keil's *Leuchtturm*, and *Planet* – the latter under a male pseudonym, 'Otto Stern', at the request of the publisher) meant that she was already experienced as a journalist. Her 'Adresse eines deutschen Mädchens' (Address to a German girl) in the *Leipziger Arbeiter-Zeitung* of 20 May 1848, in which she argued the case for working women, had considerable success, especially with her target audience among the socially underprivileged. Crucial to her success was the fact that in all her demands for equality between men and women she did not challenge the prevailing social consensus about women as devoted, deeply emotional beings, full of pious feelings and willing to make sacrifices. The *Frauen-Zeitung*, whose rallying-cry was 'Dem Reich der Freiheit werb' ich Bürgerinnen' (Women citizens, enlist in the ranks of liberty!), concentrated on material support for women whose husbands either had been killed in the revolutionary clashes in March 1848, or were victims of political persecution. Other objectives were women's rights to self-determination, and the training and educating of girls and women as a prerequisite for achieving social and economic equality, and thus the creation of a democratic society.

Louise Otto-Peters also wrote many of the articles herself. In the case of pieces written by other women, her editorial principle was to publish them unaltered – she left her women readers to judge for themselves. She invited contributions – and this was an innovation – from working-class women, too, promising them help with their articles, since otherwise they would have had no opportunity of making their concerns public. She showed that she was not merely following a modish trend but acting out of genuine conviction by publishing (in Issue 4) Louise Dittmar's poem 'Volkstümlich', which satirized the inflationary, distorted use of this term – and the popular nationalist traditionalism associated with it – for political ends by those in power. Convinced that women must claim their rights for themselves, she repeatedly demanded that women should unite. She addressed her educational and social programme principally to working women in the lowest social strata, especially those who were obliged to help support the family by working from home, without any recognition or assistance from the nascent workers' movement, let alone from the state authorities. For these women in particular she wanted to create a space in which they could express themselves and grasp the symptomatic nature of their predicament, in order to articulate their demands for equality. Otto-Peters herself wrote short stories about such women for her newspaper, for example 'Die Spitzenklöpplerin' (The lace-maker). The remedy she proposed for the hardships which she described so compassionately was education, which would in turn give rise to self-confidence and self-sufficiency, and ultimately help achieve full economic, social and political self-determination. She was convinced that women had energies and abilities which, if developed, could contribute to the well-being of the whole community. She wanted the role which women traditionally played in the family to be extended for the benefit of society as a whole.

Hard as Otto-Peters worked to combat the stereotype of dependent women who lacked any real rights, thus greatly helping to politicize public awareness, she nevertheless presented a picture of women as moral and ethical beings who were tirelessly fulfilling their obligations to the community at large for the good of society. In this way she (perhaps unwittingly) helped to create a new stereotype, since in the course of time these criteria would become a prerequisite for women's asserting any rights at all. Even so, in 1850 her report on the conditions under which political prisoners were kept under arrest caused such a sensation that solely on this account a paragraph was inserted into the Saxon Newspaper Law stipulating that newspapers could only be edited by men. She moved the editorial office from Meißen, in Saxony, to Gera in Thuringia, where the newspaper continued to appear until 1852, thus becoming the longest-lived of all the *Frauenzeitungen*.

Otto-Peters regarded Louise Dittmar as her closest ally. Dittmar had previously asked Otto-Peters to work on a newspaper with her, although the collaboration never materialized. After the first issue of Dittmar's *Sociale Reform. Eine Zeitschrift für Frauen und Männer* (Social Reform. A periodical for women and men), published in Leipzig, had appeared in January 1849, Otto-Peters reviewed it on 19 May 1849 in her *Frauen-Zeitung*. She regarded Dittmar's work as providing a philosophical basis for the struggle for equal rights. Further evidence of their shared interests is the fact that Otto-Peters's article 'Mein Programm als Mitarbeiterin an einer Frauen-zeitung' (My programme as a contributor to a women's newspaper) had appeared in the first issue of *Sociale Reform*. Like Aston, Dittmar was strongly influenced by Feuerbach's ideas; she saw human reason as an innate quality which would further the development of society. Her declared aim was to disseminate the ideas of French and German socialists; she saw her work in journalism as a means of educating people in the use of reason. She wrote most of this newspaper, which appeared monthly for four issues only, herself, with the aim of making it clear to all women what part they were to play in rebuilding society. '*I desire!* (*Ich will!*) That is my ideal, my destiny, my justification, my qualification! And the more I desire the more alive I am, the more human I am . . .' – thus ran her self-confident credo in Issue 1. It is therefore only logical that she should follow up this statement in Issues 2, 3 and 4 by publishing her views on 'Das Wesen der Ehe' (The nature of marriage), in which she characterized marriage as a repressive and disciplinarian institution. In her analysis, which encompassed the historical, legal and economic origins of marriage, Dittmar concluded that not only did the institution still remain barbaric but it was also the basis for both men's and women's misfortune. Inasmuch as it gave one person rights of possession over another, it was founded on inequality, economic dependence and, as a consequence, immorality; as such it reflected conditions in society as a whole. Dittmar's aim in her articles was to make people clearly aware of this; she believed it would have an explosive effect that would shake and transform the very foundations of society. All the efforts human beings had made hitherto to modernize society – and like Otto-Peters, Dittmar included industrial and technological advances in this – would then become freely available to all.

Even if these periodicals were short-lived and could reach only a small proportion of the women and men whom they sought to address, they nevertheless laid the foundations for a medium which specifically addressed the problems of women and a forum in which they could find their own voice. Thus literature played an important part in setting the scene for the increasing politicization of the women's movement from the second half of the nineteenth century onwards.

Translated by Anthony Vivis

Part III
_____

'Coming of age' – 1890–1945

7

The struggle for emancipation: German women writers of the *Jahrhundertwende*

By the turn of the nineteenth century the number of women writing and publishing in German was astonishing. This can be seen from the numerous lexica and anthologies of women writers that appeared between 1895 and 1910 and from the more easily accessible 1986 dtv dictionary of women writers in German from 1800 to 1945, the *Lexikon deutschsprachiger Schriftstellerinnen 1800–1945*. This lists some seventy or more writers active in this period. These women writers produced poetry, prose, drama, essays, children's literature, popular fiction and journalism. There were also many writers of political essays, pamphlets and journalism active within the bourgeois and proletarian women's movements. Important political writers included, for example, Helene Lange, Helene Stöcker, Clara Zetkin, Lily Braun and Gertrud Bäumer.

Many prose writers, in particular, had successful careers, publishing novels and short stories which appeared in large print runs and reached wide audiences. Most women wrote for financial reasons. The expansion in literacy and in newspaper, magazine and book publishing in the last quarter of the nineteenth century opened up new markets. In a society in which many middle-class women remained unmarried, writing was one of the few socially acceptable professions. It offered women an independence denied them as teachers or governesses and it was open to both unmarried and married women. In order to maximize their income many writers first published their fiction in newspapers and magazines and then in book form. With the growth in the numbers of successful women writers came the establishment of women writers' organizations, for example, the *Verein der Schriftstellerinnen und Künstlerinnen* (Union of Women Writers and Artists) founded in Vienna in 1885, the *Schriftstellerinnenverein* (Women Writers' Union), Leipzig, 1890, and the two Berlin organizations, the *Verein deutscher Schriftstellerinnen* (Union of German Women Writers), 1896 and the *Freie Vereinigung deutscher Schriftstellerinnen* (Free Organization of German Women Writers), 1898. The *Verein deutscher Schriftstellerinnen*, for example, met fortnightly and by 1911 had a membership of 230.

Like their male contemporaries, women writers employed a range of different styles of writing. Much well-received prose was influenced by Naturalism. Letters and diaries were a popular form for fiction and the successful writer Ricarda Huch came to be seen as a founding figure of New Romanticism. Depite the difficulties of entering a peculiarly male domain, a number of plays by women were performed. While many writers produced poetry, drama and essays, prose fiction remained their chief source of income. In addition to 'serious' fiction, a number of women, for example, Hedwig Courths-Mahler and Nataly von Eschstruth, wrote popular romantic fiction.

Whatever genre they chose, most women writers took women's lives as their main subject matter and wrote about the experience of being a woman and about female subjectivity. The often-used forms of the diary and letters facilitated an apparently unmediated expression of female perspectives. Much prose writing was socially critical and supported the case for women's emancipation. Hedwig Dohm, Gabriele Reuter, Helene Böhlau and Ilse Frapan, for example, all published widely read novels and short stories which were highly critical of the way middle-class society treated girls and women.

Novels, short stories and essays which were not explicitly or unproblematically feminist, for example the work of Lou Andreas-Salomé, or were indeed at times explicitly anti-feminist (Franziska zu Reventlow), none the less addressed the question of female sexuality and individual women's rights to self-fulfilment. This was something that demanded a revision of bourgeois norms of femininity and morality. Grete Meisel-Hess, who, like Reventlow, wrote novels, short stories and essays, took up the themes of female sexuality and sexual double standards. Unlike Reventlow, she wrote from a feminist perspective, although later she came to support eugenicist ideas and to see motherhood as women's natural role in life.

Bertha von Suttner achieved an international reputation in 1889 with her pacifist novel *Die Waffen nieder!* (*Lay down your arms!*). Other writers well received at the time included Ricarda Huch and Clara Viebig. One of the first German women to gain a doctorate, at Zurich University in 1891 (women were not admitted to university in Germany until 1908), Huch published an influential study of Romanticism (1899–1902), wrote poetry and prose, often with an historical content, and became one of the few writers of the period whose reputation extended into the postwar period. Clara Viebig, who was both prose writer and dramatist, established an enduring reputation for her Naturalist stories of the life of ordinary people in the Eifel and Berlin.

Most writers were either middle-class or from aristocratic families. Working-class writing was rare. One notable exception was the Austrian autobiography *Jugend einer Arbeiterin* (Youth of a working-class woman) by Adelheid Popp which first appeared anonymously in 1909. Middle-class women allied to the Social Democratic Party and the proletarian women's movement published fiction in social democratic newspapers and magazines. Minna Kautsky, for example, dealt with the problems of working-class life and the 'woman question' in her fiction, which was widely read in social democratic circles at the turn of the century and earned her the nickname 'die rote Marlitt' (red Marlitt). (Eugenie Marlitt was still one of the most-read authors of popular fiction around 1900.)

While many women writers wrote poetry, few did so exclusively or earned a living from it. Often writers first made a name for themselves with volumes of poetry but went on to write prose and drama. Such writers included Margarete Beutler, Marie Eugenie delle Grazie, Ricarda Huch, Marie Janitschek and Isolde Kurz. An important exception was Else Lasker-Schüler, well known for her bohemian lifestyle as well as her poetry, who remained primarily a poet, though she also wrote prose and drama.

Drama was the most difficult area for women to enter successfully. It was a very public medium which was widely regarded as a male domain in which women should only figure as actresses. Those women who succeeded in having plays staged often did so under male pseudonyms. Women were most successful in amateur, popular and regional theatres. The high-art theatres in the larger cities remained largely closed to them. There were, of course, a few notable exceptions. In the 1870s, Hedwig Dohm succeeded in having a number of plays staged by the Königliches Schauspielhaus in Berlin. Although not overtly feminist, they satirized men and male behaviour. The Austrian writer Emil Marriot (Emilie Mataja) had a feminist play, critical of bourgeois marriage, *Gretes Glück* (Grete's happiness), staged by the Berlin Freie Bühne (Free Theatre) in 1897. Ernst Rosmer (Elsa Bernstein-Porges) offered a feminist perspective on the education of girls in *Maria Arndt,* which was performed in Munich in 1908. Ilse Frapan took prostitution as her theme in *Der Retter der Moral* (The saviour of morality), which was performed in Hamburg in 1905. Clara Viebig's plays *Barbara Holzer* (1896) and *Das letzte Glück* (Last happiness; 1909) were performed in Berlin and Frankfurt respectively. For the most part, however, theatrical successes were rare and the authors concerned concentrated on the socially more acceptable form of prose fiction.

The intellectual climate in the metropolitan centres in Germany and Austria at the turn of the century was exciting. Feminism had become a powerful social movement, particularly with the radicalization of the middle-class women's movement between 1895 and 1908. In addition to the long-established demands for education and access to the professions, issues such as suffrage, sexual double standards and the rights of unmarried women had become important feminist issues. The impact of Ibsen and the Naturalists on writers was profound. More important still, however, was the impact of Nietzsche, whose writings, despite their misogynistic aspects, became popular with women interested in emancipation. They seemed to offer a platform from which to criticize existing bourgeois moral and social norms and to advance women's right to full self-development as individuals.

Yet for all the new ideas in circulation, the nineteenth and early twentieth centuries were dominated by dualistic theories of gender which stressed differences between women and men. The years around 1900 saw the publication of a number of conservative writings on women which sold in large numbers and demonstrate the level of interest in and strength of feelings about the 'woman question'. Numerous texts in medicine, psychology, philosophy, biology and the law argued that men and women were naturally different and suited to different social spheres and life-styles. Domesticity and motherhood were widely held to be women's primary and fundamental roles. Moreover the restrictions on women's access to education and the professions were often justified in the interests of motherhood.

The dualist model of sexual difference also dominated the German women's movement. From Louise Otto-Peters, writing in the 1840s, onwards, most feminists accepted the idea of different spheres for women and men. They argued that education and access to the professions would make women better wives and mothers and solve the problem of single women. Many feminists saw women's particular cultural mission in the extension of their mothering qualities into the public arena. Yet the years immediately around the turn of the century were exceptional. Between 1895 and 1908 the more radical wing of the women's movement gained ascendancy, demanding suffrage and a wide range of social changes particularly in the area of sexual standards as they affected single women.

One of the writers championed by the radical wing of the women's movement was Hedwig Dohm, whose radical political writings from the 1870s were reprinted in the 1890s. Dohm drew on John Stuart Mill and Anglo-American feminism, writing within a liberal tradition which regarded equal rights for women as basic human rights. She questioned traditional gender norms, arguing that rather than being natural, they were socially produced and that they served male interests. Between 1870 and her death in 1919, Dohm wrote pamphlets, articles, novels and short stories. In them she argued for civil rights, education, the right to work, the rights of single women and single mothers, a new morality and an end to sexual double standards. She was also a strong critic of the First World War.

Dohm's political writings focused on the deconstruction of traditional, conservative thinking about the nature of women. For example, in her first political text, *Was die Pastoren von den Frauen denken* (What the pastors think about women; 1872), a response to two anti-emancipatory pamphlets by men, Dohm asked why healthy, middle-class women who were well able to earn their own livings should remain dependent on their families. She asserted women's rights to self-development and work as basic human rights, going further than the women's movement in demanding these for married as well as single women.

In Dohm's view, male opponents of emancipation drew on conceptions of womanhood which were specific to the middle classes. She described the very different situation of working-class women who were forced to endure long hours of heavy work in unhealthy environments. She argued that the jobs from which women were excluded were those that brought with them status, power and influence and she reinterpreted the so-called 'natural' laws that restricted women to the roles of housewife and mother as *Männergesetze* (men's laws): laws designed by men which served their interests.

In the political texts that followed over the next few decades, Dohm took issue with conservative thinking on education, suffrage, sexuality, motherhood and the position of older women. Her rhetorical style included rational counter-argument and critiques of what currently passed for knowledge, for example history writing that excluded the achievements of women. She also resorted to pathos and irony to evoke sympathy for the feminist cause.

Dohm did not restrict her attacks on anti-feminism to male writers. She commented both on the different tendencies within the women's movement and on the arguments of writers – men and women – whose work she considered anti-feminist. For example, in *Die Antifeministen* (The Anti-feminists; 1902) she criticized Nietzsche, the views of gynaecologists, the influential work of the sociobiologist Möbius, but also what she saw as reactionary tendencies within the women's movement. She took issue with the images of women to be found in the work of Laura Marholm, author of *Das Buch der Frauen* (The book of women; 1895), *Wir Frauen und unsere Dichter* (We women and our poets; 1895) and *Zur Psychologie der Frau* (On the psychology of women; 1897); of the Swedish writer and pacifist, Ellen Key; and of the writer and friend of Nietzsche, Rilke and Freud, Lou Andreas-Salomé.

If Dohm's political writings focus on the theories, social assumptions and laws that restricted women's potential, her fiction turns its attention to women themselves. It looks at the social construction of femininity and women's apparent complicity with patriarchal social relations. Between 1890 and 1909, Hedwig Dohm published four novels and ten novellas in which she took up many of the themes found in her political writings, yet the emphasis in her fiction is different. More than anything else, the novels and short stories offer perspectives on the psychological and emotional consequences for individual middle-class women of a society that does not allow them access to education, the professions and political life. Her fiction also examines how women need to change in order to take advantage of the opportunities which emancipation offers.

Emancipation in Dohm's fiction is not restricted to questions such as education and the right to a well-paid, professional career. It touches crucially on those areas usually regarded as dimensions of private life, for example, marriage, motherhood and sexuality. Underlying her treatment of each of these issues is the need for a new set of social values and a new morality in which the rights of the individual – married or unmarried – are paramount.

Dohm's novels and short stories make extensive use of diaries, memoirs and letters which appear to give the reader privileged access to the thoughts and feelings of their protagonists. They detail the everyday life of middle-class women, the ways in which the social relations of the day make it impossible for them to realize their full potential intellectually or sexually, and their stategies of resistance. Nowhere is this waste of potential more powerfully expressed than in the 1894 novella *Werde, die Du bist* (Become yourself), which offers a powerful account of madness induced by the realization on the part of the widowed Agnes Schmidt that she has lived her life without experiencing love or self-fulfilment and that, now, as an ageing widow, she has no positive role to play in society.

The diary, which forms the substance of the novella, traces her thoughts, feelings and experiences in the period between her husband's death and the onset of her mental illness. It offers a picture of a woman whose life was defined by her husband and, before him, by her parents. It traces the development of Agnes Schmidt's increasing self-awareness and critical attitude towards herself and society. It gives a vivid picture of her feelings as she looks back on her life and recounts how she experiences life, including passion, as an elderly widow.

For Agnes Schmidt, realization of the poverty of her life comes too late. As an old woman in this society, she can only experience what she has missed in madness and her illness is marked by the attempt to inhabit a more youthful, sexual self. In contrast, the protagonists of Dohm's trilogy *Sibilla Dalmar* (1896), *Schicksale einer Seele* (Destinies of a soul; 1899) and *Christa Ruland* (1902) are all younger women who still have the chance to change their lives. All middle-class, though not all equally rich, the three protagonists span three generations. They have in common inadequate education, unhappy marriages and lives as society hostesses. They vary considerably, however, in how they manage their situations.

The novels reflect changing ideas about women. In *Schicksale einer Seele*, set in 1866, the protagonist, Marlene, is very much a victim of both family and society. Shy and ill-educated, she has internalized the negative self-image which her mother and then her husband reinforce. In contrast, Sibilla Dalmar, born a generation later, although dissatisfied with her life, is much more in control of it. She is depicted as particularly intelligent, well-read and self-confident. A successful society hostess, she is none the less still restricted by social mores which insist that she marry well, that is, a rich man whom she does not love, and remain faithful to him even though he is repeatedly unfaithful to her. Christa Ruland, the youngest of the three generations, mixes with other women who aspire to the title 'new woman'. She suffers from a loveless marriage in which she is expected to deny her own individuality. Yet this experience leads her to look to Nietzsche and his precursor Stirner for a new conception of self and to develop a new concept of marriage.

In each of the three novels, the protagonists change and develop through reading and through platonic relationships with men other than their husbands. The pressure to marry for financial reasons is seriously questioned in both *Sibilla Dalmar* and *Christa Ruland*. Over the course of three generations the alternatives to marriage do increase. For Marlene there are no other options, while for Sibilla there is the possibility of studying, not in Germany, where women are still barred from the universities, but in Zurich. Sibilla, however, rejects this idea since the professions remain closed to women even with degrees. Christa Ruland is desperate for a university education, which is now open to women, but her aspirations are thwarted by her mother and husband, both of whom still regard marriage as the only respectable career for women.

Conventional thinking in Germany at this time saw not only marriage, but more importantly motherhood within marriage, as the essence of women's role. In *Schicksale einer Seele* motherhood is the only aspect of Marlene's married life that brings her pleasure and this only while her children are young. Sibilla Dalmar eventually turns, like her mother before her, to motherhood as her salvation. She comes to view it as the one thing that can give her life meaning. Ironically she dies in childbirth. By Christa Ruland's generation, a new conception of motherhood is possible in which women retain an identity beyond their role as mother.

In the course of the three narratives, each of the heroines aquires a broadly feminist understanding of her life. Speaking in 1866, Marlene decides that her life has taken the course that it has because women are denied the right to determine their path and goal in life. Sibilla Dalmar is quite clear that she is a sad *Übergangsgeschöpf*, a transitional creature born before the Women's Movement has achieved its goals. A similar perspective is articulated by Christa Ruland:

> Die neuen Ideen sind schon lebendig, die alten in uns noch nicht tot... Wir haben die Nerven der alten Generation und die Intelligenz und das Wollen der neuen. Und gleich dem Moses, werden wir an der Schwelle des gelobten Landes sterben. (p. 307)

> New ideas are alive in us, old ones not yet dead... We have the nerves of the older generation and the intelligence and aspiration of the new. And like Moses, we will die on the threshold of the promised land.

The difficult process of emancipation is also the main theme of two novels by the Hamburg-born writer, Ilse Frapan, *Wir Frauen haben kein Vaterland* (We women have no Fatherland; 1899) and *Arbeit* (Work; 1903). After ten years as a teacher, Frapan established herself as a writer of short stories about Hamburg life. Her two feminist novels were quite different from the stories with which she generally earned her living. *Wir Frauen haben kein Vaterland* presents the diary of a young Hamburg woman who is studying law in Zurich. Drawing on autobiographical elements, it takes up many key issues under discussion in the women's movement of the day. Its heroine Lilie Halmschlag supports many of the arguments of the radical wing of the women's movement, including grammar school education for girls, changes in the law on prostitution and the vote. The novel asks how women can become fully emancipated. Is it possible in society as it exists or must society change?

Lilie, who is highly critical of traditional family norms, is herself a victim of internalized norms of femininity which render her ineffectual in a male-dominated world. While she believes that women have a special natural motherly love that can help transform society, she has to give up her own struggle for emancipation through education for lack of financial support. She becomes a manual worker and turns to social democracy. By contrast, the heroine of Frapan's *Arbeit* is much more successful in achieving the status of 'new woman'. While her husband is in prison, Josefine Geyer manages to complete a medical degree, become a successful doctor and raise four children.

The cause of women's rights is also central to the work of Helene Böhlau. Reduced by literary historians to a footnote in the history of German Naturalism, Böhlau was regarded at the turn of the century as one of the most important women writers. Between 1882 and 1939 she published over forty novels and short stories. Like Frapan she was perhaps best-known for her politically innocuous writing: her immensely popular and long-term best-selling stories about life in Weimar in the age of Goethe, *Rathsmädelgeschichten* (Stories of councillors' daughters; 1888) and *Altweimarische Liebes- und Ehegeschichten* (Stories of love and marriage in Old Weimar; 1897). Böhlau's socially critical novels, *Der Rangierbahnhof* (The marshalling yard; 1896), *Das Recht der Mutter* (The mother's right; 1896) and *Halbtier* (Semi-beast; 1899), which were influenced by Naturalism, formed a small but important part of her literary work.

Halbtier, a novel that argues that gender relations in German society reduced women to a less than human status, had an enormous impact. It tells the story of Isolde and her elder sister Marie, impoverished 'höhere Töchter' (daughters of the upper middle class) brought up in a repressive patriarchal family in which their mother firmly believes that women must do as men tell them. The family's fortunes change when the daughters inherit a substantial amount of money from an uncle. The narrative focuses on Isolde, who, in contrast to her calm and gentle older sister Marie, is depicted as highly emotional and critical of the life that they lead as women.

Like many heroines of the period, Isolde is profoundly influenced by modern art. At the age of fifteen she discovers the work of Henry Mengersen at an art exhibition in Munich, and falls in love both with the paintings and with the artist. She meets Mengersen, an extremely chauvinistic man, at a social engagement. For all his contempt for women, he shows interest in her because he sees her as different from other girls of her class and background. Yet his attraction to her is sexual and he never regards her as a fully *human* being. Misinterpreting Mengersen's interest in her as love, Isolde agrees to pose naked for him. If he did not love her, she reasons, he would not have asked her to pose. She is mistaken. Mengersen wants a wife of means, but a compliant one who will not challenge his misogynist view of women. He chooses Isolde's sister Marie and Isolde realizes for the first time how women are regarded by men in this society. Mengersen, she feels, has treated her as 'ein Wesen das nicht Mensch sondern Weib ist, ein Wesen, das nicht wie ein Mensch fühlen und handeln kann, das nur geschlechtlich ist' (a being that is not human but female, a being that cannot feel and act like a human being but is only sexual; p. 120).

In an attempt to establish her humanity, Isolde dedicates the next five years of her life to painting and becomes a recognized artist. The success that she achieves is at the expense of an emotional life, husband or children. Yet in spite of his recognition of the quality of her work, Mengersen still treats Isolde as mere sexual prey and she shoots him as he attempts to rape her. This deed and her own death are portrayed as heroic: she is made to stand for 'die Hälfte der Menschheit' (half of humanity), representing and avenging 'the idea of the eternally oppressed woman, the underdeveloped creature, robbed of her mind, who can be ordered to do everything, who accepts everything, facing every form of humiliation defenceless and without rights' (pp. 178–9).

The heroines of Böhlau's other emancipatory novels, *Der Rangierbahnhof* and *Das Recht der Mutter*, also display heroic qualities: the one in her dedication to her work as an artist, the other in her commitment to motherhood. Both are faced with social situations that require that they give up these pursuits and conform to accepted norms of how a married woman and an unmarried girl should behave. Both refuse to conform and eventually have their brave stands endorsed by men who love and respect them, though for the talented heroine of *Der Rangierbahnhof*, Olly, the man in question, is not her husband and she is terminally ill.

A bleaker picture of the effects of social pressures on women is to be found in the work of Gabriele Reuter, in particular in her controversial novel *Aus guter Familie. Leidensgeschichte eines Mädchens* (Of good family. History of a girl's sufferings 1895). Like Böhlau, Reuter was one of the most popular writers of the period, and her work included issues at the heart of the feminist agenda. Between 1888 and 1937 she published thirty-eight texts including prose, drama, children's books and studies of Ebner-Eschenbach and Droste-Hülshoff. *Aus guter Familie* tells the story of Agathe Heidling from her confirmation at the age of seventeen to her nervous breakdown in her early thirties. She is the daughter of a civil servant of limited means who married a woman with a private fortune. When this fortune is dissipated paying off the son's gambling debts, there is not enough left for a dowry for Agathe. Unable to marry, she is forced to take over the running of the household when her mother goes to pieces after her father has lost his job. Her life becomes a round of tedious tasks as her father, who has always sought to control her reading, thwarts her attempts at self-education. After her mother's death, on a holiday in Switzerland with her father, Agathe finally has a nervous breakdown.

Aus guter Familie offers a vivid picture of the social attitudes and practices that reduce an intelligent and emotional woman to a nervous breakdown and a semi-vegetative future as companion to her father. Parental attitudes, religion and education are all depicted as important factors, but perhaps most fundamental is the socially taboo question of female sexuality. Girls and women are not supposed to have sexual needs before marriage, if at all, and certainly not if they remain unmarried as Agathe does.

From the start of the novel, sexuality is signalled as the key to understanding what happens to Agathe. Repressive attitudes to female sexuality are depicted as fundamental to middle-class society. Agathe's religious education stresses qualities such as renunciation of the world of physical pleasures, yet the religious hymns sung in church use erotic language and begin what becomes for Agathe a habit of displacing the sexual and fearing and despising it while at the same time needing it – subsequently she turns to Pietism as a substitute for sexual needs, to the point where she becomes socially embarrassing.

Agathe's ambivalence towards sexuality is exemplified in her feelings towards her childhood friend Eugenie and cousin Martin, for both of whom she develops passionate feelings, combined with a horror of sensuality. Later she escapes from the world of real relationships by turning to Romanticism, as embodied by Lord Byron. Even when she falls in love with the painter Adrian Lutz, the relationship, like that with Byron, exists largely in her imagination. Nevertheless, her desire for love is matched only by fear of a life as a spinster. The desire for sexual contact with a man – to be kissed – becomes a fixed idea, and she dreams of passionate adventures while fearing physical contact.

When she is finally offered the chance of escape and a new, if uncertain, life in Switzerland, Agathe is unable to make the break. Her socialization has taught her that her own needs and desires are reprehensible and must be repressed. Her childhood sweetheart and cousin Martin Gressinger urges her to stay with him in Zurich. Yet in his concern to emancipate her from her family, he has little understanding of her position as unmarried yet dependent woman, and she looks to him in vain for love. Their newly established relationship ends in Agathe's nervous breakdown.

Aus guter Familie powerfully conveys the ways in which women internalize contradictory and often masochistic, self-destructive social values which stunt them as human beings and often lead to their downfall. The scenes in the sanatorium make it clear that Agnes is just one case among many. The women there are mostly young and can be divided into two groups: those exhausted by the demands made on them by their husbands, children and society, and the pale, young, unmarried women, ill from the effects of doing nothing, of longing and disappointment. In Agathe's case all her repressed bitterness and hatred, her sexual needs and her disappointed hopes of motherhood culminate in an attempt to murder her sister-in-law. After two years in mental hospitals, Agathe is returned to her father docile, brain-damaged, no longer knowing what she is missing in life.

Yet not all Reuter's emancipatory prose depicts women as hopeless victims of society. Some of her heroines resist more successfully, for example Ellen in *Ellen von der Weiden* and Cornelie in *Das Tränenhaus* (The house of tears). *Ellen von der Weiden* tells the story of an unconventional woman from the Harz who refuses to lose her identity in marriage and become what her husband wants her to be. He suspects her of adultery and divorces her even though she is carrying his child. Cornelie, the heroine of *Das Tränenhaus*, becomes pregnant as a result of a pre-marital relationship. Disappointed by the father of her child and full of hatred and despair, she goes to a home for unmarried mothers-to-be in the country.

Here she sees the fate of unmarried pregnant women from a range of class backgrounds and becomes determined to retain her autonomy and return to her life as a successful writer once her child is born. Strong as they are, in both cases the heroines are faced at the end of the novels with a lonely life as single mothers.

The difficulty of combining an independent life as a working woman with marriage is one of the themes of Lou Andreas-Salomé's fiction. In it she explores how women relate to men and, in the process, the nature of female desire. Two novellas, in particular, look in detail at the possibilities of full and equal relationships between men and women and the masochistic construction of much female desire. *Fenitschka* is the story of a Russian woman who has studied in Zurich and returns to St Petersburg to take up a teaching post. There she falls in love, but is forced by the social constraints of the time to choose between marriage and a career. She chooses her career, partly as a result of her lover's inability to relate to her fully as an emancipated woman.

The story is told from the perspective of a German psychologist, Max Werner, who meets Fenitschka briefly for the first time in Paris and then a year later in Russia at his sister's wedding. He is attracted to Fenitschka in Paris because she is different. To him she appears intelligent and asexual and throughout the novella an opposition is maintained between intellectual and sexual qualities in women. The two apparently cannot be mixed.

Fenitschka is depicted as unconventional in her spontaneity. She is not a slave to the social conventions that govern relationships between the sexes in the middle and upper classes. She has strong and unconventional views on love and marriage, holding the two completely distinct. Love is for her something completely natural and healthy. It should bring a sense of peace. She finds the socially imposed secrecy in which she is forced to conduct her relationship degrading. If men, as Werner claims, find secrecy engaging this is, she argues, an effect of sexual double standards which degrade women.

The novella is critical of men, showing how they refuse to see women as both intelligent and sensual. The narrator, Max Werner, for example, does not approve of educated women. The very idea of them annoys him and he is at pains to maintain distinctions between men and women who study. Educated women, for him, remain upstarts. He cannot come to terms with Fenitschka's apparent equality. His normal attitude to women is demonstrated in his relationship to his fiancée, whom he loves for her subservience and masochism.

In *Eine Ausschweifung* (An excess) the narrator, Adine, experiences a contradiction between her emancipated and self-determined life as a painter and the masochistic nature of her desire. This makes it impossible for her to have serious relationships with men. Unlike other women in the story, who are able to identify either with an emancipated conception of relations between the sexes or with a subservient masochism, Adine remains divided. Despite her unusually liberal upbringing and her father's support for her artistic aspirations, Adine grows up with a masochistic attitude to erotic relationships between women and men. She traces this back to an incident in early childhood when she saw her nanny express pleasure and satisfaction on being beaten by her husband. Adine regards masochism as an inherited attitude from which women are only beginning to liberate themselves.

After the death of her father, Adine falls passionately in love with her cousin Benno Frensdorff, to whom she becomes engaged. In an extremely masochistic relationship, which he encourages, she tries to become what he wants – a good traditional housewife – but this makes her ill. Benno eventually realizes what is happening and at great emotional cost dissolves the engagement. Adine, who is heartbroken, goes abroad with her mother and becomes a painter in Paris. Asked by both her mother and Benno to return home after six years, Adine arrives in Brieg at Christmas.

On her return she discovers that Benno still loves her, has changed and wants a marriage with her in which they are equals. Yet for Adine this is no longer possible. She does not love Benno any more; her attraction to him rests, as it did previously, on masochism, yet she knows that she could no longer ever actually live in such a masochistic relationship where she would be humiliated and her individuality denied.

If in *Eine Ausschweifung* Salomé sees masochism as an historically conditioned aspect of femininity which is in the process of changing, for Franziska zu Reventlow gender characteristics are both given and unchanging. Reventlow, who was renowned for her bohemian life-style and views on free love, wrote novels, short prose, autobiographical sketches, diaries and essays in which she took issue with aristocratic and bourgeois family life and existing moral standards.

In her autobiographical novel, *Ellen Olestjerne,* she tells the story of the childhood, adolescence and early adulthood of the daughter of an aristocratic family. Permanently in conflict with her family, Ellen eventually breaks all ties with them and with support from her fiancé goes to

Munich to become a painter. While there she becomes pregnant by another painter and returns north to marry her fiancé. The loss of the foetus is followed in due course by divorce, another pregnancy and a future as a promiscuous, single mother.

Both motherhood and free love are central to Reventlow's view of women. These are explored in some detail in her essay *Was Frauen ziemt* (What becomes women). Here she argues, with some irony, that in philistine, middle-class circles the most important thing for girls and women is the preservation of their reputation and a good marriage – a 'life of boredom' from the 'small girl well-behaved at school' through the role of 'useful object or decoration in the home' when older, to the 'blushing bride sewing her trousseau' in preparation for 'fulfilling the duties of the Christian marriage bed', to the wife 'standing by her husband … and preparing her children for the same dismal life' (p. 250).

Yet rather than endorse the women's movement's campaigns for access to education and the professions, Reventlow insists on respect for what she sees as 'natural' gender differences. These, she argues, fit women for a life as mother and luxury object. Women achieve less than men physically. Some women may study, but this costs them their femininity. There are, she says, no female thinkers, philosophers or inventors. While women have more of a sense for art and literature, even here their role is restricted to that of actress or dancer.

Woman's difference from men means that she should be allowed to live differently:

> Sie ist nicht zur Arbeit, nicht für die schweren Dinge der Welt geschaffen, sondern zur Leichtigkeit, zur Freude, zur Schönheit – ein Luxusobjekt in des Wortes schönster Bedeutung, ein beseeltes, lebendes, selbstempfindendes Luxusobjekt, das Schutz, Pflege und günstige Lebensbedingungen braucht, um ganz das sein zu können, das es eben sein kann. (pp. 257–8)

> She is not made for work or the difficult things in the world, but for ease, joy, beauty – a luxury object in the finest sense of the word. An inspired, living, luxury object which experiences itself as such, which needs protection, care and favourable living conditions in order to realize itself fully.

Given that women dedicate their lives to men and children, Reventlow argues, their lives should be made as easy as possible. Moreover, women should be sexually free and the realization of this freedom would be a worthy goal for a women's movement. However, Reventlow regards the existing women's movement as the enemy of all erotic culture because, as she sees it, it wants to make women masculine.

In *Von Paul zu Pedro. Amouresken* (From Paul to Pedro. Amouresques), fictional letters from a beautiful promiscuous woman to a male friend, Reventlow gives a picture of how a woman who believes in free love actually relates to men. She maintains a distinction between sensual attraction and personal attraction. She has relationships that function only at the level of physical attraction and personal, often platonic, friendships with men, as with her correspondent. Jealousy rarely figures in her short-lived sexual relationships. The men come and go and it is the pleasure of the moment that counts.

Reventlow insists on a distinction between love and eroticism. Men, she argues, assume that women maintain at least the illusion that they are in love when they belong to a man. She resists generalizations about women and men and wants to hold on to a plurality of ways of relating. They may involve love or 'great passion' but often the motivation is pleasure, adventure, the immediate situation, politeness or boredom.

The other fundamental aspect of women for Reventlow is motherhood. In her essay *Das Männerphantom der Frau* (Women's illusory images of men) she describes motherhood as the essence of woman. Women's desire for men is, she suggests, nothing more than a desire for motherhood. She endorses Nietzsche's aphorism that everything about women is a puzzle which has but one solution: pregnancy. She maintains that a woman who has really understood the meaning of life will not see a man who makes her pregnant and abandons her as a seducer and betrayer. She will bless the man for enabling her to experience motherhood. She will be willing to let him go since he is but a means to an end. Women, she says, should be brought up to believe this and society should make single motherhood possible, instead of rejecting illegitimate children, driving men to prostitutes and women to abortion. Normal sexual instinct is, she argues, rare in this society. It is mostly found among promiscuous women, such as prostitutes, who are also the best mothers.

Franziska zu Reventlow's writing is, like that of many feminist writers, an attack on established bourgeois sexual and social norms. Her promotion of motherhood ran parallel to campaigns within the moderate wing of the women's movement to see women's mothering qualities extended into public life. Both moderate feminists and Reventlow understood motherhood to be women's special cultural mission, but for Reventlow this transcended the restrictive bounds of bourgeois morality. She redefines women as sensual and promiscuous beings but denies them all capacities other than those connected with sex and motherhood. In restricting women, on the basis of their 'nature', to the roles of lover and mother, she dispenses with the bourgeois family. While ideally men should provide women with lives of luxury, if they do not, then the state should step in. Her position on women was guaranteed to outrage both conservatives and feminists alike. None the less, the claims that she makes for women's right to erotic relationships irrespective of marriage and her revaluation of single motherhood cannot but be seen as oddly progressive in the context of turn-of-the-century thinking on these issues.

Conclusion

As we have seen, the end of the nineteenth century was, for a number of reasons, a particularly interesting and productive period for women writers. The women's movement had raised consciousness about women's social situation and questioned existing norms of femininity, marriage and sexual double standards. In response, a wide range of conservative writings on the nature of women appeared. Moreover, other broader influences on the intellectual climate, particularly the concerns of the Naturalists and of Nietzsche, were changing how both men and women thought about themselves. Furthermore, an imbalance in the population meant that large numbers of middle-class women remained unmarried. With the expansion of publishing outlets in the last quarter of the nineteenth century, writing became a realistic means of earning a living free from the constraints and humiliations of the more usual areas of middle-class female employment such as work as governesses, teachers, companions or seamstresses. These writers found an eager reading public anxious for their work.

As contemporary histories of German literature show in their positive evaluation of women writers, by this period the latter had successfully established themselves on the literary scene. It is ironic, therefore, that almost all of the seventy or more active writers named in such works should disappear completely from later literary histories and become part of that lost history that this volume is seeking to recover.

8

Trends in writing by women, 1910–1933

Introduction

The beginning of this period is marked by a literary event: the foundation, in 1910, of the first Expressionist journals: *Der Sturm* in Berlin, edited by Herwarth Walden and August Stramm, and its Austrian counterpart, *Der Brenner*, edited by Ludwig von Ficker. The end, however, is fixed by a political event: Hitler's seizure of power in 1933. Between these dates falls one of the most significant turning-points in history, World War I, bringing with it radical changes in politics and society, as well as in art and literature. In literary-historical terms, this is an extremely varied epoch, comprising a number of diverse literary movements – neo-Romanticism, late Naturalism, Futurism, Expressionism, Dadaism, Surrealism, and *Neue Sachlichkeit* (New Objectivity).

As a result of the historical developments in Germany, and under pressure from the emerging women's movement, women's social position changed radically during the 'Expressionist decade' (1900–10), and especially during the Weimar Republic (1919–33). Women's literary and artistic production, and their participation in the artistic circles of Berlin, Munich, Zurich and Vienna, increased as their confidence grew. Indeed, it is thanks to their contacts in these circles that some of these women writers are known today, irrespective of the literary merit of their works. The importance of the poetry of Else Lasker-Schüler and the plays of Marieluise Fleißer is now widely recognized, yet it is doubtful whether even their work would have achieved a place in the German literary canon were it not for their connections both within contemporary literary circles and with eminent 'men of letters'. Some of the influential names with whom Else Lasker-Schüler was associated include the poet Georg Trakl and the satirist Karl Kraus, both connected with the Innsbruck Expressionist periodical *Der Brenner*, and the Expressionist poet Gottfried Benn; a number of her poems were included in Kurt Pinthus's famous anthology of Expressionist poetry, *Die Menschheitsdämmerung* (*Dawn of Humanity*). For Marieluise Fleißer, the decisive factors were her 'discovery' by the writer and publisher Lion Feuchtwanger, and Bertolt Brecht's staging of her first play *Fegefeuer in Ingolstadt* (*Purgatory in Ingolstadt*) in 1926.

In many other cases, however, such prominence resulted in a dubious fame at the expense of the writers' literary works, as in the cases of Emmy (Ball-)Hennings and Claire (Studer-)Goll, who have gone down in literary history as the 'wives of famous men' while their considerable literary oeuvre of lyric poetry and novels remains virtually unknown today. Emmy Hennings is well known as the lover of Ferdinand Hardekopf, Jakob von Hoddis and Erich Mühsam as well as the wife of Hugo Ball, while Claire Goll is best known as the lover of Rainer Maria Rilke and the wife of Yvan Goll, relationships she documented in her deliberately provocative *Chronique scandaleuse*, originally written in French and later published in German under the title *Ich verzeihe keinem* (I forgive no one).

Looking back at the Expressionist decade and the Weimar period, one could generalize by saying that, in conventional literary history, writing by men has been viewed in terms of the reception of their work, whereas women writers are described in terms of their biography. As a corrective to this it is necessary for a history of women's writing to focus on works and issues, rather than on biographical details. In the early years of the twentieth century, and especially after World War I, women's writing increased spectacularly, becoming a mass phenomenon. In 1930, Adrienne Thomas's *Die Katrin wird Soldat* (*Katrin becomes a Soldier*) achieved sales of 11,000 after only two weeks, and in 1933 the German works most frequently translated were the best-selling novels of Vicki Baum.

The problem therefore is not so much that of finding texts by women, as of making a meaningful selection; the traditional reference works are of little help here. Some women writers already form part of the accepted German literary canon, such as Marie-Luise Kaschnitz, Else Lasker-Schüler, Marieluise Fleißer, Ina Seidel, Ilse Langner, Annette Kolb and the early Anna Seghers, and are therefore more readily accessible; accordingly, while they are documented in the bibliography, less detailed reference will be made to them here. What follows should thus be seen as a general survey of developments in the different genres, rather than a fully comprehensive account of women's writing from 1910 to 1933.

The concept of *Frauenliteratur*

In her 1984 study of writing by women in the twenties, *Trennungs-Spuren: Frauenliteratur der Zwanziger Jahre*, Heide Soltau offers a broad definition of *Frauenliteratur* (women's writing): 'It refers to writing by women, writing which thematizes problems within the context of women's lives: it does not in the first instance have any implications as to content or aesthetic quality' (p. 111). In the early twentieth century, descriptions like *Frauenliteratur, Frauenroman* (women's novel) or *Frauenlyrik* (women's poetry) are all terms in current use.

In the early years of the century, texts written by women in a variety of genres were collected and brought before a wider readership in a series of anthologies, for example Julia Virginia's *Frauenlyrik unserer Zeit* (Contemporary poetry by women; 1907). In 1919, Christine Touaillon's 600-page work on German women's novels in the eighteenth century, *Der deutsche Frauenroman des 18. Jahrhunderts*, established women's writing as a genre in its own right. Numerous reviews of, and articles on, women's writing began to appear in newspapers and magazines, and regular columns were devoted to the subject in journals such as *Das literarische Echo*. However, the women who gained recognition in such anthologies and reviews turned out to be mainly established writers of the older generation, either publishing works in the neo-Romantic style, like Helene Voigt-Diederichs, or in the tradition of late Naturalism, like Clara Viebig, or else were authors of pietistic or Catholic novels, for example Anna Schieber and Gertrud von le Fort.

Alongside these more traditional, but no less typical writers, then, we need to seek out the avant-garde women writers in what we might call their natural habitat: Expressionist magazines, the programmes of key publishing houses and reports of literary life in clubs, *Kabaretts* and artists' cafés. For convenience, each of the main genres will be considered separately.

Lyric poetry

In 1993, Anna Rheinsberg, already well-known for her work on women writers of the Weimar period through her anthologies *Bubikopf* (Bobbed hair; 1988) and KRIEGS/LÄUFE (War/lives; 1989), published a book of poems and portraits entitled *Wie bunt entfaltet sich mein Anderssein. Lyrikerinnen der zwanziger Jahre* (How brightly my otherness unfolds. Women poets of the twenties; 1993). Rheinsberg's anthology, which she refers to as 'a subjective selection', contains poems by Emmy Hennings, Claire Goll, Henriette Hardenberg, Sylvia von Harden, Else Rüthel, Paula Ludwig, Rut Landshoff(-York) and Mascha Kaléko, while Hartmut Vollmer's 1993 anthology, *In roten Schuhen tanzt die Sonne sich zu Tod* (The Sun dances itself to death in red shoes), contains poems by thirty-six largely neglected women writers (see the bibliography, pp. 274–5). There is to date no comprehensive overview of poetry written by women in this period; thus the present survey represents a first attempt to locate the writers between the poles of Christian poetry and the Jewish tradition, between reactionary and avant-garde trends, the cult of femininity on the one hand and the atmosphere of a 'fresh start', or *Aufbruch*, evoked by the new possibilities for women to shape their own lives, on the other.

Although Christian poetry figures largely in the work of women poets of this period, one cannot in any sense speak of a 'group' of Christian women poets, the main proponents being individual writers who made names for themselves in very different contexts. One such example is Frida Bettingen, author of two volumes of poems, *Eva und Abel* (Eve and Abel; 1919), and *Gedichte* (Poems; 1922). Her poetry spans twenty-five years, from 1897 to 1922, and her very first published poem, 'Meine Seele leidet Gewalt' (My soul suffers violence), already shows originality in its use of rhyme and variation on the strophic form, while many of her later poems eschew end-rhymes and rigid strophic forms altogether. In formal terms, therefore, Frida Bettingen is a progressive writer. Instead of using Biblical subject-matter in its own right, she transmutes aspects of her personal life into Christian legend, as for instance in the *Eva und Abel* poems, in which she expresses her grief for her son, killed in action in World War I, through the image of Eve mourning Abel.

One poet who achieved recognition beyond German-speaking countries, especially in Catholic circles, is Gertrud von le Fort. Originally from a Prussian Protestant family, from 1907 onwards she made several visits to Rome, which gave rise to her interest in the Catholic faith. In 1924, two years before her conversion to Catholicism, she published the volume *Hymnen an die Kirche* (Hymns to the church). Gertrud von le Fort's view of women's role was a traditional one, firmly rooted in the context of a life of devotion to the Christian community. The *Hymnen an die Kirche* read like a confession of faith; as with all her works, these poems pose fundamental questions about existence – about the meaning of life, love, fear and death. In 1932 le Fort published a companion volume, *Hymnen an Deutschland*

(Hymns to Germany). Here, she invoked a Christian-inspired notion of empire, something which in the historical context seems ideologically dubious or, at the very least, naive – she was in fact far from sympathetic to National Socialism and its own dreams of empire.

Ein Hymnus der Erlösung (A Hymn of salvation) is the subtitle of Elisabeth Langgässer's first book, *Wendekreis des Lammes*, a volume of poems published in 1924. In choosing the most exalted form of Christian praise, the hymn, Langgässer, like Gertrud von le Fort, places herself in a poetic tradition which goes back to the Baroque period. Langgässer's cycle of poems follows the Christian year, starting with 'Advent'. The main title itself, *Wendekreis des Lammes* (Tropic of the lamb) indicates the central themes of her oeuvre: nature (astronomy), mythology (the allusions to the Tropics of Cancer and Capricorn and their significance), as well as Jewish heritage and Christian doctrine (the sacrifice of the lamb at the Jewish Feast of the Passover, and the lamb as a symbol of Christ). The first volume was followed in 1935 by the *Tierkreisgedichte* (Zodiac poems), and by *Der Laubmann und die Rose* (The leafman and the rose) in 1946. Elisabeth Langgässer is regarded as one of the most important nature poets of her day. Her preoccupation with women's issues, which she repeatedly addresses in her letters (published in 1990), found more direct expression in her prose writing, especially the short story *Proserpina* (1932; see chapter 9, pp. 153–4) and her short prose works after 1945, as well as in the 1933 anthology *Herz zum Hafen. Frauengedichte der Gegenwart* (Heart-haven. Contemporary women's poetry; 1933).

Ruth Schaumann made her literary début as one of only three women writers to be included in Kurt Wolff's illustrious series *Der Jüngste Tag* (The day of Judgement). Published between 1913 and 1921, this comprised eighty-six writers who, in the publisher's opinion, 'should be regarded as characteristic of our times and as pointing the way forward'. The two other women writers included were Emmy (Ball-)Hennings and Mechtilde Lichnowsky. The poems collected under the title *Die Kathedrale* (The cathedral) bear witness to Ruth Schaumann's religious development, which in 1924 led to her conversion to the Catholic faith. Schaumann also worked as a painter and sculptor, and her poems have an intensely visual quality, depicting colours, images and scenes captured in graphic images, and characterized by the tension between seeing in terms of the senses, and visionary experience. In 1924 Schaumann married Friedrich Fuchs, one of the editors of Carl Muth's journal *Hochland*. This brought her into close contact with Catholic intellectual circles, especially in Switzerland, and thus with the writers Hugo Ball and Emmy Hennings.

Within Austria and the countries of the Austro-Hungarian empire, Vienna was the literary centre of Christian Expressionism. As well as Paula Grogger, who explicitly embraced the tradition of women's writing characteristic of the turn of the century – as represented for example by Enrica von Handel-Mazzetti – and Paula von Preradović, we should mention here the poets Erika Mitterer and Herta Koenig, both of whom were in contact with the poet Rainer Maria Rilke as young women. Elisabeth Janstein, who also lived in Vienna before emigrating in 1938 to Paris and then England, wrote Christian Expressionist poetry. Both her volumes of poems, *Gebete um Wirklichkeit* (Prayers for reality; 1919) and *Die Landung* (Landfall; 1921), testify to a writer with her own poetic voice, distinctively musical and imbued with a conscious effort to create an unfettered yet structured lyrical form. Martina Wied, a member of the Austrian Expressionist *Brenner* circle until her emigration to England, published her collection *Bewegung* (Movement) in 1919. Like Elisabeth Janstein's *Gebete um Wirklichkeit*, published by the Strache Verlag in the same year, these poems lie somewhere between Christian subject-matter and typical Expressionist themes, beginning with 'Gedichte von Gottheit und Tod' (Poems of divinity and death), and ending with a group of poems whose common theme is the prime locus of all Expressionist poetry – 'Die Stadt' (The city).

A similar tension characterizes Emmy Hennings's volume of poems, *Helle Nacht* (Bright night; 1922). 'Ich bin so vielfach in den Nächten / Ich steige aus den dunklen Schächten / Wie bunt entfaltet sich mein Anderssein' (I am so intricate at night / I climb through shafts obscured from light / How brightly my otherness unfolds), Emmy Hennings wrote in one of her early poems. Her 'intricacy' encompasses the multiple facets of her personality, the varied personae to which she adds throughout her life, as well as her conversion from Protestantism to Catholicism after recovering from a severe attack of typhoid. Her early poems, published in 1913 as volume 5 of the series *Der Jüngste Tag*, already contain, in embryo, the religious themes which were to become so important in her later poetry. Moreover, Emmy Hennings's multi-faceted personality encompasses the varied roles which she played on music-hall and political cabaret stages – for example Simplizissimus in Munich and the Apollo Theatre in Berlin – as well as those roles forced upon her by the need to survive: peddling, performing in nightclubs and prostitution. Poems with titles such as 'Mädchen am Kai' (Girl on the quayside), 'Die Tänzerin' (The dancer), 'Nach dem Kabarett' (After the cabaret) thus illustrate the realities of her everyday life.

Whilst on the one hand we can place Emmy Hennings's oeuvre in the context of the Christian poetry of her day, other aspects link her to the avant-garde women writers who, like herself, were members of the literary circles centred on the Romanisches Café and the Café des Westens in Berlin, and on the Café Stefanie in Munich – writers such as Sylvia von Harden, Paula Ludwig, Bess Breck-Kalischer, Henriette Hardenberg, Else Rüthel, Rut Landshoff(-York) and Nell Walden, among others. She shared with them a tendency to role-play even in real life and to reinvent herself continually for a new audience. After the outbreak of World War I, which the Dadaist Hugo Ball, among others, saw as the logically absurd consequence of an inherently rationalistic view of the world, a sense of playfulness became established as an artistic principle. Dadaism, which arose as a protest movement, caused a break with traditional aesthetic principles, on the one hand by a return to a childlike creative spontaneity, and on the other by eliminating boundaries between the arts, as shown for example in the title of Claire Goll's 1922 volume of poetry, *Lyrische Films* (Lyrical films). Numerous women, for example Emmy Hennings, or Sophie Täuber(-Arp), with her Cubist costumes, were major contributors to Dada groups, both in the Cabaret Voltaire in Zurich, and after the war in Berlin. Art became action art, with the *Kabarett* as its stage, and its statements grew more and more explicitly political – as in the case of the *Kabarett* artist Claire Waldoff.

While Else Lasker-Schüler, in common with the Dada artists, adopted a number of different public personae, her principal sphere of activity remained the written word. By contrast with her playful style of presentation, her subjects are deadly serious: war, love and death; her book *Der Malik* (Malik; 1919) has been seen as an attempt to sublimate the experiences of World War I in a homage to the Expressionist painter Franz Marc, her fallen *Blauer Reiter*. Between 1910 and 1933 she published at least six volumes of poetry and short prose, including *Meine Wunder* (My miracles) in 1911, *Hebräische Balladen* (*Hebrew Ballads*; 1913/1920) and *Konzert, Prosa und Gedichte* (*Concert*) in 1932, the year in which she was awarded the Kleist prize. The leading Expressionist poet Gottfried Benn, who figures in her works in the guise of 'Giselheer der Barbar' (Giselheer the barbarian) and 'Der Tiger', described his fellow writer as 'Germany's greatest woman poet ever'. In her poetry, Else Lasker-Schüler creates worlds of the imagination which she peoples with characters who have the attributes of friends and literary figures she knows personally. She herself appears on this imaginary stage in the roles of Princess Tino of Baghdad and Prince Youssuf of Thebes. Silvia Schlenstedt sees these projections as utopian designs for an imaginary world which represents an alternative to real life under the Wilhelmine monarchy (*Bilder neuer Welten*, p. 302). The inner freedom to create a new system of values within an invented world is also linked to the way she transgresses the boundaries of fixed gender roles. Now as a prince, now as a princess, in her works Else Lasker-Schüler adopts male or female characteristics at will.

Also characteristic of Lasker-Schüler's poetry is her highly individual portrayal of her Jewish heritage – not by stressing differences from Christianity, but by returning to Old Testament themes as the common source of religious faith (Bauschinger, *Else Lasker-Schüler*, pp. 161–89). Her view of the world contrasted starkly with real historical developments. In 1933 Lasker-Schüler, persecuted as a Jew, left Germany, never to return.

The Jewish poet Gertrud Kolmar was less fortunate. She was deported to Auschwitz in March 1943, after which there are no further records. Her first volume of poems (*Gedichte*) was published in 1917. However, many of her early poems, written before 1933, not only remained unpublished during her lifetime but did not see the light of day until they were discovered among her papers in 1980 by her biographer, Johanna Woltmann-Zeitler. Kolmar's oeuvre is only now beginning to receive the recognition it deserves. She started writing as young as sixteen, and her early poems, consisting of nursery rhymes and songs, and collected under the blanket heading of 'Mutter und Kind' (Mother and child), are still derivative in formal terms. They are followed by love poems – 'Mann und Weib' (Man and woman), 'Zeit und Ewigkeit' (Time and eternity), and 'Früher Zyklus I, II, and III' (Early cycle I, II and III). After 1933, Kolmar wrote poems on historical and political subjects. Although her early poems are well worth reading, her most intense and mature poems date from after 1933.

Mascha Kaléko occupies a special place among women writers of the Weimar period, combining as she did poetic form with the subject-matter of prose to create a new genre. In 1929 her *Feuilleton-Gedichte* (feuilleton poems) or *Lyrik-Feuilletons* (poem-feuilletons) began appearing in the major Berlin daily newspapers. When, in 1933, Rowohlt published her collected works in book form, Mascha Kaléko rapidly became well known, for no one documents with more humour and greater sureness of touch everyday life in Berlin, whether it be office work, a rented room, unemployment or the longing for domestic bliss. *Das Lyrische Stenogramm-heft* (The lyrical shorthand-notebook) captured the flavour of the times, and this led Hermann Hesse to review the poems in the following terms: 'a mixture of sentiment and flippancy, the mocking style of the poetry . . . is full of self-irony, capricious and playful . . .' (Zoch-Westphal, *Aus den sechs Leben*, p. 38). In 1935, with the publication of her *Kleines Lesebuch für Große. Gereimtes und Ungereimtes* (A small book for grown-ups. Rhymes and non-sense), Mascha Kaléko was able to repeat the success of her *Lyrisches Stenogrammheft*; but thereafter, as a Jewish writer, she was forbidden to publish, and emigrated first to New York in 1938, and then to Israel. She remains one of the women writers whose personal and literary brilliance account for the 'flair' of the 1920s. With her commitment to everyday issues and her realistic subject-matter, which for her took precedence over aesthetic considerations, Mascha Kaléko had more in common with the women novelists of her day than with other women poets.

Prose and drama

In Germany the years from 1910 to 1933 were a time of enormous political and social upheaval, spanning the last years of the Wilhelmine era, World War I, the first tentative steps towards parliamentary democracy and finally the emergence of National Socialism. Everyday life and working conditions – especially conditions of cultural production – underwent radical change after the end of the war, and a short phase of great political and social tolerance set in. The liberal climate meant that reforms in the legal status of women, towards which the women's movement had been working since its inception, were at last implemented, and these developments were mirrored closely in the *Frauenliteratur* of the time.

One significant step towards equal rights for women was the repeal of the *Vereinsgesetz*, the Prussian law governing the right of association, in 1908, enabling women to become members of political parties. This amendment helped give legal force to a development which had begun in Germany in 1873 with a public speech by Hedwig Dohm, and which had by 1919 resulted in the introduction of women's suffrage. At the Reichstag elections of 19 January 1919, thirty-seven women were elected to parliament – the highest proportion anywhere in the world. Among them were numerous representatives of the *Frauenbewegung* (women's movement) – though not of the *Stimmrechtsbewegung* (suffrage movement) itself. Along with women's attempts to gain public recognition in the political sphere, various central demands of the women's movement, especially those to do with education and the workplace, gradually became reality. In Berlin in 1908, Alice Salomon established the first non-denominational Social School for Women; reform of girls' schools made it possible for young women to stay at school until the *Abitur*, and thus to qualify for university study; and, also in 1908, the Prussian state took the logical step of opening higher education to women. The education of women teachers improved markedly from 1903 onwards. In 1919 the law enforcing celibacy for women teachers (*Lehrerinnenzölibat*) was repealed. In the following year it finally became legal for women to exercise a profession – something which affected middle-class women in particular. During the war, men's jobs were often taken by women, and so not even the most hardened sceptic could doubt their abilities any longer. Now, in view of the high number of war-widows and fatherless daughters, employment had become an absolute necessity for middle-class women.

As women's legal status gradually altered, so their role in society became less clearly defined. This new freedom allowed women to experiment with new forms of living, both in their everyday lives and in literature. In the novel, especially, women writers explored new roles for women; the extent to which these were a radical departure can be fully appreciated today only when they are set against the background of contemporary political events, and viewed against the stereotyped roles allotted to women in works by male authors. As well as dealing with traditional material, such as Christian or historical themes – for example Clara Viebig's novel *Unter dem Freiheitsbaum* (Beneath the tree of liberty; 1922), Alma Johanna Koenig's *Der heilige Palast* (The holy palace; 1922) or Gertrud von le Fort's novels of this period – women novelists concerned themselves with key contemporary issues.

From the very beginning of the war, women had actively promoted pacifism in countless speeches, appeals, essays and conference reports. Among the women activists for peace included in Gisela Brinker-Gabler's anthology *Frauen gegen den Krieg* (Women against war), we find texts by Claire Goll, Rosa Mayreder and Berta Lask. Annette Kolb, who campaigned for Franco-German reconciliation in her 1916 *Briefe einer Deutschfranzösin* (Letters from a Franco-German woman), and who opposed World War I from the very beginning, as is shown in her volume of anti-war essays, *Die Last. Antikriegsaufsätze* (The burden; 1918), was forced to emigrate because of her commitment to pacifism. Similarly, Ilse Langner made the emancipation of women during the war the main theme of her anti-war play *Frau Emma kämpft im Hinterland* (Frau Emma fights a rearguard action), first performed in 1929. In 1918, Claire Goll dedicated her novel *Die Frauen erwachen* (Women awake; 1918) to 'all sisters'. This book describes the suffering war inflicts on women, but Goll also implicates her 'sisters', who made no attempt to oppose the slaughter. In her pacifist writings, Claire Goll depicts women in a manner which, on closer inspection, turns out to be inconsistent. On the one hand, she takes issue with the passivity and humility that have been instilled into women, but on the other hand, in *Der gläserne Garten* (The glass garden) she rehearses the traditional stereotypes of the rational male and the emotional female: 'The man was the head, the woman the heart of the world' (p. 156).

Whilst Emmy Hennings agrees with Goll that women have a special part to play in preventing war, she avoids reiterating the conventional stereotypes. However, concrete alternatives are less readily available, as the following quote from Editha von Münchhausen (thought to be a pseudonym for Emmy Hennings) shows:

> European culture as it has developed under male hegemony over the past nineteen hundred years has bankrupted itself with its striving in this war ... since men have shown themselves incapable of steadily raising European culture and civilization to new heights, it is fair to ask whether women, who have been suppressed until now, should not be called upon to marshal their wealth of hitherto untapped energies to make good the loss, and save what can be salvaged from it; then to devote their fresh powers to building up a new culture from the fragments of the old.
>
> (EDITHA VON MÜNCHHAUSEN (= Emmy Hennings?),
> *Das neue Recht der Frau* (The new rights of women), pp. 22–3)

Another way of coming to terms with the experience of war is to be found in autobiographical writings by Jo Mihaly, Adrienne Thomas and Paula Schlier. Claire Goll and Emmy Hennings experienced the war from the safety of Swiss emigration. This may help explain why they were able to present the war in a more detached and theoretical manner than other women writers. Jo Mihaly spent World War I in Berlin, and her diary of the years 1914–18 documents her change of attitude from an unthinking young girl – at the outbreak of war she was barely twelve years old – to a committed opponent of the war.

Adrienne Thomas's semi-fictional diary *Die Katrin wird Soldat. Ein Roman aus Elsaß-Lothringen* (*Katrin becomes a Soldier*; 1930) tells the story of Katrin Lentz, who volunteers as a nurse in a field hospital at the age of seventeen after her lover, Lucien, has been conscripted. Working in the

Red Cross Headquarters at the railway station in Metz, she sees both sides of the war: the initial enthusiasm of troops marching off to battle, and the returning wounded. At the end of the novel Katrin dies, having experienced the loss of friends and ultimately her lover as a process of spiritual mutilation which gradually destroys her: 'The ostensible cause of death was pneumonia. In reality, as they hacked off one friend after another, ending with her Lucien, she probably bled to death' – this is how Adrienne Thomas herself describes the death of her protagonist.

Paula Schlier, though only fifteen years old at the time, also worked as an assistant nurse in a field hospital. She described her experiences in her autobiographical book *Petras Aufzeichnungen oder Konzept einer Jugend nach dem Diktat der Zeit* (Petra's jottings or the idea of a youth spent under the dictates of the times; 1926). This book makes it clear that the medical corps cannot be regarded simply as a source of humanitarian assistance, but also serves the war machine by patching up 'human *matériel*'.

Whereas Adrienne Thomas initially wrote only popular fiction after the war, only returning to more political writing with her experience of emigration, Paula Schlier remained an acute observer. She described the social deprivation of the 1923 inflation, the rise of the *Völkische Bewegung* (Nationalist movement), mass marches and Hitler's attempted *Putsch* on 8 November 1923. By her own account, she published anti-National Socialist articles in a Nuremberg daily newspaper, while working as a secretary in the NSDAP Party Headquarters in order to observe their work at first hand.

Whereas Schlier chose the medium of the press to express her political commitment, other women writers opted for the stage. Few women writers in this period succeeded in having their work performed, but there are notable exceptions, for example Lu Märten, Else Lasker-Schüler, Anna Gmeyner, Marieluise Fleißer, Ilse Langner, and Berta Lask. Ilse Langner and Marieluise Fleißer take up the issue of women's place in society in their plays: 'Obviously, I could only depict something going on between men and women', Marieluise Fleißer said (Kord, 'Fading Out', p. 57). The political starting-point, manifested here in repeated attempts to dramatize class differences, is common to all these writers, even if approaches to it vary greatly. In *Die Wupper* (The river Wupper; 1909, first performed 1919), Else Lasker-Schüler highlighted social tensions by depicting psychologically convincing friendships and erotic relationships between middle-class and working-class characters. By contrast, the plays of Berta Lask, a socialist writer who was also a member of the KPD (Kommunistische Partei Deutschlands), should be seen rather in terms of political agitation. Plays such as Lu Märten's *Bergarbeiter* (Mineworkers; first performed 1911) and Anna Gmeyner's *Heer ohne Helden* (Army without heroes; first performed 1930) – belong to the Naturalist tradition of plays about miners. In her non-fiction, Lu Märten, a journalist and from 1920 onwards also a member of the KPD, concentrated on women's issues and on socialism. In *Bergarbeiter*, she lends her voice to the downtrodden characters who have to risk their lives to earn enough for their families to survive, at the same time making her Naturalist approach explicit within the play:

> When one of our sort goes among writers he has to obey the law of depicting the truth about his life. And when one of our sort depicts the truth about his life, the strongest aspects . . . are the pain, the injustice. The pain . . .,

says Hermann to Gretje, and she continues his train of thought:

> Tell me . . . after all, you know more about the books and all the things people out there think and know . . . it seems to me they don't know what we know; what we have to put up with.

(Bergarbeiter; 1924, p. 27)

Both this drama and Anna Gmeyner's play about miners are based on actual mining disasters, and both highlight social suffering by depicting a form of labour which gives stark expression to the hopelessness faced by the under-privileged workers. Anna Seghers is the best-known woman writer to treat class differences in the form of a novel – *Aufstand der Fischer* (*The Revolt of the Fishermen*; 1928), and the Communist writer Hermynia Zur Mühlen is the most politically extreme – in 1924 she was accused of high treason for her short story *Schupomann Karl Müller* (Policeman Karl Müller).

With the establishment of the 1919 Constitution, women were able to take advantage of another opportunity for political action. They could vote and be voted for. On the stage the *Kabarett* artist Claire Waldoff would sing 'Raus mit den Männern aus dem Reichstag / und rein mit den Frauen in den Reichstag' (Get the men out of the Reichstag / and get the women into the Reichstag). Despite the relatively high proportion of women in Parliament, the influence of female deputies remained slight. In both Germany and Austria, conservatively inclined women Members of Parliament, in particular, saw party work as a good opportunity for pursuing their political objectives. Against this background it comes as no surprise that a writer like Josephine Widmar, who can nowadays be considered one of the literary precursors of fascism, wrote a novel about the parliamentary system: *Drei gehen aus dem Parlament* (Three leave Parliament; 1931). Other writers also touched on this theme in their works, such as Herta van Delden's *Das Heer der Heimat* (The army of the home front; 1930), Marieluise Fleißer's *Mehlreisende Frieda Geier* (Frieda Geier, Travelling Flour Representative) and Gabriele Tergit's *Käsebier erobert den Kurfürstendamm* (Käsebier conquers the Kurfürstendamm), both from 1931. The female representatives of all parties only collaborated on two issues: abolishing state regulation of prostitution, and raising unemployment benefit for women workers. Even so, problems as crucial as the new divorce laws, or the repeal of Section 218 on abortion, remained unresolved by legislation. No overall policy on women (*Frauenpolitik*) was agreed, and while debates continued in Parliament it was, in fact, women writers who redefined women's social position by means of their protagonists. This emerges especially clearly in novels taking women and work as their subject.

Some female protagonists of women's novels in the Weimar period earned their own living, for example in Martha Niggli's *Zwischen zwanzig und dreißig* (Between twenty and thirty; 1930) and Fleißer's *Mehlreisende Frieda Geier*. Other roles and occupations were also represented in fiction. Vicki Baum's *Stud. chem. Helene Willfüer* (Chemistry student Helene Willfüer; 1925) portrays the life of a student, while doctors and pharmacists feature in Hilde Marie Kraus, *Ärztinnen* (Women doctors; 1929) and Juliane Karwarth, *Marie Duchanin* (1928). The acting profession is the subject of novels by Emmy Hennings (*Das Brandmal* (The stigma; 1919)), Tilla Durieux (*Eine Tür fällt ins Schloß* (A door slams shut; 1928)), and Joe Lederer (*Das Mädchen George* (Girl George; 1928)). Secretaries – at that time known as *Schreibfräulein* or 'writing girls' – also figure largely, for example in Christa Brück's *Schicksale hinter Schreibmaschinen* (Destinies behind typewriters; 1930), Irmgard Keun's *Das kunstseidene Mädchen* (*The Artificial Silk Girl*; 1932) as well as in Kaléko's *Kleines Lesebuch für Große*, for example 'Mädchen an der Schreibmaschine' (Girl at a typewriter; pp. 88–92). Working-class women are depicted in Maria Leitner, *Eine Frau reist durch die Welt* (A woman travels the world; 1932), and teachers are the subject of novels by Grete von Urbanitzky: *Der wilde Garten* (The wild garden; 1927) and Clara Viebig: *Die mit den tausend Kindern* (*The Woman with a Thousand Children*; 1929).

Many of these novels revolve around the question of whether love and marriage can be combined with a career. Since it was still obligatory, in the early 1920s, for women teachers to leave the profession if they married, this problem emerges most clearly in the novels featuring women teachers. Financial security and independence constituted the arguments for continuing in paid employment after getting married, but there were a number of arguments against this. The first was the impossibility of combining the role of wife with a career: 'The idea was preposterous: being a doctor's wife and a teacher at the same time! She – his wife – teach at that wretched school?! No, that would not do at all, he'd never ever agree to that!...' (Viebig, p. 187) Moral misgivings also stood in the way of women teachers getting married. A colleague of the protagonist Marie-Luise, with the expressive name Cläre Halbhaus, née Spiegel, while initially fighting hard to keep her job despite getting married, succumbs both to the double burden and to the moral pressure:

> They don't respect me any more. A teacher who's expecting a baby – hunh – she's just like all the rest, first, people will sneer, then just laugh at her. A teacher must be a single woman, a woman who's different from the rest.
>
> (VIEBIG, *Die mit den tausend Kindern*, p. 208)

Grete von Urbanitzky and Clara Viebig both depict protagonists who ultimately dedicate their lives to their pupils and sacrifice their right to love and be loved to the more exalted task of educating children at school. In *Die mit den tausend Kindern* Marie-Luise explicitly voices this decision:

> It can't possibly work. I belong here with these children. They need me more than you need me. Weak lambs who have gone astray, I have to carry them, and I'm happy I can hold them. And where my flock is, that's where my heart is, too. And so this can never work out, and so: goodbye!
>
> (VIEBIG, p. 320)

In one respect Marie-Luise's decision is progressive, since she values her career more highly than her marriage. On the other hand, however, her role as a loving woman providing for others' needs whilst subordinating her own corresponds to the traditional female stereotype.

Other problems encountered at work by female protagonists are lack of recognition on the part of superiors, and sexual harassment. Both emerge most clearly in texts about the situation faced by secretaries, for example in Paula Schlier, *Petras Aufzeichnungen*:

> The test of my suitability for this work took the form of my taking down ten lines in shorthand, then typing ten lines. No one asked where I came from or who I was, still less did anyone show any interest in what I thought about the area in which I was about to work. The opinions of a shorthand typist in a large editorial office are of no account whatever; a typist belongs with her typewriter – she has one function only: to operate the carriage return and shiftkey.
>
> (SCHLIER, pp. 98–9)

Working in the editorial office makes Paula Schlier's Petra feel like an object and she becomes merely a part of the furniture. By contrast, Fräulein Brückner in Brück's *Schicksale hinter Schreibmaschinen* is exposed to continuous verbal and physical abuse. Moreover, the difficult job market prevents her putting her position at risk by fighting back: 'I'm really not asking for a lot. Just a living. Just a job which stops me being afraid of the future . . . Perhaps there are some professions in which a woman's erotic worth . . . doesn't determine her career prospects, doesn't count at all, in fact. Insofar as her work is subordinated to men, I suppose that one way or another a woman's career will always be influenced by her sexual identity – for good or ill' (Brück, pp. 253–4).

Sexual harassment of women in the workplace remains an unresolved problem and is once again the subject of public debate. The same applies to other problems, highlighted again by the women's movement of the 1970s and 80s but already discussed by women writers of the Weimar period. These include issues such as prostitution (Hennings), and especially child prostitution (Viebig). The issue of father–daughter incest surfaces in Friderike (Zweig)-Winternitz, *Vögelchen* (Little birds) and Emmy Hennings, *Gefängnis* (Prison), both 1919, while lesbian love is shown in Viebig and von Urbanitzky as well as novels such as Maximiliane Ackers, *Freundinnen* (Women friends), Anna Elisabeth Weirauch, *Der Skorpion* (The scorpion) and Christa Winsloe, *Das Mädchen Manuela* (The girl Manuela; 1933), better known as the film *Mädchen in Uniform* (Girls in uniform). After the sexologist Magnus Hirschfeld's theory about the existence of the 'third sex' had liberated homosexuality from the stigma of the pathological, lesbian women gained in self-confidence and became more visible, both in real life and in the literature of the time.

Female homosexuality was already a public issue, since conservative politicians had attempted to extend the anti-homosexuality Paragraph 175, which declared homosexuals to be criminals and which had hitherto applied only to men, to include lesbians. The debate about the abortion laws, and the problems of single motherhood – as current today as they were then – were given literary form by Emmy Hennings in *Gefängnis* and by Herta van Delden *in Das Heer der Heimat*. In 1930 Ilse Langner dramatized the subject in her play *Katharina Henschke*. For heterosexual women protagonists – then as now – marriage is where sexuality can best be fulfilled. Alternatives to marriage are either unhappiness (Lederer, *Das Mädchen George*) or abstinence (Viebig, *Die mit den tausend Kindern*). Because there was in any case no socially acceptable form in which homosexual women could express their sexuality, lesbian novels were an opportunity (perhaps the only opportunity) for depicting fulfilling sexual encounters outside marriage. Thus, lesbian protagonists are the first to exercise the right to define their own sexuality. To do this they first have to leave home, claiming for themselves in the process a freedom which seems unattainable to other women, who are able only to think 'in terms of alternatives: marriage or career, sexuality or abstinence' (Soltau, *Trennungs-Spuren*, p. 342).

For women, then, freedom is possible only in certain settings. The lesbian couple in Grete von Urbanitzky's *Der wilde Garten* finds happiness on a Greek island which, as a location outside society, is described as a Utopia. The big city – and in the twenties this is generally Berlin – becomes the scene of women's attempts to liberate themselves in everyday life, the starting-point for their quest for professional independence and/or sexual freedom. Another kind of freedom is reflected in travel writing by women, as for instance in Mechtilde Lichnowsky's book on Egypt, *Götter, Könige und Tiere in Ägypten* (Gods, kings and animals in Egypt; 1913), in the travel reports which Erika Mann wrote with her brother Klaus, *Rundherum. Abenteuer einer Weltreise* (Roundabout. Adventures during a journey around the world; 1929) and *Das Buch von der Riviera* (The book of the Riviera; 1931), as well as in books about America by Marta Karlweis: *Eine Frau reist durch Amerika* (A woman travels through America; 1928) and Maria Leitner: *Eine Frau reist durch die Welt* (1932). While Marta Karlweis depicts both people and places in an unsophisticated way, and her style reveals a superficial view of real social conditions, Leitner, a professional journalist, describes social conditions from the viewpoint of low earners and the dispossessed.

Conclusion

Looking back, Mascha Kaléko once described the twenties as 'die paar leuchtenden Jahre vor der großen Verdunkelung' (those few years of light before the great darkness; quoted in Zoch-Westphal, p. 42). Yet despite their political commitment, only a handful of women writers recognized the beginnings of National Socialism for what it was and described it accordingly. Paula Schlier, with her observations about the Nationalist Movement in *Petras Aufzeichnungen*, represents something of an exception here. The end of the women's movement and its attempts to liberate women in everyday life became apparent only gradually, since certain aspects of National Socialist ideology regarding the position of women in society were already prefigured by some representatives of the women's movement. It is only a small step from the view of an essential difference between the sexes, based on the premise that women are biologically pre-destined for motherhood, to the Nazis' *Mutterkult* (cult of the mother). The exclusion of Jewish women from German women's organizations, the *Gleichschaltung* (enforced uniformity) of the Nazi Women's League, and the 'voluntary' disbanding of the Bund Deutscher Frauenvereine (Federa-tion of German Women's Associations) put an end to the political efforts for women's emancipation in the Weimar Republic. Women writers began to be divided. While the reactionary climate tended to favour pub-lications by women writers of the older generation and supporters of Nazi ideology came to prominence, critical writers fell silent, choosing the path of *innere Emigration* (inner emigration), and émigrée writers had to fight for survival. Many writers remaining in Germany or already flee-ing from it – Gertrud Kolmar and Maria Leitner, for example – did not escape with their lives.

Translated by Anthony Vivis

9

Women's writing under
National Socialism

It would be quite wrong to suppose that with the coming to power of the National Socialists the cultural and ideological orientation of German literature was radically changed. Many writers, whether men or women, who had been publishing successfully since the end of the First World War carried on doing so throughout the Hitler years. Indeed, as far as *Trivialliteratur* is concerned, the interwar period was a time in which women novelists in particular came into their own. As cheaper editions of fiction of all kinds became more readily available, the readership of female *Bildungsromane*, from the trite to the innovative, increased spectacularly. Popular novelists of the Weimar period, such as Hedwig Courths-Mahler, Clara Viebig, Margarete Böhme or Lena Christ in Germany, and Enrica von Handel-Mazzetti and Paula Grogger in Austria, continued to be read throughout the 1930s. Many of their characteristic preoccupations such as love and self-sacrifice, the continuity of the family, the child and particularly the idea of *Heimat* dominate these fictions before and after Hitler.

A book which reiterates these themes in a particularly evocative way is Ina Seidel's *Das Wunschkind* (*The Wish Child*; 1930), a novel which was to become one of the most successful pieces of woman's fiction of the period. Set at the time of the Napoleonic Wars, it devotes more than a thousand pages to the fortunes of Cornelie, a Prussian war-widow stranded in French-occupied Mainz, and her relationship to her son who, like his father, will die on the battlefield. The plot revolves around three central issues: the status and role of woman in society, Germany's history and Christian heritage, and the importance of the German homeland. In essence, *Das Wunschkind* is the portrait of a German woman, drawn at a moment of political, social and moral turbulence. Frau Cornelie grapples valiantly with the tensions between German Protestantism and Catholicism and with the ideas emanating from post-revolutionary France which threaten the old German order. As she loses first her husband and then her father, her lover and her son, she assumes the stature of a kind of archetypal mother, tending the poor, the sick and the wounded and drawing solace and strength from life on her native estate.

The 'German Land' as the source of life itself, the symbol of eternal continuity, is also an important notion in many of the tales of village life and novels about the fatherland (*Heimatsromane*) which had been popular for generations before Hitler. In Austria especially, the genre flourished in the hands of Enrica von Handel-Mazzetti, Maria Grengg and Paula Grogger. Many of Clara Viebig's best-known novels of the 1920s are set in the author's native Eifel, while the poet Lulu von Strauß und Torney hit a popular vein with her tales of contemporary peasant life. The earlier novels *Die Rumplhanni* (Messy Hanna; 1916) and *Madam Bäuerin* (Madam Farmer; 1920) by Lena Christ are based upon her first-hand knowledge of her native Bavarian countryside and they remained firm favourites with the reading public throughout the 1930s. Clearly it would be inappropriate to identify these authors with the cultural policies of German fascism. On the other hand there is the case of Agnes Miegel, who had become famous in the 1920s for her ballads, fairytales and historical studies on Eastern Prussia. Under Hitler, she became a celebrated exponent of 'true German art' and, in 1934, replaced the departing rebel Ricarda Huch as the only woman member of the Preußische Akademie der Künste.

It is with Josefa Berens-Totenohl's *Der Femhof* (The lynch farm; 1934) and *Frau Magdlene* (1935) that the *Heimatsroman* takes on the unmistakable hues of fascist ideology. Her narratives are set in the fourteenth century in her native Westphalia and focus on the woman Magdlene, who quietly resists her father's tyrannical ways by choosing an outlaw on the run from the lynchers to be the father of her child. After the death of her father and her lover, Magdlene goes on to manage the homestead successfully, raising her child in readiness for a dawning new age. These are atmospheric, easy-to-read tales about a woman's triumph over an out-of-date patriarchal order, and it is not difficult to understand why Berens-Totenohl's books were so popular with the young female reader of the time. Her stories draw upon flattering images of German womanhood as proud, forward-looking, independent and supremely competent. Magdlene is a woman fighting the good fight against a defunct power-system and against daemonic forces which are invariably represented by dark-skinned, exploitative foreigners and sinister gypsy-women.

In 1936 the officially-backed publishing house, the Raabe Stiftung in der NS-Kulturgemeinde, published the anthology *Deutsche Frauendichtung der Gegenwart* (German women's writing of today). It contained extracts from the recent work of thirty-six women writers, including, for example, a passage from *Vanadis* (Vanadis; 1930), the last novel of the long-established, neo-classical writer, the octogenarian Isolde Kurz, who by no stretch of the imagination could be labelled an exponent of National Socialist ideology. It also contained a very few poems and ballads, evocations of German landscapes and legends, by Lulu von Strauß und Torney and Agnes Miegel. The bulk of the anthology was however devoted to prose extracts by authors like Berens-Totenohl, Marie Diers, Anne-Marie Koeppen, Edith Salburg, Irma von Drygalski, Kuni Tremel-Eggert and Lene Bertelsmann, all writers explicitly or implicitly aligned with National Socialist ideology. They write books in which, in atmospheric evocations of the German past, we meet heroines who are deeply rooted in a German landscape and who understand their roles in terms of an essential 'Muttersein der Seele' (motherhood of the soul). In an often single-handed struggle against war, famine, and the invasion of 'red hordes' these heroines protect the purity of their race against all kinds of opposition from outsiders, people of 'different race' or 'different ideas'. It is a notion of womanhood which found its exegesis in the treatise *Die deutsche Frau und der Nationalsozialismus* (German women and National Socialism; 1933) by Guida Diehl, who had been working for the National Socialist movement as early as the 1920s and in 1932 became the Party's spokeswoman for cultural affairs, appointed by the Führer.

At the 1942 *Literaturkonferenz* in Weimar, Josef Goebbels voiced his grave disappointment that the National Socialist movement had thus far failed to produce a contemporary novel of any stature. The lack he identified was even more glaring when one looks at the productions of the women writers. It is true that Kuni Tremel-Eggert, an enthusiastic supporter of Hitler, claimed that in her *Barb. Der Roman einer deutschen Frau* (Barb. Novel of a German woman) of 1933 she had fashioned a new kind of authentic *Zeitroman* (novel of the times). The novel tells the story of two lovers, Barb and Büchner, and their struggles as they move through war and revolution to the National Socialist dawn. Their tale reaches its climax with the heroine sewing a German flag, and an epilogue to the book ends with the Hitler salute. Predictably, the book was enormously successful while Hitler was in power but was soon forgotten afterwards. In a similar vein, the Austrian Edith Salburg, who had earlier published bitter tales about the loss of her homeland after the war, now extols, in *Die Unverantwortlichen* (The irresponsible ones; 1936), the 'genuine nobility' of the German peasant as opposed to an urban bourgeoisie endangered by its misguided deference to a bankrupt German aristocracy. Her later novel *Eine Landflucht* (Emigration from the land; 1939) carries the subtitle: 'A Book of our Time'. In it she sees the solution to present ills in the *Anschluß* – the recent annexation of Austria – when the Führer presides over the integration of Austria, 'the land of his inheritance', into the Reich. Details of everyday reality portrayed in such novels were strongly coded, indeed, distorted so as to accommodate the political dream of a National Socialist future. Yet even Goebbels himself, by so publicly condemning the tawdriness and narrowness of contemporary fiction, acknowledged that such writing was hardly likely to earn its place in the great tradition of the German novel. Meanwhile women writers like Annette Kolb, Irmgard Keun and Adrienne Thomas, who in the 1920s had made their reputation with distinguished fiction about everyday life in Weimar Germany, had, by the time Goebbels made his lament, long since vanished into exile. Those demanding fictional works which could still be published in Germany, on the other hand, such as Editha Klipstein's novels *Anna Lunde* (1935) and *Der Zuschauer* (The onlooker; 1942), were in real danger of sinking without trace for lack of public interest.

Given the punitive interventions in all cultural affairs of the new state literary academy, the Reichsschrifttumskammer – its burning of books, its summary censorship and the threat of prohibition for anyone whose writings might be seen as avant-garde, or, worse, 'decadent' – it is not surprising that writers shied away from experimenting with ideas and forms capable of rendering a true image of the times. Historical novels, on the other hand, now flourished as never before. By situating a narrative in the past, a writer could engage with any subject and portray a German reality without being obliged to comment upon the actual present. Especially popular were novels concerning Germanic tribal life in ancient times. The novels of Lydia Kath, *Aud. Geschichte einer Wikingerfrau* (Aud. Story of a Viking woman) and *Urmutter Unn* (Great mother Unn), set in an imagined Nordic realm of prehistory, were to be found in schools and libraries across Germany, together with the writings of Agnes Miegel, whose novella *Die Fahrt der sieben Ordensbrüder* (The journey of the seven monks) conjures up a fascinating vision of a great German Dark

Age similar to that which forms the backdrop to the stories of Berens-Totenohl.

Among the most impressive historical narratives of the 1930s are Enrica von Handel-Mazzetti's *Die Waxenbergerin: Ein Roman aus dem Kampf-jahr 1683* (The woman from Waxberg. A novel from the year of struggle 1683; 1934), Ina Seidel's *Lennacker* (1938) and Gertrud von le Fort's *Magdeburgische Hochzeit* (Wedding in Magdeburg; 1938). In these novels the authors' investment in the past is clearly suggestive of a certain unease about the present. In le Fort's novel especially, clear parallels are drawn between the ideological totalitarianism rampant in the Thirty Years War and that of Hitler's Germany. The same may also be said of the Austrian Erika Mitterer, whose first novel, *Fürst der Welt* (Prince of the world; 1940), offers a portrayal of the Spanish Inquisition which is a thinly disguised critique of contemporary National Socialist rule.

As in the case of Mitterer, the determining theme in the oeuvre of Gertrud von le Fort is spiritual experience within a society in moral decline. A committed Christian, le Fort shared to some extent the essentialist notion of womanhood, the belief in the fundamental dichotomy between man and woman, which underpinned the National Socialist view of women. In her theological essay *Die ewige Frau. Die Frau in der Zeit. Die zeitlose Frau* (*The Eternal Woman*; *Woman in Time*; *Timeless Woman*; 1934) she argues that, in order to fulfil the will of God, the noble woman must remain veiled, passive and silent, bringing redemption to an aggressive male world through her charity and the love of God. Given such deeply traditionalist religious views, it was possible for le Fort to embody a spirit of conservative resistance to Hitler, without ever quite falling foul of the Nazi regime.

Unlike Gertrud von le Fort, who took no overt stand in the face of political developments, Ina Seidel had made her *Treuegelöbnis* (declaration of allegiance) to Hitler in 1933. The success of *Das Wunschkind* had secured her position as the foremost woman writer under National Socialism. Her next novel, *Lennacker*, is however more problematic. Like its predecessor, it is in essence a historical novel in which the evolution of German Protestantism is a dominant theme. But unlike *Das Wunschkind*, *Lennacker* has a modern setting. The hero, Hansjakob Lennacker, returns from the front on Christmas Eve 1918 to visit his aged aunt, a deaconess presiding over a home full of impoverished and elderly religious women. During the night the young man falls ill with influenza and over the twelve nights of Christmas has twelve feverish dreams in which he revisits the twelve generations of his Saxon forebears, all of them Protestant pastors. In this way the novel engages in an exploration of German Protestantism, from its origins up to what is perceived to be its decline in the twentieth century. The book was received with some unease, for a number of critics rightly sensed that the book was a coded critique of the spiritual life of contemporary Germany.

In the context of preoccupation with the German past, it is interesting to note the date of publication of Ricarda Huch's major historical treatise on the Thirty Years War, *Der dreißigjährige Krieg* (1937). At the time of Hitler's accession to power in 1933, Huch, then almost seventy years old, was one of the first cultural celebrities publicly to criticize the regime's cultural policies and to dissociate herself from them by resigning from the Preußische Akademie der Künste. It was not in scholarship, or in fiction, but in poetry that she found a medium which allowed her to speak of her times. Many of the poems published in her *Herbstfeuer* (Autumn fires; 1944) combine intimations of personal mortality with a lament about the deadly tide of barbarism engulfing the land.

Many other women writers who were at odds with Hitler's regime nevertheless remained in Germany throughout the Third Reich. In 1936 Elisabeth Langgässer was prohibited from publishing, not so much because of the nature of her work but simply because she was a 'half-Jew', a fate shared by Ruth Hoffmann, who was married to a Jew and whose Silesian family saga, *Pauline aus Kreuzberg* (Pauline from Kreuzberg; 1935) was banned a year later. Ilse Langner, on the other hand, had her works thrown on Hitler's bonfires because of their content, for her subject matter includes such themes as women's emancipation, pacifism and the exploration of other cultures. The powerful control which the National Socialists exerted over cultural matters, their excessive encouragement of ideologically 'correct' literature and their ruthless suppression of all dissent, inevitably resulted in most writers exerting some sort of conscious or unconscious self-censorship.

Feminine retreats into the spiritual dimension or worlds of the imagination are another recurring feature of women's writing in the later years of National Socialist rule in Germany. We have already noted a preoccupation with ancient conflicts between German Protestantism and Catholicism in the novels of Seidel and le Fort, to which may be added the works of the Austrians Handel-Mazzetti and Grogger, as well as the scholarly writings of Ricarda Huch. In the works of a devout Catholic like Ruth Schaumann, piety and deeply conservative visions of womanhood remain characteristic, from her early Expressionist lyrics and her writings for children to her wartime tale *Die Silberdistel* (The carline thistle) of 1941, which evokes a mystical feminine idyll in a mountain setting remote from the tumult of war.

One of the most successful books in this mode was Luise Rinser's semi-autobiographical account of a girl's awakening to spiritual independence, *Die gläsernen Ringe* (*Rings of Glass*; 1940). With her father away at war, the young heroine begins to develop her own value system in the seclusion of a wild vicarage garden somewhere in rural Southern Germany. Hidden by the garden walls from the watchful eyes of her mother, her aunt and her great-uncle, the Catholic village priest, she embarks on a process of solitary learning. The 'rings of glass' which she sees developing as she throws stones into the ancient garden pond become the central motif of a quest which has, thus far, no clear objective. The second part of the novella traces the adolescent's experiences at a boarding school in town. Here her rebellion against the petty authority of parents and teachers gathers momentum as she becomes aware of the power and danger of female sexuality and of the mystique of Eastern philosophy. Today it is hard to account for the contemporary reaction to this dreamy, only mildly subversive celebration of individuality. The book's success was a cause of much concern for the Nazis: after its first edition had gone out of print within months, a second edition was banned. Moreover, Luise Rinser was placed under police surveillance and her husband, a conductor, was virtually debarred from all further concerts. Accused of high treason in 1944, Rinser spent the last nine months of the war in prison.

In the case of Ilse Langner, the retreat within or *innere Emigration* took on a different dimension. As the previous chapter shows, she had achieved notoriety in the late 1920s with the anti-war play *Frau Emma kämpft im Hinterland* (1929), along with *Katharina Henschke* (1930), a play advocating the right of women to self-determination and to birth-control; a further play *Die Heilige aus USA* (The saint from America; 1933) explored the achievements of the Christian Scientist Mary Baker-Eddy. When in 1933 the Nazis cancelled a first performance of Langner's new comedy *Die Amazonen* (The Amazons) and banned all further publications, she left on an extended tour of the Far East.

From this period dates her novel *Die purpurne Stadt* (The purple city; 1937), a *Bildungsroman*, in which a young heroine ventures forth into the mysteries of the forbidden city of Peking. The lure of the East, with its heady mixture of mysticism and sexual promise, embroils the heroine

Gloria in complex intrigues, from which she emerges to return to Germany, chastened and mature. The novel is a delightful, somewhat traditionalist, interlude for a writer who had previously broken new ground in her critique of contemporary issues. In the late 1930s, Langner returned to her earlier themes, albeit in coded form, in her dramatized reinterpretations of Greek myths, notably *Der Mord in Mykene* (Murder in Mycenae), *Iphigenie kehrt heim* (Iphigenia returns home), *Dido* and *Orpheus findet Eurydike* (Orpheus finds Eurydice).

As has been suggested above, a preoccupation with myth, the exotic, with religion and imaginary worlds of all kinds, a phenomenon generally identified as the 'inner emigration' of Germany's artistic community under Hitler, dominates what is best in German writing of the period. Among one of the most intriguing works in this vein to be produced by a woman writer is Marie Luise Kaschnitz's *Elissa* (1937). Her first novel, *Liebe beginnt* (Love's beginning; 1933), had been a finely honed psychological account of a young woman's relationship to her lover on a journey through a hazily perceived contemporary Italy. The Mediterranean landscape is again the backdrop against which the story of *Elissa* unfolds. But now the scenery has receded into the mythic distance of an archaic past. The heroine Elissa grows up on an immense country estate run by women but dominated by an irascible, brutish and promiscuous father. Elissa's story is the lyrical account of a young woman's dream-like quest for the ideal man. It culminates in a reworking of the tale of Dido and Aeneas when, instead of immolating herself on the funeral pyre, as does Virgil's Dido, Kaschnitz's heroine sets fire to the ships on which Aeneas, the father of her child, is planning his escape. The book ends with Elissa setting out on a long journey to meet her true lover, the wise and gentle Sicheus. Although somewhat muted and too flawed to be a genuinely subversive feminine text, the novel acquires a new dimension when read as a message of rebellion against contemporary masculine power.

Myths and mystic experience likewise inform the work of Elisabeth Langgässer. Her novels *Proserpina. Welt eines Kindes* (Proserpina. A child's world; 1932) and *Der Gang durch das Ried* (The walk through the reeds; 1936) are so deeply steeped in nature imagery, both Christian and pagan, that they convey a sense of mythic permanence despite the fact that the action is set in the contemporary world of the author's native Rhine-Hessen. As its title suggests, *Proserpina* is the recreation of an ancient myth of fertility and seasonal change, and tells of a frail young girl who acquires strange and dangerous strengths through her closeness to nature and the world of dreams.

During the ten years of enforced silence and harassment by the authorities because of her status as 'half-Jew', Langgässer produced works which rank amongst the finest of the German literature of *innere Emigration*. When, in 1946, she was at last able to publish the major novel she had been writing throughout the 1930s, *Das unauslöschliche Siegel* (*The Indelible Seal*), it immediately established her as one of the foremost literary figures in Germany. On a primary level the book deals with the spiritual odyssey of a frivolous modern man, Lazarus Belfontaine, a Jew who converts to Catholicism upon his marriage. The 'indelible seal' of the Christian baptism acts as a *leitmotif* representing the unwavering divine promise of redemption even as the hero struggles in the grip of insidious daemonic forces. The non-linear narrative and the book's associative, free-flowing prose gesture towards a mythic reality which transcends not just the narrow confines of the hero's story but also those of orthodox Catholic dogma. As a piece of experimental writing, the novel is virtually unique for its time and cultural origins, and was certainly unpublishable under Nazism. In the posthumously published essay *Rechenschaftsbericht an meinen Leser* (Self-justification to my reader. A report), Langgässer discusses her personal concept of art and acknowledges her debt to James Joyce and Graham Greene, as well as to painters like Matisse and Picasso, names which would not have impressed the National Socialist censors.

In 1933 Langgässer, in collaboration with Ina Seidel, brought out the anthology *Herz zum Hafen* (Heart in harbour), to which twenty-six contemporary women poets contributed. Alongside well-known writers from the 'old guard' (e.g. Isolde Kurz and Ricarda Huch) were works by the 'new guard' (Agnes Miegel and Ina Seidel), as well as by individuals such as Else Lasker-Schüler, and four early poems by the virtually unknown Jewish poet Gertrud Kolmar. As with Langgässer, a recurrent theme in Kolmar's poetry is a vision of the natural world as a sinister and irreducible presence. *Die Frau und die Tiere* (The woman and the animals; 1938) contains poems with titles such as 'Die Unke' (The toad), 'Teichfrosch' (Frog), 'Der Hamadryas' (The sacred baboon) or 'Ein altes Pferd' (An old horse), all extremely intense pieces which resemble Rilke's *Dinggedichte* inasmuch as the poet, by evoking the very essence of animal being, assumes its characteristics. With Kolmar, the creatures thus evoked also become emblems of female experience. The glance of an old horse turns into the tired eyes of a mother searching for her son. In 'Arachne', the spider draws the reader in from the second-person *Du* to the first-person *Ich* until the latter itself becomes the victim. Often Kolmar's poetry evokes an image of the female poet as sick or blind, a troglodyte, hyena or toad. Yet the hateful attributes of lowliness are triumphantly transformed into defiant anthems to 'otherness', to being female, and indeed to being Jewish.

Thus as well as being one of the great German poets of the twentieth century, Kolmar is also one of the most tragic. Born into a Jewish family in Berlin, she remained there to care for her ailing father throughout the Hitler years, fully realizing what this was likely to mean. Poems like 'Ewiger Jude' (The eternal Jew) or 'Wir Juden' (We, the Jews) of 1933 are passionate declarations of love for her people and also a clear-sighted acceptance of the inevitability of suffering. Her letters to her sister in Switzerland tell of her enforced labour in a factory and of the imposed lodgers who are taking over the family's flat until she is reduced to sharing a bedroom with her father. After his deportation to Theresienstadt in 1942, Kolmar's letters become less frequent. Her last communication dates from 21 February 1943, and was presumably written on the eve of her own journey to the concentration camp.

Other Jewish poets narrowly avoided a similar fate. While Kolmar spent the last years of her life a virtual prisoner of the regime in Berlin, Rose Ausländer sat hiding in the cellars of the ghetto of Czernowitz and only escaped deportation in 1944 through a stroke of luck. Nelly Sachs, who spent the 1930s living quietly in Berlin, was able at the eleventh hour to flee with her mother to Sweden in 1940, thanks to the intervention of the Swedish writer Selma Lagerlöf. It was not until twenty years after the end of the war that the poetry of Kolmar and Sachs was published and could begin to reach a reading public.

Invaluable for today's assessment of the period are women's first-hand accounts of their recent experiences, as they appeared in the immediate post-war period. Luise Rinser's *Gefängnistagebuch* (*Prison Journal*) of 1946, for example, offers an evocative account of the last nine months of the war, which the author spent in the women's prison at Traunstein; Else Behrend-Rosenfeld's *Ich stand nicht allein – Erlebnisse einer Jüdin in Deutschland 1933–1944* (I was not alone – experiences of a Jewish woman in Germany, 1933–44) of 1949 records her undercover activities helping Jewish refugees. In contrast, Charlotte Beradt's *Das dritte Reich des Traums* (*The Third Reich of Dreams*; 1966), a record of the dreams emanating from the experience of life under National Socialism which continued to haunt the author for years after the war, seems to belong more appropriately to the new post-war endeavour to come to terms with the past. But even today, over fifty years after the death of Hitler, first-hand chronicles by women of the catastrophe that befell Germany are still being found. It was as late as 1984, for example, that Ilse Langner's autobiographical account of the last days of the war, *Flucht ohne Ziel. Tagebuch-Roman. Frühjahr 1945* (Flight to nowhere. A diary-novel. Spring 1945) was finally published, while writers like Veza Canetti or Editha Klipstein are only now beginning to find recognition for their work of the 1930s. The year 1991 saw the publication of Ilse Weber's *In deinen Mauern wohnt das Leid* (Sorrow dwells within your walls), a compilation of the arresting poems written between 1942 and 1944 in the concentration camp of Theresienstadt, where Weber perished in the gas chamber together with her ten-year-old son Tommy. Many more such writings may still await discovery.

10

Writing in exile

The National Socialists forced more than half a million people to leave Germany. Persecution and murder of political opponents began immediately after the Reichstag fire in February 1933 and the victory of the National Socialists in the March elections. The continuing erosion of liberal and critical culture, starting with the book-burnings of May 1933, drove opponents of fascism into exile. After 1933, some 30,000 political refugees fled Germany, along with around 5,500 creative artists and approximately 2,500 writers and journalists. The largest group of exiles were people of Jewish origin and those declared 'non-Aryans' according to Nazi race laws. Emigration, though it was a route into an uncertain and unsafe future, was often the only alternative to disenfranchisement and death. German émigrés were not welcome anywhere. European countries were in the grip of economic recession, xenophobic and anti-Semitic feelings were rife, and, in some countries, immigration controls and work permits were extremely restrictive. Most émigrés lived on the breadline, dependent on support from welfare organizations and generally tolerated only on sufferance. Initially, countries prepared to receive émigrés included France, Austria, Czechoslovakia, Belgium, the Netherlands, Denmark and Switzerland, but as more countries came under National Socialist domination after 1938, increasing numbers were driven out or interned in the occupied countries, handed over to the Gestapo, and deported to concentration camps. The outbreak of war led to the establishing of émigré communities outside Europe – primarily in Palestine, the USA and Mexico. After the November pogrom in 1939, Jewish émigrés in particular sought to escape overseas, their situation exacerbated by increasingly stringent immigration policies in the host countries. Life was very hard, and for many émigrés, exile was to outlast fascism and the war. As German citizens, they often met with a hostile response in the host countries, because the indigenous population did not distinguish between Nazis and refugees from Nazi Germany. They were thus also vulnerable to depression, brought on by isolation and homesickness, poverty, loss of social status, and battles with the bureaucracy of the country in which they sought asylum.

Literary and journalistic production

The people whom the National Socialists drove out of Germany were a highly heterogeneous group. What ultimately united them was their opposition to fascism, and – especially in the case of those who emigrated for political reasons – their claim to represent the 'other Germany', as opposed to Nazi Germany. Anti-fascist socialist writers lost no time in becoming organized in Paris and Prague. In conjunction with the International Congresses for the Defence of Culture, they created a focus for support of the Popular Front in France and the struggle of the International Brigades in Spain, where German émigrés were also fighting. The loss of the German language, their separation from their readers, and the extremely limited openings they had for publication all drastically reduced opportunities for writers and journalists to work and so to exercise influence. Only a handful were able to make a living through their publications, and the vast majority existed in extremely harsh material circumstances. Magazines and newspapers offered some – albeit limited – scope for publication, and a few publishers, such as Querido in Amsterdam, which in 1933 set up a German section specifically to publish books banned in Germany, published books by émigrés, including world bestsellers such as Anna Seghers's 1942 novel, *Das siebte Kreuz* (*The Seventh Cross*). Only a very few exiled writers succeeded in becoming culturally assimilated in their host countries – for example Vicki Baum, already a successful author in the Weimar Republic, who continued her career as a novelist and screenwriter in the USA.

By far the most common genre in exile literature is narrative prose, with two dominant trends: the contemporary novel, or *Zeitroman*, subdivided into the *Deutschlandroman* (novel about Germany) and the *Exilroman* (exile novel); and the *historischer Roman*, or historical novel. In the first phase of exile, the aim of enlightening people about fascism is apparent in the frequent choice of documentation, reportage and accounts of personal experience, as for example in Lili Körber's novel *Eine Jüdin erlebt das neue Deutschland* (A Jewish woman experiences the new Germany), first published in Vienna in 1934. In the second phase, the juxtaposition of contemporary and historical material predominates. For example, the early development of the Third Reich is depicted in Anna Seghers's *Der Kopflohn* (*A Price on his Head*; 1933) and *Die Rettung* (The rescue; 1937), and in Anna Gmeyner's 1938 novel *Manja*, while the literary representation of everyday life under fascism is shown in, for example, Irmgard Keun's *Nach Mitternacht* (*After Midnight*; 1937). All of these appeared first in Amsterdam, published by Querido.

Examples of the *Exilroman*, depicting the often harsh circumstances of exile, include *Reisen Sie ab, Mademoiselle!* (Leave now, Mademoiselle; 1944), by Adrienne Thomas; *Der Umbruch oder Hanna und die Freiheit* (The upheaval, or Hanna and freedom), by Alice Rühle-Gerstel; and *Transit* by Anna Seghers – a novel which appeared first in Spanish, English and French in 1944, and in German only in 1948. In the third and final phase of exile the autobiographical element increases markedly, the *Deutschlandroman* disappears, and in the *Exilroman*, as writers become aware of a new age dawning, they deal with the years of exile in autobiographies, family sagas and novels about successive generations, such as Anna Seghers's *Die Toten bleiben jung* (*The Dead Stay Young*; 1949), or in allegories about Germany.

The majority of women writers who published prose works in exile were already writing in the twenties and early thirties, for example Anna Seghers, Irmgard Keun, Adrienne Thomas and Maria Leitner. It is striking that the protagonists of these works – which are frequently (auto)biographical – are almost always female; their authors favour novels set in Germany with either a politically committed, educational slant, or else a psychological emphasis, over the genre of the historical novel, which tends to be more of a male preserve. They also depict the circumstances and difficulties of everyday life in exile, especially internment and flight, with great vividness and precision. In many respects, narrative prose by exiled women writers was typified by the novel *Der Umbruch oder Hanna und die Freiheit* by Alice Rühle-Gerstel, who was born in Prague in 1894 and committed suicide in Mexico in 1943. Trained as a social psychologist, while in exile in Prague and later in Mexico she worked, illegally, as a journalist and translator. Her novel is the only one written in exile that is at once anti-fascist *and* anti-Stalinist; it was not published until 1984. By means of a dialectic of liberation and loss, the author depicts an identity crisis within her main character, a German communist émigrée, on three levels: as a woman, as an intellectual and as a socialist. In a mixture of reportage, autobiographical account and fictional narrative, Alice Rühle-Gerstel reworks her own experience of the loss of her home, both political and geographical.

Aside from prose writing in exile (an area which has been extensively researched in recent years), women were also strongly represented in the genres of children's literature and journalism. Women writers like Berta Lask, Hermynia Zur Mühlen, Ruth Rewald, Lisa Tetzner and Erika Mann all began writing for children, primarily for the children of émigrés. After spending 1937–8 in Republican Spain, Ruth Rewald, a Jewish writer born in Berlin in 1906, wrote a book for young people called *Vier spanische Jungen* (Four Spanish boys), based on a true incident in the Spanish Civil War. In 1942 Ruth Rewald was deported from occupied France to Auschwitz, where she died; the book was not published until 1987.

Whilst very little has been written to date on journalists who emigrated, the amount of journalistic writing by exiled women writers is extensive, ranging from editorial articles for the exile press, essays, reportage, reviews, travel descriptions, reports on Nazi Germany, and very varied accounts of personal experience, through non-fiction and feature articles, to short prose works and serialized novels. In 1933 Ika Halpern, a key contributor to the *Schwarzbuch über die Lage der Juden in Deutschland. Tatsachen und Dokumente* (Black book on the situation of the Jews in Germany. Facts and documents; 1934), emigrated with her future husband, Rudolf Olden, to London by way of Prague and Paris. In 1933–4, together with Olden, she wrote the book *Von Hitler vertrieben. Ein Jahr deutsche Emigration* (Driven out by Hitler. A year in the life of German émigrés), with a preface by the well-known Jewish writer Lion Feuchtwanger. Although it was one of the first books to take stock of the situation facing anti-fascist émigrés, especially in France, it was not published until 1994, under the title *In tiefem Dunkel liegt Deutschland* (Germany lies in total darkness). Ika Olden perished in a torpedo attack on the English ship in which she was trying to escape to American exile in 1940.

The circumstances of exile were especially problematic for dramatists. Anna Gmeyner turned to writing narrative prose instead, while Ilse Langner, Hilde Rubinstein and Christa Winsloe, who did write plays while in exile, had no prospect of their being published or performed.

Compared to prose written in exile, the range of poetry written and published by exiled writers is modest in scale. Some 200 volumes of poetry by individual writers were published abroad, though most poetry written in exile did not appear until after 1945. Poetry written in exile tends to be dominated by those writers who had emerged as poets before 1933, such as the well-established Bertolt Brecht, Johannes R. Becher and the Jewish poet Else Lasker-Schüler. Lasker-Schüler left Germany in 1933 at the age of sixty-four, spending her remaining years in exile in Switzerland and Jerusalem. Her last volume of poetry, *Mein blaues Klavier* (My blue piano), appeared in 1943 in Jerusalem, where she died in 1945. In one of her posthumously published poems she wrote:

> Man muß so müde sein wie ich es bin
> Es schwindet kühl entzaubert meine Welt aus meinem Sinn
> Und es zerrinnen meine Wünsche tief im Herzen.
>
> Gejagt und wüßte auch nicht mehr wohin
> Verglimmen in den Winden alle meine Kerzen
> Und meine Augen werden dünn.

(Sämtliche Gedichte, p. 256)

> You need to feel as weary as I do today
> My world, grown cold, has been bewitched away
> Deep in my heart desire runs dry.
>
> Hunted and failing to find the way
> My candles flicker in the wind and die
> My eyes grow dim in my dismay.

(tr. AV)

Silence in exile

In her documentary text *Frauen und Kinder* (Women and children), written in exile in France, Anna Seghers vividly demonstrated that traditional gender-specific divisions of everyday work became even more sharply defined in exile. Irrespective of social origin, religion, professional training or age, women had to take the main responsibility for day-to-day living. Whilst the men (writers included) generally tried to continue working in their chosen profession, their female partners were responsible for food and accommodation, as well as for obtaining visas and providing financial support. They cleaned other people's homes, looked after other people's children, worked in other people's households – and above all, they learnt the foreign language, in order to be able to work and get by. In other words, the women repressed their own desires and potential and devoted all their strength and energy to coping with everyday life, supporting their husbands and children both materially and spiritually.

Neither Ernst Bloch nor Lion Feuchtwanger nor Bertolt Brecht – to name only a few examples – could have been as productive in exile as their works attest, had not their wives and companions – Karola Bloch and Marta Feuchtwanger; Elisabeth Hauptmann, Margarete Steffin and Ruth Berlau – made their own time and energy available to them.

Where, on the other hand, women had already made a name for themselves as writers during the Weimar Republic, or had begun to write at that time, it could not by any means be assumed, if they were married or had a family, that their male partners would make it possible for them to write. Apart from Anna Seghers, who had two small children and whose husband worked as an economist, almost no woman writer with a family was able to continue writing and publishing in exile. In other words, for the vast majority of women writers, exile also meant an interruption, if not an end, to their writing career.

The necessity of concentrating on survival left little room for other concerns or ambitions. On the one hand this resulted in a great loss of productivity and creativity, of self-assurance and self-confidence, whilst on the other it shows how much energy, courage and strength such a role demanded. This enforced return to traditional female roles is one of the main reasons why exile literature written and published between 1933 and 1945 features relatively few works by women writers. A typical example is that of the Jewish poet Mascha Kaléko, who had made a name for herself as a writer in the early thirties. It was not until 1938 that Kaléko emigrated to the USA, together with her husband, the composer Chemjo Vinaver, and her small son. Although Kaléko lived in New York for almost thirty years, she remained unknown there. The main reason why she was able to publish only one volume of poetry while exiled in America – *Verse für Zeitgenossen* (Verses for contemporaries; 1945) – is that she took upon herself the organizational problems of everyday life: above all earning a living for the family, supporting her husband's work, attending his concerts, and translating and negotiating for him. She gave ironic expression to this perpetual dilemma in her poem *Die Leistungen der Frau in der Kultur* (A woman's contribution to culture): 'Was uns Frauen fehlt, ist "Des Künstlers Frau" / Oder gleichwertiger Ersatz' (*In meinen Träumen läutet es Sturm*, p. 96) – 'We women, though, have no "artist's wife" / Or any substitute of equal weight.'

The themes of the poetry she wrote in exile are alienation and loneliness, the problems of adjusting to a new life, and above all unremitting homesickness. The short poem *Der kleine Unterschied* (A slight difference) addresses this:

Es sprach zum Mister Goodwill
ein deutscher Emigrant:
'Gewiß, es bleibt dasselbe,
sag ich nun *land* statt Land,
sag ich für Heimat *Homeland*
und *poem* für Gedicht.
Gewiß, ich bin sehr *happy*:
Doch glücklich bin ich nicht.'

(In meinen Träumen läutet es Sturm, p. 52)

A German emigrant
explained to Mr Goodwill:
'Sure, you will understand
if I translate *Land* as "land",
Heimat as "my homeland"
Gedicht as "poetry".
Sure, I am very "happy" here
But *glücklich* I cannot be.'

(tr. AV)

In 1966 Mascha Kaléko and her husband emigrated to Israel, where working conditions were better for Vinaver. Whilst her volumes of poetry were reprinted in Europe, Kaléko's emigration to Israel only served to emphasize her isolation. She died there alone in January 1975.

Post-war oblivion

All too often the silence imposed by exile turned into permanent neglect. Post-war attitudes in West Germany were a contributory factor; people forgot about the émigrés, who were part of the history of fascism, which soon became distorted and suppressed. The situation was different in what was to become the GDR, where returning émigrés helped build the 'other' Germany; Anna Seghers and Hedda Zinner, in particular, made major contributions to GDR *Frauenliteratur*. A separate issue, which lies outside the scope of the present study, is the situation in the Soviet Union. Attitudes to the Nazi past and the returning émigrés in West Germany may be characterized by the titles of two key psychology texts on the subject: *Die Unfähigkeit zu trauern* (The inability to mourn), by Alexander and Margarete Mitscherlich, and *Die zweite Schuld* (The second guilt), by Ralph Giordano. A typical fate is that of Irmgard Keun, who had had a sensational success with her first novel, *Gilgi – eine von uns* (Gilgi – one of us) in 1931, which she followed with *Das kunstseidene Mädchen* (*The Artificial Silk*

Girl) in 1932. After 1933, however, her books were banned; in 1935 she emigrated to Belgium, and with Joseph Roth travelled to Paris, Warsaw and New York, before returning to Germany illegally in 1940. In these few years, from 1935 to 1940, she published four more novels, whose style of composition – associative juxtaposition of scenes and dramatic dialogue, reminiscent of edited film footage – continues in the tradition of social criticism in contemporary novels of the Weimar Republic. *Nach Mitternacht*, which gives an atmospherically dense picture of everyday life in fascist Germany, filled other exiles with both delight and terror because it conveyed to them authentic, up-to-date impressions from the Nazi-dominated homeland from which they were excluded. In his review in *Die neue Weltbühne* (April 1937) Klaus Mann gave a telling account of Keun's book: 'The air through which these people move is thick with tension – an atmosphere somewhere between that of a prison and a lunatic asylum. Sombre shadows flit across all the faces; some people are destroyed, others flee and liberate themselves; still others grow despondent and give up all hope. None of them is happy. No one in a totalitarian fascist state is ever happy.' Irmgard Keun was forgotten in post-war Germany, and she died in Cologne in 1982. Only in the last few years have her books been reprinted.

Autobiographical texts

Characteristic features of women's autobiographical texts published since the war are that their main thematic focus is on the period of exile – either exclusively, or else as a key episode within the story of their lives; that in general only a minority of the women authors in question had written and published work previously; and that the main purpose behind writing the texts is to structure and come to terms with the caesura in the pattern of everyday life caused by persecution, exile, and attempts, whether successful or otherwise, to adapt to a new culture. Furthermore, these women writers bear witness to a period which, although crucial in their own lives and for the history of their country, has yet to be addressed adequately by society as a whole.

Women's autobiography tends to differ significantly from that of men in the inclusion of personal, even intimate, details. This emerges very vividly from, for example, the memoirs of Karola Bloch. *Aus meinem Leben* (From my life; published posthumously, 1981) is at once an outstanding cultural-historical document and an openly self-critical account of one woman's individual development. The number of autobiographies by women addressing the experience of exile is now vast, though unfortunately this does not always mean that their books, whose dates of publication range from the end of the war right up to the present day, are readily available; some of their names are listed in the bibliography. It is difficult to say how many autobiographical texts by women remain unpublished for each one which has appeared in print.

Jewish poetry

Rose Ausländer and Nelly Sachs, both of whom escaped death by emigrating, continued to write and publish poems in their respective countries of exile, the USA and Sweden, during the Holocaust and World War II. Other Jewish women spent all their lives attempting – by means of writing – to come to terms with the stigma of having been saved whilst relatives and friends were murdered and other Jewish people perished, along with their culture and the places where they lived. Here we should mention in particular Ilse Blumenthal-Weiss, Stella Rotenberg and Hilde Domin. Coming to terms with the Holocaust, and also to some extent with the experience of exile, is of central importance in their poetry.

Stella Rotenberg was forced to abandon her medical studies because of her Jewish origins, and she emigrated via Holland to England, where she worked as a nurse, doctor's assistant and office clerk. She married a doctor, a Polish émigré. From 1940 onwards she wrote poems in German. After the war she discovered that her parents and nearly all her relatives had perished in Nazi extermination camps. Since 1948 she has been living in Leeds. As well as two volumes of poetry she has also published a volume of poetry and prose. The central themes of her poems – published in the collections *Gedichte* (Poems; 1972); *Die wir übrig sind* (Those of us who are left; 1978); and *Scherben sind endlicher Hort* (Fragments are a finite treasure; 1991) – are mourning and suffering, the incomprehensibility of the Holocaust, and writing in order not to forget, as in the 1972 poem *Vermächtnis aus Auschwitz* (Testimony from Auschwitz):

> Daß du, Mensch, uns nicht vergißest,
> und vergiß unsre Mörder nicht!
> Das Unheil, das uns vernichtet,
> Steht auch vor deinem Gesicht.
>
> Verhülle nicht deine Augen
> und halt' deine Ohren nicht zu!

Sonst sind wir für nichts gestorben,
heute ich und morgen du.

(Scherben, p. 57)

Humanity, do not forget us
or the murderers of our race!
The evil that will wipe us out
Also stares you in the face.

Look at it squarely, do not flinch
and keep your ears wide open, too!
Or we have died for nothing,
I today, tomorrow, you.

(tr. AV)

Nowadays such a reminder is more necessary than ever.

Most of the Jewish women who emigrated – frequently to Israel – never returned to Germany. The majority wrote in German; Jenny Aloni may serve as an example here. Born in 1917, she had started writing before emigrating, and she was able to resume this later, publishing several novels, radio plays, stories and poems. As a young woman she joined the Zionist movement, worked in a youth camp, and in November 1939 managed to escape on one of the last ships sailing to Palestine, though her parents and sister remained behind. Jenny Aloni studied Hebrew at the University in Jerusalem, and later joined the army. In her autobiographical novel *Zypressen zerbrechen nicht* (Cypresses do not break; 1961), she described her experiences in the years when Palestine, where she made a new home, was developing as a country. Autobiographical themes find their way into almost all her works, and self-analysis is an important aspect of her writing. In her poems, she formulates the ever-recurring thoughts of a sorrow rich in images, as in the volume *In den schmalen Stunden der Nacht* (In the small hours; 1980): '. . . roter Regen tropft / von den Ästen des Korallenbaumes / und an den Zweigen der Trauerweide / hängen rote Tränen' (p. 81) (. . . red rain drips / from the branches of the coral tree / and on the boughs of the weeping willow / red tears hang).

Her work probably represents most clearly the full range of women's writing in exile: from grief at all that was lost, through attempts to begin afresh, to the unrelenting struggle against forgetting.

Translated by Anthony Vivis

Part IV

Post-war, East and West

11

Restoration and resistance: women's writing 1945–1970

If the notion of *Nullpunkt* (tabula rasa) in 1945 has long outlived its usefulness and been replaced with a focus on continuities in the post-war German literary tradition, there is also a case for correcting the view of the the 1950s and 1960s as a period virtually devoid of significant women authors. This image is due both to the male domination of the forum of the new West German literature, the *Gruppe 47*, in the narrative of post-war literary history (with only passing reference to its 'token' women), and to the self-image of second wave feminism as a radical break with the conservatism of the immediate post-war years. To a young generation of women, politicized by the students' movement but dissatisfied with its failure adequately to address the politics of gender, the 1950s appeared to represent a period of stagnation in the social and cultural emancipation of women.

Whilst there can be no doubt that the women's movement provided the institutional base for a specifically feminist discourse and thus a feminist literature, since the late 1980s there has been a revival of critical interest in the less obviously political writing of the 1950s. This includes revisionist readings of the work of established authors such as Ingeborg Bachmann, Ilse Aichinger and Marie Luise Kaschnitz, but is also signalled by new editions of the work of forgotten writers such as Marlen Haushofer, Johanna Moosdorf and Unica Zürn.

This is in part a result of the growing sophistication and pluralism of theoretical debates within feminist literary criticism, producing a shift in emphasis from the representation of positive images of femininity towards an analysis of textual strategies for the articulation of dissent. Thus it is possible to detect in the work of the older generation of women writers a significant critique of patriarchal culture which has yet to theorize its structures of oppression, or to formulate positive alternatives to the status quo. The conflict experienced between social integration and self-realization emerges in what Sigrid Weigel has called the 'schielender Blick', the double focus resulting from a critical awareness combined with practical complicity in an oppressive social order.

The more politicized generation of women starting to publish in the 1960s (for example Barbara König, Gabriele Wohmann, Gisela Elsner, Erika Runge, Angelika Mechtel), whilst more outspoken in their social criticism, tend to be less sensitive to the role of gender in the socio-economic inequalities they deplore. In terms of aesthetic innovation and radical potential, their writing holds less interest for feminist literary criticism in the 1990s than that of the preceding generation, on which the focus of this survey will lie.

The achievements of women writers in the early post-war years must be considered against the background of the social transformation of women's lives from the end of the war to the 1950s. Much of what we now know about the reality of women's lives at this time derives from their own accounts in published diaries and chronicles such as those of Susanne Kerkhoff, Ursula von Kardorff, Karla Höcker and Margret Boveri (see also Rapisarda, 'Anfang' (1986), pp. 91f.). These reflect women's active participation in public and professional life, in addition to their role as head of the household, and reinforce the impression of Germany in 1945 as a *Frauengesellschaft* (women's society) in a very real sense.

The 1950s saw an almost total reversal of this state of affairs, with the restoration of traditional notions of femininity and the affirmation of women's primarily domestic role. Government policies which actively promoted this included the *Doppelverdienerkampagne* (campaign against female dual income earners) and the establishment in 1953 of the first Ministry for the Family under the conservative Minister Franz Wuermeling. Government legislation to support the institution of the family was endorsed by the Roman Catholic Church, both church and state being concerned to uphold family values as the moral and economic foundation on which the new German prosperity would be built.

A glance at the literary landscape in the late 1940s reveals a clear correlation between these social developments and the short-lived prominence of women writers in cultural life after the war. The first (and only united) German Writers' Congress in Berlin (1947) was chaired by Ricarda Huch, a powerful unifying force rallying behind her writers of all political persuasions, including writers of *innere Emigration* such as Elisabeth Langgässer, and those returned from exile such as Anna Seghers. The leadership role of such women at the conference was doubtless a source of the confidence with which many younger women writers and journalists also participated. Yet at the second major cultural congress in the West, the Congress for Cultural Freedom in 1950, only 6 of the 118 invited guests were female.

Whilst established women writers in Austria and German-speaking Switzerland such as Paula von Preradović and Cécile Lauber may have done little to raise women's profile in public life, critical voices such as that of the Swiss lawyer and journalist Iris von Roten do provide a contemporary analysis of the oppressive structure of the nuclear family as an obstacle to Swiss women's emancipation (*Frauen im Laufgitter. Offene Worte zur Stellung der Frau*; 1958). Meanwhile the new post-war West German literature was gaining European recognition with novels such as Wolfgang Koeppen's *Tauben im Gras* (*Pigeons on the Grass*; 1951), with its representation of the family as the only point of stability in an increasingly precarious reality.

In view of the apparently universal dominance of the discourses of the church and family life in German-speaking Western Europe in the 1950s, it is important to consider whether women's writing reinforced or challenged the definitions of femininity they endorsed. This will be explored first in women's 'religious' writing of the period, encompassing ideas from the *renouveau catholique* to feminist theology. The focus will then move to representations of motherhood, relations between the sexes and family life in writing of the 1950s and 1960s, with particular attention to deviations from the norm in the treatment of working women, androgyny and homosexuality. In addition to these thematic considerations, it is important to note the formal innovation in women's writing, with its challenge to conventional notions of subjectivity prefiguring more recent theories of a feminine aesthetic. Notably, however, this is less evident in the work of the generation whose publishing careers started in the 1960s, when aesthetic considerations were increasingly subordinated to political concerns.

From 'religious' writing to feminist theology

Religious writing by women has a long and established tradition, but whereas that of the medieval mystics has been reinterpreted as a site for the legitimate articulation of female desire, that of writers such as Elisabeth Langgässer, Christine Lavant and Gertrud von le Fort is still regarded as fundamentally conservative, merely perpetuating repressive images of femininity reinforced in the Third Reich and subjected to no significant revision in the post-war years. Yet much of the writing of Langgässer and le Fort can be read as a critique of institutionalized religion and a positive affirmation of female spirituality, with Christ portrayed as 'the most feminine of men'.

Gertrud von le Fort, a Roman Catholic convert and representative of conservative resistance to National Socialism, was not as uncontroversial an 'establishment' figure after the war as is generally assumed. Accused of blasphemy in 1951 for her novel *Der Kranz der Engel* (Garland of angels; 1946), her choice of historical and Biblical themes was often intended to cast a critical light on her own time. Far from endorsing female subordination, her narratives of the 1950s can be seen as affirming traditionally feminine qualities which contemporary society neglects at its peril. Hence the short story *Die Frau des Pilatus* (*The Wife of Pilate;* 1950) implies a critique of the church for privileging justice over compassion, in the story of Claudia Procula's premonition of Christ's suffering at the hands of her husband. In *Die Tochter Farinatas* (Farinata's daughter; 1950) set in thirteenth-century Florence, the very survival of humanity seems dependent on the redefinition of masculinity and femininity, not as hierarchically opposed poles, but existing in a relationship of equal and mutual supplementarity.

Le Fort's essay 'Die Frau des christlichen Abendlandes' (Women in Western Christendom; 1951) is an analysis of contemporary society which, while not questioning dominant definitions of gender, does locate power relations between the sexes as an important site of potential social change. The warlike and destructive forces in the world are attributed to the dominance of masculinity and the process of secularization, although motherhood is still seen as the principal means whereby femininity can exercise its salutary influence. Nevertheless, in 'Das Gebet der Frauenseele' (The prayer of the female soul; 1951), which is far from a conventional account of natural female piety, 'femininity' becomes virtually synonymous with 'a capacity for devotion', and a potentiality in all people, regardless of sex. Elisabeth Langgässer is another writer whose religious, Catholic world view and commitment to the notion of justification by faith ran counter to the dominant secular, existentialist aesthetic discourse of the *Junge Generation*. Her novel of *innere Emigration, Das unauslöschliche Siegel* (*The Indelible Seal;* 1946), has thus been read as an apologia for passive resistance to National Socialism, with its implicitly untragic representation of mankind as a pawn tossed between the forces of good and evil. Yet as the first speaker at the Berlin Writers' Congress after Ricarda Huch's opening address, Langgässer was to emphasize the responsibility of all German intellectuals for the crimes of National Socialism (Langgässer, 'Schriftsteller' (1947), pp. 36–41). Younger women writers who have attempted to rehabilitate her writing include voices as diverse as Luise Rinser and Ingeborg Drewitz, the latter pointing to the vivid sensuousness of her prose, too often overlooked by critics who reject her on political grounds. Indeed, it was the all-too-graphic portrayal of compulsive eroticism alongside spirituality which caused the controversy surrounding the posthumously published *Märkische Argonautenfahrt* (*The Quest;* 1950). It is arguably precisely her treatment of sexuality which defies simplistic dualistic interpretation, as erotic experience is presented as both a profane and a mystical dimension of experience.

The narrative of *Märkische Argonautenfahrt* is overlaid with mythological discourse which may be read as the culmination of an ongoing exploration in her work of the tensions between the classical and the Judaeo-Christian traditions. It is seen also in her poetry and in stories such as 'Die getreue Antigone' (Faithful Antigone; 1947) in which the mythological dimension introduces ambiguity into an otherwise conventional portrayal of femininity, as subordinate to the Law of the Father embodied by the church. As the daughter of an assimilated Jewish father, who felt herself to be Catholic yet had her writing banned in 1936 on racial grounds, Langgässer's treatment of female identity is often more complex than her reputation would suggest. Stories such as 'Untergetaucht' (Under cover; 1948) and 'An der Nähmaschine' (At the sewing machine; 1956) are good examples of unheroic *Vergangenheitsbewältigung*, coming to terms with the Nazi past, which highlight the differences and power inequalities between women, rather than their solidarity, whilst 'Glück haben' (Lucky; 1948) adopts the narrative position of female hysteria to articulate a disturbing critique of the wartime discourses of fortitude and stoicism (see Meyer (1997), pp. 35ff.).

As these examples illustrate, the use of a Biblical or mythological framework, even in the work of older writers of this period, need not imply a reinforcement of oppressive cultural archetypes. Indeed, the Gospels and stories of the early church form the basis of the more explicitly anti-clerical critique of writers such as Geno Hartlaub, Johanna Moosdorf and Luise Rinser, whose later writing focuses on the church as the primary locus of patriarchy and source of women's oppression. Moosdorf's essay 'Religion ohne Glaube?' (Religion without faith?; 1986[1]) proposes a feminization of Christianity, opposing the writings of female medieval mystics to church dogma, and articulating in theoretical terms the androgynous ideal of Christ she constructs in the stories 'Frauen am Brunnen' (Women at the well) and 'Sieben Jahre nach Ostern' (Seven years after Easter; 1974: both stories are reprinted in Moosdorf, *Die Tochter*; 1991). A similar emphasis on the androgyny of Christ marks the writing of Geno Hartlaub, more recently focusing on the prominence of women in the early church in the fictionalized letters of a woman of the Nazarenes in *Freue dich, du bist eine Frau. Briefe der Priscilla* (Rejoice, you are a woman. Letters from Priscilla; 1983). Whilst Moosdorf's and Hartlaub's religious writing may be read in the context of 1980s feminist theology and the peace movement, that of Luise Rinser forms a link between them and the generation of Langgässer and le Fort.

Long spurned by critics as a didactic writer, with the attendant associations of a moralizing, apolitical voice, the close connection between Rinser's views on gender politics and the church is stated already in her essays *Zölibat und Frau* (Women and celibacy; 1967) and *Unterentwickeltes Land Frau* (Underdeveloped land: woman; 1970). In the latter essay, like Moosdorf she differentiates between the values embodied by Jesus and those upheld by the church, identifying St Paul as the major source of misogynist tendencies leading to the exclusion of women from education and ecclesiastical office.

Relating this analysis to the contemporary reality of women's lives, Rinser identifies the central persisting myth governing definitions of femininity and upheld by the church as that of motherhood. She warns against all systems of thought which seek to fix women in their maternal role, thus excluding them from the public and political sphere. The essay concludes with a call for a new concept of partnership in place of the hierarchical relationships between men and women perpetuated by the institutional framework of the family.

Motherhood, the family and androgyny

One of the most significant contributions to the discursive redefinition of gender, both in terms of theoretical statements on women and art, and in her interrogation of women's role in the reconstruction of Germany, was undoubtedly that of the dramatist Ilse Langner. Already known for her pacifist plays in the Weimar Republic, and scorned as an 'amazon' in the male-dominated world of theatre, she continued writing mythological dramas which were published after 1945 (*Klytämnestra* (Clytaemnestra; 1947), *Iphigenie kehrt heim* (Iphigenia returns home; 1948)), and was one of the most politically active women writers of the immediate post-war years.

When invited by the German Academy for Language and Literature to comment on 'Das Besondere der Frauendichtung' (The feminine literary voice),[2] she gave an account of how women's affinity for drama rests on an assertion of gender difference, and a view of 'feminine language' not far removed from more recent theories of 'writing the body', according to which the female writing subject has privileged access to the unconscious impulses repressed by symbolic language. Yet parallels may also be drawn with Virginia Woolf in Langner's commitment to an ideal of the androgynous creative mind. Her thinking is characteristic of the time in attempting to reconcile positions which would diverge radically within the women's movement.

Langner's contribution to the debate about women's post-war social role can be found in a fictional address by Berlin, a mythological mother-figure, to her female inhabitants, 'Mutter Berlin an ihre Töchter' (Mother Berlin to her daughters; 1947).[3] She points to the debasement by National Socialism of concepts such as 'Mutterliebe' (mother love) and 'Vaterland' (Fatherland), proposing instead an inclusive notion of 'Elternland' (parent country). Whilst not absolving women of the guilt of complicity, her analysis of the evil perpetrated by the Germans rests on the definition of masculinity in terms of nationalism and militarism.

Her post-war drama *Heimkehr. Ein Berliner Trümmerstück* (Homecoming: Berlin in ruins; 1949) addresses the problems of readjustment to conventional gender roles when the POWs returned from captivity, and hers was one of the earliest voices to warn of the dangers of nuclear technology in the play *Cornelia Kungström* (1955) and the novel *Die Zyklopen* (The Cyclopes; 1960). The consistent focus on women's experience, their resilience in wartime, the question of childlessness and the survival of the race, and her interest in the cultural construction of femininity from antiquity to the present make Langner an important precursor of second wave feminism, as well as an inspiration to younger female dramatists of the early post-war years.

Johanna Moosdorf's insistent focus on National Socialism is also inextricably related to her critique of masculinity. A prodigious and versatile literary talent whose career was dogged by personal tragedy and political obstructions to her publishing in three different German regimes, her work has still to receive the critical acclaim it deserves. She is eloquent on the problems of female authorship after 1945, and on the courage required to make a woman the subject of a literary text. Her novels of the 1950s, *Flucht nach Afrika* (Flight to Africa; 1952) and *Die Nachtigallen schlagen im Schnee* (The nightingales sing in the snow; 1953), are narrated from a male perspective, which she herself admits was a form of 'internalized conformism'. This changed in the 1960s, as seen in the revision of the early 1948 story 'Das Mädchen Margret' (The girl Margaret), published in 1963 as 'Ruth und Rose' (Ruth and Rose; reprinted Moosdorf, *Die Tochter*) without the framework male narrator of the original version. It is the story of a woman haunted by the memory of a childhood friendship with a Jewish girl, and horrified to find the trauma reproduced in her husband's brutal treatment of their own daughter. It combines a lament for past female solidarity with a critique of the patriarchal power exercised in the nuclear family, and suggests the continuation of the structures of dictatorship in post-war reality.

These are central themes also of the novels of the 1960s, *Nebenan* (Next door; 1961) and *Die Andermanns* (The Andermanns; 1969). The former, narrated in part by the 'madwoman' Dorothea, committed to an asylum by her husband, a former concentration-camp doctor, to rid him of her 'whining voice', is both an indictment of National Socialist atrocities and the institution of marriage. In *Die Andermanns* it is a son who cannot come to terms with his father's Nazi past, but women are still the guardians of memory, and men the creators of a brutal and bureaucratic 'Mörderwelt' (world of murderers). Surprisingly violent forms of female revenge are a frequent theme in early works, such as *Schneesturm in Worotschau* (Snowstorm in Worotschau; 1957), but in the 1960s and 1970s the representation of relationships between women is striking in its variety. Already in *Nebenan* there is the supportive friendship between Agathe Steinbach and her younger companion Elena, but the unacceptability of lesbianism as a literary theme at this time is seen in the eight-year delay between completion and publication of the novel *Die Freundinnen* (The girlfriends; 1977).

In addition to the critique of masculinity in this novel, there is also a utopian vision of the 'new man' in the androgynous figure of Peter Heuck. An earlier attempt to construct an alternative model of masculinity is seen in the novel for which Moosdorf won the Nelly Sachs prize, *Die lange Nacht* (Long is the night; 1963). It is largely the inner monologue of a man blinded in the war who, deprived of the masculine prerogative of sight, develops a new sensitivity which extends to the suspension of normal subject–object relations and of the linear experience of time. Moosdorf's writing in all literary genres from the late 1940s to the autobiographical novel *Jahrhundertträume* (Dreams of the century; 1989) charts an increasingly political awareness of the need for a transformation of definitions of gender as a prerequisite for social change.

A similar claim could be made for the dramatist and novelist Ingeborg Drewitz, whose literary and political essays demonstrate a commitment both to the promotion of women's writing and to the political responsibility of literature. Her work on Bettina von Arnim (1969) as well as essays on contemporary women authors and women's drama are themselves a contribution to the construction of a female literary tradition. Her active involvement in projects promoting young dramatists and actors in post-war Berlin is reflected in the recollections of the narrator of her novel *Oktoberlicht. Ein Tag im Herbst* (October light. A day in autumn; 1969), a woman whose convalescence from an operation gives rise to reflections on her own life and on the recent history of the divided city. Political and professional disillusionment is here inextricably linked with personal disappointments: the failure of her marriage and her problems in relating to the political radicalism of her daughter's generation.

Drewitz's reputation as a political dramatist was established in the first post-war decade, but in her short stories of the 1950s she also combines an acute political vision with a critical perspective on the institutions of marriage and the family. The topos of the 'madwoman narrator' appears in the story 'Auch so ein Leben' (Just another life), in which a woman is in psychiatric hospital after having murdered her husband. Her dislocated memories of the daily cruelties, humiliation and boredom of her marriage alternate with the rational perspective of the psychiatrist which criminalizes her deed. 'Ponte della Libertà' consists mainly of the disillusionment and escape-fantasies of a middle-aged wife on a 'second honeymoon' in Venice after twenty-six years of marriage.

In her 1971 essay 'Gespaltenes oder Gedoppeltes Leben? Zur Emanzipationsdiskussion in der Bundesrepublik Deutschland' (Divided or doubled lives? On the emancipation debate in the Federal Republic of Germany), Drewitz identifies the nuclear family as the single most important structure preventing the transformation of female consciousness, formulating in psychological terms the failure of women's emancipation in the 1960s. However, she laments the pessimism of women's writing in the 1960s, the lack of hope invested in relationships and the renunciation of children in the pursuit of women's liberation. Like many others of her generation, Drewitz calls for a new notion of partnership, a non-confrontational resolution of the inequalities between the sexes.

A similar ideal of re-negotiated partnership is found in Hilde Domin's only novel, *Das zweite Paradies* (The second Paradise; 1968), the story of a crisis in the marriage of a couple who have returned to the FRG from exile. The shared memories of exile reveal the roots of the crisis, which lie less in the couple's extramarital affairs than in the redefinition of their roles, when the wife begins to question the expectation that she will bear sole emotional responsibility for their relationship. Starting to write in exile in the Dominican Republic in 1951, Hilde Domin became known on her return to the FRG for her poetry collections, and her volume of poetry and interpretation *Doppelinterpretationen. Das zeitgenössische Gedicht zwischen Autor und Leser* (Double interpretations. Contemporary poetry between writer and reader; 1966) remains an important landmark among the vexed aesthetic debates of the 1960s.

A prolific essayist as well as a poet, Domin's statements on art and gender manifest the same tensions found in others of her generation, between the assertion and denial of difference. Her association of creative, intellectual work with masculinity in *Von der Natur nicht vorgesehen* (Not as Nature intended; 1974) coexists uneasily with her views on the 'hermaphrodite' nature of the poetic imagination, set out in her 1988 *Frankfurter Vorlesungen* (Frankfurt Poetry Lectures), *Das Gedicht als Augenblick der Freiheit* (The poem as moment of freedom). Of more immediate interest to feminist aesthetic debates is the lucid account in her introduction to *Doppelinterpretationen* of the unresolved dialectic of poetic response. Her analysis of the autonomy of the text and the plurality of meaning has resonances in recent feminist theoretical writing, as do the metaphors of fluidity and solidity, which she uses to describe the interaction of affective and rational responses in the reception of poetry.

An altogether darker picture of relations between the sexes emerges from the novels of Geno Hartlaub, whose idyllic memories of childhood and privileged access to intellectual and literary circles in no way cloud her critical perspective on marriage and the remaining obstacles in the way of women's emancipation. Like Drewitz, her more recent writing shows awareness of the psychological factors which militate against political solidarity among women, but even her earliest work offers a challenge to the gender roles dictated by marriage and the nuclear family.

Although *Die Tauben von San Marco* (The pigeons of St Mark's Square;

1953) is based on the predictable topos of an older man's quest to regain his innocence through marriage to a young, inexperienced bride, there is a note of resistance to the clichéd gender stereotypes with which the narrative works, and a hint of the need for female solidarity if marriage is to be survived at all. This finds more extreme expression in *Der große Wagen* (The Big Dipper; 1954), which envisages the potentially idyllic ménage of two women bringing up a baby, dispensing with its male progenitor altogether. Society's indifference to women's need for self-realization is presented in the most brutal terms in the story 'Rot heißt auch schön' (Red means beautiful too; 1969), the inner monologue of a woman whose response to the desperate tedium of her loveless marriage manifests itself in clinical claustrophobia, against which the medical profession prescribes pregnancy.

Hartlaub combines criticism of the institution of the family with the intensely personal process of mourning the loss of her own brother in the semi-surreal story of the love between a brother and sister, *Der Mond hat Durst* (The thirsty moon; 1963). It is narrated by Nini, a young woman in a psychiatric ward, where she inhabits the fantasy of living on the moon until she reaches the age of her brother when he died. Androgyny is an ambiguous ideal in this text, at once a revolt against the bourgeois heterosexual norm, and only possible at the expense of female identity. The tension at the centre of this strange tale could be seen as that between female subjecthood and female desire within a patriarchal symbolic order.

Working women – emancipated women?

A notable correlation to women's albeit often critical focus on marriage and motherhood in the 1950s is the dearth of textual representations of women in the workplace. Where these do occur, the effect is often to reinforce the fact that women's participation in the post-war economic miracle under Adenauer's government did nothing to alter the definition of femininity in relation to the structures of family life. The devaluation of women's work in the public sphere is treated by Drewitz in the story 'Every day (gesungen: ev'ry deii)' (publ. 1985), which explores from three different narrative perspectives the status of an unmarried, middle-aged female office employee. It bears comparison with Ruth Rehmann's novel *Illusionen* (*Saturday to Monday*; 1959), in that both juxtapose three generations of women in the office and reveal the veiled rivalry between them. This is largely based on their sexual power to attract men, which stands in inverse proportion to their relations of professional seniority. (For a detailed discussion of *Illusionen*, see Meyer, 'The early novels of Ruth Rehmann'; in Weedon (1997) pp. 61–76.) Rehmann's critical analysis of gender becomes more explicit in her later, more widely known work of the 1970s and 1980s, but it is significant that two chapters of this early novel are incorporated virtually unchanged in the short story volume *Paare* (Couples; 1978).

There are very few truly emancipated women in the novels of these years, and for them there is always the costly choice: between love and independence, intimacy and isolation. A case in point is Nina, the protagonist of Luise Rinser's *Mitte des Lebens* (*Nina*; 1950), a writer who achieves professional success and personal independence, combining a sensuous passionate nature with uncompromising integrity and intellectual rigour. Despite Rinser's elitist idealization of the female artist, and her tendency towards moralizing abstraction, *Mitte des Lebens* retains its resonance largely because of the complexity of its representation of emancipation, not excluding motherhood, but contingent on a partnership which allows for personal development and change.

Critique of heterosexuality and utopian visions

The Austrian Marlen Haushofer has enjoyed only belated recognition by feminist criticism, probably because she represents the inability of women to escape the constraints of married domesticity. Yet women are not pure victims in her work; as mothers they are often complicit in even the most shocking abuses of patriarchy. The very title of the novella *Wir töten Stella* (We kill Stella; 1958) implicates the female narrator in her husband's seduction of their foster-daughter and the girl's subsequent suicide.

The thirty-year-old protagonist of *Die Tapetentür* (*The Jib Door*; 1957) gives up her career and independence for a marriage which stifles her most fundamental instincts, and finds herself expecting a child she cannot love. The dual narrative voice exposes the strategies of self-deception by which she denies to herself the damage being done to her personality and the subordination of her erotic needs to those of her husband. The ambiguous metaphor of the concealed door in an imaginary wall which appears at the end of the novel prefigures Haushofer's most ambitious work, *Die Wand* (*The Wall*; 1963), the dystopian novel of a woman's sole survival of the end of civilization. This presents a wide-ranging exploration of the elusive boundary between culture and nature. The analysis of gender extends from a radical critique of marriage to a probing interrogation of the integrity of the self, in which it anticipates postmodern feminist writing of the 1980s. The tension between the protagonist's diminishing sense of her own 'femininity', and her apparently primeval urge to nurture all life points again to the 'schielender Blick' (double focus) of this generation, whose dissatisfaction with the institutions of marriage and the family stopped short of the renunciation of love and procreation.

Haushofer's last novel, *Die Mansarde* (The attic; 1969), relocates her cultural criticism within the context of bourgeois marriage, depicting a woman's strategies of escape into forms of non-symbolic meaning, and ending on a utopian note with her drawing of a dragon, the mythological creature which can embody femininity or, more broadly, the 'Other' of human culture. Whether in the sinister, cold atmosphere of many of her novels, or in the laconic humour of the short stories in the volume *Schreckliche Treue* (Dreadful faithfulness; 1968), Haushofer illuminates the agonies underlying conventional family life, as well as exploring variations on relations between the sexes.

Throughout her work there is an extraordinarily differentiated view of female sexuality. It is not just men's incapacity to love but their different libidinal desires which make heterosexual relationships so problematic for her female characters. Thus in *Die Tapetentür* Annette longs for an intimacy with her husband which would not be merely a preliminary to genital sex. She opposes to his goal-directed love-making a plural, diffuse sexual pleasure verging on autoeroticism.

Surprisingly it is only in her first novel, *Eine Handvoll Leben* (A handful of life; 1955), that relationships between women are given more prominent treatment than those with men, and the female protagonist actively rejects marriage and motherhood. In the extended flashbacks to her convent education it becomes clear that the stirrings of lesbian sexuality were crushed by a rigidly heterosexual socialization, teaching the girls to despise their own bodies and alienating them from their own desire. More important even than the thematic treatment of lesbian love is the novel's implication that female subjectivity is only available to women in the prevailing social order as the objects of male desire.

It is this aspect of Haushofer's work which invites comparison with her more famous Austrian contemporary Ingeborg Bachmann. Having won critical acclaim as the 'new star in the constellation of German poets' with her two collections *Die gestundete Zeit* (Time on hold; 1953) and *Anrufung des Großen Bären* (Invocation of the Great Bear; 1956), Bachmann made a prose debut in 1961 that was in part a reaction against the de-politicizing reception of her poetry. In the altered critical climate of the 1980s and 1990s it is her exposure of the politics of the private, her exploration of the linguistic construction of the psyche and her radical view of the suppression of femininity in our culture which ensure her continuing prominence as the most significant precursor of second wave feminist writing.

The interrogation of masculinity and its destructive potential is already present in the early stories (collected in the 1978 volume *Die Fähre* (The ferry)), and is central to the volume *Das dreißigste Jahr* (*The Thirtieth Year*; 1961) in stories such as 'Unter Mördern und Irren' ('Among Murderers and Madmen'). The figures in these stories demonstrate that social integration is always bought at the expense of personal integrity, and that the social order is held in place by language. Hence the insights of the father in 'Alles' ('Everything'; 1961) who resists initiating his son into language, and of the male narrator of the title story that the creation of a better world depends on the creation of a new symbolic order. The two stories in *Das dreißigste Jahr* narrated from a female perspective are those which articulate the clearest resistance to cultural gender stereotypes. In 'Undine geht' ('Undine Goes'), the eponymous figure of the water nymph – herself a mythological male invention – asserts her 'otherness', not craving a human soul but calling her male lover to join her in her own element of speechlessness and fluidity. In 'Ein Schritt nach Gomorrha' ('A Step Towards Gomorrha'), Bachmann explores the possibility of love between two women in the absence of a language in which to articulate lesbian desire. It is in spontaneous, non-verbal communication that an unexpected intimacy is established, and only in the semi-consciousness of approaching sleep can some alternative to the existing binary order be envisaged.

The most devastating and complex portrayal of the 'eternal battle' between the sexes to emerge from this period is undoubtedly Bachmann's unfinished *Todesarten* (Ways of death) trilogy. The fascination of the one completed novel *Malina* (1971) lies in the fragmented identity of the narrator/protagonist, which has clear resonances with late twentieth-century theories of the subject as a linguistic and cultural construct. Far from a conventional narrative, the text includes dream fantasies, musical motifs, operatic 'recitative', prophetic and fairy-tale passages, the last incorporating the utopian dimension of the novel: the vision of a time beyond the deadly antagonism of gender difference. However violent her nightmare visions of the slaughter of the feminine in patriarchal culture, this ideal of absolute, unconditional love, depicted most clearly in the radio play *Der gute Gott von Manhattan* (*The Good God of Manhattan*; 1958), is the single feature separating Bachmann from the feminist writing of the 1970s, in which all such hope seems to disappear.

Formal innovation: from Surrealism to *écriture féminine*

One of the many features of *Malina* which invites feminist interpretation is its focus on language as both collective phenomenon and structure of the individual psyche. Whilst Bachmann was perhaps the first to relate such ideas so specifically to a critique of patriarchy, she was not alone among women writers of her time in beginning to explore the aesthetic consequences of new notions of identity and the self. These include a wide range of writers, from those influenced by French Surrealism or the Austrian avant garde to those, like Marie Luise Kaschnitz, schooled in the German classical tradition.

Kaschnitz began her writing career in the 1930s, but it is no coincidence that her literary reputation since the war has been based on her poetry, rather than on her autobiographical and theoretical prose which charts an astonishing aesthetic development. She moves from an absolute faith in the transforming power of love and the stability of individual identity to a position of radical doubt in the integrity of the subject. Her immediate response to the collapse of German society in 1945 was to affirm the self as the single remaining certainty in a dislocated world, as in *Menschen und Dinge 1945* (People and things 1945; 1946). By the early 1960s, in *Dein Schweigen, meine Stimme* (Your silence my voice; 1962) and *Wohin denn Ich* (Whither I?; 1963), this confidence had been replaced by a belief in the self only as a textual construct. Her view of femininity also undergoes remarkable revision, from the opposition of archetypal female experience to male politico-historical experience still seen in *Griechische Mythen* (Greek myths; 1943) and *Engelsbrücke* (Ponte Sant'Angelo; 1955), towards a more universal notion of political *engagement*, reflected in her poetry cycles 'Tutzinger Gedichtkreis' (Tutzingen poems) and 'Hiroshima', both included in *Neue Gedichte* (New poems; 1957).

Her characterization of *Frauendichtung* (women's poetry) in 1957 (Kaschnitz et al., Frauendichtung', 1958, pp. 59–63), focusing on mythological aspects of women's love-poetry, contrasts with the more formal reflections on 'feminine writing' in the essay volume *Zwischen Immer und*

Nie (Between always and never; 1971), in particular when she considers her own preference for the immediacy of the diary form in the novel *Das Haus der Kindheit* (The house of childhood; 1956). Indeed, it is the destabilizing, interpolated narrative of this fictionalized autobiography which accounts for the plurality of possible psychological interpretations. The female narrator's experience of re-living her childhood in the mysterious 'H.D.K.' has been read as a successful Jungian voyage of self-discovery, but is also open to Lacanian interpretation as a disturbing account of female identity acquisition. Kaschnitz's stories and radio plays also call into question linear notions of individual identity and human history. The plays 'Spiel vom Kreuz' (Play of the cross; 1953) and 'Tobias oder das Ende der Angst' (Tobias or the end of fear; 1961) both challenge received ideas about causality and progress.

A non-teleological understanding of human development is central to the story 'Spiegelgeschichte' ('Mirror Story'), printed in *Der Gefesselte* (*The Bound Man*; 1953), for which the Austrian Ilse Aichinger won the prize awarded by the *Gruppe 47* for outstanding new writing in 1952. Aichinger's concern with the problematic relationship of language to the self is made explicit in theoretical terms in 'Meine Sprache und ich' (My language and I; 1968) and *Schlechte Wörter* (Bad words; 1973). Initial reception of her first novel *Die größere Hoffnung* (*Herod's Children;* 1948) was muted, its disorientating blurring of the boundaries between dream and reality, victim and oppressor, apparently saying little to contemporary readers struggling to come to terms with the reality of the Holocaust.

Her political statement 'Aufruf zum Mißtrauen' (Call for suspicion; 1946[4]) also stands out from the pathos of the contemporary discourse of German guilt, with its focus on the moral ambivalence of human subjectivity, rooted in the structures of language itself. Whilst some of the stories and plays of the 1950s can be seen as a direct response to the war and post-war reality, her writing becomes increasingly abstract and challenging in its interrogation of meaning. Unlike Franz Kafka, with whom she is often compared, her prose narratives since the 1960s rarely acquire the firm contours of an allegorical world. The surreal images of the texts in *Wo ich wohne* (Where I live; 1963) or *Eliza Eliza* (1965) have the multiple associations of poetry and the autonomy of painted figures, prompting from one critic the epithet 'Austrian Chagall'. Visual images such as the kaleidoscope or the medieval frieze are also central to Aichinger's aesthetic statements, implying the decentring of textual meaning.

A more radical challenge still to conventional reader expectations is offered by the non-narrative prose of Aichinger's compatriot Friederike Mayröcker. Influenced by French Surrealism, Dada and Constructivism, her texts are governed by a dream logic which confounds all notions of a rational perceiving subject. Thus in *Larifari. Ein konfuses Buch* (Larifari. A confused book; 1956), the narrating subject of 'Schöner Garten' (Beautiful garden) shifts in and out of the familiar landscapes it lovingly evokes. The subjects of 'Mythologische Stücke' (Mythological pieces) are female figures such as Medea, Ariadne and Nausicaa, giving vivid, sensual expression to their transgressive, unending desire. The power of love occupies a central position for Mayröcker as for Bachmann, Aichinger, Haushofer, Kaschnitz and others, but as both the inspiration of literature and the raw material of the text itself. In the 1980s she herself used the terms 'verfehlte Liebko-sung' (misdirected caress) and 'platonischer Coitus' (platonic sex) to describe writing as a textual act of love, and leading one critic to designate her poem 'Rosenfragment' (Rose fragment) as 'écriture érotique'.

The difficulty of categorizing Mayröcker's work has doubtless contrib-uted to her critical neglect. Similar uncertainties surround the position of writers whose work crosses national and linguistic boundaries such as Claire Goll and Unica Zürn, in addition to the fact of being overshadowed by the more prominent Yvan Goll and Hans Bellmer. Of an older genera-tion than Aichinger, Mayröcker, and Hertha Kräftner, they form a link between this experimental post-war Austrian women's writing and its roots in the European avant garde. Having published extensively in the 1920s, both in her own right and in collaboration with Yvan Goll, after his death in 1950 Claire Goll devoted herself to editing and translating his work into German, becoming known herself in Germany for stories such as 'Chinesische Wäscherei' (Chinese laundry; 1952) and the autobiographi-cal novels *Der gestohlene Himmel* (The stolen Heaven; 1962), *Traumtänzerin* (Dreamdancer; 1971) and *Ich verzeihe keinem. Eine literarische Chronique scanda-leuse* (I forgive no one. A scandalous literary chronicle; 1978). In an uncom-promising infringement of the taboo surrounding mother-love, the first two document the tortures of cruelty and sexual humiliation at the hands of her mother, which drove her brother to suicide at the age of sixteen. The highly specific hatred of her mother extends to a more generalized miso-gyny in the final volume, set against the literary stylization of her mar-riage to Yvan Goll, an idealized union of souls in which her own literary talent and sexual desire are virtually effaced. Long dismissed by women readers and feminist critics alike, her work in its conscious enactment of conventional definitions of femininity can be read as a defiant gesture, which throws into sharp relief the limited range of contradictory positions open to women of her generation (see Littler, 'Madness', 1997).

Unica Zürn, who left Berlin to live in Paris with the artist Hans Bellmer in 1953 and always published first in German, then in French translation, was better known in France as an artist, and exhibited her work alongside that of Hans Arp, André Breton, Marcel Duchamp and Man Ray at the last major Surrealist exhibition at Galérie Cordier in 1959. However, she continued publishing in Germany, not merely experimenting with Surrealist imagery, but recording in the text *Der Mann im Jasmin* (*The Man of Jasmine*; 1966, published in Germany 1977) the progression of her own mental illness. *Dunkler Frühling* (Dark spring; 1969, published in Germany 1977) is the more controlled but equally disturbing autobiographical narrative of a young girl's psycho-sexual development, including her mother's attempted sexual abuse, rape by her brother, and prefigures the manner of her own suicide.

In addition to the thematic link with the *Krankheitsberichte* of the 1970s, 'sickness reports' in which physical symptoms are construed as a form of resistance to female socialization, there is also in *Der Mann im Jasmin* and in the dream-like text 'Das Weiße mit dem roten Punkt' ('The Whiteness with the Red Spot'; 1959) a utopian vision of union with a reconstructed, unaggressive masculine 'other', comparable with the angel evoked in Hertha Kräftner's 'Beschwörung eines Engels' (Conjuring up an angel; 1950), who combines the sensual and reproductive qualities required in both sexes to ensure the survival of the race.

The extraordinary subject matter of Zürn's prose is matched by the virtuosity of her *Anagrammdichtung* (anagram poetry), which seeks every possible variation of meaning in a single sentence, working to discover the 'meaning behind the words'. In *Der Mann im Jasmin* this poetry is described as both the product of intense concentration and the spontaneous articulation of her body, whilst Hans Bellmer described it as as 'new unity of form, meaning and emotional state'. Doubly marginalized by the rationalist, male discourses of post-war literary criticism, her work is now finding recognition as one of the most original expressions of repressed femininity in the post-war cultural order.

The 1960s: the myth of emancipation

Recent sociological research has done much to qualify the myth of the 1960s as a golden age of women's emancipation, with the availability of the contraceptive pill and labour-saving devices in the home. There was still no doubt as to whose labour was being saved and who bore primary responsibility for childcare. Until 1977, article 1356 (1) of the Federal Republic's legal code still allowed women's paid employment outside the home only in so far as it could be reconciled with their conjugal and domestic duties. Gender issues were not high on the political agenda until the end of the decade, the radical journal *Kursbuch* devoting a volume to women's social position for the first time in 1969.

The principal concerns of women writers who started publishing in the sixties were largely the same as those of men: the critique of materialism, of the affluent society, and of the failures of democratic and social restructuring since the war. The socially critical and politically engaged mood of the time is captured in the documentary *Protokolliteratur* of Erika Runge, co-founder of the *Werkkreis Literatur der Arbeitswelt* (Working Group on Literature of the Workplace) and member of *Gruppe 61* along with Gisela Elsner and Angelika Mechtel. The *Bottroper Protokolle* (Bottrop protocols; 1968) and *Frauen. Versuche zur Emanzipation* (Women. Attempts at emancipation; 1970) document the optimism and disillusionment of the decade, confirming, as Runge's postscript points out, the lack of progress which had been made towards women's liberation.

The alienation of individuals through work is the theme of Helga Novak's early prose, its detached reportage-style narrative reflecting the depersonalizing effect of the industrial environment. Her short stories in *Aufenthalt in einem irren Haus* (Sojourn in a mad house; 1971) identify the free market economy and the corruption of big business as destructive of individual consciousness, working with clichés to expose the linguistic abuse of power. The literary debut of Novak and Renate Rasp coincided with the demise of *Gruppe 47*. Rasp scandalized its last meeting in 1967 with her explicit poetry, and was dubbed 'the Amazon with the evil eye' for her satirical attack on bourgeois family life in the novel *Ein ungeratener Sohn* (A Family Failure; 1967). Her poetry collection *Eine Rennstrecke* (A racetrack; 1969) posed a challenge to West German norms of decency, as did the outrageous *Chinchilla* text (1973), which aimed to present marriage as a form of legalized prostitution. All notions of romantic love are absent, sexual relations merely veiling male acts of violence encouraged by women's masochistic complicity.

Equally uncompromising in its grotesque exposure of the uglier side of West German middle-class prosperity is Gisela Elsner's *Die Riesenzwerge* (The Giant Dwarfs; 1964). *Der Nachwuchs* (The young ones; 1968) bears comparison with Rasp's *Ungeratener Sohn*, as a critique of the nuclear family, whereas *Das Berührungsverbot* (Touching forbidden; 1970) exposes the brutal reality of the 1960s sexual revolution, in a world still structured by class and gender hierarchies. Whilst her later novels *Abseits* (*Offside*; 1982) and *Die Zähmung* (The taming; 1984) focus specifically on women's oppression in the nuclear family, Elsner herself was vehemently opposed to being banished to what she saw as the 'literary ghetto' of *Frauenliteratur*. Her stand on this issue in the early 1980s is a telling response to the continuing critical prejudice against women writers such as Elsner, Mechtel and Gabriele Wohmann, whose writing fails to conform to conventional expectations of 'feminine' style. Their resistance to contemporary definitions of femininity is expressed in a rejection of harmonious language and conciliatory narratives, but also of the notion that women bear responsibility for interpersonal relationships and the survival of the human race.

Where issues of identity and relations between the sexes are addressed by these writers, they lack any positive sense of the 'otherness' of femininity, often appearing merely to reproduce cultural stereotypes of gender identity. Barbara König still enjoys little recognition for her novels *Das Kind und sein Schatten* (The child and its shadow; 1958), *Kies* (Gravel; 1961) or *Die Personenperson* (The personperson; 1965), all centrally concerned with the search for identity. Her playful treatment of social clichés and gender stereotypes lacks sociological or psychological analysis, and thus identifies no potential sites for change. *Die Personenperson* never addresses the origin of the protagonist's incompatible personalities, nor how they relate to the imaginary, unified identity of 'Nadine'.

Gabriele Wohmann focuses relentlessly on the functioning of oppressive social mechanisms in the private sphere, representing personal relationships in terms of the most brutal generalities. As with König, however, it is often difficult to determine where parody ends and reproduction of clichés begins. The novel *Abschied für länger* (A final farewell; 1965) is the story of an unsatisfactory affair between the female protagonist and an older, married man. The obsessive reiteration of inconsequential detail signals the abundance of what remains repressed and unsaid, both in their relationship and in the narrator's consciousness: even what appears to be an attempt to murder her lover is repressed beneath her masochistic self-deception.

The title story of the volume *Ein unwiderstehlicher Mann* (An irresistible man; 1966) constructs a stereotypical female academic, tormented by sexual jealousy and observing the unattainable object of her desire from the 'sterility of her college life'. Wohmann's representation of lesbian love in the story 'Eine großartige Eroberung' (A fantastic conquest), in the same volume, both reproduces the absurd cliché of lesbian relationships based on an extreme heterosexual model, and exposes satirically the incompatibility of contemporary definitions of masculinity and femininity.

Whilst there can be no denying the prominence of women writers emerging in the 1960s, few of them gained the lasting recognition of Gabriele Wohmann, and her reputation is not due in the main to feminist readings of her work. In the political climate of the 1960s, gender difference was subordinated to class difference to such an extent that even its women writers lost sight of what can now be seen as the more radical impulses of the 1950s. Instead of asserting and positively reappropriating qualities traditionally associated with femininity, the women politicized by the students' movement were understandably more concerned with effacing gender difference to achieve political and economic equality. The lasting literary achievements of these years can be found, however, in the exploration of productive tensions between the critical and the utopian moment in women's writing. These include the rejection of oppressive limitations on female self-realization, and the reluctance to renounce traditionally feminine values such as the commitment to love and peace, tensions encapsulated in the words of the Austrian poet Christine Lavant: 'Sag mir ein Wort, und ich stampfe dir / aus dem Zement eine Blume heraus, / denn ich bin mächtig geworden vor Schwäche / und vom sinnlosen Warten' (Just say the word, and I will stamp / a flower for you out of the cement, / for I have grown powerful through weakness / and waiting in vain).

NOTES

1. Printed in Martin Gregor-Dellin (ed.), *Die Botschaft hör ich wohl. Schriftsteller zur Religion*, Stuttgart: Kreuz Verlag, 1986, pp. 16–27.
2. Marie Luise Kaschnitz, Ilse Langner, Oda Schaefer, 'Das Besondere der Frauendichtung', *Deutsche Akademie für Sprache und Dichtung Jahrbuch 1957*, Darmstadt, 1958, pp. 59–76 (Langner, pp. 63–70).
3. Ilse Langner, 'Mutter Berlin an ihre Töchter', *Berliner Almanach 1947*, ed. W. G. Oschilewski and L. Blanvalet, Berlin: Blanvalet Verlag, 1947, pp. 18–30.
4. Ilse Aichinger, 'Aufruf zum Mißtrauen', *Der Plan* (Vienna) 1 (1946), p. 588.

12

GDR women writers: ways of writing for, within and against Socialism

Among the writers who returned full of hope after the war to the Russian sector of occupied Germany (which became the GDR in 1949) was Anna Seghers, the most prominent female exile. A communist since 1928, Seghers had been awarded many literary prizes and had become famous for her novel *Das siebte Kreuz* (*The Seventh Cross*; 1942), which depicted resistance to fascism and expressed the hope of a liberated, humane – which for her meant communist – Germany. The GDR welcomed her as an internationally acclaimed author who was to be a moral and literary authority both at home and abroad, whose voice was to lend support to the development of communism, and who was to help create a new socialist culture.

But the cultural politics of the GDR were determined less by Anna Seghers than by Moscow. In all Eastern bloc countries, Socialist Realism, originally promoted by Stalin in the 1930s, was raised to the status of a dogma in the arts. With regard to literature, the doctrine of Socialist Realism was influenced by the literary scholar Georg Lukács. His theories of what socialist literature should be like were based on his studies of nineteenth-century French realist novelists, whose style he took as a model. According to Lukács, art was to penetrate surface appearances and portray the essence and totality of society through typical characters in typical situations, using simple forms that would be immediately accessible to the masses. Art was to mirror reality objectively and thus make visible the progression of history towards communism; this historical process, according to the Marxist world view, was one of teleological necessity and therefore already visible in its germination, especially to the mind trained in historical materialism. Lukács had developed this normative and conservative position in the so-called debate on Expressionism, in which Bertolt Brecht, as his most prominent opponent, had argued for formal experimentation as the appropriate artistic response to new problems and new realities. Seghers had taken an intermediate position, defending writers who did not conform to Lukács's views. However, in the Soviet Union in the Stalinist 1930s and later in the GDR, Socialist Realism was adopted by state functionaries and pushed through relentlessly. Once in the GDR, Seghers herself felt that she had to toe the party line. The experience of her friend Walter Janka's imprisonment for alleged counter-revolutionary activities, at which she did not raise her voice despite knowing the falsity of the accusations, may have frightened her into submission. She did write a novella in 1957 based on Janka's imprisonment, but until her death in 1983 she never tried to publish it. It appeared only posthumously, and after the publication of Janka's autobiography, as *Der gerechte Richter* (The just judge; 1990). Unable to give up her lifelong belief in socialism in the face of its perverted practice, she sacrificed her artistic integrity. In the two novels she published in the GDR, *Die Entscheidung* (The decision; 1959) and *Das Vertrauen* (Trust; 1968), and in those stories of the collection *Die Kraft der Schwachen* (1965; translated in *Benito's Blue and Nine Other Stories*) which are set in the GDR, she portrayed socialist life in the way expected of her. The traditional omniscient narrator gives the reader clear guidance as to what is good and what is evil in this allegedly realistic portrayal of typical representatives of post-war German society. The good are all the upright socialist workers who sacrifice their time, health and happiness to the advancement of socialist production. The evil are the capitalists in the West who are still nearly all fascists. Some devious people do exist in Seghers's GDR, but they confirm their wickedness by defecting to the West for purely selfish and base motives. Seghers's often noted conservative portrayal of women can be seen as an integral part of her general political orthodoxy.

Apart from conforming to party expectations of how the GDR should be portrayed in literature, Seghers also tried to support belief in socialism by means of historical analogy. She wrote stories about the eighteenth-century struggle against slavery in the Caribbean, *Karibische Geschichten* (Caribbean stories). By going back to a historical issue in which a cause can be seen, with hindsight, to be clearly vindicated and in which wrong was overcome long ago, Seghers suggests by analogy that socialism will one day overcome capitalism which is implied to be on the same level as slavery.

Within the confines of Socialist Realism, the socialist forms of industrial production were to be the main topic of GDR writing. To this end, the Sozialistische Einheitspartei Deutschlands (the ruling communist party) initiated a conference in the industrial town of Bitterfeld in 1959. There it was decided that the gap between workers and intellectuals was to be bridged from two directions: writers were to gain practical work experience on the shop floor in order to develop their capacity to write about manual labour; manual workers were to write down their experiences, helped and advised by the writers who were working in their factory.

Brigitte Reimann, who had already put her literary talent at the service of the party in her early stories *Die Frau am Pranger* (The pilloried woman; 1956) and *Das Geständnis* (The confession; 1960), was one of the many GDR writers who followed this so-called 'Bitterfeld Path' (*Bitterfelder Weg*) for a while. Her novel *Ankunft im Alltag* (Arrival in everyday; 1961) gave its name to a period of literature in the GDR. *Ankunftsliteratur* ('arrival literature') faced up to the existence of conflicts and difficulties in socialist society, acknowledged that there was still a long and hard way to go, but was confident of reaching the pre-determined Marxist goal. Yet beyond giving a name to a period in GDR literature, Reimann's novel with its clichéd language and plot, its industrial romanticism, and its simplistic faith in harmony, perfectibility and progress is rightly forgotten. While Christa Wolf's first novel *Der geteilte Himmel* (*Divided Heaven*; 1963) also belonged to this genre, it did begin to use more sophisticated literary techniques, which, however, Wolf only managed to develop fully in stories from 1965 onwards (see *Gesammelte Erzählungen* (Collected stories)), and above all in *Nachdenken über Christa T.* (*The Quest for Christa T.*; 1968). *Christa T.* succeeded in liberating itself from the doctrine of Socialist Realism and was the beginning of that part of GDR literature which would survive the dissolution of the GDR.

Wolf's aesthetic innovation and political criticism in *Christa T.* earned her a lot of praise from the West and a great deal of criticism and difficulty in her own country. In this novel, Wolf replaces the traditional plot and representative protagonist by a narrator's reflections on a friend, Christa T., who died prematurely. The friend's life story, for which the narrator draws on Christa T.'s letters and notes as well as on her own memory and imagination, is not presented as objective truth, but rather as conjecture. The author's 'subjective authenticity' (a term Wolf herself created to describe her way of writing – see the volume of essays *Lesen und Schreiben* (Reading and writing; 1972; English versions in *The Writer's Dimension*)), which manifests itself in the narrator's deliberately contemplating, evaluating and even inventing aspects of her friend's life against the backdrop of her own experience, is the decisive mediator of the fictional text. Wolf thus rejects the Marxist claim that artists were merely to mirror an objective reality. Subjectivity becomes not only the content of the novel, but also its form. Often blurring the boundaries between narrator, author and character by an ambiguous use of pronouns, the novel explores the fluidity of subjectivity rather than constructing a rigidly closed self-identical subject. Serious, reflective and questioning in tone, the narrator merges the essayistic and the fictional in her analysis of what her friend's search for identity and for harmony between the individual and society tells us about socialist society. Rather than praising the achievements of socialism as Seghers did, Wolf's novel focuses on those values which contemporary socialism rejected at its peril: individual responsibility, integrity, honesty, imagination, love, striving after the utopian absolute. It criticizes conformism, utilitarianism and cold efficiency, but never leaves any doubt that, despite these criticisms, socialism is the morally superior political system for both the protagonist and the narrator. In fact, the novel ends with the optimistic view that GDR socialism is already on its way to overcoming the shortcomings explored in the text.

Another major novel, also published in 1968, breaks with the dogma of Socialist Realism in a completely different way: Irmtraud Morgner's *Hochzeit in Konstantinopel* (Wedding in Constantinople). Morgner's previous novel, *Rumba auf einen Herbst* (Autumn rumba), had not only been censored in 1963 and 1965; the manuscript was never returned to her. Only in 1992 were pieces of this work which Morgner had integrated into other novels, together with fragments found posthumously, reconstructed into what the novel might have been. *Hochzeit*, however, passed the censor and even received great praise. The apparently unpolitical nature of the novel's theme may have contributed to making it seem harmless to the state, although its episodic open form was highly unorthodox. It involves a *Rahmenhandlung* (framework narrative) consisting of a day-by-day account of a package holiday in Yugoslavia which the protagonists Bele and Paul take as their honeymoon trip – prior to the wedding! – and, inserted in this, the nightly stories which Bele tells Paul in Sheherezadic fashion. While the *Rahmenhandlung* is already funny in its laconic narrative of incongruous details of everyday holiday life, the nightly tales often exaggerate the real into the exuberant, the grotesque and the fantastic. The novel derides narrow-minded, pedantic, bureaucratic, ambitious behaviour, without, however, commenting on it in essayistic fashion as

Wolf does in *Christa T.*, and without exploring discursively either the narrator's or the protagonist's psychological make-up. Rather, Morgner's way of privileging subjectivity consists in imaginatively transforming reality, showing us the funny side of things and leaving us to draw our own conclusions. Thus the reader has the pleasure of discovering the connection between Bele's stories and her holiday experience with Paul, the reason for Bele's leaving her lover just before the wedding, and the wider implications of this apparently private experience. The strong comic sense of this novel, carried by a laconic style and exuberant imagination, the open structure and the active role thrust on the reader break new ground in GDR literature and make this a work which is both modern and delightful.

While GDR writers had practised literary styles going beyond Socialist Realism since the second half of the 1960s, it was only in 1971, with Erich Honecker's coming to power, that the dogma of Socialist Realism was officially lifted. Honecker's famous pronouncement that there should be no taboos in literature and art, provided artists started from a firm socialist position, did lead to a more liberal atmosphere, although his conditional clause could be, and in fact was, used for the continued repression of 'undesirables'.

The more open climate in their country encouraged women writers in the GDR, at about the same time as the feminist movement was getting under way in Western countries, to measure their experiences against the promise of socialism to provide not only the equality of all men, but also that of men and women. While Anna Seghers's work had been characterized by the perpetuation of the traditional stereotypes of good mothers and bad independent women, and while the portrayal of women in the sphere of productive labour – particularly in traditionally 'masculine' jobs – had been the party's preferred image of female emancipation, women were now asking not only whether the new socialist society offered people the possibility of self-realization (as in *Christa T.*), but also what specific burdens women had to carry and whether sexual relationships in socialism had achieved a new equality.

Like their Western counterparts, GDR women writers experimented with documentary forms, for example Sarah Kirsch, *Die Pantherfrau* (*The Panther Woman;* 1973) or Maxie Wander, *Guten Morgen, du Schöne* (Good morning, beautiful; 1977), and partly autobiographical first-person narratives, tracing a quest for fulfilment, as in Gerti Tetzner, *Karen W.* (1974), and, aesthetically more complex, Brigitte Reimann's best prose text

Franziska Linkerhand (1974). Even feminist science fiction was produced, for example the stories about a sex-change in the collection *Blitz aus heiterm Himmel* (Bolt from the blue; 1975). But among these feminist-inspired texts of the early seventies, it was Irmtraud Morgner's novel *Leben und Abenteuer der Trobadora Beatriz nach Zeugnissen ihrer Spielfrau Laura* (Life and adventures of the Trobadora Beatriz as chronicled by her minstrel Laura. A novel in thirteen books and seven intermezzos; 1974) which was most innovative and influential – in West Germany too, where it was widely quoted in debates on the theory of women's writing. Morgner had created a unique hybrid: a montage novel of history and myth, documentary and science fiction, legend and fairy tale, realistic observation and fantasy. With incisive wit it created a different world from all those texts that trusted in the authority of women's individual experiences, faithfully captured. However, while the depth and breadth of Morgner's vision of the female condition and the experimental, open form of the novel were widely admired, its limitations were overlooked for some time. Morgner shared with other GDR writers of the early 1970s the conviction that only socialist countries had laid the political and legal foundations for women's emancipation and that they were morally superior to capitalist countries. Although Morgner strongly criticized sexism in the GDR, she presented it merely as a 'custom' left over from older social formations, one which would naturally disappear in the course of socialist development, rather than exploring the relationship between the paternalistic political system of GDR socialism and the patriarchal structures of private life. While criticizing some aspects of the practice of real socialism, Morgner clung to the teleological certainties of socialist theory, as is evidenced by the status of the documentary texts in *Trobadora* which confirm the cold-war division into humanitarian socialist and evil capitalist countries, thus fixing meaning rather than questioning it. The very same utopian thinking that had given rise to feminist perspectives in women's writing in the early seventies also limited its critical potential and the radicalism of its aesthetic experiment. It had inspired women to explore the shortcomings of their lives in relation to the promised socialist utopia and thus to give voice to women's marginalized perspective in literature. But it had also made them interpret their experiences and structure their texts according to the socialist model of a pre-determined historical development, thus reproducing existing patterns of closure in thinking and aesthetics.

In November 1976, the expulsion of the poet and singer Wolf Biermann dramatically changed most writers' relationship to the GDR state.

The protest of many writers and artists was suppressed by means of prison sentences and psychological pressure, in the form of open surveillance and even smear campaigns aiming at the psychological destruction of dissidents. Many writers found it impossible to continue living and working in the GDR and applied for exit visas, which were granted in order to silence criticism within the GDR. An exodus of writers began in 1977 and continued until the end of the state's existence in 1990. Among the women writers who left were Sarah Kirsch, Barbara Honigmann, Katja Lange-Müller, Christa Moog, Irina Liebmann and Monika Maron.

Those who decided to remain in the GDR had to work through their disillusionment with the state. Morgner fell into a long silence. Wolf had in 1976, prior to Biermann's expulsion, published *Kindheitsmuster* (*A Model Childhood*), arguably one of her most important novels, examining, in a fictionalized autobiography, her childhood attraction to Nazi ideology, the lasting patterns of behaviour laid down in childhood and the nature of memory. She now looked further into the past for the origin of contemporary problems. In the novella *Kein Ort. Nirgends* (*No Place on Earth*; 1979) and in her essays on Romantic women writers included in *Die Dimension des Autors* (*The Writer's Dimension*), she projects her own alienation from the state on to historical writers living around 1800, whose Romantic ideals about life, Wolf suggests, were frustrated by the utilitarian thinking which was becoming dominant with the onset of the industrial revolution.

In *Kassandra* (*Cassandra*; 1983) Wolf locates the beginning of the individual's alienation from the state even further back, at the intersection of history and myth with the transformation from matriarchy to patriarchy, which Wolf assumes to have taken place at the time of the Trojan war. Written as interior monologue in a heightened diction and rhythm reminiscent of classical German literature, the tale sets out to be as much a parable for contemporary world politics as an exploration of historical origins. Wolf develops the ideal of a model female dissident, with regard not only to GDR socialism, but also more generally to a patriarchy that has led the world to the brink of nuclear catastrophe and ecological disaster. Wolf's critique of patriarchy and her fictional endeavour to give a voice to women who have been absent from history received attention from feminists worldwide. Her conception of femininity was largely read as an attempt to deconstruct the masculine model of the closed subject and to construct a female subject beyond binary oppositions with their concomitant exclusions. What was overlooked was the fact that, as Wolf became more pessimistic about the possibility of change in the GDR, her narrative strategy aimed not so much at a recognition of the contradictions, instability and irrationality of the subject depicted in her fiction, as at overcoming negative aspects of the self in favour of a 'true' self which was then to serve as a lever for social change. Thus Kassandra in the end succeeds in raising to consciousness the whole of her unconscious formation by her society, in liberating herself completely from her social background, and in attaining a 'true' self whose value she confirms by freely choosing death rather than compromise her ideals. This 'true' self is modelled on classical, early bourgeois conceptions of the subject as noble, good and self-identical. It expresses Wolf's attempt, also paralleled in Weimar classicism, to overcome the negativity of the reality portrayed in her texts by ending them with a utopian perspective which didactically offers to her readers a positive model of meaning.

This is also the case in Wolf's diary-like text *Störfall. Nachrichten eines Tages* (*Accident. A Day's News*; 1987) which was inspired by the Chernobyl accident; in *Sommerstück* (Summer scene; 1989) which elegiacally recalls a summer with friends in which they learn to appreciate beauty (reminiscent of Schiller's *Aesthetic Education of Man*); and in her highly controversial text *Was bleibt* (*What Remains*; 1990), dealing with the writer's surveillance by the secret police. While prior to 1989 Wolf's ability to provide a positive outlook was valued as pointing the way forward, after 1989 many critics focused only on the conservative aspects of her writing. However, Wolf was more courageous and radical in her political critique, and more innovative aesthetically, than many of the other writers remaining in the GDR. But the yardstick of her critique remained the *ideal* of socialism, increasingly supplemented by the humanistic ideals of Weimar classicism. Both these sets of ideals attribute to literature the function of moral guidance, and envisage as the teleological aim of the historical process a harmonious unity between individual and society, in which the individual can realize its potential, but as a closed, self-identical subject. The events of 1989 and the revelation of the fact that Wolf had been a *Stasi* informer – though her involvement was only brief, marginal and at the very beginning of her career – but had 'forgotten' all about it, have served to highlight the fact that the implementation of such ideals requires repression and suppression, both on a social and on a personal level. This should encourage a more measured re-reading of Wolf's texts.

The substitution of one teleological system of orientation (socialism) by another (German classicism) is even more striking in Morgner's last novel *Amanda* (1983). A montage novel like its predecessor *Trobadora*, *Amanda* contains a wealth of literary forms, exploring, like Wolf's *Kassandra*, the impending nuclear and ecological disaster as an aspect of patriarchy, and positing the integration of women's experiences and feminine values into the public sphere as necessary for the survival of humanity. But here too, readers are guided in their interpretation of the (fictional) world by a utopian perspective, though this is no longer based on the authority of socialism but on that of classical authors, who are quoted extensively. Goethe in particular is explicitly named as the guarantor of a truth which anticipates a future beyond patriarchy.

While the established writers went through crises of disillusionment, new voices began to be heard. Some were sarcastic and with sharp insight (Rosemarie Zeplin); some were entertaining but harmless and naive (Christine Wolter); others served primarily a journalistic function in writing about social taboos like abortion and death (Charlotte Worgitzky), or about women's negative side (Helga Schubert), without breaking new ground in the way they wrote. Among these new voices arising from the second half of the 1970s onwards, it was the mathematician Helga Königsdorf who received most attention. Her first collection of short stories, *Meine ungehörigen Träume* (My improper dreams; 1978), was memorable for its fantastic transformation of reality. These stories on the one hand explore the repressed, unconscious part of the mind, leaving readers to draw their own conclusions from the dream images or dream-like actions. On the other hand, Königsdorf exaggerates blameworthy behaviour in satires that leave no doubt as to right or wrong. In her later work, especially in her longer story *Respektloser Umgang* (Disrespectful dealings; 1986) and her epistolary tale *Ungelegener Befund* (Inexpedient findings; 1989), she attempts a fusion of these two tendencies by demonstrating that an integration into their conscious personalities of previously repressed aspects helps the protagonists assume responsibility, not only for their own lives, but for humanity as a whole. Thus Königsdorf joins the group of GDR writers who view the function of literature as that of conscience of the nation, of teacher of ideals.

But in the 1980s there also began to appear GDR writers who attacked the repression accompanying idealism. One of the earliest and most fascinating texts of this kind – which was surprisingly also published in the GDR – was Helga Schütz's novel *Julia oder Erziehung zum Chorgesang* (Julia or education to choral singing; 1980). In the previous decade Schütz had published quasi-Schweykian stories and novels, mainly set in Nazi Ger-

many. Employing changing perspectives and association as the organizing principles, *Julia* shows (rather than tells) the reader, in vivid scenes
and images, what kind of reality has been masked behind noble ideals in
the history of the GDR. Monika Maron, none of whose work was published in the GDR although she lived there until 1988, employs Surrealism to deconstruct socialist idealism and its internalization in her novel
Die Überläuferin (*The Defector*; 1986). The techniques of the *nouveau roman*
are used by Brigitte Burmeister in *Anders oder vom Aufenthalt in der Fremde*
(Different, or on living in a foreign country; 1987). Irina Liebmann, whose
collection of short stories *Mitten im Krieg* (In wartime; 1989) also did not
appear in the GDR, tries to capture linguistically her protagonist's sense
of immobility and stasis. Writers of the younger generation like Angela
Krauß and Kerstin Hensel also discard the didactic and prophetic function of literature. Rather than pointing the reader to the future, they offer
new insights into the past and the present in stories that range from
Krauß's psychological realism in most of the texts in *Glashaus* (Glasshouse; 1988), to Hensel's interest in the monstrosity of everyday life in
Hallimasch (Honey mushroom; 1989). Although not utopian, these texts
are far from uncritical. But in giving up utopianism, they mark the end of
GDR literature, in which utopian thinking in various forms had been
dominant for nearly four decades.

13

Post-1945 women's poetry from East and West

Ways out of the rubble

The 'rubble poetry' which is most readily associated with the immediate post-war years in Germany was almost exclusively written by men. The premium placed upon the bald documentation of war and its aftermath, the naked saying of the essentials in a language cleansed and simplified, meant that the experience of men – at the front, returning from the trenches – became the dominant poetic paradigm. However, whereas this poetry served to support the myth of a fundamental post-war caesura, much German poetry (perhaps more than other genres) is striking for the continuities which established themselves across the years of the Third Reich. The 1940s and early 1950s also saw a great deal of very different poetry: much of it written by women.

There were almost no new names at first. Continuity with the pre-war years was established by the publication of the collected poems of some of the conservative poets of *innere Emigration*: Ina Seidel, Paula Ludwig and Gertrud von le Fort. Notwithstanding the highly organized mechanisms of censorship, a relatively large number of poets had been able to remain in Germany during the years of the Third Reich. After the war these poets appeared to pick up many of the debates, styles and techniques which had been current in the 1920s and 1930s. This made itself felt particularly in the dominance of traditional forms, especially the sonnet; remoteness from time and the world; religious motifs; and a preoccupation with nature as salvation.

At the time this kind of poetry was widely read and acclaimed; its striving for a universal and timeless significance and almost total retreat from empirical reality provided comfort and distraction for a people desperately evading, and 'unable to mourn', the horrors of fascism. Seidel, for example, fixed on a tradition of poetic imagery and language from the nineteenth century. Her unshakeable Protestant piety and a cult of humility and sacrifice meant that the wretchedness of the contemporary world was passed over in favour of the immanence of the afterlife. Oda Schaefer along with her friend Elisabeth Langgässer were part of the so-called 'Lehmann school' of poetry (after the poet Wilhelm Lehmann, 1882–1968), for whom the experience of nature became the source of poetic inspiration, but also a refuge where the memory of a world intact could act as a talisman against the reality around them. Seidel's 1946 collection, *Irdisches Geleit* (Earthly passage), and the later *Grasmelodie* (Grass melody; 1959) abound in images of mountain mists, larks' song and Aeolian harps. In traditional forms and with abundant use of synaesthesia and an elegiac tone she creates visions of the union of nature and soul. Langgässer was one of the best known and most respected writers in Germany after the war. Her 1947 collection *Der Laubmann und die Rose* (The leafman and the rose) fuses nature, poetic fervour, myth and symbols of Christian purity into a personal and elliptical theology.

Swiss and Austrian poetry of the period was also marked by conservative traditions. Silja Walter, Erika Mitterer, Erika Burkart and Christine Busta focus on the sufferings and longings of humankind in modest language and conventional natural imagery. Of these the most interesting is perhaps the Austrian Busta. Her first collections of the early 1950s sing of the love and mercy of God and a longing for harmony in conventional melodic tones. By *Unterwegs zu älteren Feuern* (Onwards to older fires) of 1962, her confidence in powers of salvation has given way to a darker mood of fear, melancholy and doubt, however. Humankind is presented as the 'citizens of Babel' who have not heeded, or could not comprehend, the word of God; the dominant image of ash symbolizes the dangers which threaten to extinguish the world.

Another very distinctive Austrian poet in the religious tradition is Christine Lavant. Born in a remote Carinthian village in the Lavant valley from which she took her pen-name, she grew up in extreme poverty and sickness, without a formal education. The edition published on the occasion of the fifth anniversary of her death, *Kunst wie meine ist nur verstümmeltes Leben* (Art like mine is only crippled life; 1978), gives a clue to the bleak universe of her poetry. Absence, abandonment, alienation from self, and lack are the dominant characteristics; the way to God is through martyrdom, suffering and pain. In her 1956 collection *Die Bettlerschale*

(The begging bowl) elements like the moon, earth, wind, morning star and dew are imbued with a melancholy aura of devotion and meditation. Later poetry, which continues the interest in nature, has an obsessive, confessional quality. The many minor figures which appear – witch, child, madwoman, heretic – are all decipherable as manifestations of Lavant's own isolation and suffering. Although she uses traditional forms, with echoes of Hofmannsthal and Rilke among others, it is Lavant's language which is most remarkable. It is unusual in its direct simplicity, informed at times with a bitter agitation which has been thought anarchic – even blasphemous.

Silence and the poetic word

The flight towards poetic idyll which characterized women's poetry of the immediate post-war years was made at the price of wilful historical and political ignorance. The 1950s and 1960s, however, saw a reaction against the sentiment and linguistic cliché of the early post-war years. This was precipitated, amongst other things, by Adorno's notorious polemic against 'poetry after Auschwitz'. This was not so much an embargo on poetic utterance, however, as a challenge to the insularity of a poetry which had not been contaminated by the shock of the mass-destruction. Now a new poetry was called for – adequate to its own time. Writers responded by shifting away from the poetry of experience to the poetry of reflection, strands of which were to develop into the 1970s. This process was, however, accompanied by an increasing insecurity about the role of the poet and a mistrust of the powers of poetic language. Silence became a central topos. But out of that silence came an acute awareness of the procedures of poetry itself.

Marie Luise Kaschnitz is a key representative of the paths of poetry out of the rubble of the post-war years. Her 1947 volume *Totentanz und Gedichte zur Zeit* (Dance of death and poems for the times) signalled the dawning of a belated social awareness and focused on the destruction of her home town of Frankfurt in large elegiac strophes. By the 1950s, her own commitment to her times was characterized by a ferociously honest questioning of all aspects of her contemporary world. The lyric subject appeared fragmented and threatened, and the security of rhyme was sacrificed in favour of an elliptical mode. In 'Genazzano' (1957), one of her best known and most important poems, an atmosphere of coldness and stagnation extinguishes the self in a vision of a futureless world. 'Hiroshima', another famous poem from the same collection, demonstrates her increasing anxiety and apocalyptic moods. In later works these combine with the progress towards poetic condensation and culminate in frequent compacted words like *Überallnie* (Everywherenever), the title Kaschnitz gave to her own selection of her poetry, published to mark her sixty-fifth birthday. Here her development is particularly clear: the neo-classical solemnity of her early texts seems to belong to another century in comparison with the loosened structures and the laconic, chastened vernacular mode of her later work.

For those writers who had gone into exile from the Third Reich – Rose Ausländer, Hilde Domin, Else Lasker-Schüler, Nelly Sachs – the painful meditation on the fragilities and movements of poetic language often proved even more acute. Ausländer, like Paul Celan, was born in Bukovina (now part of Romania). It was reputedly a meeting with Celan in Paris in 1957 which gave her the impetus to start writing poetry in German once more. Her homecoming in 1964, to her native language and to the poetry of Kaschnitz, Celan and Sachs, she experienced as a profound rebirth. Rhymes, regular metres and traditional imagery gradually dissolved to make way for a rhymeless poetry with irregular rhythms, striking images and a terse, closed language. Yet although problematizing the material of language, her poetry does not tend toward silence in quite the same way as that of Celan or Kaschnitz. She presents an enigmatic distillation of stages of Jewish experience – of emigration, exile and the longing for a lost geographical or spiritual homeland. In a poem 'Schallendes Schweigen' (Resounding silence) she takes up the motif of silence explicitly, but reaffirms her faith in a poetic language of remembrance and transformation, which can banish the spectre of death.

The theme of exile and return is omnipresent in the work of Hilde Domin; indeed she came to regard exile as the paradigm for the poet's position *per se*. Her poems are driven by the experience of homelessness and the nostalgia for community and sanctuary beyond time and place in a 'Wolkenbürgerschaft' (a citizenry of the clouds). For her, as for many exiles, the act of writing signifies the ultimate return home, and her 1968 volume of essays *Wozu Lyrik heute* (What purpose poetry today) demonstrates an overwhelming faith in the power of the poetic word. However, there is also a clear commitment to her contemporary world, and although her early work reflected her exposure to Spanish Surrealism during her exile in the Caribbean, *Hier* (Here) of 1964 saw a move to a much more epigrammatic style, and *Ich will dich* (I want you) of 1970 developed into a more explicitly political poetry. Domin is perhaps best known for editorial work and for her theoretical essays. Her Frankfurt poetry lectures of 1993 confirm her faith in the poetic word as an 'Augenblick der Freiheit' (a moment of freedom).

Like Domin and Ausländer, Nelly Sachs also fled the brutalities of Nazi Germany: but where they eventually returned, she chose to live in Sweden until her death in 1970. Her theme is the martyrdom of the Jewish people; the experience of persecution, suffering and murder. The locus of her work is almost inescapably 'in the dwellings of Death' (*In den Wohnungen des Todes*), the title of a 1947 collection, dedicated to 'my dead brothers and sisters'. However, she should not only be thought of as a poet of the Holocaust; for her the suffering of Israel is a paradigm of universal suffering. With recourse to language of the Bible, the Cabbala and ancient mythologies, she transcends the contours of contemporary history to create poetry embracing human and cosmic dimensions. Symbols which might be thought of as traditional are taken up and metamorphosed into mystic emblems of the spirit in ways which, at times, appear dangerously arbitrary. For her this kind of transformation offers redemption to the wanderings and suffering of the human soul. Poetry itself enacts the ultimate transformation of 'Klage' (lament) into 'Sternmusik' (music of the stars) and assumes a sacred function. But Sachs also recognized the fragility and inadequacy of language, and her late poetry becomes increasingly hermetic, compressed, and preoccupied with silence, as in *Fahrt ins Staublose* (Journey into dustlessness; 1961). Sachs was awarded the Nobel Prize for Literature in 1966, not as a German author, but as a survivor of the Holocaust, yet she belongs in a tradition which stretches from Friedrich Hölderlin in the eighteenth century, to twentieth-century poets like Georg Trakl and Sachs's friend Paul Celan, to Ingeborg Bachmann and beyond: all poets who conjure poetry out of the very limits of language and try to articulate the secret correspondences of the world.

Ingeborg Bachmann dedicated 'Ihr Worte' (You words), one of the last poems she wrote, to Sachs as 'poet and friend' in 1961. Although she published very little poetry before being overtaken by a crisis which led her away from the lyric genre, Bachmann is one of the most influential women poets of the period. Her arrival on the poetry scene with her first collection, *Die gestundete Zeit* (Time on hold) was a major media event. At the age of twenty-seven she was awarded the prize of the *Gruppe 47*, and the news magazine *Der Spiegel* ran a title story and cover photograph of her. Her work challenged the expansive consumerist thinking and restorative programmes of the 1950s by illuminating an altogether darker side of progress. Bachmann managed to create a new modern poetic language which was at once of its times yet did not obscure its roots in German tradition. Striking are the many genitive metaphors, shifting rhythms and sound-patterning. However, it is partly her linguistic virtuosity that allowed critics to miss the undertow of resignation and darkness in her work. Her second collection, *Anrufung des Großen Bären* (Invocation of the Great Bear; 1956) is structured around a number of ambiguous metaphors and shows an increased preoccupation with language as a subject. Her confidence in the utopian potential of the poetic word is indicated in her Frankfurt lectures on the problems of contemporary poetry in 1959/60, and the frequent symbols of poetic inspiration which appear in her work. But at the same time a linguistic scepticism, rooted in her studies of Wittgenstein and Heidegger, made her acutely aware of its fragility and possible contaminations. In poems like 'Nebelland' ('Fog-Land') or the celebrated 'Erklär mir, Liebe' ('Tell me, Love') it is rather isolation, loss of love and the threat to language which predominate. The links between loss of love, loss of identity, loss of language and gender are explored in gradually more disturbing variations as her work progresses. Amongst her handful of final poems 'Keine Delikatessen' (No delicacies) of 1963 records a decision to abandon the lyric mode.

That the struggle for language is also a gendered struggle is also made clear in the work of a writer whose work is unique in the period: Inge Müller. The first wife of the celebrated GDR dramatist Heiner Müller had published very little before her suicide in 1966, although a posthumous collection of her poetry published in 1987, *Wenn ich schon sterben muß* (If I have to die), has earned great acclaim. In 1945, while working as a military volunteer amongst the bomb sites, she spent three days buried in the rubble of a collapsed house, before digging out the dead bodies of her parents with her own hands. The trauma associated with this event, and her whole experience of war, become the compulsive centre of her work. It is captured in a raw, terse writing which has been influential for many younger poets, and anticipates developments of the 1980s. More than simply a direct transcription of experience, the reduction and vulnerability of the self in her poems becomes a powerful symbol for the silencing and alienation of women in history: 'Daß ich nicht ersticke am Leisesein' (Don't let me choke on swallowing my words).

UNTERM SCHUTT III[1]

Als ich Wasser holte, fiel ein Haus auf mich
Wir haben das Haus getragen
Der vergessene Hund und ich.
Fragt mich nicht wie
Ich erinnere mich nicht.
Fragt den Hund wie.

UNDER THE RUBBLE III

As I was fetching water a house fell on me
We carried the house
The forgotten dog and I.
Do not ask me how:
I do not remember.
Ask the dog how.

The poetry of revolution

The 1960s saw a fundamental paradigm shift in lyric poetry. The hermetic tendencies epitomized by Celan, but also by writers like Sachs, Ausländer, Kaschnitz and Bachmann, were now met with scepticism. Writers turned to the real, and set about recording the unpoetic experiences of the factual world. Poetry quickly developed a radical agenda. Hans Bender's anthology *Mein Gedicht ist mein Messer* (My poem is my knife) of 1961 may be taken as a useful motto for an aggressive new writing which culminated in the propaganda poetry associated with the student uprising of 1968. One interesting aspect of the new work is the renaissance of interest in *Bänkelsang* (street ballad), chanson and political song, including notable debuts by three women poets from the GDR: Christa Reinig, Helga M. Novak and Bettina Wegner.

Reinig is perhaps one of the most distinctive and underrated poets of the post-war period. Her *Die Steine von Finisterre* of 1960 (The rocks of Finisterre) contains grotesque examples of *Moritat* (broadsheet ballad), *Bänkelsang* and ballad tradition in the manner of Brecht. The ballads are laced with irony and polished parodic rhymes but also contain a strong sense of sympathy for the many social outcasts which people them: executioners, pirates, suicides, madmen. Loneliness is one of her key themes, along with the fragile belief that the poetic word can break through that isolation. Silenced in the GDR from 1951, she moved to the West in 1964, where she was influenced by the emerging women's movement. Her strong socio-political commitment sharpened into radical feminism around 1976 and her work has since become gradually both more explicit and more epigrammatic. Novak came to prominence with *Die Ballade von der reisenden Anna* (The ballad of travelling Anna) in 1963; her spare and often brutal ballad forms recall popular street forms. Like Reinig, her explicit social criticism and thematization of thwarted communication did not find favour with the GDR authorities. After expatriation from the GDR in 1966, her work in the West, although always provocative, has become increasingly self-reflexive and complex: as in her *Legende Transsib* (Trans-Siberian legend) of 1985, a resonant lyric journey through the legends and images associated with the word Siberia. Bettina Wegner, one of very few female *Liedermacher* (singer-songwriters), was prevented from performing in the East and came to the West in 1983 where she has since produced a number of records and volumes of protest songs.

'New Subjectivity', the movement which dominated German poetry during the 1970s, began as a poetic programme of the *Alltagsgedicht* (poem of the everyday) from the mid-1960s. While the 1970s saw the shift away from a vulgarized Marxist understanding of literature and a bid to rehabilitate imagination, fantasy and the utopian character of art, women's poetry of the period is conspicuous for its continuity and modulation of social concerns. Disappointed by the failure of the radical political movements of the late 1960s to address women's concerns explicitly, a large number of women explored new ways of bringing their own experience into the public domain. This was quickened by, and fed into, the emancipatory energies of the women's movement. From the middle of the 1970s onwards, poetry began to reclaim many spheres of personal experience formerly taboo, and to experiment with emancipatory forms and styles. Taboos in both East and West were challenged: fairy tales and myths were re-articulated in feminist terms; love was taken up as a vehicle for exploring the feminine consciousness; an explicit eroticism was introduced. It was perhaps this decade more than any other which established women's poetry as an independent and distinctive force in the German literary scene.

Although better known for work in other genres, celebrated writers like Verena Stefan, Angelika Mechtel, Elfriede Jelinek, Renate Rasp and Gabriele Wohmann also produced poetry which took up contemporary themes including familial and personal relationships, everyday brutality, role-playing and the search for identity. Of those who concentrated more specifically on lyric poetry, Frederike Frei's volume *Losgelebt* (Lived free) of 1977 is perhaps typical in its emphasis on aspects of the everyday life of a woman and her bid for emancipation. Karin Kiwus also fixes on the experiences of the lyric subject with laconic, often ironic, observation. Margot Schroeder, although often critical of contemporary feminism, worked at mixing fantasy and realism to vouchsafe new insights into the working lives of women, whereas Elisabeth Alexander, again an open critic of feminism, treats women's place in the social upheavals of the 1960s and beyond in blunt aphoristic style. Margarete Hannsmann, an outspoken political activist, has used her work to highlight environmental and political issues. In 1967 she began a fruitful twelve-year association with the artist HAP Grieshaber and most of her texts after that date are accompanied by illustrations or woodcuts by him.

One of the dangers of striving for an apparently artless, direct poetry of the everyday is a tendency towards cliché and triviality. Not all of the poetry of this time could rise above the banality of its origins. An exception, however, is the work of Ursula Krechel. She has produced eight volumes of poetry to date, alongside her high-profile feminist essays. Her didactic and epigrammatic debut volume *Nach Mainz!* (To Mainz!; 1977) explores a range of social and explicitly feminist concerns. Much of her work deals with the theme of women's inability to dream of a better life and to liberate themselves from the many forms of male oppression which imprison them. Her *Verwundbar wie in den besten Zeiten* (Vulnerable as in the best times) of 1979 explores individual forms of female resistance, but is notable for its more oblique manner and an undertow of disillusionment, while *Rohschnitt* (Rough-cut) of 1983 is an allegorical epic using cinematic montage techniques.

Although the dominant characteristic of women's poetry during the 1960s, 1970s and even into the 1980s was the poem of social and political comment, written with a strong subjective dimension, a number of writers developed an individual style very far from the mainstream. Never expansive or sentimental, the poetry of the Austrian Jutta Schutting (who since 1989 has become Julian Schutting) is marked by horrors of the past (Auschwitz), and the brutalities of the everyday, but also precise and vivid memories of happiness. The poems exploit the conversational and the self-consciously poetic, in order to expose and explore 'the memory of words'. Marie-Thérèse Kerschbaumer's *Neun Canti auf die irdische Liebe* (Nine cantos on earthly love), published in 1989, are love poems in a classical sense, with a rich background of literary allusions and an anarchically vital sense of *eros*. But within the disturbed syntax of the long lines one has a sense of a tentative search for identity. Ilse Aichinger's poetry is unusual in that despite the moral, even didactic tone of much of her work, she develops a highly experimental use of language. She is frequently linked with French Surrealist influences, and her attitudes to language, her use of collage and experimental techniques to expose layers of hidden meaning have earned her a reputation as a difficult poet. The 1990s, however, have seen a new interest in her work.

As a general rule those strands of 'experimental' poetry which originated in Dada and were taken up in the concrete poetry of the 1960s in the West and the underground scene of the 1980s in the GDR have traditionally attracted very few women. Two striking exceptions are Friederike Mayröcker and Elke Erb. Mayröcker's literary beginnings were linked with the avant-garde Viennese writers of the Wiener Group and concrete poetry, where she was inspired and supported by her friend and collaborator Ernst Jandl. The work which helped her to make her mark was the 1966 *Tod durch Musen* (Death by muses), a mixture of 'constellations', anti-narrative prose pieces and automatic writing. Later texts offer an eclectic mix of impulses from classical avant-garde, Expressionism, Dada and Surrealism. Even in some of the most experimental pieces, the reader of Mayröcker's texts can often construe a strong sense of a lyric consciousness and an arsenal of experience which is being processed in linguistic forms. In more recent works this aspect is even more conspicuous: Jandl has identified a number of what he calls 'self-portraits' in her 1986 volume *Winterglück* (Winter happiness), and some of the most resonant of her later texts appear to be written as a talisman against death. Central to all her work, however, is the sense of permanent movement. Her texts use collage techniques and exploit fragmentary syntax and daring associative connections to challenge dominant systems of language and thought. Inevitably the material of language itself and the act of writing become central themes.

This is also the case with Elke Erb from the former GDR, who in many ways bears comparison with Mayröcker, and has indeed edited the latter's work. Erb's *Der Faden der Geduld* (The thread of patience; 1978) presents poetic texts, supple and rhythmic prose miniatures, constellations and experimental texts of various kinds. The texts are dense and often border on the unintelligible. In a much-quoted dialogue printed at the end of the collection, Christa Wolf expresses her irritation at the hermetic nature of the texts, and Erb leads her through a reading of one striking but difficult piece, 'Memento'. The sense of following a thread and unravelling the composition of a work becomes a structural principle of her later volumes. A twenty-page text like 'Alex in M. oder Der Weg zum Ziel' (Alex in M. or the way to the goal) from *Vexierbild* (Picture puzzle) of 1983 takes Erb's 'processual writing' to its logical extreme. It lays bare the dynamics of the writing process, mixing experience, reflection, and the energies of the subconscious, linguistic games and typographical experiment and draws the reader into its own intense logic. In the GDR Erb's challenge to orthodox modes of writing put her at odds with the authorities, but inspired a younger generation of (mostly male) writers associated with the literary underground of Berlin. This again bears comparison with Mayröcker, who has exercised a considerable influence over younger poets in the West.

A contemporary of Erb who also began writing in the GDR and has developed an entirely distinctive voice and style – dubbed by a fellow poet the 'Sarah-sound' – is Sarah Kirsch. She came to prominence in the early 1960s as one of the controversial group of young poets now known as the 'Saxon school of poetry'. Although focused on nature, her work was far from the sentimental mood poetry of the early post-war years or of popular contemporaries such as Eva Strittmatter. In Kirsch's texts precise observation acts as the starting point for associative inward journeys. Although her early collections rarely touched explicitly on public issues, they nevertheless offered insights into the stresses of the private world and into the society that produces them. This brought her into conflict with the GDR authorities. A row at the Sixth Writers' Congress in 1969 centred on one of her poems, 'Schwarze Bohnen' ('Black Beans'), which fixed an everyday moment of melancholy with dead-pan humour, but was reproached for being decadent, passive and unfitting for a socialist poet. Her collections *Zaubersprüche* (Magic charms) of 1973 and *Rückenwind* (Wind at your back) of 1976 are both striking for their emotional intensity, matched with playful irony and exuberant vitality. *Zaubersprüche* is notable for its eroticism and its incantatory charm-like quality. At the centre is the figure of the witch who uses her invocation of the elements, her spells and her curses to bring revenge on a faithless lover. The second collection, *Rückenwind*, is slightly more subdued, but contains the celebrated 'Wiepersdorf cycle' in which Kirsch invokes a literary tradition for herself stretching back to Bettina von Arnim. Although there are moments of idyll, chiefly in remembered interludes of harmony in the landscape, the collection also introduces a note of spiritual desolation and symbols of an encroaching coldness which feature strongly in later collections. In 1977, under pressure from the authorities, Kirsch emigrated to the West in the wake of Wolf Biermann's expatriation. Because much of her poetry is not primarily derived from topical events, but rather from impressions of the natural world, the transition came more easily to her than to a number of other poets. Her numerous collections in the West have seen a progressive darkening of tone, as they chart the decline of a damaged natural landscape and a hunger for stability in a fractured world. This sense of dislocation finds its way into the very structure and texture of the poems, nowhere more perhaps than in her collection *Bodenlos* (Groundless) of 1996. Although she has a range of traditional forms at her disposal, her poetry is more often characterized by a sense of indeterminacy and flux. Moods shift between parody and elegy, satire and idyll. Lack of punctuation, odd syntactic shifts, frequent enjambement, collisions of nouns and phrases which may or may not be related, and the deliberate fluctuation between tenses and grammatical moods creates stylistic ambiguity which is both challenging and distinctively resonant, and has made her one of the most important German poets writing today.

Tradition and experiment

The ecological pessimism which found its way into the work of Sarah Kirsch is symptomatic of an increasing scepticism about the utopian visions of earlier decades. The late 1970s and 1980s saw a wave of poetry which chimed in with the insecurities of global politics and issued into a topos of *Abschiednehmen* or 'taking leave of a disappearing world', though with mixed poetic results. For some, lurid apocalyptic visions and a fatally dramatized rhetoric were often substituted for a serious dialogue with reality, while, for others, the pessimism brought a crisis of confidence in the legitimacy of the poetic voice. A symptomatic development can be seen in Elisabeth Borchers, whose early work was characterized by the world of dreams and children's rhymes. Her later poems warn instead of the lateness of the hour, and the collection *Wer lebt* (Who lives) of 1986 is obsessively concerned with the threat of old age and potential destruction. A much-praised debut volume of 1986 by the young writer Sabine Techel, *Es kündigt sich an* (There is a sign) offers a precise and atmospheric snapshot of the growing tensions of the period.

Perhaps because of the growing sense of menace and insecurity, the 1980s also saw a consolidation of the tradition of religious poetry written by women. Dorothée Sölle, the prolific feminist theologian, is unusual in that, as indicated by the title of her 1990 collection, *Zivil und Ungehorsam* (Civilian and disobedient), hers is also an explicitly political poetry, which does not shy away from confronting religious belief with the social issues of the day. More often, as in the work of Erika Burkart, Christine Busta, Silja Walter, Eva Zeller and the Czech émigrée Olly Komenda-Soentgerath, there is, instead, a mystical sublimation of concrete reality. Burkart, for example, writing from self-imposed isolation in rural Switzerland since 1948, has produced some fifteen collections cataloguing her love for the local people, her native moor and its myths and fairy-tales. Proceeding from traditional rhymed verse to unrhymed irregular hymns, her most recent collections are informed by reflections on time, the threat of technology, death and a mystical belief in the divine totality of nature.

Inevitably, perhaps, the instability of recent years has provoked a return to traditional forms and the apolitical stance of the immediate post-war years. In part no doubt also as a reaction to the prosaic banality of the 1970s, writers like Ulla Hahn, Doris Runge, or Karin Kiwus have developed a highly-wrought culture of form and feeling. After her successful 1981 collection *Herz über Kopf* (Heart over head) sold 40,000 copies, Hahn went on to become the most commercially successful poet of the 1980s. In the process, however, she split critics into two distinct camps. Her fans praise her craft, the virtuosity of her play with the formal canon of German tradition, her deft echoes of any number of writers from Goethe to Brecht, and her concentration on the traditional theme of poetry: love. Her critics claim that hers is a derivative rehearsal of the canon. She re-uses the classical forms – from folk-song to rondo – and borrows a rhetoric from the eighteenth century without noticing how these have changed in the intervening years. In any case, it is clear that her interest is in euphony; the inconsistencies and irritations of reality and history leave no mark on her language. Her *Unerhörte Nähe* (Extraordinary closeness) of 1988 is filled with 'the blissful music of blackbirds and old masters'.

Against this backlash, the 1980s also saw the continuation of the political impetus of the 1960s and 1970s. Writers like Krechel, Hannsmann, Novak, Reinig, Wohmann and Angelika Mechtel, for example, continued to publish, although almost all have grown slightly more oblique and self-reflexive. In the GDR, writers born in the 1940s like Christa Kožik, Christiane Grosz or Brigitte Struzyk problematized their divided experience as woman, mother, worker and writer and introduced controversial themes like abortion and suicide. This was coupled with a search to reclaim historical models and to re-create an alternative feminine tradition. The empathy with the natural world so often seen in volumes from the 1970s developed into an explicit questioning of technological progress, often expressed as equivalent with the patriarchal. In particular, the volumes by Grosz – *Blatt vor dem Mund* (Mincing words) – and Struzyk – *Leben auf der Kippe* (Life on the edge) – were important in offering a trenchant review of reality with an explicitly female consciousness.

In East and West a number of much younger writers have also established distinctive voices, often with smaller independent publishing houses. In the West the over-riding tone is one of diffidence and anxiety. All, one senses, are defensive about the possibilities of writing at all and use a bleak irony to guard against the possibility of sentiment. Brigitte Oleschinski's debut volume *Mental Heat Control* of 1990 mixes scientific language in a surrealistic flow of striking images. The Austrian Evelyn Schlag also concentrates on the technical trauma of the modern times and the search for self-realization. In laconic texts, with strong images, she explores both the female body and the deformations of patriarchal language. Eva Christina Zeller presents brief texts fixed in a single striking moment, but often with dark or violent overtones. Bettina Wiengarn, Barbara Maria Kloos, Sibylle Klefinghaus, and Liobe Happel, although their individual diction is very different, all focus on recognizable facets of the everyday but with an overt and sometimes brooding sensuality. Also of note is Meta Merz, who was born in Vienna in 1965 and died at the age of twenty-four. Her one posthumously published collection, *erotik der distanz* (erotics of distance) enacts a struggle to bring the precarious transitions between states of waking and sleeping to language in spare prosaic forms.

In the former GDR the bid for emancipation was taken up in even more radical form by poets like Uta Mauersberger, Annerose Kirchner, Elisabeth Wesuls, Gabriele Eckart, and Jayne-Ann (formerly Bernd) Igel. The loss of illusion amongst this generation brought a fundamental sobriety to the poetry which, for the most part, has continued beyond the *Wende* of 1989. Fairy tales were subverted; the lyric subject was often undermined, unmasked or withdrawn altogether; love poetry became dominated by themes of loss, division and violence. There developed a growing awareness of the nuclear threat, and a readiness to turn to larger issues, including the subject of poetry itself. This becomes most explicit in Kerstin Hensel, who, along with Kathrin Schmidt also reintroduced the sonnet form, and particularly the complex sonnet cycle, as a remarkable counterpoint to the atomization of experience. The sonnet is not, however, used in the spirit of conservative restoration (as with Hahn, for example): rather it enacts the struggle between order and the forces of disintegration brought to bear upon it. While Schmidt's recent poetry has continued with its intensely metaphorical and sensual – even visionary – explorations of female experience, Hensel's poetry since 1989 has become sparer and more overtly political. Pointed and experimental in form, her *Angestaut* (Pent up) of 1993 includes bitter reflections on the process of unification.

Besides Hensel and Schmidt, there were a large number of other women writers and artists on the margins of the underground GDR scene of the 1980s, who, as a rule, have received far less critical attention than their male counterparts, for example Róža Domašcyna, Raja Lubinetski, Annett Gröschner, Gabriele Stötzer(-Kachold). Since 1989, Stötzer in particular has gained a reputation as a provocative feminist writer, although her work clearly owes much to models from the early 1970s. Her harrowing prison experiences in the GDR are central to her first text *zügel los* (rein less) but this and her subsequent text *grenzen los fremd gehen* (bound less going astray) are as much concerned with liberating the self from the bonds of pre-ordained sexual norms, rationality and the rules of language. Concentrating on the body as locus of an emancipatory aesthetic, she combines political radicalism with a stream-of-consciousness style and a sometimes rabid denunciation of patriarchal systems. The most interesting of the young writers to emerge since 1989 is probably Barbara Köhler, fast gaining a reputation as one of the most significant poets of the contemporary German scene. She has produced two collections, *Deutsches Roulette* (German roulette) of 1991, which reflects amongst other things on the events of 1989, and *Blue Box* of 1995, which takes its title from cinematic techniques. Her work demonstrates marked formal variety, from the sonnet and rondo to characteristic 'box' poems and long cycles of dense and rhythmic prose. Köhler acknowledges a debt to the German literary tradition (particularly Hölderlin and Bachmann) and writes with a clear knowledge of contemporary feminist and psychoanalytic theory. However, her reflection on borders, rivers, mirrors and the figures of myth and fairy tale, are – perhaps first and foremost – reflections on the workings of poetry itself: 'Bilder ohne / Rahmen, Entwürfe ohne Maß, die geheime Zerstörung / der Proportionen' (Pictures without / frames, blue-prints without measure, the secret destruction / of proportions).

One of the most distinctive aspects of women's poetry since 1945 is the extent to which younger women have cultivated and drawn strength from a tradition of women's poetry. There are a large number of references to, and quotations from, Romantic writers; others again look to mystics, to writers from other traditions like Sylvia Plath, but also closer to home, particularly to Else Lasker-Schüler, Inge Müller, Nelly Sachs and Ingeborg Bachmann. A number of writers have edited selections of poetry or anthologies of respected forebears and have been active in rescuing others from obscurity. The school of feminist criticism which has so shaped our understanding of post-war women's prose writing has, however, made fewer inroads into the poetry of the same period. Although some individual writers have been the subject of critical analysis, there is a marked absence of useful work on many poets who are clearly worthy of attention. This could well be because poetry as a genre is more resistant to the kind of sociological or theoretical bent which has marked much feminist work. Equally, the conventional poetic interests of women (religious poetry, landscape and love), which have remained a constant since 1945, do not necessarily appear to lend themselves to a progressive critical agenda. A large number of women have also worked to consolidate traditional forms and conventional understandings of the lyric subject. Perhaps, as women struggled for so long for the opportunity to realize an authentic sense of self and articulate an individual voice in their work, they are more reluctant (in this genre at least) to risk that self in the playgrounds of the postmodern. As always, however, great poetry demands risks. The work of the most significant and exciting women poets of the post-war period enacts the struggle between tradition and progress and speaks distinctively of, and out of, its own time.

NOTES

1. Inge Müller, *Irgendwo; noch einmal möcht ich sehn: Lyrik, Prosa, Tagebücher*, ed. Ines Geipel, Berlin: Aufbau, 1996, p. 16. We are grateful to the Aufbau-Verlag for permission to reproduce this poem.

14

Feminism, *Frauenliteratur*, and women's writing of the 1970s and 1980s

The 1970s and 1980s saw the emergence of women's literature in a new key: not just in the generic sense of literature written by women authors or the conventionally gendered sense of literature written for a female audience, but feminist in a political sense. This was a body of literature that was programmatically woman-identified, yet at the same time challenged the very notion of woman by which it was defined. A series of interrelated, though not synchronous, events map the terrain: the formation of a new feminist politics in the context of the women's movements of the late sixties and early seventies, the publication of new forms of writing by women that both recalled previous traditions of women's literature and submitted these traditions and the gender assumptions on which they relied to critical scrutiny, and the emergence and gradual institutionalization of feminist literary scholarship in the late seventies and early eighties. What these events shared was an ultimately utopian vision of social transformation that included, but did not stop at, gender; a commitment to work towards such ends from the perspective of women's interests; and a view of culture as a primary site of feminist struggle and change.

What this alternative world would look like, how we would get there, and who 'we' were: these were the questions that constituted the grounds of debate. As they were taken up in the literary texts of a new generation of women writers, a body of literature was produced that both perceived itself and was perceived as, from the very outset, political. In the 1970s and 1980s, German-speaking women writers in the Federal Republic, Austria, and Switzerland explored such issues as the concept of self, the relationships between texts and bodies, language and sexuality, through the prism of women's experience.

The difficulties posed by this reassessment lay in the need, on the one hand, to construct a separate public sphere based on the assumption of female difference; and the simultaneous need, on the other hand, to deconstruct the very bases of gendered structures. The tension between such different positions, and the differing needs they addressed, marks the development of women's literary production and feminist scholarship in these decades.

One obvious set of historical markers for the period of contemporary German feminist writing and *Frauenliteratur* is 1968 and 1989 – the date that symbolically marks the revolt of the generation that came of age after World War II, and the year the Berlin Wall was opened up, marking the end of the divide between West and East Germany. Each of these events had significant consequences for women. However, in terms of gender there was an important structural difference between 1968 and 1989. In the wake of the movements spawned by the events of 1968 – which included, crucially, the women's movement – gender was put on the national agenda. The year 1989 and the events that followed marked a decisive shift in this regard. For even as the effects of German unification intensified still existing social, political and economic inequalities between men and women, gender as an issue of sustained public concern was eclipsed by what were officially perceived to be more pressing issues.

The call of the 'sixty-eighters', as they were known, was to break with the past and create alternative structures. This call carried special resonance for women attempting to speak and write in a new voice and make themselves heard in the public sphere. Moreover, the specific form of the generational rebellion of the late sixties and early seventies was particularly suited to the expression of women's concerns and the development of feminist cultural practices. The emphasis on personal experience as a valid source of knowledge and political agency encouraged the development of writing that reconceptualized and realigned concepts of the personal, the political, and the theoretical. In this respect, the work of writers otherwise as diverse as Verena Stefan, Marie-Thérèse Kerschbaumer, and Christa Reinig mark the emergence of a feminist writing practice in which the attempt to express women's experience from the inside out, as it were, gave rise to new forms of representation. Furthermore, the insistence on the need to create new expressive forms in order to free oneself from old ways of seeing, thinking and feeling encouraged experiments with language based in women's physical and social worlds, beginning with the female body. Sometimes, as in the work of the playwright and performance artist

Ginka Steinwachs, who elaborated a concept of expressive pleasure and dramatic tension located in women's bodies, this meant pushing language to the very limits of its ability to function as a communicative medium. At other times, as in the work of the Austrian writer and playwright, Elfriede Jelinek, it produced narratives in which the eruption into language of a hitherto silenced body (for example, the body of a woman being raped) explodes the decorum of convention by which the romance narrative works to obscure the violence that often underlies it, as for example in *Lust* (1989). Finally, the critique of the family as a primary locus of authoritarian structures and their reproduction validated the so-called private sphere – love, sexuality, domestic life and relationships – in its mundane dailiness as not just 'women's issues' but as matters of serious consequence.

An early example of such new experiments in writing are Margot Schroeder's novels *Ich stehe meine Frau* (Standing our ground; 1975) and *Der Schlachter empfiehlt noch immer Herz* (The butcher still recommends heart), published a year later. Both novels are set in Schroeder's own Hamburg working-class milieu. In *Ich stehe meine Frau*, Charlie, a working-class woman who works part-time at minimum-wage jobs and full-time at home for no pay and scant respect, becomes active in a tenants' initiative to create a safe playground for the resident children, and in the process becomes politicized herself. The second novel follows a similar plot line: Ola's involvement in a campaign to create a battered women's shelter leads her to realize the everyday forms of violence that mark her own family life at home. Schroeder's female protagonists tell their stories in their own voice; their narrative is supplemented with images (photographs, drawings and cartoons) that complement and comment on the events narrated. For women like Charlie and Ola, where their children can play or how to get the grocery shopping done before the mandated shop closing time of 6.30 p.m. are as much political issues as who the shop steward is or whom to support in the local elections. In both cases, the novels trace the coming to feminist consciousness of a woman as she struggles to balance the competing demands of her various roles: mother, worker, partner, lover and public citizen. The questions of who she 'really' is and what she wants 'for herself' are raised, but suspended as untimely; there is too much to do here and now.

Central to what some called the 'cultural revolution' of 1968 was the concept of a 'revolution in language'. Translated into the literary realm, this meant new forms of writing by new subjects in new voices. Yet, as compelling as this agenda was in theory for women, in practice it proved difficult to enact. Women, too, it turned out, were deeply invested in existing structures even when this investment served them ill. Moreover, the creation of something new was not only difficult but risky. So the dilemma remained of trying to find a language that was authentic and true *for them*.

On one point, however, feminist thinkers and writers, no matter what their differences, agreed: true female subjectivity was an experience for which there was as yet no language. As Verena Stefan put it in the foreword to *Häutungen* (*Shedding*; 1975), when she tried to write about her experience as a woman, 'bin ich wort um wort und begriff um begriff an der vorhandenen sprache angeeckt' (p. 3; every word, every idea I expressed collided with conventional language). No wonder, then, that the first anthology of German feminist theory to deal with issues of representation, Gabriele Dietze's *Die Überwindung der Sprachlosigkeit: Texte aus der neuen Frauenbewegung* (Overcoming silence: texts from the women's movement; 1979) bore the mandate to work on language in its title.

Among women writers no one represented the burden and challenge of this mandate more powerfully than Ingeborg Bachmann, in many ways the defining woman writer of her time. An inspiration for later feminist writers, her works relentlessly probe the issues that defined the agenda of women writers, feminist activists and literary scholars in these years. The relationship between writing and the body, history and gender, and the search for a usable language are all thematized in her novel *Malina* (1971), the first published instalment of her projected trilogy, *Todesarten* (Ways of death). Indeed, as much as Bachmann can be seen as the defining writer of her time, *Todesarten* is the paradigmatic work of literature. For the three parts of this triptych – *Malina*, *Der Fall Franza* (Franza, a case study; 1978) and *Requiem für Fanny Goldmann* (Requiem for Fanny Goldmann; 1978); of these only *Malina* was completed and published during her lifetime – are a sustained reflection on women's silence, its causes, consequences and forms, and an impassioned quest for new ways of speaking. Whether in private (particularly in their relationships to men) or in public engagements with power, women, Bachmann argued, seldom speak out; and when they do, they are even more seldom listened to. Their silence is thus a sign at once of passivity and of victimization. Bachmann highlights the tension between these different forms of silence by having the woman who is victimized and made an object of abuse on the level of plot tell the story and thus assume subject status on the level of narration. *Malina*, for example, tells the story of the relationship between three people, a woman and two men (one of whom, the title figure, Malina, is the woman's male alter, or super, ego). Divided within herself to the point that she does not have an actual self, the narrating woman (who, throughout the text, is never named) finally disappears into the wall. Invisible and silenced, she has become a thing that is both gone and still there, a literal embodiment of the uncanny. 'Es ist etwas in der Wand, es kann nicht mehr schreien, aber es schreit doch' (p. 355; there is something in the wall, it can't scream any more, and yet it does scream): thus *Malina* concludes.

If *Malina*, the intended first volume of the trilogy, focused on gender relations, *Der Fall Franza*, which was Bachmann's planned coda to *Todesarten*, addressed the imbrication of race and gender in German history. The protagonist, Franziska ('Franza') Ranner, comes from the Galician periphery of Austrian society; her husband, Professor Leopold Jordan, is a prominent Viennese physician. Yet, under the surface of his successful career and the glamour of their lifestyle is the barely submerged history of his involvement in Nazi medical experiments and euthanasia programmes. Now he experiments on Franza, plying her with psychotropic drugs and recording her reactions. Attempting to flee, first to Galicia, then to Egypt, Franza realizes that the murderous social policy of eliminating 'undesirable' life has gender as well as race dimensions. And what is more, this text, like all of Bachmann's work, suggests, it is a policy and a stance that did not end with Nazism.

In many ways, *Der Fall Franza* prefigured the very questions that, by the end of the 1980s, were to become defining German concerns: the meaning of racialized foreignness and ethnicized Germanness in terms of one another. The Turkish-German writer Emine Sevgi Özdamar's first collection, *Mutterzunge* (*Mother Tongue*), which was honoured with the Ingeborg Bachmann prize in 1989, is a case in point, representing a shift in focus that could be said to mark the end of this period of German women's writing much as *Malina* marked its beginning. In 1971, *Malina* gave literary form and a critically gendered inflection to the questions that Bachmann had raised programmatically in her inaugural lectures in the newly appointed chair of poetics at the University of Frankfurt a decade earlier (1959/60): how can we find a language and aesthetic forms adequate to the task of expressing the moral, social, and political issues of our time, and what will become of us if we don't find them? Özdamar's text, published in 1990, resonates with the continued urgency of these questions, but the agonistic despair of Bachmann's struggle with language gives way, in *Mutterzunge*, to a play with myriad possibilities.

Like Bachmann's texts, these stories can be read as a narrative about cultural displacement and hybridity, language and foreignness, tradition and modernity. The limitations of a concept of Germanness bounded by assumptions of German ethnicity, Christian values and Western culture were also keenly felt by women writing from *within* the bounds of normative Germanness: within their work, too, the difficulty of feeling at home in German was consistently thematized. Bachmann's Franza, for example, feels more 'at home' in the Egyptian desert than in Vienna or Galicia, while in *Malina* the female protagonist is left without any place to go; even, at the end, without language. Even though she is at home – in Austria, Vienna, and the apartment that is objectively hers – subjectively she belongs nowhere.

By contrast, Özdamar's female protagonists are neither homeless nor speechless. Whereas Bachmann's protagonists, like the author who created them, had, in the end, to disappear, the protagonists of *Mutterzunge*, though classed as foreigners in passport terms, are, like Özdamar herself, at home in more than one language and place, moving *between* different worlds and defining themselves in the freedom of this movement. Thus, in a noticeable departure from the stance that had defined German literature for two generations, the narrative perspective and historical starting-points of this text are not post-war, but post-colonial.

On the level of issues addressed thematically, *Malina* and *Mutterzunge* also point to some of the changes that took place in the landscape of German culture in these years, in relation not just to gender, but to race and ethnicity as well. For if, at the beginning of the seventies, 'women's writing' referred almost exclusively to the work of women writing from within – even if against – the normative mainstream of ethnically German and western European culture, by the end of this period, from around the mid-eighties on, a critical mass of new writers like Jeanette Lander (American-German-Jewish), Saliha Scheinhardt (Turkish-German), Libuše Moníková (Czech-German), TORKAN (*nom de plume* of the Iranian-German writer, Torkan Daneshfar-Pätzoldt), Herta Müller (Romanian-German), and Irena Brežná (Slovak-Swiss), had begun to challenge the hegemony of this cultural norm and explore its limitations.

Like the new German feminism, the new German women's literature of the seventies and eighties emerged for the most part out of the Left, both the university-based student movement informed by Marxist principles and the community-based cultural activism of socialist and social-democratic labour groups. The initial impulse was to document the lives of those who had been disenfranchised – the poor, the working-class and (as feminists added) women – and legitimate them as carriers of social, political and cultural authority. This combined effort of documentation and legitimation was to inform not only much of the new women's literature produced in these years, but also the better part of feminist literary history and criticism. Early texts included Ulrike Meinhof's short essays and polemics, *Die Würde des Menschen ist antastbar* (The dignity of human beings is violate; 1968), and Erika Runge's *Bottroper Protokolle* (Bottrop protocols; 1968), interviews with mostly working-class men and women that document the ways in which wage labour and family life create a web of interlocking dependencies that simultaneously sustain and entrap. From these beginnings, a body of documentary literature emerged that set out to map the topography of women's lives. Runge's *Frauen* (Women; 1970), interviews with seventeen German women between the ages of fourteen and eighty-four, not only recorded the ways in which women tell the stories of their lives, it measured the discrepancy between the ideal of emancipation and the experience of discrimination. Marianne Herzog's *Von der Hand in den Mund. Frauen im Akkord* (*From Hand to Mouth. Women and Piecework*; 1976) followed suit with a documentation of women's industrial piecework. Shortly thereafter, Herzog was instrumental in the publication of the first literary contribution by a woman to the emergent body of writing initially classified as *Gastarbeiterliteratur*, Vera Kamenko's *Unter uns war Krieg* (There was war between us; 1978). This 'Autobiography of a Yugoslavian Woman Worker', as the subtitle announced, traces Vera's life from her childhood and adolescence in Yugoslavia, through her sojourn as an industrial migrant worker in Germany between 1969 and 1976, to her final imprisonment for manslaughter in the beating to death of her child and her resulting deportation back to Yugoslavia. Written in several forms of German, from Herzog's editorial 'corrections' and introduction, to the 'broken' German of Kamenko's own writing, this text called into question the definition of what an appropriate literary language is, and what – or whom – it excludes.

That these questions had bearing not just for women like Vera Kamenko, for whom German literary language was foreign in virtually all respects, but for German women writers overall, is documented by the volume of work on the relationship between language, literary form and gender produced by both women writers and feminist scholars in this period. The question of how women told the stories of their lives, in what forms and to whom, led to a critical review of established genre categories. Were documentary literature, autobiographies and letters inherently 'subliterary' genres, or had they been classified as such to maintain a gendered and class-based hierarchy of literature?

The scope of this inquiry called for the resources of a broad and intersecting set of disciplines, including, most centrally, literature, history, philosophy and psychoanalysis. With their systematic attention to the relationship between language, identity and power, both the work of the French psychoanalyst Jacques Lacan, and the work of French feminist theorists (for example Hélène Cixous, Luce Irigaray and Julia Kristeva), whose works became known in Germany in the mid to late 1970s, played a formative role in the development of theoretical models for a feminist analysis of texts and critical reading practices. A specific focus of attention within German feminist circles, notably among artists, writers, and literary and art critics, was the question of whether there was such a thing as a feminine aesthetic, a way of expressing oneself, whether through writing, composing or painting, that was particular or even unique to women. The resulting debate generated some of the best and most original work to be produced within the field of German feminist theory. Significantly, Gisela Ecker's edited volume of essays from this debate, *Feminist Aesthetics* (1985), is still the only collection of German feminist theory to appear in English.

Answers to the questions raised by – and about – women's writing could only – or best – be found, women argued, if they had their own space in which to explore them. And while the radical feminist dream of a separate women's culture was not only unrealizable, but, for most, even undesirable, an alternative system for the production, distribution and reception of women's writing and feminist thought was fairly quickly put in place. By the early 1980s a remarkably autonomous and extensive network of feminist presses, journals, printers, distributors and archives, women-only bookstores and women's centres had been established, connecting women across Germany and internationally. In 1974 the first (and soon to become major) German feminist press, the Munich-based *Frauenoffensive*, was founded. A proliferation of new journals, most community-based, though some commercial, like the feminist magazine *Emma*, played a key role in the development of feminist theory and a women's cultural public sphere. Some journals were popular, others scholarly; some, like the evocatively named *Wissenschaft und Zärtlichkeit* (Science and intimacy), already envisioned a world in which new ways of being would transform what we think of as scholarship.

The degree to which writing and language were considered critical to an emancipatory politics for women from the outset is reflected in the fact that several journals, such as the Münster-based *Mamas Pfirsiche – Frauen und Literatur* (Mama's peaches – women and literature), or the Bremen-based 'Frauenliteraturzeitung' *Schreiben* (Writing) were dedicated entirely to the exploration of these issues and, as such, were venues for the publication of innovative new work, both scholarly and creative. At the same time as the basis for an alternative infrastructure of textual production was being laid, groups of women were organizing themselves locally, regionally, nationally and beyond, to explore together what 'writing as a woman' might mean. Thus, in 1976 the first 'meeting of women writing' took place in Munich, while the second Berlin Writers' Congress that year was organized around the theme 'Frauen in der Literatur' (women in literature).

The emergence of this new body of women's writing was paralleled by the production of a new body of feminist scholarship. The first of what was to become a pacesetting series of conferences on women's writing was organized in Hamburg in 1977, resulting in publications that mapped a new terrain of German feminist literary scholarship. Among the most influential series in this respect were the special issues on feminist scholarship published from the early eighties on by the Argument-Verlag. In 1978 the first anthology of German women writers, *Deutsche Dichterinnen vom 16. Jahrhundert bis zur Gegenwart* (German women poets from the sixteenth century to the present) appeared, edited by Gisela Brinker-Gabler, to be followed, a year later, by the publication of the first book-length work of feminist literary scholarship in Germany, Silvia Bovenschen's *Die imaginierte Weiblichkeit* (Imagined femininity; 1979). From 1983 onwards, the combined newsletter and journal *Frauen in der Literaturwissenschaft* (Women in literary studies), began to appear regularly. Compiled by a student and faculty collective at the University of Hamburg, it provided German feminist literary scholars with vital networking information as well as a public forum for debate and the dissemination of new scholarship.

One of the issues that became a focus of debate around this time was the meaning – and function – of the term *Frauenliteratur* itself. While some wondered whether women's writing – particularly when it was not only *by* women *for* women, but *about* 'women's issues' – could ever free

itself from the stereotype of *sentimentale Trivialliteratur* and saw it as politically anodyne in contrast to the emancipatory impulse of *feminist* literature, others saw it mainly as a marketing strategy designed to attract and
mollify women readers. As evidenced by the fact that within a few years
most of the major West German commercial presses had introduced
paperback series in this new field, *Frauenliteratur* certainly filled a marketing niche. However, as feminist literary scholars like Sigrid Weigel pointed out, the advent of the new women's writing from around the
mid-1970s on equally undeniably marked a break with the traditional
mould of German literature.

In this respect, the work of women writing in the 'other Germany', the
GDR, at this time played an important role in the expansion of the concept of *Frauenliteratur*. For, appearing in the West as soon as (sometimes
before) they were published in the East, works like Irmtraud Morgner's
virtuosic montage-novel, *Leben und Abenteuer der Trobadora Beatriz nach
Zeugnissen ihrer Spielfrau Laura. Roman in dreizehn Büchern und sieben Intermezzos* (Life and adventures of the Trobadora Beatriz as chronicled by her
minstrel Laura. A novel in thirteen books and seven intermezzos; West
publication 1977), Maxie Wander's collection of interviews, *Guten Morgen,
du Schöne. Frauen in der DDR* (Good morning, beautiful. Women in the
GDR; West publication 1978), and Christa Wolf's retelling of the story of
Cassandra and the Trojan War, *Kassandra. Erzählung* and *Voraussetzungen
einer Erzählung. Kassandra* (*Cassandra. A novel and four essays*; West publication 1983), astounded and delighted feminists in the West with their bold
and unapologetic assumption that women were – and had a right to claim
their place as – subjects of history. Thus, while GDR women writers certainly acknowledged what Christa Wolf had described as 'die Schwierigkeit, "Ich" zu sagen' (the difficulty of saying 'I'), they simultaneously
insisted on the possibility of remaking the world here and now.

Frauenliteratur, in short, embodied the contradictions of feminism
itself: for while it was conventional in terms of its continued faith in an
Enlightenment-based emancipation aesthetics (writing as a means of
'finding one's self'), it simultaneously broke with this convention by
defining emancipation in female terms. The subject of history in the new
Frauenliteratur was, at least narratively, reconceptualized.

In this respect, as the Swiss feminist literary scholar Erika Tunner proposed, perhaps the more interesting question was not what *Frauenliteratur*
was, but what it did to our reading practice. Its significance, in other
words, lay less in the gender of the writer than in the gendered position

from which we read. In this light, the basic definition of *Frauenliteratur* as literature by women writing *as women* had to be expanded to include the equally critical dimension of reading from a gendered position.

What all this might mean was put to the test by a small, pocket-size paperback published in 1975 by the Frauenoffensive press, Verena Stefan's *Häutungen (Shedding)*. This text, defined generically as 'Autobiografische Aufzeichnungen Gedichte Träume Analysen' (Autobiographical jottings poems dreams analyses) tells the story of a young woman (the barely disguised autobiographical persona of the author) in contemporary Berlin, her feminist activism and coming-to-consciousness through her dysfunctional encounters with men and growing intimacy in relationships with women. In the process, she begins to explore what and who she wants to be under the layers of socialized femininity. At the end of the text, the protagonist is alone, but at peace with herself. The success of *Häutungen*, which became a virtual cult book within the new German women's movement, marked it as exemplary within an emergent body of texts that blended the confessional, the testimonial, and the programmatic around the narrative construction of a female 'I' known as *Identifikationsliteratur*. The expected identification of the woman reader with – and as – this 'I' was based on the assumption that, as women, she and the narrator inhabited the same worlds, socially and psychologically. The goal of this literature was to render the truth of women's lives, with 'truth' defined less in terms of 'what really happened' than in terms of 'what it felt like' in a given woman's experience. The success of texts like Karin Struck's autobiographical novel *Klassenliebe* (Class love; 1973), Angelika Mechtel's short stories *Die Träume der Füchsin* (The dreams of the vixen; 1976), or Brigitte Schwaiger's bestselling novel *Wie kommt das Salz ins Meer* (*Why is there salt in the sea?*; 1977), was a measure of their ability to convey this subjective dimension compellingly.

Texts such as these were as much part of the general shift in German literature of the 1970s towards what was hailed as the 'New Subjectivity' as they were part of the new feminist politics of solidarity among women, autonomy and self-discovery. What distinguished feminist *Identifikationsliteratur* from the general literary trend at the time towards subjective self-analysis was the degree to which it politicized subjectivity – what it means for a woman to say 'I' – within the broader framework of women's history. To the extent that it linked self-discovery and activism, feminist *Identifikationsliteratur* was thus commonly seen as the literary embodiment of the new feminist politics. Its political intent was clear: to affirm and legitimate women's experience. The challenge lay in translating this intent into practice without unwittingly falling back into conventional antithetical gender categories.

This question of sexual difference – whether it really existed, where it came from, how it was constructed, and what effects it had – was the defining issue not only for feminist thinkers of this time, but also for women writers. Among the latter, few grappled with this question as doggedly as Christa Reinig, who continued to probe the assumptions underlying 'man'/'woman' constructs until she pushed them over the edge in the form of satire. *Entmannung* (Unmanning), which appeared in 1976, is Reinig's *tour de force* in this regard. This novel, a dizzying mix of historical psychodrama-cum-modernist-narrative-cum-radical-feminist-manifesto, tells the story of the surgeon Otto Kyra ('Herr Profes-sor Doktor... Playboy und Chirurg') and the women who surround him: Doris (Dr. Dankwart), assistant to Kyra at the clinic; Menni (Klytemnes-tra von der Leyden), mad housewife and mother of unruly sons; and Thea (Gutsman), the embodiment of whorish femininity. As they engage, amidst shifting alliances, in struggle, seduction, war and play (with other figures, from Freud and Hitchcock to Valerie Solanas, entering the fray at times), it becomes evident that they are all, without exception, playing roles. But, Reinig reminds us, it is a play for life or death. This is the point of departure of *Der Wolf und die Witwen* (The wolf and the widows), a collection of short stories and essays by Reinig published in 1979. The opening short story, 'Die Witwen' (The widows), a sketch of which had appeared in *Entmannung* as a nightmare fantasy of Otto Kyra's, responds to the questions the women in this earlier text had raised as to whether men were either necessary or permissible, and hypothesizes a radical solution. In 'Die Witwen' the men are wiped out by a fatal, viral Y-chromosome attack, leaving the women to their own devices. What would the world – and we – be like without our gender constraints, Reinig's texts muse. Who knows, they respond, but it is worth finding out. What is more, and here the black humour of Reinig's satire turns deadly serious, we fail to do so at the risk of our own survival.

To know what freedom from gender constraints might mean would require understanding the degree to which gender marks not just who we think we are, but how and what we think. As feminist scholars looked for clues to such understanding in the history of women's writ-ing, literature by women that had been forgotten or thought lost was rediscovered, reissued and reassessed. Texts like Bettina von Arnim's bold interventions in the political culture of her day, *Dies Buch gehört dem König* (This book belongs to the King; 1843) or Hedwig Dohm's 1894 novella, *Werde, die Du bist* (Become yourself), were reprinted, while more recent women's literature of the post-1945 period was reread for its pre- or proto-feminist resonances. At the same time as feminist scholars began their revisions of literary history, women writers went about the business of reimagining women's lives. In *Die neue Sophie, oder Der Beginn einer längst fälligen Gattung der Literatur* (The new Sophie, or the beginning of a long overdue literary genre; 1972), Ursula Erler presented a female *Bildungsroman* in which the 'new' Sophie, unlike her conventional counterpart in Rousseau's classical *Emile*, rejects her role as the subordinate other to the normative, male subject. In Erler's version, Sophie is the subject of her own story. In *Was geschah, nachdem Nora ihren Mann verlassen hatte* (*What Happened After Nora Left Her Husband*), presented first as a play on stage (1977/78) and then on radio (1979), Elfriede Jelinek took up the story of Nora where Ibsen left off and continued it as Nora might have shaped it. Christine Brückner's *Wenn du geredet hättest, Desdemona: Ungehaltene Reden ungehaltener Frauen* (*Desdemona – If You Had Only Spoken! Eleven Uncensored Speeches of Eleven Incensed Women*; 1983) adopted a similar strategy, rewriting history by imagining how it could have been otherwise had women had their say; the German original begins with Christiane von Goethe, the poet's wife and former mistress, talking to his former mentor and companion, Charlotte von Stein.

At issue, in part, in these revisions of past women's work was a question of particular urgency to the generation of 1968, namely how to conceptualize the 'political' from a women's perspective. *Vorabend* (The night before; 1975), the first novel of the Swiss writer Gertrud Leutenegger (published the same year as *Häutungen*, by her compatriot, Verena Stefan), thematizes this question on the level of plot. On the eve of a major demonstration, a young woman charts its course by walking its projected route. As her meanderings through different streets trigger memories from her past, she ponders the meaning of political agency for someone like herself, torn between the conflicting pulls of solidarity within groups and her need for autonomy as a woman. These are the dilemmas the narrator struggles to resolve.

Writing as a member of the new cohort of Swiss women writers who began publishing in the 1970s and thus added a cultural presence to their recent enfranchisement in the political public sphere (Swiss women were only granted the right to vote in 1971), Leutenegger is representative of her generation in yet another way, namely in her insistence on the importance of literature as a counterforce to the press of prevailing exigencies. This is precisely the ground on which the avant-garde staked its claim. Arguing that language is not a window onto experience, but an aesthetic rendering of experience, writers and artist-theorists like Ginka Steinwachs, Eva Meyer, Elfriede Jelinek and Friederike Roth countered the attempt to discover female-specific forms with an attempt to deconstruct 'woman'. Friederike Roth's 1983 novel, *Das Buch des Lebens* (The book of life), is a reflection of the ways in which 'experience' is unavoidably always, in part, a reinscription of ourselves into the already-written – 'everything that's always been written about love, here it is again, freshly stolen', is how Roth describes her novel. In her plays, meanwhile, she works with open drama forms to explore the dynamics of male/female relationships, as in *Klavierspiele* (*Piano Plays*; 1980) or the possibilities of women's self-realization, for example in *Ritt auf die Wartburg* (*The Donkey-Ride*; 1981). Toward the same ends, the Austrian Elfriede Jelinek creates a dramatic montage form in her plays, juxtaposing dramatic text with intertextual allusions to create new possibilities of interpretation.

This strategy of disjunctures is, of course, not without risk, for the logical conclusion of such dislocation is madness. In this sense, the reception of the avant-garde writer Unica Zürn on the part of West German feminists in the 1980s may be seen as symptomatic. Simultaneously experimental and autobiographical, Zürn's work became an important point of reference for German feminist readers and literary scholars in this period, embodying the search for a radical break with the bounds of realist conventions and signalling a shift in emphasis in women's writing, from the communication of women's experience to a deconstruction of the very categories on which the previous agenda had been based.

Thus the work of this generation of women writers and feminist scholars was defined by the dual impulses of *construction* – of a space in which women could be free to fully know and express themselves – and *deconstruction* – of the structures that stood in the way, from social institutions through modes of representation to conscious and unconscious structures of feeling. In the process, several issues emerged as defining sites of debate: the relationship between aesthetic structures of representation (including language and conventions of narrative) and the embodied experience of gender; the difference between what men and women have done (and what has been done in their name) and the bearing this difference has on what 'history' means and on how we experience agency and responsibility; who is counted as 'German', on what grounds, and the consequences of the exclusions.

Obviously, these issues and debates overlap, with each new work readjusting the focus. In Anne Duden's long prose narrative *Übergang* (*Opening of the Mouth*; 1982), for example, the focus is so tight (we are, narratively speaking, inside the body of an injured woman) that all else, even things directly related to the injury – like the issue of race in post-war Germany – fade into chimerical vagueness. In Jutta Heinrich's *Das Geschlecht der Gedanken* (*The Gender of Thoughts*; 1977) or Elfriede Jelinek's *Lust* (1989) a similiar telescoping on bodily trauma has much the same effect: the world virtually disappears. And while this focuses our attention, it also blinkers our view. It is perhaps for this reason that some writers like Ingeborg Bachmann, Marie-Thérèse Kerschbaumer, and Erica Pedretti created narratives in which voice and perspective continually change. Pedretti's *Valerie oder Das unerzogene Auge* (Valerie or the untrained eye; 1986) is a fitting case in point. Valerie is the object of the gaze of her lover, Franz, who obsessively paints the progression of her cancer; at the same time, Franz is the object of Valerie's gaze, as she watches him flee from the vulnerability he fears into the safety of images; finally, through it all, she watches herself being watched. She is body and image, subject and object, all at once; the self that is Valerie – or 'I' – lies in the balance.

Other works widen the focus to an almost panoramic scope, as in the case of the Austrian writer, documentarist, and textual scholar Marie-Thérèse Kerschbaumer. In her monumental work on women in Austria during the years of Nazi rule, *Der weibliche Name des Widerstands. Sieben Berichte* (*Woman's Face of Resistance. Seven Reports*; 1980), Kerschbaumer employs a combination of documentary research and fictional reconstruction to tell the story of Austrian fascism from the perspective of different women. Similarly, Elizabeth Reichart, in *Februarschatten* (*February Shadows*; 1984), revisits the past of war and Holocaust from the perspective of two women as a daughter's insistence on knowing her mother's life gradually draws out the repressed memories of violence that the latter had witnessed in the war and been complicitous in covering in silence. Rahel Hutmacher's *Tochter* (Daughter; 1983) tells its story of the daughter from the perspective of her mother; in contrast to the dominant accusatory or recriminatory mode in German-language literature of this post-war generation, this is a story of love, separation and reconnection between a parent and her child from symbiotic infancy to respectfully separate adulthood.

Finally, the question of who we are and what it has to do with the history of the places we pass through – the localities of our birth, displacement or settlement – is thematized in the work of writers like Jeanette Lander and Herta Müller. The Slovak-Swiss writer Irena Breźna thematizes the attractions and anxieties of the encounters between people culturally foreign to one another and the degree to which such foreignness is often cast in racial terms. In *Die Schuppenhaut* (Scaling skin; 1989), for example, the narrator tells the story of her involvement with a man with psoriasis whom she meets doing research for a study on this illness. While the issue of race is not raised explicitly in this text, in contrast to Breźna's subsequent collection of stories and essays, *Karibischer Ball* (Caribbean ball), it is metaphorically expressed in the focus on skin as a marker of otherness. At the end of the narrative in *Schuppenhaut*, the man with psoriasis turns into a reptile and slithers off, while his lover returns to her 'normal' life with husband, job and children.

Taken as a whole, German women's literature of this period of feminist organization and debate is marked by a particular kind of energy: often passionate, sometimes wild, with little in the way of humour or contemplative calm; there is anger and an often despairing undertow.

The difficulties this generation of women writers faced were immense. They were also time- and place-specific. On the one hand, there was the historical difficulty of finding a way out of the particular nexus of gender and Germanness established in reaction to Nazi history, with its limited categories of either victim or perpetrator. The result is a body of literature marked by violence of all kinds. Indeed, the perversions of violence are played out in these texts as a theme with infinite variations, from the quiet madness of the protagonists in the work of Angelika Mechtel, Ingeborg Bachmann or Unica Zürn; through the sadistic fury unleashed in the narratives of Jutta Heinrich, Anne Duden or Elfriede Jelinek; to the final withdrawal in death – typically, that of the female characters.

On the other hand, there was the strategic difficulty of finding a new language in which to simultaneously write women as subjects *into* literary discourse and free women *from* the constraints of gender. This dilemma remained largely unresolved. Recourse to existing formulae and conventional tropes (with woman-as-innocent-victim-at-the-hands-of-men by far the prevailing one at this time) was as predictable as it was common. At the same time, there is a wide variety of experiments with new subjects, new genres, new ways of writing, reading and producing literature.

It is too early to determine the extent to which this generation of women writers produced literary works of enduring value. Perhaps, though, this is not important. For beyond this or that individual work that will succeed in speaking for its time and place in a voice that carries over to other times and places elsewhere, what is most significant and historically memorable about this period is the richness and energy of feminist cultural production: the formative and often transformative work of women writers, artists, film-makers, scholars, publishers, bookstore and distribution collectives, together with the network of other projects specifically for women, such as women's refuges and counselling centres, coffee houses and health projects, that had an enduring impact on the possibilities of women's lives.

15

Women's writing in Germany since 1989: new concepts of national identity

Literary reactions to the *Wende*

The surprising turn of the East German 'revolution' was linguistically captured in the term *Wende* (turning point), a term coined by East Germans which subsequently became common currency to describe the events of 1989 and 1990 in the GDR. The *Wende*, the failure of the 'revolution' to institute an alternative 'third way', left the GDR's intelligentsia confused and frustrated. Leading writers like Christa Wolf, long revered as spokespersons for their generation, were astounded by the chasm suddenly separating them from the populace and were forced to confront the fact that they had deluded themselves about their leading intellectual role in GDR society. More importantly, the ongoing revelations about corruption brought home the realization that even writers critical of the government would have to examine the degree to which any stance short of outright dissidence had helped sustain East Germany's repressive system.

Attempts at *Gegenwartsbewältigung* (coming to terms with the GDR past – by analogy with *Vergangenheitsbewältigung*, coming to terms with the Nazi past) on the part of well-known writers date back to the hectic, historic days of autumn 1989. Significantly, these first ventures were not cast in traditional literary forms. Instead, writers like Christa Wolf and Helga Königsdorf turned to shorter, more immediate genres, such as the essay, letter and interview, as they struggled to process the impressions, thoughts and emotions aroused by the unprecedented succession of events that would ultimately topple the communist regime. Thus volumes such as Christa Wolf's *Im Dialog: Aktuelle Texte* (In dialogue: contemporary texts) and *Angepaßt oder mündig: Briefe an Christa Wolf im Herbst 1989*

(Conformity or maturity?: Letters to Christa Wolf, autumn 1989) and Helga Königsdorf's *1989 oder ein Moment der Schönheit* (1989 or a moment of beauty), *Aus dem Dilemma eine Chance machen* (Making an opportunity out of the dilemma) and *Adieu DDR: Protokolle eines Abschieds* (Adieu GDR: protocols of a parting), all published in 1990, document the euphoria, confusion, frustration and disillusionment of two loyal socialists convinced of the viability of a socialist renewal.

Two further volumes, *'Die Geschichte ist offen.' DDR 1990: Hoffnungen auf eine neue Republik* ('History is open'. GDR 1990: hopes for a new republic) and *Gute Nacht, du Schöne: Autorinnen blicken zurück* (Good night, beautiful: women writers look back), offer the reactions of a broad array of women writers to the demise of the GDR. Appearing within one year of each other, in 1990 and 1991 respectively, these collections document the abrupt change in mood that characterized the GDR in this period. The obvious allusion of the title *Gute Nacht, du Schöne* to Maxie Wander's influential 1977 collection of interviews with GDR women, *Guten Morgen, du Schöne* (Good morning, beautiful), further underscores the sense of finality and closure that informs the remarks of the GDR women writers who contributed to this volume.

In June 1990 Christa Wolf published *Was bleibt* (*What Remains*), a short narrative text written in 1979 and reworked in 1989, that was received extremely acrimoniously by the West German press. Wilfully misreading Wolf's first halting attempt to come to terms with the GDR past in literary form, critics interpreted this first-person narrative about a writer under surveillance by the GDR secret police, the *Stasi*, as Wolf's attempt to claim victim status for herself and thereby exonerate herself for her complicity with the corrupt SED (= Sozialistische Einheitspartei Deutschlands) state. The ensuing literary debate, known as the *deutsch–deutscher Literaturstreit*, can be read as a thinly veiled attempt to write GDR literature out of the German literary canon by totally discrediting its leading writer. Dubbing Wolf a 'state poet', the West German literary establishment's *ad feminam* attack sought to recast this committed, yet increasingly critical, socialist writer in the role of deluded handmaiden of the hated SED regime.

By consistently (mis)reading *Was bleibt* as a straightforward autobiographical text about *Stasi* surveillance, critics failed to see that Wolf's narrative in fact addressed precisely those issues which they faulted her for suppressing. Ignoring the debilitating sense of disorientation, despair, alienation and guilt which the text exudes, they remained oblivious to the fact that Wolf's writer-narrator, acutely aware both of her privileged status and of her shortcomings, is full of self-doubt. Her discomfort manifests itself most clearly in a meeting with a young dissident writer (modelled on Gabriele Stötzer-Kachold), who fearlessly and authentically articulates her criticisms of the regime, despite the likelihood of severe political reprisals, including renewed imprisonment. Confronted with this young woman, the narrator feels compelled to justify herself; yet she can only defend her privileged position and console herself through a future-oriented commitment to writing in a different, more authentic language, one free of self-censorship and rationalization.

Christa Wolf remained uncharacteristically silent throughout the *Was bleibt* controversy. Just when the media attacks had abated somewhat, she revealed that from 1959 to 1962 she had been an *Inoffizielle Mitarbeiterin* (unofficial collaborator) of the *Stasi*. In the wake of a second round of attacks, she encouraged the publication of her entire *Stasi* file, along with the public debate it had engendered. Only 117 pages of the 337-page volume *Akteneinsicht Christa Wolf: Zerrspiegel und Dialog* (A look into the files on Christa Wolf: distortion and dialogue; 1993) constitute Wolf's *Stasi* file, a document that makes clear how limited, indeed ultimately insignificant, Wolf's interactions with *Stasi* agents had been.

Wolf's decision to break the silence she had maintained since the publication of *Was bleibt* marked an important step towards confronting her GDR past. Her next major publication, in 1994, was *Auf dem Weg nach Tabou: Texte 1990–1994* (*Parting from Phantoms. Selected Writings, 1990–1994*). A heterogeneous volume comprised of essays, diary entries, correspondence and speeches, as well as the stories 'Nagelprobe' ('Trial by Nail') and 'Befund' ('Clinical Findings'), it contains several entries indicative of a painful process of self-scrutiny regarding the GDR past, analogous to Wolf's earlier confrontation with the Nazi past in *Kindheitsmuster* (*Patterns of Childhood*).

Her 1996 narrative, *Medea Stimmen* (*Medea: A Modern Retelling*), on the other hand reads more like a self-justification than a self-examination. As with her Cassandra project, Wolf again indirectly addresses contemporary political issues by historically displacing them onto classical antiquity and by psychologizing myth. In her rewriting of the Medea story, Wolf eschews the received image of Medea as child murderess, presenting her as the victim of a systematic campaign of projection and defamation on the part of the Greeks. Wolf's description of the interaction between Medea, from the 'barbarian' Eastern kingdom of Colchis, and the Western 'civilized' Greeks functions as a thinly-veiled autobiographical account of her position in the *Literaturstreit* and captures the tense East–West social relations operative at the time of the *Wende*. By unearthing the secret crime (infanticide) upon which the city of Corinth is built, the erstwhile

Colchian princess jeopardizes her position in Greek society. Perceived as a threat to the polis, Medea, who had initially been admired as the exoticized Other, is gradually marginalized and ultimately ostracized. By commemorating the fabricated story of Medea's infanticide the Greeks ensure that Medea will be misrepresented in perpetuity. Thus *Medea Stimmen* emerges as a parable of the colonization of the East by the West.

Wolf's recent collection of texts, *Hierzulande Andernorts: Erzählungen und andere Texte 1994–1998* (At home abroad: stories and other texts, 1994–1998), published in 1999, is in many ways a sequel to *Auf dem Weg nach Tabou*. Reflecting in large part her experiences in the United States during her 1993 fellowship year at the Getty Center in Santa Monica, California, the heterogeneous texts which comprise *Hierzulande andernorts* continue Wolf's ruminations on post-*Wende* Germany, documenting her profound sense of displacement and loss in the wake of the demise of the GDR, her distress at the defamatory *Literaturstreit* and her attempt to insert herself into the German émigré tradition. Drawing heavily on quotations by Brecht and Thomas Mann, Wolf warns of Germany's continued need to confront its Nazi past. While offering an important corrective to the neo-conservative stance of writers such as Martin Walser and Botho Strauss, Wolf, by stylizing herself as victim and exile of (re)unified Germany, leaves herself open to the criticism of self-aggrandizement. Yet Wolf's text makes poignantly clear the pain of those GDR thinkers currently without an intellectual home(land) and the East–West tensions still operative in contemporary Germany; her plea for broad-based tolerance and respect can be disregarded only with peril.

Since the *Wende*, Helga Königsdorf, who shares many of Christa Wolf's political convictions, has published three narrative texts and several volumes of essays. The epistolary novel *Ungelegener Befund* (Inexpedient findings), which appeared in 1989, deals with an East German academic's contemplation of his father's possible implication in National Socialism. The narrative's open ending (the protagonist learns that incriminating letters may have been written by someone else) mitigates Königsdorf's criticism, allowing her more easily to call into question the GDR's official national narrative of a radical caesura between Hitler's Germany and the GDR anti-fascist state. However, the novel's unresolved ambiguity could be seen as raising the question as to which 'committed' communist in the GDR (of a certain age) is above suspicion of having also been a committed Nazi. The degree to which people can substitute one ideology with another is, of course, also a burning issue today, as East Germans confront the need to make the transition from communism to capitalism.

Königsdorf's narrative texts *Gleich neben Afrika* (Right next to Africa; 1992) and *Im Schatten des Regenbogens* (In the shadow of the rainbow; 1993) portray the effects of the demise of communism and (re)unification on the lives of her East German characters. Echoing sentiments that Königsdorf had expressed earlier in her essays, the narrator of *Gleich neben Afrika* offers astute insights into the contemporary German scene, even as she spins a fantastic tale of adventure, passion and greed, revolving around 'laundered' money and escape to an unspoiled tropical island. Ultimately, the adventure plot serves as a convenient device that allows Königsdorf to articulate her (veiled) critique of West Germany's 'colonization' of the GDR.

Im Schatten des Regenbogens features a diverse and colourful cast of characters, forced by economic exigencies into establishing a communal household. Anxiety, depression, fear of unemployment and uncertainty about the future also unite these characters, several of whom are, or were, employed by an academic institute. Königsdorf's ironic depiction of *Abwicklung* – the ideological process, initiated by West Germany after (re)unification, by which the intellectual merits of East German academics were reviewed to determine whether they could continue in their posts – gives the text its historical specificity and its socio-critical bite. Like *Gleich neben Afrika*, *Im Schatten des Regenbogens* juxtaposes citizens of the former GDR and West Germans, with Königsdorf pitting against each other two brothers who had been separated after the war – the East German intellectual about to be *abgewickelt*, and the commissioner from the West who will determine his professional fate. By having East and West Germans confront each other in the person of these two mirror images, Königsdorf forces readers to confront their prejudices about the German Other, even as she reveals her own biases.

As in most of Königsdorf's texts, gender plays an important role in *Im Schatten des Regenbogens*. By having only the situation of the male character from the East improve, while the situation of the female characters deteriorates, Königsdorf's text accurately reflects the far more negative consequences of the current socio-political situation for GDR women, who have emerged as the real losers of (re)unification.

The playfulness and self-irony so characteristic of Helga Königsdorf's writings is utterly missing from Helga Schubert's *Judasfrauen* (Judas women; 1990). Schubert, who worked on the *Judasfrauen* project from 1985 to 1990, frames her carefully researched 'Ten Case Studies of Female Denunciation in the Third Reich', as the book is subtitled, with an autobiographical excursus in which her narrator-researcher relays how GDR *apparatchiks* sought to hamper her investigation of women's complicity in

Nazism. Such resistance was consistent with the national ideology of the GDR, whose foundation myth was posited on the notion of widespread resistance to fascism, and for whom therefore a project intent on recuperating yet more former Nazis could only be anathema. Calling her case study narratives 'parables of betrayal', Schubert encourages readers to draw connections between fascism and communism.

Although only twelve years younger than Christa Wolf and three years younger than Helga Königsdorf, Monika Maron in many ways belongs to a different generation, one too young to have consciously experienced Nazism or the foundation of the East German state. Whereas both Wolf and Königsdorf enthusiastically (if somewhat naively) embraced socialism as *the* alternative to fascism after the war, Monika Maron, as the stepdaughter of a high East German official, was weaned on communist rhetoric. Recognizing the unbridgeable gap between theory and praxis, Maron ultimately rebelled against both her authoritarian father and the state he represented. From the outset, Maron's writings have been far more overtly critical of the GDR than either Wolf's or Königsdorf's, and her first two novels, *Flugasche* (*Flight of Ashes*) and *Die Überläuferin* (*The Defector*), were suppressed in East Germany.

Maron's 1991 narrative *Stille Zeile Sechs* (*Silent Close No. 6*) juxtaposes Nazism and communism. The novel derives its force from the conflict between the 42-year-old Rosalind Polkowski, a true child of the GDR, and her surrogate father Beerenbaum, one of the founding fathers of the East German state. Projecting onto Beerenbaum her unresolved conflicts with her biological father, Rosalind enters into a life and death struggle with the infirm old man. By pressing him for information about the notorious Hotel Lux, that ostensible Soviet haven for persecuted European communists in the forties, which was in reality often a death trap, she hastens his demise. In contrast to Schubert's facile, dualistic perspective, Maron's more nuanced presentation shows how an individual can alternately be a victim and a perpetrator, or indeed be both simultaneously.

The *Wende* serves as the backdrop for an all-consuming love affair between a West German man and an East German woman in Maron's 1996 narrative, *Animal triste* (Sad animal). Narrated by the woman, whose life effectively came to a standstill when she was abandoned by her lover, the novel interweaves personal and socio-political history. While on the surface a story of obsessive love and loss, the novel also documents the working through of national and political loss, offering a gendered perspective on (re)unification.

Among the younger generation of GDR writers, the texts of Angela Krauß and Gabriele Stötzer-Kachold stand out. Krauß, who made her writing debut in 1984 with the story of a working-class woman, *Das Vergnügen* (The diversion), also published the narrative *Glashaus* (Glasshouse; 1988) and a collection of short stories, *Kleine Landschaft* (Little landscape; 1989), before making her mark on the Western literary establishment with her father–daughter narrative *Der Dienst* (The mission; 1990), for which she received the Ingeborg Bachmann prize.

Told from the daughter's perspective, the lyrical narrative of *Der Dienst* metaphorically embeds the first-person narrator's memories of her childhood within the mountainous landscape of the Erzgebirge on the GDR–Czech border. Focusing on the seemingly calm and static early 1950s, the text depicts the deluded naiveté of those years, a time when radium baths, believed to have healing qualities, were commonly administered spa treatments and when children's feet were regularly X-rayed to assure proper fitting shoes, with the dangers of radioactivity not recognized until the first Soviet H-bomb tests.

The narrator's father, often away from home on some clandestine military assignment, also turns out to be endangered. His initial enthusiasm for his post and commitment to the communist state gradually give way to despondency and alienation and he ultimately kills himself; his suicide, though, bears the hallmarks of an execution. The reasons for this are never stated; however, the timing of the death, on a military mission in October 1968, allows readers to infer that his suicide-execution is atonement for his involvement in the Soviet-led invasion of Czechoslovakia, in which GDR troops participated. As the first literary attempt to (re)address the question of the GDR's complicity in the oppression of communist comrades, *Der Dienst* marks an important step in coming to terms with East Germany's Stalinist past.

Compared to Krauß's oblique lyricism, the writings of Gabriele Stötzer-Kachold are combatively direct. Loosely connected to the literary subculture of the Prenzlauer Berg which developed in East Berlin in the 1980s, Kachold's texts combine formalist experimentation with biting political and social criticism. A courageous and outspoken critic of the SED regime, Kachold was expelled from the University of Erfurt for her anti-government activism and later imprisoned for her vocal criticism of the poet-songwriter Wolf Biermann's expatriation in 1976. Known in the GDR before the *Wende* through underground publications, illegal readings and performance art, she became known in the West only after the publication of the boldly experimental texts *zügel los* (rein less; 1989) and *grenzen los fremd gehen* (bound less going astray; 1992), which in both form and content represent a conscious affront to Socialist Realist aesthetics. Kachold's vitriolic criticism makes clear the extent to which she conceives of the GDR state as a patriarchal institution, and her texts, with their strongly autobiographical impulse, are marked by an insistence on the articulation and validation of subjective experience.

Accompanied by the author's provocatively sexualized drawings of both the male and female body, in *grenzen los fremd gehen* Stötzer-Kachold dismantles East German constructions of femininity, replacing them with an insistence on women's right to orgasmic pleasure, be it heterosexually, homoerotically or autoerotically derived. In their celebration of unbridled female sexuality, Stötzer-Kachold's texts fly in the face of the GDR's heterosexist and rather prudish sexual politics, and are among the most challenging and provocative contributions of the new generation of GDR women writers.

Another leading voice of the younger generation of East German women writers to emerge recently is Kerstin Hensel, born in 1961, and thus a member of the 'Wall generation', who, never having known the GDR as anything but a cordoned-off, insular state, experienced the stagnation, confinement and hypocrisy of East German society in ways that previous generations had not. Hensel began her career as a lyric poet, but since the *Wende* she has made her mark as a prose writer of great originality and biting social commentary.

Her first collection of short stories, *Hallimasch* (1989), met with general critical acclaim. Matter-of-factly intermingling the grotesque, fantastic and bizarre with trivial, everyday experiences of figures positioned within the specific historical context of Imperial Germany, the Nazi period and/or East German socialism, these early stories display features that have become the hallmark of Hensel's prose style. The title story, in which the twin sisters Liese and Lotte Möbius meet Hitler, derives its effect from its interface between the real and the grotesque, while in 'Grus' (Detritus) the real *is* the grotesque. The story recounts Maikel Koserczek's unsuccessful attempts to organize his fellow residents in his Leipzig neighbourhood to protest against and improve the inhumane living conditions in their attic apartments. The graphic descriptions of these attics, suffocatingly hot in summer and freezing in winter, are a biting commentary on prevalent social conditions during the last years of the GDR and might help explain why so many citizens from Leipzig took to the streets in 1989. In Hensel's story nothing changes; everything remains the same, an indication of the GDR citizenry's scepticism about the possibility of effecting change from within the system.

Hensel's more recent narrative *Im Schlauch* (The tube; 1993) deals with everyday GDR reality in the mid 1980s. Set in the fictive town of Stinopel (the GDR slang term '*Stino*' is short for *stinknormal*, stinkingly normal), it recounts Natalie Kulisch's thwarted attempt to escape the stultifying boredom of her family life. On her sixteenth birthday, Natalie decides to run away from home, and briefly occupies a dilapidated, deserted old house before ending up in a seedy theatre pub, 'Der Schlauch'. On her second day of freedom, she is locked out of her new home by the police, who inform her that the house is unsafe and will be torn down. The third day finds her back in the bosom of her family, who have not even noticed her absence. Interspersed into the story of Natalie's short-lived 'emancipation' is the narrative of her parents' life, specifically their sex life – their unimaginative, routine marital couplings being contrasted with their rather flamboyant infidelities. Switching without transition between the two narrative strands, between past and present, the text presents readers with a mosaic of several decades of GDR life. Hensel's unrelentingly perceptive gaze and her biting irony make this satirical account of life in the GDR highly entertaining.

Like *Im Schlauch*, Hensel's 1993 narrative *Tanz am Kanal* (Dance by the canal) is a testimony to the fact that it is possible to write GDR literature even after the demise of the GDR. In writing down her autobiography, the homeless Gabriela von Haßlau also recounts the history of East Germany's failed socialist experiment, documenting the corruption, cynicism and hypocrisy that led to the demise of the communist state.

Excursus: lesser-known GDR writers

By contrast with Maron, a number of women writers who were well-established in East Germany were not known to readers in the West before 1989. Often focusing on the problematic of gender relations in the GDR, their writings give the lie to the Marxist notion of the all-round developed personality, documenting how difficult it was for women to realize themselves in GDR society.

Taken together, the writings of Renate Apitz, Helga Schütz, Maria Seidemann, Angela Stachowa, Charlotte Worgitzky, and Rosemarie

Zeplin, to name but a few, present readers with a vivid portrait of the difficulties of everyday life for women under GDR socialism, thereby offering an important corrective to the official (falsely) positive image of women in GDR society, with its simplistic notions of emancipation as legal equality. In addition, writers like Renate Apitz, whose novel *Hexenzeit* (Time of witches; 1984) clearly alludes to Morgner's monumental work *Amanda, Ein Hexenroman* (Amanda, a witch novel), and Rosemarie Zeplin, whose 1990 narrative *Der Maulwurf oder fatales Beispiel weiblicher Gradlinigkeit* (The mole, or fatal example of feminine consistency) picks up motifs from Christa Wolf's *Sommerstück*, bear witness to the cultivation of a tradition of women's writing in the GDR.

In her 1995 novel *Vom Glanz der Elbe* (The glow of the Elbe River) Helga Schütz takes up the story from her 1986 novel *In Annas Name* of the twins Anna and Adam Brühl, who grew up in East and West Germany respectively. This time the narrative focus is on Adam, who returns to East Germany after the fall of the Wall to look for his sister, whom he has not seen since childhood. Using the trope of the journey, the text unfolds Adam's story, telling of his emigration to the United States and his happy familial and successful professional life there. Adam's search for Anna is of course also a quest for home, the attempt of a man in mid-life to reassess his past and to integrate that which he has rejected/ repressed back into his life.

Schütz's earlier narrative *Heimat, süße Heimat* (Home sweet home; 1992) focuses on the fate of 'ethnic Germans' in the Soviet Union, addressing the complexly intertwined issues of homeland, national identity and multiculturalism, concerns relevant for contemporary German society with the problems of assimilation faced by its own immigrant population. The work is comprised of the diary entries Schütz made on a trip to Kazakhstan in the (former) Soviet Union to research a West German television film on the life of the actor Helmut Damerius, together with an abstract of the projected film *Kasalinsk*. Like many Soviet 'ethnic Germans', Damerius was sent by Stalin to a Soviet Gulag after the German invasion of the Soviet Union, then deported to the remote city of Kasalinsk (near the Aral Sea) in Kazakhstan in 1945, where he remained until Stalin's death in 1953. In addition to problematizing notions of multiculturalism and national identity, *Heimat, süße Heimat*, like Angela Krauß's *Der Dienst*, raises the issue of Stalin's irresponsible nuclear experimentation policies (Kazakhstan was one of the areas most directly affected by Soviet underground testing). Writing after the collapse of communism, Schütz voices her criticisms directly and forcefully, taking care to relegate responsibility for these afflictions not solely to Stalin, but rather to those who refused to acknowledge what was going on around them as well. In addressing the issue of complicity, this work repeatedly draws connections between the collapsing Soviet Union and the situation in the GDR.

'Minority' women's writings

Contemporary Germany is a multicultural society. Many of the so-called *Gastarbeiter*, or guest-workers, who were brought to the Federal Republic in the 1960s from Italy, Yugoslavia and Turkey to do the West Germans' menial labour decided to settle in their new homeland, as did some of their East German counterparts from Vietnam after (re)unification. In addition to these multiethnic groups, Germany, by virtue of its colonialist and militaristic heritage, has an Afro-German population that further adds to its cultural diversity.

Both quantitatively and qualitatively, Turkish women living in Germany have produced some of that country's finest minority literature, leading to a re-evaluation of what constitutes 'German' literature. Zehra Cirak, Renan Demirkan, Emine Özdamar, Saliha Scheinhardt, and Alev Tekinay all write in German, though ironically the prose writings of the Turkish writer perhaps best known in Germany, Aysel Özakin, have been translated from the Turkish, or, more recently, from English. She has, however, written two volumes of poetry in German, *Du bist willkommen* (You are welcome; 1985), and *Zart erhob sie sich bis sie flog* (Tenderly she lifted herself up until she flew; 1986), texts that poignantly capture the dilemma of being caught between two cultures and mirror her own situation, that of a Turkish woman living in Germany.

Saliha Scheinhardt, the most prolific of these Turkish women writers and the first one to publish in Germany, has to date produced eight 'docufictional' novels, that is fictionalized accounts of case histories. Having emigrated to the Federal Republic with her German husband – whom she had met in Turkey – in 1967, at the age of seventeen and against her family's wishes, she considers the Federal Republic her 'linguistic and intellectual home' and describes herself as a 'German-language author of texts written by a generation of foreigners living in this country'. Fearing that censorship in Turkey will render her works unrecognizable, she has refused to allow her books to be translated into Turkish and thus writes for a German-speaking audience.

With the exception of *Von der Erde bis zum Himmel Liebe* (From earth to heaven, love; 1988) all of Scheinhardt's protagonists are minority women caught between two cultures. Scheinhardt began her writing career with a trilogy about Turkish women and migration. Based on fieldwork for her doctoral thesis on the role of Islam in the Turkish 'diaspora', *Frauen, die sterben, ohne daß sie gelebt hätten* (Women who die without having lived; 1983) and *Drei Zypressen* (Three cypresses; 1984) focus on the plight of Turkish women caught between repressive Islamic and patriarchal familial structures and an unwelcoming foreign environment. *Und die Frauen weinten Blut* (And the women wept blood; 1985) depicts the plight of rural women who leave their villages for the city slums, from whence they hope to follow family members who have emigrated, or hope to emigrate, to Germany as *Gastarbeiter*.

Scheinhardt has also published two fictionalized autobiographical texts, *Träne für Träne werde ich heim zahlen. Kindheit in Anatolien* (I'll pay back tear for tear: childhood in Anatolia; 1987) and a 'sequel', *Die Stadt und das Mädchen* (The city and the girl; 1993), which tells of a Turko-German woman living in Germany whose repressed childhood memories help precipitate a severe emotional crisis and who returns to her Turkish homeland in an attempt to work through the trauma. Documenting the brutality and misogyny that inform Islamic family life, these texts powerfully reiterate the criticism of repressive structures expressed in her earlier texts.

Von der Erde bis zum Himmel Liebe is unusual in having a male figure at the centre of the narrative. Set in Ankara during the military *Putsch* of 1980, this portrait of a male Turkish resistance fighter is a tribute to the Turkish writer and publisher Ilhan Erdost, who was tortured to death by the military junta. Scheinhardt's sympathetic portrayal of the protagonist as a caring (albeit jealous) lover, husband, brother and son, as well as a courageous and upright citizen, somewhat counterbalances and relativizes the negative image of Muslim men presented in her other stories.

In *Liebe, meine Gier, die mich frißt* (Love, the desire that devours me; 1992) Scheinhardt again depicts oppressive gender relations, this time focusing on a Sicilian woman whose life under Italian Catholic patriarchy is not dissimilar from that of Turkish women under Islamic patriarchy. Finally, in *Sie zerrissen die Nacht* (They demolished the night; 1993), she depicts the beleaguered situation of the Kurds in Turkey.

Unlike Saliha Scheinhardt, Aysel Özakin was an established writer before leaving Turkey in 1981. As a leftist intellectual and political refugee, Özakin speaks from a position of privilege, emphatically distancing herself from the notion of *Gastarbeiter*-literature and insisting that her writings be judged on purely aesthetic grounds. Özakin's writings stand in sharp contrast to those of Scheinhardt, whose partisan championing of Turkish women places them in the ranks of *littérature engagée*. Her largely autobiographical texts often explore dilemmas she herself faces as a Turkish feminist writer, with issues of identity and authorship constituting the overarching themes of her work. Repudiating the cultural specificity of her writing and stylizing herself into a unique and gifted individual, Özakin's concept of authorship is clearly informed by (Western) Enlightenment notions of identity and aesthetics.

Özakin spent about ten years in the Federal Republic before moving to England in the early 1990s. In texts written since emigrating to the West, Özakin often employs the topos of the journey as a vehicle to problematize the concept of *Heimat*. Writing from the position of the Other, she depicts her female writer-narrators' struggle to find a place for themselves in a new, foreign land. *Die Leidenschaft der anderen* (The passion of the others; 1983) and *Die blaue Maske* (The blue mask, 1988; German translation 1989) each deal with the experiences of a Turkish woman writer on a reading tour in Europe and poignantly evoke the state of homelessness. At home neither in Turkey nor in Germany, both protagonists ultimately conclude that home is not geographically determined, but rather to be found in writing. Since moving to England Özakin has written two novels in English. Both *Glaube, Liebe, Aircondition* (Faith, lust and airconditioning; 1991) and *Die Zunge der Berge* (The tongue of the mountains; 1994), have been translated into German and published by major German presses, but to my knowledge have not yet appeared in English. Paradoxical as it may seem, the fact remains that, whether she is writing in Turkish, German or English, Aysel Özakin forms an established part of the contemporary German literary scene.

Alev Tekinay, arguably the most assimilated of the Turkish writers living in Germany, was educated at the German School in Istanbul before emigrating to Germany and obtaining her doctorate at the University of Munich. Her first three volumes of short stories, *Über alle Grenzen* (Beyond all borders; 1986), *Die Deutschprüfung* (The German exam; 1989) and *Es brennt ein Feuer in mir* (A fire burns in me; 1990), deal with issues of transnationalism and hybrid identity. Whereas Scheinhardt and Özakin tend to stress cultural differences, in texts such as 'Jakob and Yakkup' (*Es brennt ein Feuer in mir*) Tekinay, playing with the *Doppelgänger* motif, emphasizes cultural similarities between Germans and Turks. The story of two students of *Germanistik*, one German, the other Turkish, with so much in common that they ultimately are able to assume each other's identity

(Jakob returns to Turkey in Yakkup's stead, while Yakkup remains in Germany), helps dismantle notions of Otherness and alterity. 'Achterbahn' (Rollercoaster), in the same collection, playfully transgresses national border demarcations, while at the same time subverting cultural stereotypes about Turks. Tekinay's fascination with Romanticism manifests itself in this magical realist text about a fictional character who frees himself from his author, determined to write his own story, devoid of the cultural clichés about Turks he accuses his creator of perpetuating.

In her neo-romantic novel *Der weinende Granatapfel* (The weeping pomegranate; 1990), the story of a German Orientalist who goes to Turkey, Tekinay inverts her own biography, putting a contemporary, multicultural spin on the Romantic trope of the quest for self-recognition in the story of Ferdinand Tauber's search for his Turkish alter ego, the writer Ferdi T. The 1993 text *Nur der Hauch vom Paradies* (Only a breath of Paradise) focuses on the second generation of Turks living in Germany. Like so much of her writing, this novel is characterized by a playfulness often lacking in other minority women's writings.

As a Kurd, Emine Sevgi Özdamar, the newest woman writer from Turkey to appear on the German literary scene, belonged to an ethnic minority group in her native Turkey. She studied acting in Turkey before going to East Berlin to work with Benno Besson, a pupil of Brecht's, at the *Volksbühne*. Well known in the German theatre world, she has also worked with the director Claus Peymann in Bochum and has appeared in Hark Bohm's film *Yasemin* and Doris Dörrie's film *Happy Birthday, Türke*. Like Özakin and Tekinay, Özdamar is also interested in the notion of a transnational identity, deterritorializing the concept of *Heimat*, exploring its relationship to the 'mother tongue' which provides the title to her short story collection *Mutterzunge* (1990).

In 1991 Özdamar was the first writer from a non-German-speaking country to receive the coveted Ingeborg Bachmann prize, for *Das Leben ist eine Karawanserei. hat zwei Türen. aus einer kam ich rein. aus der anderen ging ich raus* (*Life is a caravanserai has two doors I came in one I went out the other*; 1992), a monumental semi-autobiographical novel about a girl's childhood and youth in Turkey. A linguistic *tour de force* whose poetic vitality stems in no small part from Özdamar's ability to combine German colloquial speech with transliterations and literal translations (particularly of aphorisms) from the Turkish, *Karawanserei* begins before the nameless first-person narrator's birth and ends with her departure as a nineteen-year-old for Germany, referred to as *Bitterland*. In telling her story, the narrator also relays the story of her extended family's decline, while at the same time painting a vivid picture of rural and cosmopolitan Turkey in the 1950s and 1960s.

The German reception of *Karawanserei*, which makes clear that Özdamar is viewed not as a 'foreign' writer, but as one whose remarkable linguistic and narrative talents will help revitalize German literature, also marks a watershed in contemporary German letters. In looking to the Turkish-born Özdamar for literary inspiration and modelling, German critics have come a long way from marginalizing literature written by Turks as mere *Gastarbeiter* literature.

In her autobiographical novel of 1998, *Die Brücke vom goldenen Horn* (The bridge of the Golden Cape), Özdamar recounts the experiences of a young Turkish *Gastarbeiterin* caught between two cultures. The first part, 'Der beleidigte Bahnhof' (The insulted train station), set in Berlin during the turbulent 1960s, vividly describes the living and working conditions of Germany's guest workers and the chilly reception they receive from their 'hosts'. The second part, 'Die Brücke von goldenen Horn', which takes place after the narrator's return to Turkey in 1968, is set in Istanbul and documents the brutal political confrontation between the Left and the Right in Turkey during the late 1960s. The novel's title, which refers to the bridge spanning the Bosporus which unites Turkey and Europe, reflects the narrator's position in the text: she, too, is suspended between Turkey and Europe, between the 'Orient' and the Occident.

Although she comes from a different cultural context, there are many overlaps between the autobiographical novels of Torkan Daneshfar-Pätzoldt, an Iranian woman living in Germany and writing in German under the name of TORKAN, and Turkish women writers. Like them, she stems from a predominantly Muslim country and must therefore contend with restrictive Islamic religious and social practices, and is similarly ambivalent about her 'in between' status.

Written from the perspective of an Iranian woman living in Germany, TORKAN's *Tufan: Brief an einen islamischen Bruder* (Tufan: Letter to an Islamic brother; 1983) represents the most differentiated account of Muslim familial relations extant among ethnic women's writings in Germany. Far from presenting stable, unchanging power relations, divided along traditional patriarchal gender lines, TORKAN's text shows how these relations fluctuate. In common with much minority writing, *Tufan* confounds notions of national identity. Its most compelling section, however, is the depiction of the narrator's return to Iran – by virtue of having internalized many Western values and customs during her stay in Germany, she has essentially become a foreigner in her homeland as well.

The same sense of alienation and lack of belonging is to be found in the writings of Afro-German women. In 1986 Katharina Oguntoye, May Opitz and Dagmar Schultz published *Farbe bekennen* (*Showing our Colors*), a groundbreaking book comprised of sociological studies, interviews, testimonials and poems which eloquently bears witness to the exclusion experienced by Afro-German women, who are often the offspring of a German mother and black father – either of Africans from Germany's former colonies, or foreign soldiers who fought in Germany during World War I or World War II.

Opitz's analysis from the outset establishes a connection between racism and sexism, arguing that Afro-German women, by virtue of their gender, must confront even more prejudices than their male counterparts. Tracing the representation of Blacks in Germany from the precolonial period to the present, Opitz uses excerpts from her sociological thesis on the subject to discuss, among other things, the negative connotation of the colour black for medieval Christianity, and the image of Africa in German precolonial, colonial and Nazi Germany. A section devoted to the treatment of Afro-Germans during the Weimar Republic and the Third Reich includes interviews with Afro-German women who lived at this time. By far the most space, however, is devoted to statements by the so-called occupation children (*Besatzungskinder*), Afro-Germans born during the Allied occupation of Germany. A common lament is that, although born and raised in Germany, they are almost invariably considered foreigners; thus for them the 'compliment' that they speak German well is perceived as an insult. The final section of *Farbe bekennen* contains poems by Afro-German women in which they eloquently give voice not only to their alienation and frustration, but also to the advantages of a hybrid identity.

In 1995 May Ayim (also known as May Opitz) published *blues in schwarz weiss* (blues in black white), a volume of poems which registers her reactions to racial inequalities and other social injustices in Germany. In 1997 another poetry volume, *nachtgesang* (nightsong), and a collection of essays, *grenzenlos und unverschämt* (borderless and outrageous), appeared posthumously.

The publication in 1998 of the *Besatzungskind* Ika Hügel-Marshall's autobiography, *Daheim unterwegs: Ein deutsches Leben* (At home on the go: a German life), offers the most intimate and detailed extant account of what it was like for a *Mischlingskind* (child of mixed race) to grow up in postwar Germany and constitutes one of the most significant contributions to Afro-German women's writing. Among the contributors to *Farbe bekennen*, Hügel-Marshall fleshes out in her autobiographical narrative the sense of alienation and displacement she had expressed in her earlier text. Her shattering description of life as the child of an (absent) Black American GI and a German mother in a small Bavarian town in the 1950s makes the reader privy to the racism and cultural displacement she experienced, while her account of her trip to the United States in search of her father in her late thirties leaves open the possibility for a reconciliation and a productive acceptance of her racial and cultural hybridity.

'Ethnic German' women's writings

The minority perspective offered by ethnic women living in Germany is augmented by the writings of so-called 'ethnic Germans', that is, by those writers whose 'mother tongue' is German but who were born or live outside Germany's national borders. The most important contemporary woman writer in this group is Herta Müller, who was born in a small village in the German-speaking Banat, a region in northwestern Romania. Müller, who has emerged as one of the leading writers of German-Romanian literature, wrote three books of short prose about life in the Banat before emigrating to West Germany in 1987. Taken together, they present a devastating portrait of intolerance, brutality, corruption and moral bankruptcy and leave little doubt about the legacy of fascism among Romania's minority German population.

The autobiographical short story collection *Niederungen* (*Nadirs*; 1982) documents the backwardness and provinciality of the rural enclaves of the Banat. Told from the perspective of an emotionally abused and neglected child, the individual stories present case studies in alienation and demonstrate that the proverbial values of the Swabians who settled there – industriousness, frugality, a sense of community and tradition: values that ostensibly still drive family life – have in fact become meaningless among the current population.

In *Der Mensch ist ein großer Fasan auf der Welt* (Man is a large pheasant in the world; 1986, translated as *The Passport*), Müller addresses the phenomenon of emigration among Romania's German minority population, now reaching epidemic proportions; from a pre-World War II population of 900,000, fewer than 300,000 remain. In describing the endeavours of the miller Windisch, his wife Katharina, and his daughter Amalia to emigrate to West Germany, the episodic tableaux that comprise *Der Mensch ist ein großer Fasan auf der Welt* vividly portray the greed and corruption that is part of everyday life in the Banat village. The book's title, a literal translation of a Romanian proverb, casts humankind in the role of a pheasant, which for the Romanians, as a bird that is unable to fly, is the eternal prey, the natural loser.

While *Der Mensch ist ein großer Fasan auf der Welt* is written from the perspective of those who desperately want to leave Romania, *Reisende auf einem Bein* (*Travelling on One Leg*; 1989), written after Müller herself emigrated, has been read as Müller's reckoning with the Federal Republic. It relates the story of Irene, who succeeds in leaving the country, but for whom emigration to the German *Heimat* fails to alleviate feelings of emptiness and despair. As is so often the case in her writings, sexuality is inextricably linked to power and the erotic serves as a vehicle for articulating alienation; the affair Irene had with a West German who visited Romania disintegrates upon her arrival in the Federal Republic. Dispirited by the overabundance of consumer goods she encounters in Berlin, which she is unable to afford, Irene recognizes the material gap that separates her from the affluent West Germans.

In *Der Fuchs war damals schon der Jäger* (The fox was already the hunter back then; 1992), a story of intrigue and surveillance which represents her most overt attempt to come to terms with Romania's Stalinist past, Müller depicts life in Romania in the final months of the Ceauşescu dictatorship. If the perspective on Romanian society under Ceauşescu seems bleak, the conclusion of the novel leaves little hope for substantive change in the foreseeable future. What links this novel to her earlier examinations of rural life among the Banat Swabians is the text's attention to issues of oppression and repression. In Müller's work, as in that of many writers from the (former) GDR, coming to terms with the Stalinist past is also linked with an interest in probing the legacy of fascism, in turn related to issues of identity politics and questions of home.

Towards a transnational literature?

While Herta Müller's writings graphically capture the specificity of a peculiar Romanian milieu, many texts of the Czech writer Libuše Moníková are informed by Czech politics, specifically by the failed uprising of 1968, while others transcend geographic boundaries to create an imaginative aesthetic space. As a Central European, Moníková is less likely to be regarded as a 'foreigner' in Germany than are other non-German writers discussed here. Indeed, by virtue of her Czech background she has close ties to German culture; Bohemia did, after all, belong to the Habsburg Empire from medieval times until the collapse of the Austro-Hungarian Empire in 1918 and it has been a bilingual society since the High Middle Ages. Thus the figure of Franz Kafka looms large in Moníková's writings, as does the atmosphere of alienation and *Angst* that we have come to call 'Kafkaesque'.

Moníková's *Eine Schädigung* (A violation; 1981), a case study of the debilitating psychological and psychic effects of rape, makes it unequivocally clear that rape is motivated not by sexual desire, but by power and control. The story of a young woman who, after having being brutally beaten and raped by a police officer, bludgeons him to death and dumps his body into the river, the text conflates individual (male) power with the power of the state. By having her protagonist replay the rape over and over in her mind, Moníková effectively replicates the psychological trauma of this violation. Her repeated invocations also repeatedly conjure up the site of the rape, with the mysterious, cordoned-off citadel, located high on a hill overlooking the town, clearly identifying the city as Prague. In dedicating *Eine Schädigung* to Jan Palach, who immolated himself in Wenceslas Square in January 1969 to protest against the Soviet invasion of Czechoslovakia, Moníková makes clear that this ostensibly personal narrative about rape is also a deeply political novel, that the female body and the body politic have both been inscribed and violated by the brutal exercise of power.

The title of Moníková's second novel, *Pavana für eine verstorbene Infantin* (Pavane for a deceased Infanta; 1983), is taken from Maurice Ravel's famous piano piece *Pavane pour une infante défunte*. Despite allusions to Queen Libuše (the founder of Prague and subject of a number of German literary works) and to Ingeborg Bachmann's *Der Fall Franza*, *Pavana* is ultimately a homage to Franz Kafka. Not only is Kafka repeatedly evoked, he actually appears as a figure in the novel. Continuing in his tradition, *Pavana*, like all of Moníková's texts, is a narrative of profound alienation. Told from the perspective of a Czech professor of literature who teaches at a West German university, the text reflects the disorientation of someone suspended between two cultures. For no compelling physical reasons, the narrator voluntarily relegates herself to a wheelchair, thereby making visible the marginalization she experiences. But her outsider position also affords her unique insights into her surroundings, and her isolation becomes a badge of defiance. In what amounts to a definition of postmodern identity, the narrator states: 'My life is a series of literary and cinematic scenes, random quotes that I sometimes cannot place right away' (p. 19).

Whereas Moníková's earlier narratives documented acts of resistance on the part of individuals, *Die Fassade: M.N.O.P.Q.* (*The Façade: M.N.O.P.Q.*; 1987) presents the collaborative resistance of two painters and two sculptors who are assigned the never-ending task of restoring the façade of a

Renaissance castle in Friedland in northern Bohemia (familiar to German readers from Schiller's *Wallenstein*) in preparation for a festival celebrating the composer Bedřich Smetana. In those places where the façade has been so ravaged as to render the iconography undecipherable, the four 'restorers' invent new symbols, incorporating into the Renaissance allegories a broad and imaginative array of references to contemporary history and literature.

In contrast to the atmosphere of rage and mourning which characterized *Die Schädigung* and *Pavana*, *Die Fassade* is a satirical and humorous text, whose original subtitle was to have been 'a collective picaresque novel'. The second part of the novel, in which Moníková allows her fantasy to run wild, consists of an extravagant and hilarious interlude in which five characters strike out for Japan, only to end up stranded in Siberia. Yet there is political bite to what on the surface appears to be an endless play of signifiers: thus, for example, Moníková, bringing together elements from the *Odyssey* and contemporary history, has a feminist Circe transform recalcitrant communist officials into reindeer; and a matriarchal community appears more successful at creating an egalitarian society than was the international brotherhood championed by Eastern-bloc communism.

Die Fassade ends with a return to Friedland: the final image of the four artists reconstructing, revising and amending the symbols of the castle's Renaissance façade becomes symbolic of the never-ending process of historiography. Ultimately, *Die Fassade*, like all of Moníková's texts, is about history and memory; it is about the moral imperative to remember and to record, for, as Moníková's compatriot Milan Kundera noted, 'The struggle of human beings against power is the struggle of memory against forgetting.'

Conclusion

It is hardly surprising that in times of great historical upheaval writers should seek to (re)assess the past, even as they attempt to situate themselves within evolving or significantly altered societal structures. The collapse of the GDR was profoundly disorienting for established writers like Christa Wolf and Helga Königsdorf, who had to come to grips with the loss of what they had perceived to be their social(ist) utopia. Writing against their pain, they must now come to terms with the GDR's communist past, just as they had earlier to come to terms with Germany's Nazi past, if they are to find a place in their new homeland.

Younger, less established writers like Angela Krauß, Gabriele Stötzer-Kachold and Kerstin Hensel seem to have found change – in particular the lifting of aesthetic prescriptions – exhilarating, as witnessed by their experimentation with innovative forms and their production of a variety of highly original texts.

Despite massive stylistic and ideological differences, a common denominator of many texts by writers from the (former) GDR is their attention to the history of the Nazi period, with a view to discerning possible similarities in institutional structures between German fascism and East German communism. Interestingly, the examination of possible points of contiguity between Nazism and (in this case, Romanian) Stalinism also informs the writings of the Romanian-German writer Herta Müller. Thus questions about the legacy of Nazism still loom large for contemporary writers of German extraction.

The collapse of Eastern-bloc communism has understandably precipitated a crisis of national and personal identity for Central European writers. The articulation of this crisis links their writings with texts by German minority writers. Different as their point of departure might be, the texts of Turkish writers Saliha Scheinhardt, Aysel Özakin, Alev Tekinay and Emine Özdamar, with their foregrounding of issues of national and cultural hybridity, stand in dialogue with the writings of Central European women. Among the many strands that make up the rich fabric of women's writing in Germany since 1989, those dealing with issues of identity and *Heimat* form a recurrent pattern.

As is readily discernible from the discussion of contemporary women's writing since the *Wende*, the notion of what constitutes German literature is in great flux. With the writings of such 'foreign' authors as Emine Özdamar and Libuše Moníková being heralded by the literary establishment as exemplary texts of German literature, it is clear that traditional categories, such as origin and national borders, can no longer be regarded as the primary determinants in defining the parameters of 'German' literature. The situation becomes more complex when we consider the increasingly significant role of literature translated into German: for many years Aysel Özakin has produced texts written in Turkish – and most recently in English – which, translated into German, have become part of the German literary scene. These more fluid, more permeable categories may be seen as heralding a move to a transnational model of literature that can only be applauded in an increasingly multicultural world.

16

Writing about women writing in German:
postscript and perspectives

Historical narrative

A History of Women's Writing in Germany, Austria and Switzerland: each element presents dilemmas which are compounded in combination. The term history refers both to an object of study, the past, and to the product of that study, historiography, an ambiguity which can sometimes obscure the fact that historical narrative does not simply inhere in past events but is the product of agendas and choices, of inclusions and exclusions. The rise of history as an academic discipline accompanied the rise of the nation state and women entered national histories only in so far as they achieved equality with men in the institutions of bourgeois society, which is to say that they remained largely absent, and even in oppositional Marxist history, as Patricia Howe notes above, women were largely construed as passive beneficiaries of class struggle, while patriarchy was seen as a side-effect of class division which would automatically wither away in communist society. German history has been a particularly contentious arena of battles over national identity, so that the competing interpretations of the Third Reich, for example, are as much about current politics as past history. Thus historiography resounds to the noise of axes being ground, a weapon which Christa Reinig has accused women of being too sparing with: 'Beil oder nicht Beil, das ist hier die Frage' (To wield or not wield, that is the question; *Entmannung*, p. 153). Women too must grind axes: the contestation of the meaning of the past contributes to present empowerment and can have future effects in making new kinds of action seem possible. But women need to make as explicit as possible the moral and political ground from which we are working, the formal devices we are deploying, the exclusionary moves we are making and, above all, who 'we' are.

Literary history

Women's historiography is oppositional. It gives voice to those who have been excluded. That is not, however, to suggest a Manichean vision of the all-powerful versus the absolutely powerless. To write history at all entails access to professional skills, to libraries and to publishing houses. Neither were nor are the women studied here simply victims: some, such as Hildegard of Bingen, the Mother Superior of a Benedictine convent, held positions of considerable power; and women have participated in the political struggles of modern times, as Patricia Howe and Chris Weedon amply demonstrate. But because women, if not wholly excluded, stood at the margins of the institutions of literacy, not only is there less published writing by women but, as Helen Watanabe notes, their work could also be easily contaminated or swallowed up by male collaborators. Even in the twentieth century, the biography of women such as Lou Andreas-Salomé, Veza Canetti or Claire Goll, the companions of famous men, continues to overshadow their own work as writers. So much is out of print and there may be no historiographical springboard to work from: as Sabine Werner-Birkenbach notes, there has been scarcely any assessment of women poets of the Expressionist generation. Modern historiography developed in the nineteenth century in tandem with nationalism and hysterical assertions of bourgeois patriarchy, so that women's writing was suppressed or half-consigned to the anthropological domain in a sexist aesthetics based on the polarized gender categories which Lesley Sharpe analyses. German national identity was shaped through a heroic discourse which devalued women's writing and deployed femininity as a denigrating metaphor, as, for example, in the downgrading of the feminine, Frenchified rococo in favour of the heroic sublimity of the German *Sturm und Drang*.

The dense tissue of a literary culture gives rise to the phenomenon of intertextuality, into which texts enter via authors who are also readers and via readers who are also co-producers of meaning. The intertextual fabric is, however, full of holes: producing a history of women's writing is more like the criss-cross work of darning than the spinning of a continuous thread. Women arrive, but drop out again – La Roche was much admired by Goethe but ignored by generations of Germanists. Women achieve power, but are swept aside again – as Margaret Littler documents, the first post-war all-German writers' congress of 1947 was chaired by Ricarda Huch and attended by a host of prominent women writers, but at the second such meeting in West Germany in 1950, only 6 out of the 118 invited guests were female. Women's historiography thus cannot and should not emulate nationalistic literary history in which the building of a canon paralleled the building of cannons, but narrative can proceed through cooperative work, as in this multi-authored volume which aims to show a variety of often contradictory tendencies and modes of appropriation or subversion of literary norms and conventions.

Historically changing value judgements make criteria of selection and exclusion problematic. Paralleling post-structuralist attacks on the ideological agendas of narrative history has been criticism of women's literary history for merely producing an alternative canon biased towards the experience of an educated elite yet claiming to represent all women and for being naively essentialist in failing to recognize the constructed, historically culturally disparate nature of gender identities. Post-structuralism, by contrast, aims to dismantle the binary opposition between 'Woman' defined as the negative to Man as the universal human norm, and to explore 'the feminine in writing' whether the author be male or female, so running counter to the socio-historical study of women's writing. But these different approaches need not be antagonistic. As Chris Weedon (1987) has argued, post-structuralism can offer the historian radical tools for uncovering the metaphors underpinning historically changing discourses of power. It would thus be folly in the name of deconstruction to leave silent the female voices silenced in the master-narratives; rather we can write history which takes critical account of the changing gender discourses within which women's literary work is embedded but which it may also subvert or radically contest. Our volume thus retains something of an emancipatory feminism: it aims to recover forgotten achievements, without, however, either uncritically celebrating a female perspective merely for being female or repeating the myth of progress which would devalue past writing because it had not reached present feminist consciousness. The dialogue between history and theory, between bringing alive a past culture in its historical specificity but also addressing current interests, leads to different emphases. Thus Margaret Ives and Almut Suerbaum place visionary writing by women in medieval context but also in a mystical tradition and a theology of the feminine stretching through to the twentieth century, a theme taken up by Margaret Littler in commenting on the work of Langgässer, Lavant and le Fort.

The criteria are in part pragmatic: whereas English studies long included women writers such as Austen and Eliot in the canon, German studies in English-speaking institutions commonly included no texts by women (with the occasional exception of Droste-Hülshoff's *Die Juden-buche*). This volume aims to recover forgotten texts and indicate research fields still to be developed. But it also celebrates the rich vein of recent writing to which the metaphors of marginality or the 'sub'-cultural in no way apply. The volume leans towards literary rather than cultural studies and gestures towards a canon of complex texts; thus Sabine Werner-Birkenbach, for example, discusses established authors such as Else Lasker-Schüler or Marieluise Fleißer. But it also interrogates the politics of canon-building: as Patricia Howe notes, the canonical works by Droste-Hülshoff were those which most conformed to dominant aesthetic values whereas feminist critics have turned to her hitherto neglected ballads. Non-canonical modes of writing such as letters and diaries, so significant for women, as Lesley Sharpe and Judith Purver note, are explored as are other non-fictional modes such as the travel writing on which Patricia Howe comments or Hedwig Dohm's feminist essays which Chris Weedon includes. The contributors make explicit the aesthetic and political grounds of value judgements, as when Ricarda Schmidt discriminates between conformist writing and critically experimental work liable to survive the demise of the GDR. As that example suggests, gender politics necessarily engages with other aspects of the exercise of power.

'Woman' or women?

In the Oedipal history of male-authored literature, so Harold Bloom (1973) has argued, the anxiety of influence drives poets to vie with mighty predecessors. But the pre-literary anxiety of transgressing limits set not by literary mothers (who too often languished out of print and unknown) but by social conventions and taboos weighed on woman writers and entered their texts. Thus a history of women's writing cannot be purely literary, but must address material and cultural forces which shape, but also change gender identity. Nor can it be surgically divided from writing by men, which dominated the formation of aesthetic conventions, determining supposedly masculine and feminine values in writing. If male authors vie with their literary fathers, writing by women has been perceived either as different but minor to the male-authored canon or as but mimicking male forms: a mere rib in the forward-striding body of literary history. Women's literary history must question such judgements and, as Patricia Howe argues, find new ways of reading to uncover the defiant subtexts in women's writing. And we can now celebrate not Oedipal battles, but the richly intertextual dialogues between contemporary women writers – Wolf with Bachmann, for example – or the building of bridges to bring past work into the present – again Wolf and women of the Romantic generation or Drewitz and Bettina von Arnim spring to mind. Nor, despite all the discontinuities, are such dialogues new: as Helen Watanabe notes, Caritas Pirckheimer, writing in the fifteenth century, was known as the new Hrotsvit after the writer of the tenth century, and in the eighteenth century, as Lesley Sharpe tells us, Sidonia Zäunemann looked to Christina Ziegler as a mentor.

Feminist literary history builds up and revalues women's writing, but in producing a separate history it could be accused of tacitly underwriting the biological discourse of either/or sexual difference which is used to justify women's subjection, to stigmatize lesbian and gay identity, and to pathologize hermaphroditic bodies or transsexuals. Judith Butler (1990) has indeed turned that commonplace of feminist theory, the distinction between biological sex which precedes but does not determine socially constructed gender, upside down: she argues that social gender comes first and gives rise to pressures to sex all bodies at birth as either male or female, to stigmatize deviations from the norm, and to define women by the reproductive role of motherhood. Yet granted the need to avoid reductive biological definitions, there remains a history to be told of embodied identities which can chart the highly complex relations between writing and the changing social practices – material and symbolic – of reproduction. A feminism which ceased to address relations of reproduction would be as futile as a feminism which reinscribed motherhood as the female essence. Thus the institution of monastic chastity deserves our attention as does that of post-Reformation marriage: the former did not expunge the sexuality of those who practised it, as Ives and Suerbaum's analysis of mystic poetry shows, nor did the latter the capacity for literary self-reflection, as witness Margaretha von Kuntsch's poems on the death of children on which Watanabe comments. And in later periods, the peculiar intensity of patriarchal ideology in post-Enlightenment German culture – from the anti-feminism of the idealists Fichte or Hegel, the irrationalist misogyny of Schopenhauer or Nietzsche, through Wilhelmine family ideology, the perceived crisis of masculinity in the age of Freud and Weininger, to the crass attacks on sexual 'degeneracy' by National Socialist ideologues – has made of gender a never innocent and always contested category. The struggle for homosexual rights goes back to the nineteenth century (Fadermann and Eriksson 1990). And more recently, as Margaret Littler shows, much post-war writing before the debates of the 1970s and 1980s is marked by subversive androgynous or homoerotic subtexts and fluid gender identities.

Feminism and German identity

The last thirty years of feminist debates have seen a shift from emphasis on common identity as women to differences between women. Women never have constituted a homogeneous group: literacy was once the prerogative of the few so that 'women's' writing cannot give voice to all women of a period, still less universally to all women. Different kinds of writing addressed and still address different kinds of women: as Weedon notes, Marlitt and the 'red Marlitt', Minna Kautsky, addressed the different class interests of different readerships. The additional category of 'German' adds multiple and competing bases of identity such as paternal or maternal lineage, geographical place of birth or of residence, political state, native language(s), regional or metropolitan loyalties, national, sub- or supra-national cultural community, ethnic or religious adherence, mystical folk-identity, and biologistically defined race. As the naming of three separate countries in our title suggests, the notion of 'German literature' refers not to one nationality, but to a common language spoken, albeit in a great range of dialectal varieties, in countries and regions whose boundaries have changed many times in the ebb and flow of population movements and political upheavals. Written in a medium which flowed across national boundaries but which also expressed the local and particular, literature provided an anchor of identity in difference, solving in imagination the tensions between region and nation and transcending state boundaries.

For good or ill, the rise of literary history was integral to the building of German identity, whether in the humane and liberal mode of a Gervinus or the violent polemics of a Menzel. Literary history could underpin a cultural identity independent of nation states and power politics and it could further anti-feudal and democratic aspirations. But it could also fuel an ambiguous pan-Germanism based on the claimed universality of the Germans, in whom the best qualities of others were supposedly subsumed, a seemingly generous spiritual vision, which, however, overlay all too material expansionist ambitions. Just as 'German' identity did not easily fit the political map of nation states, neither did 'non-German', which might designate peoples of other nations, but also 'alien' bodies within German communities. Language too failed to provide a stable basis: in anti-semitic ideology Jews were held to lack that seamless fusion of the linguistic with the ethnic which constituted identity and to be capable only of speaking German as a foreign language, even though they might speak and write a German indistinguishable from their neighbours'. Yet people who knew no German were held to be true Germans on grounds of lineage: to this day Volga Germans have stronger citizenship rights than people of Turkish descent, born and educated in the Federal Republic, who speak and write 'native' German.

Literary history is a deeply political affair, then, as the bitter debates of the 1960s on *Germanistik* in the Third Reich testify. That a conservative phalanx of professors of *Germanistik* excluded women writers from the canon and would gladly have excluded women students from their classes and women scholars from their ranks does not mean, however, that women were simply victims to be absolved from political responsibility. As Agnès Cardinal documents, women writers occupied a range of positions on the political spectrum. Support for National Socialism was strong among women: the ideology of motherhood took up old themes from the right wing of the women's movement and acted for many women as a boost to self-worth, just as the iconography of the powerful female body and the earth goddesses of the *Heimat* offered imaginary pleasures. Such a history should make us sensitive now to inclusions and exclusions. None of the criteria – whether birth, residence, nationality, language, culture or ethnicity – can ever be absolute. Thus Ives and Suerbaum examine the Latin works of Hrotsvit or Hildegard and include Eleonore of Scotland as a German author, while Watanabe includes Glickel von Hameln's Yiddish memoirs. Sonja Hilzinger's chapter is devoted to the authors who fled into exile during the Third Reich, and Margaret Littler includes Claire Goll and Unica Zürn, writers who cross national and linguistic borders. In the post-war period the key themes of contrast or convergence of the two Germanies, all the more fascinating in post-unification retrospect, should not block out Austrian or Swiss-German writing or the wider complexities of nationality, class and ethnicity as gendered formations in the 'New Europe' of which unified Germany is part. Geography and economics have long made of the German-speaking lands a place of border traffic which has often taken the form of wars, conquest and persecution of minorities. The most alarming development in Europe following the end of the Cold War – compounded in Britain and France by post-imperial racism – has been the rise of a racialized ethnic consciousness which turns those deemed to be different into an alien species to be excluded or even exterminated. But the border traffic has also brought immense enrichment.

Writing across borders

Now more than ever the weave of cultural identity is frayed at its edges, the patterns in the weave more shifting than ever. My metaphor of a fabric always in the making joins a multiplicity of terms which have been proposed to convey the interplay of cultural identity and difference. The term 'border' is a further metaphor borrowed from Maggie Humm (1991). A place on the border allows for mobility along intersecting geographical, historical, economic, linguistic and psychic axes so that border writing is marked by an interplay of difference with identity of aspects of self distinct from or shared by others. Border writing usefully opens up the notion of 'German' and celebrates the current diversity of women's writing.

I cannot here do more than offer a few suggestions complementing Anna Kuhn's survey in the previous chapter. In the past an inestimable contribution to German culture has come from Jewish writers. A deep gulf divides young Jewish writers from the terrible history of their parents, and that horror in turn forms an abyss cutting off the still earlier history of German Jewry. These are the borders which Esther Dischereit's novel *Joëmis Tisch. Eine jüdische Erzählung* (Joëmi's table. A Jewish tale; 1988) crosses as the protagonist seeks to recuperate her Jewishness through a dialogue with her dead mother while also looking to a woman-centred Jewish cultural tradition going back to the Romantic salons of women such as Rahel Varnhagen. Another Jewish writer is Barbara Honigmann, who was born in East Berlin and lived there until 1984, when she moved across two borders to Strasbourg. Her collection of stories *Roman von einem Kinde* (Novel of a child; 1986) mixes Jewish legend with contemporary experience, laments division from the past but also celebrates the survival of Jewish identity. Thomas Nolden (1994) has noted differences between recent writing by male German-Jewish writers and their female colleagues, who, he suggests, write more strongly from within a Jewish tradition which is also consciously female. This tradition looks back to the diary and epistolary forms of women's writing in the Romantic age on which Judith Purver comments here. Besides

Dischereit and Honigmann, Nolden cites work by Ronnith Neumann and Irene Dische.

Less than ever do language, thematics or an author's place of residence coincide to give a singular identity: Honigmann, who lives in Strasbourg and writes in German, juxtaposes at the beginning of her autobiographical *Eine Liebe aus nichts* (A love made of nothing; 1991) her father's return from exile in Russia to the very heart of classical German culture, to Weimar, and her own departure many years later for France in a multiple crossing of temporal and spatial borders. Or there is Aysel Özakin, whose work, as Anna Kuhn notes, exemplifies the frayed edges of 'German literature'. In Özakin's collection *Deine Stimme gehört dir* (Your voice is your own; 1992) exile is both physical and linguistic. In the story 'Soll ich in Berlin alt werden' (Am I to grow old in Berlin), a postcard from Büyükada, an island near Istanbul, brings the narrator news of the death of her Greek friend, Danay, who, though she was born and brought up in Turkey, had never felt at home in the Turkish language, but who loved French and English poetry and to whom the narrator had given a Turkish translation of Seferis's poetry. Here the Greek woman dying in Turkey mirrors the Turkish woman living and fearing to die in Berlin. As I read the German edition of Özakin's stories, the linguistic borders multiply: a native speaker of Anglo-Scottish, I am reading the German translation of a story written in Turkish about a Turkish woman in Berlin remembering giving a Greek woman a Turkish translation of a Greek poet. The experience is exhilarating: for all its grief the story closes with the scent of orange marmalade and an invitation by the narrator to her dead friend to come in, an invitation which crosses language borders to address the reader too.

As its title signals, Emine Sevgi Özdamar's *Mutterzunge* (*Mother Tongue*; 1990) is another collection with language as a theme. The title story opens: 'In meiner Sprache heißt Zunge: Sprache' (In my language tongue means language; p. 7). But, sitting in Berlin 'mit meiner gedrehten Zunge' (with my turned tongue), the narrator wonders when it happened that she lost her mother tongue so that her mother's sentences sound in her memory like a foreign language. And in the next story 'Großvaterzunge' (Grandfather tongue) she sets out to find the way into her mother's tongue by way of her grandfather's Arabic script, abolished in 1928 by Atatürk. Her teacher in Berlin, Ibni Abdullah, teaches Arabic to a Western 'Orientalistin' (female student of orientalism), but now helps an 'Orientalin' (Eastern woman), whose career hitherto, however, might be described as Occidentalism: the woman who has crossed borders to enter the Western theatre and now seeks a way across closed linguistic and cultural borders to the lost worlds of her grandfather and mother. (Özdamar works in film and theatre; the sketch *Karagöz in Alamania* (Blackeye in Germany) was first produced as a play in the Schauspielhaus Frankfurt in 1987.) The way across the borders is not, however, a reactionary way back to an idealized homeland, for the narrator's wish to recover her Turkish mother tongue is connected to her solidarity with persecuted political prisoners in Turkey, and her quest for access to Arabic does not entail rejection of Atatürk's reforms or a turning against German. *Karagöz in Alemania* deploys the forked tongue of bilingualism in a hybridized German shot through by transliterations of Turkish idiom to subversive effect. The patches of standard *Hochdeutsch* quite fail in their task of normative control over the jostling linguistic inventions of the characters passing back and forth through 'die Tür von Deutschland' (the door of Germany). Özdamar's novel *Das Leben ist eine Karawanserei*, on which Anna Kuhn comments, takes further such intentional linguistic hybridity, to brilliant effect.

Renan Demirkan's best-seller, *Schwarzer Tee mit drei Stück Zucker* (Black tea with three sugars; 1991), may serve as a last example of Turkish–German border crossings. The narrative structure dramatizes the constant moving across geographical, generational, cultural and psychic borders. An unnamed woman lies in hospital awaiting what will be the difficult birth by caesarean section of her first child – a first physical crossing fraught with symbolic meaning – and remembers in a loose episodic sequence, with constant returns to the present, her nomadic family history. The woman remains anonymous and the narration is in the third person. The effect is in part alienating. The reader is held at a distance from 'die Frau' (the woman) to whose memories we yet have intimate access, just as the German nurse and surgeon have to her body. On the other hand, an identity, perhaps never to be fixed yet always emergent, breaks through briefly into the first person when the protagonist remembers the village woman 'Eier-Tatta' (Egg-aunty) who lived in the same building (pp. 101–6): Germans just as Turks have crossed borders between rural and urban life. Difficulties with the first person have been a *leitmotif* in women's writing, expressing the problematic relation of women to the position of speaking and writing subject in a civil society from which they were traditionally excluded, and conveying also other more specific political problems such as the collective ideology of the GDR or the perversion of German during the Third Reich: Wolf's protagonist Christa T. expressed the difficulty in achieving subjecthood in the now famous phrase 'die Schwierigkeit "ich" zu sagen'; in Monica Maron's *Flugasche* (*Flight of Ashes*) the first-person narration gives way to the third person; the first-person narrator of Bachmann's *Malina* is finally displaced/ murdered by her masculine alter ego and the novel closes in the third person. In Demirkan's novel a disturbed relation to language is related to geographical and linguistic exile. A friend in Dortmund who came from the Black Sea coast no longer knows 'who it was who could say "I" back then in Sinop'. Nor is he at home in Germany: his German wife learnt Turkish, but to no avail; they got divorced and he married a woman from his home village who feels alienated in Germany. As the novel's title suggests, aromatic black tea is the Proustian stimulus to the recovery of lost time which is also a lost language. But the man from the Black Sea drinks tea-bag tea with a few drops of lemon from a plastic container and cannot integrate past and present. The narrator seeks to find the lost time of a collective past: on a country road in Anatolia the young woman driving through the desert in her car is relieved to see another human being, an old man on a donkey to whom she offers the word of greeting: 'merhaba'. But the old man 'from somewhere or other' raises his hands not in greeting but in prayer, saying only an amen and gazing into the distance and as if the young woman did not exist, while conversely 'merhaba' and 'amin' stand isolated in the surrounding desert of the German text. But along with bitterness are many moments of communion across borders and lament is mixed with comedy. The black Turkish tea has its counterpart in the bacon pancakes Cologne-style which the narrator so enjoys: the crossing of borders is also a transgression of rules whether dietary or linguistic. The lines which women must cross in order to write have been a limiting force, but their crossing has produced the wealth of literature which this volume documents and which continues in today's changing world with its multiple border-crossings.

Bibliography

The bibliography is arranged in three sections: a select bibliography by subject, containing works relevant to several chapters; a general bibliography by chapter; and an alphabetically arranged 'Bibliographical guide to women writers and their work' with dates of individual writers, their principal works, works translated into English where known, and suggestions for further reading.

NB: Secondary literature on individual writers and their works will be found in the Bibliographical guide.

Select bibliography by subject

Works of reference and general works

Brinker-Gabler, Gisela (ed.), *Deutsche Literatur von Frauen*, 2 vols., Munich: Verlag C. H. Beck, 1988
    Vol. I *Vom Mittelalter bis zum Ende des 18. Jahrhunderts*
    Vol. II *19. und 20. Jahrhundert*
Brinker-Gabler, Gisela, Karola Ludwig and Angela Wöffen, *Lexikon deutschsprachiger Schriftstellerinnen 1800–1945*, Munich: dtv, 1986
Frederiksen, Elke P. (ed.), *Women Writers of Germany, Austria and Switzerland. An Annotated Bio-Bibliographical Guide*, Bibliographies and Indexes in Women's Studies, 8, New York; Westport, Connecticut; London: Greenwood 1989
Friedrichs, Elisabeth, *Die deutschsprachigen Schriftstellerinnen des 18. und 19. Jahrhunderts: ein Lexikon*, Stuttgart: Metzler, 1981
Fürstenwald, Maria, and Jean M. Woods, *Schriftstellerinnen, Künstlerinnen und gelehrte Frauen des deutschen Barock. Ein Lexikon*, Stuttgart 1984
Gnüg, Hiltrud, and Renate Möhrmann (eds.), *Frauen Literatur Geschichte. Schreibende Frauen vom Mittelalter bis zur Gegenwart*, Stuttgart: Metzler, 1985; repr. Frankfurt am Main: Suhrkamp, 1989
Schmid-Bortenschlager, Sigrid, and Hanna Schnedl-Bubenicek, *Österreichische Schriftstellerinnen 1880–1938. Eine Bio-Bibliographie*, Stuttgart: Heinz 1982
Stump, Doris, Maya Widmer and Regula Wyss, *Deutschsprachige Schriftstellerinnen in der Schweiz, 1700–1945. Eine Bibliographie*, Zurich: Limmat Verlag, 1994

Selected further reading

Becker-Cantarino, Barbara, *Der lange Weg zur Mündigkeit. Frauen und Literatur in Deutschland von 1500 bis 1800*, Stuttgart: Metzler, 1987

Bird, Stephanie, *Recasting Historical Women: Female Identity in German Biographical Fiction*, Oxford: Berg, 1998

Bovenschen, Silvia, *Die imaginierte Weiblichkeit. Exemplarische Untersuchungen zu kulturgeschichtlichen und literarischen Präsentationsformen des Weiblichen*, Frankfurt am Main: Suhrkamp, 1979

Cocalis, Susan L., and Kay Goodman (eds.), *Beyond the Eternal Feminine; Critical Essays on Women and German Literature*, Stuttgart: Akademischer Verlag Hans-Dieter Heinz, 1982

Diethe, Carol, *Towards Emancipation: German Women Writers of the Nineteenth Century*, Oxford: Berghahn, 1997

Ecker, Gisela (ed.), *Feminist Aesthetics*, tr. Harriet Anderson, Boston: Beacon Press; London: The Women's Press, 1985

Fiddler, Allyson (ed.), *'Other' Austrians: Post-1945 Austrian Women's Writing*, Bern: Peter Lang, 1998

Goodman, Katherine R., and Edith Waldstein (eds.), *In the Shadow of Olympus: German Women Writers around 1800*, Albany: State University of New York Press, 1992

Herminghouse, Patricia (ed.), *Frauen im Mittelpunkt: Contemporary German Women Writers*, New York: Feminist Press at City University of New York, 1987

Kosta, Barbara, and Helga Kraft, 'Critical Interventions: German Women Writing after 1945', in *Beyond 1989: Re-reading German Literature since 1945*, ed. Keith Bullivant, Providence and Oxford: Berghahn, 1997, pp. 69–88

Littler, Margaret (ed.), *Gendering German Studies: New Perspectives on German Literature and Culture*, Oxford: Blackwell, 1997

Vansant, Jacqueline, *Against the Horizon: Feminism and Postwar Austrian Women Writers*, New York; Westport, Connecticut; London: Greenwood Press, 1988

Weedon, Chris, 'The Limits of Patriarchy: German Feminist Writers', in Forsås-Scott (ed.), p. 267 below, pp. 74–99

Weedon, Chris (ed.), *Postwar Women's Writing in German. Feminist Critical Approaches*, Oxford: Berghahn, 1997

Women in German Yearbook: Feminist Studies in German Literature and Culture (various editors), Lincoln and London: University of Nebraska Press, 1984–

Women Writers of the Age of Goethe (ed. Margaret Ives), Occasional Papers in German Studies, Lancaster University, vols. I–IX, 1988–98

Literary and historical context

Battersby, Christine, *Gender and Genius. Towards a Feminist Aesthetics?*, London: Women's Press, 1989

Boa, Elizabeth and Janet Wharton (eds.), *Women and the 'Wende': Social Effects and Cultural Reflections of the German Unification Process*, German Monitor 19, Amsterdam: Rodopi, 1994

Duby, Georges, and Michelle Perrot (eds.), *A History of Women in the West*, vols. I–V, Cambridge, Massachusetts, and London: Harvard University Press, 1996 (first published in Italian, Rome and Bari: Laterza, 1992)

Eigler, Friederike, and Susanne Kord (eds.), *The Feminist Encyclopedia of German Literature*, Westport, Connecticut, and London: Greenwood Press, 1997

Evans, Richard J., *The Feminist Movement in Germany, 1894–1933*, London and Beverly Hills: Sage Publications, 1976

Forsås-Scott, Helena (ed.), *Textual Liberation. European Feminist Writing in the Twentieth Century*, London and New York: Routledge, 1991

Fout, John C. (ed.), *German Women in the Nineteenth Century. A Social History*, New York and London: Holmes & Meier, 1984

Frevert, Ute, *Women in German History: From Bourgeois Emancipation to Sexual Liberation*, tr. Stuart McKinnon-Evans, New York, Oxford, and Munich: Berg, 1989, repr. 1993; 1997

Good, David, Margarete Grander and Mary Jo Maynes (eds.), *Frauen in Österreich: Beiträge zu ihrer Situation im 19. und 20. Jahrhundert*, Vienna: Böhlau, 1993

Heilbrun, Carolyn G., *Writing A Woman's Life*, New York: Ballantine Books, 1988

Joeres, Ruth-Ellen B., and Mary Jo Maynes (eds.), *German Women in the Eighteenth and Nineteenth Centuries. A Social and Literary History*, Bloomington: Indiana University Press, 1986

Moi, Toril, *Sexual/Textual Politics*, London: Methuen, 1985

Sagarra, Eda, and Peter Skrine (eds.), *A Companion to German Literature: From 1500 to the Present*, Oxford: Blackwell, 1997

Todd, Janet, *Feminist Literary History: A Defence*, Cambridge: Polity Press, 1988

Watanabe-O'Kelly, Helen (ed.), The *Cambridge History of German Literature*, Cambridge: Cambridge University Press, 1997

Woolf, Virginia, *A Room of One's Own*, first published London: Hogarth Press, 1929 (numerous reprints, e.g. St Albans; London etc.: Granada, 1977ff.)

Anthologies of women's writing in German

Borchers, Elisabeth (ed.), *Deutsche Gedichte von Hildegard von Bingen bis Ingeborg Bachmann*, Frankfurt am Main: Suhrkamp, 1987

Brinker-Gabler, Gisela (ed.), *Deutsche Dichterinnen vom 16. Jahrhundert bis zur Gegenwart*, Frankfurt am Main: Fischer, 1978

Kubli, Sabine, and Doris Stump, *Viel Köpfe, viel Sinn. Schweizer Schriftstellerinnen von 1800–1945. Eine Textsammlung*, Zurich: eFeF, 1994

See also editions by Reichart, *Österreichische Dichterinnen* (1993); Langgässer and Seidel, *Herz zum Hafen* (1933); and Schaefer, *Unter dem Sapphischen Mond* (1957) (see below, pp. 280, 274 and 361 respectively)

Anthologies in English translation

Altbach, Edith Hoshino, et al. (eds.), *German Feminism. Readings in Politics and Literature*, Albany: State University of New York Press, 1984

Blackwell, Jeannine, and Zantop, Susanne (eds.), *Bitter Healing. German Women Writers 1700–1830. An Anthology*, Lincoln, Nebraska 1990 (second volume planned)

Case, Sue-Ellen (ed.), *The Divided Home/Land: Contemporary German Women's Plays*, Ann Arbor: University of Michigan Press, 1992

Cocalis, Susan L. (ed.), *The Defiant Muse. German Feminist Poems from the Middle Ages to the Present. A Bilingual Anthology*, New York: Feminist Press, 1986

Herrmann, Elisabeth Rütschi, and Edna Huttenmaier Spitz (eds.), *German Women Writers of the Twentieth Century*, Oxford: Pergamon Press, 1978

Ives, Margaret C., and Anthony J. Harper (eds.), *Sappho in the Shadows. Essays on the Work of Some German Women Poets of the Age of Goethe (1749–1832), with Translations of Their Poetry into English*, Bern: Peter Lang, 1999

Rosenberg, Dorothy, and Nancy Lukens (eds. and tr.), *Daughters of Eve: Women's Writing from the GDR*, Lincoln: University of Nebraska Press, 1993

Selected general anthologies containing works by German women writers in English translation

Bankier, Joanna et al. (eds.), *The Other Voice. Twentieth Century Women's Poetry in Translation*, foreword by Adrienne Rich, New York: Norton, 1976

Cardinal, Agnès, Dorothy Goldman and Judith Hattaway (eds.), *Women's Writing of the First World War*, Oxford: Oxford University Press, 1999

Cosman, Carol, Joan Keefe and Kathleen Weaver (eds.), *The Penguin Book of Women Poets*, Harmondsworth: Penguin, 1981 (English only)

Gutzschhahn, Uwe-Michael (ed.), *Young Poets of Germany. An Anthology*, tr. Raymond Hargreaves, London: Forest Books, 1994 (English only)

Hamburger, Michael (ed.), *German Poetry 1910–1975*, Manchester: Carcanet, 1977 (parallel text) (includes poems by Aichinger, Bachmann, Borchers, Busta, Domin, Kirsch, Kolmar, Lasker-Schüler, Lavant, Sachs)

Hamburger, Michael, and Christopher Middleton (eds.), *Modern German Poetry 1910–1960*, London: MacGibbon and Kee, 1966 (parallel text)

Holton, Milne and Herbert Kuhne (editors and translators), *Austrian Poetry Today/Österreichische Lyrik heute*, New York: Schocken Books, 1985 (parallel text) (includes poems by Aichinger, Bachmann, Busta, Kräftner, Lavant, Mayröcker, Schutting)

Mulford, Wendy (ed.), *The Virago book of Love Poetry*, London: Virago, 1990 (English only)

Ungar, Frederick (ed.), *Austria in Poetry and History*. Bilingual. English translations by Lowell A. Bangerter et al., New York: Frederik Ungar Publishing Co., 1984 (parallel text) (includes poems by Bachmann, Busta, Ebner-Eschenbach, Greiffenberg, Alma Johanna Koenig, Preradović, Wied, Willemer)

General bibliography by chapter

1 The Middle Ages

Anthologies

Deutsche Gedichte von Hildegard von Bingen bis Ingeborg Bachmann (see p. 267 above)

Deutsche Mystik, ed. Louise Gnädiger, Zurich: Manesse, 1989

see also Dronke, Wilson (pp. 268, 269 below)

Secondary literature

Beer, Frances, *Women and Mystical Experience in the Middle Ages*, Woodbridge: The Boydell Press, 1992

Brinker-Gabler, *Deutsche Literatur von Frauen* (1988) (see p. 265 above)

Classen, Albrecht (ed.), *Women as Protagonists and Poets in the German Middle Ages. An Anthology of Feminist Approaches to Middle High German Literature*, Göppingen: Kümmerle, 1991

Dinzelbacher, Peter, and Dieter R. Bauer (eds.), *Religiöse Frauenbewegung und mystische Frömmigkeit im Mittelalter*, Cologne: Böhlau, 1988

Dinzelbacher, Peter, *Mittelalterliche Frauenmystik*, Paderborn: Schöningh, 1992

Dronke, Peter, *Women Writers of the Middle Ages*, Cambridge: Cambridge University Press, 1984 (contains some texts, including Latin texts by Hildegard von Bingen)

Ennen, Edith, *Frauen im Mittelalter,* Munich: Verlag C. H. Beck, 1984
Finnegan, Mary Jeremy OP, *The Women of Helfta: Scholars and Mystics,* Athens, Georgia, and London: The University of Georgia Press, 1991
Gnüg/Möhrmann, *Frauen Literatur Geschichte* (1985) (see p. 265 above)
Grundmann, Herbert, 'Die Frauen und die Literatur im Mittelalter. Ein Beitrag zur Frage der Entstehung des Schrifttums in der Volkssprache', *Archiv für Kirchen-Geschichte* 26 (1936), 129–61
Lewis, Gertrud Jason, *Bibliographie zur deutschen Frauenmystik des Mittelalters. Mit einem Anhang zu Beatrijs van Nazareth und Hadewijch von Frank Willlaert und Marie-José Govers,* Berlin: E. Schmidt Verlag, 1989
Monson, C. A., *The Crannied Wall. Women, Religion and the Arts in Early Modern Europe,* Ann Arbor: The University of Michigan Press, 1992
Peters, Ursula, *Religiöse Erfahrung als literarisches Faktum. Zur Vorgeschichte und Genese frauenmystischer Texte des 13. und 14. Jahrhunderts,* Tübingen: Niemeyer Verlag, 1988
Ruh, Kurt, *Geschichte der abendländischen Mystik,* vol. II: 'Frauenmystik und Franziskanische Mystik der Frühzeit', Munich: Verlag C. H. Beck, 1993
Wilson, Katharina (ed.), *Medieval Women Writers,* Manchester: Manchester University Press 1984 (contains some texts)

2 Women's writing in the early modern period

Anthologies

Brinker-Gabler, *Deutsche Dichterinnen* (1978) (see p. 267 above)
Freybe, Peter (ed.), *Frauen mischen sich ein,* Wittenberg 1995 (contains articles on, among others, Katharina Luther, Katharina Melanchthon, Katharina Zell and Hille Feicken)

In translation

Blackwell and Zantop, *Bitter Healing* (1990) (see p. 267 above)
Cocalis, *The Defiant Muse* (1986) (contains poems by Argula von Grumbach, Hoyers, Greiffenberg, Kuntsch and Susanna Elisabeth Zeidler) (see p. 267 above)
Wilson, Katharina M. (ed.), *Women Writers of the Renaissance and Reformation,* Athens, Georgia, 1987 (includes translations of writing by Pirckheimer, Hoyers, Kottanner and Margaret of Austria)
Wilson, Katharina M. and Frank J. Warnke (eds.), *Women Writers of the Seventeenth Century,* Athens, Georgia, 1989 (includes translations of writing by Greiffenberg, Schwarz and Ludamilia Elisabeth von Schwarzburg-Rudolstadt)

General and reference works; secondary sources

Becker-Cantarino, Barbara, *Der lange Weg zur Mündigkeit. Frau und Literatur 1500–1800,* Stuttgart, 1987
'Die Böse Frau und das Züchtigungsrecht des Hausvaters in der frühen Neuzeit', in *Der Widerspenstigen Zähmung. Studien zur bezwungenen Weiblichkeit in der Literatur vom Mittelalter bis zur Gegenwart,* ed. Sylvia Wallinger and Monika Jonas, Innsbruck, 1986
(ed.), *Die Frau von der Reformation zur Romantik. Die Situation der Frau vor dem Hintergrund der Literatur- und Sozialgeschichte,* Bonn, 1980
Bepler, Jill, 'Women in German Funeral Sermons: Models of Virtue or Slice of Life?', in *German Life and Letters* 44/5 (1991), 392–403
Blackwell, Jeannine, 'Die Zunge, der Geistliche und das Weib: Überlegungen zur

struktureller Bedeutung der Hexenbekenntnisse 1500–1700', in *Der Widerspenstigen Zähmung* (as above).

Brandes, Ute, 'Baroque Women Writers and the Public Sphere', *Women in German Yearbook 7*, (1991), 43–63

Cunitz, Maria: see Guentherodt, p. 270 below

Daly, Peter M., 'Emblematic Poetry of Occasional Meditation', *German Life and Letters* 25, (1972), 126–39

Fürstenwald, Maria, and Woods, Jean M., *Schriftstellerinnen, Künstlerinnen und gelehrte Frauen des deutschen Barock. Ein Lexikon*, Stuttgart, 1984

Gössmann, Elisabeth (ed.), *Das wohlgelahrte Frauenzimmer*, Archiv für philosophie- und theologiegeschichtliche Frauenforschung, vol. I, Munich, 1984f.

Guentherodt, Ingrid, 'Maria Cunitia: Urania Propitia. Intendiertes, erwartetes und tatsächliches Lesepublikum einer Astronomin des 17. Jahrhunderts', *Daphnis* 20/2 (1991), 311–53

Jordan, Constance, *Renaissance Feminism. Literary Texts and Political Models*, New York, 1990

Kastinger Riley, Helen M., 'Liebe in der Sicht der Frau des 17. Jahrhunderts', *Daphnis* 17/3 (1988), 441–56

Lorenz, Dagmar, 'Vom Kloster zur Küche: Die Frau vor und nach der Reformation Dr. Martin Luthers', in Becker-Cantarino (1980) (p. 269 above)

Marshall, Sherrin (ed.), *Women in Reformation and Counter-Reformation Europe*, Bloomington, Indiana, 1989

Niekus Moore, Cornelia, *The Maiden's Mirror. Reading Material for German Girls in the Sixteenth and Seventeenth Centuries*, Wolfenbütteler Forschungen 36, Wiesbaden, 1987

'The Poetess Aramena and her Novel *Margaretha von Oesterreich*. Women Writing Novels', *Daphnis* 17/3 (1988), 481–91

Pörnbacher, Hans, 'Biographisches und Autobiographisches: Ansätze zur Beschreibung einer Gattung in Bayern', in *Probleme und Perspektiven bayerischer Geschichte (Festgabe für Max Spindler zum 90. Geburtstag)*, ed. Andreas Klaus, Munich, 1984, pp. 157–80

'Von der Fürtrefflichkeit der Frauenzimmer: Über Schriftstellerinnen der Barockzeit in Bayern', in *Land und Leute*, Munich, 1992

Roper, Lyndal, *The Holy Household. Women and Morals in Reformation Augsburg*, Oxford, 1989

Simon, Sunka, '"Als sie ihr Bildniss schildern sollte". Die sprachliche Struktur der Innen- und Aussenporträts in der Lyrik Christiana Mariana von Zieglers', *Daphnis* 19/2 (1990), 247–65

Smart, Sara, *Doppelte Freude der Musen. Court Festivities in Brunswick-Wolfenbüttel 1642–1700*, Wiesbaden, 1989 (chapter 2 deals with the theatrical works of Sophie Elisabeth of Braunschweig-Lüneburg)

Tatlock, Lynne (ed.), *The Graph of Sex and the German Text: Gendered Culture in Early Modern Germany 1500–1700*, Chloe, Beihefte zum *Daphnis*, 19, Amsterdam, 1994

Wiesner, Merry E., *Working Women in Renaissance Germany*, New Brunswick: Rutgers University Press, 1986

Woods, Jean M., '"Die Pflicht befihlet mir / zu schreiben und zu tichten": Drei literarisch tätige Frauen aus dem Hause Baden-Durlach', in Becker-Cantarino (1980) (see p. 269 above)

Wunder, Heide, *'Er ist die Sonn', sie ist der Mond'. Frauen in der Frühen Neuzeit*, Munich, 1992

Zemon Davis, Natalie, *Women on the Margins. Three Seventeenth-Century Lives*, Cambridge, Massachusetts, 1995

3 The Enlightenment
General studies and anthologies

Battersby, Christine, *Gender and Genius. Towards a Feminist Aesthetics?* London: Women's Press, 1989

Beaujean, M. *Der Trivialroman in der zweiten Hälfte des 18. Jahrhunderts*, Bonn: Bouvier, 1969

Becker-Cantarino, Barbara, *Der lange Weg zur Mündigkeit. Frauen und Literatur in Deutschland von 1500 bis 1800*, Stuttgart: Metzler, 1987

Blackwell and Zantop, *Bitter Healing* (1990) (contains extracts in English from L. A. V. Gottsched, Karsch, La Roche and Naubert) (see p. 267 above)

Blochmann, Elisabeth, *Das 'Frauenzimmer' und 'die Gelehrsamkeit'. Eine Studie über die Anfänge des Mädchenschulwesens in Deutschland*, Heidelberg: Quelle und Meyer, 1966

Bovenschen, Silvia, *Die imaginierte Weiblichkeit*, Frankfurt am Main: Suhrkamp, 1979

Brinker-Gabler, *Deutsche Literatur von Frauen* (1988) (see p. 265 above)

Charlton, D. G., *New Images of the Natural in France. A Study in European Cultural History 1750–1800*, Cambridge: Cambridge University Press, 1984

Devrient, Eduard, *Geschichte der deutschen Schauspielkunst*, revised edn by Willy Stuhlfeldt, Berlin and Zurich: Eigenbrödler, 1929

French, Loreley, *German Women as Letter Writers: 1750–1850*, Cranbury, New Jersey, and London: Associated University Presses, 1996

Gallas, Helga, and Magdalene Heuser (eds.), *Untersuchungen zum Roman von Frauen un 1800*, Tübingen: Niemeyer, 1990

Hausen, Karin, 'Die Polarisierung der "Geschlechtscharaktere" – Eine Spiegelung der Dissoziation von Erwerbs- und Familienleben', in Werner Conze (ed.), *Sozialgeschichte der Familie in der Neuzeit Europas. Neue Forschungen*, Stuttgart: Klett, 1976, pp. 363–93

Heuser, Magdalene, 'Das Musenchor mit neuer Ehre zieren. Schriftstellerinnen zur Zeit der Frühaufklärung', in Brinker-Gabler, *Deutsche Literatur von Frauen* (1988) (see p. 265 above), vol. I, pp. 293–313

Kord, Susanne, *Ein Blick hinter die Kulissen. Deutschsprachige Dramatikerinnen im 18. und 19. Jahrhundert*, Stuttgart: Metzler, 1992

Martens, Wolfgang, *Die Botschaft der Tugend. Die Aufklärung im Spiegel der deutschen Moralischen Wochenschriften*, Stuttgart: Metzler, 1968/1971

Meise, Helga, *Die Unschuld und die Schrift: Deutsche Frauenromane im 18. Jahrhundert*, Berlin: Guttandin & Hoppe, 1983; repr. Frankfurt am Main: Ulrike Helmer, 1992

Nickisch, R. 'Die Frau als Briefschreiberin im Zeitalter der deutschen Aufklärung'. *Wolfenbütteler Studien zur Aufklärung 3* (1976), 29–66

Touaillon, Christine, *Der deutsche Frauenroman des 18. Jahrhunderts*, Vienna: Braumüller, 1919; repr. with preface by Enid Gajek, Bern: Lang, 1979

Wurst, Karin (ed.). *Frauen und Drama im 18. Jahrhundert*, Cologne and Vienna: Böhlau, 1991 (contains Sophie Albrecht's *Theresgen*, Marianne Ehrmann's *Leichtsinn und gutes Herz*, Christiane Karoline Schlegel's *Düval und Charmille* and Wilhelmine von Gersdorf's *Die Zwillingsschwestern*)

Journals and periodicals (selected)

Die Vernünftigen Tadlerinnen, ed. J. C. Gottsched. Halle: Spörl 1725, Leipzig: Brauns Erben, 1726

Pomona für Teutschlands Töchter, ed. Sophie La Roche. Speyer, 1783, 1784; reprinted in 4 vols. with a foreword by J. Vorderstemann, Munich: Sauer, 1987

Amaliens Erholungsstunden. Teutschlands Töchtern geweiht, ed. Marianne Ehrmann, 6 vols., Tübingen: Cotta, 1790–2

Die Einsiedlerin aus den Alpen, Zurich: Orell, 1793–5

Secondary literature

Krull, E. *Das Wirken der Frau im frühen deutschen Zeitschriftenwesen*, Beiträge zur Erforschung der deutschen Zeitschrift vol. V, Charlottenburg: Lorentz, 1939

Schumann, S. 'Das "lesende Frauenzimmer": Frauenzeitschriften im 18. Jahrhundert', in Becker-Cantarino (ed.), *Die Frau von der Reformation bis zur Romantik* (1980) (see p. 269 above), pp. 138–69

4   Revolution, Romanticism, Restoration (1789–1830)

General studies and anthologies

Blackwell and Zantop, *Bitter Healing* (1990) (see p. 267 above)

Burkhard, Marianne (ed.), *Gestaltet und gestaltend: Frauen in der deutschen Literatur*. Amsterdamer Beiträge zur neueren Literatur 10. Amsterdam: Rodopi, 1980

Drewitz, Ingeborg, *Berliner Salons: Gesellschaft und Literatur zwischen Aufklärung und Industriezeitalter*, Berlin: Haude & Spener, 1965

Friedrichs, Elisabeth, *Die deutschsprachigen Schriftstellerinnen des 18. und 19. Jahrhunderts: ein Lexikon*, Stuttgart: Metzler, 1981

Hardin, James and Christoph E. Schweitzer (eds.), *German Writers in the Age of Goethe, 1789–1832*. Dictionary of Literary Biography 90, Detroit: Gale Research Inc., 1989

Hoock-Demarle, Marie-Claire, *Die Frauen der Goethezeit*. Munich: Fink, 1990

Ives, M. C. (ed.), *Women Writers of the Age of Goethe*, vols. I–IX, Lancaster University, 1988–98

Joeres, Ruth-Ellen Boetcher and Marianne Burkhard (eds), *Out of Line/Ausgefallen: The Paradox of Marginality in the Writings of Nineteenth-Century German Women*, Amsterdam: Rodopi, 1989

Kluckhohn, Paul, *Die Auffassung der Liebe in der Literatur des 18. Jahrhunderts und in der deutschen Romantik*, Halle: Niemeyer, 1922

Purver, Judith. '"Zufrieden mit stillerem Ruhme"? Reflections on the Place of Women Writers in the Literary Spectrum of the Late Eighteenth and Early Nineteenth Centuries', *Publications of the English Goethe Society* 64–5, 1993–5 (1996), 72–93

Riley, Helene M. Kastinger, *Die weibliche Muse: Sechs Essays über künstlerisch schaffende Frauen der Goethezeit*. Columbia: Camden House, 1993

Walter, Eva, *Schrieb oft, von Mägde Arbeit müde: Lebenszusammenhänge deutscher Schriftstellerinnen um 1800 – Schritte zur bürgerlichen Weiblichkeit. Mit einer Bibliographie zur Sozialgeschichte von Frauen 1800–1914 von Ute Daniel*, ed. Annette Kuhn, Düsseldorf: Schwann, 1985

Wiese, Benno von, *Deutsche Dichter der Romantik: ihr Leben und Werk*, 2nd edn, Berlin: Schmidt, 1983

Drama

Dawson, Ruth P., 'Frauen und Theater: vom Stegreifspiel zum bürgerlichen Rührstück', in Brinker-Gabler, *Deutsche Literatur von Frauen* (1988) (see p. 265 above), vol. I, pp. 421–33

Hoff, Dagmar von, *Dramen des Weiblichen: deutsche Dramatikerinnen um 1800*, Opladen: Westdeutscher Verlag, 1989

Kord, Susanne, *Ein Blick hinter die Kulissen* (1992) (see p. 271 above)

Wurst, Karin (ed.), *Frauen und Drama im 18. Jahrhundert* (1991) (see p. 271 above)

Lyric poetry

Brinker-Gabler, *Deutsche Dichterinnen* (1978) (see p. 267 above)

Treder, Uta, 'Das verschüttete Erbe. Lyrikerinnen im 19. Jahrhundert', in Brinker-Gabler, *Deutsche Literatur von Frauen* (1988) (see p. 265 above), vol. II, pp. 27–35

Prose fiction

Dangel, Elsbeth, 'Lyrische und dramatische Auflösungen in den Briefromanen *Amanda und Eduard* von Sophie Mereau und *Die Honigmonathe* von Caroline Auguste Fischer', *Aurora* 51 (1991), 63–80

Fetting, Friederike, *'Ich fand in mir eine Welt': eine sozial- und literaturgeschichtliche Untersuchung zur deutschen Romanschriftstellerin um 1800: Charlotte von Kalb, Caroline von Wolzogen, Sophie Mereau-Brentano, Johanna Schopenhauer*, Munich: Fink, 1992

Gallas, Helga, and Anita Runge, *Romane und Erzählungen deutscher Schriftstellerinnen um 1800: eine Bibliographie mit Standortnachweisen*, Stuttgart: Metzler, 1993

Kammler, Eva, *Zwischen Professionalisierung und Dilettantismus: Romane und ihre Autorinnen um 1800*, Opladen: Westdeutscher Verlag, 1992

Touaillon, Christine, *Der deutsche Frauenroman des 18. Jahrhunderts* (1919/1979) (see p. 271 above)

Letters

Behrens, Katja (ed.), *Frauenbriefe der Romantik*, Frankfurt am Main: Insel, 1981

Hahn, Barbara, '"Weiber verstehen alles la lettre": Briefkultur im beginnenden 19. Jahrhundert', in Brinker-Gabler, *Deutsche Literatur von Frauen* (1988) (see p. 265 above), vol. II, pp. 13–27

Runge, Anita, and Liselotte Steinbrügge, *Die Frau im Dialog: Studien zu Theorie und Geschichte des Briefes,* Stuttgart: Metzler, 1991

5 Women's writing 1830–1890

Secondary literature:

[Boetcher]-Joeres, Ruth Ellen and Marianne Burkhard, *Out of Line/Ausgefallen* (1989) (see p. 272 above)

Brinker-Gabler et al., *Lexikon deutschsprachiger Schriftstellerinnen 1800–1945* (1986) (see p. 265 above)

Cocalis, Susan L., and Kay Goodman (eds.), *Beyond the Eternal Feminine* (1982) (see p. 266 above)

Fout, John C., *German Women in the Nineteenth Century* (1984) (see p. 267 above)

Goodman, Katherine, *Dis/closures. Women's Autobiography in Germany between 1790 and 1914*, New York: New York University, 1986

Pataky, Sophie, *Lexikon deutscher Frauen der Feder. Eine Zusammenstellung der seit dem Jahre 1840 erschienen Werke weiblicher Autoren*, 2 vols., Berlin: Schuster & Löffler, 1898; repr. Bern: Lang, 1971; Pforzheim: Antiquariat Peter Kiefer, 1987

Schwarz, F. H. C., *Grundsätze der Tochtererziehung*, Jena, 1836

6 Political writing and women's journals: the 1848 revolutions

Boetcher-Joeres, Ruth-Ellen, and A. Kuhn (eds.), *Frauen in der Geschichte IV: Frauenbilder und Frauenwirklichkeiten. Interdisziplinäre Studien zur Frauengeschichte in Deutschland im 18. und 19. Jahrhundert*, Düsseldorf, 1985

Gerhardt, Ute, *Verhältnisse und Verhinderungen. Frauenarbeit, Familie und Recht der Frauen im 19. Jahrhundert*, Frankfurt am Main, 1980

Koepcke, Cordula, *Frauenbewegung zwischen den Jahren 1800 und 2000*, Heroldsberg bei Nürnberg, 1979

Möhrmann, Renate, *Die andere Frau. Emanzipationsansätze deutscher Frauen im Vorfeld der 48er Revolution*, Stuttgart, 1977

Frauenemanzipation im deutschen Vormärz. Texte und Dokumente, Stuttgart, 1978

Twellmann, Margrit, *Die deutsche Frauenbewegung im Spiegel repräsentativer Frauenzeitschriften. Ihre Anfänge und erste Entwicklung 1843–1889*, 2 vols., Meisenhain am Glan: Verlag Anton Hein, 1972

Die deutsche Frauenbewegung. Ihre Anfänge und Entwicklung, Meisenhain, 1972

7 The struggle for emancipation: German women writers of the *Jahrhundertwende*

Brinker-Gabler et al., *Lexikon deutschsprachiger Schriftstellerinnen 1800–1945* (1986) (see p. 265 above)

Engel, Eduard (ed), *Geschichte der deutschen Literatur von den Anfängen bis in die Gegenwart*, vol. II, Leipzig: Baedeker, 1906

Historische Comission bei der Königlich Bayrische[n] Akademie der Wissenschaften, *Allgemeine Deutsche Biographie*, Leipzig, 1875–1912

Pataky, *Lexikon deutscher Frauen der Feder* (1898) (see p. 273 above)

Plothow, Anna, *Die Begründerinnen der deutschen Frauenbewegung*, Leipzig, 1907

Reed, Philippa, *'Alles was ich schreibe, steht im Dienst der Frauen.' Zum essayistischen und fiktionalen Werk Hedwig Dohms*, Frankfurt am Main: Peter Lang, 1987

Twellmann, *Die deutsche Frauenbewegung* (1972) (see p. 274 above)

8 Trends in writing by women, 1910–1933

Anthologies of works by women writers

Beuttenmüller, Hermann (ed.), *Deutsches Frauenbuch*, Leipzig: Walther, 1912

Klaiber, Theodor (ed.), *Dichtende Frauen der Gegenwart*, Stuttgart: Strecker und Schröder, 1907

Langgässer, Elisabeth and Ina Seidel (eds.), *Herz zum Hafen. Frauengedichte der Gegenwart*, Leipzig: Voigtländer, 1933

Leipziger Schriftstellerinnenverband (ed.), *Dichtung und Prosa Leipziger Frauen*, Leipzig: Naschke, 1914

Rheinsberg, Anna (ed.), *Bubikopf. Aufbruch in den Zwanzigern*, Darmstadt: Luchterhand, 1988

Wie bunt entfaltet sich mein Anderssein. Lyrikerinnen der zwanziger Jahre. Gedichte und Portraits, Mannheim: Persona, 1993

KRIEGS/LÄUFE. Namen. Schrift. Über Emmy Ball-Hennings, Claire Goll, Else Rüthel, Mannheim: Persona, 1989

Virginia, Julia (ed.), *Frauenlyrik unserer Zeit*. Berlin, Leipzig: Schuster & Löffler, 1907

Vollmer, Hartmut (ed.), *'In roten Schuhen tanzt die Sonne sich zu Tod'. Lyrik expressionistischer Dichterinnen*, Zurich: Arche, 1993 (includes works by, and bibliographical information on, the following writers: Lulu Albert-Lazard, Maria Benemann, Trude Bernhard, Frida Bettingen, Bess Brenck-Kalischer, Hedwig Caspari, Erna Gerlach, Claire [Studer-]Goll, Sylvia von Harden, Henriette Hardenberg, Emmy

[Ball-]Hennings, Annemarie Jacob, Elisabeth [von] Janstein, Elisabeth Joest,
    Cläre Jung, Mimi Korschelt, Erna Kröner, Margarete Kubicka, Ingeborg Lacour-
    Torrup, Lola Landau, Berta Lask, Else Lasker-Schüler, Sophie van Leer,
    Mechtilde [von] Lichnowsky, Paula Ludwig, Käte März, Elisabeth Meinhard, i.e.
    Elisabeth Frantz, Marie Pukl, Ruth Schaumann, Hilde Stieler, Henny Stock,
    Franziska Stoecklin, Nadja Strasser, Nell Walden[-Heimann], Maria Luise
    Weissmann, Martina Wied, i.e. Alexandrine Martina Weisl née Schnabel,
    Charlotte Wohlmuth)
Zöllner, Flora (ed.), *Deutscher Frauengeist in Dichtung und Wissenschaft. Eine Auswahl des
    Frauenschaffens der Gegenwart*. Lahr in Baden: Verlag für Volkskunst und
    Volksbildung Keutel, 1928

Works of reference and secondary literature
Adams, Marion, 'Der Expressionismus und die Krise der deutschen Frauenbewegung',
    in *Expressionismus und Kulturkrise*, Heidelberg: Winter, 1983, pp. 105–30
    Frauen gegen den Krieg, Frankfurt am Main: Fischer, 1980
Brinker-Gabler, *Deutsche Literatur von Frauen* (1988) (see p. 265 above)
Brinker-Gabler et al., *Lexikon deutschsprachiger Schriftstellerinnen 1800–1945* (1986) (see
    p. 265 above)
Gerhard, Ute, *Unerhört. Die Geschichte der deutschen Frauenbewegung*, Reinbek bei
    Hamburg: Rowohlt 1992
Gnüg/Möhrmann, *Frauen Literatur Geschichte* (1985) (see p. 265 above)
Keith-Smith, Brian (ed.), *German Women Writers 1900–1933. Twelve Essays*, Lewiston,
    Queenston and Lampeter: Edwin Mellen, 1993
Lexikon der Frau in zwei Bänden, Zurich: Encyclios 1953
Raabe, Paul (ed.), *Index Expressionismus. Bibliographie der Beiträge in den Zeitschriften und
    Jahrbüchern des literarischen Expressionismus*, 18 vols., Nendeln/Liechtenstein:
    Kraus-Thomson 1972–
Soden, Kristine von, and Maruta Schmidt (eds.), *Neue Frauen. Die zwanziger Jahre*, Berlin:
    Elefanten-Press, 1988
Soltau, Heide, *Trennungs-Spuren. Frauenliteratur der Zwanziger Jahre*, Frankfurt am Main:
    Extrabuch, 1984
Stephan, Inge, and Sigrid Weigel, *Die verborgene Frau. Sechs Beiträge zu einer feministischen
    Literaturwissenschaft*, Berlin: Argument, 1983
Weiland, Daniela, *Geschichte der Frauenemanzipation in Deutschland und Österreich.
    Biographien, Programme, Organisationen*, Düsseldorf: Econ 1983

Contemporary review articles of works by women writers
[anon.], 'Betrachtungen zur Frauendichtung', *Die literarische Welt* 9, Nr. 20/21 (1933), 1
Fürst, Rudolf, 'Frauenbücher', *Das literarische Echo* 18 (1915/16), cols. 610–19
    'Frauen-Romane', *Das literarische Echo* 19 (1916/17), cols. 94–100
Knobloch, Adolf, 'Sendung und Werk weiblicher Prosadichtung', *Hochland* 27/2
    (1929/30), 57–75
Langgässer, Elisabeth, 'Wege heutiger Frauendichtung', *Die literarische Welt* 9, Nr. 20/21,
    (1933), 1
Plothow, Anna, 'Frauenromane', *Literarische Rundschau. Beilage zum Berliner Tageblatt*
    398 (7 August 1912).
Wigher, F., 'Frauen, die Dramen dichten', *Hochland* 14/2 (1916/17), 631–3

General sources: Expressionist journals, anthologies and other documentation

Die Aktion. Zeitschrift für freiheitliche Politik und Literatur, ed. Franz Pfemfert, Berlin: Verlag der Wochenschrift Die Aktion, 1911–

Der Brenner, ed. Ludwig von Ficker, Innsbruck 1910–

Die Fackel, ed. Karl Kraus, Vienna: Die Fackel 1899–

Hochland. Zeitschrift für alle Gebiete des Wissens, der Literatur und der Kunst, ed. Carl Muth, Kempten; Munich: Kösel, 1903–

Die Kolonne. Zeitschrift für Dichtung, ed. Artur Kunert et al., Dresden: Jess, 1930–

Menschen. Monatsschrift für neue Kultur. Jüngste Literatur, Graphik, Musik, Kritik, ed. Felix Stiemer et al., Dresden: Dresdner Verlag, 1918–

Revolution, ed. Hans Leybold, Munich: Bachmair, 1913–

Der Sturm. Wochenshrift für Kultur und Künste, ed. Herwarth Walden, Berlin: Verlag Der Sturm, 1910–

Die Weissen Blätter. Eine Monatsschrift, ed. Erik Ernst Schwabach und René Schickele, Leipzig: Verlag der Weissen Blätter, 1913–

Anz, Thomas und Michael Stark (eds.), *Manifeste und Dokumente zur deutschen Literatur 1910–1920*, Stuttgart: Metzler 1982

Pinthus, Kurt (ed.), *Menschheitsdämmerung, Symphonie jüngster Dichtung*. Berlin: Rowohlt 1920; reissued as *Menschheitsdämmerung. Ein Dokument des Expressionismus. Mit Biographien und Bibliographien*, Hamburg: Rowohlt 1959ff.

9 Women's writing under National Socialism
Anthologies

Raabe Stiftung in der NS-Kulturgemeinde (ed.), *Deutsche Frauendichtung der Gegenwart: 36 Dichterinnen*, in *Jahrbuch der deutschen Dichtung 1936*, Berlin: Volkschaft-Verlag, 1936

Secondary literature

Denkler, Horst, and Karl Prümm (eds.), *Die deutsche Literatur im Dritten Reich*, Stuttgart: Reclam, 1976

Ketelsen, Uwe-K., *Literatur und Drittes Reich*, Schernfeld: SH-Verlag GmbH, 1992

Ritchie, J. M., *German Literature under National Socialism*, London: Croom Helm, 1983

Schoeps, Karl-Heinz Joachim, *Literatur im Dritten Reich*, Langs Germanistische Lehrbuch Sammlung, Band 43, Berlin: Peter Lang, 1992

10 Writing in exile
Anthologies

An den Wind geschrieben. Gedichte 1933–1945, ed. and intr. Manfred Schlösser, first publ. 1960; 4th edn Berlin, 1982

Lyrik des Exils, ed. Wolfgang Emmerich and Susanne Heil, Stuttgart, 1985

Schoppmann, Claudia (ed.), *Im Fluchtgepäck die Sprache. Deutschsprachige Schriftstellerinnen im Exil*. Berlin: Orlanda Frauenverlag 1991; rev. paperback edn Frankfurt am Main: Fischer, 1995 (contains works by and short biographies of Jenny Aloni, Ruth Landshoff-Yorck, Ilse Losa, Erika Mann, Hilde Rubinstein, Lessie Sachs, Anna Siemsen, Christa Winsloe and Hedda Zinner)

General and secondary sources

Benz, Wolfgang (ed.), *Das Exil der kleinen Leute. Alltagserfahrungen deutscher Juden in der Emigration*, Munich, 1991

Dick, Jutta, and Marina Sassenberg (eds.), *Jüdische Frauen im 19. und 20. Jahrhundert. Lexikon zu Leben und Werk*, Reinbek, 1993
Heinemann, Marlene, *Gender and Destiny. Women Writers and the Holocaust*, Westport, Connecticut, 1986
Keenan, Deborah and Roseann Lloyd (eds.), *Looking for Home. Women writing about Exile*, Minneapolis, 1991
Melzwig, Brigitte, *Deutsche sozialistische Literatur 1918–1945. Bibliographie der Buchveröffentlichungen*, Berlin and Weimar, 1975
Rohlf, Sabine, and Susanne Rockenbach, 'Auswahlbibliographie Frauen und Exil', in *Frauen und Exil. Zwischen Anpassung und Selbstbehauptung*, Munich, 1993 (= *Exilforschung. Ein internationales Jahrbuch Bd. 11*), pp. 239–77
Schmid-Bortenschlager and Schnedl-Bubenicek, *Österreichische Schriftstellerinnen* (1982) (see p. 265 above)
Sternfeld, Wilhelm and Eva Tiedemann: *Deutsche Exil-Literatur 1933–45. Eine Bio-Bibliographie*, 2nd edn, Heidelberg, 1970
Wall, Renate, *Lexikon deutschsprachiger Schriftstellerinnen im Exil, 1933–1945*, 2 vols., 3rd edn., Freiburg im Breisgau: Kore, 1995

Secondary literature

Hans, Jan, 'Historische Skizze zum Exilroman', in *Der deutsche Roman im 20. Jahrhundert*, ed. Manfred Brauneck, Bamberg, 1976, pp. 240–59
Hilzinger, Sonja, '"An Stelle von Heimat / halte ich die Verwandlungen der Welt" (Nelly Sachs). Jüdische Lyrikerinnen im Exil', in Renate von Bardeleben and Patricia Plummer (eds.), *Perspektiven der Frauenforschung*, Tübingen: Stauffenburg, 1998
'"Ich hatte nur zu schweigen" (Anni Sauer). Strategien des Bewältigens und Verdrängens der Erfahrung Exil in der Sowjetunion am Beispiel autobiographischer Texte von Frauen', in Rohlf and Rockenbach, *Frauen und Exil* (1993) (see p. 277 above), pp. 31–52
'Frauenbilder, Faschismusanalyse und Exilerfahrung in antifaschistischen Zeitromanen von Schriftstellerinnen der dreißiger und vierziger Jahre', in *Von Poesie und Politik. Zur Geschichte einer dubiosen Beziehung*, ed. Jürgen Wertheimer, Tübingen, 1994, pp. 138–70
'"Das Wort der Stummen" (Gertrud Kolmar). Deutschjüdische Lyrik in Nazi-Deutschland', in *Menora. Jahrbuch für deutsch-jüdische Geschichte 9*, Munich and Zurich: Piper, 1998
Klapdor, Heike, 'Überlebensstrategie statt Lebensentwurf. Frauen in der Emigration', in Rohlf and Rockenbach, *Frauen und Exil* (1993) (see p. 277 above), pp. 12–30; also published in *Zwischen Aufbruch und Verfolgung. Künstlerinnen der zwanziger und dreißiger Jahre*, ed. Denny Hirschbach and Sonia Nowoselsky, Bremen, 1993.
Kreis, Gabriele, *Frauen im Exil. Dichtung und Wirklichkeit*, Darmstadt: Luchterhand, 1988 (contains interviews with Charlotte Beradt, Karola Bloch, Marta Feuchtwanger, Elisabeth Freundlich, Irmgard Keun, Margarete Kollisch, Lili Körber-Grave, Vera Lachmann; Adrienne Thomas; Elisabeth Viertel-Neumann among others).
Kunst und Literatur im antifaschistischen Exil 1933–1945, ed. Akademie der Wissenschaften der DDR/Zentralinstitut für Literaturgeschichte und Akademie der Künste der DDR, 6 vols., Leipzig, 1979ff.
Lemke, Ute, 'Autorinnen und ihre Publikationen im "Pariser Tageblatt/Pariser Tageszeitung" – ein Überblick', in *Pariser Tageblatt/Pariser Tageszeitung (Décembre 1933 – Février 1940). Beiträge der Tagung des Forschungsprojekts der Universität*

Paris 8 zur deutschen Exilpresse in Frankreich (1933–1940) vom 16.–17.
    Dezember 1988 in Paris, ed. Hélène Roussel, Lutz Winckler,
    Universitätsdruckerei Bremen, n.d., pp. 103–13
Lixl-Purcell, Andreas (ed.), *Women of Exile. German-Jewish Autobiographies since 1933*, New
    York, 1988 (German edition: *Erinnerungen deutsch-jüdischer Frauen 1900–1990*,
    Leipzig, 1992)
Mittag, Gabriele, 'Erinnern, Schreiben, Überliefern. Über autobiographisches
    Schreiben deutscher und deutsch-jüdischer Frauen', in Rohlf and Rockenbach,
    Frauen und Exil (1993) (see p. 277 above), pp. 53–67
Mittag, Gabriele (ed.), *Deutsche Emigrantinnen im französischen Exil*, Berlin, 1990
Mülsch, Elisabeth-Christine, '"Die Romane unserer Zeit sind die Romane unserer
    Kinder". Deutschsprachige jüdische Kinder- und Jugendbuchautoren im
    amerikanischen Exil', in *Exil. Forschung, Erkenntnisse, Ergebnisse* (1/1990), pp. 65–73
Nieraad, Jürgen, 'Deutschsprachige Literatur in Palästina und Israel', in *Fluchtpunkte des
    Exils*, Munich, 1987 (= *Exilforschung. Ein internationales Jahrbuch* vol. 12), pp. 90–110
Pazi, Margarita, 'Staub und Sterne. Deutschschreibende Autorinnen in Erez-Israel und
    Israel', in Brinker-Gabler, *Deutsche Literatur von Frauen* (1988), vol. II, pp. 317–33
Ritchie, J. M., 'Women in Exile in Great Britain', *German Life and Letters* 47 (January 1984),
    51–66
Rotermund, Erwin, 'Exilliteratur', in *Moderne Literatur in Grundbegriffen*, ed. Dieter
    Borchmeyer and Viktor Žmegač, Frankfurt 1987, pp. 115–26
Siegel, Eva-Maria, '"Vorläufiges Leben". Emigrationsalltag in Prag 1933–1939', in *Exil.
    Forschung, Erkenntnisse, Ergebnisse* (1/1994), 23–38
Stern, Guy, 'Exil-Jugendbücher als Politikum', in *Wider den Faschismus. Exilliteratur als
    Geschichte*, ed. Sigrid Bauschinger and Susan L. Cocalis, Tübingen and Basel 1993,
    pp. 41–60
Stürzer, Anne, *Dramatikerinnen und Zeitstücke. Ein vergessenes Kapitel der Theatergeschichte
    von der Weimarer Republik bis zur Nachkriegszeit*, Stuttgart and Weimar, 1993

11 Restoration and resistance: women's writing 1945–1970

Becker, Bärbel (ed.), *Unbekannte Wesen. Frauen in den 60er Jahren*, Berlin: Elefanten Press,
    1987
Buchebner, Walter, *Das Schreiben der Frauen in Österreich seit 1950*, Vienna: Böhlau, 1950
Fliedl, Konstanze, *Zeitroman und Heilsgeschichte. Elisabeth Langgässers 'Märkische
    Argonautenfahrt'*, Vienna: Wilhelm Baumüller, 1986
Frederiksen, Elke, 'Literarische (Gegen-)Entwürfe von Frauen nach 1945: Berührungen
    und Veränderungen', in Gerd Labroisse and Mona Knapp (eds.), *Frauen-Fragen in
    der deutschsprachigen Literatur seit 1945*, Amsterdam: Rodopi, 1989, pp. 83–110
Littler, Margaret, 'Madness, Misogyny, and the Feminine in Aesthetic Modernism:
    Unica Zürn and Claire Goll', in E. Roberston and R. Vilain (eds.), *Yvan Goll – Claire
    Goll. Texts and Contexts*, Amsterdam: Rodopi, 1997, pp. 153–73
'The Cost of Loving: Love, Desire, and Subjectivity in the Work of Marlen
    Haushofer', in A. Fiddler (ed.), *Other Austrians: Post-1945 Austrian Women's Writing*,
    Bern: Peter Lang, 1998
Lühe, Irmela von der, 'Schriftstellerinnen der Gruppe 47', in *Dichter und Richter. Die
    Gruppe 47 und die deutsche Nachkriegsliteratur*, ed. Deutsche Akademie der Künste,
    Berlin (W), 1988, pp. 94–102
Marti, Madeleine, *Hinterlegte Botschaften. Die Darstellung lesbischer Frauen in der
    deutschsprachigen Literatur seit 1945*, Stuttgart: Metzler, 1992

Meyer, Franziska, 'The early novels of Ruth Rehmann', in Weedon, *Postwar Women's Writing* (1997) (see p. 279 below), pp. 61–76

'Women's writing in Occupied Germany, 1945–1949', in Weedon, *Postwar Women's Writing*, (1997), pp. 25–43.

Rapisarda, Cettina, 'Anfang, Zwischenreich, Zukunft. Autorinnen im Berlin der Nachkriegszeit', in Franziska Meyer et al. (eds.), *Eine Kulturmetropole wird geteilt. Literarisches Leben in Berlin (West) 1945 bis 1961*, Berlin: Berliner Kulturrat, 1987, pp. 88–101

Roten, Iris von, *Frauen im Laufgitter. Offene Worte zur Stellung der Frau*, Bern: Hallwag, 1958

Stephan, Inge, Regula Venske and Sigrid Weigel (eds.), *Frauenliteratur ohne Tradition? Neun Autorinnenporträts*, Frankfurt am Main: Fischer, 1987

Venske, Regula, *Mannsbilder-Männerbilder. Konstruktion und Kritik des Männlichen in zeitgenössischer Literatur von Frauen*, Hildesheim: Olms, 1988

Das Verschwinden des Mannes in der weiblichen Schreibmaschine, Hamburg: Luchterhand, 1991

Weigel, Sigrid, 'Der schielende Blick. Thesen zur Geschichte weiblicher Schreibpraxis', in Inge Stephan and Sigrid Weigel (eds.), *Die verborgene Frau*, Berlin: Argument, 1983; tr. as 'Double Focus: On the History of Women's Writing', in Ecker, *Feminist Aesthetics* (1985) (see p. 266 above)

Weedon, Chris (ed.), *Postwar Women's Writing in German. Feminist Critical Approaches*, Oxford: Berghahn, 1997

12 GDR women writers: ways of writing for, within and against Socialism

Anthology

Anderson, Edith (ed.), *Blitz aus heiterm Himmel*, Rostock: Hinstorff Verlag, 1975

Secondary literature

Anz, Thomas (ed.), *'Es geht nicht um Christa Wolf'. Der Literaturstreit im vereinten Deutschland*, Munich: edition spangenberg, 1991

Deiritz, Karl and Hannes Krauss (eds.), *Der deutsch–deutsche Literaturstreit oder 'Freunde, es spricht sich schlecht mit gebundener Zunge'*, Hamburg: Luchterhand, 1991

Emmerich, Wolfgang, *Kleine Literaturgeschichte der DDR*, Frankfurt am Main: Luchterhand, 1989 (expanded and revised version of the 1981 edition)

Janka, Walter, *Schwierigkeiten mit der Wahrheit*, Reinbek: Rowohlt, 1989

Kane, Martin (ed.), *Socialism and the Literary Imagination. Essays on East German Writers*, Oxford: Berg, 1991

Mittenzwei, Werner, 'Die Brecht-Lukács-Debatte', *Sinn und Form* 19 (1967), 235–69

Raddatz, Fritz J. (ed.). *Marxismus und Literatur. Eine Dokumentation in drei Bänden*, vol. II, Reinbek: Rowohlt, 1969

13 Post-1945 women's poetry from East and West

Anthologies

Borchers, Elisabeth (ed.), *Deutsche Gedichte von Hildegard von Bingen bis Ingeborg Bachmann* (1987) (see p. 267 above)

Cocalis, *The Defiant Muse* (1986) (see p. 267 above)

Göbelsmann, Ch. (ed.), *Mörikes Lüfte sind vergiftet: Lyrik von Frauen*, Munich: dtv, 1982

Graves, Peter (ed.), *Three Contemporary German Poets: Wolf Biermann, Sarah Kirsch, Reiner Kunze*, Leicester: Leicester University Press, 1985

Gutzschhahn, *Young Poets of Germany* (1994) (see p. 268 above), contains English
    translations of the following women poets: Lioba Happel, Kerstin Hensel,
    Barbara Maria Kloos, Brigitte Oleschinski, Evelyn Schlag, Sabine Techel, Bettine
    Wiengarn, Eva Christina Zeller
Hamburger, *German Poetry 1910–1975* (1977) (see p. 268 above)
Rosenkranz, Jutta (ed.), *Wenn wir den Königen schreiben. Lyrikerinnen aus der DDR*,
    Darmstadt: Luchterhand, 1988
Taylor, Andrew, and Beate Josephi (eds.), *Miracles of Disbelief: Selected Poems from the
    German of Christine Lavant, Ingeborg Bachmann, Sarah Kirsch, Ursula Krechel*,
    Canberra: The Leros Press, 1985

Secondary literature in English
Foot, Robert, *The Phenomenon of Speachlessness [sic] in the Poetry of Marie Luise Kaschnitz,
    Günter Eich, Nelly Sachs and Paul Celan*, Bonn: Bouvier, 1982
Hamburger, Michael, *After the Second Flood: Essays in Modern German Literature*, New York:
    St Martin's Press, 1986

Secondary literature in German
Berendse, Gerrit-Jan, *Die 'Sächsische Dichterschule': Lyrik der DDR der sechziger und siebziger
    Jahre*, Frankfurt am Main: Peter Lang, 1990
Braun, Michael, 'Lyrik', in Klaus Briegleb and Sigrid Weigel (eds.), *Gegenwartsliteratur
    seit 1968* (= Hansers Sozialgeschichte der deutschen Literatur), Munich and
    Vienna: Hanser dtv 1992, pp. 424–54
Beil, Claudia, *Sprache als Heimat: Jüdische Tradition und Exilerfahrung in der Lyrik von Nelly
    Sachs und Rose Ausländer*, Munich, 1988
Castein, Hanne, 'Scherz, Satire, Ironie und tiefere Bedeutung: Zur Thematik der
    Frauenlyrik in der DDR', in John Flood (ed.), *Ein Moment des erfahrenen Lebens. Zur
    Lyrik der DDR*, Amsterdam: Rodopi, 1987 (GDR Monitor Special Series No.5),
    pp. 99–119
Dahlke, Birgit, '"Am Brunnen vor dem Tore". Autorinnen in inoffiziellen Zeitschriften
    der DDR 1979–90', in Walter Delabar, Werner Jung and Ingrid Pergande (eds.),
    Neue Generation – Neues Erzählen: Deutsche Prosa-Literatur der 80er Jahre, Opladen:
    Westdeutscher Verlag, 1993, pp. 177–94
Domin, Hilde (ed.), *Doppelinterpretation*, Frankfurt am Main: Athenäum, 1966.
Emmerich, Wolfgang, *Kleine Literaturgeschichte der DDR*. Erweiterte Neuausgabe,
    Leipzig: Gustav Kiepenheuer Verlag, 1996
Heukenkamp, Ursula, 'Poetisches Subjekt und weibliche Perspektive. Zur Lyrik', in
    Gnüg and Möhrmann, *Frauen Literatur Geschichte* (1985/89) (see p. 265 above),
    pp. 354–66
Jürgensen, Manfred, *Deutsche Frauenautoren der Gegenwart: Bachmann, Reinig, Wolf,
    Wohmann, Struck, Leutenegger, Schwaiger*, Bern: Francke, 1983
Korte, Hermann, *Geschichte der deutschen Lyrik seit 1945*, Stuttgart: Metzler, 1989
Labroisse, Gerd, 'Frauenliteratur-Lyrik in der DDR', in *DDR Lyrik im Kontext*, ed.
    Christine Cosentino, Wolfgang Ertl and Gerd Labroisse, Amsterdam: Rodopi,
    1988, pp. 145–94
Naaijkens, Ton, 'Härte, Herz und Auge: Zur Lyrik der Gegenwart', in Brinker-Gabler,
    Deutsche Literatur von Frauen (1988) (see p. 265 above), vol. II, pp. 477–86
Reichart, Elisabeth (ed.), *Österreichische Dichterinnen*, Salzburg and Vienna: Otto Müller,
    1993

Schlenstedt, Silvia, 'Bilder neuer Welten', in Gnüg and Möhrmann, *Frauen Literatur Geschichte* (1985/89) (see p. 265 above), pp. 300–17

Schmölzer, Hilde (ed.), *Frau sein und schreiben: Österreichische Schriftstellerinnen definieren sich selbst*, Vienna: Österreichischer Bundesverlag, 1982

Schnell, Ralf, *Geschichte der deutschsprachigen Literatur seit 1945*, Stuttgart and Weimar: Metzler, 1993

Venske, Regula, and Sigrid Weigel, '"Frauenliteratur" – Literatur von Frauen', in Klaus Briegleb and Sigrid Weigel (eds.), *Gegenwartsliteratur seit 1968* (= Hansers Sozialgeschichte der deutschen Literatur), Munich and Vienna: Hanser dtv, 1992, pp. 245–76

Wolf, Ruth, 'Wandlungen und Verwandlungen: Lyrikerinnen des 20. Jahrhunderts', in Brinker-Gabler, *Deutsche Literatur von Frauen* (1988) (see p. 265 above), vol. II, pp. 334–52

14   Feminism, *Frauenliteratur*, and women's writing of the 1970s and 1980s

Anthology

Geyer-Ryan, Helga (ed.), *Was geschah, nachdem Nora ihren Mann verlassen hatte? Acht Hörspiele*, Munich: dtv, 1982

Histories of literature, works of reference, theory

alternative 108/109 (1976): 'Das Lächeln der Medusa: Frauenbewegung, Sprache, Psychoanalyse'

Adelson, Leslie, *Making Bodies, Making History: Feminism and German Identity*, Lincoln: University of Nebraska Press, 1993

Altbach, Edith Hoshino, Jeanette Clausen, Dagmar Schultz, and Naomi Stephan (eds.), *German Feminism: Readings in Politics and Literature*, Albany: SUNY Press, 1984

Ästhetik und Kommunikation 25 (1976): 'Frauen, Kunst, Kulturgeschichte'
      47 (1982): 'Weibliche Produktivität'

Beck, Evelyn Torton, and Patricia Russian, 'Die Schriften der modernen Frauenbewegung', in *Neues Handbuch der Literaturwissenschaft*, ed. Jost Hermand, Wiesbaden: Athenaion, 1979

Beck, Evelyn Torton, and Biddy Martin, 'Westdeutsche Frauenliteratur der siebziger Jahre', in *Deutsche Literatur in der Bundesrepublik seit 1965*, ed. Paul Michael Lützeler and Egon Schwarz, Königstein: Athenäum, 1980

Berger, Renate, Monika Hengsbach, Maria Kublitz, Inge Stephan and Sigrid Weigel (eds.), *Frauen – Weiblichkeit – Schrift*, Berlin: Argument, 1985

Bovenschen, Silvia, 'Über die Frage: Gibt es eine "weibliche" Ästhetik?' *Ästhetik und Kommunikation* 25 (1976), 60–75; tr. Beth Weckmueller as 'Is There a Feminine Aesthetic?' *New German Critique* 10: 111–37; also in Ecker, *Feminist Aesthetics* (1985) (see p. 282 below), pp. 23–50

Die imaginierte Weiblichkeit, Frankfurt am Main: Suhrkamp, 1979

Brinker-Gabler, *Deutsche Dichterinnen* (1978) (see p. 267 above)

Cella, Ingrid, '"Das Rätsel Weib" und die Literatur: Feminismus, feministische Ästhetik und die neue Frauenliteratur in Österreich,' in *Studien zur österreichischen Erzählliteratur der Gegenwart*, ed. Herbert Zemann, Amsterdam: Rodopi, 1982, pp. 189–228

Dietze, Gabriele (ed.), *Die Überwindung der Sprachlosigkeit. Texte aus der neuen Frauenbewegung*, Darmstadt: Luchterhand, 1979

Ecker, Gisela (ed.), *Feminist Aesthetics*, tr. Harriet Anderson, Boston: Beacon Press;
    London: The Women's Press, 1985
Export, Valie, 'Überlegungen zum Verhältnis von Frau und Kreativität', In
    Künstlerinnen international, 1877–1977. Exhibition catalogue, ed. Frauen in der
    Kunst, Berlin: Neue Gesellschaft für bildende Kunst, 1977
Ferree, Myra Marx, 'Equality and Autonomy: Feminist Politics in the United States and
    West Germany', in *The Women's Movements of the United States and Western Europe*,
    ed. Mary Katzenstein and Carol Mueller, Philadelphia: Temple University Press,
    1987
Frevert, Ute, *Frauen-Geschichte. Zwischen bürgerlicher Verbesserung und neuer Weiblichkeit*,
    Frankfurt am Main: Suhrkamp, 1986; tr. as *Women in German History*, New York,
    Oxford and Munich: Berg, 1989
Heuser, M., 'Literatur von Frauen/Frauen in der Literatur', in Pusch, *Feminismus* (1983)
    (see p. 282 below)
Jurgensen, Manfred, *Deutsche Frauenautoren der Gegenwart*. Bern: Francke, 1983
    Frauenliteratur: Autorinnen – Perspektiven – Konzepte, 1983
Kerschbaumer, Marie-Thérèse, *Für mich hat Lesen etwas mit Fließen zu tun ... Gedanken zum
    Lesen und Schreiben von Literatur*, Vienna: Frauenverlag, 1989
Kleiber, Carine and Erika Tunner (eds.), *Frauenliteratur in Österreich von 1945 bis heute*,
    Bern: Peter Lang, 1986
Knapp, Mona, and Gerd Labroisse (eds.), *Frauen-Fragen in der deutschsprachigen Literatur
    seit 1945*, Amsterdam: Rodopi, 1989
Künstlerinnen international, 1877–1977, Berlin: Neue Gesellschaft für bildende Kunst, 1977
Lühe, Irmela von der (ed.), *Entwürfe von Frauen in der Literatur des 20. Jahrhunderts*, Berlin:
    Argument, 1982
Martin, Biddy, 'Weiblichkeit als kulturelle Konstruktion', tr. Cornelia Holfelder-von der
    Tann, *Das Argument* 25 (March/April 1983), 210–15.
Meyer, Eva, *Zählen und Erzählen. Für eine Semiotik des Weiblichen*, Vienna: Medusa, 1983
    Versprechen: ein Versuch ins Unreine. Berlin: Stroemfeld/Roter Stern, 1984
Moffit, Gisela, *Bonds and Bondage: Daughter-Father Relationships in the Father Memoirs of
    German-Speaking Women Writers of the 1970s*, New York: Peter Lang, 1993
Möhrmann, Renate, 'Feministische Trends in der deutschen Gegenwartsliteratur', in
    Deutsche Gegenwartsliteratur: Ausgangspositionen und aktuelle Entwicklungen. ed.
    Manfred Durzak, Stuttgart: Reclam, 1981, pp. 336–57
Oguntoye, Katharina, May Opitz, and Dagmar Schultz (eds.), *Farbe bekennen: Afro-
    deutsche Frauen auf den Spuren ihrer Geschichte*, Berlin: Orlanda Frauenverlag, 1986;
    tr. Anne V. Adams as *Showing Our Colors: Afro-German Women Speak Out*, Amherst:
    University of Massachusetts Press, 1986
Puknus, Heinz, *Neue Literatur von Frauen: Deutschsprachige Autorinnen der Gegenwart*,
    Munich: Beck, 1980
Pulver, Elsbeth (ed.), *Zwischenzeilen: Schriftstellerinnen der deutschen Schweiz*, 2nd rev. edn,
    Bern: Zytglogge Verlag, 1989
Pusch, Luise, *Feminismus: Inspektion der Herrenkultur*, Frankfurt am Main: Suhrkamp,
    1983
    Das Deutsche als Männersprache: Aufsätze und Glossen zur feministischen Linguistik,
    Frankfurt am Main: Suhrkamp, 1984
Schenk, Herrad, *Die feministische Herausforderung. 150 Jahre Frauenbewegung in Deutschland*,
    Munich: C. H. Beck, 1980

Schmidt, Ricarda, *Westdeutsche Frauenliteratur in den 70er Jahren*, Frankfurt am Main: Rita
  G. Fischer, 1982; 2nd edn 1990
Schwarzer, Alice, *Der 'kleine Unterschied' und seine großen Folgen. Frauen über sich. Beginn einer
  Befreiung*, Frankfurt am Main: Fischer, 1975
Stephan, Inge, *Feministische Literaturwissenschaft*, Berlin: Argument, 1984
Stephan, Inge, and Sigrid Weigel, *Die verborgene Frau: Sechs Beiträge zu einer feministischen
  Literaturwissenschaft*, Berlin: Argument, 1983
Stephan, Inge, Regula Venske and Sigrid Weigel (eds.), *Frauenliteratur ohne Tradition?
  Neun Autorinnenporträts*, Frankfurt am Main: Fischer, 1987
Strobl, Ingrid, *Frausein allein ist kein Programm*, Freiburg: Kore, 1989
Thurmer-Rohr, Christina, *Vagabundinnen: Feministische Essays*, Berlin: Orlanda, 1987;
  tr. Lise Weil as *Vagabonding: Feminist Theory Cut Loose*, Boston: Beacon Press, 1991)
Trömel-Plötz, Senta, *Frauensprache: Sprache der Veränderung*, Frankfurt: Fischer, 1982
Vansant, Jacqueline, *Against the Horizon: Feminism and Postwar Austrian Women Writers*,
  Westport, Connecticut: Greenwood Press, 1988
Wartmann, Brigitte, 'Schreiben als Angriff auf das Patriarchat', *Literaturmagazin* 11
  (1979): 'Schreiben oder Literatur', 108–32
'Weiblichkeitsbilder', Discussion between Herbert Marcuse, Silvia Bovenschen and
  Marianne Schuller, in *Gespräche mit Herbert Marcuse*, ed. Jürgen Habermas, Silvia
  Bovenschen et al., Frankfurt am Main: Suhrkamp, 1978
Weigel, Sigrid, 'Der schielende Blick: Thesen zur Geschichte weiblicher Schreibpraxis',
  in Stephan and Weigel, *Die verborgene Frau* (1983) (see p. 283 above), pp. 83–137;
  tr. as 'Double Focus: On the History of Women's Writing', in Ecker, *Feminist
  Aesthetics* (1985) (see p. 282 above), pp. 59–80
'"Woman Begins Relating to Herself": Contemporary German Women's Literature
  (Part One)', tr. Luke Springman, *New German Critique* 31 (1984), 53–94
'Overcoming Absence: Contemporary German Women's Literature (Part Two)', tr.
  Amy Kepple, *New German Critique* 32 (1984), 3–22
Die Stimme der Medusa. Schreibweisen in der Gegenwartsliteratur von Frauen, Duelmen-
  Hiddingsel: tende, 1987
von Wysocki, Gisela, *Die Froste der Freiheit*, Frankfurt am Main: Syndicat, 1980

15 **Women's writing in Germany since 1989:
    new concepts of national identity**
    See bibliography for previous and following chapters.

16 **Writing about women writing in German:
    postscript and perspectives**
    Anthologies

Ackermann, Irmgard, *Türken deutscher Sprache: Berichte, Erzählungen, Gedichte*, Munich:
  dtv, 1984
Esselborn, Karl, *Über Grenzen: Berichte, Erzählungen, Gedichte von Ausländern*, Munich: dtv,
  1987
Friedrich, Heinz (ed.), *Chamissos Enkel: Literatur von Ausländern in Deutschland*, Munich:
  dtv, 1986
Harnisch, Antje, Anne-Marie Stokes and Friedemann Weidenauer (eds.), *Fringe Voices:
  An Anthology of Minority Writing in the Federal Republic of Germany*, Oxford: Berg,
  1999

Kummer, Irmela, et al. (eds.), *Fremd in der Schweiz: Texte von Ausländern*, Muri bei Bern: Francke/Cosmos, 1987

Ney, Norbert (ed.), *Sie haben mich zu einem Ausländer gemacht ... ich bin einer geworden. Ausländer schreiben vom Leben bei uns*, Reinbek: Rowohlt, 1984

Özkan, Hülya, and Andrea Wörte, *Eine Fremde wie ich: Berichte, Erzählungen, Gedichte von Ausländerinnen*, Munich: dtv, 1985

Schierloh, Heimke, *Das alles für ein Stück Brot: Migrantenliteratur als Objektivierung des Gastarbeiterdaseins*, Bern: Lang, 1984

Secondary literature on theoretical issues

Adelson, Leslie A., *Making Bodies, Making History: Feminism and German Identity*, Lincoln and London: University of Nebraska Press, 1993

Bloom, Harold, *The Anxiety of Influence: A Theory of Poetry*, Oxford: Oxford University Press, 1973

Butler, Judith, *Gender Trouble: Feminism and the Subversion of Identity*, London: Routledge, 1990

Fadermann, Lillian, and Brigitte Eriksson, *Lesbians in Germany 1890s-1920s*, Tallahassee: Naiad Press, 1990

Gaul-Ferenschild, Hartmut, *National-völkisch-konservative Germanistik. Kritische Wissenschaftsgeschichte in personengeschichtlicher Darstellung*, Bonn: Bouvier, 1993

Humm, Maggie, *Border Traffic: Strategies of Contemporary Women Writers*, Manchester: Manchester University Press, 1991

Maier, Charles S., *The Unmasterable Past: History, Holocaust, and German National Identity*, Cambridge, Massachusetts: Harvard University Press, 1988

Todd, Janet, *Feminist Literary History: A Defence*, Cambridge: Polity Press, 1988

Weedon, Chris, *Feminist Practice and Poststructuralist Theory*, Oxford: Blackwell, 1987

White, Hayden, *The Content of the Form: Narrative Discourse and Historical Representation*, Baltimore and London: Johns Hopkins University Press, 1987

Worton, Michael and Judith Still, *Intertextuality: Theories and Practice*, Manchester: Manchester University Press, 1990

Young, Robert J. C., *Colonial Desire: Hybridity in Theory, Culture and Race*, London: Routledge, 1995

Secondary literature on multi-cultural literature in Germany

Chiellino, Gino, *Literatur und Identität in der Fremde: zur Literatur italienischer Autoren in der Bundesrepublik*, Kiel: Neuer Malik Verlag, 1989

Fischer, Sabine, and Moray McGowan, 'From Pappkoffer to Pluralism: Migrant Writing in the German Federal Republic' in Russel King, John Connel and Paul White (eds.), *Writing across Worlds: Literature and Migration*, London: Routledge, 1995, pp. 39–56

Frederking, Monika, *Schreiben gegen Vorurteile: Literatur türkischer Migranten in der BRD*, Berlin: Express, 1985

Gohrisch, Jana, 'Differenzen um das Eigene und das Fremde. Überlegungen zum Ethnozentrismus', in *Rasse – Klasse – Geschlecht*, Heft 2, *Studien zur feministischen Theorienentwicklung*, ed. Hanna Behrend, Jana Gohrisch, Susan Arndt and Stefan Lieske, Berlin: Gesellschaftswissenschaftliches Forum e. V., 1994, pp. 23–37

Hamm, Horst, *Fremdgegangen – freigeschrieben: eine Einführung in die deutschsprachige Gastarbeiterliteratur*, Würzburg: Königshausen und Neumann, 1988

Heinze, Hartmut, *Migrantenliteratur in der Bundesrepublik Deutschland: Bestandsaufnahme und Entwicklungstendenzen zu einer multikulturellen Literatursynthese*, Berlin: EXpress, 1988

Horrocks, David, and Eva Kolinsky, *Turkish Culture in German Society Today*, Oxford: Berghahn, 1996

New German Critique 46 (1989): Special Issue on Minorities in German Culture, ed. Russel A. Bermann, Aazade Seyhan and Arlene Akiko Teraoka

Nolden, Thomas, 'Contemporary German Jewish Literature', *German Life and Letters* 57 (1994), 77–93

Oguntoye, Katherina, 'Die Schwarze deutsche Bewegung und die Frauenbewegung in Deutschland', *Afrekete: Zeitung von afro-deutschen und schwarzen Frauen* 4 (1989), 3–5, 33–7

Reeg, Ursula, *Schreiben in der Fremde. Literatur nationaler Minderheiten in der Bundesrepublik Deutschland*, Essen: Klartext Verlag, 1988)

Riemann, Wolfgang, *Über das Leben in Bitterland: Bibliographie zur türkischen Deutschland-Literatur und zur türkischen Literatur in Deutschland*, Wiesbaden: Harrassowitz, 1990

Rösch, Heidi, *Migrationsliteratur im interkulturellen Kontext*, Frankfurt am Main: Verlag für Interkulturelle Kommunikation, 1992

Suhr, Heidrun, 'Ausländerliteratur: Minority Literature in the Federal Republic of Germany', *New German Critique* 46 (1989), 71–103

Bibliographical guide to women writers and their work

Note: Entries in this guide are arranged alphabetically, using the name by which each writer is most commonly known: other names are listed in the Index where appropriate. Dates and place of birth and death are given where these are available. Works are mainly listed in chronological order; in the case of large entries, however, collected works have been listed first. For the sake of convenience, in some cases works have been grouped according to genre (prose, poetry, etc.).

For further information on biography, publications, and works in English translation, the following works of reference may be useful:

Brinker-Gabler, Gisela, Karola Ludwig and Angela Wöffen, *Lexikon deutschsprachiger Schriftstellerinnen 1800–1945*, Munich: dtv, 1986

Buck, Claire (ed.), *The Bloomsbury Guide to Women's Literature*, London: Bloomsbury, 1992

Dictionary of Literary Biography, ed. James Hardin et al., Detroit: Gale Research Inc., 1987–; see in particular vols. 56, 66, 69, 75, 81, 85, 90, 94

Frederiksen, Elke P. (ed.), *Women Writers of Germany, Austria and Switzerland. An Annotated Bio-Bibliographical Guide*, Bibliographies and Indexes in Women's Studies 8, New York; Westport, Connecticut; London: Greenwood, 1989

Frederiksen, Elke P., and Elizabeth G. Ametsbichler (eds.), *Women Writers in German-Speaking Countries: A Bio-Bibliographical Critical Sourcebook*, New York; Westport, Connecticut; London: Greenwood Publishing Group, 1998

Resnick, Margery, and Isabelle de Courtivron, *Women Writers in Translation. An Annotated Bibliography, 1945–1982*, New York: Garland, 1984 (difficult to locate in the UK)

Wilson, Katharina M. (ed.), *An Encyclopedia of Continental Women Writers*, 2 vols., Chicago, London: St. James, 1991

Translation bibliographies

Gerber, Margy and Judith Pouget, *Literature of the German Democratic Republic in English Translation. A Bibliography,* Lanham and London: University Press of America, 1984

Keenoy, Ray, Mike Mitchell, Maren Meinhardt et al., *The Babel Guide to German Fiction in English Translation (Germany, Austria, Switzerland)*, London: Boulevard Books, 1997

Mönnig, Richard (ed.), *Translations from the German*, Göttingen: Vandenhoeck and Ruprecht, 1968

Morgan, Bayard Quincey, *A Critical Bibliography of German Literature in English Translation, 1481–1927*, 2nd edn, New York and London: Scarecrow Press, 1965 (first published 1938)

Morgan, Bayard Quincey, *A Critical Bibliography of German Literature in English Translation*, Supplement Embracing the Years 1928–1955, New York and London: Scarecrow Press, 1965

O'Neill, Patrick, *German Literature in English Translation. A Select Bibliography*, Toronto, Buffalo and London: University of Toronto Press, 1981

Smith, Murray F., *A Selected Bibliography of German Literature in English Translation, 1956–1960*, Methuen, New Jersey: Scarecrow Press, Inc., 1972

In addition, the recently founded periodical *New Books in German* (ed. Rosemary Smith), published by The Society of Authors, now lists, by year, translations from German, starting with 1997.

List of abbreviations

a = autobiographical writings
ch = children's literature
d = dramatic works (including radio plays)
e = essays, non-fiction
l = letters
n = novel
p = poetry
r = religious writings
s = short story, short prose fiction
t = travel writing

   Where there is an entry on a particular author in one of the reference works immediately above, it is indicated as follows: entries in the *Dictionary of Literary Biography* (**DLB**) are given with full bibliographical reference; 'Frederiksen' indicates that this writer has an entry in the *Bio-Bibliographical Critical Sourcebook* (1998); 'Wilson' indicates an entry in the *Encyclopedia of Continental Women Writers* (1991); 'Morgan' indicates an entry in the *Critical Bibliography of German Literature in English Translation* (1965) (S=Supplement); and so on. Other short titles refer to the English or bilingual anthologies on pp. 267–8 above.

Ackers, Maximiliane (Saarbrücken 1896 – 1982 Glonn, Bavaria)

Freundinnen. Ein Roman (unter Frauen). Hannover: Steegemann, 1925; Berlin: Steegemann 1927 (n)

Secondary literature

'Maximiliane Ackers', *Juni. Magazin für Literatur und Politik* 21 (December 1994), 137–45

Aichinger, Ilse (Vienna 1921–)

Werke (8 vols.), ed. Richard Reichensperger, Frankfurt am Main: Fischer, 1991
Selected short stories and dialogues, ed. James C. Alldridge, Oxford: Pergamon Press, 1966
    (texts in German, introduction and notes in English)
Die größere Hoffnung, Amsterdam: Bermann-Fischer, 1948; Frankfurt am Main: Fischer,
    1976; 1983 (= *Werke* 1) (n)
Der Gefesselte, Frankfurt am Main: Fischer, 1953 (= *Werke* 2) (s)
Wo ich wohne: Erzählungen, Dialoge, Gedichte. Frankfurt am Main: Fischer, 1963 (s, d, p)
Eliza, Eliza, Frankfurt am Main: Fischer, 1965 (= *Werke* 3) (s)
Schlechte Wörter: Lyrische Kurzprosa und ein Hörspiel. Frankfurt am Main: Fischer, 1976
    (=*Werke* 4) (a, e, d)
Meine Sprache und ich, Frankfurt am Main: Fischer, 1978 (e, s)
Kleist, Moos, Fasane, Berlin: Wagenbach, 1979; Frankfurt am Main: Fischer, 1987 (= *Werke*
    5) (e, s)
Verschenkter Rat, Frankfurt am Main: Fischer, 1978 (= *Werke* 8) (p)
Spiegelgeschichte. Erzählungen und Dialoge, Weimar: Kiepenheuer, 1979 (e, d)
Knöpfe, Düsseldorf: Eremiten Presse, 1980 (d)

Works in English translation

Selected Poetry and Prose, ed. and tr. Allen H. Chappel, Durango: Longbridge-Rhodes, 1983
    (also contains drama *The Jouet Sisters* (= *Die Schwestern Jouet*))
Alldridge, J. C. (ed.), *Ilse Aichinger*, London: Wolff, 1969 contains stories, dialogues and
    poems in English translation, as well as a bibliography
Herod's Children (= *Die größere Hoffnung*; tr. Cornelia Schaeffer), New York: Athenaeum,
    1963 (n)
The Bound Man and Other Stories (= *Der Gefesselte*; tr. Eric Mosbacher), London: Secker &
    Warburg, 1955; New York, Noonday Press, 1956
Herrmann and Spitz, *German Women Writers* (1978)

Secondary literature

Moser, Samuel (ed.), *Ilse Aichinger: Materialien zu Leben und Werk*, Frankfurt am Main:
    Fischer, 1990
Frederiksen; Wilson

Albrecht, Sophie, née Baumer (Erfurt 1757 – 1840 Hamburg)

Works in 3 volumes: I: *Gedichte und Schauspiele*. (p, d); II: *Gedichte und prosäische Aufsätze* (p,
    e), Erfurt: Albrecht und Compagnie, 1781, 1785; III: *Gedichte und prosäische Aufsätze*,
    Dresden: Richter, 1791. (p, e)
*Ida von Duba das Mädchen im Walde: eine romantische Geschichte aus den grauenvollen Tagen der
    Vorwelt*, Altona: Friedrich Bachthold, n.d. (c. 1805) (n)
Theresgen (d), repr. in Karin Wurst (ed.), *Frauen und Drama im 18. Jahrhundert*, Cologne and
    Vienna: Böhlau, 1991

Alexander, Elisabeth (FRG 1932–)

Poetry includes

Bums: 50 Gedichte, Hamburg: Merlin, 1971
Ich bin kein Pferd, Leverkusen: et cetera, 1976
Zeitflusen, Heidelberg: Heidelberger Verlagsanstalt, 1986

Has also written novels

Translation (extracts): in Altbach, *German Feminism* (1984)

Aloni, Jenny (Paderborn 1917 – 1993 Gane Jehuda)

Gesammelte Werke in Einzelausgaben, ed. Friedrich Kienecker and Hartmut Steinecke, Paderborn: Schöningh, 1990–5

In den schmalen Stunden der Nacht, Tel Aviv: Achdut Press, 1980; included in *Gedichte* (= *Gesammelte Werke*, vol. VII), Paderborn: Schöningh, 1995 (p)

Zypressen zerbrechen nicht (= *Gesammelte Werke*, vol. II), Paderborn: Schöningh, 1990 (n)

Aloni, Jenny/Hartmut Steineke, '. . . *man müßte einer späteren Generation Bericht geben': Ein literarisches Lesebuch und eine Einführung in Leben und Werk Jenny Alonis*, Paderborn: Schöningh, 1995

Secondary literature

Schoppmann, Claudia, 'Portrait Jenny Aloni', in Claudia Schoppmann (ed.), *Im Fluchtgepäck die Sprache*, Berlin: Fischer, 1991, pp. 161–8

Amalie Marie Friederike Auguste, Prinzessin von Sachsen (=Amalie Heiter) (1794–1870)

Dramatische Werke, 6 vols., ed. Robert Waldmüller Leipzig: Edouard Duboc, 1873 (d; includes brief biography)

Lüge und Wahrheit (1833) (d)

Works in English translation

Six Dramas (The Uniformed Girl; The Heir of Scharfeneck; The Irresolute Man; Captain Firnewald; The Son's Return; The Young Lady from the Country), London: Parker, 1848

Social life in Germany, illustrated in the acted dramas of the princess A— of Saxony, tr. Mrs Anna Jameson, 2 vols., London: Saunders and Otley, 1840

Andreas-Salomé, Lou (St Petersburg 1861 – 1937 Göttingen)

Works of fiction include

Im Kampf um Gott, Leipzig and Berlin: Friedrich, 1885 (n)

Ruth, Stuttgart: Cotta, 1896 (s)

Aus fremder Seele. Eine Spätherbstgeschichte; Fenitschka. Eine Ausschweifung, Stuttgart: Cotta, 1898; repr. Frankfurt am Main: Ullstein, 1983 (s)

Menschenkinder, Stuttgart: Cotta, 1899 (s)

Ma. Ein Porträt, Stuttgart and Berlin: Cotta, 1901 (s)

Works in English translation

The Freud Journal (= *In der Schule bei Freud*; tr. Stanley A. Leavy), London: Quartet, 1987 (a)

Ibsen's Heroines (=*Henrik Ibsens Frauen-Gestalten*; ed. and tr. Siegfried Mandel), Redding Ridge, Connecticut: Black Swan Books, c. 1985 (e)

Fenitschka and *Deviations: Two Novellas* (= *Fenitschka. Eine Ausschweifung*; tr. Dorothee Einstein Krahn), Lanham: University Press of America, 1989 (s)

Sigmund Freud and Lou Andreas-Salomé. Letters, tr. W. and E. Robson Scott, 1972

Looking Back. Memoirs (= *Lebensrückblick*, ed. Ernst Pfeiffer, 1973; tr. Breon Mitchell), New York: Paragon House, 1991 (a)

Secondary literature

Martin, Biddy, *Woman and modernity: the (life)styles of Lou Andreas-Salomé*, Ithaca and
    London: Cornell University Press, 1991
Livingstone, Angela, *Lou Andreas-Salomé*, London: Gordon Fraser Gallery, 1984
Resch, Margit, 'Lou Andreas-Salomé', in James Hardin (ed)., *German Fiction Writers,
    1885–1913*, Detroit, 1988, pp. 3–17
Frederiksen; Wilson

Anneke, Mathilde Franziska (nr. Blankenstein 1817 – 1884 Milwaukee, USA)

*Mathilde Franziska Anneke: Die gebrochenen Ketten. Erzählungen, Reportagen und Reden
    (1861–1873)*, ed. Maria Wagner, Stuttgart, 1983 (s, e)
Der Erbe von Morton Park, 3 vols., 1845 (n)
Producte der rothen Erde, Münster 1846 (almanac)
Das Weib im Konflikt mit den socialen Verhältnissen, Münster 1847 (e)
Das Geisterhaus in New York, 1863 (n)

Secondary literature

Gerlach, M., *Mathilde Franziska Anneke. Biographie*, Berlin, 1988
Henkel, Martin and Rolf Taubert, *'Das Weib im Konflikt mit den socialen Verhältnissen'.
    Mathilde Franziska Anneke und die erste deutsche Frauenzeitung*, Bochum, 1976
Wagner, Maria, *Mathilde Franziska Anneke in Selbstzeugnissen und Dokumenten*, Frankfurt
    am Main: Fischer, 1981
Frederiksen

Selected translations: see Morgan

Apitz, Renate (1939?–)

Evastöchter, Rostock: Hinstorff, 1981 (n)
Hexenzeit, Rostock: Hinstorff, 1984 (n)
Herbstzeitlose, Rostock: Hinstorff, 1989 (n)
Wilson

Arnim, Bettina von, née Brentano (Frankfurt 1785 – Berlin 1859)

Sämtliche Werke, ed. W. Oehlke, 7 vols., Berlin: Propyläen-Verlag (1920–2)
Werke und Briefe, vols. I–IV, ed. G. Konrad; vol. V *Briefe*, ed. J. Müller, Frechen: Bartmann-
    Verlag, 1959–63
Schmitz, Walter and Sibylle von Steinsdorff (eds.), *Werke und Briefe in vier Bänden*,
    Frankfurt am Main: Deutsche Klassiker Verlag, 1986–
Goethe's Briefwechsel mit einem Kinde: seinem Denkmal, 3 vols., Berlin: Dümmler, 1835; repr.
    Frankfurt am Main: Insel, 1984 (n/l/a)
Die Günderode: den Studenten, Grünberg: Levysohn, 1840; repr. with afterword by Christa
    Wolf as *Die Günderode*, Frankfurt am Main: Insel, 1982 (n/l)
Dies Buch gehört dem König, 2 vols., Berlin: Schröder, 1843; repr. Frankfurt am Main: Insel,
    1983 (n)
Clemens Brentano's Frühlingskranz aus Jugendbriefen ihm geflochten, Charlottenburg: Bauer,
    1844; repr. Frankfurt am Main: Insel, 1985 (n)

Works in English translation

Goethe's Correspondence with a Child, translated by herself and Mrs. Austin, 1837–9, 3 vols., Berlin: Trowitzsch, 1837–38; London: Longman etc., 1837–9; 2 vols., Lowell, Massachusetts: Bixby, 1841; more recently tr. W. S. Murray in Franke (ed.), *The German Classics*, vol. vii, New York; 1913–15; AMS Press, 1969

Günderode (= *Die Günderode*; tr. (incomplete) Margaret Fuller Ossoli), Boston: Peabody, 1842; completed by Minna Wesselhoeft as *Correspondence of Fräulein Günderode and Bettine von Arnim*, Boston: Burnham, 1861

'The Queen's Son' (fairy tale) and 'The Report on Günderode's Suicide', etc., in Blackwell and Zantop, *Bitter Healing* (1990), pp. 443–72

Secondary literature

Drewitz, Ingeborg, *Bettine von Arnim: Romantik, Revolution, Utopie: eine Biographie*, Düsseldorf: Diederichs, 1969; 2nd edn Düsseldorf: Claassen, 1984

Frederiksen, Elke P., and Katherine R. Goodman (eds.), *Bettina Brentano-von Arnim: Gender and Politics*, Detroit: Wayne State University, c. 1995

Härtl, Heinz (ed.), *Bettina von Arnim: eine Chronik: Daten und Zitate zu Leben und Werk*, Weimar: Schöpfel, 1984

Helps, Arthur, and Elizabeth Jane Howard, *Bettina: A Portrait*, London: Chatto and Windus, 1957

Internationales Jahrbuch der Bettine von Arnim-Gesellschaft, Berlin (1987–).

Ives, Margaret (ed.), *Women Writers of the Age of Goethe*, vol. vi (special number on B. von Arnim)

Purver, Judith, 'Bettina von Arnim', in Lesley Henderson (ed.), *Reference Guide to World Literature*. 2nd edn, Detroit: St James Press, 1995, vol. i, pp. 61–3

Riley, Helene M. Kastinger, 'Bettina von Arnim', in James Hardin and Christoph Schweitzer (eds.), *German Writers in the Age of Goethe*, Detroit: Gale Research Inc., 1989, pp. 19–26

Waldstein, Edith. *Bettine von Arnim and the Politics of Romantic Conversation*, Columbia, South Carolina: Camden House, 1988

Wolf, Christa, 'Nun ja! Das nächste Leben geht aber heute an: ein Brief über die Bettine', in Wolf, *Lesen und Schreiben: neue Sammlung*, Darmstadt: Luchterhand, 1980, pp. 284–318; tr. Jan van Heurck as 'Your Next Life Begins Today: A Letter about Bettine', in *The Writer's Dimension* (see Wolf entry, p. 377 below), pp. 187–216

Frederiksen

Artner, Therese von (1772–1829)

Die That, Leipzig, 1817; 2nd edn Leipzig: Hartleben, 1820 (d)

Gedichte, Leipzig: Hartleben, 1818 (p)

Aston, Louise (later Louise Aston-Meier) (nr. Halberstadt 1814 – 1871 Wangen/Allgäu)

Ein Lesebuch. Gedichte Romane Schriften in Auswahl (1846–1849), ed. Karlheinz Fingerhut, Stuttgart: Akademischer Verlag, 1983 (p, n, e)

Wilde Rosen. Zwölf Gedichte, Berlin: W. Moeser & Kühn, 1846 (p)

Meine Emancipation, Verweisung und Rechtfertigung, Brussels, C. G. Vogler, 1846 (a, e)

Aus dem Leben einer Frau, Hamburg: Hoffmann & Campe, 1847; repr. Stuttgart: Akademischer Verlag, 1982

Lydia, Magdeburg: Emil Bänsch, 1848 (n)
Revolution und Conterrevolution, Mannheim: J. P. Grohe, 1849 (n)
Freischärlerreminiscenzen. Zwölf Gedichte, Leipzig: E. O. Weller, 1850 (p)
Also edited *Der Freischärler. Für Kunst und sociales Leben*, 1. Jg., 1848, numbers 1–7, 1
    November to 16 December

    Translation: Cocalis, The Defiant Muse (1986)

Secondary literature
Goetzinger, G., *Für die Selbstverwirklichung der Frau: Louise Aston*, Frankfurt am Main, 1983
Frederiksen

Ausländer, Rose (Czernowitz 1901 – 1988 Düsseldorf)
Poetry
Gesammelte Werke in sieben Bänden und einem Nachtragsband, ed. Helmut Braun. 8 vols.,
    Frankfurt am Main: Fischer, 1984–90
Der Regenbogen, Czernowitz: Literaria, 1939
Gesammelte Gedichte, Leverkusen: Literarischer Verlag Braun, 1976; Cologne: Braun, 1977
Immer zurück zum Pruth: Ein Leben in Gedichten, ed. Helmut Braun, Frankfurt am Main:
    Fischer, 1988
The Forbidden Tree: Englische Gedichte, ed. Helmut Braun, Frankfurt am Main: Fischer,
    1995 (poems written in English during exile)

    Numerous reissues and anthologies published by Fischer since 1988, mostly ed.
    Helmut Braun
Mein Atem heißt jetzt: Porträt einer Lyrikerin im Exil, Frankfurt am Main: Fischer, 1994

Works in English translation
Selected Poems, ed. Ewald Osers, London: London Magazine editions, 1977
Mother Tongue: Selected Poems, tr. Anthony Vivis and Jean Boase-Beier, Todmorden: Arc,
    1995

Secondary literature
Braun, Helmut, *Rose Ausländer: Materialien zu Leben und Werk*, Frankfurt am Main:
    Fischer, 1991
Beil, Claudia, *Sprache als Heimat: Jüdische Tradition und Exilerfahrung in der Lyrik von Nelly
    Sachs und Rose Ausländer*, Munich, 1988
Hilzinger, Sonja, '"Ich will wohnen im Menschenwort". Zur Lyrik Rose Ausländers', in
    Jörg Thunnecke (ed.), *Deutschsprachige Exillyrik 1933–1945*, Amsterdam: Rodopi,
    1998
Werner-Birkenbach, Sabine, '"Durch Zeitgeräusch wandern von Stimme zu Stimme . . ."
    Die Lyrikerin Rose Ausländer', *German Life and Letters* 45 (1992), 345–57
Frederiksen

Ava (Frau Ava) (Austria, early twelfth century)
Die Dichtungen der Frau Ava, ed. Kurt Schacks, Graz: Akademische Druck- und
    Verlagsanstalt 1986

Ayim, May (formerly known as May Opitz) (1960–96)
blues in schwarz weiss, Berlin: Orlanda Frauenverlag, 1995 (p)

nachtgesang, Berlin: Orlanda Frauenverlag, 1997 (p)
grenzenlos und unverschämt, Berlin: Orlanda Frauenverlag, 1997 (p)

Bacheracht, Therese von (pseud.: Therese) (Stuttgart 1804 – 1852 Java)

Briefe aus dem Süden, Braunschweig, 1841 (l/t)
Ein Tagebuch, Braunschweig: Vieweg & Sohn, 1842 (a)
Falkenberg, 1843 (n)
Am Teetisch, 1844 (n)
Lydia, 1844 (n)
Weltglück, 1845 (n)
Heinrich Burkart, Braunschweig: Vieweg & Sohn, 1846 (n)
Eine Reise nach Wien, Leipzig: Brockhaus, 1848 (t)
Alma, Braunschweig: Vieweg & Sohn, 1848 (n)
Sigismund, 1848 (n)
Novellen 1.u.2.Tl., Leipzig: Brockhaus, 1849 (s)

English translation
Heinrich Burkhart (tr. Hugh Powell), Columbia, South Carolina: Camden House, 1997

Secondary literature
Powell, Hugh, *Fervor and Fiction: Therese von Bacheracht and her Works*, Columbia, South
     Carolina: Camden House, c. 1996

Bachmann, Ingeborg (Klagenfurt 1926 – 1973 Rome)

Werke, ed. Christine Koschel, Inge von Weidenbaum and Clemens Münster, 4 vols.,
     Munich, Zurich and Piper, 1978
Die gestundete Zeit, Frankfurt am Main: Frankfurter Verlagsanstalt, 1953 (p)
Anrufung des Großen Bären, Munich: Piper, 1956 (p)
Der gute Gott von Manhattan, Munich: Piper, 1958 (d)
Das dreißigste Jahr, Munich: Piper, 1961 (s)
Malina, Frankfurt am Main: Suhrkamp, 1971 (n)
Der Fall Franza. Requiem für Fanny Goldmann, Munich: Piper, 1979 (n)
Frankfurter Vorlesungen: Probleme zeitgenössischer Dichtung, Munich: Piper, 1980/82 (e)
Simultan, Munich: Piper, 1982 (s)
Die Fähre, Munich: dtv, 1982 (s)
Sämtliche Gedichte, Munich and Zurich: Piper, 1983 (p)
Liebe: Dunkler Erdteil. Gedichte aus den Jahren 1942–1967, Munich: Piper, 1984 (p)

Works in English translation
In the Storm of Roses: Selected Poems by Ingeborg Bachmann, tr. Mark Anderson, Princeton:
     Princeton University Press, 1986
The Good God of Manhattan (= *Der gute Gott von Manhattan*; tr. Faith Wilding), in *German
     Radio Plays*, New York: Continuum, 1991
Three Paths to the Lake (= *Simultan*; tr. Mary Fran Gilbert), New York and London: Holmes
     and Meier, 1989 (s)
The Thirtieth Year (= *Das dreißigste Jahr*; tr. Michael Bullock), New York: Holmes & Meier,
     1987 (s)
Malina. A Novel (= *Malina*; tr. Philip Boehm), New York and London: Holmes and Meier,
     1990 (n)
Song above the Dust, tr. Eveline L. Kanes, Princeton: Princeton University Press, 1977 (p)

Songs in Flight: The Collected Poems, tr. Peter Filkins, New York: Marsilio, 1998 (bilingual
edition)
*Three Radio Plays (A Deal in Dreams; The Cicadas; The Good God of Manhattan) (=Ein Geschäft
mit Träumen; Die Zikaden; Der gute Gott von Manhattan*; tr. Lilian Friedberg),
Riverside, California: Ariadne, 1999
Herrmann and Spitz, *German Women Writers* (1978)

Selections: Cocalis, *The Defiant Muse* (1986); Hamburger, *German Poetry 1910–1975*
(1977); Taylor, *Miracles of Disbelief* (1985) (see p. 280 above)

Secondary literature
Achberger, Karen R., *Understanding Ingeborg Bachmann*, Columbia: University of South
Carolina Press, 1995
Bartsch, Kurt, *Ingeborg Bachmann*, Stuttgart: Metzler, 1988
Höller, Hans, *Ingeborg Bachmann: Das Werk. Von den frühesten Gedichten bis zum 'Todesarten'-
Zyklus*, Frankfurt am Main: Athenäum, 1987
Lennox, Sara, 'The Feminist Reception of Ingeborg Bachmann', in *Women in German
Yearbook* 8 (1993), 73–111
Pichl, Robert, and Alexander Stillmark (eds.), *Kritische Wege der Landnahme: Ingeborg
Bachmann im Blickfeld der Neunziger Jahre*, Londoner Symposium 1993 zum 20.
Todestag der Dichterin (17.10.1973), Vienna: Hora Verlag, 1994; publ.
simultaneously (with a bibliography) as vol. LX of Publications of the Institute of
Germanic Studies (University of London)
Frederiksen

Bacsányi, Gabriele, née Baumberg (1766–1839)
Gedichte. Mit einer Abhandlung über die Dichtkunst, von F.W.M., Vienna: Degen, 1805 (p, e)

Secondary literature
Ives, M., 'In Praise of Marriage: Reflections on a poem by Gabriele Baumberg', in Ives
(ed.), *Women Writers of the Age of Goethe*, vol. VII (1995), pp. 3–17

Bandemer, Susanne von, née von Frencklin or
von Franklin (1751–1828)
Sidney und Eduard, oder Was vermag die Liebe? Hannover, 1792 (d)

Baum, Vicki (Vienna 1888 – 1960 Hollywood);
emigrated to USA in 1930s; later wrote in English
Frühe Schatten. Das Ende einer Kindheit, Berlin: Reiss 1914 (n)
Stud. Chem. Helene Willfuer, Berlin: Ullstein 1929; first publ. 1925 (n)
Der Weg. Novelle. Stuttgart, Berlin and Leipzig: DVA 1925 (s)
Menschen im Hotel, Ein Kolportageroman mit Hintergründen, Berlin: Ullstein 1929 (n)
Zwischenfall in Lohwinkel, Berlin: Ullstein 1930 (n)
Leben ohne Geheimnis, Berlin: Ullstein 1932 (n)

Numerous other works of fiction in German and English

Works in English translation
Falling Star (= Leben ohne Geheimnis, tr. Ida Zeitlin), New York, 1937
Grand Hotel (= Menschen im Hotel; tr. Basil Creighton), London: Bles, 1930; repr. Pan
Books, 1977

Helene (= *Stud. Chem. Helene Willfuer*; tr. Ina Zeitlin), New York, 1933
Results of an Accident (= *Zwischenfall in Lohwinkel*; tr. Margaret Goldsmith), London: Bles, 1931
It Was All Quite Different: The Memoirs of Vicki Baum, New York: Funk and Wagnalls, 1964

    Further works and translations: see Frederiksen; Wilson; Morgan; Mönnig

Secondary literature
King, Lynda J., *Best-sellers by Design: Vicki Baum and the House of Ullstein*, Detroit: Wayne State University Press, 1988

Beradt, Charlotte (Lausitz 1907 – 1986 New York)

Das Dritte Reich des Traums, Munich: Nymphenburger Verlagshandlung GmbH, 1966 (a)

English translation
The Third Reich of Dreams: The Nightmares of a Nation 1933–1939, tr. Adriane Gottwald, with an essay by Bruno Bettelheim. Wellingborough: Aquarian, 1985

Berens-Totenohl, Josefa (Grevenstein, Sauerland 1891 – 1969 Meschede)

Der Femhof, Cologne: Eugen Diederichs, 1934 (n)
Frau Magdlene, Cologne: Eugen Diederichs, 1935 (n)
(Both re-issued as *Die Leute vom Femhof*, 1958) (n)
Das schlafende Brot, 1936 (p)
Die Frau als Schöpferin und Erhalterin des Volkstums, Jena: Diederichs, 1938 (e)
Einer Sippe Gesicht, Jena: Diederichs, 1941 (p)
Der Fels, 1943 (n)
Im Moor, 1944 (n)

Bettingen, Frida (1865–1924)

Eva und Abel, Düsseldorf: Bagel, 1919 (p)
Gedichte, Munich: G. Müller, 1922 (p)

Secondary literature
Keith-Smith, Brian, 'Frida Bettingen and Bess Brenck-Kalischer', in Keith-Smith (1993) (see p. 275 above), pp. 225–54

Beutler, Margarete (Gollnow, Pomerania 1876 – 1949 nr. Tübingen)

Gedichte, Berlin: M. Lilienthal, 1902–3 (p)
Neue Gedichte, Berlin: B. Cassirer, 1908 (p)
Leb wohl, Boheme! Ein Gedichtbuch, Munich: G. Müller, 1911 (p)

    Selections translated in: Cocalis, *The Defiant Muse* (1986)

Binzer, Emilie von (pseud.: Ernst Ritter) (Berlin 1801 – 1891 Munich)

Williams Dichten und Trachten, n.d. (d)
Die Gauklerin, n.d. (d)
Erzählungen und Novellen, 1836 (s)
Mohnkörner, 2 vols., 1846 (s)
Karoline Neuber, 1847 (d)
Erzählungen, 2 vols., 1850
Charaktere, 1855 (s)

Ruth, 1868 (d)
Drei Sommer in Löbichau. *1819–1821*, Stuttgart: Spemann, 1877

Birch-Pfeiffer, Charlotte (Stuttgart 1800 – 1868 Berlin)
Gesammelte dramatische Werke, 23 vols., Leipzig, 1863–80 (d)
Gesammelte Novellen und Erzählungen, 3 vols., Leipzig, 1863–5 (s)

Wrote c. 74 plays and numerous works of short fiction

English translation
Twixt Axe and Crown; *Jane Eyre* (see Wilson)
Frederiksen; Wilson

Blumenthal-Weiss, Ilse (Berlin 1899 – 1987 Connecticut, USA)
Ohnesarg. Gedichte und ein dokumentarischer Bericht. Mit einer Einführung von Günter Kunert,
    ed. Alfred Pfaffenholz, Hannover, 1984 (p, e)

Secondary literature
Niers, Gert, *Frauen schreiben im Exil: zum Werk der nach Amerika emigrierten Lyrikerinnen*
    Margarete Kollisch, Ilse Blumenthal-Weiss, Vera Lachmann, Frankfurt am Main: P.
    Lang, 1988
Pfaffenholz, Alfred, '"Erbschaft der Scheiterhaufen". Über Ilse Blumenthal-Weiss', in
    Denny Hirschbach and Sonia Nowoselsky (eds.), *Zwischen Aufbruch und Verfolgung.*
    Künstlerinnen der zwanziger und dreißiger Jahre, Bremen, 1993, pp. 144–8
Wilson

Böhlau, Helene (Weimar 1859 – 1940 Bavaria)
Rathsmädelgeschichten, Minden: J. C. C. Bruns, 1888 (s)
Der Rangierbahnhof, Berlin: F. Fontane, 1896 (n)
Das Recht der Mutter, Berlin: F. Fontane, 1896 (n)
Altweimarische Liebes- und Ehegeschichten, Stuttgart: Engelhorn, 1897 (s)
Ratsmädel- und Altweimarische Geschichten, Stuttgart: Engelhorn, 1897 (s)
Halbtier, Berlin: F. Fontane, 1899 (n)

English translation
The Ball of Crystal (= *Die Kristallkugel*; tr. A. I. du P. Coleman), in Franke (ed.), *The German*
    Classics, New York (1913–15)

Secondary literature
Singer, Sandra L., *Free Soul, Free Woman?: A Study of Selected Fictional Works by Hedwig Dohm*,
    Isolde Kurz, and Helene Böhlau, New York: P. Lang, c. 1995

Bölte, Amely (Amalie) (Mecklenburg 1811 – 1891 Wiesbaden)
Numerous works of fiction and travel literature, including
Luise, oder Die Deutsche in England, Bautzen: Schlüssel, 1846 (s)
Erzählungen aus der Mappe einer Deutschen in London, Leipzig: Grunow, 1848 (s)
Visitenbuch eines deutschen Arztes in London, Berlin: Duncker & Humblot, 1852 (s)
Eine deutsche Palette in London, Leipzig: Duncker & Humblot, 1853 (s)
Männer und Frauen, Dresden: L. Wolf, 1854 (s)
Liebe und Ehe, Braunschweig: Verlags-Comptoir, 1857 (s)
Frau von Staël, Leipzig: E. J. Günther, 1859 (n)

Winkelmann, oder: Von Stendal nach Rom, Berlin: Gerschel, 1861 (n)
Frauenbrevier, Vienna: C. A. Müller, 1862 (e)
Fanny Tarnow. Ein Lebensbild, Berlin: Wegener, 1865 (biog.)
Elisabeth, oder eine deutsche Jane Eyre, Vienna: Hartleben, 1873 (n)
Neues Frauenbrevier, Leipzig: Abel, 1876 (e)

English translation
Madame de Staël: an historical novel (= *Frau von Staël*; tr. Theodore Johnson), New York: G. P. Putnam, 1869

Bonin, Elsa von (Berlin 1882 – 1965 West Berlin)
Das Leben der René von Catte. Berlin: Fleischel 1911

And several later novels

Borchers, Elisabeth (Homberg, Niederrhein, FRG, 1926–)
Poetry
Gedichte, ed. Jürgen Becker, Frankfurt am Main: Suhrkamp, 1961; 1976
Wer lebt, Frankfurt am Main: Suhrkamp, 1986
Von der Grammatik des heutigen Tages, Frankfurt am Main: Suhrkamp, 1992

Also writes d; ch; s

Works in English translation
Poems, tr. Ruth and Matthew Mead, Santa Barbara, Unicorn Press, 1969
Fish Magic: Selected Poems, tr. Annelise Wagner, London: Anvil Press, 1989
Wilson

Brachmann, Louise (Rochlitz 1777 – 1822 Halle)
Auserlesene Dichtungen, ed. Friedrich Karl Julius Schütz, 2 vols. Leipzig: Weygand, 1824; 2nd edn 1834 (p)
Brinker-Gabler, *Deutsche Dichterinnen* (1978) (see p. 265 above), pp. 153–7 (contains biographical information and work selections)

Translations: see Morgan
Wilson

Braunschweig-Lüneburg, Sophie Elisabeth von (1613–76)
Sophie Elisabeth, Herzogin von Braunschweig-Lüneburg, Dichtungen, vol. 1: *Spiele* (5 more volumes planned), ed. Hans-Gert Roloff, Frankfurt am Main, 1980 (d, n, p)

Secondary literature
Roloff, Hans-Gert, 'Absolutismus und Hoftheater. Das *Freudenspiel* der Herzogin Sophie Elisabeth zu Braunschweig und Lüneburg', in Jörg Jochen Berns (ed.), *Höfische Festkultur in Braunschweig-Wolfenbüttel 1590–1666*, Amsterdam, 1982
Smart, Sara, *Doppelte Freude der Musen. Court Festivities in Brunswick-Wolfenbüttel 1642–1700*, Wiesbaden, 1989 (chapter 2 deals with theatrical works of Sophie Elisabeth of Braunschweig-Lüneburg)

Brenck-Kalischer, Bess (Rostock 1878 – 1933 Berlin)
Dichtung, Dichtung der Jüngsten 1., Dresden: Dresdner Verlag von 1917, 1917 (p)
Die Mühle. Eine Kosmee, Berlin: Hirsch 1922 (n)

Secondary literature
Keith-Smith, Brian, 'Frida Bettingen and Bess Brenck-Kalischer', in Keith-Smith (1993) (see p. 275 above), pp. 225–54

Breźna, Irena (Switzerland; writing 1980s)
Die Schuppenhaut, Zurich: efef, 1989
Karibischer Ball, Erzählungen und Reportagen, Zurich: efef, 1991

Brück, Christa Anita (Liegnitz [now Poland] 1899 – 1858 Königstein)
Schicksale hinter Schreibmaschinen, Berlin: Sieben Stäbe, 1931 (n)

Brückner, Christine (Waldeck 1921 – 1996 Kassel)
Wenn du geredet hättest, Desdemona. Ungehaltene Reden ungehaltener Frauen, Hamburg: Hoffmann und Campe, 1983 (s)

And numerous works of fiction

Works in English translation
Desdemona – if you had only spoken! Eleven uncensored speeches of eleven incensed women (= *Wenn du geredet hättest, Desdemona*; tr. Eleanor Bron), London: Virago, 1992
Gabrielle (= *Ehe die Spuren verwehen*; tr. Paul Selver), London: Hale, 1956
Katarina (= *Katharina und der Zaungart*; tr. Mervyn Savill), London: Hale, 1988
Gillyflower Kid (= *Jauche und Levkojen*, 1975; tr. Ruth Hein) New York: Fromm International Publishers, 1982
Flight of Cranes (= *Nirgendwo ist Pönichen*, 1982; tr. Ruth Hein), New York: Fromm, 1982
The Time of the Leonids (= *Die Zeit der Leoniden (Der Kokon)*, 1966; tr. Marlies I. Comjean), Boston: Charles River Books, 1984
Wilson

Brun, Friederike, née Munter (Saxony 1765 – 1835 Copenhagen)
Gedichte von Friederike Brun, geb. Münter, ed. Friedrich Matthisson, Zurich: Orell, Geßner, Füßli & Comp., 1795; further edns 1798, 1803, 1806 (p, s)
Prosäische Schriften, 4 vols., Zurich: Orell, Füßli und Compagnie, 1799–1801 (e, s, p)
Wahrheit aus Morgenträume (sic), Aarau: Sauerländer, 1810–24 (a)
Briefe aus Rom, ed. R. U. Böttger, Dresden, 1816 (e)

Selected translations and song settings: see Morgan

Secondary literature
Keith-Smith, Brian, 'Friederike Brun and her contemporaries', in Ives (ed.), *Women Writers of the Age of Goethe*, vol. I (1988), pp. 8–35
Wilson

Büchner, Luise (Darmstadt 1821–77)
Die Frauen und ihr Beruf. Ein Buch der weiblichen Erziehung, Leipzig: Thomas, 1856 (e)
Aus dem Leben. Erzählungen aus Heimat und Fremde, Leipzig: Thomas, 1861 (s)
Frauenherz, Halle: Herm. Gesenius, 1862 (p)
Das Schloß zu Wimmis, Leipzig: Thomas, 1864 (n)
Weihnachtsmärchen für Kinder, Glogau: Flemming, 1868 (s)
Praktische Versuche zur Lösung der Frauenfrage, Berlin: Janke, 1870 (e)
Über weibliche Berufsarten, Darmstadt: Köhlers-Verlag, 1872 (e)

Über Verkaufs-und Vermittlungsstellen für weibliche Handarbeit, Leipzig: Thomas, 1873
    (lecture)
Klara Dettin, Leipzig: Thomas, 1874 (p)
Deutsche Geschichte von 1815–1870, Leipzig: Thomas, 1875 (20 lectures)

Bürger, Elise, née Hahn (1769–1833)
Adelheit Gräfinn von Teck, Hamburg, 1799 (d)
Lilien-Blätter, Offenbach: Hauch, 1823 (p)
Gedichte, Hamburg, 1912 (p)

Secondary literature
Schiefer, Karl. 'Elise Bürger: ein Beitrag zur deutschen Literatur- und
    Theatergeschichte', diss., Frankfurt am Main, 1921

Burkart, Erika (Aarau, Switzerland, 1922–)
Poetry
Der dunkle Vogel, St. Gallen: Tschudy, 1953
Sterngefährten, St. Gallen: Tschudy, 1955
Bann und Flug, St. Gallen: Tschudy, 1956
Sommersonnenwende, Sins: Borgis, 1957
Geist der Fluren, St. Gallen: Tschudy, 1958
Die gerettete Erde, St. Gallen: Tschudy, 1960
Mit den Augen der Kore, St. Gallen: Tschudy, 1962
Ich lebe, Zurich, Stuttgart: Artemis, 1964 and 1977
Die weichenden Ufer, Zurich, Stuttgart: Artemis, 1967
Das Licht im Kahlschlag, Zurich, Munich: Artemis, 1977
Augenzeuge: Ausgwählte Gedichte, Zurich, Munich: Artemis, 1978
Die Freiheit der Nacht, Zurich, Munich: Artemis, 1981

And several more recent volumes

Secondary literature
Vogt-Baumann, Frieda, *Von der Landschaft zur Sprache: Die Lyrik der Erika Burkart*, Zurich,
    Munich: Artemis, 1977

Burmeister, Brigitte (Posen 1940 – GDR)
Anders oder Vom Aufenthalt in der Fremde, Berlin: Verlag der Nation, 1987; Darmstadt:
    Luchterhand, 1988
Unter dem Namen Nora, Stuttgart: Klett, 1994 (n)

Busta, Christine (Vienna 1915–87)
Many volumes of poetry, including
Der Regenbaum, Vienna: Thomas Morus Presse, 1951; repr. Salzburg: Otto Müller, 1977
Unterwegs zu älteren Feuern, Salzburg: Otto Müller, 1962
Konfigurationen, Salzburg: Otto Müller, 1971
Christine Busta 1915–1987, Vienna: Österreichische Nationalbibliothek, 1990
Der Atem des Wortes: Gedichte aus dem Nachlaß, ed. Anton Gruber, Salzburg, Vienna: Otto
    Müller, 1995
Wilson

Canetti, Veza (Vienna 1897 – 1963 London)

Die gelbe Straße, Munich and Vienna: Hanser, 1990 (n)
Der Oger. Ein Stück, Munich and Vienna: Hanser, 1991 (d)
Geduld bringt Rosen. Erzählungen, Munich and Vienna: Hanser, 1992 (s)

Works in English translation
Yellow Street: a novel in five scenes (= *Die gelbe Straße*; tr. Ian Mitchell), with a foreword by
    Elias Canetti, London: Halban, 1990
The Ogre (= *Der Oger*; tr. Richard Dixon) in *Anthology of Contemporary Austrian Folk Plays*,
    Riverside, California: Ariadne Press, 1993

Secondary literature
Lorenz, Dagmar C., 'Women's Concerns – Women's Popular Drama? Veza Canetti and
    Marieluise Fleißer', *Modern Austrian Literature* 26/3–4 (1993), 115–28

Chézy, Wilhelmine (Helmina) von, née von Klen(c)ke (also Helmina von Chézy, pseud. Sylvandra(y)) (Berlin 1783 – 1856 Geneva)

Euryanthe: große romantische Oper in drei Akten: in Musik gesetzt von Carl Maria von Weber,
    Bremen: Heyse, 1824 (libretto); repr. as *Euryanthe. Romantische Oper von Karl Maria
    von Weber. Dichtung von H.v.C, Vollständiges Buch*, ed. Karl Wittmann, Leipzig: Ph.
    Reklam jun., 1890
Leben und Kunst in Paris seit Napoleon dem Ersten. Von Helmina von Hastfer, geb. von Klenck (sic),
    2 vols., Weimar: Verlag des Landes Industrie-Comptoirs, 1805–7 (e)
Unvergessenes. 2 vols., Leipzig: Brockhaus, 1858; Facsimile repr. ed. William T. Parsons,
    Collegeville, Pennsylvania, 1982 (a)
Herzenstöne auf Pilgerwegen, Sulzbach, 1833 (p)
Erinnerungen aus meinem Leben, Schaffhausen: Hurter, 1863) (a)

    Numerous works of fiction and non-fiction, also translations

Works in English translation
Euryanthe translated into English six times between 1841 and 1887, performed at Drury
    Lane Theatre 1841–2; see Morgan
Manual for travellers to Heidelberg and its Environs, Heidelberg: F. Engelmann, 1825

Secondary literature
Götze, Alfred, 'Frau von Staël, Chamisso und Helmina von Chézy', *Archiv* 189 (1952–3),
    145–71
Wilson

Christ, Lena (nr. Munich 1881 – 1920 Munich)

Sämtliche Werke, ed. Walter Schmitz, 3 vols., Munich: Süddeutscher Verlag, 1990
Die Rumplhanni, Munich: Lange, 1916; repr. Munich: dtv, 1988 (n)
Madam Bäurin, 1919; repr. Munich: dtv, 1989 (n)
Wilson

Christen, Ada (pseud. for Christi(a)ne von Breden) (Vienna 1839–1901)

Lieder einer Verlorenen, Hamburg: Hoffmann & Campe, 1868 (p)
Aus der Asche, Hamburg: Hoffmann & Campe, 1870 (p)

Ella, Vienna and Pest: Martin, 1869 (n)
Faustina, Drama, Vienna: Dirnböck, 1871 (d)
Schatten, Hamburg: Hoffmann & Campe, 1872 (p)
Vom Wege, Skizzen, Hamburg: Hoffmann & Campe, 1874 (e)
Aus dem Leben. Skizzen, Leipzig: Berlin, Nicolais Sortiment, 1876 (a)
Aus der Tiefe, Hamburg: Hoffmann & Campe, 1878 (p)

Selected translations: see Morgan

Cirak, Zehra (Istanbul 1960 – FRG from 1963; Berlin)

Fremde Flügel auf eigener Schulter. Gedichte, Cologne: Kiepenheuer & Witsch, 1991 (p)
Vogel auf dem Rücken eines Elefanten. Gedichte, Cologne: Kiepenheuer & Witsch, 1991 (p)

Courths-Mahler, Hedwig (Thuringia 1867 – 1950 Tegernsee)

Scheinehe, Berlin, Eisenach and Leipzig: Hillger, 1905 (n)
Auf falschem Boden, Würzburg: Memminger, 1910 (n)
Es irrt der Mensch, Würzburg: Memminger, 1910 (n)

And numerous other works of popular fiction (listed Wilson)

For works in English translation see Morgan, e.g.
The String of Pearls (tr. anon.), Philadelphia: Lippincott, 1929
Wilson

Delden, Herta van (writing in 1920s and 1930s)

Das Heer der Heimat, Berlin: Behrs 1930 (n)

Delle Grazie, Marie Eugenie (Hungary 1864 – 1931 Vienna)

Wrote numerous works of prose and poetry, collected as
Sämtliche Werke, 9 vols., Leipzig: Breitkopf & Härtel, 1903–4

For further details, see Wilson (entry under **G**razie); also
Johns, Jorun B., 'Marie Eugenie delle Grazie', in James Hardin and Donald Daviau
(eds.), *Austrian Fiction Writers, 1875-1913*, Detroit, 1989, pp. 78–85

Demirkan, Renan (Ankara 1955; moved to Germany 1962)

Schwarzer Tee mit drei Stück Zucker, Cologne: Kiepenheuer & Witsch, 1991; repr. Munich: Goldmann, 1993 (n)
Die Frau mit Bart, Cologne: Kiepenheuer & Witsch, 1994 (s)

Diehl, Guida (Southern Russia 1868 – 1958 Giessen)

Erlösung vom Wirrwahn. Wider die von Dr Mathilde Ludendorff beeinflußte 'Deutschgläubigkeit', Eisenach: Neuland-Verlag, 1931 (e)
Die deutsche Frau und der Nationalsozialismus, Eisenach: Neuland-Verlag, 1933 (e)

Diers, Marie (Mecklenburg 1867 – 1949 Sachsenhausen nr. Berlin)

Freiheit und Brot. Roman einer Arbeiterfamilie, Berlin, 1933 (n)
Die Erbschaft der Magd. Eine Erzählung, Bremen, 1935 (s)
Die Doktorin von Bullenberg, Berlin: Paul Franke, 1937 (n)

And numerous other works of fiction 1902–43

Dischereit, Esther (Heppenheim/Bergstraße 1952 – FRG)

Joëmis Tisch – Eine jüdische Geschichte, Frankfurt am Main: Suhrkamp, 1988 (n)
Merryn, Frankfurt am Main: Suhrkamp, 1992 (prose)

Dittmar, Louise (1807–84)

Brutus Michel. Gedichte, Darmstadt: Leske, 1848 (p)
Bekannte Geheimnisse, Satire, Darmstadt, 1845
Vier Zeitfragen. Beantwortet in einer Versammlung des Montag-Vereins, Offenbach am Main, 1847 (e)
Lessing und Feuerbach oder Auswahl aus G. E. Lessings theologischen Schriften nebst Originalbeiträgen und Belegstellen aus L. Feuerbach's Wesen des Christenthums, Offenbach am Main, 1847 (e)
Wühlerische Geschichte eines Wahrhaftigen, Mannheim, 1848 (s)
Das Wesen der Ehe nebst einigen Aufsätzen über die sociale Reform der Frauen, Leipzig: O. Wigand 1849 (e)

Secondary literature

Louise Dittmar (1807–1884): un-erhörte Zeitzeugnisse, ed. and intr. Gabriele Käfer-Dittmar, Darmstadt: J. von Liebig, 1992

Dohm, Hedwig (Berlin 1831 – 1919 Berlin)

Numerous works of fiction, drama and non fiction, including
Was die Pastoren von den Frauen denken, Berlin: Schlingmann, 1872; repr. Zurich: ala, 1977; 1986 (e)
Der Jesuitismus im Hausstande. Ein Beitrag zur Frauenfrage, Berlin: Wedekind & Schwieger, 1873; reprinted in *Falsche Madonnen*; Zurich: ala, 1990 (e)
Die wissenschaftliche Emancipation der Frau, Berlin: Wedekind & Schwieger, 1874; repr. as *Emanzipation*, Zürich: ala, 1982 (e)
Der Frauen Natur und Recht, Berlin: Wedekind & Schwieger, 1876; Zurich: ala, 1986 (e)
Der Seelenretter, Vienna: Wallishausser, 1876 (d)
Vom Stamm der Asra, Berlin: Lassar's Buchhandlung, 1876 (d)
Ein Schuß ins Schwarze, Erfurt: Wallner's Schaubühne, 1878 (d)
Die Ritter vom goldenen Kalb, Bloch's Theater-Correspondenz, 1879 (d)
Wie Frauen werden. Werde die Du bist, Breslau: Schottländer, 1894; Zurich: ala, 1988 (s)
Sibilla Dalmar. Berlin: S. Fischer, 1896 (n)
Schicksale einer Seele, Berlin: S. Fischer, 1899; Munich: Frauenoffensive, 1988 (n)
Christa Ruland, Berlin: S. Fischer, 1902 (n)
Die Antifeministen. Ein Buch der Verteidigung, Berlin: F. Dümmler, 1902 (e)
Die Mütter. Beitrag zur Erziehungsfrage, Berlin: S. Fischer, 1903 (e)
Erziehung zum Stimmrecht der Frau, Berlin: Preussischer Landesverein für Frauenstimmrecht, 1909 (e)

Works in English translation

Women's Nature and Privilege (= *Der Frauen Natur und Recht*; tr. Constance Campbell), Westport: Hyperion, 1976

Secondary literature

Reed, Philippa, *'Alles was ich schreibe, steht im Dienst der Frauen.' Zum essayistischen und fiktionalen Werk Hedwig Dohms*, Frankfurt am Main: Peter Lang, 1987

Singer, Sandra L., *Free Soul, Free Woman?: A Study of Selected Fictional Works by Hedwig Dohm, Isolde Kurz, and Helene Böhlau*, New York: P. Lang, c.1995
Weedon, Chris, 'The Struggle for Women's Emancipation in the Work of Hedwig Dohm', *German Life and Letters* 47 (1994), 182–92
Frederiksen

Domašcyna, Róša (GDR 1951–)
Zaungucker: gedichte, texte, Berlin: Janus press, BasisDruck, 1992

Domin, Hilde (i.e. Hilde Palm, née Löwenstein) (1912 – FRG)
Nur eine Rose als Stütze.,Frankfurt am Main: Fischer, 1959 (p)
Rückkehr der Schiffe, Frankfurt am Main: Fischer, 1962 (p)
Hier, Frankfurt am Main: Fischer, 1964 and 1990 (p)
(ed.) *Doppelinterpretationen*, Frankfurt am Main: Athenäum, 1966 (crit)
Das zweite Paradies. Roman in Segmenten, Munich, Piper, 1968 (amended version publ. as *Das zweite Paradies. Eine Rückkehr*, Frankfurt am Main, Fischer, 1980; 2nd amended version, without the *Spiegel* quotations, with the dreams, Munich, Piper, 1986) (n)
Ich will dich. Munich: Piper, 1970; revised and expanded edition Frankfurt am Main: S. Fischer, 1992 (p)
Von der Natur nicht vorgesehen. Autobiographisches, Munich: Piper, 1974 (a)
Wozu Lyrik heute: Dichtung und Leser in der gesteuerten Gesellschaft, Munich: Piper, 1968; new edn 1975 (e)
Aber die Hoffnung: Autobiographisches aus und über Deutschland, Munich: Piper, 1982 (a)
Gesammelte Gedichte, Frankfurt am Main: Fischer, 1987 (p)
Das Gedicht als Augenblick der Freiheit: Frankfurter Poetik-Vorlesungen, Frankfurt am Main: Fischer, 1993 (e/theory)

Works in English translation
Four German Poets: Günter Eich, Hilde Domin, Erich Fried, Günter Kunert, ed. and tr. Agnes Stein, New York: Dust, 1979

Secondary literature
Braun, Michael, *Exil und Engagement: Untersuchungen zur Lyrik und Poetik Hilde Domins*, Frankfurt am Main: Peter Lang, 1993
Stern, Dagmar C., *Hilde Domin, from Exile to Ideal*, Bern: P. Lang, 1979
Wangenheim, Bettina von (ed.), *Heimkehr ins Wort: Materialien zu Hilde Domin*, Frankfurt am Main: Fischer, 1982
Frederiksen

Drewitz, Ingeborg (Berlin 1923 – 1986 West Berlin)
Bettine von Arnim. Romantik, Revolution, Utopie, Düsseldorf and Cologne: Diederichs, 1969 (e)
Oktoberlicht, Munich: Nymphenburger, 1969 (n)
Gestern war heute. Hundert Jahre Gegenwart, Düsseldorf: Claassen, 1978 (a/n)
Auch so ein Leben. Erzählungen aus den 50er Jahren, Göttingen: Herodot, 1985 (s)
And numerous other works

Works in English translation
Drewitz (ed.), *The German Women's Movement: The Social Role of Women in the 19th Century and the Emancipation Movement in Germany*, tr. Patricia Crompton, Bonn: Hohenwacht, 1983

Secondary literature

Kuntz, Liselotte, 'Ingeborg Drewitz', in Wolfgang D. Elfe and James Hardin (eds.), *Contemporary German Fiction Writers: Second Series*, Detroit, 1988, pp. 50–3

Frederiksen

Droste-Hülshoff, Annette von (Münster 1797 – 1848 Meersburg)

Annette von Droste-Hülshoff. Historisch-kritische Ausgabe, ed. Winfried Woesler, Tübingen: Niemeyer Verlag, 1978–

Gedichte von Annette Elisabeth v. D ... H ..., Münster, 1838 (p)

Gedichte von Annette Freiin von Droste-Hülshoff, Stuttgart: Cotta, 1844 (p)

Annette von Droste-Hülshoff. Briefe. Gesamtausgabe, ed. Karl Schulte Kemminghausen, 2 vols., Jena, 1944; repr. Darmstadt, 1968 (l)

Annette von Droste-Hülshoff. Poems, ed. Margaret Atkinson, London: Clarendon German Series, 1968

Annette von Droste-Hülshoff. Sämtliche Werke in zwei Bänden, ed. Günther Weydt and Winfried Woesler, Munich, 1973, 1978

Annette von Droste-Hülshoff. Werke in einem Band, ed. Clemens Heselhaus, Munich, 1984

Works in English translation

The Jew's Beech (= Die Judenbuche); tr. Lionel and Doris Thomas, London: Calder, 1958; 1963; tr. Michael Bullock as 'The Jew's Beech Tree', in: *Three Eerie Tales from 19th Century Germany*, New York, 1975; tr. Michael Fleming, in *Eight German Novellas*, Oxford: OUP, 1997

'Ledwina', in Blackwell and Zantop, *Bitter Healing* (1990) (s)

Cocalis, *The Defiant Muse* (1986); see also Morgan; O'Neill

Secondary literature

Guthrie, John, *Annette von Droste-Hülshoff: A German Poet between Romanticism and Realism*, Oxford: Berg, 1989

Morgan, Mary, *Annette von Droste-Hülshoff: A Woman of Letters in a Period of Transition*, Bern: P. Lang, 1981

Pickar, Gertrud Bauer, *Ambivalence Transcended: A Study of the Writings of Annette von Droste-Hülshoff*, Columbia, South Carolina: Camden House, c. 1997

Niethammer, Ortrun, and Claudia Belemann (eds.), *Ein Gitter aus Musik und Sprache: feministische Analysen zu Annette von Droste-Hülshoff*, Paderborn: Schöningh, c. 1993

Frederiksen; Wilson

Duden, Anne (Oldenburg 1942 – FRG)

Übergang, Berlin: Rotbuch, 1982 (s)

Das Judasschaf, Berlin: Rotbuch, 1985 (n)

Der wunde Punkt im Alphabet, Berlin: Rotbuch, 1985 (prose)

Steinschlag, Cologne: Kiepenheuer & Witsch, 1993 (p)

Wimpertier, Cologne: Kiepenheuer & Witsch, 1995 (p and prose)

Works in English translation

Opening of the Mouth (= Übergang; tr. Della Couling), London: Pluto Press, 1985

Durieux, Tilla, pseud. for Ottilie Godeffroy (Vienna 1880 – 1971 Berlin)

Eine Tür fällt ins Schloß, Berlin-Grunewald: Horen, 1928 (n)

Spielen und Träumen, Berlin: Verlag der Galerie Flechtheim, 1922 (e/a)

Meine ersten neunzig Jahre. Erinnerungen, Reinbek bei Hamburg: Rowohlt, 1976 (a)

Düringsfeld, Ida (later von Reinsberg, pseud.: Thekla)
(Silesia 1815 – 1876 Stuttgart)

Gedichte, 1835 (p)
Schriften, 7 vols., Breslau: Kern, 1845
Byrons Frauen, Breslau: Kern, 1845 (criticism)
Margarethe von Valois und ihre Zeit. Memoiren-Roman (1847 (n)
Am Canal Grande, Dresden: Meinhold & Söhne, 1848 (t, p)
Antonio Foscani, Stuttgart: Metzler, 1850 (n)
Eine Pension am Genfersee, Breslau: Kern, 1851 (n)
Reiseskizzen, vols. I–II, Leipzig: Haessel, 1851; vols. III–VI, Prague: Bellmann, 1857;
    vol. VII, Merano: Plant, 1868 (t)
Für Dich. Lieder, Leipzig: Weber, 1851, 1865 (p)
Amimone. Alpenmärchen, Breslau: Trewendt, 1852 (s)
Esther, Breslau: Trewendt, 1852 (n)
Die Literaten, Vienna, Leipzig: E. J. Günther, 1863 (n)

    Numerous other works of fiction, non-fiction and translations

    Translation: see Cocalis, *The Defiant Muse* (1986)
Wilson (under Reinsberg)

Ebner, Christine (1277–1353)
Büchlein von der Gnaden Überlast, ed. Karl Schröder, Tübingen: Literarischer Verein, 1871 (r)
Leben und Gesichte der Christina Ebnerin, Klosterfrau zu Engelthal, ed. Georg Wolfgang Karl
    Lochner, Nuremberg: F. Schmid, 1872 (r)

Ebner, Jeannie (Sydney, Australia 1918 – Austria)
Poetry
Sämtliche Gedichte 1940–1993. Wiener Neustadt: Merbod, 1993

    Also novels, short stories

Works in English translation
Three Flute Notes (= *Drei Flötentöne* (n; 1981); tr. Lowell A. Bangerter), Riverside, California:
    Ariadne, 1993
The Bengal Tiger (= *Der Königstiger* (s; 1959); tr. Lowell A. Bangerter), Riverside, California:
    Ariadne, 1992
Wilson

Ebner-Eschenbach, Marie von (Moravia 1830 – 1916 Vienna)
Kritische Texte und Deutungen, ed. Karl Konrad Polheim, Bonn: Bouvier, 1978– (vol. I:
    Unsühnbar; vol. II: *Das Gemeindekind*; vol. III: *Tagebücher*, Tübingen, 1989)
Sämtliche Werke, 12 vols., Leipzig, 1928
Erzählungen. Autobiographische Schriften, 3 vols., Munich: Winkler, 1956–8 (s/a)

    Prodigious output of plays, narrative fiction, essays and critical works

Works in English translation
Beyond Atonement (= *Unsühnbar*); tr. Mary A. Robinson, New York: Worthington, 1892; tr.
    Vanessa van Ornam, Columbia, South Carolina: Camden House, 1997
Aphorisms, tr. Mrs. Annie Lee Wister, Philadelphia: Lippincott, 1883; tr. G. H. Needler,
    Toronto: Burns & MacEachern, 1959; tr. David Scrase and Wolfgang Mieder,
    Riverside, California: Ariadne, 1994

The Child of the Parish (= *Das Gemeindekind*; tr. Mary A. Robinson), New York: R. Bonner's
  Sons, 1893
'The District Doctor' (= 'Der Kreisphysikus'; tr. Julia Franklin) and 'Krambambuli'; tr.
  A. Coleman, in Franke (ed.), *The German Classics* (1913–15), vol. XIII (see also *Seven
  Stories*)
The Two Countesses (= *Zwei Comtessen*; tr. Mrs. Ellen Waugh), The Pseudonym Library,
  vol. XXVII, 1893 (see also *Seven Stories*)
Seven Stories, tr. and intr. Helga W. Harriman, Columbia, South Carolina: Camden
  House, 1986 ('Krambambuli', 'Jacob Szela', 'Countess Muschi', 'Countess Paula',
  'The Wake', 'The Finch', 'The Travelling Companions')
Their Pavel (= *Ihr Pavel*; tr. Lynne Tatlock), Columbia, South Carolina: Camden House, 1996

Further translations listed in:
Resnick and Courtivron; Morgan; and Donald G. Daviau (ed.), *Major Figures of Turn of the
  Century Austrian Literature*, Riverside, California: Ariadne Press, 1991, pp. 131–2
Cocalis, *The Defiant Muse* (1986)

Secondary literature
Bramkamp, Agatha C., *Marie von Ebner-Eschenbach: The Author, Her Time, and Her Critics*,
  Bonn: Bouvier, 1990
Johns, Jorun B., 'Marie von Ebner-Eschenbach', in James Hardin and Donald Daviau
  (eds.), *Austrian Fiction Writers, 1875–1913*, Detroit, 1989, pp. 86–94
Rose, Ferrell V., *The Guises of Modesty: Marie von Ebner-Eschenbach's Female Artists*,
  Columbia, South Carolina: Camden House, c. 1994
Steiner, Carl, *Of Reason and Love: The Life and Works of Marie von Ebner-Eschenbach*, Riverside,
  California: Ariadne, 1994
Frederiksen

Eckart, Gabriele (GDR/FRG, 1954–)
Tagebuch: Gedichte, Berlin: Buchverlag Der Morgen, 1978 (p)
Per Anhalter, Berlin: Verlag neues Leben, 1982 (n)
So sehe ick die Sache: Protokolle aus der DDR, Cologne: Kiepenheuer & Witsch, 1984
  (interviews/e)
Sturzacker: Gedichte 1980–1984, Berlin: Buchverlag Der Morgen, 1985 (p)
Wie mag ich alles was beginnt, Cologne: Kiepenheuer & Witsch, 1987 (p)
Frankreich heißt Jeanne, Berlin: Buchverlag der Morgen, 1990
Der gute fremde Blick: eine (Ost)deutsche entdeckt Amerika, Cologne: Kiepenheuer & Witsch,
  c. 1992 (t/a)

English translation
Hitchhiking (= *Per Anhalter*; tr. Wayne Kram), Lincoln: University of Nebraska Press, 1992
Wilson

Ehrmann, Marianne (Rapperswil, Switzerland 1755 – 1795 Stuttgart)
Leichtsinn und gutes Herz, repr. Karin Wurst (ed.), *Frauen und Drama im 18. Jahrhundert*,
  Cologne and Vienna: Böhlau, 1991 (d)

Also edited the following journals
Amaliens Erholungsstunden. Teutschlands Töchtern geweiht, 6 vols., Tübingen: Cotta, 1790–2
Die Einsiedlerin aus den Alpen, Zurich: Orell, 1793–5

For more details see Wilson

Elisabeth von Nassau-Saarbrücken (France, after 1393 – 1456 Saarbrücken)

Hug Schapel, in *Romane des 15. und 16. Jahrhunderts*, ed. Jan-Dirk Müller, Frankfurt: Deutscher Klassiker Verlag, 1990, pp. 177–339 (prose romance)
Herpin, in *Die deutschen Volksbücher*, ed. Karl Simrock, Basel, 1892. repr. Hildesheim and New York: Olms, 1974, 213–445 (prose romance)
Loher und Maller, ed. Karl Simrock, Strassburg: Cotta, 1868 (prose romance)
Sibille, in *Der Roman von der Königin Sibille in 3 Prosafassungen des 14. u. 15. Jahrhunderts*, ed. Hermann Tiemann, Hamburg: Hauswedell, 1977, pp. 117–86 (prose romance)
Wilson

Elsner, Gisela (Nuremberg 1937 – 1992 Munich)

Die Riesenzwerge, Reinbek: Rowohlt, 1964 (n)
Der Nachwuchs, Reinbek: Rowohlt, 1968 (n)
Das Berührungsverbot, Reinbek: Rowohlt, 1970 (n)
Die Zähmung. Chronik einer Ehe, Reinbek: Rowohlt, 1984 (n)

Works in English translation

The Giant Dwarfs (= *Die Riesenzwerge*; tr. Joel Carmichael), New York: Grove Press, 1965
Offside (= *Abseits*, tr. Anthea Bell), London: Virago, 1985
Herrmann and Spitz, *German Women Writers* (1978)

Engel, Regula, née Egli (Fluntern nr. Zurich 1761 – 1853 Zurich)

Lebensbeschreibung der Wittwe des Obrist Florian Engel, Zurich, 1821; part 1 only repr. Zurich: Rascher & Co., 1914 (a)
Die schweizerische Amazone: Abentheuer Reisen und Kriegszüge einer Schweizerinn, vol. II: *Abentheuer Reisen durch die Schweiz mit merkwürdigen Schicksalen und Anmerkungen begleitet*. Zug: Blunschi, 1828 (a)
Frau Oberst Engel: von Cairo bis Neuyork, von Elba bis Waterloo: Memoiren einer Amazone aus napoleonischer Zeit. Zurich: Limmat Verlag, 1982 (based on the 1825 edition) (a)

Secondary literature

Stump, Doris, '"So gewiß ist es, daß wo wir Brod finden, unser Vaterland ist": die Lebensbeschreibung der Schweizer Offiziersgattin Regula Engel-Egli (1761–1853)', in Joeres, *Out of Line* (see p. 272 above), pp. 77–92

Erb, Elke (Eifel 1938 – GDR)

Poetry

Gutachten: Poesie und Prosa, Berlin and Weimar: Aufbau, 1975 (p/s)
Einer schreit 'Nicht!': Geschichten und Gedichte, Berlin: Wagenbach, 1976 (p/s)
Der Faden der Geduld, Berlin and Weimar: Aufbau, 1978
Trost: Gedichte und Prosa, ed. Sarah Kirsch, Stuttgart: DVA, 1980 (p/s)
Vexierbild, Berlin and Weimar: Aufbau, 1983
Kastanienallee: Texte und Kommentare, Berlin and Weimar: Aufbau, 1987
Winkelzüge oder nicht vermutete aufschlussreiche Verhältnisse, Berlin: Galrev, 1990
Unschuld, du Licht meiner Augen, Göttingen: Steidl, 1994
Wo das Nichts explodiert: Gedichte, Berlin: Mariennenpresse, 1994

Editions

Annette von Droste-Hülshoff, *Gedichte. Mit einem Essay*, Leipzig: Insel-Verlag, 1989
Friederike Mayröcker, *Veritas: Lyrik und Prosa*, Leipzig: Reclam, 1993

with Sascha Anderson, *Berührung ist nur eine Randerscheinung: Neue Literatur aus der DDR*,
    Cologne: Kiepenheuer & Witsch, 1985

    Translations: see Gerber and Pouchet
Wilson

Erler, Ursula (Cologne 1946–)

Die neue Sophie, oder Der Beginn einer längst fälligen Gattung der Literatur. Starnberg: Werner
    Raith, 1972

    Other works listed in Wilson

Eschstruth, Nataly von (Hofgeismar 1860 – 1939 Schwerin)

Illustrierte Romane und Novellen, Leipzig: P. List, 1899–1909 (5 series: 53 vols. in all)

    Numerous short stories and novels listed in Wilson

Works in English translation
A Priestess of Comedy (= *Comödie*; tr. Elise L. Lathrop), New York: Bonner, 1893
The Erl Queen (= *Erlkönigin*; tr. Emily S. Howard), New York: Worthington, 1892
Polish Blood (= *Polnisch Blut*; tr. Cora L. Turner), New York: Alden, 1889

    Further works listed in Morgan

Fischer, Caroline Auguste, née Venturini (Braunschweig 1764 – 1842 Frankfurt)

Die Honigmonathe, 2 vols., Posen: Kühn, 1802; repr. (ed. Anita Runge), Hildesheim: Olms,
    1987 (n)
Der Günstling, Posen: Kühn, 1808 (1809); repr. (ed. Anita Runge), Hildesheim: Olms, 1988 (n)
Margarethe, ein Roman, Heidelberg: Mohr und Zimmer, 1812; repr. (ed. Anita Runge),
    Hildesheim: Olms, 1989 (n)
Kleine Erzählungen und romantische Skizzen, Posen: Kühn, 1818; repr. (ed. Anita Runge),
    Hildesheim: Olms, 1988 (s)

Works in English translation
'William the Negro' (= 'William der Neger', from *Erzählungen*) in Blackwell and Zantop,
    Bitter Healing (1990), pp. 351–67

Secondary literature
Purver, Judith, 'Caroline Auguste Fischer: An Introduction', in Ives (ed.), *Women Writers
    of the Age of Goethe*, vol. IV (1991), pp. 3–30
Purver, Judith, 'Passion, Possession, Patriarchy: Images of Men in the Novels and Short
    Stories of Caroline Auguste Fischer (1764–1842)', *Neophilologus* 79 (1995), 619–28
Runge, Anita, 'Die Dramatik weiblicher Selbstverständigung in den Briefromanen
    Caroline Auguste Fischers', in Runge and Steinbrügge, *Die Frau im Dialog* (see
    p. 273 above), pp. 93–114
Zantop, Susanne. 'Karoline Auguste Ferdinandine Fischer', in James Hardin and
    Christoph E. Schweitzer (eds.). *German Writers of the Age of Goethe: Sturm and Drang
    to Classicism*, DLB 94, Detroit: Gale Research Inc., 1990, pp. 31–6

Fleißer, Marieluise (Ingolstadt 1901–74)

Gesammelte Werke, ed. Günther Rühle, 4 vols., Frankfurt am Main: Suhrkamp, 1972–89
Ingolstädter Stücke (*Fegefeuer in Ingolstadt*; *Pioniere in Ingolstadt*), Frankfurt am Main:
    Suhrkamp, 1977 (d)

Pioniere in Ingolstadt, repr. with an introduction, notes and vocabulary by David Horton, Manchester: Manchester German Texts, 1992 (d)

Mehlreisende Frieda Geier. Roman vom Rauchen, Sporteln, Lieben und Verkaufen. Berlin: Kiepenheuer 1931; repr. as *Eine Zierde für den Verein. Roman vom Rauchen, Sporteln, Lieben und Verkaufen,* Frankfurt am Main: Suhrkamp, 1987

Works in English translation

Purgatory in Ingolstadt (= *Fegefeuer in Ingolstadt*) and *Pioneers in Ingolstadt* (*Pioniere in Ingolstadt*; 1968 version; tr. Elisabeth Bond-Pablé and Tinch Minter), in *Plays by Women: Nine,* ed. Annie Castledine, London: Methuen, 1991

Purgatory in Ingolstadt, tr. Gitta Honegger, in Case, *The Divided Home/Land* (1992)

Secondary literature

Beicken, Peter, 'Marieluise Fleißer', in James Hardin (ed.), *German Fiction Writers 1914–1945,* Detroit, 1987, pp. 94–101

Hoffmeister, Donna L., *The Theater of Confinement. Language and Survival in the Milieu Plays of Marieluise Fleißer and Franz Xaver Kroetz,* Columbia, South Carolina: Camden House, 1983

Kord, Susanne, 'Fading out: Invisible Women in Marieluise Fleißer's Early Dramas'. *Women in German Yearbook* 5 (1989), 57–72

Lorenz, Dagmar C., 'Women's Concerns – Women's Popular Drama?' (see p. 299 above, under Canetti)

Tax, Sissi, *marieluise fleißer. schreiben überleben – ein biographischer versuch,* Basel and Frankfurt am Main: Stroemfeld/Verlag Roter Stern, 1984

Frederiksen; Wilson

Fouqué, Caroline de la Motte, née von Briest (nr. Rathenow 1774–1831)

Rodrich: ein Roman in zwey Theilen, vol. I Berlin: Hitzig, 1806; vol. II. Berlin: Dümmler, 1807 (n)

Die Frau des Falkensteins: ein Roman von der Verfasserin des Rodrich, 2 vols. Berlin: Hitzig, 1810 (n)

Magie der Natur: eine Revolutions-Geschichte, Berlin: Hitzig, 1812 (n)

Das Heldenmädchen aus der Vendee, 2 vols, Leipzig: Fleischer, 1816 (n)

Neue Erzählungen, Berlin: Dümmler, 1817 (s)

Kleine Romane und Erzählungen: neue Sammlung, 2 vols., Jena: Schmid, 1820 (n, s)

Die Vertriebenen: eine Novelle aus der Zeit der Königin Elisabeth von England, 3 vols., Leipzig: Hartmann, 1823 (s)

Weihnachtsgabe: drei Erzählungen, Berlin: Herbig, 1827 (s)

Geschichte der Moden, vom Jahre 1785 bis 1829, als Beytrag zur Geschichte der Zeit, Stuttgart: Cotta, 1830, repr. (ed. Dorothea Böck) Berlin: Union Verlag, 1987 (e)

Works in English translation

'The Curse: A Tale' (= 'Die Verwünschung' from *Neue Erzählungen*; tr. N. Stenhouse), Edinburgh: privately printed, 1825

The Outcasts: A Romance (= *Die Vertriebenen*; tr. George Soane), 2 vols., London: Printed for G. and W. G. Whittaker, 1824

The Physician of Marseilles, The Revolutionists, Etc.: Four Tales from the German, tr. anon., London: Burns, 1845 (includes 'The Revolutionists', and 'The Christmas Tree' and 'Valerie' from *Weihnachtsgabe*)

The Castle of Scharffenstein: German Stories, Selected from the Works of Hoffmann, de la Motte

Fouqué, Pichler, Kruse, and Others by R. P. Gillies, Edinburgh: W. Blackwood, 1826
   (includes translation of 'Der Scharffenstein' from *Kleine Romane*)
*The Castle on the Beach: A Tale. Foreign Tales and Traditions, Chiefly Selected from the Fugitive
   Literature of Germany by G. Godfrey Cunningham*., 2 vols., Glasgow: Blackie,
   Fullarton, 1830
The Cypress Crown (= *Der Cypressenzweig*; tr. anon.), c. 1820

Secondary literature
Hofacker, Erich P., Jr., 'Caroline de la Motte Fouqué', in James Hardin and Christoph
   Schweitzer (eds.), *German Writers in the Age of Goethe*, Detroit: Gale Research, Inc.,
   1989, pp. 78–83
Purver, Judith, 'Caroline de la Motte Fouqué', in Lesley Henderson (ed.), *Reference Guide
   to World Literature*, 2nd edn, Detroit: St James Press, 1995, vol. I, pp. 430–2
Wilde, Jean T., *The Romantic Realist: Caroline de la Motte Fouqué*, New York: Bookman
   Associates, 1955

François, Louise von (Herzberg, Saxony 1817 – 1893 Weißenfels, Saxony)
Gesammelte Werke in 5 Bänden, Leipzig: Insel (1918)
Gesammelte Werke in 2 Bänden, Leipzig: Minerva (1924)

Numerous novels and short stories including
Die letzte Reckenburgerin (1871), numerous reprints, e.g. Berlin: Greve, 1925; Cologne:
   Atlas, 1957; Leipzig: G. Fischer, 1965; Bonn: J. Latka, 1988 (n)
Frau Erdmuthens Zwillingssöhne, repr. Zurich: Manesse, 1954 (n)

Works in English translation
The Last von Reckenburg (= *Die letzte Reckenburgerin*; tr. 'J. M. Percival'), Boston: Cupples and
   Hurd, 1887; London: Gardner, 1888; tr. Mary Joanna Safford, ed. and intr. Tiiu V.
   Laane, Columbia, South Carolina: Camden House, 1995
Wilson

Frapan, Ilse (Hamburg 1849 – 1908 Geneva)
Hamburger Novellen, Hamburg: O. Meißner, 1886 (s)
Wir Frauen haben kein Vaterland. Monologe einer Fledermaus, Berlin: F. Fontane, 1899 (n)
Arbeit, Berlin: Gebrüder Paetel, 1903 (n)
Die Retter der Moral, Leipzig: Reclam, 1905 (d)

Works in English translation
'Heavy Laden' (= 'Die Last') and 'Old Fashioned Folk' (= 'Altmodische Leute'), tr. Helen
   A. McDonell, London: Unwin, 1892
God's will, and other stories, tr. Helen A. McDonell, London and New York: Cassell, 1893

Frei, Frederike (1944 – FRG)
Losgelebt, Hamburg: Dölling & Galitz, and Cologne: Braun, 1977 (p)

   Translation: Cocalis, *The Defiant Muse* (1986)

Gallitzin, Amalie Fürstin von, née von Schmettau (1748–1806)
*Frauen der Goethezeit in Briefen, Dokumenten und Bildern: von der Gottschedin bis zu Bettina von
   Arnim: eine Anthologie,* ed. Helga Haberland and Wolfgang Pehut, Stuttgart:
   Reclam, 1960, pp. 107–27 (l)

Gertrud von Helfta (Gertrude the Great, St Gertrude) (1256 – 1302 Helfta); wrote in Latin

Works in English translation

The Life and Revelations of Saint Gertrud. By a Religious Order of Poor Clares, London: Burns and Oates, 1865; 2nd edn 1871

Spiritual Exercises (= *Exercitia spiritualia*); translation, introduction, notes, and indexes by Gertrud Jaron Lewis and Jack Lewis, Kalamazoo, Michigan: Cistercian Publications, 1989

The Herald of God's Loving-Kindness: Books One and Two (=*Legatus divinae pietatis*), tr. with an introduction and notes by Alexandra Barratt, Kalamazoo, Michigan: Cistercian Publications, c. 1991; as *The Herald of Divine Love*, tr. and ed. Margaret Winkworth, intr. Sister Maximilian Marnau, preface by Louis Bouyer, New York: Paulist Press, c. 1993

Secondary literature

Finnegan, Mary Jeremy OP, *The Women of Helfta: Scholars and Mystics*, Athens, Georgia and London: The University of Georgia Press, 1991

Wilson

Gleit, Maria (Crimmitschau, Saxony 1909 – 1981 Zollikon, Switzerland)

Junges Weib Veronika, 1936 (n)

And other works of fiction and ch.; later wrote in English, e.g.

Paul Tiber, Forester, Chicago: Scribner, 1949

Works in English translation

Child of China (= *Sa Tu Sai führt Krieg*; tr. E. F. Peeler), London: OUP, 1958 (ch)

Glickl bas Judah Leib (also known as Glückel von Hameln) (Hamburg 1645 or 1647 – 1724 Metz); wrote in Yiddish

Die Memoiren der Glückel von Hameln, tr. Bertha Pappenheim and ed. Viola Roggenkamp, Weinheim, 1994 (a)

Works in English translation

The Life of Glückel of Hameln 1646–1724. Written by Herself, tr. from the original Yiddish and ed. Beth-Zion Abrahams, London: Horovitz, 1962

The Memoirs of Glückel of Hameln, tr. from the German (Feilchenfeldt edition of 1913) Marvin Löwenthal, New York: Schocken, 1977 (first publ. 1923)

Secondary literature

Feldman, Linda Ellen, 'Converging Difference: Reflections on Marginalism, Postmodernism and the Memoirs of Glückel von Hameln', *Daphnis* 22 (1993), 669–700

Wilson

Gmeyner, Anna (Vienna 1902 – 1991 York, GB) (pseud.: Anna Reiner); wrote in English (as Anna Morduch) after 1960

Heer ohne Helden, first performed Berlin, 1929 (d)

Automatenbufett. Ein Spiel in drei Akten mit einem Vorspiel und einem Nachspiel, Berlin: Arcadia, 1932 (d)

Manja. Ein Roman um fünf Kinder, first publ. Amsterdam: Querido, 1938 (under the pseudonym Anna Reiner); repr. Mannheim: Persona Verlag, 1984 (with a preface by Heike Klapdor-Kops) (n)

Works in English translation

Five Destinies (= *Manja*; tr. Philip Ownes), New York: Knopf, 1939; appeared as *The Wall*, London: Secker and Warburg, 1939

Café du Dôme, tr. T. and P. Blewitt, London: Hamilton, 1941; also publ. as *The Coward Heart*, New York: Knopf 1941(?) (n)

Secondary literature

Klapdor-Kops, Heike, "'Und was die Verfasserin betrifft, laßt uns weitersehen." Die Rekonstruktion der schriftstellerischen Laufbahn Anna Gmeyners', in *Gedanken an Deutschland und andere Themen* (= *Exilforschung*, vol. III, Munich, 1985), pp. 313–38

Goll, Claire, also known as (Studer-)Goll (Nuremberg 1891 – 1977 Paris): German Jew, associated with French Surrealism (also wrote in French); poetry, prose and autobiographical writings published in German throughout her life

Die Frauen erwachen. Novellen (von) Claire Studer, Frauenfeld: Huber, 1918 (s)

Lyrische Films. Gedichte, Basel, Leipzig: Rhein-Verlag 1922; Nendeln, Liechtenstein: Kraus-Reprint, 1973 (p)

Der Neger Jupiter raubt Europa, Basel: Rhein-Verl., 1925; Berlin: Argon, 1987; repr. Munich: dtv, 1992 (n)

Ein Mensch ertrinkt (= *Une perle*), Leipzig 1931 (n)

Arsenik, Paris and Vienna: Bergis 1933; first publ. in French as *Un crime en province*, 1932; repr. as *Arsenik oder Jedes Opfer tötet seinen Mörder*, Reinbek: Rowohlt 1980 (n)

Der gläserne Garten. Prosa 1917–1939, ed. Barbara Glauert-Hesse, Berlin: Argon 1989 (s, a, e)

Chinesische Wäscherei, Zurich: Pflugverlag, 1953 (s)

Klage um Ivan, Wiesbaden: Limes, 1960 (p)

Der gestohlene Himmel, Munich: List, 1962 (a)

with Ivan Goll, *Die Antirose: Gedichte im Dialog mit Yvan Goll*, Wiesbaden: Limes, 1967; Munich: Heyne, 1979; (French) Paris: Seghers, 1965 (p)

Traumtänzerin. Jahre der Jugend, Munich, List, 1971 (a)

Ich verzeihe keinem. Eine literarische Chronique scandaleuse unserer Zeit, Munich: Droemer 1976; repr. Bern and Munich: Scherz, 1978 (title of French original: *La poursuite du vent*)

Works in English translation (mainly translated from French)

Diary of a horse (= *Journal d'un cheval*), drawings by Marc Chagall, New York: T. Yoseloff, c. 1956

Love Poems (Claire and Yvan Goll) = *Poèmes d'amour* (Paris, 1925), tr. the authors, drawings by Chagall, New York: Hemispheres, 1947

The Jewel (= *Une Perle*, 1929; tr. Pierre Loving), New York: Knopf 1931

Secondary literature

Rheinsberg, Anna. *KRIEGS/LÄUFE. Namen. Schrift. Über Emmy Ball-Hennings, Claire Goll, Else Rüthel.* Mannheim: Persona 1989

Robertson, E. and R. Vilain (eds.), *Yvan Goll – Claire Goll. Texts and Contexts*, Amsterdam: Rodopi, 1989

Wilson

Gottsched, Luise Adelgunde Victorie (Danzig 1713 – 1762 Leipzig)

Dramas

Die Pietisterey im Fischbein-Rocke; Oder die Doctormäßige Frau. In einem Lust-Spiele vorgestellet. Rostock [in fact Leipzig: Breitkopf], 1736; repr. (ed. W. Martens) Stuttgart: Reclam, 1968

Die ungleiche Heirath. Die Deutsche Schaubühne, vol. IV, ed. J. C. Gottsched. Leipzig: Breitkopf, 1743

Die Hausfranzösinn oder Die Mamsell and *Panthea. Die Deutsche Schaubühne,* vol. V, Leipzig: Breitkopf, 1744.

Das Testament and *Der Witzling. Die Deutsche Schaubühne,* vol. VI, Leipzig: Breitkopf, 1745. (All repr. in *Die Deutsche Schaubühne,* Stuttgart: Metzler, 1972).

Der Witzling. Ein deutsches Lustspiel in 1 Aufzuge [with J. E. Schlegel's *Die Stumme Schönheit*]. *Komedia,* Deutsche Lustspiele vom Barock bis zur Gegenwart, Berlin: de Gruyter, 1962.

Letters

Briefe der Frau Louise Victorie Gottsched gebohrene Kulmus, 3 vols., Dresden: Hartung, 1771–2

Also numerous translations from French and English, including Pope's *The Rape of the Lock* (1792); listed Wilson

Works in English translation

Pietism in Petticoats and Other Comedies (= *Die Pietisterey im Fischbein-Rocke,* and other works; tr. and intr. T. Kerth and J. R. Russell). Columbia, South Carolina: Camden House, 1994

'The Witling' (= *Der Witzling*), and selected letters, in Blackwell and Zantop, *Bitter Healing* (1990)

Secondary literature

Bohm, A., 'Authority and Authorship in Luise Adelgunde Gottsched's *Das Testament*', *Lessing Yearbook* 18 (1986), 129–40

Critchfield, R., 'Beyond Luise Gottsched's *Die Pietisterey im Fischbein-Rocke oder die Doctormäßige Frau*', *Jahrbuch für Internationale Germanistik* 17/2 (1985), 112–20

Petig, W. E., 'Forms of Satire in Antipietistic Dramas', *Colloquia Germanica* 18 (1985), 257–63

Richel, V. C., *Luise Gottsched. A Reconsideration,* Bern: Lang, 1973

Waters, M. 'Frau Gottsched's *Die Pietisterey im Fischbein-Rocke*: Original, Adaptation or Translation?' *Forum for Modern Language Studies* 11 (1975), 252–67

see also Renate Feyl's novel, *Idylle mit Professor,* Berlin: Verlag Neues Leben, 1986

Frederiksen; Wilson

Greiffenberg, Catharina Regina von (Seysenegg, Austria 1633 – 1694 Nuremberg)

Sämtliche Werke, ed. Martin Bircher and Friedhelm Kemp, New York, 1983 (p, r, l)

Geistliche Sonette, Lieder und Gedichte, ed. Heinz-Otto Burger, Darmstadt, 1967 (p, r)

Translation: Cocalis, *The Defiant Muse* (1986)

Secondary literature

Frank, Horst-Joachim, *Catharina Regina von Greiffenberg. Leben und Welt der barocken Dichterin,* Göttingen, 1967

Foley-Beining, Kathleen, *The Body and Eucharistic Devotion in Catharina Regina von Greiffenberg's 'Meditations',* Columbia, South Carolina: Camden House, c. 1997

Frederiksen; Wilson

Grengg, Maria (Stein an der Donau, Austria 1889 – 1963 Rodaun, nr. Vienna)

Numerous poems and works of fiction, including
Die Liebesinsel, 1934 (n)
Der murrende Berg, 1936 (s)
Niederösterreich, das Land unter der Enns, 1937 (e)
Die Kindlmutter, Berlin, 1938 (n)
Wilson

Grogger, Paula (Öblarn, Austria 1892–1984)

Das Grimmingtor, Breslau: Ostdeutsche Verlagsanstalt, 1926 (n)
Das Gleichnis von der Weberin, Breslau: Ostdeutsche Verlagsanstalt, 1929 (n)
Der Lobenstock, 1935; repr. Munich: Albert Langen/Georg Müller, 1982 (s)
Unser Herr Pfarrer, 1946 (s)
Das Bauernjahr. Steierische Mundart, 1947; 1982 (s)

Also wrote plays, poems

Works in English translation
The Door in the Grimming (= *Das Grimmingtor*; tr. Caroline Cunningham), 1936
Wilson

Gröschner, Annett (1964–)

Herzdame Knochensammler, Berlin: KONTEXTverlag, 1993 (p)

Grosz, Christiane (GDR 1944 – FRG)

Scherben, Berlin and Weimar: Aufbau, 1978 (p)
Blatt vor dem Mund, Berlin and Weimar: Aufbau, 1983 (p)
Die Tochter, Berlin and Weimar: Aufbau, 1987
Die asoziale Taube, Berlin and Weimar: Aufbau, 1991 (p)

Grumbach, Argula von (Seefeld, Bavaria 1495 – 1563 nr. Schweinfurt) (r; p)

Classen, Albrecht, 'Woman Poet and Reformer: The 16th-Century Feminist Argula von Grumbach', *Daphnis* 20, (1991/2), 167–97
Halbach, Silke, *Argula von Grumbach als Verfasserin reformatorischer Flugschriften*, Bern 1992
Matheson, Peter (ed.), *Argula von Grumbach: a woman's voice in the Reformation*, Edinburgh: T & T Clark, 1995

Translation: see Cocalis, *The Defiant Muse* (1986); Wilson, *Women Writers of the Renaissance* (see p. 269 above)
Wilson

Günderrode, Karoline von (pseud.: Tian; Ion) (Karlsruhe 1780 – 1806 Winkel am Rhein)

Sämtliche Werke und ausgewählte Studien. Historisch-kritische Ausgabe, ed. Walter Morgenthaler with Karin Obermeier and Marianne Graf, 3 vols., Basel: Stroemfeld/Roter Stern, 1990–1
Gedichte und Phantasien, as Tian, Hamburg: Hermann, 1804 (p, d, s)

Poetische Fragmente, as Tian, Frankfurt am Main: Wilmans, 1805 (d, p)
Melete, as Ion, Heidelberg: Mohr, 1806; repr. ed. Leopold Hirschberg, Berlin: Harrwitz,
    1906 (p, l, s, d)
Der Schatten eines Traumes: Gedichte, Prosa, Briefe, Zeugnisse von Zeitgenossen, ed. Christa
    Wolf, Darmstadt: Luchterhand, 1979; 6th edn 1986 (p, l, e)

Works in English translation
Blackwell and Zantop. *Bitter Healing* (1990), pp. 417–42: selected letters, poems, and a
    prose fragment
Cocalis, *The Defiant Muse* (1986)
Morgan (see under Bettina von Arnim, *Günderode*)

Secondary literature
Diab, Susan, 'Karoline von Günderrode and Her Poetry', in Ives (ed.), *Women Writers of the
    Age of Goethe*, vol. I (1988), pp. 36–59
Lazarowicz, Margarete, *Karoline von Günderrode: Porträt einer Fremden*, Frankfurt am
    Main: Lang, 1986
Riley, Helene M. Kastinger. 'Caroline von Günderrode', in James Hardin and Christoph
    Schweitzer (eds.), *German Writers of the Age of Goethe*, Detroit: Gale Research, Inc.,
    1989, pp. 114–19
Wolf, Christa, 'The Shadow of a Dream: A Sketch on Karoline von Günderrode', tr. Jan
    van Heurck, in *The Writer's Dimension*, pp. 131–71 (see Wolf entry, p. 377 below, for
    full bibliographical details)
Frederiksen

Hahn, Ulla (Sauerland 1946 – FRG)
Poetry
Herz über Kopf, Stuttgart: DVA, 1981
Spielende, Stuttgart: DVA, 1983
Freudenfeuer, Stuttgart: DVA, 1985
Unerhörte Nähe: Gedichte mit einem Anhang für den, der fragt, Stuttgart: DVA, 1988 (p/e)
Liebesgedichte, Stuttgart: DVA, 1993
Klima für Engel, Munich: DTV, 1993
Epikurs Garten. Stuttgart: DVA, 1995
(ed.), Gertrud Kolmar, *Gedichte*, Frankfurt am Main: Suhrkamp, 1983

Hahn-Hahn, Ida (Mecklenburg 1805 – 1880 Mainz)
Gesammelte Schriften, 21 vols., Berlin: Paetel (1851)

Numerous poems, novels, stories and travel literature, e.g.
Gräfin Faustine, Berlin: Duncker, 1841; repr. Bonn: Bouvier, 1986 (n)
Aus der Gesellschaft. Gesamtausgabe der Romane derselben, Berlin: Duncker (1844)
Reisebriefe, Berlin: Duncker (1844) (t/l)
Orientalische Briefe, Berlin: Duncker (1844) (t/l)
Von Babylon nach Jerusalem, Mainz: Kirchheim, 1851 (t/l)
Aus Jerusalem, Mainz: Kirchheim (1851) (t)
Zwei Schwestern, Mainz: Kirchheim (1863) (n)
Eudoxia, die Kaiserin. Ein Zeitgemälde aus dem 5. Jahrhundert, Mainz: Kirchheim (1867)
Meine Reise nach England, ed. Bernd Goldmann, Mainz, 1981 (t)

Works in English translation

The Countess Faustina, A Novel (= *Gräfin Faustine*); tr. A. E. I., London: John Olliver, 1845;
  tr. H. N. S., Clarke's Cabinet Series, London 1844; *Faustina. A Novel*, New York:
  Carleton, 1872; London: Low, 1872

From Babylon to Jerusalem (= *Von Babylon nach Jerusalem*; tr. Elizabeth Atcherley), London:
  T. C. Newby, 1851

Letters of a German Countess Written during her Travels in Turkey, Egypt, the Holy Land, Syria,
  Nubia, etc. in 1843–1844 (= *Orientalische Briefe*), London: H. Colburn, 1845; also tr. as
  Letter from the Orient, tr. Samuel Phillips, 2nd edn London, 1845; *Adventures and*
  Travels of Ida, Countess Hahn-Hahn in Turkey, Egypt, the Holy Land, etc., London: H.
  Colburn, 1845

Travels in Sweden: Sketches of a Journey to the North, tr. J. B. S., London (1845)

Dorothea Waldegrave. A tale, tr. Lady Herbert, London (1875)

From Jerusalem (= *Aus Jerusalem*; tr. E. Atcherley), London: T. C. Newby, 1852

Society: or High Life in Germany (= *Aus der Gesellschaft*), London: Piper, Stephenson etc., 1854

Eudoxia: A Picture of the Fifth Century, Baltimore: Kelly, Piet & Co., 1869

  Further translations: see Morgan + S; Cocalis, *The Defiant Muse* (1986)
Frederiksen; Wilson

Haidenbucher, Maria Magdalena (1576–1650)

Geschicht Buech de Anno 1609 biß 1650. Das Tagebuch der Maria Magdalena Haidenbucher
  (1576–1650), Äbtissin von Frauenwörth, ed. Gerhard Stalla, Amsterdam, 1988 (a, r)

Handel-Mazzetti, Enrica Freiin von (Vienna 1871 – 1955 Linz)

Die arme Margaret. Ein Volksroman aus dem alten Steyr. Kempten, München: Kösel 1910 (n)

Deutsche Passion. Des Rosenwunders zweiter Teil. Ein deutscher Roman, Münich: Kösel 1925 (n)

Jesse und Maria. Ein Roman aus dem Donaulande, Kempten, Munich: Kösel 1911 (n)

Die Waxenbergerin: Ein Roman aus dem Kampfjahr 1683, Munich: Kösel, 1934 (n)

Graf Reichard, der Held vom Eisernen Tor. Roman aus dem deutschen Siegesjahr 1691, 2 vols.,
  Munich: Kösel, 1939/40 (n)

  And numerous other plays, short stories, novels and poems

Works in English translation

Jesse and Maria (= *Jesse und Maria. Ein Roman aus dem Donaulande*; tr. G. N. Schuster), New
  York: Holt, 1931

Secondary literature

Schmidt, Josef, 'Enrica von Handel-Mazzetti', in James Hardin and Donald G. Daviau
  (eds.), *Austrian Fiction Writers, 1875–1913*, Detroit, 1989, pp. 113–18
Wilson

Hannsmann, Margarete (Heidenheim, Württemberg, 1921–)

Poetry: many volumes, including

Tauch in den Stein, Darmstadt: Bläschke, 1964

Zwischen Urne und Stier, Hamburg, Düsseldorf: Claassen, 1971

Das andere Ufer vor Augen, Hamburg, Düsseldorf: Claassen, 1972

Aufzeichnungen über Buchenwald: Deutsch – Englisch – Français, Frankfurt am Main:
  Röderberg, 1978 (p/e)

Engel der Geschichte. Folge 24: Landkarten, Düsseldorf: Claassen, 1980
Spuren: Ausgewählte Gedichte 1960–1980, ed. Franz Fühmann, Leipzig: Reclam, 1980 and Düsseldorf: Claassen, 1981
(Pseud. S. Pansa) *Abschied von HAP G. Gedicht mit zwei Malbriefen von HAP Greishaber*, Düsseldorf: Eremiten-Presse, 1981
Du bist in allem: Elegie auf Lesbos, Freiburg im Breisgau: Kerle, 1983
Purpuraugenblick: Gedichte aus 25 Jahren, Stuttgart: Klett-Cotta, 1991

Happel, Lioba (Aschaffenburg 1957 – FRG)
vers reim und wecker, West Berlin: Literarisches Colloquium, 1987 (p)
Grüne Nachmittage. Frankfurt am Main: Suhrkamp, 1989 (p)
Ein Hut wie Saturn, Frankfurt am Main: Suhrkamp, 1991 (n)
Der Schlaf überm Eis: Gedichte, Frankfurt am Main: Schöffling & Co., 1995 (p)

Translation: Gutzschhahn, *Young Poets of Germany* (1994)

Harden, Sylvia von (Hamburg 1894 – 1964 nr. London)
Verworrene Städte, Das neue Gedicht 35, Dresden: Kämmerer, 1920 (p)
Robespierre. Eine Novelle, Berlin, 1924 (s)

Hardenberg, Henriette (Berlin 1894 – 1993 London)
Neigungen. Gedichte, Die neue Reihe 12, Munich: Roland, 1918 (p)
Dichtungen, ed. Hartmut Vollmer, Zurich: Arche 1988 (p)
Südliches Herz. Nachgelassene Dichtungen, ed. Hartmut Vollmer, Zurich: Arche, 1994

Hartlaub, Geno(veva) (Mannheim, 1915–)
Die Tauben von San Marco, Frankfurt am Main: Fischer, 1953 (n)
Der große Wagen, Frankfurt am Main: Fischer, 1954 (n)
Der Mond hat Durst, Hamburg: Claassen, 1963 (n)
Rot heißt auch schön, Hamburg: Claassen, 1969 (s)
Freue dich, du bist eine Frau. Briefe an die Priscilla. Erzählt von G. H., Freiburg im Breisgau, Basel and Vienna: Herder, 1983 (s)
Wilson

Hauptmann, Elisabeth (Westfalen 1887 – 1973 E. Berlin); collaborated with Bertolt Brecht
Julia ohne Romeo. Geschichten, Stücke, Aufsätze, Erinnerungen. Berlin und Weimar: Aufbau-Verlag, 1977 (includes *Happy End*)
(as 'Dorothy Lane') 'Happy End: A Criminal Case Based on The Comedy with the Same Name by Dorothy Lane: Filmfassung von Manfred Werkwerth', in *Brecht Women and Politics, Brecht-Jahrbuch* 12, 1983; Detroit and Munich: Wayne State University Press/edition text + kritik, 1985

Translated into German numerous works later 'adapted' by Brecht, e.g.:
Die Dreigroschenoper: ein Stück mit Musik nach John Gay's 'The Beggar's Opera' von Elisabeth Hauptmann/Kurt Weill; Deutsche Bearbeitung von Bertold Brecht, Vienna: Universal-Edition, c. 1956, first publ. 1928 (libretto/adaptation)

Secondary literature
Fuegi, John, *The Lives and Lies of Bertolt Brecht*, London: Harper Collins, 1994

Hanssen, Paula, *Elisabeth Hauptmann: Brecht's Silent Collaborator*, Bern and New York:
   Peter Lang, c. 1995
Horst, Astrid, *Prima inter pares: Elisabeth Hauptmann, die Mitarbeiterin Bertolt Brechts*,
   Würzburg: Königshausen & Neumann, 1992
Kebir, Susanne, *Ich fragte nicht nach meinem Anteil: Elisabeth Hauptmanns Arbeit mit Bertolt
   Brecht*, Berlin: Aufbau, 1997
Willett, John, 'Bacon ohne Shakespeare? – The Problem of Mitarbeit', in *Brecht Women
   and Politics, Brecht-Jahrbuch* 12, 1983; Detroit and Munich: Wayne State University
   Press/ edition text + kritik, 1985

Haushofer, Marlen (née Marie Helene Frauendorfer) (Frauenstein, Austria 1920–70)

Eine Handvoll Leben, Vienna: Zsolnay, 1955 (n)
Die Tapetentür, Vienna: Zsolnay, 1957 (n)
Wir töten Stella. Novelle, Vienna: Bergland, 1958 (s/n)
Die Wand, Gütersloh: Mohn, 1963 (n)
Schreckliche Treue, Düsseldorf: Claassen, 1968 (s)
Die Mansarde, Düsseldorf: Claassen, 1969 (n)

Works in English translation
The Wall (= *Die Wand*; tr. Shaun Whiteside), London: Quartet, 1990; Pittsburgh, Cleis
   Press, 1990
The Jib Door (= *Die Tapetentür*; tr. Jerome C. Samuelson), Riverside, California: Ariadne,
   1998

Secondary literature
Littler 'The Cost of Loving' (1998) (see p. 278 above)
Wilson

Heinhold, Agnes (1642–1711)
Poems reprinted in
Neugebauer, Birgit, 'Agnes Heinhold (1642–1711) – ein Beitrag zur Literatur von Frauen
   im 17. Jahrhundert', *Daphnis* 20/3-4 (1991), 601–702

Heinrich, Jutta (1940 – FRG)
Das Geschlecht der Gedanken, Munich: Frauenoffensive, 1978 (n)
Mit meinem Mörder Zeit bin ich allein, Munich: Frauenoffensive, 1981 (a, e, s, p)
'Im Revier der Worte': Provokationen, Gegenreden, Zwischenrufe. Frankfurt am Main: Fischer,
   1994

English translation
The Gender of Thoughts (excerpt from *Das Geschlecht der Gedanken*; tr. Jeanette Clausen), in
   Altbach, *German Feminism* (1984), pp. 276–83

Helvig, Amalie von, née von Imhoff (Weimar 1776 – 1831 Berlin)
Die Schwestern von Lesbos, in Friedrich von Schiller (ed.), *Musenalmanach für 1800*, Book edn
   Heidelberg, 1801 (p)
Die Schwestern auf Corcyra, Amsterdam, 1812 (d)
Die Tageszeiten, Amsterdam, 1812 (d)
Wilson

Hennings, Emmy; also known as (Ball-) Hennings (Flensburg 1885 – 1948 Lugano)

Betrunken taumeln alle Litfaßsäulen. Frühe Texte und autobiographische Schriften 1913–1922, ed. Bernhard Merkelbach, Hanover: Postskriptum, 1990

Die letzte Freude, Der jüngste Tag 5, Leipzig: Wolff, 1913 (p)

'Das neue Recht der Frau', *Der Revolutionär* 10 (1919), 19–23 (e)

Gefängnis. Berlin: Reiss 1919; repr. Wetzlar: Büchse der Pandora 1981; Frankfurt am Main, Berlin and Vienna: Ullstein, 1985 (n)

Das Brandmal. Ein Tagebuch, Berlin: Reiss, 1920 (a)

Helle Nacht. Gedichte, Berlin: Reiss, 1922 (p)

Das ewige Lied, Berlin: Reiss, 1923 (p)

Secondary literature

Rheinsberg, Anna, *KRIEGS/LÄUFE* (1989) (see p. 311 above)

Teubner, Ernst (ed.), *Hugo Ball Almanach 1994. Emmy Hennings zum 100. Geburtstag*, Pirmasens: Stadt Pirmasens, 1985

Werner-Birkenbach, Sabine, 'Emmy Hennings. A Women Writer of Prison Literature', in Keith-Smith (1993) (see p. 275 above), pp. 167–202

Wilson

Hensel, Kerstin (Chemnitz 1961 – GDR)

Poesiealbum, Berlin: Verlag Neues Leben, 1986 (p)

Stilleben mit Zukunft, Halle and Leipzig: Mitteldeutscher Verlag, 1988 (p)

Hallimasch, Halle: Mitteldeutscher Verlag, 1989; repr. Frankfurt am Main: Luchterhand, 1989 (s)

Schlaraffenzucht, Frankfurt: Luchterhand, 1990 (p)

Gewitterfront, Leipzig: Mitteldeutscher Verlag, 1991 (p)

Ab tritt Fraulein Jungfer! Liebesgedichte, Berlin: Günther, 1991 (p)

Angestaut. Aus meinem Sudelbuch, Halle: Mitteldeutscher Verlag, 1993 (p)

Tanz am Kanal, Frankfurt am Main: Suhrkamp, 1994 (n)

Translation: Gutzschhahn, *Young Poets of Germany* (1994)

Hensel, Luise (Brandenburg 1798 – 1876 Paderborn)

Lieder, ed. Christoph Bernhard Schlüter. Paderborn: Schöningh, 1869; eleven further editions to 1922 (p)

Secondary literature

Freund, Winfried, *Müde bin ich, geh' zur Ruh. Leben und Werk der Luise Hensel*, Wiedenbrück: Güth & Etscheidt, 1984

Harper, Anthony J. 'Luise Hensel: Profile of a Romantic Poetess', in Ives (ed.), *Women Writers of the Age of Goethe*, vol. III (1991), pp. 35–51

Translated selections: see Morgan

Wilson

Herwegh, Emma (Berlin 1817 – 1904 Paris)

Zur Geschichte der deutschen demokratischen Legion aus Paris von einer Hochverräterin, Grünberg: Levysohn, 1849; reissued as *Im Interesse der Wahrheit*, ed. Horst Brandstätter, Lengwil: Libelle, 1998 (e)

Eine Erinnerung an Georg Herwegh (1875) (biog.)

Secondary literature

Krausnick, Michail, *Nicht Magd mit den Knechten – Emma Herwegh, eine biographische Skizze*, Marbacher Magazin 83, Marbach am Neckar: Deutsche Schillergesellschaft, 1998

Herz, Henriette, née Lemos (Berlin 1764–1847)

Putzel, Max J. (ed.), *Letters to Immanuel Bekker from Henriette Herz, S. Pobeheim and Anna Horkel*, Bern: Lang, 1972 (German texts with English commentary)

Schmitz, Rainer (ed.), *Henriette Herz in Erinnerungen, Briefen und Zeugnissen*, Frankfurt am Main: Insel, 1984 (a, l)

Works in English translation

'Memoirs of a Jewish Girlhood' (tr. of selected autobiographical writings) in *Bitter Healing* (1990), pp. 297–331

Secondary literature

Davies, Martin. 'Portraits of a Lady: Variations on Henriette Herz (1764–1847)', in Ives (ed.), *Women Writers of the Age of Goethe*, vol. v (1992), pp. 45–75

Hertz, Deborah S., *Jewish High Society in Old Regime Berlin*, New Haven: Yale University Press, 1988

Wilson

Herzog, Marianne (Mecklenburg 1940 – FRG)

Von der Hand in den Mund. Frauen im Akkord, Berlin: Rotbuch, 1976

See also **Kamenko** (p. 324 below)

English translation

From Hand to Mouth: Women and Piecework, tr. Stanley Mitchell, Harmondsworth: Penguin, 1980

Altbach, *German Feminism* (1984) (extracts)

Hildegard von Bingen (Rheinhessen 1098 – 1179 nr. Bingen); wrote in Latin

Scivias, ed. Adelgundis Führkötter and Angela Carlevaris, Turnhout, 1978

Das Buch von den Steinen (= De lapidibus), German translation and commentary by Peter Riethe, Salzburg: O. Müller, c. 1979

Works in English translation

Scivias (Know the Ways) [English translation of Latin original], tr. Bruce Hozeski. Santa Fe: Bear and Company 1986

Scivias, tr. Mother Columba Hart and Jane Bishop, intr. Barbara J. Newman, preface by Caroline Walker Bynum, New York: Paulist Press, c. 1990

The Book of the Rewards of Life (= Liber vitae meritorum; tr. Bruce W. Hozeski), New York and Oxford: Oxford University Press, 1997 (first publ. New York and London: Garland, 1994)

Symphonia: A Critical Edition of the Symphonia armonie celestium revelationum [Symphony of the Harmony of Celestial Revelations], with introduction, translations, and commentary by Barbara Newman, Ithaca and London: Cornell University Press, 1988 (English and Latin)

Bowie, Fiona, and Oliver Davies (eds.), *Hildegard of Bingen: An Anthology*, with new translations by Robert Carver, London: SPCK, 1990

The Letters of Hildegard of Bingen, tr. Joseph L. Baird and Radd K. Ehrman, vol. I, New York
    and Oxford: Oxford University Press 1994

Secondary literature
Newman, Barbara, *Sister of Wisdom. St. Hildegard's Theology of the Feminine*, Aldershot:
    Scolar Press, 1987
Bobko, Jane (ed.), *Vision: The Life and Music of Hildegard von Bingen*, with text by Barbara
    Newman and commentary by Matthew Fox, New York and London: Penguin
    Studio, 1995
Flanagan, Sabina, *Hildegard of Bingen, 1098–1179: A Visionary Life*, London: Routledge, 1990;
    2nd edn 1998
Frederiksen; Wilson

**Hirsch, Jenny (pseud.: F. Arnefeld etc.) (Zerbst, Saxony 1829 – 1902
Berlin)**
Numerous works of fiction and translations from English, Swedish and
French, including
Über die Hörigkeit der Frau, 1872 (translation of John Stuart Mill, *Vindication of the Rights of
    Women* (1869))

Hoffmann, Ruth (Breslau 1893 – 1974 Berlin)
Various works of poetry and narrative fiction, including
Pauline aus Kreuzberg, 1935; 1973 (n)
Dunkler Engel, 1946 (p)
Meine Freunde aus Davids Geschlecht, 1947 (s)
Franziska Lauterbach, 1947; 1975 (n)

Honigmann, Barbara (East Berlin 1949–; moved to FRG in 1984)
Roman von einem Kinde. Sechs Erzählungen, Hamburg: Luchterhand, 1989 (n/s)
Eine Liebe aus nichts, Reinbek: Rowohlt, 1993 (s)

Hoyers, Anna Ovena (Holstein 1584 – 1655 Sweden)
Geistliche und Weltliche Poemata, ed. Barbara Becker-Cantarino, Tübingen 1986 (p, r)

English translations
Cocalis, *The Defiant Muse* (1986); Wilson, *Women Writers of the Renaissance* (see p. 269
    above)
Wilson

**Hrotsvit von Gandersheim (also Hroswitha, Roswitha)
(Saxony, c. 935 – 973, Gandersheim, Saxony); wrote in Latin**
Hrosvitae opera (Latin), ed. Helene Homeyer, Paderborn: Schöningh, 1970
Hrosvita von Gandersheim: Werke in deutscher Übertragung, tr. Helene Homeyer, Paderborn:
    Schöningh 1973 (German translation)

Works in English translation
The Plays of Hrosvita of Gandersheim, tr. Larissa Bonfante and Alexandra Bonfante-Warren,
    Oak Park: Bolchazy-Carducci, 1986
The Plays of Hrotsvit of Gandersheim, tr. Katharina Wilson, New York and London:
    Garland, 1989

The Non-Dramatic Works of Hrosvitha, tr. Sister M. Gonsalva Wiegand, St Louis: St Louis
University Press, 1936

For other translations see Morgan

Secondary literature

Wilson, Katharina, *Hrosvit of Gandersheim. The Ethos of Authorial Stance,* Leiden, New York,
Copenhagen and Cologne: Brill, 1980

Frederiksen; Wilson (under **G**andersheim)

Huber, Therese (Göttingen 1764 – 1829 Augsburg); also translated from French

Die Familie Seldorf: eine Erzählung aus der französischen Revolution, 2 vols., Tübingen: Cotta,
1795–6; repr. ed. Magdalene Heuser, 1 vol., Hildesheim: Olms, 1989 (n)

Luise – oder ein Beitrag zur Geschichte der Konvenienz, Leipzig: Wolf, 1796, repr. with a
postscript by M. Heuser, Hildesheim: Olms, 1991 (n)

Erzählungen, as L. F. Huber, 3 vols., Brunswick: Vieweg, 1801–2 (s)

Bemerkungen über Holland aus dem Reisejournal einer deutschen Frau, as Therese H., Leipzig:
Fleischer, 1811 (t)

L. F. Hubers gesammelte Erzählungen, fortgesetzt von Therese Huber geb. Heyne, 2 vols. Stuttgart
and Tübingen: Cotta, 1819 (s)

Ellen Percy, oder Erziehung durch Schicksale, 2 vols., Leipzig: Brockhaus, 1822; repr. ed.
Magdalene Heuser with extracts from Mary Brunton, *Discipline* (London, 1832), 2
vols. in 1, Hildesheim: Olms, 1996 (n)

Die Ehelosen, 2 vols., Leipzig: Brockhaus, 1829 (n)

*Therese Huber. Die reinste Freiheitsliebe, die reinste Männerliebe: ein Lebensbild in Briefen
zwischen Aufklärung und Romantik*, ed. Andrea Hahn, Munich: Henssel, 1989 (l)

*Schriftstellerinnen und Schwesterseelen. Der Briefwechsel zwischen Therese Huber und Karoline
Pichler (1769–1843)*, ed. Brigitte Leuschner, Marburg: Tectum, 1995 (l)

Works in English translation

'Female Experience' (= 'Ueber die Weiblichkeit in der Kunst, in der Natur und in der
Gesellschaft'; tr. Miss Eliza C.), in *The German Novellist: A Choice Collection of Novels*.
Görlitz: Anton, 180–? (s)

Francis and Josepha: A Tale, tr. W. Fardely, Leeds: 1807

Adventures on a Journey to New Holland, and The Lonely Deathbed (= *Bemerkungen über Holland*;
tr. Rodney Livingstone), ed. Leslie Bodi, Melbourne: Lansdowne Press, 1966 (e)

Secondary literature

Becker-Cantarino, Barbara, 'Revolution im Patriarchat: Therese Forster-Huber
(1764–1829)', in Joeres, *Out of Line* (see p. 272 above), pp. 235–53

Blackwell, Jeannine. 'Therese Huber', in James Hardin and Christoph Schweitzer
(eds.), *German Writers in the Age of Goethe*, Detroit: Gale Research, Inc., 1989
pp. 187–92

Gokhale, Vibha Bakshi, *Walking the Tightrope: A Feminist Reading of Therese Huber's Stories*,
Columbia, South Carolina: Camden House, c. 1996

Kontje, T., 'Under the Spell: Patriarchy versus Patriotism in Therese Huber's *Die Familie
Seldorf*', *Seminar* 28/1 (1992), 17–32

Worley, Linda Kraus. 'The Body, Beauty, and Woman: The Ugly Heroine in Stories by
Therese Huber and Gabriele Reuter', *The German Quarterly* 64 (1991), 368–78

Wilson

Huch, Ricarda (pseud.: Richard Hugo)
(Braunschweig 1864 – 1947 Schönberg)

Gesammelte Werke, ed. Wilhelm Emrich, 11 vols., Cologne: Kiepenheuer & Witsch, 1966–74 (comprehensive bibliography in vol. XI, though does not list all translations)

Gedichte (as Richard Hugo), Dresden: E. Pierson, 1891 (p)

Erinnerungen von Ludolf Ursleu dem Jüngeren, Berlin: Besser, 1893 (n)

Blütezeit der Romantik, Leipzig: H. Haessel, 1899; *Ausbreitung und Verfall der Romantik*, Leipzig: H. Haessel, 1902; repr. in 1 vol. as *Die Romantik*, Leipzig: H. Haessel, 1924

Der Einfluß von Studium und Beruf auf der Persönlichkeit der Frau, Vienna: Verein für erweiterte Frauenbildung, 1903 (e)

Die Geschichte von Garibaldi in drei Teilen, 2 vols., Stuttgart: Verlags-Anstalt, 1906–7 (e)

Der Dreißigjährige Krieg, 2 vols., Leipzig: Insel, 1937; Frankfurt am Main: Insel, 1974 (hist)

Herbstfeuer, 1944 (p)

And much more

Works in English translation

Recollections of Ludolf Ursleu the Younger (= *Erinnerungen von Ludolf Ursleu dem Jüngeren*; tr. (abridged) Muriel Almon), in Franke (ed.), *The German Classics*, 1913–15; as *Eros Invincible*, tr. William A. Drake, New York: The Macaulay Company, 1931; Fertig, 1984; republ. as *Unconquered Love*, London: Eyre and Spottiswode, 1931

The Deruga Trial (= *Der Fall Deruga*; 1917, tr. Lorna Dietz), New York: The Macaulay Company, 1930

Garibaldi and the New Italy (= *Die Geschichte von Garibaldi*; tr. Catherine Alison Phillips), 2 vols (*Defeat* and *Victory*), New York: Knopf, 1928

The Romantic Character (= chapter from *Die Romantik*; tr. Anne Garrison), East Lansing, 1945

'Romantic Marriage' (= 'Romantische Ehe'), in H. A. Keyserling (ed.), *The Book of Marriage*, New York: Harcourt/Brace, 1926

Herrmann and Spitz, *German Women Writers* (1978)

Secondary literature

Bubser, Reinhold K., 'Ricarda Huch', in James Hardin (ed.), *German Fiction Writers, 1885–1913*, vol. I, Detroit, 1988, pp. 231–40

Wilson

Hutmacher, Rahel (Zurich, 1944–)

Tochter, Darmstadt: Luchterhand, 1983; repr. 1987 (prose)

Wildleute, Darmstadt: Luchterhand, 1986 (s)

Igel, Jayne-Ann (GDR, 1954–); Bernd Igel up to 1989

Gedichte, Berlin: Verlag Neues Leben, 1989 (p)

Das Geschlecht der Häuser gebar mir fremde Orte, Frankfurt am Main: Fischer, 1989 (p)

Fahrwasser: eine innere biographie in ansätzen, Leipzig: Reclam, 1991 (a, p)

Janitschek, Maria (nr. Vienna 1859 – 1927 Munich)

Im Kampf um die Zukunft, Stuttgart: Spemann, 1887 (p)

Verzaubert. Eine Herzensfabel in Versen, Stuttgart and Munich, 1888 (p)

Irdische und unirdische Träume, Stuttgart: Union, 1889 (p)

And many other novels and short stories; see Wilson

Translation: Cocalis, *The Defiant Muse* (1986)

Wilson

Janstein, Elisabeth (von) (Moravia 1893 – 1944 Winchcombe, GB)

Gebete um Wirklichkeit, Vienna, Prague and Leipzig: Strache, 1919 (p)
Die Kurve, Vienna, Prague and Leipzig: Strache, 1920
Die Landung, Munich: Drei Masken, 1921 (p)

Jelinek, Elfriede (Steiermark, Austria, 1946–)

Lisas Schatten, Munich: Relief, 1967 (p)
Ende: Gedichte von 1966–1968, Schwifting: Schwiftinger Galerie-Verlag, 1980 (p)
Die Liebhaberinnen, Reinbek: Rowohlt, 1975 (n)
Die Klavierspielerin, Reinbek: Rowohlt, 1983 (n)
Theaterstücke, Reinbek: Rowohlt, 1984 (d)
Lust, Reinbek: Rowohlt, 1989 (n)
Malina. Ein Filmbuch, Frankfurt am Main: Suhrkamp, 1991 (screenplay for Werner
        Schroeter's 1986 film adaptation of Bachmann's novel)
Die Kinder der Toten, Reinbek: Rowohlt, 1995 (n)
Stecken, Stab und Stangl/Raststätte oder Sie machens alle/Wolken. Heim, Reinbek: Rowohlt,
        1997 (d)
Ein Sportstück, Reinbek: Rowohlt, 1998 (d)

Works in English translation

The Piano Teacher (= *Die Klavierspielerin*; tr. Joachim Neugroschel), London: Serpent's Tail,
        1988
Wonderful, Wonderful Times (= *Die Ausgesperrten*; tr. Michael Hulse), London: Serpent's Tail,
        1990
Lust (= *Lust*; tr. Michael Hulse), London: Serpent's Tail, 1992
Women as Lovers (= *Die Liebhaberinnen*; tr. Martin Chalmers), London: Serpent's Tail, 1994

Drama
'What happened after Nora left her husband' (= 'Was geschah, nachdem Nora ihren
        Mann verlassen hatte?' tr. Tinch Minter), in *Plays by Women: Ten*, ed. Annie
        Castledine, London: Methuen, 1994
'Totenauberg – Death/Valley/Summit' (= 'Totenauberg'; tr. Gitta Honegger), in *Drama
        Contemporary: Germany*, ed. Carl Weber, Baltimore: Johns Hopkins Press, 1996
Services (= *Raststätte*; tr. Nick Grindell), London: Methuen (Gate Theatre Productions), 1996
Clara S. (= 'Clara S.: musikalische Tragödie', in *Theaterstücke*; tr. Anthony Vivis),
        Theaterbibliothek des Goethe-Instituts (Deutsches Theater der Gegenwart),
        Cologne: Theaterverlag Ute Nyssen/J. Bansemer, 1997; also forthcoming in
        Modern European Plays by Women, ed. Alan Barr

Excerpts in Altbach, *German Feminism* (1984)

Secondary literature

Fiddler, Allyson, *Rewriting Reality: An Introduction to Elfriede Jelinek*, Oxford: Berg, 1994
Johns, Jorum B., and Katherine Arens (eds.), *Elfriede Jelinek: Framed by Language*,
        Riverside, California: Ariadne Press, 1994
Frederiksen; Wilson

Kalb, Charlotte von, née Marschalk von Ostheim
(Walthershausen, Franconia 1761 – 1843 Berlin)

Cornelia: für Freunde der Verewigten, Manuscript, Berlin, 1851 (n)

Secondary literature

Naumann, Ute, *Charlotte von Kalb. Eine Lebensgeschichte (1761–1843)*, Stuttgart: Metzler, 1985

Kaléko, Mascha (Schidlow, Poland 1912 – 1975 Zurich)

Das lyrische Stenogrammheft. Verse vom Alltag, Berlin: Rowohlt, 1933; repr. Reinbek:
    Rowohlt, 1956 (p)
Kleines Lesebuch für Große. Gereimtes und Ungereimtes, Berlin: Ullstein 1935 (p)
Verse für Zeitgenossen, first pub. Cambridge, Massachusetts: Schoenhof Verlag, 1945; repr.
    Reinbek: Rowohlt, 1958; Düsseldorf: Eremitenpresse, 1978; edited with an
    afterword by Gisela Zoch-Westphal, Reinbek: Rowohlt, 1980 (p)
In meinen Träumen läutet es Sturm. Gedichte und Epigramme aus dem Nachlaß, ed. and intr.
    Gisela Zoch-Westphal, Munich: dtv, 5th edn 1981 (p)

    Translation: Cocalis, *The Defiant Muse* (1986)

Secondary literature

Wellershoff, Irene, 'Vertreibung aus dem "kleinen Glück". Das lyrische Werk der
    Mascha Kaléko', Diss., Aachen 1982
Zoch-Westphal, Gisela, *Aus den sechs Leben der Mascha Kaleko. Biographische Skizzen, ein
    Tagebuch und Briefe*, Berlin: Arani, 1987
Wilson

Kamenko, Vera (Sombor, Yugoslavia 1947 – FRG)

(with Marianne Herzog, ed.), *Unter uns war Krieg. Autobiografie einer jugoslawischen
    Arbeiterin*, Berlin: Rotbuch, 1978 (a)
Wilson

Karlweis, Martha (Vienna 1889 – 1965 Lugano, Switzerland)

Amor und Psyche auf Reisen, Berlin: Volksverband der Bücherfreunde Wegweiser Verlag,
    1928
Eine Frau reist durch Amerika, Berlin: S. Fischer, 1928 (t)
Schwindel. Geschichte einer Realität, Berlin: S. Fischer, 1931

Works in English translation

'Marriage and the Changing Woman' (= 'Die Ehe und die verwandelte Frau'), in
    Keyserling (ed.), *Book of Marriage*, 1926 (see p. 322 above)

Karsch, Anna Louisa [also Luise] (also known as Karschin)
(Brandenburg 1722 – 1791 Berlin)

Auserlesene Gedichte, Berlin: Winter, 1764 (p)
Neue Gedichte der Anna Louise Karschin, Mietau and Leipzig: Hinz, 1772 (p)
*Gedichte. Von Anna Louisa Karschin. Nach der Dichterin Tode nebst ihrem Lebenslauff hersg. von
    C. L. von Klenke*. Berlin: Maurer, 1792 (p)
Die Karschin. Friedrich des Großen Volksdichterin. Ein Leben in Briefen, ed. E. Hausmann,
    Frankfurt am Main: Societäts-Verlag, 1933 (l)
O, mir entwischt nicht, was die Menschen fühlen. Anna Louisa Karschin. Gedichte und Briefe.

Stimmen der Zeitgenossen, ed. Gerhard Wolf, East Berlin: Buchverlag Der Morgen, 1981 (l, p)

Gedichte und Lebenszeugnisse, ed. Alfred Anger, Stuttgart: Reclam, 1987 (l, p)

'Mein Bruder in Apoll': Briefwechsel zwischen Anna Louisa Karsch and Johann Wilhelm Ludwig Gleim, ed. Regina Nörtemann, 2 vols., Göttingen: Wallstein, 1996 (l)

Selected translations: see Morgan; Blackwell and Zantop, *Bitter Healing* (1990); Cocalis, *The Defiant Muse* (1986)

Secondary literature

Bennholdt-Thomsen and Anita Runge (eds.), *Anna Louisa Karsch (1722–1791). Von schlesischer Kunst und Berliner 'Natur'. Ergebnisse des Symposions zum 200. Todestag der Dichterin*. Göttingen: Wallstein, 1992

Frederiksen; Wilson

Karwath, Juliane (1877–1931)

Marie Duchanin. Die Apothekerin und ihr Weg, Stuttgart, Berlin and Leipzig: DVA, 1928 (n)

Die Droste. Der Lebensroman der Annette von Droste-Hülshoff, Stuttgart, Berlin and Leipzig: DVA, 1929 (n)

Kaschnitz, Marie Luise (Freifrau von Kaschnitz-Weinberg) (Karlsruhe 1901 – 1974 Rome)

Gesammelte Werke, ed. Christian Büttrich und Norbert Miller, 7 vols., Frankfurt am Main: Insel, 1981–89

Liebe beginnt, Berlin: Cassirer, 1933; repr. *GW* 1; Frankfurt am Main: Suhrkamp, 1984 (n)

Elissa, Berlin: Universitas, 1937; repr. Berlin: Deutsche Buchgemeinschaft, 1938; *GW*; Frankfurt am Main: Suhrkamp, 1984 (n)

Griechische Mythen, Hamburg: Claassen & Goverts, 1946; repr. Munich: Deutscher Taschenbuch Verlag, 1975, 1984, 1986 (e)

Menschen und Dinge 1945. Zwölf Essays, Heidelberg: Schneider, 1946 (e)

Gedichte, Hamburg: Claassen & Goverts, 1947 (p)

Totentanz und Gedichte zur Zeit, Hamburg: Claassen & Goverts, 1947 (p)

Engelsbrücke. Römische Betrachtungen, Hamburg, Claassen, 1955; repr. Munich: dtv, 1995 (e/a)

Das Haus der Kindheit, Hamburg, Claassen, 1956 (n)

Neue Gedichte, Hamburg: Claassen, 1957 (p)

'Das besondere der Frauendichtung', in *Deutsche Akademie für Sprache und Dichtung, Darmstadt. Jahrbuch 1957*, Heidelberg, Darmstadt: Schneider, 1958 (e)

Lange Schatten, Hamburg, Claassen, 1960 (s)

Dein Schweigen – meine Stimme, Gedichte 1958–1961, Hamburg: Claassen, 1962 and Munich: Heyne, 1978 (p)

Wohin denn ich. Aufzeichnungen, Hamburg: Claassen, 1963 (e/a)

Zwischen Immer und Nie. Gestalten und Themen der Dichtung, Frankfurt am Main, Insel, 1971; repr. 1992 (e)

Ein Wort weiter, Hamburg: Claassen, 1965

Überallnie. Ausgewählte Gedichte 1928–1965, Hamburg: Claassen, 1965 and Frankfurt am Main: Fischer, 1984

Kein Zauberspruch, Frankfurt am Main: Insel, 1972 and Frankfurt am Main: Suhrkamp, 1986

Works in English translation

Selected Later Poems of Marie Luise Kaschnitz, tr. Lisel Mueller, Princeton: Princeton
    University Press, 1980 (parallel German text and English translation)
Lange Schatten – Long Shadows, tr. Kay Bridgwater, Munich: Hueber, 1966 (s)
Long Shadows: Stories, tr. Anni Whissen. Columbia, South Carolina: Camden House, 1995
Cocalis, *The Defiant Muse* (1986)
Herrmann and Spitz, *German Women Writers* (1978)

Secondary literature

Foot, Robert, *The Phenomenon of Speachlessness [sic] in the Poetry of Marie Luise Kaschnitz,
    Günter Eich, Nelly Sachs and Paul Celan*, Bonn: Bouvier, 1982
Pulver, Elsbeth, *Marie Luise Kaschnitz*, Munich: Beck, 1984
Schweikert, Uwe, *Marie Luise Kaschnitz*, Frankfurt am Main: Suhrkamp, 1984
Joeres, Ruth-Ellen B., 'Marie Luise Kaschnitz', in Wolfgang D. Elfe and James Hardin
    (eds.), *Contemporary German Fiction Writers (First Series)*, Detroit, 1988, pp. 174–82
Frederiksen; Wilson

Kath, Lydia (writing in 1930s)

Aud. Geschichte einer Wikingerfrau, Berlin-Steglitz: Verlag Junge Generation, 1934 (n)
Urmutter Unn. Geschichten um altnordische Frauen, Berlin-Steglitz: Verlag Junge
    Generation, 1935 (s)

Kautsky, Minna (Graz 1837 – 1912 Berlin)

Herrschen und Dienen, 2 vols., Leipzig; Reißner, 1882 (n)
Die Alten und die Neuen, 2 vols., Leipzig: Reißner, 1884 (n)
Victoria, 2 vols., Zurich: Verlags-Magazin, 1889 (n)
Helene, 3 vols., Stuttgart: Dietz, 1894 (n)

Kerschbaumer, Marie-Thérèse (nr. Paris 1936 – Austria)

Gedichte, Bucharest: Krition, 1970 (p)
Liebesgedichte, Klagenfurt and Salzburg: Wieser Verlag, 1970 (p)
Der weibliche Name des Widerstands: Sieben Berichte, Olten and Freiburg im Breisgau:
    Walter, 1980 (e)
Neun Canti auf die irdische Liebe, Klagenfurt and Salzburg: Wieser Verlag, 1989 (p)
Für mich hat Lesen etwas mit Fließen zu tun: Gedanken zu Lesen und Schreiben von Literatur,
    Vienna: Wien Frauenverlag, 1989 (e)
bilder immermehr: Gedichte (1964–1987), Salzburg and Vienna: Otto Müller Verlag, 1997 (p)

Works in English translation

Woman's Face of Resistance (= *Der weibliche Name des Widerstands*; tr. with afterword by
    Lowell A. Bangerter), Riverside, California: Ariadne, 1996
Frederiksen; Wilson

Keun, Irmgard (Berlin 1910 – 1982 Cologne)

Gilgi, eine von uns, Berlin: Universitas, 1931; repr. Düsseldorf: Claassen, 1980; Munich:
    dtv, 1989 (n)
Das kunstseidene Mädchen, Berlin: Universitas, 1932; repr. Munich: dtv, 1989 (n)
Das Mädchen mit dem die Kinder nicht verkehren durften, 1936; 1982 (n)

Nach Mitternacht, Amsterdam: Querido, 1937; repr. Düsseldorf: Claassen, 1980; Stuttgart:
   Klett, 1982; Munich: dtv, 1991 (n)
D-Zug dritter Klasse, first publ. 1938; repr. Düsseldorf: Claassen, 1983; Munich: dtv, 1990
   (n)
Ferdinand, der Mann mit dem freundlichen Herzen, first publ. 1950; repr. Düsseldorf:
   Claassen, 1981 (n)
Wenn wir alle gut wären, ed. Wilhelm Unger, Cologne: Kiepenheuer & Witsch, 1983

Works in English translation

The Artificial Silk Girl (= *Das kunstseidene Mädchen*; tr. Basil Creighton), London: Chatto, 1933
The Bad Example (= *Das Mädchen mit dem die Kinder nicht verkehren durften*; tr. Leila Berg and
   Ruth Baer), New York, 1955; republ. as *Grown-ups Don't Understand*, London:
   Parrish, 1955
After Midnight (= *Nach Mitternacht*); tr. James Cleugh, New York: Knopf; London: Secker,
   1938; tr. Anthea Bell, London: Gollancz, 1985; repr. Sceptre, 1987

Secondary literature

Beutel, Heike, and Anna Barbara Hagin (eds.), *Irmgard Keun. Zeitzeugen, Bilder und
   Dokumente erzählen*, Cologne, 1995
Kreis, Gabriele, *Was man glaubt, gibt es. Das Leben der Irmgard Keun*, Zurich, 1991
Rosenstein, Doris, *Irmgard Keun. Das Erzählwerk der dreißiger Jahre*, Frankfurt am Main:
   P. Lang, 1991
Sautermeister, Gerd, 'Irmgard Keuns Roman *Nach Mitternacht*, in Christian Fritsch and
   Lutz Winckler (eds.), *Faschismuskritik und Deutschlandbild im Exilroman*, Berlin
   1981, pp. 15–35
Horsley, Rita Jo, 'Irmgard Keun', in Wolfgang D. Elfe and James Hardin (eds.),
   Contemporary German Fiction Writers (First Series), Detroit, 1988, pp. 182–8
Frederiksen; Wilson

Kinkel, Johanna (Bonn 1810 – 1858 London)

Hans Ibeles in London, Stuttgart, 1860; repr. Frankfurt am Main: Ulrike Helmer-Verlag,
   1988 (n)
(with Johann Gottfried Kinkel) *Erzählungen*, Stuttgart and Tübingen, 1849 (s)

   Translations: see Morgan, also Frederiksen (1989)
Wilson

Kirsch, Sarah (Limlingerode, Harz 1935; moved from GDR to FRG in 1977)

Gespräch mit dem Saurier (with Rainer Kirsch), Berlin: Verlag Neues Leben, 1965 (p)
Landaufenthalt, Berlin and Weimar: Aufbau 1967, and Ebenhausen: Langewiesche-
   Brandt, 1969 (p)
Die Pantherfrau. Fünf unfrisierte Erzählungen aus dem Kassetten-Recorder, Berlin: Aufbau-
   Verlag, 1973; repr. Reinbek: Rowohlt, 1978 (documentary prose)
Zaubersprüche, Berlin and Weimar: Aufbau, 1973 and Ebenhausen: Langewiesche-
   Brandt, 1974 (p)
Rückenwind, Berlin and Weimar: Aufbau 1976 and Ebenhausen: Langewiesche-Brandt,
   1977 (p)
Katzenkopfpflaster, Munich: dtv, 1978 (p)

Drachensteigen, Ebenhausen: Langewiesche-Brandt, 1979 (p)

La Pagerie, Stuttgart: DVA, 1980 (p/e/a)

Erdreich, Stuttgart: DVA, 1982 (p)

Katzenleben, Stuttgart: DVA, 1984 (p)

Landwege: eine Auswahl 1980–1985, Stuttgart: DVA, 1985 (p)

Erklärung einiger Dinge: Dokumente und Bilder, with comments by Elke Erb and Urs
    Widmer, Munich: Langewiesche-Brandt, 1978; Reinbek: Rowohlt, 1981 (a)

Schneewärme, Stuttgart: DVA, 1989 (p)

Erlkönigs Tochter, Stuttgart: DVA, 1992 (p)

Das simple Leben, Stuttgart: DVA, 1994 (p/prose)

Bodenlos. Gedichte, Stuttgart: DVA, 1996 (p)

Luftspringerin. Ein Sarah-Kirsch-Lesebuch, Stuttgart: DVA, 1997 (p, e: selections)

(ed.), Elke Erb, *Trost: Gedichte und Prosa*. Stuttgart: DVA, 1980 (p/s)

(ed.), *Annette von Droste-Hülshoff*, Cologne: Kiepenheuer & Witsch, 1986

Works in English translation

The Panther Woman. Five Tales from the Cassette Recorder (= *Die Pantherfrau*; tr. Marion Faber),
    Lincoln: University of Nebraska Press, 1989

Conjurations. The Poems of Sarah Kirsch, tr. Wayne Kram, Columbus: Ohio University Press,
    1985 (English and German, with notes)

The Brontës Hats, tr. Wendy Mulford and Anthony Vivis, Cambridge: Street Editions, 1991
    (parallel German texts and English translations)

Catlives (= *Katzenleben*; tr. and ed. Marina Roscher and Charles Fishman), Texas Tech
    University Press, 1991

Winter Music: Selected Poems, tr. Margitt Lehbert, London: Anvil Press, 1995

T, tr. Wendy Mulford and Anthony Vivis, Saxmundham: Street Editions, 1995

'Five pieces from *Marshland Grass*' (= excerpts from *Schwingrasen*; tr. Anthony Vivis),
    Storm 5 (1992), 4–12

Altbach, *German Feminism* (1984)

Taylor, *Miracles of Disbelief* (see p. 280 above)

Gerber and Pouchet

Secondary literature

Arnold, Heinz Ludwig (ed.), *Sarah Kirsch*, Munich: Text + Kritik, 1989

Cosentino, Christine, *'Ein Spiegel mit mir darin': Sarah Kirschs Lyrik*, Tübingen: Franke,
    1990

Fehn, Ann Clark, 'Sarah Kirsch', in Wolfgang D. Elfe and James Hardin (eds.),
    Contemporary German Fiction Writers (Second Series), Detroit, 1988, pp. 146–56; (also
    lists poems tr. in periodicals; with bibl.)

Graves, Peter J. (ed.), *Three Contemporary German Poets: Wolf Biermann, Sarah Kirsch, Reiner
    Kunze*, Leicester: Leicester University Press, 1985

Hopwood, Mererid, and David Basker (eds.), *Sarah Kirsch*, Cardiff: University of Wales
    Press, 1997

Frederiksen; Wilson

Kiwus, Karin (W. Berlin 1942–)

Von beiden Seiten der Gegenwart, Frankfurt am Main: Suhrkamp, 1976 (p)

Angenommen später, Frankfurt am Main: Suhrkamp, 1978 (p)

Zweifelhafter Morgen, Leipzig: Philipp Reclam jun., 1987 (p)
Das Chinesische Examen, Frankfurt am Main: Suhrkamp, 1992 (p)

> Translation: Cocalis, *The Defiant Muse* (1986)

Wilson

Klipstein, Editha (Kiel 1880 – 1953 Laubach, Hessen)

Anna Lunde, Hamburg: H. Goverts, 1935 (n)
Der Zuschauer, Hamburg: H. Goverts, 1942 (n)

> And other essays and works of fiction

Wilson

Kloos, Barbara Maria (FRG 1958–)

SOLO, Munich: Piper, 1986 (p)
with Birgit Kempker and Kristin T. Schneider, *61 Grad über dem Horizont*, ed. Dietger
> Pforte, Berlin: Literarisches Colloquium, 1986 (p)
Die Tage waren wie Ballons, Munich: Franz Schneekluth Verlag, 1991 (p)

Klopstock, Margarete (Meta) (Hamburg 1728–58)

Hinterlassene Schriften, ed. F. G. Klopstock. Hamburg: Bohn, 1759 (d, p, s)
Meta Klopstock geborene Moller. Briefwechsel mit Klopstock, ihren Verwandten und Freunden, ed.
> Hermann Tiemann, 3 vols., Hamburg: Maximilian-Gesellschaft, 1956 (l)

Works in English translation

Memoirs of Frederick and Margaret Klopstock, tr. Miss Elizabeth Smith, Bath: R. Crutwell;
> London: Cadell & Davies 1808 and various edns.; Microopaque: Worcester,
> Massachusetts: American Antiquarian Society, 1971

Secondary literature

Trunz, E. 'Meta Moller und das 18. Jahrhundert', in *Briefwechsel mit Klopstock* (above),
> vol. III: pp. 955–74

Wilson

Koenig, Alma Johanna (Prague 1887 – 1942? Minsk)

Der heilige Palast, 1922 (n)
Die Geschichte von Half, dem Weibe. Ein Wikingerroman, 1924 (n)

> And other works; see Wilson

Works in English translation

Passion in Algiers (= *Leidenschaft in Algier*, 1932; tr. J. H. Lepper), London: Cassell, 1933
Gudrun (tr. Anthea Bell), Harmondsworth: Kestrel Books, 1979 (ch)

Secondary literature

Kerschbaumer, *Der weibliche Name des Widerstands* (1980) (see p. 326 above)

Koenig, Hertha (Gut Boeckel, Westphalia 1884–1976)

Sonnenuhr, Gedichte, Munich: Beck, 1910 (p)
Emilie Reinbeck, Berlin, 1913 (n)
Die kleine und die große Liebe, Berlin: S. Fischer, 1917

Sonette, Leipzig: Insel, 1917 (p)

Blumen, Leipzig: Insel 1919 (p)

Alles ist Anfang geworden. Gedichte 1938–1945, Iserlohn: Holzwarth, 1946 (p)

And later works of fiction and memoirs

Köhler, Barbara (Chemnitz 1959 – GDR)

Deutsches Roulette: Gedichte 1984–1989, Frankfurt am Main: Suhrkamp, 1991 (p)

Blue Box, Frankfurt am Main: Suhrkamp, 1995 (p)

Kolb, Annette (Munich 1870–1967)

Das Exemplar, Roman. Berlin: S. Fischer, 1913 (n)

Wege und Umwege, Leipzig: Verlag der Weissen Bücher, 1914

Briefe einer Deutsch-Französin, Berlin: Reiss, 1916 (l)

Die Last, Zurich: Rascher, 1918 (e)

Daphne Herbst, Berlin: S. Fischer, 1928 (n)

Further works listed Wilson. Also translated from French.

Works in English translation

Mozart (= *Mozart. Sein Leben*, 1937; tr. Phyllis and Trevor Blewitt), London: Gollancz, 1939; repr. 1948; reissued London: Prion Books, 1998

Secondary literature

Fetzer, John Francis, 'Annette Kolb', in James Hardin (ed.), *German Fiction Writers, 1885–1913*, vol. I, Detroit, 1988, pp. 258–67

Kolmar, Gertrud (Berlin 1894 – ?1943 Auschwitz)

Weibliches Bildnis. Sämtliche Gedichte, Munich: dtv, 1987

Das lyrische Werk, Munich: Kösel, 1960 (p)

Gedichte, Berlin: Fleischel, 1917 (p)

Preussische Wappen. Gedichte, Rabenpresse, 1934 (p)

Die Frau und die Tiere, Berlin: Erwin Löwe, 1938 (p)

Eine Mutter, 1965; reissued as *Eine jüdische Mutter*, Munich: Kösel, 1978; Frankfurt am Main: Ullstein, 1981 (s)

Briefe an die Schwester Hilde (1938–1943), ed. Johanna Zeitler, Munich: Kösel, 1970 (l)

Gedichte, ed. Ulla Hahn, Frankfurt am Main: Suhrkamp, 1983, 1986 (p)

Gertrud Kolmar. Briefe, ed. Johanna Woltmann, Göttingen: Wallstein, 1997

Works in English translation

Dark Soliloquy. The Selected Poems of Gertrud Kolmar, tr. and intr. Henry A. Smith, foreword by Cynthia Ozick, New York: Seabury, 1975

Selected Poems, tr. David Kipp, London: Magpie Press, 1970

The Shimmering Crystal: Poems from 'Das lyrische werk', tr. Elizabeth Spencer, London: Millennium, c. 1995 (parallel German text and English translation)

A Jewish Mother from Berlin, and *Susanna* (=*Eine Mutter*; *Susanna*; tr. Brigitte M. Goldstein), New York: Holmes and Meier, 1998

Cocalis, *The Defiant Muse* (1986)

Secondary literature

Eichmann-Leutenegger, Beatrice, *Gertrud Kolmar: Leben und Werk in Texten und Bildern*, Frankfurt am Main: Jüdischer Verlag, 1993

Woltmann-Zeitler, Johanna, *Gertrud Kolmar, Leben und Werk*, Göttingen: Wallstein, 1995
Woltmann, Johanna, *Gertrud Kolmar*. Marbacher Magazin 63, Marbach: Deutsche
 Schillergesellschaft, 1993
Frederiksen

Komenda-Soentgerath, Olly (Czechoslovakia 1923 – FRG)

Wasserfall der Zeit, ed. Hans Hinterhöfer and Roswitha Hlawatsch, Eisingen: Horst-
 Heiderhoff Verlag, 1981 (p)
Das schläft mir nachts unter den Lidern, ed. Roswitha Hlawatsch and Horst Heiderhoff.
 Eisingen: Hans-Heiderhoff Verlag, 1981; 1990 (p)
Mit weniger kann ich nicht leben, ed. Roswitha Hlawatsch and Horst Heiderhoff, Eisingen:
 Horst-Heiderhoff Verlag, 1983 (p)
Ein Strahl von deinem Licht: Gedichtzyklus zum Vaterunser, Munich: Claudius 1986 (p)
Unerreichbar nahe, ed. Roswitha and Horst Heiderhoff, Eisingen: Horst-Heiderhoff
 Verlag, 1986 (p)
Erst wenn die Boten kommen, ed. Roswitha Heiderhoff and Viktor Mundt, Eisingen: Horst-
 Heiderhoff Verlag, 1992 (p)

Works in English translation

Under my Eyelids: Poems of Olly Komenda-Soentgerath, tr. Tom Beck, London: Forest Books, 1994
In the Shadow of Prague (= *Im Schatten Prags*; tr. Tom Beck), London: Forest, 1996
Only When the Messengers Come, tr. Tom Beck (= *Erst wenn die Boten kommen*), London:
 Forest, 1995 (parallel English and German text)

König, Barbara (Bohemia 1925–)

Das Kind und sein Schatten, Munich: Hanser, 1958 (n)
Kies, Munich: Hanser, 1961 (n)
Die Personenperson, Munich, Hanser: 1965 (n)

Works in English translation

The Beneficiary (= *Der Beschenkte*, 1980; tr. R. Theobald), Evanston, Illinois: Northwestern
 University Press, 1993; repr. Hydra Books, 1998
Our House, tr. Roslyn Theobald, Hydra Books, 1998
Herrmann and Spitz, *German Women Writers* (1978)

Königsdorf, Helga (Gera 1938 – GDR)

Meine ungehörigen Träume, Berlin: Aufbau-Verlag, 1978; repr. in abbrev. form as *Mit
 Klischmann im Regen*, Darmstadt: Luchterhand, 1983 (s)
Respektloser Umgang, Berlin: Aufbau-Verlag, 1980; repr. Darmstadt: Luchterhand, 1988 (s)
Ungelegener Befund, Berlin: Aufbau-Verlag, 1989; repr. Frankfurt am Main: Luchterhand,
 1990 (s)
Adieu DDR. Protokolle eines Abschieds, Reinbek: Rowohlt, 1990 (a, e, interviews)
Aus dem Dilemma eine Chance machen. Reden und Aufsätze, Hamburg: Luchterhand, 1990 (e)
1989 oder ein Moment Schönheit: Eine Collage aus Briefen, Gedichten, Texten, Berlin and
 Weimar: Aufbau, 1990 (e. l, p)
Gleich neben Afrika, Berlin: Rowohlt, 1992 (s)
Im Schatten des Regenbogens, Berlin: Aufbau, 1993 (n)
Über die unverzügliche Rettung der Welt, Berlin and Weimar: Aufbau, 1994 (e)
Die Entsorgung der Großmutter, Berlin: Aufbau, 1997 (n)
Frederiksen; Wilson

**Königsmark, Aurora von (Agathenburg,
Stade 1662 – 1728 Quedlinburg)**
Selection of poems repr. Jean M. Woods 'Nordischer Weyrauch: The Religious Lyrics of
Aurora von Königsmark and Her Circle', *Daphnis* 17/2 (1988), 267–326 (p)
Die Drei Töchter Cecrops, reprinted in *Die Hamburger Oper. Eine Sammlung von Texten der
Hamburger Oper aus der Zeit 1678–1730*, ed. Reinhart Meyer, 3 vols., Munich, 1980,
vol 1., pp. 125–70 (libretto)

Secondary literature
Olsen, Solveig, 'Aurora von Königsmarck's Singspiel *Die drey Töchter Cecrops*', *Daphnis* 17/3
(1988), 467–80
Seelbach, Ulrich, 'Maria Aurora von Königsmarck's Stanzen über ihren Bruder Philipp
Christoph', *Daphnis* 20/2, (1991), 403–22
Woods, Jean M., 'Aurora von Königsmarck; Epitome of a "Galante Poetin"', *Daphnis* 17/3,
(1988) 457–65

Körber, Lili (Moscow 1897 – 1982 New York)
Eine Frau erlebt den roten Alltag, Berlin, 1932 (n)
Eine Jüdin erlebt das neue Deutschland, first publ. Vienna, 1934; repr. as *Die Ehe der Ruth
Gompertz*, Mannheim: Persona, 1984, repr. 1987; Leipzig and Weimar, 1988 (ed.
Viktoria Hertling)

Works in English translation
Night over Vienna (= *Eine Österreicherin erlebt den Anschluß*; tr. Viktoria Hertling and Kay M.
Stone, with glossary and commentary by Viktoria Hertling), Riverside,
California: Ariadne Press, 1990
Life in a Soviet Factory (= *Eine Frau erlebt den roten Alltag*; tr. C. W. Sykes), London: Lane, 1933
Adventures in the East (= *Begegnungen im Fernen Osten*, Budapest 1936; tr. K. S. Shelvankar),
London: Lane, 1937

Kożik, Christa (GDR 1941–)
Gedichte, Berlin: Verlag Neues Leben, 1980 (p)
Tausendundzweite Nacht, Berlin: Verlag Neues Leben, 1988 (p)
Also writes ch

**Kräftner, Hertha (Vienna 1928–51; committed suicide aged twenty-
three)**
Das Werk: Gedichte, Skizzen, Tagebücher, ed. Otto Breicha and Andreas Okopenko,
Eisenstadt: Roetzer, Burgenländische Bibliothek, 1977
Kühle Sterne: Gedichte und Prosa aus dem Nachlaß, ed. Gerhard Altmann and Max Bläulich,
Klagenfurt and Salzburg: Wieser, 1997
Das blaue Licht. Lyrik und Prosa, Darmstadt: Luchterhand, 1981 (p, e/s)
Wilson

Kraus, Hilde Maria (Vienna 1904–?)
Villa Bedlam, Prague: Kohl, 1928
Ärztinnen, Breslau: Bergstadt, 1929 (n)
Neun Monate, Breslau: Bergstadt, 1931 (n)

Krauß, Angela (Chemnitz 1950 – GDR)

Das Vergnügen, Berlin: Aufbau-Verlag, 1984; repr. Frankfurt am Main: Suhrkamp, 1988;
1990 (s)
Glashaus, Berlin: Aufbau-Verlag, 1988; 9 of the stories repr. as *Kleine Landschaft*,
Frankfurt am Main: Suhrkamp, 1989 (s)
Der Dienst, Frankfurt am Main: Suhrkamp, 1990 (n)
Die Überfliegerin, Frankfurt am Main: Suhrkamp, 1995 (n)

Krechel, Ursula (Trier 1947–)

Selbsterfahrung und Fremdbestimmung: Bericht aus der neuen Frauenbewegung, Darmstadt:
Luchterhand, 1975; revised edn, 1983 (e)
Nach Mainz! Darmstadt: Luchterhand, 1977 and Munich: dtv, 1983 (p)
Verwundbar wie in den besten Zeiten, Darmstadt: Luchterhand, 1979 (p)
Zweite Natur. Szenen eines Romans, Darmstadt and Neuwied: Luchterhand, 1981 (n)
Rohschnitt: Gedicht in sechzig Sequenzen, Darmstadt: Luchterhand, 1983 (p)
Vom Feuer Lernen, Darmstadt: Luchterhand, 1985 (p)
Landläufiges Wunder, Frankfurt am Main: Suhrkamp, 1995 (p)

Also essays, prose fiction

Translation: Taylor, *Miracles of Disbelief* (see p. 280 above); Cocalis, *The Defiant
Muse* (1986)
Wilson

Kuntsch, Margaretha Susanna von (Allstedt, Saxony 1651 – 1717 Eisenach)

Sämmtliche Geist- und Weltliche Gedichte, 1720 (p, r, a)
Brinker-Gabler, *Deutsche Dichterinnen* (1978) (see p. 267 above)

Secondary literature
Carrdus, Anna, 'Consolation Arguments and Maternal Grief in Seventeenth Century
Verse: the Example of Margarethe Susanna von Kuntsch', *German Life and Letters*
47/2 (1994), 135–51
Hedstrom, Elke O., 'Margarethe Susanne von Kuntsch (1651–1717): Eine unbekannte
deutsche Dichterin aus der Barockzeit', *Daphnis* 19/2 (1990), 223–46
Cocalis, *The Defiant Muse* (1986)
Wilson

Kurz, Isolde (Stuttgart 1853 – 1944 Tübingen)

Gesammelte Werke, 6 vols., Munich: Georg Müller, 1925–

Poetry and numerous works of fiction, including
Nächte von Fondi. Eine Geschichte aus dem Cinquecento, Munich: Beck, 1922 (n)
Die Liebenden und der Narr. Eine Renaissance-Novelle, Nuremberg: Schrag, 1924 (s)
Vanadis. Der Schicksalsweg einer Frau. Tübingen: Wunderlich, 1931; 1986 (n)

Works in English translation
Tales of Florence (= *Florentiner Novellen*; tr. Lilian Dundas), London: Melrose, 1919
see also Wilson

Secondary literature

Bennett, Timothy A., 'Isolde Kurz', in James Hardin (ed.), *German Fiction Writers, 1885–1913*, vol. I, Detroit, 1988, pp. 280–4

Singer, Sandra L., *Free Soul, Free Woman?: A Study of Selected Fictional Works by Hedwig Dohm, Isolde Kurz, and Helene Böhlau*, New York: P. Lang, c. 1995

Lander, Jeannette (New York 1931 – Berlin)

Ein Sommer in der Woche der Itke K., Frankfurt am Main: Suhrkamp, 1971 (n)
Die Töchter, Frankfurt am Main: Insel, 1976 (n)
Ich, allein, Munich: AutorenEdition, 1980 (n)

Landshoff(-Yorck), Rut[h] (Berlin 1909 – 1966 New York; emigrated to USA in 1937)

Die Vielen und der Eine, Berlin: Rowohlt, 1930 (n)
Klatsch, Ruhm und kleine Feuer. Biographische Impressionen, Cologne, Berlin: Kiepenheuer 1963 (a)

Also wrote in English after 1937, e.g.

The man who killed Hitler, London, 1939 (n)
Sixty to go, New York, 1944 (n)
Lili Marlene, New York, 1945 (n)
So cold the night, New York: Harper, 1948 (n)

Secondary literature

Schoppmann, *Im Fluchtgepäck* (see p. 276 above), pp. 72–100

Lange-Müller, Katja (Berlin, GDR 1951–)

Wehleid: Wie im Leben. Erzählungen, Frankfurt am Main: Fischer, 1986 (s)
Kasper Mauser: Die Feigheit vorm Freund. Cologne: Kiepenheuer & Witsch, 1988 (s)

Langgässer, Elisabeth (Alzey, Rheinhessen 1899 – 1950 Rheinzabern)

Gesammelte Werke in Einzelausgaben, 5 vols., Hamburg: Claassen, 1959–64
Gedichte, Frankfurt am Main, Berlin and Vienna: Ullstein, 1981 (p)
Der Wendekreis des Lammes. Ein Hymnus der Erlösung, Mainz: Matthias Grünewald, 1924 (p)
Proserpina. Welt eines Kindes, Leipzig: Hesse & Becker, 1932; *Proserpina. Eine Kindheitsmythe* (original version), Hamburg: Claassen 1949; repr. Frankfurt am Main, Berlin and Vienna: Ullstein, 1982 (n)
(ed. with Ina Seidel), *Herz zum Hafen. Frauengedichte der Gegenwart*, Leipzig: R. Voigtländer Verlag, 1933 (p)
Tierkreisgedichte, Leipzig: Hegner, 1935 (p)
Der Gang durch das Ried, Leipzig: Hegner, 1936; Frankfurt am Main, Berlin and Vienna: Ullstein, 1981 (n)
Das unauslöschliche Siegel, Hamburg: Claassen & Goverts, 1946; Darmstadt & Neuwied: Luchterhand, 1979 (n)
Der Laubmann und die Rose. Ein Jahreskreis, Hamburg: Claassen & Goverts, 1947 (p)
... soviel berauschende Vergänglichkeit. Briefe 1926–1950, ed. Wilhelm Hoffmann, Hamburg: Claassen, 1954; Frankfurt am Main, Berlin and Vienna: Ullstein 1981 (l)
Märkische Argonautenfahrt, Hamburg, Claassen, 1950 (n)

Works in English translation

The Quest (= *Märkische Argonautenfahrt*; tr. Jane Bannard Greene), New York: Knopf, 1953
The Indelible Seal (= *Das unauslöschliche Siegel*, tr.?)
Herrmann and Spitz, *German Women Writers* (1978)

Secondary literature

Fliedl, *Zeitroman und Heilsgeschichte* (1986) (see p. 278 above)
Metzger, Erika A., 'Elisabeth Langgässer', in Wolfgang D. Elfe and James Hardin (eds.),
    Contemporary German Fiction Writers (First Series), Detroit, 1988, pp. 216–25
Frederiksen; Wilson

Langner, Ilse (i.e. Ilse Siebert) (Breslau 1899 – 1988 Darmstadt)

Dramen, 2 vols., ed. Eberhard Günter Schulz, Würzburg: Bergstadt Verlag W. G. Korn,
    1983 (contains bibliography)
Frau Emma kämpft im Hinterland. Chronik in drei Akten (1918), Berlin: Fischer, 1930;
    Darmstadt: Lehrdruckerei der TH, 1979
Katharina Henschke, 1930 (d)
Die Heilige aus U.S.A. Ein Drama, Berlin: S. Fischer, 1931 (d)
Amazonen. Komödie, Berlin: 1932; Frankfurt am Main: Fischer, 1953 (d)
Der Mord an Mykene, 1934 (1936); publ. as *Klytämnestra. Tragödie in drei Akten*, Hamburg:
    Mölich, 1947; Berlin: Aufbau, 1949 (d)
Das Gionsfest. Eine japanische Novelle, 1934 (s)
Die purpurne Stadt, Berlin: Fischer, 1937; Stuttgart: Cotta, 1952; Munich: Langen-Müller,
    1983 (n)
Flucht ohne Ziel. Tagebuch-Roman. Frühjahr 1945, Würzburg: Bergstadtverlag Korn,
    1984 (a)
Zwischen den Trümmern, 1948 (p)
Iphigenie kehrt heim, Berlin, Aufbau, 1948 (d)
Heimkehr, 1949 (d)
Die Zyklopen, Hamburg, Christian Wegner, 1960 (n)
Wilson

Secondary literature

Stürzer, *Dramatikerinnen* (see p. 278 above)

La Roche, Sophie von (Kaufbeuren 1730 – 1807 Offenbach)

*Geschichte des Fräuleins von Sternheim. Von einer Freundin derselben aus Originalpapieren . . .
    gezogen*, ed. C. M. Wieland, Parts 1 and 2, Leipzig: Weidmann, 1771; repr. (ed.
    Günter Häntzschel) Munich: Winkler, 1976; (ed. Barbara Becker Cantarino)
    Stuttgart: Reclam, 1983 (n)
Rosaliens Briefe an ihre Freundin Mariane von St***, 3 vols., Altenburg: Richter, 1779–81 (n)
Neuere moralische Erzählungen, Altenburg: Richter, 1786 (s)
Journal einer Reise durch Frankreich, Altenburg: Richter, 1787 (a/t)
Geschichte von Miß Lony und der schöne Bund, Gotha: Ettinger 1789 (n)
Erscheinungen am See Oneida, 3 vols., Leipzig: Gräff, 1798 (n)
Melusinens Sommer-Abende, ed. C. M. Wieland. Halle: Societäts-Buch- und
    Kunsthandlung, 1806 (s)

Ich bin mehr Herz als Kopf. Sophie von La Roche. Ein Lebensbild in Briefen, ed. M. Maurer,
    Munich: Beck, 1983 (l)

Works in English translation

'Two Sisters' (= 'Die zwey Schwestern') in Blackwell and Zantop, *Bitter Healing* (1990) (s)
Memoirs of Miss Sophy Sternheim (= *Geschichte des Fräuleins von Sternheim*; tr. Edward
    Hardwood), 2 vols. London: T. Becket, 1776
The History of Lady Sophia Sternheim (= *Geschichte des Fräuleins von Sternheim*), tr. Joseph
    Collyer, ed. James Lynn, London: Pickering & Chatto, 1991; New York: New
    York University Press, 1992; ed., tr. and intr. Christa Bagus Britt, Albany: SUNY,
    1991
Sophie in London, 1786: Being the Diary of Sophie von La Roche (= *Tagebuch einer Reise*, extracts;
    tr. Claire Williams), London: Cape, 1933

Secondary literature

Becker-Cantarino, B., '"Muse" und "Kunstrichter". Sophie La Roche und Wieland'. *MLN*
    99 (1984), 571–88
Blackwell, Jeannine, 'Sophie von La Roche', in James Hardin and Christoph E.
    Schweitzer (eds.), *German Writers in the Age of Goethe*, Detroit: Gale Research, Inc.
    1989, pp. 154–61
Heidenreich, B., *Sophie La Roche – eine Werkbiographie*, Frankfurt am Main, Bern: Lang,
    1986
Joeres, R-E. B., '"That girl is an entirely different character!". Yes, but is she a feminist?
    Observations on Sophie von La Roche's *Geschichte des Fräuleins von Sternheim*', in
    Joeres and Maynes, *German Women in the Eighteenth and Nineteenth Centuries* (1986)
    (see p. 267 above), pp. 137–56
Lange, V., 'Visitors to Lake Oneida: An Account of the Background of Sophie von La
    Roche's Novel *Erscheinungen am See Oneida*', *Symposium* 2 (1948), 48–78
Langner, M., *Sophie von La Roche – die empfindsame Realistin*. Heidelberg: Winter, 1995
Maurer, M., 'Das Gute und das Schöne. Sophie von La Roche (1730–1807) wieder-
    entdecken?', *Euphorion* 79 (1985), 111–38
Nenon, M., *Autorschaft und Frauenbildung. Das Beispiel Sophie von La Roche*, Würzburg:
    Königshausen und Neumann, 1988
Wiede-Behrendt, I., *Lehrerin des Schönen, Wahren, Guten. Literatur und Frauenbildung im
    ausgehenden 18. Jahrhundert am Beispiel Sophie von La Roche*, Frankfurt am Main and
    Bern: Lang, 1987
Winkle, S. A., *Woman as Bourgeois Ideal. A Study of Sophie von La Roche's 'Geschichte des
    Fräuleins von Sternheim' and Goethe's 'Werther'*, New York, Bern and Frankfurt am
    Main: Lang, 1988
See also the novel by Renate Feyl, *Die profanen Stunden des Glücks*, Munich: Heyne, 1996
Frederiksen

Lask, Berta (Wadowice, Galicia 1878 – 1967 Berlin, GDR)

Stimmen, Hannover: Steegemann, 1919 (p)
Rufe aus dem Dunkel. Auswahl 1915–1921, Berlin: Buchverlag der Arbeiter-Kunst-
    Ausstellung, 1921 (p)
*Auf dem Flügelpferde durch die Zeiten. Bilder vom Klassenkampf der Jahrtausende. Erzählungen
    für junge Proletarier*, Berlin: Vereinigung Internationaler Verlagsanstalten,
    1925 (s)

Leuna 1921. Drama der Tatsachen, Berlin: Vereinigung Internationaler Verlagsanstalten, 1927 (d)

Numerous other works, including ch

Works in English translation
'The Boy Who Wanted to Fight with a Dragon' (= 'Die Geschichte von dem Jungen, der mit einem Drachen kämpfen wollte', from *Proletarischer Kindergarten*; tr. Jack Zipes) in Zipes (ed.), *Utopian Tales from Weimar*, Edinburgh: Polygon, 1990
Cocalis, *The Defiant Muse* (1986)

Secondary literature
Cardinal, Agnès, 'A Voice out of Darkness: Berta Lask's Early Poetry', in Keith-Smith (1993) (see p. 275 above), pp. 203–24
Wilson

Lasker-Schüler, Else (Wuppertal-Elberfeld 1869 – 1945 Jerusalem)

Gesammelte Werke in 8 Bänden, 8 vols., Munich: dtv, 1986
Gesammelte Werke in drei Bänden, ed. Friedhelm Kemp, Werner Kraft and Margarete Kupper, Munich: Kösel Verlag, 1959–69
Meine Wunder. Gedichte, Karlsruhe and Leipzig: Dreililien, 1911 (p)
Hebräische Balladen, Berlin-Wilmersdorf: A. R. Meyer 1913 (p)
Der Prinz von Theben, Ein Geschichtenbuch, Leipzig: Verlag der Weissen Bücher, 1914 (s)
Der Malik. Eine Kaisergeschichte mit Bildern und Zeichnungen von Else Lasker-Schüler, Berlin: Cassirer, 1919 (n)
Die Wupper. Schauspiel in 5 Aufzügen, Berlin: Cassirer, [1919] (d)
Konzert, Berlin: Rowohlt, 1932
Arthur Aronymus. Die Geschichte meines Vaters, Berlin: Rowohlt, 1932 (d)

Works in English translation
Hebrew Ballads and other poems, tr., ed. and intr. Audri Durchschlag and Jeanette Litman-Demestre, Philadelphia: The Jewish Publication Society of America, 1980
Concert (= *Konzert*; tr. Jean M. Snook), Lincoln and London: University of Nebraska Press, 1994
Your Diamond Dreams Cut open my Arteries: Poems by Else Lasker-Schüler, tr. and ed. Robert P. Newton, Chapel Hill: University of North Carolina Press, 1982
IandI (= *IchundIch*; tr. Beate Hein Bennett), in Case, *The Divided Home/Land* (1992), pp. 137–79 (d)
Curtis, Jane Elisabeth, 'Else Lasker-Schüler's Drama *Dark River* [= *Die Wupper*]: A Translation into English and a Critical Commentary', diss., The Catholic University of America, 1982 (University Microfilms International, Ann Arbor, Michigan 1982)

Secondary literature
Bauschinger, Sigrid, *Else Lasker-Schüler. Ihr Werk und ihre Zeit*, Heidelberg: Stiehm, 1980
Cohn, Hans W., *Else Lasker-Schüler: The Broken World*, Cambridge: Cambridge University Press, 1974
Schwertfeger, Ruth, *Else Lasker-Schüler: Inside this Deathly Solitude*, New York: Berg, 1991
Resch, Margit, 'Else Lasker-Schüler', in James Hardin (ed.), *German Fiction Writers, 1885–1913*, vol I., Detroit, 1988, pp. 285–305
Frederiksen; Wilson

Lavant, Christine (i.e. Christine Habernig, née Thonhauser)
(St. Stefan, Lavant Valley, Austria 1915–73)
Poetry
Gedichte, ed. Thomas Bernhard, Frankfurt am Main: Suhrkamp, 1987
Gedichte: Der Pfauenschrei/Die Bettlerschale/Spindel im Mond, 3 vols., Salzburg: Otto Müller,
    1993
Die Bettlerschale, Salzburg: Otto Müller Verlag, 1956
Spindel im Mond, Salzburg: Otto Müller Verlag, 1959
Sonnenvogel, Wülfrath, Rheinland: Atteln, 1960 and Waldbrunn: Heiderhoff, 1982
Der Pfauenschrei, Salzburg: Otto Müller Verlag, 1962
*Kunst wie meine ist nur verstümmeltes Leben: Nachgelassene und verstreut veröffentlichte Gedichte,
    Prosa, Briefe*, ed. Johann Strutz and Arnim Witgotschnig, Salzburg: Otto Müller
    Verlag, 1978. (s, e, l, p)

Translations: see Taylor, *Miracles of Disbelief* (see p. 280 above) and O'Neill

Secondary literature
Lübbe-Grothues, Grete, and Hilde Domin (eds.), *Über Christine Lavant: Leseerfahrung,
    Interpretationen, Selbstdeutungen*, Salzburg: Otto Müller, 1984.
Strutz, Johann, *Poetik und Existenzproblematik: Zur Lyrik Christine Lavants*, Salzburg: Otto
    Müller, 1979
Wilson

Lederer, Joe (Vienna 1907 – 1987 Munich)
Das Mädchen George, Berlin: Universitas, 1928 (n)
Drei Tage Liebe. Berlin: Universitas, 1931 (n)

And many other works of fiction

Works in English translation
Late Spring (= *Letzter Frühling*, 1957; tr. D. Hardie), London: Cape, 1958
Fafan in China (=*Fafan in China*, 1938; tr. Margaret Rounds), New York: Holiday House
    1939 (ch)
A Leaf in the Wind (=*Blatt im Wind*, 1935; tr. Basil Creighton), London: Jenkins, 1938; repr.
    1939, 1940 (n)
Flowers for Cornelia (= *Blumen für Cornelia*, 1936; tr. Basil Creighton), London: Jenkins, 1939
    (n)
Over-night (= *Musik der Nacht*, 1930; tr. Guy Endore), New York: Farrar, 1931

**le Fort, Gertrud von (Minden, Westfalen 1876 – 1971 Oberstdorf,
    Allgäu); wrote critical essays until 1910 under pseud. Gerta von Stark;
    Huguenot family, Catholic convert 1926; from 1941 lived in Bavarian
    Alps (Oberstdorf)**
Lieder und Legenden, Leipzig: Eckardt, 1912 (p)
Hymnen an die Kirche, Munich: Theatiner, 1924 (p)
Das Schweißtuch der Veronika, Munich, 1924 (n)
Der Papst aus dem Ghetto. Die Legende des Geschlechts Pier Leone, Munich: Ehrenwirth, 1930 (n)
Die Letzte am Schafott, Munich: Kösel, 1931; Pustet, 1931; Munich: Ehrenwirth, 28th edn
    1983; Stuttgart: Reclam, 1983 and 1985 (s)
Hymnen an Deutschland, Munich: Kösel, 1932 (p)

Die ewige Frau. Die Frau in der Zeit. Die zeitlose Frau, Munich: Kösel & Pustet, 1934; 20th edn
  1962 (e)
Das Gericht des Meeres, Leipzig: Insel 1934; 1966 (s)
Die Magdeburgische Hochzeit, Leipzig: Insel, 1938; repr. Frankfurt am Main: Insel,
  1987 (n)
Der Kranz der Engel, Munich, Michael Beckstein, 1946 (n)
Die Tochter Farinatas, Wiesbaden: Insel, 1950 and Leipzig: Insel, 1951 (s)
Die Frau des Pilatus. Novelle, Wiesbaden: Insel, 1955 (n/s)
Annette von Droste-Hülshoff, Berlin: Propyläen, 1956 (e)
Gedichte und Aphorismen, Munich: Franz Ehrenwirth Verlag, 1970 (p/c)
Gertrud von le Fort erzählt, Frankfurt am Main, Leipzig: Insel, 1993

Works in English translation
The Veil of Veronica (= *Das Schweißtuch der Veronika*; tr. Conrad M. R. Bonacina), London:
  Sheed & Ward, 1932
The Pope from the Ghetto (= *Der Papst aus dem Ghetto*; tr. Conrad M. R. Bonacina), London:
  Sheed & Ward, 1934
The Eternal Woman; Woman in Time; Timeless Woman (Die ewige Frau . . .; tr. Marie Cecilia
  Buehrle), Milwaukee: Bruce, 1954
Hymns to the Church (= *Hymnen an die Kirche*; tr. Margaret Chanler), London: Sheed &
  Ward, 1938
The Judgement of the Sea. Four Novellas (= *Das Gericht des Meeres*; tr. Isabel and Florence
  McHugh, intr.: Karl Stern), Chicago: Regnerey, 1962
Song at the Scaffold (= *Die Letzte am Schafott*; tr. Olga Marx), New York: Sheed and Ward,
  1951; London: Sheed and Ward, 1953; repr. New York: Doubleday, 1961
The Wife of Pilate (= *Die Frau des Pilatus*; tr. Marie C. Buehrle), Milwaukee: Bruce Publ.,
  1957
Herrmann and Spitz, *German Women Writers* (1978)

Secondary literature
Ives, Margaret, 'Gertrud von le Fort's *Hymnen an die Kirche*', in Keith-Smith (1993) (see
  p. 275 above), pp. 279–92
O'Boyle, Ita, *Gertrud von le Fort: An Introduction to the Prose Work*, New York: Fordham
  University Press, 1964
Schmidt, Josef, 'Gertrud von le Fort', in James Hardin (ed.), *German Fiction Writers,
  1885–1913*, vol. I, Detroit, 1988, pp. 306–10
Wilson (entry under **G**ertrud von Le Fort(!))

Leitner, Maria (Varasdin, Croatia 1892 – 1941? S. France or concentration camp)
Eine Frau reist durch die Welt, Berlin: Agis, 1932; Berlin: Dietz, 1988 (t)
Elisabeth, ein Hitlermädchen. Erzählende Prosa, Reportagen und Berichte, ed. and with an
  afterword by Helga Schwarz. Berlin and Weimar, 1985 (n)
Hotel Amerika. Ein Reportage-Roman, Berlin: Neuerde Verlag, 1930; repr. Dresden, 1950;
  Berlin: Dietz, 1960 (n)

Secondary literature
Siegel, Eva-Maria, *Jugend, Frauen, Drittes Reich: Autorinnen im Exil, 1933–1945*, Pfaffenweiler:
  Centaurus-Verlagsgesellschaft, 1993

Leutenegger, Gertrud (Schwyz, Switzerland 1948–)
Vorabend, Frankfurt am Main: Suhrkamp, 1975
And other works
Translation: see Frederiksen (1989)

Secondary literature
Boa, Elizabeth, 'Gertrud Leutenegger: A Feminist Synthesis', in Michael Butler and
Malcolm Pender (eds.), *Rejection and Emancipation: Women in German-Speaking
Switzerland 1945–1991*, New York and Oxford: Berg, 1991, pp. 202–21
Zinggeler, Magrit Verena, *Literary Freedom and Social Constraints in the Works of Swiss Writer
Gertrud Leutenegger*, Amsterdam and Atlanta, Georgia: Rodopi, 1995

Lewald, Fanny (Fanny Lewald-Stahr) (1811–89)
Gesammelte Werke, 12 vols., Berlin: O. Janke, 1871
Gesammelte Novellen, Berlin: Gerschel, 1862 (s)
Jenny, Leipzig: Brockhaus, 1843; repr. *Gesammelte Werke*, vol. IX; Frankfurt am Main:
Ulrike Helmer-Verlag, 1993 (n)
Der dritte Stand, Ein Zeitbild im Berliner Kalender für 1845, 1846 (n)
Diogena. Roman von Iduna Gräfin H . . . H . . ., Leipzig: Brockhaus, 1847 (n)
Italienisches Bilderbuch, Berlin: Duncker, 1847 (t)
Prinz Louis Ferdinand, Breslau: Joseph Max und Comp, 1849; Berlin: Hoffmann & Co.,
1859 (n)
Erinnerungen aus dem Jahre 1848, Braunschweig: Vieweg & Sohn, 1850 (a)
Wandlungen, Berlin: O. Janke, 1853 (n)
England und Schottland, Braunschweig: Vieweg, 1851; Berlin: O. Janke, 1864 (t)
Deutsche Lebensbilder. Erzählungen von Fanny Lewald, Braunschweig: Vieweg, 1856 (includes
Die Hausgenossen, Das große Los, Kein Haus, Die Tante) (s)
Meine Lebensgeschichte, Berlin: O. Janke, 1861–2; repr. Frankfurt am Main: Fischer, 1980;
Frankfurt am Main: Ulrike Helmer-Verlag, 3 vols., 1988–89 (a)
Politische Schriften für und wider die Frauen (contains *Osterbriefe für die Frauen*; repr. and *Für
und wider die Frauen*) Frankfurt am Main: Ulrike Helmer-Verlag, 1993 (e)
Adèle, Braunschweig: Vieweg und Sohn, 1855, Berlin: O. Janke, 1864 (n)
Römisches Tagebuch (1865), ed. H. Spiero, Leipzig: Klinkhardt & Biermann, 1927 (e)
And many other works

Works in English translation
The Italians at Home (= *Italienisches Bilderbuch*; tr. Countess D'Avigdor), 1848
A Year of Revolutions. Fanny Lewald's 'Recollections of 1848' (=*Erinnerungen aus dem Jahre 1848*;
tr. and ed. Hanna Ballin Lewis), Providence and Oxford: Berghahn, 1997
(contains a complete list of English translations of Lewald's works)
Frederiksen

**Lichnowsky, Mechtild[e] von (Schloß Schönburg,
Lower Bavaria 1879 – 1958 London)**
Götter, Könige und Tiere in Ägypten, Leipzig: Wolff, 1914 (t, e)
Gott betet. Der jüngste Tag 56, Leipzig: Wolff, 1918 (prose poems)
Der Kinderfreund. Schauspiel in 5 Akten, Berlin: Reiss 1919 (d)
Geburt, Berlin: Reiss, 1921 (n)

Das Rendez-vous im Zoo. Querelles d'amoureux, Vienna and Leipzig: Jahoda, 1928 (s)
An der Leine, Berlin: S. Fischer, 1930 (n)
Kindheit, 1934; 1984 (a)
Delaide, Berlin, 1935; 1984 (n)
Der Lauf der Asdur, Vienna: Bermann-Fischer, 1936; 1982 (a; sequel to *Kindheit*)
Gespräche in Sybaris. Tragödie einer Stadt in 21 Dialogen, 1946 (d)
    And other works

Works in English translation
On the Leash (= *An der Leine*; tr. Hugh Hare), London: Cape, 1930

Secondary literature
Hemecker, Wilhelm, *Mechtilde Lichnowsky*. Marbacher Magazin 64, Marbach: Deutsche
    Schillergesellschaft, 1993
Wilson

Liebmann, Irina (Moscow 1943 – GDR; moved to FRG in 1988)
Berliner Mietshaus. (Begegnungen und Gespräche), Halle: Mitteldeutscher Verlag, 1982; repr.
    Frankfurt am Main: Frankfurter Verlagsanstalt, 1990 (documentary fiction)
Mitten im Krieg, Frankfurt am Main: Frankfurter Verlagsanstalt, 1989 (s)

Ludecus, Karoline, née Kotzebue (1757–1827?)
Johanne Gray, Berlin, 1806, in *Theater der Deutschen: Eine Sammlung aller seit dem Anfange des
    achtzehnten Jahrhunderts für die deutsche Bühne herausgegebenen Werke*, part 106, vol.
    II. 1817– (d)

Ludwig, Paula (Vorarlberg, Austria 1900 – 1974 Darmstadt)
Gedichte. Gesamtausgabe, ed. Kristian Wachinger and Christian Peter, Ebenhausen:
    Langewiesche-Brandt, 1986 (p)
Die selige Spur, Munich: Roland, 1920 (p)
Der himmlische Spiegel, Berlin: S. Fischer, 1927 (p)
Dem dunklen Gott. Ein Jahresgedicht der Liebe, Dresden: Jess 1932; repr. Ebenhausen bei
    München: Langewiesche & Brandt, 1974 (p)

Mann, Erika (Munich 1905 – 1969 Zurich)
Rundherum, Berlin: S. Fischer, 1929 (t)
(with Klaus Mann) *Das Buch von der Riviera*, Munich: Piper, 1931; Berlin: Silver u.
    Goldstein, 1989 (t)
Escape to Life: deutsche Kultur im Exil, 3rd edn Munich: Edition Spangenberg, 1992

Works in English translation
School for Barbarians (= *Zehn Millionen Kinder*; tr. anon.), New York: Modern Age, 1938;
    publ. as *Education under the Nazis*, London: Drummond, 1939
The Lights Go Down, tr. Maurice Samuel, New York: Farrar, 1940
Gang of Ten, tr. anon., L. B. Fischer, 1942
The Last Year: a Memoir of my Father; tr. Richard Graves [London]: Secker & Warburg,
    1958
(with Klaus Mann) *Escape to Life* (first publ. in English), Boston: Riverside Press, 1939;
    London: T. Allen, 1939

The Other Germany, tr. H. Norden

Case, *The Divided Home/Land* (1992) (see p. 267 above): poems, pp. 218–28

Secondary literature

von der Lühe, Irmela, 'Die Publizistin Erika Mann im amerikanischen Exil', in *Publizistik im Exil und andere Themen*, Munich 1989 (= *Exilforschung* 7) pp. 65–84

von der Lühe, Irmela, *Erika Mann. Eine Biographie*, Frankfurt am Main and New York, 1994

Schoppmann, *Im Fluchtgepäck* (see p. 276 above), pp. 153–83

Marholm, Laura (i.e. Laura Hansson) (Riga, Latvia 1854–1928)

Das Buch der Frauen, Paris and Leipzig: Langen, 1895 (translated into 6 languages)

Zur Psychologie der Frau, 2 vols., Berlin: Duncker, 1903 (e)

> Numerous works of fiction, political and psychological writings (see also Wilson)

Works in English translation

Modern Women (= *Das Buch der Frauen*; tr. Hermione C. Ramsden), London: Lane and Boston: Roberts, 1896; another version publ. as *Six Modern Women: Psychological Sketches*, Boston: Roberts, 1896

We Women and our Authors (= *Wir Frauen und unsere Dichter*; tr. Hermione C. Ramsden), London and New York: Lane, 1899

Studies in the Psychology of Woman (= *Zur Psychologie der Frau*; tr. Georgia A. Etchison), Chicago and New York: Stone, 1899; as *The Psychology of Women*, London: Richards, 1899

Secondary literature

Brantly, Susan, *The Life and Writings of Laura Marholm*, Basel: Helbing & Lichtenhahn, 1991

Marlitt, Eugenie (pseud.: Eugenie John) (Arnstadt 1825–87); extremely popular fiction writer of her day

Gesammelte Romane und Novellen, 10 vols., Leipzig: E. Keils Nachfolger, 1891–94 (n, s)

Individual titles, with first date of publication, include

Reichsgräfin Gisela (vol. III of Collected Works), 1870; repr. Frankfurt am Main: Fischer, 1974; Berlin: Verlag Neues Leben, 1992

Im Hause des Kommerzienrates (vol. V of Collected Works), 1877; repr. Klagenfurt: Eduard Kaiser, 1973; Berlin: Verlag Neues Leben, 1991

Goldelse (vol. VIII of Collected Works), 1867; repr. Berlin: Verlag Neues Leben, 1991

Works in English translation

(numerous translations and reprints; for further details see Wilson, and Morgan + S), e.g.:

The Old Mam'sell's Secret (= *Das Geheimnis der alten Mamsell*; tr. Mrs A. L. Wister), Philadelphia: Lippincott, 1868

The Little Moorland Princess (= *Das Heideprinzeßchen*; tr. Mrs A. L. Wister), Philadelphia: Lippincott, 1876

The Countess Gisela (= *Reichsgräfin Gisela*; tr. A. Nahmer), New York: Harper, 1872–6; also tr. Mrs Wister, as above

In the Schillingscourt (= *Im Schillingshof*; tr. Mrs A. L. Wister), Philadelphia: Lippincott, 1879

At the Councilor's; Or, A Nameless History (= *Im Hause des Kommerzienrates*; tr. Mrs A. L.
  Wister), Philadelphia: Lippincott, 1879
The Lady with the Rubies (= *Die Frau mit den Karfunkelsteinen*; tr. Mrs A. L. Wister),
  Philadelphia: Lippincott, 1885
The Second Wife: A Romance (= *Die zweite Frau*; tr. Mrs A. L. Wister), Philadelphia:
  Lippincott, 1874
Gold Elsie (= *Goldelse*; tr. Mrs A. L. Wister) Philadelphia: Lippincott, 1868 (this text
  translated over 20 times)
The Owl's Nest (= *Das Eulenhaus*; tr. Mrs A. L. Wister), Philadelphia: Lippincott, 1888
The Bailiff's Maid: A Romance (= *Amtmanns Magd*; tr. Mrs A. L. Wister), Philadelphia:
  Lippincott, 1881

Maron, Monika (Berlin 1941 – GDR)

Flugasche, Frankfurt am Main: Fischer, 1981 (n)
Das Mißverständnis. Vier Erzählungen und ein Stück, Frankfurt am Main: Fischer, 1987 (1982)
  (s, d)
Die Überläuferin, Frankfurt am Main: Fischer, 1986 (n)
Stille Zeile sechs, Frankfurt am Main: Fischer, 1991 (n)
Animal triste, Frankfurt am Main: Fischer, 1996 (n)

Works in English translation

Flight of Ashes (= *Flugasche*; tr. David Newton Marinelli), London: Readers International,
  1986
The Defector (= *Die Überläuferin*; tr. David Newton Marinelli), London: Readers
  International, 1988
Silent Close No. 6 (= *Stille Zeile sechs*; tr. David Newton Marinelli), Columbia, Louisiana,
  and London: Readers International, 1993
Frederiksen; Wilson

Marriot, Emil (pseud.: Emilie Mataja) (Vienna 1855–1938)

Gretes Glück, Trier: Theater-Bibliothek, 1897 (d)

  And many works of fiction and non-fiction

Secondary literature

Byrnes, John, *Emil Marriot: a Re-evaluation Based on her Short Fiction*, Bern and New York: P.
  Lang, c. 1983
Wilson (under Mataja)

Märten, Lu (Berlin 1879 – 1970 West Berlin)

Die Künstlerin. Eine Monographie, 1910 (e)
Bergarbeiter. Schauspiel in einem Akt, Frankfurt am Main, Berlin and Leipzig: Taifun,
  1924 (d)

  Also poems, novels, essays

Mayröcker, Friederike (Vienna 1924–)

Gedichte. Gesamtausgabe, ed. Kristian Wachinger and Christiane Peter, Ebenhausen, 1986
  (p)
Larifari. Ein konfuses Buch, Vienna: Bergland, 1956

Tod durch Musen. Poetische Texte, Reinbek: Rowohlt, 1966; Darmstadt: Luchterhand, 1973 (p)

Blaue Erleuchtungen. Erste Gedichte, Düsseldorf: Eremiten-Presse, 1973 (p)

Ausgewählte Gedichte 1944–1978, Frankfurt am Main: Suhrkamp, 1979 (p)

Die Abschiede, Frankfurt am Main: Suhrkamp, 1980 (n)

Gute Nacht, guten Morgen. Gedichte 1978–1981, Frankfurt am Main: Suhrkamp, 1982 (p)

Reise in die Nacht, Frankfurt am Main: Suhrkamp, 1984 (n)

Winterglück: Gedichte 1982–1985, Frankfurt am Main: Suhrkamp, 1986 (p)

Das besessene Alter: Gedichte 1986–1991, Frankfurt am Main: Suhrkamp, 1992 (p)

Veritas: Lyrik und Prosa 1950–1992, ed. Elke Erb, Leipzig: Reclam, 1993 (p, prose)

Lection, Frankfurt am Main: Suhrkamp, 1994 (prose)

das zu Sehende, das zu Hörende, Frankfurt am Main: Suhrkamp, 1997 (d)

English translation

Night Train (= *Reise in die Nacht*; tr. Beth Bjorklund), Riverside, California: Ariadne, 1992

Secondary literature

Arnold, Heinz Ludwig (ed.), *Friederike Mayröcker,* Munich: Text + Kritik, 1984

Beyer, Michael, *Friederike Mayröcker: Eine Bibliographie 1946–1990*. Frankfurt am Main: Suhrkamp, 1984

Schmidt, Siegfried J. (ed.), *Friederike Mayröcker,* Frankfurt am Main: Suhrkamp, 1984

Wilson

Mechtel, Angelika (Dresden 1943 – FRG)

Gegen Eis und Flut. Dülmen: Laumann, 1963 (p)

Das gläserne Paradies, Bergisch-Gladbach: Bastei-Verlag, 1973 (n)

Die Träume der Füchsin, Stuttgart: Deutsche Verlagsanstalt, 1976 (s)

Wir sind arm, wir sind reich, Stuttgart: Deutsche Verlagsanstalt, 1977

Wir in den Wohnsilos, Pforzheim: Harlekin Verlag, 1978 (p)

Himmelsvögel, Pforzheim: Hertenstein, 1986 (p)

Die Prinzipalin, Frankfurt am Main: S. Fischer, repr. Fischer Taschenbuch, 1994; 1997 (n)

And numerous other works

English translations

Altbach, *German Feminism* (1984); Cocalis, *The Defiant Muse* (1986); Herrmann and Spitz, *German Women Writers* (1978)

Mechthild von Hackeborn (nr. Magdeburg 1241 – 1299 Helfta); wrote in Latin

Das buch. geistlicher gnaden. offenbarunge. wunderliches vnde beschawlichen lebens. der heiligenn iungfrawen. Mechtildis vnd Gertrudis. Closter iungfrawen. des closters Helffede . . . (early German translation of *Liber specialis gratie*), ed. Marcus von Weida, Leyptzk [=Leipzig]: [Melchior Lotter the elder], 1503 (r)

Works in English translation

Love of the Sacred Heart, New York: Benziger, 1892

The booke of gostlye grace of Mechtild of Hackeborn (= Middle English translation of *Liber specialis gratiae*), ed. Theresa A. Halligan, Toronto: Pontifical Institute of Mediaeval Studies, 1979

Secondary literature

Finnegan, Mary Jeremy, *The Women of Helfta: Scholars and Mystics*, Athens, Georgia, and
    London: University of Georgia Press, 1991
Wilson (under **H**ackeborn)

Mechthild von Magdeburg (Magdeburg c. 1210–94)

Mechthild von Magdeburg: Das fließende Licht der Gottheit, ed. Hans Neumann and Gisela
    Vollmann-Profe, vol. I Munich: Artemis, 1990, vol. II 1993 (r)
Ich tanze, wenn du mich führst [modern German translation], tr. Margot Schmidt,
    Freiburg: Herder 1988 (r)

Works in English translation

Flowing Light of the Divinity (=*Das fließende Licht der Gottheit*; tr. Christiane Mesch Galvani),
    New York and London: Garland Publishing Inc. 1991; tr. Frank Tobin as *The
    Flowing Light of the Godhead*, Panlin Press, 1998
Bowie, Fiona (ed.), *Beguine Spirituality. An Anthology*, tr. Oliver Davies, London: SPCK,
    1989 (contains works by Mechthild von Magdeburg, Beatrice of Nazareth and
    Hadewijch of Brabant)
The Revelations of Mechthild, tr. Lucy Menzies, London: Longmans, 1953
Cocalis, *The Defiant Muse* (1986)

Secondary literature

Beer, Frances, *Women and Mystical Experience in the Middle Ages*, Woodbridge: Boydell
    Press, c. 1992
McGinn, Bernard (ed.), *Meister Eckhart and the Beguine mystics: Hadewijch of Brabant,
    Mechthild of Magdeburg, and Marguerite Porete*, New York: Continuum, 1994
Tobin, Frank, *Mechthild von Magdeburg: a Medieval Mystic in Modern Eyes*, Columbia, South
    Carolina: Camden House, c. 1995
Frederiksen; Wilson (under Magdeburg)

Meinhof, Ulrike Marie (Oldenburg 1934 – 1976
Stammheim prison nr. Stuttgart)

Die Würde des Menschen ist antastbar. Aufsätze und Polemiken, Berlin: Klaus Wagenbach, 1968
Wilson

Mereau, Sophie, née Schubart (Altenburg 1770 – 1806 Heidelberg)

Gedichte von Sophie Mereau, 2 vols. Berlin: Unger, 1800–1802; 2nd edn in 1 vol., Vienna:
    Haas, 1805 (p)
Das Blüthenalter der Empfindung, Gotha: Justus Perthes, 1794; repr. ed. Herman Moens,
    Stuttgart: Heinz, 1982 (n)
Amanda und Eduard: ein Roman in Briefen, 2 vols., Frankfurt am Main: Willmans, 1803;
    modern edn by Bettina Bremer and Angelika Schneider, Freiburg: Kore, 1993 (n)
Kalathiskos, 2 vols., Berlin: Frölich, 1801–2, repr. ed. Peter Schmidt, Heidelberg: Lambert
    Schneider, 1968 (journal ed. by Mereau and including poems, stories, and
    translations by her)
Die Flucht nach der Hauptstadt, in U. Spazier (ed.), *Taschenbuch für das Jahr 1806: der Liebe und
    Freundschaft gewidmet*, Frankfurt am Main: Willmans, 1806, pp. 137–84 (s)
Lebe der Liebe und liebe das Leben: der Briefwechsel von Clemens Brentano und Sophie Mereau, ed.
    Dagmar von Gersdorff, Frankfurt am Main: Insel, 1981 (l)

Works in English translation
Blackwell and Zantop, *Bitter Healing* (1990)

Secondary literature
Bürger, Christa, '"Die mittlere Sphäre". Sophie Mereau – Schriftstellerin im klassischen
Weimar', in Brinker-Gabler, *Deutsche Literatur von Frauen* (see p. 265 above), vol. I,
pp. 366–88
Gersdorff, Dagmar von, *Dich zu lieben kann ich nicht verlernen. Das Leben der Sophie Brentano-
Mereau*, Frankfurt am Main: Insel, 1984
Harper, Anthony, 'The novels of Sophie Mereau (1770–1806)', in Ives (ed.), *Women Writers
of the Age of Goethe*, vol. VII (1995), pp. 32–56
Treder, Uta, 'Sophie Mereau: Montage und Demontage einer Liebe', in Gallas and
Heuser, *Untersuchungen* (see p. 271 above), pp. 172–83
Frederiksen; Wilson

Merz, Meta (Vienna 1965–89)
erotik der distanz: prosa, ed. Anthon Thuswaldner, Vienna: Wiener Frauenverlag, 1990 (e/s)

Miegel, Agnes (Königsberg 1879 – 1964 Bad Nenndorf)
Gesammelte Werke, 7 vols., 3rd edn Düsseldorf and Cologne: Diederichs, 1952–65
Deutsche Balladen, Jena: Diederichs, 1935 (p)
Das Bernsteinherz, Berlin: Reclam, 1937, 1963 (s)
Mein Bernsteinland und meine Stadt, Königsberg: Gräfe & Unzer, 1944 (p)

Translation: see Morgan

Secondary literature
Aulls, Katharina, 'Agnes Miegel', in James Hardin (ed.), *German Fiction Writers 1914–1945*,
Detroit, 1987, pp. 206–12

**Mihaly, Jo (= Elfriede Steckel) (Posen 1902 – 1989 nr. Starnberg,
Bavaria)**
'... *da gibt's ein Wiedersehn'. Kriegstagebuch eines Mädchens 1914–1918*, Freiburg and
Heidelberg: Kerle, 1982 (a)
Kasperltheater und andere nachdenkliche Geschichten mit Tuschezeichnungen von Jo Mihaly,
Stuttgart: Gundert, 1929 (s)

Secondary literature
Hahn, Andrea, 'Jo Mihaly and her War Diary "... *da gibts ein Wiedersehn!*" From the Game
"Krieg" to the Dance "Der tote Soldat"; from the Child Who Welcomed War to
the Pacifist', in Keith-Smith (1993) (see p. 275 above), pp. 117–44

Mitterer, Erika (Vienna 1906–)
Dank des Lebens. Gedichte, Frankfurt am Main: Rütten und Löning 1930 (p)
Höhensonne, 1935 (s)
Gesang der Wandernden, 1935 (p)
Der Fürst der Welt, 1940 (n)
Begegnung im Süden, 1941 (s)
Die Seherin, 1942 (s)
Wir sind allein, Roman zwischen zwei Zeiten, 1945 (n)
Gesammelte Gedichte, Vienna: Luckmann 1956 (p)

Entsühnung des Kain, Freiburg: Johannes Verlag, 1974 (p)
Gedichte, Vienna: Faecher, 1984 (p)
Das verhüllte Kreuz: Neue Gedichte, Vienna: Niederösterreichisches Pressehaus, 1985 (p)

Works in English translation

All our Games (= *Alle unsere Spiele*; tr. Catherine Hutter), Columbia, South Carolina:
  Camden House, 1988
Wilson

Moníková, Libuše (Prague 1945 – Berlin 1998)

Eine Schädigung, Berlin: Rotbuch, 1981 (s)
Pavane für eine verstorbene Infantin, Berlin: Rotbuch, 1983; Munich: dtv, 1988 (n)
Die Fassade M.N.O.P.Q., Munich and Vienna: Hanser, 1987 (n)
Schloß, Aleph, Wunschtorte. Essays, Munich and Vienna: Carl Hanser, 1990 (e)
Unter Menschenfressern: Ein dramatisches Menü in vier Gängen, Frankfurt am Main: Verlag
  der Autoren, 1990 (d)
Treibeis, Munich and Vienna: Carl Hanser Verlag, 1992 (n)

English translation

The Facade: M.N.O.P.Q. (= *Die Fassade M.N.O.P.Q.*; tr. John E. Woods), London: Chatto &
  Windus, 1992
Frederiksen

Moosdorf, Johanna (Leipzig 1911–; moved to W. Berlin in 1950)

Flucht nach Afrika, Freiburg im Breisgau: Klemm, 1952 (n)
Die Nachtigallen schlagen im Schnee, Büchergilde Gutenberg, 1954 (n)
Schneesturm in Worotschau. Novelle, Gütersloh: Bertelsmann, 1957 (n)
Nebenan, Frankfurt am Main: Suhrkamp, 1961 (n)
Die lange Nacht, Frankfurt am Main: Suhrkamp, 1963 (n)
Die Andermanns, Stuttgart: Goverts, 1969 (n)
Die Freundinnen, Munich: Nymphenburg, 1977 (n)
Jahrhundertträume, Frankfurt am Main: Fischer, 1989 (n)
Die Tochter, Afterword by Regula Venske, Frankfurt am Main: Fischer, 1991 (s)

Works in English translation

Next Door (= *Nebenan*; tr. Michael Glenny), New York: Knopf and London: Gollancz, 1964
Flight to Africa (= *Flucht nach Afrika*; tr. Richard and Clara Winston), London: M. Joseph,
  1955; New York: Harcourt, Brace, 1954
Wilson

Morgner, Irmtraud (Chemnitz 1933 – 1990 Berlin GDR)

Hochzeit in Konstantinopel, Berlin: Aufbau-Verlag, 1968; repr. Frankfurt am Main:
  Luchterhand, 1989 (n)
Die wundersamen Reisen Gustavs des Weltfahrers. Lügenhafter Roman mit Kommentaren, Berlin:
  Aufbau-Verlag, 1972; repr. Frankfurt am Main: Luchterhand, 1989 (n)
Leben und Abenteuer der Trobadora Beatriz nach Zeugnissen ihrer Spielfrau Laura, Berlin:
  Aufbau-Verlag, 1974; repr. Darmstadt: Luchterhand, 1977 (n)
Amanda. Ein Hexenroman, Berlin: Aufbau-Verlag, 1983; repr. Darmstadt: Luchterhand,
  1983 (n)
Rumba auf einen Herbst, Frankfurt am Main: Luchterhand, 1992 (n)

English translation (excerpts)

'Life and Adventures of the Trobadora Beatriz as Chronicled by her Minstrel Laura (Twelfth Book)', tr. Karen and Friedrich Achberger, *New German Critique* 15 (1978), 121–46

Altbach, *German Feminism* (1984)

Gerber and Pouchet

Secondary literature

Gerhardt, Marlis (ed.). *Irmtraud Morgner. Texte, Daten, Bilder*, Frankfurt am Main: Luchterhand, 1990

Lewis, Alison, *Subverting Patriarchy: Feminism and Fantasy in the Novels of Irmtraud Morgner*, Oxford: Berg, 1995

Linklater, Beth, '. . . *Und immer zügelloser wird die Lust'. Constructions of Sexuality in East German Literatures with Special Reference to Irmtraud Morgner and Gabriele Stötzer-Kachold*, Bern and Frankfurt am Main: Peter Lang, 1998

Slessarev, Helga, 'Irmtraud Morgner', in Wolfgang D. Elfe and James Hardin (eds.), *Contemporary German Fiction Writers (Second Series)*, Detroit, 1988, pp. 197–203

Frederiksen; Wilson

Mühlbach, Louise (pseud. for Klara Mundt) (Neubrandenburg 1814 – 1873 Berlin)

Kleine Romane, 21 vols., Altona: Hammerich, 1860–6

Ausgewählte Werke, 15 vols., Berlin: O. Janke, 1867–9

Ein Roman in Berlin, Berlin: Mylius, 1846 (n)

Eva. Ein Roman aus Berlins Gegenwart, Berlin: Morin, 1844, republ. as *Frau Meisterin*, Berlin: Janke, 1859 (n)

Aphra Behn, Berlin: Simion, 1849 (n)

Friedrich der Große und sein Hof, Berlin, 1853–4 (hist. n.)

Numerous nineteeth-century translations: see Morgan + S

Müller, Herta (Nitzkydorf, Banat, Romania 1953 – FRG)

Niederungen. Februar, Bucharest: Kriterion, 1992; publ. in Germany by Berlin: Rotbuch, 1984

Drückender Tango, Berlin: Rotbuch, 1984

Der Mensch ist ein großer Fasan auf der Welt, Berlin: Rotbuch, 1986

Barfüssiger Februar, Berlin: Rotbuch, 1987

Reisende auf einem Bein, Berlin: Rotbuch, 1989

Der Teufel sitzt im Spiegel, Berlin: Rotbuch, 1991

Der Fuchs war damals schon der Jäger, Reinbeck: Rowohlt, 1992

Herztier, Reinbek: Rowohlt, 1994 (n)

Hunger und Seide. Essays, Reinbek: Rowohlt, 1995 (e)

Heute wär ich mir lieber nicht begegnet, Berlin: Rowohlt, 1997 (n)

Works in English translation

Nadirs (=*Niederungen*; tr. Sieglinde Lug), Lincoln: University of Nebraska Press (European Writers Series), 1999

The Passport. A Surreal Tale of Life in Romania Today (= *Der Mensch ist ein großer Fasan auf dieser Welt*; tr. Martin Chalmers), London: Serpent's Tail, 1989

The Land of Green Plums (= *Herztier*; tr. Michael Hofmann), New York: Metropolitan
  Books, 1996; London: Granta, 1998
Travelling on One Leg (=*Reisende auf einem Bein*; tr. Valentina Glajar and André Lefevre),
  Evanston, Illinois: Northwestern University Press, 1998

Secondary literature
Haines, Brigid (ed.), *Herta Müller*, Swansea: University of Wales Press, 1998

Müller, Inge (1925 – 1966 GDR)
Gedichte, ed. Bernd Jentsch. Berlin: Verlag Neues Leben, 1976 (p)
Wenn ich schon sterben muß, ed. Richard Pietraß, Darmstadt: Luchterhand, 1986; Berlin
  and Weimar: Aufbau, 1987 (p)
Ich bin eh ich war. Gedichte, ed. Blanche Kommerell, Giessen: Literarischer Salon, 1992 (p,
  e, interview, crit)
Irgendwo; noch einmal möcht ich sehn. Lyrik, Prosa, Tagebücher, ed. Ines Geipel, Berlin and
  Weimar: Aufbau, 1996 (p, e, a)

Naubert, Christiane Benedikte (Leipzig 1756–1819)
Heerfort und Klärchen: Etwas für empfindsame Seelen, 2 vols., Frankfurt: Reiffenstein, 1779;
  repr. with postscript by G. Sauder, Hildesheim: Gerstenberg, 1982 (n)
Die Amtmännin von Hohenweiler, Leipzig: Weygand, 1787 (n)
Geschichte der Gräfin Thecla von Thurn, Leipzig: Weygand, 1788 (n)

And numerous other novels and stories, listed Wilson

English translation
'The Mantle', tr. George Sloane, in *Specimens of German Romance, vol. 3*. London:
  Whittaker, 1826 ('Der kurze Mantel – Märchen'); as 'The Cloak', Blackwell and
  Zantop, *Bitter Healing* (1990)

Contemporary translations: see Morgan + S

Secondary literature
Blackwell, J., 'Fractured Fairy Tales: German Women Authors and the Grimm
  Tradition', *Germanic Review* 62 (1987), 162–74
Wilson

Neuber, Friederike Caroline (also known as die Neuberin) (Reichenbach, Vogtland 1697 – 1760 Laubegast)
Ein Deutsches Vorspiel, ed. A. Richter, in series *Deutsche Litteraturdenkmale des 18. und 19.
  Jahrhunderts*, Leipzig, 1897 (d)
Das Schäferfest, in F. Brüggemann (ed.), *Gottscheds Lebens- und Kunstreform in den zwanziger und
  dreißiger Jahren. Gottsched, Breitinger, die Gottschedin, die Neuberin*, Leipzig: Reclam,
  1935; repr. Darmstadt: Wissenschaftliche Buchgesellschaft, 1966 (d)

Secondary literature
Heckmann, Hannelore, 'Theaterkritik als Unterhaltung. Die Vorreden und Vorspiele
  der Neuberin', *Lessing Yearbook* 18 (1986), 111–27
Reden-Esbeck, F. von, *Caroline Neuber und ihre Zeitgenossen. Ein Beitrag zur deutschen Kultur-
  und Theatergeschichte*, Leipzig: Barth 1881; repr. with afterword and bibliography
  by W. Günther, Leipzig, 1985
Sharpe, L., 'Reform of the German Theatre: Frau Neuber and Frau Gottsched', in E.

Woodrough (ed.), *Women in European Theatre*, (Europa 1/4), Oxford: Intellect,
    1995, pp. 55–64
See also novel by Angelika Mechtel, *Die Prinzipalin* (1994) (see p. 344 above)
Wilson

Niendorf, Emma (later von Suckow) (Pappenheim, Bavaria 1807 – 1876 Rome)

Wanderungen durch die interessantesten Gegenden der Schweiz und des Elsasses, Stuttgart: Ebner
    & Seubert, 1840 (t)
Erzählungen, Stuttgart: Mäcken, 1853 (s)
Aus dem heutigen Paris, Stuttgart: Mäcken, 1854 (t)
Aus London. Dissolving Views, Berlin: Schotte & Co, 1855; Berlin: F. Stage, 1856 (t)
Liebesgabe. Märchen, Darmstadt: Zernin, 1858 (s)
Einfache Geschichten, Pforzheim: Riecker, 1860 (s)

> Translation: see Morgan

Niggli, Martha (writing in 1920s and 30s)

Zwischen zwanzig und dreißig. Roman einer Berufstätigen, Freiburg im Breisgau: Herder,
    1930 (n)

Novak, Helga (Berlin/Köpenick 1935–)

Die Ballade von der reisenden Anna, Berlin and Neuwied: Luchterhand 1963 (p)
Collquium mit vier Häuten: Gedicht und Balladen, Darmstadt: Luchterhand, 1967 (p)
Geselliges Beisammensein, Neuwied and Berlin: Luchterhand, 1968 (s)
Aufenthalt in einem irren Haus, Neuwied and Berlin: Luchterhand, 1971 (s)
Ballade vom kurzen 'Prozeß', Berlin: Rotbuch, 1975 (p)
Margarete mit dem Schrank, Berlin: Rotbuch, 1978 (p)
Grünheide Grünheide. Gesammelte Gedichte 1955–1980, Darmstadt: Luchterhand, 1983 (p)
Legende Transsib, Darmstadt: Luchterhand, 1985 (p)
Märkische Feemorgana, Frankfurt am Main: Luchterhand, 1989 (p)

English translation

Chappel, Alan H., *Selected Poetry and Prose of Helga M. Novak*, New York etc.: Peter Lang,
    1989
Cocalis, *The Defiant Muse* (1986)
Altbach, *German Feminism* (1984)
Herrmann and Spitz, *German Women Writers* (1978)
and see Wilson

Olden, Ika (writing in exile in 1930s, d. 1940)

'In tiefem Dunkel liegt Deutschland.' *Rudolf und Ika Olden: Von Hitler vertrieben – Ein Jahr
    deutsche Emigration*. Vorwort von Lion Feuchtwanger, ed. and intr. Charmian Brinson
    and Marian Malet, Berlin, 1994

Oleschinski, Brigitte (FRG 1955–)

Mental Heat Control: Gedichte, Reinbek: Rowohlt, 1990 (p)
Your Passport is not Guilty. Gedichte. Reinbek: Rowohlt, 1997 (p)

> Translations: Gutzschhahn, *Young Poets of Germany* (1994)

Otto, Louise (Louise Otto-Peters, pseud.: Otto Stern) (Meißen 1819 – Leipzig 1895)

Aus der neuen Zeit. Novellen und Erzählungen, Leipzig: Wienbrack, 1845 (s)
Westwärts. Lieder, Meissen: Klinkicht und Sohn, 1849 (p)
Aus der alten Zeit. Historische Erzählungen, Leipzig: Plauen, Schröter, 1860 (s)
Die Idealisten, Jena: Hermsdorf, 1867 (n)
Gedichte, Leipzig: Rötschke, 1868 (p)
Schloß und Fabrik, 2nd edn Leipzig: Matthes, 1869 (n)

Translation: Cocalis, *The Defiant Muse* (1986)

Secondary literature

Gerhard, Ute, Elisabeth Hannover-Drück and Romina Schmitter (eds.), *'Dem Reich der Freiheit werb' ich Bürgerinnen': die Frauen-Zeitung von Louise Otto*, Frankfurt am Main: Syndikat, 1980
Joeres, Ruth-Ellen Boetcher, 'An Introduction to the Life and Times of Louise Otto', in Avriel H. Goldberger (ed.), *Women as Mediatrix. Essays on Nineteenth-Century European Women Writers*, New York; Westport, Connecticut; and London: Greenwood Press, 1987
Frederiksen; Wilson

Özakin, Aysel (Urfu, Turkey 1942 – W. Berlin from 1981); writing in Turkish, English and German

Soll ich hier alt werden? (tr. from Turkish by H. A. Schmiede), Hamburg: Buntbuch, 1982
Die Preisvergabe (tr. from Turkish by Heike Offen), Hamburg: Buntbuch, 1983
Die Leidenschaft der anderen (tr. from Turkish by Hanne Egghardt), Hamburg: Buntbuch, 1983
Du bist willkommen. Gedichte, Hamburg: Buntbuch, 1985 (p)
Das Lächeln des Bewußtseins (tr. from Turkish by Hanne Egghardt), Hamburg: Buntbuch, 1985
Zart erhob sie sich bis sie flog, Hamburg: Galgenberg, 1986 (p)
Die blaue Maske (tr. from Turkish by Carl Koß), Frankfurt am Main: Luchterhand, 1989
Glaube, Liebe, Aircondition: Eine türkische Kindheit (tr. from English by Cornelia Holfelder-von der Tann), Hamburg and Zurich: Luchterhand, 1991
Die Vögel auf der Stirn (tr. from Turkish by Carl Voß), Frankfurt am Main: Luchterhand, 1991
Deine Stimme gehört dir. Erzählungen, Hamburg: Luchterhand, 1992 (s)
Die Zunge der Berge (tr. from English by Jeremy Gaines and Klaus Binder), Munich: Luchterhand, 1994

Works in English translation

The Prizegiving (German title *Die Preisvergabe*; tr. from Turkish by Celia Kerslake), Women's Press, 1988

Özdamar, Emine (Malataja, Turkey 1946–; moved to Berlin in 1971)

Mutterzunge. Erzählungen, Berlin: Rotbuch, 1990; repr. Cologne: Kiepenheuer & Witsch, 1998 (s)
Das Leben ist eine Karawanserei. hat zwei Türen. aus einer kam ich rein. aus der anderen ging ich raus, Cologne: Kiepenheuer & Witsch, 1992 (n)
Die Brücke vom goldenen Horn, Cologne: Kiepenheuer and Witsch, 1998 (n)

English translation

Mother Tongue (= *Mutterzunge*; tr. Craig Thomas), Toronto: Coach House Press, 1994
Life is a caravanserai has two doors I came in one I went out the other (=*Das Leben ist eine Karawanserai . . .*; tr. with afterword by Luise von Flotow), London: Middlesex University Press, World Literature Series (forthcoming)

Paoli, Betty (pseud. for Elisabeth Glück)
(Vienna 1814 – 1894 Baden nr. Vienna)

Gedichte, 1841 (p)
Nach dem Gewitter, Budapest: G. Heckenast Nachfolger R. Drodtleff, 1843 (p)
Die Welt und mein Auge. Novellen, Pressburg: G. Heckenast Nachfolger R. Drodtleff, 1844 (s)
Romancero. Gedichte, Leipzig, Pressburg: G. Heckenast Nachfolger R. Drodtleff, 1845 (p)
Neue Gedichte, Pressburg: G. Heckenast, 1850 (p)
Lyrisches und Episches, Pressburg: G. Heckenast, 1855 (p, s)
Wiens Gemäldegalerien in ihrer kunsthistorischen Bedeutung, Vienna: Gerolds Sohn, 1865 (e)
Neueste Gedichte, Vienna: Gerolds Sohn, 1870 (p)
Grillparzer und seine Werke, Stuttgart: Cotta, 1875 (e)
Gedichte. Auswahl und Nachlass, Stuttgart: J. G. Cotta Nachfolger, 1895 (p)

Translation: see Morgan; Cocalis, *The Defiant Muse* (1986)

Secondary literature

Scott, Alice Annie, *Betty Paoli: An Austrian Poetess of the Nineteenth Century*, London: Routledge, 1926
Wilson (under **G**lück)

Pedretti, Erica (Steinberg, Moravia 1930 – Switzerland)

Valerie oder Das unerzogene Auge. Frankfurt am Main: Suhrkamp, 1986 (n)

And other works

English translation

Stones, or, The destruction of the child Karl and other characters (= *Veränderung*; tr. Judith L. Black), London: John Calder, 1982
Frederiksen; Wilson

Petersen, Johanna Eleonora (Frankfurt am Main 1644 – 1724 Thyman)

Johanna Eleonore Petersen, 'Selbstbiographie', in *Der deutsche Pietismus. Eine Auswahl von Zeugnissen, Urkunden und Bekenntnissen aus dem 17., 18. und 19. Jahrhundert*, ed. Werner Mahrholz, Berlin, 1921 (a)

English translation

Blackwell and Zantop, *Bitter Healing* (1990), pp. 51–78, tr. Cornelia Niekus-Moore

Pfeiffer, Ida (Vienna 1797–1858)

Travel writing

Reise einer Wienerin in das heilige Land, Vienna, 1844
Reise nach dem skandinavischen Norden und der Insel Island im Jahre 1845, Budapest: Heckenast, 1846

Eine Frauenfahrt um die Welt. Reise von Wien nach Brasilien, Chili, Otaheiti, China, Ostindien,
    Persien und Kleinasien, Vienna: Gerold, 1850
Meine zweite Weltreise, Vienna: Gerold, 1856
Reise nach Madagaskar, Vienna: Gerolds Sohn, 1861; repr. (abridged and edited) as
    Verschwörung im Regenwald. Ida Pfeiffers Reise nach Madagaskar, Hanover and Basel:
    Schönbach, 1991

Works in English translation
Visit to the Holy Land, Egypt and Italy (= *Reise einer Wienerin in das heilige Land*; tr. H. W.
    Dulcken), London: Ingram, Cooke, 1852
A Lady's Voyage round the World: A Selected Translation from the German of Ida Pfeiffer (= *Eine
    Frauenfahrt um die Welt*; tr. Mrs Percy Sinnett), London: Longman, Brown, Green
    and Longmans, 1851; *A Lady's Travels Round the World*, tr. W. Hazlitt, London:
    Routledge, 1852
Journey to Iceland: And Travels in Sweden and Norway (= *Reise nach dem skandinavischen Norden*;
    tr. Charlotte Fenimore Cooper), London: Richard Bentley, 1852
*A Lady's Second Journey round the World: From London to the Cape of Good Hope, Borneo, Java,
    Sumatra, Celebes . . . California, Panama, Peru, Ecuador and the United States* (= *Meine
    zweite Weltreise*) London: Longman, Brown, Green and Longmans, 1855
*The Last Travels of Ida Pfeiffer: Inclusive of a Visit to Madagascar. With a Biographical Memoir of
    the Author* (= *Reise nach Madagaskar*; tr. H. W. Dulcken), London: Routledge, 1861

Further translations: see Morgan

Pichler, Caroline, née Greiner (Vienna 1769–1843)
Sämmtliche Werke, 60 vols., Vienna: Pichler, 1828–45
Heinrich von Hohenstauffen, König der Deutschen, 1813 (d)

Works in English translation
The Siege of Vienna (= *Belagerung Wiens*), Philadelphia: Key & Biddle, 1835; London: Elder &
    Smith, 1838
The Swedes in Prague, or the Signal Rocket: A Romance of the Thirty Years War (= *Die Schweden in
    Prag*; tr. James D. Haas), London: Lumley, 1845
see Morgan + S, and Fouqué, *The Castle of Scharffenstein*, p. 308 above

Secondary literature
Becker-Cantarino, Barbara, 'Caroline Pichler und die "Frauendichtung"', *Modern
    Austrian Literature* 12/3-4 (1979), 1–23
Garrard, Malcolm, '"Der Herrscher geheiligtes Haus": Caroline Pichler and Austrian
    Identity', in Ives (ed.), *Women Writers of the Age of Goethe,* vol. VIII (1996), pp. 3–25
Wilson

Pirckheimer, Caritas (1466 – 1532 Nuremberg)
Pirckheimer, Caritas, '*Die Denkwürdigkeiten' der Äbtissin Caritas Pirckheimer des St. Klara-
    Klosters zu Nürnberg,* ed. Georg Deichstetter and Benedicta Schrott, St. Ottilien,
    1983 (l, a)

Secondary literature
Wailes, Stephen L., 'The Literary Relationship of Conrad Celtis and Caritas
    Pirckheimer', *Daphnis* 17/3 (1988) 423–40

Plönnies, Louise (Hanau 1803 – 1872 Darmstadt)

Ein fremder Strauß, Gedichte, Heidelberg: C. Winter, 1844 (p)
Gedichte, Darmstadt: Leske, 1844 (p)
Reise-Erinnerungen aus Belgien, Berlin: Duncker & Homblot, 1845 (t)
Abälard und Heloise. Ein Sonettenkranz, Darmstadt: Jonghaus, 1849 (p)
Neue Gedichte, Darmstadt: Jonghaus, 1851 (p)
Die sieben Raben. Gedicht, Munich: Merhoff, 1862 (p)
Joseph und seine Brüder, Stuttgart, Gotha: Schloessmann, 1866 (epic poem)
Englische Lyriker des 19. Jahrhunderts. Ins Deutsche übertragen, Munich: Merhoff, 1867
       (translation)
Sawitri. Dichtung, Munich: Merhoff, 1867 (d)
Maria Magdalena. Ein geistliches Drama in 5 Aufzügen, Heidelberg: C. Winter, 1871 (d)
David. Ein biblisches Drama in 5 Aufzügen, Heidelberg: C. Winter, 1873 (d)
Sagen und Legenden nebst einem Anhang vermischter Gedichte, Heidelberg: C. Winter, 1874 (s,p)

   And numerous other volumes of poetry

   Translations: see Morgan
Wilson

Popp, Adelheid (nr. Vienna 1869 – 1939 Vienna)

Die Jugendgeschichte einer Arbeiterin von ihr selbst erzählt, Munich: Reinhardt, 1909; repr.
       Berlin; Dietz, 1983 (a)

   Also wrote political treatises

English translation
The Autobiography of a Working Woman (= *Die Jugendgeschichte einer Arbeiterin*, 3rd edn; tr. E.
       C. Harvey; intr. August Bebel and J Ramsey Macdonald; foreword by A.P.),
       London: Fisher Unwin, 1912; new edn Westport: Hyperion, 1983
Wilson

Preradović, Paula (Vienna 1887–1951)

Gesammelte Werke, Vienna: Fritz Modden, 1967
Südlicher Sommer. Gedichte, Munich: Kösel, 1929 (p)
Wilson

Quernheim, Anna von (before 1520–90)

Angermann, Gertrud, *Anna von Quernheim (vor 1520–1590). Die erste bekannte Liededichterin
       Westfalens und 25 ihrer geistlichen Gesänge in niederdeutscher Sprache*, Bielefeld, 1996 (p)

Rasp, Renate (Berlin 1935 – FRG)

Ein ungeratener Sohn, Cologne, Berlin: Kiepenheuer & Witsch, 1967 (n)
Eine Rennstrecke, Cologne, Berlin: Kiepenheuer & Witsch, 1969 (p)
Junges Deutschland, Munich and Vienna: Hanser, 1978; Munich: Heyne, 1981 (p)
Chinchilla. Leitfaden zur praktischen Ausübung, Reinbek: Rowohlt, 1973 (prose – satirical
       guidelines for prostitution)

Works in English translation
A Family Failure (= *Ein ungeratener Sohn*; tr. Eva Figes), New York: Orion Press, 1970;
       London: Calder & Boyers, 1970

Recke, Elisabeth von der (Schönberg, Kurland 1754 – 1833 Dresden)

Tagebuch einer Reise durch einen Teil Deutschlands und durch Italien in den Jahren 1804 bis 1806, 1815–17 (t, e)
Tagebücher und Selbstzeugnisse, Munich: Beck, 1984 (a, e)

Also wrote poetry
Wilson

Rehmann, Ruth (Siegburg 1922 – FRG)

Illusionen, Frankfurt am Main: Suhrkamp, 1959 (n)
Paare, Munich: Ehrenwirth, 1978 (s)
Der Mann auf der Kanzel. Fragen an einen Vater, Munich: Hanser, 1979 (a/n)

Works in English translation

Saturday to Monday (= *Illusionen*; tr. Catherine Hutter), London: Heinemann; New York: Viking, 1962
The Man in the Pulpit: Questions for a Father (= *Der Mann auf der Kanzel*, tr. Christoph and Pamela Lohmann), Lincoln: University of Nebraska Press, 1995; 1997
Travelling in Alien Dreams (= *Unterwegs in fremden Träumen*; 1993), excerpts, tr. Christoph Lohmann, *Dimension*² 1 (1994), 470–95 (translation forthcoming, University of Nebraska Press)

Secondary literature

Meyer, Franziska, 'The Early Novels of Ruth Rehmann', in Weedon (1997) (see p. 279 above), pp. 61–76

Reichart, Elizabeth (nr. Linz, Austria 1953–)

Februarschatten, Vienna: Edition S., 1984 (n)
(ed.) *Österreichische Dichterinnen* (1993) (see p. 280 above)

English translation

February Shadows, tr. Donna L. Hoffmeister, Riverside, California: Ariadne Press, 1989; London: The Women's Press (afterword by Christa Wolf), 1988

Reimann, Brigitte (Magdeburg 1933 – 1973 Berlin/GDR)

Die Frau am Pranger, Berlin: Verlag Neues Leben, 1956; repr. Munich: dtv, 1987 (s)
Das Geständnis, Berlin: Aufbau-Verlag, 1960; repr. in *Die Geschwister. Das Geständnis. Zwei Erzählungen*, Munich: dtv, 1988 (s)
Ankunft im Alltag, Berlin: Verlag Neues Leben, 1961; repr. Munich: dtv, 1986 (n)
Die Geschwister, Berlin: Aufbau-Verlag, 1963; repr. as *Die Geschwister. Das Geständnis. Zwei Erzählungen*, Munich: dtv, 1988 (s)
Franziska Linkerhand, Berlin: Verlag Neues Leben, 1974; repr. Munich: dtv, 1990 (n)
Elten-Krause, Elisabeth, and Walter Lewerenz (eds.), *Brigitte Reimann in ihren Briefen und Tagebüchern*, Berlin: Verlag Neues Leben, 1983; repr. as *Die geliebte, die verfluchte Hoffnung. Tagebücher und Briefe 1947–1972*, Darmstadt: Luchterhand, 1986 (a, l)

Secondary literature

Cox, Judith H., 'Brigitte Reimann', in Wolfgang D. Elfe and James Hardin (eds.), *Contemporary German Fiction Writers (Second Series)*, Detroit, 1988, pp. 224–8
Wilson

Reinig, Christa (Berlin 1926 – GDR/FRG)

Die Steine von Finisterre, Stierstadt: Eremiten-Presse, 1960 and Düsseldorf: Eremiten-Presse, 1974; Munich: dtv, 1980 (p)
Gedichte, Frankfurt am Main: Fischer, 1963 (p)
Entmannung: Die Geschichte Ottos und seiner vier Frauen, Darmstadt: Luchterhand, 1977 (n)
Müßiggang ist aller Liebe Anfang, Düsseldorf: Eremiten-Presse, 1979 (p)
Die Prüfung des Lächlers: Drei Gedichtsammlungen, Munich: dtv, 1980 (p)
Der Wolf und die Witwen. Erzählungen und Essays, Munich: Frauenoffensive, 1981 (s, e)
Sämtliche Gedichte: 1959–1976, ed. Horst Bienek, Düsseldorf: Eremiten-Presse, 1984 (p)
Feuergefährlich: Gedichte und Erzählungen für Frauen und Männer, Berlin: Wagenbach, 1985 (p/s)

Has also translated from Russian, e.g. Marina Tsvetayeva

Works in English translation
The Tightrope Walker (= *Steine von Finisterre,* selections; tr. Ruth and Matthew Mead),
       Edinburgh: published for SATIS by Malcolm Rutherford, 1981 (limited edn)
Idleness is the Root of All Love (= *Müßiggang ist aller Liebe Anfang,* 1979; tr. Ilze Mueller),
       Corvallis: Oregon State University Press, 1991
Altbach, *German Feminism* (1984): extracts from *The Wolf and the Widows* (= *Der Wolf und die Witwen*)
Herrmann and Spitz, *German Women Writers* (1978)
Frederiksen

Reinshagen, Gerlind (Königsberg 1926–)

Gesammelte Stücke, Frankfurt am Main: Suhrkamp, 1986 (contains *Doppelkopf; Leben und Tod der Marilyn Monroe; Kann das Theater noch aus seiner Rolle fallen; Himmel und Erde; Sonntagskinder; Das Frühlingsfest; Tanz, Marie!; Eisenherz; Die Clownin*) (d)
Rovinato, oder Die Seele des Geschäfts, Frankfurt am Main: Suhrkamp, 1981 (n)
Die flüchtige Braut, Frankfurt am Main: Suhrkamp, 1984 (n)
Zwölf Nächte, Frankfurt am Main: Suhrkamp, 1989 (s)
Drei Wünsche frei: chorische Stücke, Frankfurt am Main: Suhrkamp, 1992 (d)
Jäger am Rand der Nacht, Frankfurt am Main: Suhrkamp, 1993 (n)
Am Großen Stern, Frankfurt am Main: Suhrkamp, 1996 (n)

Has also written ch

Works in English translation
Heaven and Earth (= *Himmel und Erde*; tr. Estella Schmid and Anthony Vivis: London
       [Rosica Colin], 1976) (typescript)
Heaven and Earth (= *Himmel und Erde*; tr. Carl Weber), New York, 1977 (typescript)
Ironheart (= *Eisenherz*; tr. Sue-Ellen Case, Arlene A. Teraoka), in Case, *The Divided Home/Land* (1992)
The Life and Death of Marilyn Monroe (= *Leben und Tod der Marilyn Monroe,* in *Drei Wünsche frei*;
       tr. Anthony Vivis), draft version (typescript: London [Rosica Colin]), 1970
Sunday's Child (= *Sonntagskinder*; tr. Hans Werner), Goethe Institut, Toronto; no
       publication details
Sunday's Children (= *Sonntagskinder*; tr. Tinch Minter and Anthony Vivis: London [Rosica
       Colin], 1988) (typescript; Goethe Institut London); also forthcoming in *Modern European Plays by Women* ed. Alan Barr
Frederiksen; Wilson

Reuter, Gabriele (Alexandria, Egypt 1859 – 1941 Weimar)

Aus guter Familie. Leidensgeschichte eines Mädchens, Berlin: Fischer, 1895 (n)
Ellen von der Weiden. Ein Tagebuch, Berlin: Fischer, 1900 (n)
Frauenseelen, Berlin: Fischer, 1902 (s)
Das Tränenhaus, Berlin: Fischer, 1909 (n)

Works in English translation
Daughters. A Story of Two Generations (= *Töchter*, 1927; tr. Roberto Tapley), New York:
   Macmillan, 1930
see Morgan; Frederiksen (1989)

Secondary literature
Schneider, Georgia A., *Portraits of Women in Selected Works of Gabriele Reuter*, Frankfurt am
   Main: Peter Lang, c. 1988
Goodman, Katherine R., 'Gabriele Reuter', in James Hardin (ed.), *German Fiction Writers,
   1885–1913*, vol. II. Detroit, 1988, pp. 411–17
Frederiksen

Reventlow, Franziska Gräfin zu (Husum 1871 – 1918 Muralto, Tessin)

Das Männerphantom der Frau, Zurich: Verlag der Zürcher Diskussionen, 1898; repr. in *Der
   Selbstmordverein*. Berlin: Verlag der Nation, 1991; repr. in Franziska zu
   Reventlow, *Autobiographisches*, ed. Else Reventlow, Frankfurt am Main: Ullstein,
   1986 (e)
Ellen Olestjerne, Munich: Marchlewski, 1903; repr. Frankfurt am Main: Fischer, 1985 (n)
Von Paul zu Pedro. Amouresken, Munich: A. Langen, 1912; repr. Frankfurt am Main:
   Ullstein, 1987 (n)
Herrn Dames Aufzeichnungen oder Begebenheiten aus einem merkwürdigen Stadtteil, Munich:
   A. Langen, 1913; repr. Frankfurt am Main: Ullstein, 1987 (n)
Der Geldkomplex, Munich: A. Langen, 1916; repr. in *Der Selbstmordverein*, 1991 (n)

Secondary literature
Schoolfield, George C., 'Franziska Gräfin zu Reventlow', in James Hardin (ed.), *German
   Fiction Writers, 1885–1913*, vol I. Detroit, 1988, pp. 418–25
Wilson

Rewald, Ruth (Berlin 1906 – 1942 Auschwitz)

Janko, der Junge aus Mexiko, Strasbourg: Sebastian Brant-Verlag, 1934; repr. Mannheim:
   P. Wagener, 1994 (n)
Vier spanische Jungen, ed. and with afterword by Dirk Krüger, Cologne, 1987 (n)

Secondary literature
Krüger, Dirk, *Die deutsch-jüdische Kinder- und Jugendbuchautorin Ruth Rewald im Exil*,
   Frankfurt, 1990

Rheinsberg, Anna (Berlin 1956 – FRG)

Marlene in den Gassen, Hamburg: Kellner, 1979 (p)
Bella Donna, Hamburg: Kellner, 1981 (p)
Annakonda. Hamburg: Kellner, 1986 (p)
KRIEGS/LÄUFE. Namen. Schrift. Über Emmy Ball-Hennings, Claire Goll, Else Rüthel,
   Mannheim: Persona Verlag, 1989 (e)

(ed.) *Bubikopf. Aufbruch in den Zwanzigern* (1988) (see p. 274 above)
(ed.) *Wie bunt entfaltet sich mein Anderssein* (1993) (see p. 274 above)

Rinser, Luise (Pitzling, Upper Bavaria 1911 – Rocca di Papa, nr. Rome)

Die gläsernen Ringe, Berlin: Fischer, 1941; Frankfurt am Main: Fischer 1961 (s)
Gefängnistagebuch, Munich: Zinnen, 1946; repr. Berlin (GDR): Union, 1966; Frankfurt am Main: Fischer, 1973 and 1983 (a)
Jan Lobel aus Warschau, 1948; repr. 1984 (s)
Mitte des Lebens, Frankfurt am Main, Fischer, 1950 (n); 1961
Abenteuer der Tugend, Frankfurt am Main, Fischer, 1957; 1961 (n)
Magische Argonautenfahrt. Eine Einführung in die gesammelten Werke von Elisabeth Langgässer, Hamburg: Claassen, 1959 (crit)
Nina. Mitte des Lebens. Abenteuer der Tugend, Frankfurt am Main: Fischer, 1961 (n)
Zölibat und Frau, Würzburg: Echter, 1967 (e)
Unterentwickeltes Land Frau, Würzburg: Echter, 1970 (e)

And many later works including *Abaelards Liebe*, Frankfurt am Main: Fischer, 1991 (n)

Works in English translation
Rings of Glass (= *Die gläsernen Ringe*; tr. Richard and Clara Winston), Chicago: Regnery, 1958
A Woman's Prison Journal (= *Gefängnistagebuch*; tr. Michael Hulse), New York: Schocken Books, 1987; as *Prison Journal*, London: Macmillan, 1987; Harmondsworth: Penguin, 1989
Jan Lobel from Warsaw (= *Jan Lobel aus Warschau*; tr. Michael Hulse), and 'Luise Rinser interviewed by Michael Hulse', Edinburgh: Polygon, 1991
Nina (= *Nina. Mitte des Lebens*; tr. Richard and Clara Winston) Chicago: Regnery, 1956
Abelard's Love (=*Abaelards Liebe*; tr. Jean M. Snook), Lincoln: University of Nebraska Press, 1998
Herrmann and Spitz, *German Women Writers* (1978)

Secondary literature
Frederiksen, Else, 'Luise Rinser', in Wolfgang D. Elfe and James Hardin (eds.), *Contemporary German Fiction Writers (First Series)*, Detroit, 1988, pp. 255–62
Frederiksen; Wilson

Rosmer, Ernst (pseud. for Else Bernstein-Porges) (Vienna 1866 – 1949 Hamburg)

Maria Arndt, Berlin: S. Fischer, 1908 (d)

Works in English translation
Maria Arndt, tr. and intr. Susanne T. Kord, in *Modern Drama by Women 1880s-1930s: an international anthology*, ed. Katherine E. Kelly, London and New York: Routledge, 1996, pp. 80–107
The King's Children: A Fairy Tale in 3 Acts (libretto for Humperdinck opera *Die Königskinder*), various tr.; see Morgan

Rotenberg, Stella (Vienna 1916 – Leeds, GB)

Scherben sind endlicher Hort, Vienna, 1991 (selected poetry and prose)

English translation

6 poems tr. Donal McLaughlin and Stephen Richardson in *Zwischenwelt 4. Literatur und Kultur des Exils in Großbritannien*, ed. Siglinde Bolbecher et al., Vienna: Theodor-Kramer-Gesellschaft, 1995, pp. 28–9

Secondary literature

Wallas, Armin A., '"Dennoch schreibe ich" – Eine Annäherung an das literarische Werk von Stella Rotenberg, in *Stella Rotenberg: Scherben sind endlicher Hort. Ausgewählte Lyrik und Prosa*, Vienna, 1991, pp. 179–87

Wilson

Roth, Friederike (Sindelfingen 1948 – FRG)

Tollkirschenhochzeit, Darmstadt: Luchterhand, 1978 (p)
Schieres Glück, Darmstadt: Luchterhand, 1980 (p)
Das Buch des Lebens, Darmstadt and Neuwied: Luchterhand, 1983f. (n)
Schattige Gärten, Frankfurt am Main: Suhrkamp, 1987 (p)
Ritt auf die Wartburg/ Klavierspiele, Frankfurt am Main: Verlag der Autoren, 2nd edn, 1991 (d)
Krötenbrunnen, Frankfurt am Main: Suhrkamp, 1984 (d)
Wiese und Macht: Ein Gedicht, Frankfurt am Main: Suhrkamp, 1993 (p)

Also translations from English
e.g. Sylvia Plath, *Three Women,* Frankfurt am Main: Fischer, 1994

Drama in English translation

The Donkey-Ride (= *Ritt auf die Wartburg*; tr. Tinch Minter and Anthony Vivis), London [Rosica Colin], 1988 (typescript: Goethe Institut London)
Piano Play (= *Klavierspiele*; tr. David Roger), in *Gambit. International Theatre Review* 39/40, German Theatre Issue
Piano Plays (= *Klavierspiele*; tr. Andra Weddington), in Case, *The Divided Home/Land* (1992)

Rühle-Gerstel, Alice (Prague 1894 – 1943 Mexico)

Das Frauenproblem der Gegenwart, 1932; repr. as *Die Frau und der Kapitalismus*, 1972 (e)
Der Umbruch oder Hanna und die Freiheit. Written in exile in Mexico, 1937/38; first published Frankfurt, 1984 with an introduction by Ingrid Herbst and Bernd Klemm and an afterword by Stephen S. Kalmar (n)

Also works on Marxism and psychology; translations

Secondary literature

Hilzinger, Sonja, '"Ins Leere fallen". Alice Rühle-Gerstels Exilroman *Der Umbruch oder Hanna und die Freiheit*', in *Exil. Forschung, Erkenntnisse, Ergebnisse* (1/1990), pp. 43–52

Runge, Doris (Carlow, Mecklenburg 1943 – FRG)

jagdlied, Stuttgart: DVA, 1985 (p)
kommt zeit, Stuttgart: DVA, 1988 (p)
wintergrün, Stuttgart: DVA, 1991 (p)

And other volumes of poetry

Runge, Erika (Halle/Saale 1939 – FRG)

Bottroper Protokolle, Frankfurt am Main: Suhrkamp, 1968 (e; documentary)
Frauen. Versuche zur Emanzipation, Frankfurt am Main, Suhrkamp, 1970 (e)

Wilson

Rüthel, Else (Cologne 1899 – 1938 Brno, Czechoslovakia)

Anbruch des Tags, Gedichte, Prague and Vienna: Verlag Der Monat, 1936 (p)
'Die Kunst der Bergner', in Rheinsberg, *KRIEGS/LÄUFE* (1989) (see p. 357 above) (s/e)
'Backfischnovelle' and 'Eine Dreißigjährige', in Rheinsberg, ed., *Bubikopf* (1988) (see
     p. 358 above) (s)

Sachs, Nelly (Berlin 1891 – 1970 Stockholm)

Fahrt ins Staublose. Die Gedichte der Nelly Sachs, vol. I, Frankfurt am Main: Suhrkamp, 1961,
     re-issued 1991 (p)
Suche nach Lebenden. Die Gedichte der Nelly Sachs, vol. II, Frankfurt am Main: Suhrkamp,
     1971, re-issued 1988 (p)
In den Wohnungen des Todes, Berlin: Aufbau, 1947 (p)
Sternverdunkelung, Amsterdam: Bermann-Fischer/Querido Verlag, 1949 (p)
Flucht und Verwandlung, Stuttgart: DVA, 1959 (p)
Zeichen im Sand. Die szenischen Dichtungen der Nelly Sachs, Frankfurt am Main: Suhrkamp,
     1962 (p/d)
Die Suchende. Gedichtzyklus, Frankfurt am Main: Suhrkamp, 1966 (p)
Verzauberung. Späte szenische Dichtungen, Frankfurt am Main: Suhrkamp, 1970 (p/d)
Gedichte, ed. Hilde Domin, Frankfurt am Main: Suhrkamp, 1977 (p)

Works in English translation

O The Chimneys. Selected Poems including Eli, a Verse Play, tr. Michael Hamburger et al., New
     York: Farrar Straus and Giroux, 1967; as *Selected Poems*, London: Cape, 1968
The Seeker and Other Poems, tr. Ruth and Matthew Mead and Michael Hamburger, New
     York: Farrar Straus and Giroux, 1970
Selected Poems [of] Abba Kovner and Nelly Sachs; the latter tr. Michael Hamburger [et al.];
     selected and intr. by Stephen Spender, Harmondsworth: Penguin, 1971
Beryl Sees in the Night or the Alphabet Lost and Regained (= *Beryll sieht in die Nacht*; tr. Ida Noval
     Myers and Erhard Bahr), Austin, Texas: University of Texas Press, 1969
Paul Celan, Nelly Sachs: Correspondence, ed. Barbara Wiedemann, tr. Christopher Clark,
     intr. John Felstiner, New York: Sheep Meadow, 1995

Secondary literature

Bahti, Timothy and Marilyn Sibley Fries (eds.), *Jewish Writers and German Literature: The
     Uneasy Example of Nelly Sachs and Walter Benjamin*, Ann Arbor: Michigan
     University Press, 1995
Berendsohn, Walter A., *Nelly Sachs: Einführung in das Werk der Dichterin jüdischen Schicksals*,
     Darmstadt: Agora, 1974
Foot, Robert, *The Phenomenon of Speachlessness [sic] in the Poetry of Marie Luise Kaschnitz,
     Günter Eich, Nelly Sachs and Paul Celan*, Bonn: Bouvier, 1982
Beil, Claudia, *Sprache als Heimat: Jüdische Tradition und Exilerfahrung in der Lyrik von Nelly
     Sachs und Rose Ausländer*, Munich, 1988
Dinesen, Ruth, *Nelly Sachs. Eine Biographie*, Frankfurt am Main 1992
Fritsch-Vivié, Gabriele, *Nelly Sachs in Selbstzeugnissen und Bilddokumenten*, Reinbek bei
     Hamburg: Rowohlt, 1993
Frederiksen; Wilson

Salburg, Edith (Schloß Leonstein, Austria 1868–?)

Die Unverantwortlichen. Roman einer Ehe, Berlin: Falkenstein, 1936 (n)
Deutsch zu Deutsch. Deutschland und Oesterreich, zwei Völker? – ein Blut! Leipzig, 1938 (e)
Eine Landflucht. Ein Buch aus der Zeit, Leipzig: Hase & Köhler, 1939 (n)

Schaefer, Oda (Berlin 1900 – 1988 Munich)

Irdisches Geleit, Munich: Desch, 1946 (p)
Kranz des Jahres, Munich: Desch, 1948 (p)
(ed.), *Unter dem sapphischen Mond. Deutsche Frauenlyrik seit 1900*, Munich: Piper, 1957 (p)
Grasmelodie, Munich: Desch, 1959 (p)
Der grüne Ton: Späte und Frühe Gedichte, Munich: Desch, 1973 (p)
Die leuchtenden Feste über der Trauer: Erinnerungen an der Nachkriegszeit, Munich and Zurich:
    Piper, 1977 (a)
Wiederkehr: Ausgewählte Gedichte, ed. W. Fritsche, Munich and Zurich: Piper 1985 (p)

Also wrote s, e, a

Schaumann, Ruth (Hamburg 1899 – 1975 Munich)

Die Kathedrale, Munich: Wolff, 1920 (p)
Die Rose, Munich: Kösel, 1927 (p)
Der blühende Stab. Neun Geschichten, Munich: Kösel, 1929 (s)
Die Kinder und die Tiere, Munich: Kösel, 1929 (p)
Die Tenne, Munich: Kösel, 1931 (p)
Amei. Eine Kindheit, Berlin: Grote, 1932 (a)
Yves. Roman, Munich: Kösel, 1933 (n)
Der Kreuzweg. Die vierzehn Stationen, gemalt, 1934 (r/p)
Ecce Homo. Eine Passion in Meisterbildern. Dichtung von Ruth Schaumann, 1935 (r/p)
Der Major, Berlin: Grothe, 1935 (n)
Die Silberdistel, Berlin: Grothe, 1940 (s)
Die Übermacht, 1940 (n)

And numerous other novels, poems and stories, listed Wall (see p. 277 above)

Translation: Morgan

Scheinhardt, Saliha (Konya, Anatolia 1946–; moved to FRG in 1967)

Frauen, die sterben, ohne daß sie gelebt hätten, Berlin: EXpress Edition, 1983 (s)
Drei Zypressen, Berlin: EXpress Edition, 1984 (s)
Und die Frauen weinten Blut, Berlin: EXpress, 1985 (s)
Träne für Träne werde ich heimzahlen. Kindheit in Anatolien, Reinbek: Rowohlt, 1987 (a/n)
*Von der Erde bis zum Himmel Liebe: Eine Erzählung vom Leben und Sterben des aufrechten Bürgers
    C.*, Frankfurt am Main: Büchergilde Gutenberg, 1988; repr. Reinbek: Rowohlt,
    1990 (s)
Sie zerrissen die Nacht, Freiburg, Basel and Vienna: Herder, 1993 (s)
Die Stadt und das Mädchen, Freiburg, Basel and Vienna: Herder, 1993 (a/n)
Liebe, meine Gier, die mich frißt, Freiburg, Basel and Vienna: Herder, 1994 (n)

Schieber, Anna (Esslingen 1867 – 1945 Tübingen)

Wachstum und Wandlung, Tübingen; Wunderlich, 1936 (n)

And numerous other works (n, ch) from 1903 on; listed Wilson

Schlag, Evelyn (Waidhofen, Austria 1952–)

Beim Hüter des Schattens, Frankfurt am Main: S. Fischer, 1984 (s)
Einflüsterung nahe seinem Ohr, Vienna: Edition Maioli, 1986 (p)
Ortswechsel des Herzens: Gedichte, Frankfurt am Main: Fischer, 1989 (p)
Elegien, Frankfurt am Main: Fischer, 1991 (p)
Der Schnabelberg, Frankfurt am Main: Fischer, 1992 (p)

Keiner fragt mich wozu ich diese Krankheit denn brauche: Grazer Poetik-Vorlesungen, Graz: Droschel, 1993 (e)
Touché, Frankfurt am Main: Fischer, 1994 (s)
Unsichtbare Frauen, Salzburg and Vienna: Residenz Verlag, 1995 (s)

Translation: Gutzschhahn, *Young Poets of Germany* (1994)

Schlegel, Dorothea, née Brendel Mendelssohn (Berlin 1763 – 1839 Frankfurt am Main)

Schlegel, Friedrich (ed.), *Florentin: ein Roman*, vol. I, Lübeck: Bohm, 1801 [no more published]. Modern edns: ed. Liliane Weissberg: *Florentin: Roman, Fragmente, Varianten*, Frankfurt am Main: Ullstein, 1987; ed. Wolfgang Nehring, *Florentin*, Stuttgart: Reclam, 1993 (n)

Works in English translation
Camilla: a novella, tr. Edwina Lawler Lewiston intr. Hans Eichner, New York: E. Mellen Press, c. 1990
Florentin: a novel, tr., annotated, and intr. Edwina Lawler and Ruth Richardson Lewiston, New York: Edwin Mellen Press, 1988
Correspondence: The Berlin and Jena Years (1764–1802), ed. Ruth Richardson and Hans Eichner, tr. Edwina Lawler Lewiston, New York: E. Mellen, forthcoming
Blackwell and Zantop, *Bitter Healing* (1990) (l)

Secondary literature
Blackall, Eric A., *The Novels of the German Romantics*, Ithaca: Cornell University Press, 1983, pp. 44–50
Hibberd, John, 'Dorothea Schlegel's *Florentin* and the Precarious Idyll', *German Life and Letters* 30 (1977), 198–207
Scholz, Joachim J, 'Dorothea Schlegel', in: Hardin and Schweitzer, *German Writers in the Age of Goethe* (see p. 272 above), pp. 271–4
Stephan, Inge, 'Weibliche und männliche Autorschaft: zum *Florentin* von Dorothea Schlegel und zur *Lucinde* von Friedrich Schlegel', in Inge Stephan, Weigel and Wilhelms (eds.), *'Wen kümmert's, wer spricht'*, Cologne: Böhlau, 1991, pp. 83–98
Stern, Carola, *'Ich möchte mir Flügel wünschen': das Leben der Dorothea Schlegel*, Reinbek: Rowohlt, 1990; repr. 1995
Frederiksen

Schlegel-Schelling, Caroline, née Michaelis (Göttingen 1763 – 1809 Maulbronn)

Schmidt, Erich (ed.), *Caroline: Briefe aus der Frühromantik*, 2 vols., Frankfurt am Main: Insel, 1913 and 1921; repr. Bern: Lang, 1970 (l)
Damm, Sigrid (ed.), *'Lieber Freund, ich komme weit her schon an diesem frühen Morgen': Caroline Schlegel-Schelling in ihren Briefen*, Darmstadt: Luchterhand, 1980; reissued as *Die Kunst zu leben*, Frankfurt am Main: Insel, 1997 (l)

Translation: Blackwell and Zantop, *Bitter Healing* (1990) (l)

Secondary literature
Kleßmann, Eckart, *'Ich war kühn, aber nicht frevelhaft': Das Leben der Caroline Schlegel-Schelling*, 2nd edn., Bergisch Gladbach: Lübbe, 1992
McCullar, Sylvia Yvonne, *'Ideal' versus 'Real': Womanhood as Portrayed in the Literature and*

Correspondence of Early German Romanticism, diss. Rice University, 1979; Ann Arbor: University of Michigan Press, 1979
Frederiksen; Wilson

Schlier, Paula (Neuburg an der Donau 1899 – Austria)

Choronoz. Ein Buch der Wirklichkeit in Träumen, Munich: Wolff, 1928
Petras Aufzeichnungen oder Konzept einer Jugend nach dem Diktat der Zeit, Innsbruck: Brenner, 1926 (a)
Wilson

Schmidt, Kathrin (Gotha, GDR, 1958–)

Gedichte, Berlin: Verlag Neues Leben, 1982 (p)
Ein Engel fliegt durch die Tapetenfabrik, Berlin: Verlag Neues Leben, 1987 (p)
Flußbild mit Engel, Frankfurt am Main: Suhrkamp, 1995

Schopenhauer, Adèle (Hamburg 1797 – 1849 Bonn)

Haus-, Wald-, und Feldmärchen, 1844 (s)
Anna, 1845 (n)
Eine dänische Geschichte, 1848 (n)
(ed.) *Jugendleben und Wanderbilder, Aus Johanna Schopenhauers Nachlass*, 1839

Translations: see Morgan S

Schopenhauer, Johanna (Danzig 1766 – 1838 Jena)

Sämtliche Schriften, 24 vols., Leipzig: Brockhaus; Frankfurt am Main: Sauerländer, 1830–1
Gabriele: ein Roman, 3 vols., Leipzig: Brockhaus, 1819–20; modern edn by Stephan Koranyi, Munich: dtv, 1985 (n)
Sidonia: ein Roman, 3 vols., Frankfurt am Main: Wilmans, 1827–8 (n)
Reise durch England und Schottland, Stuttgart: Steingruben Verlag, 1965 (t)

Works in English translation

A Lady Travels: Journeys in England and Scotland. From the diaries of Johanna Schopenhauer; tr. and ed. Ruth Michaelis-Jena and Willy Merson, London: Routledge, 1988
see also Morgan + S

Secondary literature

Goodman, Katherine R., 'Johanna Schopenhauer (1766–1838), or Pride and Resignation', in Joeres, *Out of Line* (see p. 272 above), pp. 187–209
Köhler, Astrid, 'Geselligkeit als Lebensform und literarisches Konzept: Johanna Schopenhauers Roman *Gabriele* im Kontext ihrer Weimarer Salons', in Ives (ed.), *Women Writers of the Age of Goethe* vol. VIII (1996), 26–45
Pickett, T. H., 'Johanna Schopenhauer', in Hardin and Schweitzer, *German Writers in the Age of Goethe* (see p. 272 above), pp. 299–302
Frederiksen

Schroeder, Margot (Hamburg 1937–)

Ich stehe meine Frau, Frankfurt am Main: Fischer, 1975 (n)
Der Schlachter empfiehlt noch immer Herz, Munich: Frauenbuchverlag, 1976 (n)
Die Angst ist baden gegenagen. Poem, Berlin: Fietkau, 1976 (p)

Wiederkäuer: Lyrik und Kurzprosa, Hamburg: Svato, 1977 (p, s)
Nachts fällt nach oben. Poem, Berlin: Fietkau, 1981 (p)
Haltlose Tage, Düsseldorf: Verlag Sabine Königs, 1993 (p)

> Translation: Altbach, *German Feminism* (1984); Cocalis, *The Defiant Muse* (1986)

Schubert, Helga (Berlin 1940–)

Lauter Leben, Berlin: Aufbau, 1975; repr. as *Anna kann Deutsch*, Frankfurt am Main:
> Luchterhand, 1989 (e)
Blickwinkel, Berlin: Aufbau, 1984; repr. (with some additional stories) as *Das verbotene*
> *Zimmer*, Frankfurt am Main: Luchterhand, 1990 (s)
Judasfrauen. Zehn Fallgeschichten weiblicher Denunziation im Dritten Reich, Berlin and
> Weimar: Aufbau, 1990; Frankfurt am Main: Luchterhand, 1990
Die Andersdenkende, Munich: dtv, 1994 (e)
Wilson

Schutting, Jutta (Amstetten, Austria 1937)
[after 1989 Julian Schutting]

In der Sprache der Inseln, Salzburg: Otto Müller, 1973 (p)
Lichtungen, Salzburg: Otto Müller, 1976 (p)
Stechenpferde: Sprachpoetische Texte, Vienna: Rhombus, 1977 (p)
Liebesgedichte, Salzburg and Vienna: Residenz Verlag, 1982 and Munich: dtv, 1983 (p)
Traumreden, Salzburg and Vienna: Residenz Verlag, 1987 (p)
Flugblätter, Salzburg: Otto Müller, 1990 (p)
Zuhörerbehelligungen: Vorlesungen zur Poesie, Graz and Vienna: Droschl, 1990 (e)

> Also writes prose fiction

> Translation: Altbach, *German Feminism* (1984)
Wilson

Schütz, Helga (Falkenhain, Silesia 1937 – GDR)

Vorgeschichten oder Schöne Gegend Probstein, Berlin: Aufbau, 1970 (s)
Das Erdbeben bei Sangerhausen, Berlin: Aufbau, 1972; repr. as *Vorgeschichten oder Schöne Gegend*
> *Probstein/Das Erdbeben bei Sangerhausen und andere Erzählungen*, Munich: dtv, 1977 (s)
Festbeleuchtung, Berlin: Aufbau, 1974; repr. Darmstadt: Luchterhand, c. 1987 (n)
Jette in Dresden, Berlin: Aufbau, 1977 (n)
Julia oder Erziehung zum Chorgesang, Berlin: Aufbau, 1980; repr. Darmstadt: Luchterhand,
> 1988 (n)
In Annas Namen, Berlin: Aufbau, 1986; repr. Frankfurt am Main: Luchterhand, 1989 (n)
Heimat süße Heimat: Zeit-Rechnungen in Kasachstan, Berlin and Weimar: Aufbau, 1992 (n)
Vom Glanz der Elbe, Cologne: Kiepenheuer & Witsch, 1995 (n)

> Translation: see Gerber and Pouchet
Wilson

Schwaiger, Brigitte (Freistadt, Austria 1949–)

Wie kommt das Salz ins Meer, Reinbek bei Hamburg: Rowohlt, 1979 (n)
Lange Abwesenheit, Vienna: Paul Zsolnay, 1980

> And other works of fiction and drama

Works in English translation

Why is there salt in the sea? (= *Wie kommt das Salz ins Meer*, tr. Sieglinde Lug), Lincoln and
   London: University of Nebraska Press, 1989
Plays (*Yes, my Führer, The Galizian Jewess, The Inconvenience*) tr. Penny Black, London:
   Oberon, 1998

Schwarz, Sibylle (Greifswald 1620–38)

Gedichte, ed. Helmut W. Ziefle, Bern, 1980 (p)

Also wrote n, d

Secondary literature

Ziefle, Helmut W., *Sibylle Schwarz. Leben und Werk*, Bonn, 1975
Wilson

Seghers, Anna (Mainz 1900 – 1983 Berlin, GDR)

Gesammelte Werke in Einzelausgaben, 10 vols., Darmstadt and Neuwied: Luchterhand, 1977
Aufstand der Fischer von St. Barbara, Berlin: Kiepenheuer, 1929; repr. Berlin: Aufbau, 1951;
   1993 (s)
Der Kopflohn. Roman aus einem deutschen Dorf im Spätsommer 1932, Amsterdam: Querido,
   1933; repr. in GDR: Berlin: Aufbau, 1995 with afterword by Sonja Hilzinger (n)
Die Rettung, Amsterdam: Querido, 1937; repr. in GDR: Berlin: Aufbau, 1996 with
   afterword by Sonja Hilzinger (n)
Das siebte Kreuz, Mexico City: Editorial El Libro Libre, 1942; repr. Darmstadt:
   Luchterhand, 1988; *Das siebte Kreuz. Texte, Daten, Bilder*, ed. Sonja Hilzinger,
   Frankfurt, 1990 (n)
Transit, first published in Spanish, English and French in 1944, first German edn 1948;
   repr. Berlin and Weimar: Aufbau, 1993, with an afterword by Sonja
   Hilzinger (n)
Die Toten bleiben jung, 1949, Berlin and Weimar: Aufbau, 1964, repr. 1967 (n)
Die Entscheidung, Berlin: Aufbau-Verlag, 1959; repr. Darmstadt: Luchterhand, 1977 (n)
Das Licht auf dem Galgen. Eine karibische Geschichte aus der Zeit der Französischen Revolution,
   Berlin: Aufbau, 1961; repr. in *Die Hochzeit von Haiti* (s)
Karibische Geschichten, Darmstadt: Luchterhand, 1976 (s)
Die Kraft der Schwachen, Berlin: Aufbau, 1965; repr. Neuwied and Berlin: Luchterhand,
   1966 (s)
Das Vertrauen, Berlin: Aufbau, 1968; repr. Darmstadt: Luchterhand, 1977 (n)
Der gerechte Richter. Eine Novelle, Berlin: Aufbau, 1990 (s)

Works in English translation

The Seventh Cross (= *Das siebte Kreuz*; tr. James A. Galston), Boston: Little Brown & Co.,
   1942; London: Eyre and Spottiswode, 1950
The Dead Stay Young (= *Die Toten bleiben jung*; tr. anon.), Boston: Little, Brown; London:
   Eyre and Spottiswode, 1950
The Revolt of the Fishermen (= *Der Aufstand der Fischer von St. Barbara*; tr. Margaret
   Goldsmith), London: E. Matthews and Marot, 1929; tr. Jack and Renate Mitchell
   and published with *A Price on his Head* (= *Der Kopflohn*, tr. Eva Wulff), ed. Valerie
   Stone; Berlin: Seven Seas, 1960; London: Collet, 1961 as *Two Novelettes*
Benito's Blue and Nine Other Stories (= *Das wirkliche Blau + Kraft der Schwachen*; tr. Joan
   Becker), East Berlin: Seven Seas, 1973

'Excursion of the Dead Girls' (= 'Der Ausflug der toten Mädchen'), in Herrmann and
    Spitz, *German Women Writers* (1978)
Transit (= *Transit*; tr. James A. Galston), Boston: Little, 1944

  Further translations: see Morgan + S; Gerber and Pouchet

Secondary literature
Bangerter, Lowell A., *The Bourgeois Proletarian. A Study of Anna Seghers*, Bonn: Bouvier,
    1980
'Frauen und Kinder in der Emigration', in *Anna Seghers / Wieland Herzfelde: Ein Briefwechsel
    1939–1946*, ed. Ursula Emmerich and Erika Pick, Berlin and Weimar 1985,
    pp. 112–26
Gutzmann, Gertraud, 'Anna Seghers (Netty Reiling Radványi)', in Wolfgang D. Elfe and
    James Hardin (eds.), *Contemporary German Fiction Writers (First Series)*, Detroit,
    1988, pp. 297–310
Hilzinger, Sonja, *Anna Seghers. Monographie*, Stuttgart: Reclam, 1999
Kane, Martin, 'Beyond Ideology: The Early Work of Anna Seghers', in Keith-Smith
    (1993) (see p. 275 above), pp. 255–78
Lorisika, Irene, *Frauendarstellung bei Irmgard Keun und Anna Seghers*, Frankfurt am Main:
    Haag und Herchen, 1985 (e)
Zehl Romero, Christiane, *Anna Seghers in Selbstzeugnissen und Bilddokumenten*, Reinbek bei
    Hamburg: Rowohlt, 1993
Frederiksen; Wilson

Seidel, Ina (Halle 1885 – 1974 Ebenhausen nr. Munich)

Numerous works, including
Das Labyrinth. Ein Lebenslauf aus dem 18. Jahrhundert, Jena: Diederichs, 1922 (n)
Die Fürstin reitet, Berlin and Leipzig: DVA, 1926 (s)
Das Wunschkind, 2 vols., Stuttgart and Berlin: Neue Verlags-Anstalt, 1930; Stuttgart:
    DVA, 1975/1985; Munich: dtv, 1980 (n)
Lennacker. Das Buch einer Heimkehr, Stuttgart and Berlin: DVA 1938; 1979; Berlin: Ullstein,
    1982 (n)
Deutsche Frauen. Bildnisse und Lebensbeschreibungen, Berlin: Steinmeyer Verlag, 1939 (e)
Gedichte, Festausgabe, Stuttgart: DVA, 1955 (p)
Frau und Wort, 1941; Stuttgart: DVA, 1965 (e)
(ed. with Elisabeth Langgässer) *Herz zum Hafen* (see p. 274 above) (1933) (p)

Works in English translation
The Labyrinth (= *Das Labyrinth*; tr. Oakley Williams), New York: Farrar; London: Lane,
    1932; 1939
The Wish Child (= *Das Wunschkind*; tr. G. Dunning Gribble), New York: Farrar; London:
    Lane, 1935

Secondary literature
Stohler Bennett, JoAnn, 'Ina Seidel', in James Hardin (ed.), *German Fiction Writers
    1914–1945*, Detroit, 1987, pp. 241–7
Wilson

Sölle, Dorothée (1929 – FRG)

Die revolutionäre Geduld, Berlin: Fietkau, 1974 (p)
spiel doch von brot und rosen, Berlin: Fietkau, 1981 (p)

fliegen lernen, Berlin: Fietkau, 1982 (p)
verrückt nach licht, Berlin: Fietkau, 1984 (p)
Ich will nicht auf tausend Messern gehen, Stuttgart: dtv, 1986 (p)
Zivil und Ungehorsam, Berlin: Fietkau, 1990 (p)

Also numerous theological works, some available in English

Spyri, Johanna (Hirzel, nr. Zurich 1827 – 1901 Zurich)

Geschichten für Kinder und auch solche, welche Kinder lieb haben, 16 vols. (1879–1895)
including *Heidis Lehr- und Wanderjahre* and *Heidi kann brauchen, was es gelernt hat*
(1880) (n; ch)
Editions of *Heidi*, her most popular story, are too numerous to mention individually; it
has been widely translated, as have other of her works: see Morgan + S. for
details; also Wilson

Stefan, Verena (Bern 1947–)

Häutungen: Autobiografische Aufzeichnungen Gedichte Träume Analysen, Munich:
Frauenoffensive, 1975 and Frankfurt am Main: Fischer, 1990 (n; a; p)
mit Füssen mit Flügeln. Gedichte und Zeichnungen, Munich: Frauenoffensive, 1986 (p)
Wortgetreu ich träume: Geschichten und Geschichte, Zurich: Arche, 1987 (s/e)

Works in English translation
Shedding (= *Häutungen*; tr. Johanna Moore and Beth Weckmueller), New York: Daughters
Press, 1978; repr. in *Shedding and Literally Dreaming*, New York: The Feminist
Press, 1994
Literally Dreaming (= *Wortgetreu ich träume*; tr. Johanna Albert and Tobe Levin), in *Shedding
and Literallly Dreaming* (1994)
Foreword to *Shedding* tr. in Altbach, *German Feminism* (1984), pp. 53–5
Cocalis, *The Defiant Muse* (1986)
Frederiksen; Wilson

Steffin, Margarete (Berlin-Lichtenberg 1908 – 1941 Moscow). Collaborated with Bertolt Brecht

Konfutse versteht nichts von Frauen. Nachgelassene Texte, ed. Inge Gellert, Berlin: Rowohlt,
1991

Secondary literature
Hilzinger, Sonja, 'Schreiben im Exil. Margarete Steffins Erzählungen und Stücke für
Kinder', in Walter Delaber and Jörg Döring (eds.), *Bertolt Brecht (1898–1956)*,
Berlin: Weidler, 1998

Stein, Charlotte von (Eisenach 1742 – 1827 Weimar)

Dramen, ed. Susanne Kord, Hildesheim: Olms, 1996 (d)
Dido, 1796, in Adolf Schöll, *Goethes Briefe an Frau von Stein*, 2nd edn, 2 vols., Frankfurt am
Main, 1883–5, vol. II, pp. 488–534. (d)
Die zwei Emilien, 1803 (d, p)
Wilson

Steinwachs, Ginka (Göttingen 1942–)

marylinparis. montageroman, Vienna: Rhombus, 1978; Basel and Frankfurt am Main:
Stroemfeld/Roter Stern, 1979 (n)

George Sand: eine frau in bewegung, die frau von stand, Berlin: Medusa, 1980; Frankfurt am
   Main, Berlin and Vienna: Ullstein, 1983 (d)

English translation
'George Sand', tr. Jamie Owen Daniel, Katrin Sieg and Sue-Ellen Case in Case (ed.), *The
   Divided Home/Land* (1992), pp. 287–339

Stötzer, Gabriele (GDR 1953–) [Gabriele Kachold until 1990; Stötzer-Kachold until 1992]

zügel los: prosatexte, Berlin and Weimar: Aufbau, Außer der Reihe, 1989 and Frankfurt am
   Main: Luchterhand, 1990 (prose)
grenzen los fremd gehen: aufzeichnungen 1988–1991, Berlin and Weimar: Aufbau, 1992; Berlin:
   Janus press, Basisdruck, 1992 (p/a/e)

Secondary literature
Linklater, *Constructions of Sexuality* (1998) (see p. 348 above)

Strauß und Torney, Lulu von (Bückeburg 1873 – 1956 Jena)

Vom Biedermeier zur Bismarckzeit. Aus dem Leben einer Neunzigjährigen, Jena: Diederichs, 1932
   (hist.)
Auge um Auge (extract from *Sieger und Besiegte*, 1909), Jena: Diederichs, 1933 (n)
Erde der Väter. Ausgewählte Gedichte, Jena: Diederichs, 1936 (p)
Das verborgene Angesicht. Erinnerungen, Jena: Diederichs, 1943 (a)

   And many other poems and short stories

   Translation: see Morgan
Wilson

Strittmatter, Eva (Neuruppin 1930 – GDR)
Ich mach ein Lied aus Stille, Berlin and Weimar: Aufbau, 1973 (p)
Ich schwing mich auf die Schaukel: Bilderbuch, Berlin: Der Kinderbuchverlag, 1975 (p/ch)
Mondschnee liegt auf den Wiesen, Berlin and Weimar: Aufbau, 1975 (p)
Die eine Rose überwältigt alles, Berlin and Weimar: Aufbau, 1977 (p)
Zwiegespräch, Berlin and Weimar: Aufbau, 1980 (p)
Heliotrop, Berlin and Weimar: Aufbau, 1983 (p)
Poesie und andere Nebendinge, Berlin and Weimar: Aufbau, 1985 (p, e)
Atem, Berlin and Weimar: Aufbau, 1988 (p)
Die heimliche Freiheit der Einsamkeit, Darmstadt und Neuwied: Luchterhand, 1989 (p)
Unter wechselndem Licht: Ausgewählte Gedichte, Berlin and Weimar: Aufbau, 1990 (p)

   Has also written ch

   Translation: see Gerber and Pouchet
Wilson

Struck, Karin (nr. Greifswald 1947 – GDR; moved to FRG in 1953)
Klassenliebe, Frankfurt am Main: Suhrkamp, 1973 (n)
Die Mutter, Frankfurt am Main: Suhrkamp, 1975 (n)
Lieben, Frankfurt am Main: Suhrkamp, 1977 (n)
Trennung, Frankfurt am Main: Suhrkamp, 1978 (s)
Wilson

Struzyk, Brigitte (Thuringia 1946 – GDR)

Gedichte, Berlin: Verlag Neues Leben, 1978 (p)
Leben auf der Kippe, Berlin and Weimar: Aufbau, 1984 (p)
Der wild gewordene Tag, Berlin and Weimar: Aufbau, 1989 (p)
Caroline unter dem Freiheitsbaum: Ansichtssachen, Darmstadt: Luchterhand, 1988 (e/n/crit.)

Suttner, Bertha von (Prague 1843 – 1914 Vienna)

Gesammelte Schriften, 12 vols., Dresden: E. Pierson, 1906–7
Gesammelte Novellen, 1874 (s, p)
Daniela Dormes, Munich: Heinrichs, 1886 (n)
Die Waffen nieder! Eine Lebensgeschichte, Dresden: E. Pierson, 1890; repr. Berlin: Verlag der
    Nation, 1990 (e)
Vor dem Gewitter, Vienna: Breitenstein, 1894 (n)
Krieg und Frieden. Erzählungen, Aphorismen und Betrachtungen, 1896 (s, e)
High Life, Dresden: E. Pierson, 1896 (n)
Memoiren, 1908 (a)
Der Menschheit Hochgedanken, 1911 (n)

Works in English translation

Ground Arms! (= Die Waffen nieder; tr. Alice H. Abbott), 1892; *Lay Down Your Arms!* tr. T.
    Holmes, London and New York: Garland, 1892; repr. 1972; *Disarm! Disarm!* tr. and
    adapted, 1913
Memoirs of Bertha von Suttner (= Memoiren, tr. Boston Publ. for the International School of
    Peace), New York: Garland, 1972; *Memoirs of Bertha von Suttner: The Record of an
    Eventful Life.* 2 vols. Boston: Ginn, 1910

Secondary literature

Pauli, Hertha, *Cry of the Heart. The Story of Bertha von Suttner*, tr. Richard and Clara
    Winston, New York: Washburn, 1957
Wilson

Tarnow, Fanny (Güstrow, Mecklenburg 1779 – 1862 Dessau)

Ausgewählte Schriften, 15 vols., 1830
Gesammelte Erzählungen, 4 vols., Leipzig: Kollmann, 1840–2 (s)
Natalie: ein Beitrag zur Geschichte des weiblichen Herzens, Berlin: Hitzig, 1811 (n)

Secondary literature

Heer, Birgit, 'Liebe und Krankheit als Schlüsselbegriffe im Werke von Fanny Tarnow',
    in Ives (ed.) *Women Writers of the Age of Goethe*, vol. v (1992), pp. 28–44

Techel, Sabina (FRG 1953–)

Es kündigt sich an, Frankfurt am Main: Suhrkamp, 1986 (p)

    Translation: Gutzschhahn, *Young Poets of Germany* (1994)

Tekinay, Alev (Izmir 1951–; moved to FRG in 1971)

Es brennt ein Feuer in mir. Erzählungen, Frankfurt am Main: Brandes & Apsel, 1990 (s)
Nur der Hauch vom Paradies, Frankfurt am Main: Brandes & Apsel, 1993 (n)
Das Rosenmädchen und die Schildkröte. Märchen, Frankfurt am Main: Brandes & Apsel, 1991 (s)
Der weinende Granatapfel, Frankfurt: Suhrkamp, 1990 (n)

Tergit, Gabriele (Berlin 1894 – 1982 London)

Käsebier erobert den Kurfürstendamm, Berlin: Rowohlt, 1931; Frankfurt am Main: Krüger
    1977 (n)
Etwas Seltnes überhaupt. Erinnerungen, 1983 (a)
Wilson

Tetzner, Gerti (Thuringia 1936 – GDR)

Karen W., Halle: Mitteldeutscher Verlag, 1974; repr. Darmstadt: Luchterhand, 1975;
    1979 (n)
Eines schönen Sonntags, Halle and Leipzig: Mitteldeutscher Verlag, 1993
with Reiner Tetzner, *Im Lande der Fähren*, Halle and Leipzig: Mitteldeutscher Verlag,
    1988
Wilson

Thomas, Adrienne, née Hertha Strauch; pseud.: Deutsch, A. Hertha (Lorraine 1897 – 1980 Vienna)

Die Katrin wird Soldat. Ein Roman aus Elsaß-Lothringen, Berlin: Propyläen 1930 (n)
Dreiviertel Neugier, Amsterdam: De Lange 1934 (n)
Katrin, die Welt brennt! Amsterdam: De Lange 1938 (n)
Reisen Sie ab, Mademoiselle! first published Stockholm 1944; repr. 1982 (Hamburg) and
    1985 (Frankfurt, with Adrienne Thomas's preface to the first edition) (n)

Works in English translation
Katrin Becomes a Soldier (= *Die Katrin wird Soldat*; tr. Margaret Goldsmith), Boston: Little &
    Brown, 1931; *Catherine Joins Up*, London: E. Matthews & Marot, 1931

Secondary literature
Moens, Hermann, '*Die Katrin wird Soldat*: A Fictionalized Diary of the First World War',
    in Keith-Smith (1993) (see p. 275 above), pp. 145–66

Tieck, Dorothea (Jena 1799–1841)

Collaboration in *Shakspeare's [sic] dramatische Werke. Uebersetzt von August Wilhelm von
    Schlegel, ergänzt und erläutert von Ludwig Tieck*, 9 vols., Berlin: Reimer, 1825–33
    (translation)

    Also translated from Spanish

Secondary literature
Hoffmann, G., 'Zur Shakespear-Übersetzung Dorothea Tiecks', *Deutsche Shakespear-
    Gesellschaft West: Jahrbuch* (1971), 69–84
Paulin, Roger, *Ludwig Tieck. A Literary Biography,* Oxford: Clarendon, 1985

Tieck, Sophie (Neukölln 1775 – 1833 Estonia) [later Bernhardi, then von Knorning]

(ed.) Ludwig Tieck, *St. Evremond*. 3 vols., Breslau: Josef Max und Komp., 1836; 2nd edn
    1845 (n)
de Bruyn, Günter (ed.), *Ludwig Tieck. Die männliche Mutter und andere Liebes-, Lebens-, Spott-
    und Schauergeschichten*, Frankfurt am Main: Fischer, 1984. Includes stories by S.T.
    and a biographical sketch by the editor, pp. 392–11 (s)
Trainer, James (ed.), '*Bei aller brüderlichen Liebe . . .': The Letters of Sophie Tieck to her Brother
    Friedrich*, Berlin: de Gruyter, 1991 (l)

Trainer, James (ed.), *A Weimar Correspondence: The Letters of Friedrich and Sophie Tieck to Amalie von Voight, 1804–1837*, Columbia, South Carolina: Camden House, 1995 (l)

Secondary literature
Zimnowodzki, Jasmin, 'The Life and Works of Sophie Tieck (1775–1833)', in Ives (ed.), *Women Writers of the Age of Goethe*, vol. V (1992), pp. 3–27

TORKAN (= Torkan Daneshfar-Pätzoldt; writing in 1980s/90s)
Tufan: Brief an einen islamischen Bruder, Hamburg: perspol-verlag, 1983 (a/n)
Kaltland: Wah'schate Ssard, Hamburg: perspol-verlag, 1984 (a/n)

Tremel-Eggert, Kuni (writing in 1930s)
Barb. Der Roman einer deutschen Frau, 1933 (n)
Sonnige Heimat, Munich, 1941 (s)

Ullmann, Regina (St Gallen, Switzerland 1884 – 1961 Ebersberg, Bavaria)
Gesammelte Werke, 2 vols., Einsiedeln: Benziger Verlag, 1960; repr. Munich: Kösel Verlag, 1978
Ausgewählte Erzählungen, ed. Friedhelm Kemp, Frankfurt am Main: Suhrkamp, 1979 (s)

Secondary literature
Stephens, Don Steve, 'Regina Ullmann: Biography, Literary Reception, Interpretation', diss., Austin, Texas, 1980
Wilson

Unger, Friederike Helene (1741–1813)
Julchen Grünthal. Eine Pensionsgeschichte, 2 vols., with an afterword by Susanne Zantop, Hildesheim: Olms, 1991 (repr. of the 3rd edn. Berlin: Unger, 1798) (n)

Also translated from French, e.g. works by Rousseau

Secondary literature
Zantop, Susanne, 'Friederike Helene Unger', in James Hardin and Christoph E. Schweitzer (eds.), *German Writers in the Age of Goethe: Sturm und Drang to Classicism*, Detroit, 1990, pp. 288–93 (lists other works)

Urbanitzky, Grete von (Linz 1893 – 1974 Geneva)
Der wilde Garten, Leipzig: Hesse und Becker, 1927; repr. Wiesbaden: Feministischer Buchverlag, 1995 (n)

Varnhagen von Ense, Rahel, née Levin (Berlin 1771–1833)
Gesammelte Werke, ed. Konrad Veilchenfeldt, Uwe Schweikert and Rahel E. Steiner, 10 vols., Munich: Matthes & Seitz, 1983 (l)
Varnhagen von Ense, Karl August (ed.), *Rahel: ein Buch des Andenkens für ihre Freunde*, Berlin: Duncker & Humblot, 1833; enlarged edn, 3 vols., 1834

Works in English translation
Rahel: Her Life and Letters (= *Rahel: ein Buch des Andenkens*; tr. Mrs Vaughan Jennings), London: King, 1876 (l)
Blackwell and Zantop, *Bitter Healing* (1990), pp. 401–16 (l)

Secondary literature

Arendt, Hannah, *Rahel Varnhagen: The Life of a Jewess*, London: Leo Baeck Institute, 1957; rev. edn New York, 1974

Goodman, Kay, 'The Impact of Rahel Varnhagen on Women in the Nineteenth Century', in Burkhard (ed.), *Gestaltet und gestaltend* (see p. 272 above), pp. 125–53

Goodman, Kay, 'Poesie and Praxis in Rahel Varnhagen's Letters', *New German Critique* 27 (1982), 123–39

Guilloton, Doris Starr, 'Rahel Varnhagen von Ense', in Hardin and Schweitzer, *German Writers in the Age of Goethe* (see p. 272 above), pp. 340–4

Stern, Carola, *Der Text meines Herzens: das Leben der Rahel Varnhagen*, Rowohlt: Reinbek, 1994

Waldstein, Edith, 'Identity as conflict and conversation in Rahel Varnhagen (1771–1833)', in Joeres, *Out of Line* (see p. 272 above). pp. 95–113

Frederiksen

Viebig, Clara (Trier 1860 – 1952 W. Berlin)

Barbara Holzer, Berlin: E. Fleischel, 1897 (d)

Kinder der Eifel, Berlin: Fontane, 1897 (s)

Rheinlandstöchter, Berlin: E. Fleischel, 1897 (n)

Das Weiberdorf, Berlin: E. Fleischel (n)

Die vor den Toren, Berlin: Fleischel, 1910 (n)

Unter dem Freiheitsbaum, Stuttgart and Berlin: DVA 1922 (n)

Die Passion, Stuttgart, Berlin and Leipzig: DVA 1925 (n)

Die mit den tausend Kindern, Berlin and Leipzig: DVA 1929; repr. Rastatt: Pabel-Moewig, 1989 (n)

Insel der Hoffnung, Stuttgart and Berlin: 1933 (n)

Der Vielgeliebte und die Vielgehaßte, 1935 (n)

And numerous other novels and collections of short stories, a number of them translated into English, including:

Works in English translation

Our daily Bread (= *Das tägliche Brot*, 1902; tr. Margaret L. Clarke), New York: Lane, 1909

Burning Love (= *Brennende Liebe*; tr. William Guild Howard), in Franke (ed.), *The German Classics*, XIX, 1914

The Golden Hills (= *Die goldenen Berge*; tr. Graham Rawson), New York: The Vanguard Press, 1930

The Woman with a Thousand Children (= *Die mit den tausend Kindern*; tr. Brian Lunn), New York and London: Appleton & Co., 1937

see also Morgan + S

Secondary literature

Hofacker, Erich P., 'Clara Viebig', in James Hardin (ed.), *German Fiction Writers, 1885–1913*, vol. II, Detroit, 1988, pp. 470–9

Voigt-Diederichs, Helene (Marienhoff 1875 – 1961 Jena)

Wandertage in England, Munich: Langen, 1912 (a, t)

Zwischen Himmel und Steinen. Pyrenäenfahrt mit Esel und Schlafsack, Munich: Langen, 1919 (t)

Auf Marienhoff. Vom Leben und von der Wärme einer Mutter, Jena: Diederichs, 1925 (a)

Ring um Roderich, Jena: Diederichs, 1929 (n)

Aber der Wald lebt, Jena, 1935 (s)
Gast in Siebenbürgen, Jena, 1936 (a)
Vom alten Schlag, Jena, 1937 (s)
Das Verlöbnis, Jena, 1942 (n)

Walden(-Heimann), Nell (1887–1975)

Unter Sternen, Berlin: Stössinger 1933 (p)

Wallenrodt, Isabella von, née von Koppy (1740–1814)

Das Leben der Frau von Wallenrodt in Briefen an einen Freund: ein Beitrag zur Seelenkunde und Weltkenntniß, 2 vols., Leipzig: Stillersche Buchhandlung, 1797; repr., ed. Anita Runge, Hildesheim: Olms, 1992 (a)
Karl Moor und seine Genossen nach der Abschiedsscene beim alten Thurm: ein Gemälde erhabner Menschennatur als Seitenstück zum Rinaldo Rinaldini, Mainz: Gottfried Vollmer, 1801 (d)

Walter, Silja (Olten, Switzerland 1919–)

Gedichte, Zurich: Arche, 1950 (p)
Gesammelte Gedichte, Zurich: Arche, 1956 (p)
Die Feuertaube. Für meinen Brüder: Neue Gedichte, Zurich: Arche, 1985 (p)

Wander, Maxie (Vienna 1933 – 1977 Berlin, GDR)

Guten Morgen, du Schöne, Berlin: Buchverlag Der Morgen, 1977; repr. Darmstadt: Luchterhand, 1980 (documentary prose)
Leben wär eine prima Alternative, Darmstadt and Neuwied: Luchterhand, 1980 (a/l)
Ein Leben ist nicht genug, ed. Fred Wander, Hamburg, Zurich: Luchterhand, 1990; reissued Munich: dtv, 1996 (a/l)

Translation: Altbach, *German Feminism* (1984); Gerber and Pouchet Wilson

Weber, Ilse (Moravia 1903 – 1944 Auschwitz)

Jüdische Kindermärchen, 1928 (ch)
In deinen Mauern wohnt das Leid. Gedichte aus dem KZ Theresienstadt, Gerlingen: Bleicher Verlag, 1991 (p)

Wegner, Bettina (GDR 1947 – FRG) [also publishes as Bettina Schlesinger]; singer-songwriter

Sind so kleine Hände, 1978: CBS 83507 (recording)
Wenn meine Lieder nicht mehr stimmen, Reinbek: Rowohlt, 1979 (p)
Wenn meine Lieder nicht mehr stimmen, 1980: CBS 84523. (recording)
Traurig bin ich sowieso: Lieder und Gedichte, Reinbek: Rowohlt, 1981 (p)
Traurig bin ich sowieso, 1981: CBS 85133 (recording)
Von Deutschland nach Deutschland ein Katzensprung, Reinbek: Rowohlt, 1986 (p)
Als ich zuende war: Lieder und Gedichte aus Ost und West in Nachdichtungen. Hamburg: Rowohlt, 1986 (p)
(with Rainer Lindner and Peter Meier) *Lieder Texte Noten,* Gemünden: Lindner Gemünden, 1991 (p)

Translation: Gerber and Pouchet

Weirauch, Anna Elisabeth (Galatz, Romania 1887 – 1970 W. Berlin)

Der Skorpion, Berlin: Askanischer Verlag, 1919 (vol. I), 1921 (vol. II) and 1930 (vol. III); repr.
Haroldsweisach: Feministischer Buchverlag, 1992 (vol. I) and 1993 (vols. II and III)

Numerous other works listed in Wilson

Works in English translation

The Scorpion (= *Der Skorpion*; tr. Whittaker Chambers), New York: Greenberg, 1932, repr.
Wiley, 1948; repr. as *Of Love forbidden*, Greenwich, Connecticut: Fawcett Publ.,
1964

Outcast (= *Der Skorpion*, vol. III; tr. G. Endore), New York: Greenberg, 1932; repr. Wiley,
1948

Secondary literature

Schoppmann, Claudia, '*Der Skorpion*'. *Frauenliebe in der Weimarer Republik*, Berlin:
Frühlings Erwachen, 1985

Wilson

Weißenthurn, Johanna von, née Grünberg (1773–1847)

Schauspiele, 6 vols., Vienna, 1804–10 (d)

Das letzte Mittel, Leipzig: Ph. Reklam jun., n. d. (d)

Hermann, 1813 (d)

Many other published and unpublished dramas

Widmar, Josefine (1886–1975)

Drei gehen aus dem Parlament, Innsbruck: Throlia, 1931 (n)

**Wied, Martina, pseud. for Alexandrine Martina Weisl, née Schnabel
(Vienna 1882–1957)**

Bewegung, Vienna, Prag, Leipzig: Strache, 1919 (p)

Also wrote a number of n, d, e

Wilson (under **S**chnabl)

Wiengarn, Bettina (FRG 1959–)

Alles nocheinmal, Hamburg: Verlag Michael Kellner, 1984 (p)

Kuckuckskinder, Bergen/Holland: Verlag Erich van der Wal, 1989 (p)

Translation: Gutzschhahn, *Young Poets of Germany* (1994)

Wildermuth, Ottilie (Rottenburg 1817 – 1877 Tübingen)

Gesammelte Werke, 10 vols., ed. A. Wildermuth, Stuttgart: Union, 1891–4

Jugendschriften, 14 vols., Stuttgart: Kröner, 1871

Ausgewählte Erzählungen für die Jugend, 22 vols., 1910 (s)

Bilder und Geschichten aus Schwaben mit den 'Schwäbischen Pfarrerhäusern', ed. R.
Wildermuth, 1977 (s, e)

Der Prinz aus Mohrenland. Und andere Geschichten aus Schwaben, ed. R. Wildermuth, 1981 (s)

Numerous n, s, ch

Numerous works in English translation, e.g.

Household Stories (= Heiratsgeschichten, incl. *Der Prinz aus Mohrenland*; tr. Eleanor

Kimmont), Cincinnati: Hitchcock and Walden; New York: Nelson and Phillips,
1872
Stories for the Little Folks (= *Vom Berg zu Tal. Erzählungen für die Jugend*; tr. Anna B. Cooke),
Boston: Dutton, 1866
see also Morgan
Wilson

Willemer, Marianne von (Linz, Austria 1784 – 1860 Frankfurt am Main)

See *Goethes Werke*, Hamburger Ausgabe, ed. Erich Trunz, 14 vols., Munich: Beck, 1949–;
vol. II (*West-Östlicher Divan*), 11th edn (1978), pp. 64, 80, 82 and notes pp. 544,
593–4, 603, 605
Pyritz, Hans, *Marianne von Willemer*, Berlin, 1944, includes appendix containing poems
by M. v. W
Wilson

Winsloe, Christa (Darmstadt 1888 – 1944 Cluny)

Das Mädchen Manuela. Der Roman von 'Mädchen in Uniform', Amsterdam: De Lange,
1933 (n)
Ritter Nerestan. Schauspiel in drei Akten, Vienna and Berlin: Marton, 1930,
Bühnenmanuskript (d)

Works in English translation
The Child Manuela (= *Das Mädchen Manuela*; tr. Agnes Neill Scott), intr. Alison Hennegan,
London: Chapman and Hall, 1934; repr. London, Virago, 1994

Other translations: see Morgan S

Secondary literature
Schoppmann, *Im Fluchtgepäck* (see p. 276 above)
Wilson

Wobeser, Wilhelmine Karoline von (dates uncertain; eighteenth century)

Elisa oder das Weib wie es seyn sollte, Leipzig: Gräff, 1795; repr. of 4th (1799) edn with a
postscript by Lydia Schieth, Hildesheim: Olms, 1990 (n)

English translation
Eliza, or, The Pattern of Women: a Moral Romance, tr. Ma. Regina Roche, Lancaster, PA:
Hutter, 1802; tr. John Ebers, Leipzig: H. Gräff, 1799 [microform], Wildberg:
Belser Wissenschaftlicher Dienst (Edition Corvey), 1989–90

Secondary literature
Menhennet, A., '"Elisa steht wie eine Gottheit da": Heroic Femininity in the Popular
Novel of the *Goethezeit*', *German Life and Letters* 39/4 (1986), 253–67
Schieth, L., '*Elisa oder das Weib wie es seyn sollte*. Zur Analyse eines Frauen-
Romanbestsellers', in Gallas and Heuser (1990) (see p. 271 above), pp. 114–31

Wohmann, Gabriele (née Guyot) (Darmstadt 1932 – FRG)

Gesammelte Erzählungen aus 30 Jahren, 3 vols., Munich: dtv, 1986 (s)
Abschied für länger, Olten: Walter, 1965 (n)

Ein unwiderstehlicher Mann, Munich, 1966; Reinbek: Rowohlt, 1975 (s)
Ausgewählte Gedichte 1964–1982, Darmstadt: Luchterhand, 1983 (p)
Erzählen Sie mir was vom Jenseits: Gedichte, Erzählungen, Gedanken, Munich: Matthias-
   Grünewald, 1994 (p, e, s)
Numerous other works of prose fiction and poetry; also d

Works in English translation
The Cherry Tree (= *Der Kirschbaum*; tr. Jeanne Willson), Austin, Texas: Dimension Press,
   c. 1994
'The Sisters' (= *Die Schwestern*; tr. Edna Spitz and Elisabeth Rütschi-Hermann),
   Dimension 7/3 (1974), 450–9; repr. in Herrmann and Spitz, *German Women Writers*
   (1978)
Everything for the Gallery and Other Stories (= *Alles für die Galerie*; tr. Ingeborg McCoy),
   Dimension 4/1 (1971), 118–43
more poems and stories in *Dimension* listed in Stern, 'Gabriele Wohmann' (under
   'Secondary literature' below)
Cocalis, *The Defiant Muse* (1986) (p)

Secondary literature
Wohmann, Gabriele, *Materialienbuch*, ed. Thomas Scheffelen, Darmstadt: Luchterhand,
   1977
Knapp, Gerhard and Mona (eds.), *Gabriele Wohmann*, Königstein: Athenäum, 1981
Stern, Guy, 'Gabriele Wohmann', in Wolfgang D. Elfe and James Hardin (eds.),
   Contemporary German Fiction Writers (Second Series), Detroit, 1988, pp. 249–57
Frederiksen; Wilson

Wolf, Christa (Landsberg, Warthe 1929 – GDR)
Der geteilte Himmel, Halle: Mitteldeutscher Verlag, 1963; repr. Munich: dtv, 1973; repr. ed.
   Agnès Cardinal, London: Methuen's Twentieth Century Texts, 1987 (s)
Nachdenken über Christa T., Halle: Mitteldeutscher Verlag, 1968; repr. Darmstadt:
   Luchterhand; Munich: dtv, 1993 (n)
Lesen und Schreiben. Aufsätze und Betrachtungen, Berlin: Aufbau, 1972; repr. Darmstadt:
   Luchterhand, 1972 (e)
Unter den Linden. Drei unwahrscheinliche Geschichten, Berlin: Aufbau, 1974; repr. Darmstadt:
   Luchterhand, 1977 (s)
Kindheitsmuster, Berlin: Aufbau, 1976; repr. Darmstadt: Luchterhand, 1979 (n)
Kein Ort. Nirgends, Berlin: Aufbau, 1979; repr. Darmstadt: Luchterhand, 1979 (n)
Gesammelte Erzählungen, Darmstadt: Luchterhand, 1981 (s)
Kassandra. Erzählung. Darmstadt: Luchterhand, 1983; in censored form (together with
   Voraussetzungen) as *Kassandra. Vier Vorlesungen. Eine Erzählung*, Berlin: Aufbau,
   1983 (s)
Voraussetzungen einer Erzählung: Kassandra, Darmstadt: Luchterhand, 1983 (a, e)
Die Dimension des Autors. Aufsätze, Essays, Gespräche, Reden, vols. I and II. Berlin: Aufbau,
   1986; repr. Darmstadt: Luchterhand, 1987 (e)
Störfall. Nachrichten eines Tages, Berlin: Aufbau, 1987; repr. Darmstadt: Luchterhand,
   1987 (n)
Sommerstück, Berlin: Aufbau, 1989; repr. Frankfurt am Main: Luchterhand, 1989 (n)
Was bleibt, Berlin: Aufbau, 1990; repr. Frankfurt am Main: Luchterhand, 1990 (s)
Angepaßt oder mündig? Briefe an Christa Wolf, Frankfurt am Main: Luchterhand, 1990 (l)
Christa Wolf im Dialog, Frankfurt am Main: Luchterhand, 1990 (interviews, e/a)

Akteneinsicht Christa Wolf: Zerrspiegel und Dialog, ed. Hermann Vinke, Hamburg:
Luchterhand, 1993 (a/documentary)
Auf dem Weg nach Tabou: Texte 1990–1994, Cologne: Kiepenheuer & Witsch, 1994 (e)
Medea. Stimmen, Luchterhand, 1996 (n)
Hierzulande Andernorts: Erzählungen und andere Texte 1994–1998, Cologne: Kiepenheuer &
Witsch, 1999 (e)

Works in English translation

Divided Heaven (= *Der geteilte Himmel*; tr. Joan Becker), East Berlin: Seven Seas, 1965; New
York: Adler's Foreign Books, 1976
The Reader and the Writer: Essays, Sketches, Memories (= *Lesen und Schreiben*; tr. Joan Becker),
East Berlin: Seven Seas; New York: International Publishers, 1977
The Quest for Christa T. (= *Nachdenken über Christa T.*; tr. Christopher Middleton), London:
Hutchinson, 1971; repr. London: Virago, 1982
A Model Childhood (= *Kindheitsmuster*; tr. Ursule Molinaro and Hedwig Rappolt), London:
Virago, 1983; more recent editions have the title *Patterns of Childhood*
No Place on Earth (= *Kein Ort. Nirgends*; tr. Jan van Heurck), New York: Farrar, Straus and
Giroux, 1982; London: Virago, 1983
Accident/A Day's News (= *Störfall*; tr. Heike Schwarzbauer and Rick Takvorian), London:
Virago, 1989
Cassandra. A Novel and Four Essays (= *Kassandra. Vier Vorlesungen. Eine Erzählung*; tr. Jan van
Heurck), London: Virago, 1984
The Fourth Dimension: Interviews with Christa Wolf (= *Die Dimension des Autors* (excerpts); tr.
Hilary Pilkington), intr. Karin McPherson, London: Verso, 1988
The Writer's Dimension: Selected Essays (= *Die Dimension des Autors*; tr. Jan van Heurck),
London: Virago, 1993
What Remain and other stories (= *Gesammelte Erzählungen*; tr. Heike Schwarzbauer and Rick
Takvorian), London: Virago, 1993
Parting from Phantoms. Selected Writings, 1990–1994 (= *Auf dem Wege nach Tabou*; tr. and
annotated by Jan van Heurck), Chicago and London: University of Chicago
Press, 1997
Medea (= *Medea. Stimmen*; tr. John Cullen), London: Virago, 1998
'Change of Perspective' (= *Blickwechsel*), in Herrmann and Spitz, *German Women Writers*
(1978)
Altbach, *German Feminism* (1984); Gerber and Pouchet; Frederiksen (1989)

Secondary literature

Drescher, Angela (ed.), *Dokumentation zu Christa Wolf 'Nachdenken über Christa T.'*
Hamburg: Luchterhand, 1991
Kuhn, Anna, K., *Christa Wolf's Utopian Vision. From Marxism to Feminism*, Cambridge:
Cambridge University Press, 1988
Wallace, Ian (ed.), *Christa Wolf in Perspective* (=German Monitor, 30), Amsterdam and
Atlanta, Georgia: Rodopi, 1994
Sevin, Dieter, 'Christa Wolf', in Wolfgang D. Elfe and James Hardin (eds.), *Contemporary
German Fiction Writers (Second Series)*, Detroit, 1988, pp. 258–64
Frederiksen; Wilson

Wolter, Christine (Königsberg 1939 – GDR)

Meine italienische Reise, Berlin and Weimar: Aufbau, 1973 (t/a)
Wie ich meine Unschuld verlor, Berlin and Weimar: Aufbau, 1976 (s)

Juni in Sizilien, Berlin and Weimar: Aufbau, 1977 (t/a)
Die Hintergrundsperson oder Versuche zu lieben, Berlin and Weimar: Aufbau, 1979 (n)
Stückweise leben, Zurich: Benziger Verlag, 1980 (n)
Die Alleinseglerin, Berlin and Weimar: Aufbau, 1982 (n)
Straße der Stunden – 44 Ansichten von Mailand, Berlin and Weimar: Aufbau, 1987 (s)

English translation
'I have married again' (= 'Ich habe wieder geheiratet', from *Wie ich meine Unschuld verlor*;
tr. Friedrich Achberger) in Altbach, *German Feminism* (1984), pp. 220–5

Wolzogen, Caroline von, née von Lengefeld (Rudolfstadt 1763 – 1847 Jena)
Gesammelte Schriften, ed. Peter Boerner, 3 vols., Hildesheim: Olms, 1988 (n)
Der leukadische Fels, in Schiller, Friedrich (ed.), *Neue Thalia* II, Leipzig, 1792 (d)
Agnes von Lilien, in Schiller, Friedrich (ed.), *Die Horen*, 2 vols., Tübingen: Cotta, 1796–7.
Berlin: Unger, 1798
Cordelia, Leipzig: Brockhaus, 1840 (n)

Secondary literature
Kahn-Wallerstein, Carmen, *Die Frau im Schatten: Schillers Schwägerin Karoline von Wolzogen*,
Bern, 1970

Translation: see Morgan (under Woltmann!)

Worgitzky, Charlotte (Erzgebirge 1934 – GDR)
Die Unschuldigen, Berlin: Buchverlag der Morgen, 1975 (n)
Vieräugig oder blind, Berlin: Buchverlag der Morgen, 1978
Meine ungeborenen Kinder, Berlin: Buchverlag der Morgen, 1982; repr. 1992 (n)
Heute sterben immer nur die andern, Berlin: Buchverlag der Morgen, 1986 (s)
Traum vom Möglichen, Berlin: Buchverlag der Morgen, 1991 (n)
Wilson

Wörishöffer, Sophie (pseuds.: W. Höffer, Sophie von der Horst, K. Horstmann, S. Fischer, S. Wörishoffer) (Pinneberg, Holstein 1838 – 1890 Hamburg)
Aus den Erfahrungen einer Hausfrau, Würzburg: Keller, 1874 (n)
Am Abgrund, Görlitz: Vierling, 1878 (s)
Robert des Schiffsjungen Fahrten und Abenteuer auf der deutschen Handels- und Kriegsflotte,
Bielefeld: Velhagen und Klasing, 1877 (n)
Das Buch vom braven Mann. Bilder aus dem Seeleben. Der reifen Jugend gewidmet, Leipzig: Hirt
und Sohn, 1883 (n)
*Kreuz und quer durch Indien. Irrfahrten zweier deutscher Leichtmatrosen in der indischen
Wunderwelt*, Bielefeld: Velhagen und Klasing, 1886 (n)
And many other tales of adventure

Zäunemann, Sidonia Hedwig (Erfurt 1714 – 1740 nr. Plauen)
Poetische Rosen in Knospen. Mit einem Anhang, Erfurt: Cuno, 1739 (p)

Secondary literature
Brinker-Gabler, G, 'Das weibliche Ich. Überlegungen zur Analyse von Werken
weiblicher Autoren mit einem Beispiel aus dem 18. Jahrhundert: Sidonia

Hedwig Zäunemann', in *Die Frau als Heldin und Autorin*, ed. W. Paulsen, Bern and
Munich: Francke, 1979, pp. 55–65

Translation: Cocalis, *The Defiant Muse* (1986)

Wilson

Zeller, Eva (Eberswalde nr. Berlin 1923 – GDR/FRG)

Poetry

Sage und schreibe, Stuttgart: DVA, 1971
Fliehkraft, Stuttgart: DVA, 1975
Auf dem Wasser gehn: Ausgewählte Gedichte, Stuttgart: DVA, 1979
Unveränderliche Kennzeichen, ed. Karl Bonngardt, Berlin: Union Verlag, 1983
Stellprobe, Stuttgart: DVA, 1989
Ein Stein aus Davids Hirtentasche, Freiburg, Basel and Vienna: Herder, 1992

Zeller, Eva Christina (FRG 1960–)

Das Meer kennt kein Meer, Tübingen: Edition Skarabäus Verlag Gudrun Paul, 1985 (p)
Folg ich dem Wasser, Eggingen: Edition Klaus Isele, 1988 (p)
Requiem: Zwölf Gedichte, Dresden: edition cordeliers / edition cadre, 1988 (p)

Translation: Gutzschhahn, *Young Poets of Germany* (1994)

Zeplin, Rosemarie (Bützow, E. Germany 1939 – GDR)

Schattenriß eines Liebhabers, Berlin: Aufbau, 1980; repr. Frankfurt am Main, Berlin,
Vienna: Ullstein, 1984 (s)
Alpträume aus der Provinz, Berlin and Weimar: Aufbau, 1986
Der Maulwurf oder fatales Beispiel weiblicher Gradlinigkeit, Berlin and Weimar: Aufbau, 1990

Wilson

Ziegler, Christiana Mariana von (Frankfurt an der Oder 1695 – 1760 Frankfurt am Main)

Versuch in gebundener Schreib-Art, 2 vols., Leipzig: Hilscher, 1728–30 (p)
Moralische und Vermischte Send-Schreiben, An einige Ihrer vertrauten und guten Freunde gestellet,
Leipzig: Hilscher, 1731 (l)
Vermischte Schriften in gebundener und ungebundener Rede, Göttingen: Schmidt, 1739 (p)

Translation: Cocalis, *The Defiant Muse* (1986)

Wilson

Zitz-Halein, Kathinka (wrote under many pseudonyms, including: K. Th. Zianitzka, Theophile Christlieb, Emeline, August Enders, Johann Golder, Rosalba, Stephanie, Tina, Viola etc.) (Mainz 1801–77)

Numerous short stories, novels, and volumes of poetry including

Erzählungen und Novellen. Fremd und eigen, Nuremberg: Fr. Campe, 1845 (s)
Herbstrosen. Poesie und Prosa, Mainz: Faber, 1846 (p, s)
Rheinsandkörner. Ein Novellen-Cyklus, Mainz: Faber, 1851 (s)
Champagnerschaum. Erzählungen und Novellen, Mainz: Faber, 1854 (s)
Strohfeuer. Neue Erzählungen, Mainz: Faber, 1855 (s)
Schillers Laura, nebst anderen Erzählungen und Novellen, Mainz: Faber, 1855 (s)
Dur- und Molltöne, Neue Gedichte, 1859 (p)
Der Roman eines Dichterlebens (Goethe), 1863 (n)

Heinrich Heine, der Liederdichter, 1864 (n)
Rahel, oder Dreiunddreißig Jahre aus einem edlen Frauenleben, 1864 (e/biog.)
Lord Byron, 1867 (n)

> Translation: Cocalis, *The Defiant Muse* (1986)

Secondary literature
Zucker, Stanley, *Kathinka Zitz-Halein and Female Civic Activism in Mid-Nineteenth-Century Germany*, Carbondale: Southern Illinois University Press, c. 1991

Zur Muehlen, Hermynia (Vienna 1883 – 1951 Radletts, Hertfordshire, England)

Licht, Konstanz: Seeverlag, 1922 (n)
Ali, der Teppichweber. 5 Märchen, Berlin: Malik, 1923 (s)
Schupomann Karl Müller. Eine Erzählung, Berlin: Vereinigung Internationaler Verlagsanstalten, 1924 (s)
Der Deutschvölkische. Eine Erzählung, Berlin: Vereinigung Internationaler Verlagsanstalten, 1924 (s)
Lina. Erzählung aus dem Leben eines Dienstmädchens, Berlin: Vereinigung Internationaler Verlagsanstalten, 1926 (s)
Ende und Anfang. Ein Lebensbuch, Berlin: S. Fischer, 1929 (a)
Das Riesenrad, Stuttgart: Engelhorn, 1932 (n)
Nora hat eine famose Idee, Bern and Leipzig: Gotthelf, 1933 (n)
Reise durch ein Leben, Bern and Leipzig: Gotthelf, 1933 (a)
Ein Jahr im Schatten, Zurich: Humanitas Verlag, 1935 (n)
Unsere Töchter die Nazinnen, 1935 (n)
Fahrt ins Licht. Autobiographie, 1936 (a)

> And numerous other works, some later ones in English, e.g.

We Poor Shadows, London, 1943
Came the Stranger, London, 1946

> Also translated from English, e.g. works of Upton Sinclair

Works in English translation
Fairy Tales for Workers' Children (= *Märchen*; tr. Ida Dailes), Chicago: Daily Worker, 1925
The Runaway Countess (= *Ende und Anfang. Ein Lebensbuch*; tr. Frank Barnes), New York: Cape and Smith, 1930
The Wheel of Life (= *Das Riesenrad*; tr. Margaret Goldsmith), London: Barker; New York: Stokes, 1933
A Life's Journey (= *Reise durch ein Leben*; tr. Phyllis and Trevor Blewitt), London: Cape, 1935
A Year under a Cloud (= *Ein Jahr im Schatten*; tr. Ethel K. Houghton and H. E. Cornides), London: Selwyn and Blount, 1937
'The Fence', 'The Servant', 'The Glasses' (= 'Der Zaun', in *Das Schloß der Wahrheit*, 1924; 'Der Knecht' and 'Die Brillen', in *Ali, der Teppichweber*, 1923; tr. Jack Zipes), in Zipes (ed.), *Utopian Tales from Weimar*, Edinburgh: Polygon, 1990

Secondary literature
King, Linda J., 'Hermynia Zur Mühlen', in James Hardin (ed.), *German Fiction Writers 1914–1945*, Detroit, 1987, pp. 317–24
Altner, Manfred, *Hermynia Zur Mühlen. Eine Biographie*, Bern etc.: Peter Lang, 1997

Zürn, Unica (Nora Berta Unica Ruth Zürn) (Berlin 1916 – 1970 Paris)

Gesamtausgabe in 5 Bänden, ed. Günter Bose and Erich Brinkmann, Berlin: Brinkmann und Bose, 1988–92

Das Weiße mit dem roten Punkt, ed. Inge Morgenroth Berlin: Lilith, 1981 (s)

Der Mann im Jasmin. Dunkler Frühling, Frankfurt am Main and Berlin: Ullstein, 1982 (first publ. 1977 and 1969)

Das Haus der Krankheiten, Berlin: Lilith, 1986 (prose)

Das Meer unter meinem Kopfkissen, Kiel: Neuer Malik Verlag, 1995 (p)

Works in English translation

The Man of Jasmine and Other Texts (= *Der Mann im Jasmin*; tr. Malcolm Green), London: Atlas Press, 1994

The House of Illnesses (= *Das Haus der Krankheiten*; tr. M. Green), London: Atlas, 1997

Zweig, Friederike Maria (= Friderike Maria Winternitz) (Vienna 1882 – 1971 Stamford, Connecticut)

Der Ruf der Heimat, 1914; repr. 1931

Vögelchen, Berlin, Vienna: S. Fischer 1919 (n)

Also translated from French, e.g. Verlaine

English translation

Greatness Revisited, ed. and intr. Harry Zohn, Boston: Branden Press, 1982 (e)

Index

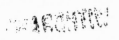